Exploring Transmedia Journalism in the Digital Age

Renira Rampazzo Gambarato
National Research University Higher School of Economics, Russia

Geane C. Alzamora
Federal University of Minas Gerais, Brazil

A volume in the Advances in Multimedia and Interactive Technologies (AMIT) Book Series

IGI Global
DISSEMINATOR OF KNOWLEDGE

Published in the United States of America by
IGI Global
Information Science Reference (an imprint of IGI Global)
701 E. Chocolate Avenue
Hershey PA, USA 17033
Tel: 717-533-8845
Fax: 717-533-8661
E-mail: cust@igi-global.com
Web site: http://www.igi-global.com

Library of Congress Cataloging-in-Publication Data

Names: Gambarato, Renira Rampazzo editor. | Alzamora, Geane editor.
Title: Exploring transmedia journalism in the digital age / Renira Rampazzo Gambarato and Geane C. Alzamora, editors.
Description: Hershey : Information Science Reference, 2018.
Identifiers: LCCN 2017022528| ISBN 9781522537816 (hardcover) | ISBN 9781522537823 (ebook)
Subjects: LCSH: Online journalism. | Journalism--Technological innovations. | Digital media. | Social media.
Classification: LCC PN4784.O62 E97 2017 | DDC 070.4--dc23 LC record available at https://lccn.loc.gov/2017022528

This book is published in the IGI Global book series Advances in Multimedia and Interactive Technologies (AMIT) (ISSN: 2327-929X; eISSN: 2327-9303)

British Cataloguing in Publication Data
A Cataloguing in Publication record for this book is available from the British Library.

Advances in Multimedia and Interactive Technologies (AMIT) Book Series

Joel J.P.C. Rodrigues
National Institute of Telecommunications (Inatel), Brazil & Instituto de Telecomunicações, University of Beira Interior, Portugal

ISSN:2327-929X
EISSN:2327-9303

Mission

Traditional forms of media communications are continuously being challenged. The emergence of user-friendly web-based applications such as social media and Web 2.0 has expanded into everyday society, providing an interactive structure to media content such as images, audio, video, and text.

The **Advances in Multimedia and Interactive Technologies (AMIT) Book Series** investigates the relationship between multimedia technology and the usability of web applications. This series aims to highlight evolving research on interactive communication systems, tools, applications, and techniques to provide researchers, practitioners, and students of information technology, communication science, media studies, and many more with a comprehensive examination of these multimedia technology trends.

Coverage

- Gaming Media
- Digital Communications
- Social Networking
- Mobile Learning
- Multimedia Streaming
- Digital Watermarking
- Internet Technologies
- Web Technologies
- Audio Signals
- Digital Images

The Advances in Multimedia and Interactive Technologies (AMIT) Book Series (ISSN 2327-929X) is published by IGI Global, 701 E. Chocolate Avenue, Hershey, PA 17033-1240, USA, www.igi-global.com. This series is composed of titles available for purchase individually; each title is edited to be contextually exclusive from any other title within the series. For pricing and ordering information please visit http://www.igi-global.com/book-series/advances-multimedia-interactive-technologies/73683. Postmaster: Send all address changes to above address.

Titles in this Series

For a list of additional titles in this series, please visit: www.igi-global.com/book-series

Handbook of Research on Advanced Concepts in Real-Time Image and Video Processing
Md. Imtiyaz Anwar (National Institute of Technology, Jalandhar, India) Arun Khosla (National Institute of Technology, Jalandhar, India) and Rajiv Kapoor (Delhi Technological University, India)
Information Science Reference • copyright 2018 • 504pp • H/C (ISBN: 9781522528487) • US $265.00 (our price)

Transforming Gaming and Computer Simulation Technologies across Industries
Brock Dubbels (McMaster University, Canada)
Information Science Reference • copyright 2017 • 297pp • H/C (ISBN: 9781522518174) • US $210.00 (our price)

Feature Detectors and Motion Detection in Video Processing
Nilanjan Dey (Techno India College of Technology, Kolkata, India) Amira Ashour (Tanta University, Egypt) and Prasenjit Kr. Patra (Bengal College of Engineering and Technology, India)
Information Science Reference • copyright 2017 • 328pp • H/C (ISBN: 9781522510253) • US $200.00 (our price)

Mobile Application Development, Usability, and Security
Sougata Mukherjea (IBM, India)
Information Science Reference • copyright 2017 • 320pp • H/C (ISBN: 9781522509455) • US $180.00 (our price)

Applied Video Processing in Surveillance and Monitoring Systems
Nilanjan Dey (Techno India College of Technology, Kolkata, India) Amira Ashour (Tanta University, Egypt) and Suvojit Acharjee (National Institute of Technology Agartala, India)
Information Science Reference • copyright 2017 • 321pp • H/C (ISBN: 9781522510222) • US $215.00 (our price)

Intelligent Analysis of Multimedia Information
Siddhartha Bhattacharyya (RCC Institute of Information Technology, India) Hrishikesh Bhaumik (RCC Institute of Information Technology, India) Sourav De (The University of Burdwan, India) and Goran Klepac (University College for Applied Computer Engineering Algebra, Croatia & Raiffeisenbank Austria, Croatia)
Information Science Reference • copyright 2017 • 520pp • H/C (ISBN: 9781522504986) • US $220.00 (our price)

Emerging Technologies and Applications for Cloud-Based Gaming
P. Venkata Krishna (VIT University, India)
Information Science Reference • copyright 2017 • 314pp • H/C (ISBN: 9781522505464) • US $195.00 (our price)

IGI Global
DISSEMINATOR OF KNOWLEDGE

701 East Chocolate Avenue, Hershey, PA 17033, USA
Tel: 717-533-8845 x100 • Fax: 717-533-8661
E-Mail: cust@igi-global.com • www.igi-global.com

Table of Contents

Detailed Table of Contents

Social networks have modified the activities of the press, the actions of audiences, and the perceptions of societies. The strategies displayed to avoid losing consumers aim at fulfilling the audience's needs and the gap between the producers' and the consumers' interests tends to widen. This leads to a crisis point in news financing, affecting the traditional logic of the media industry; while advertisers are now able to reach their audiences without its mediation, viralization and instantaneity force the media to publish information incompatible with the public interest as considered by the press. In this way, traditional newsworthiness criteria are replaced by other criteria that redefine the concept of information. The aim of this chapter is to analyze the way in which instantaneity and viralization have affected not only the journalistic activity but also the information selection criteria and the audiences' input on the web.

Among all factors that compose the journalistic routine, time plays an important role. It delimitates the period to produce content. Transmedia projects often need a faster pace than usual articles, mostly because the reporters need to plan before they leave newsrooms to capture content and, depending on the media used, work on different platforms to deliver the whole content. This chapter discusses the process behind three transmedia journalistic cases: Black Hawk Down (published by Philadelphia Enquirer, in 1997), Inside Disaster (released by PTV, in 2010), and Harvest of Change (published by Des Moines Register, in 2014). Using the case study method, they will be discussed, analyzing the process behind their publication. This reflection highlights how the adoption of tools and usage of paths to connect or publicize content on different media increased the relevance not only of time to create but the effort dedicated to plan the transmedia strategy.

The purpose of this chapter is to contribute to the theoretical frame of transmedia journalism by proposing a question-based model that focuses on transmedia design when an immersive journalism piece is integrated into a transmedia space. Immersive journalism is a new medium that could be effectively used to foster social empathy by means of virtual reality stories in journalism. The chapter is guided by the following ideas: (1) narrative strategies that may be useful in the design of immersive journalism experiences; (2) aesthetic principles of immersive experiences; and (3) inclusion of an immersive experience in a transmedia space. Thus, this chapter reviews the narrative techniques and aesthetics of immersive experiences that might contribute to the design of both the immersive piece and the transmedia space.

This chapter explores the design and execution of transmedia journalism projects to inform professional production and academic experimentation. It draws on the author's current project to illustrate real-world production planning. The chapter opens with a discussion of how design thinking and audience targeting apply to this task and contribute to project success. The chapter then elaborates the flow of decisions required for a thorough transmedia plan and finally presents the Refuge project as a design example. This pilot transmedia story network focuses on the single issue of refugees: those who migrate by force, either to escape suffering and deprivation or to build new, more hopeful lives elsewhere. It is the first in a networked series of similar projects that will explore the issues that polarize the electorate in the American West, from economic stratification to religious identity, environment, and gun ownership rights.

Multi-channel structures within the convergence era, both as crossmedia and transmedia phenomena, have become increasingly important, and have completely changed the role of the audience, undermining the notions of authority and authorship, shaping society, and influencing media habits. This has created a mediascape in which readers can vicariously enter fictional and non-fictional spaces that can be explored through multiple media windows. Starting from the assumption that transmedia design can address not only the entertainment market but also the non-fictional field, this chapter aims at exploring journalism through the design lens. The first part of the work is devoted to a description of the contemporary communication scenario, and the second part aims to suggest guidelines for the application of a transmedia approach within the Italian news business, in the form of a conceptual and operational tool.

The news coverage of the 2016 Rio Summer Olympics in Brazil encompassed multiple media platforms and the flow of information in the intersection between mass media (especially television) and social media (especially Snapchat and Instagram). The 2016 Rio Olympics was the Games of Snapchat stories and filters along with Instagram stories for news coverage. This chapter aims to investigate how transmedia features are structured and implemented in the news coverage of the 2016 Olympics by the official Brazilian broadcaster, Globo Network. The theoretical framework focuses on transmedia journalism of planned events, and the methodology is based on the analytical model for transmedia news coverage of planned events developed by Gambarato and Tárcia. The research findings indicate that the coverage presented systematic content expanded throughout various media platforms (a core characteristic of transmedia journalism) but involved limited mechanisms of audience engagement, particularly in terms of citizen participation.

This chapter discusses the participatory flair of transmedia journalism within the concreteness of urban spaces by examining The Great British Property Scandal (TGBPS), a transmedia experience designed to inform and engage the public and offer alternative solutions to the long-standing housing crisis in the United Kingdom. The theoretical framework is centered on transmedia storytelling applied to journalism in the scope of urban spaces and participatory culture. The methodological approach of the case study is based on Gambarato's transmedia analytical model and applied to TGBPS to depict how transmedia strategies within urban spaces collaborated to influence social change. TGBPS is a pertinent example of transmedia journalism within the liquid society, integrating mobile technologies into daily processes with the potential for enhanced localness, customization, and mobility within the urban fabric.

The National Geographic Society (NGS) has always sought to incorporate new ways of media production into its working routine, thus defining standards of journalism both in technical and narrative terms. As a logical result, the NGS also relies on cross media strategies, focusing on transmedia storytelling in order to connect its audience. The "Future of Food" project is one of the largest transmedia projects in journalism. The chapter first outlines the concept of transmedia storytelling and discusses 10 qualities in the context of journalism. Secondly, the authors systematically discuss the case study "Future of Food" by applying the transmedia qualities to the project. This provides insights into the modes and combinations of story elements and allows to draw attention to challenges and opportunities for researchers, producers, and users.

This chapter analyzes the transmediality of the record-breaking podcast Serial with regard to three specific contexts: organizational structures and innovation, journalistic production, and user engagement. This case study shows that the transmedia approach of Serial cannot only revitalize long-form journalism, particularly in the case of investigative journalism, but it can also strengthen forms of slow and networked journalism. This case allows us to look at fan communities not only as an engaged audience, useful for commercial purposes, but also as a source for story development and production—even if both the journalistic production and the user engagement are confronted with specific ethical issues with regard to selective transparency and participation.

In the last few years, sociopolitical events have been marked by the presence of hashtags on social networks, creating a direct dialogue with street protests. This chapter aims to investigate how media activism movements appropriate hashtags to expand the narrative through social engagement. In this sense, hashtags appear as signic processes that perform a mediating function. They articulate common positioning that creates hybrid and transmedia storytelling using online and offline dynamics. From the theoretical-methodological support of semiotics by Charles Sanders Peirce and the principles of transmedia, this study analyzes the news production by the Brazilian media activism group Mídia Ninja [Ninja Media]. The results point to a transmedia journalism anchored to the social use of hashtags by the association of new signs to semiosis, generating provisional action habits from collateral experience.

The newscast "Especial 9-N," produced by TV3 (Catalonia) in association with TV3's news channel 3/24, presents transmediatic components by combining multiplatform journalistic coverage and citizen participation in online social media. The program aired on November 9, 2014, the date of the non-binding referendum on the sovereignty of Catalonia, held by Generalitat, the regional government. This chapter discusses in what measure the editorial strategy adopted optimized social engagement with the news and favored the circulation of broadcast journalism on online social media. The analysis was based on the systematic observation of the program and its records on online social media, to assess the nature and the intensity of the communicational activity. It was concluded that TV3's institutional identification with aspects related to the region's sovereignty, in the context of significant social mobilization around the theme, fostered transmedia circulation and social engagement with the news story.

This chapter proposes a journey through an experience of transmedia journalism developed by the multimedia communication team at the National University of Rosario, Argentina, focusing on the transformation of the current media ecosystem, the characteristics assumed by transmedia storytelling in a nonfictional field, and the development of the transmedia script for the project Women for Sale, a transmedia documentary that addresses the trafficking of people for the purposes of sexual exploitation. The creation of a complex narrative universe and the definitions of stories, platforms, user experiences, and the execution of a transmedia project are analyzed in light of what has been learned in this experience of journalistic production.

One of the main features of television is its appeal to transmediation—a production model oriented for the distribution of additional and/or associated content of a specific production in different media and technology platforms. In each field of television production (entertainment, journalism, advertising, etc.), transmediation takes various demonstrations and functions. The interest of the authors here is to show how transmedia strategies are part of the construction of the éthos in TV journalism, based on the analysis of Jornal da Record News, the first Brazilian newscast to be introduced as a transmedia production.

Foreword

TRANSMEDIA JOURNALISM: A WILD WEST?

It was over a decade ago when transmedia storytelling was first beginning to be talked about in industrial and academic circles as something that essentially encapsulated what digitally networked media platforms could accomplish. There was an unlimited sense of possibility for the idea of telling stories across multiple platforms. And yet, at least for the most part, these possibilities were in fact limited to commercial practices and film or television examples from an Anglo-American origin. "It is transmedia storytelling," as *Fast Company*'s David Kushner put it back in 2008, "that ultimately lures the audience into buying more stuff—today, DVDs; tomorrow, who knows what" (Kushner, 2008). It is certainly true that commerce is closely aligned with the ethos of transmedia storytelling; after all, spreading media content across a spectrum of delivery channels and encouraging audiences to migrate repeatedly across those various channels has opened to door for innovation in the digital marketing sector, particularly in the United States and United Kingdom where transmedia sits alongside related principles of branded content as the lynchpin for engaging consumers across platforms.

But commerce is far from being the sole driving factor behind transmedia; nor is it its only function. Across the globe, people now engage with all sorts of media content across multiple platforms, following stories, characters and worlds—but also brands, charities and, indeed, news stories—across a spectrum of media channels. And so perhaps the biggest challenge and the biggest opportunity for understanding this transmedia phenomenon right now is the sheer breadth of its interpretation. As I have written for *Global Convergence Cultures: Transmedia Earth*, a forthcoming edited collection of mine, "while scholarship continues to dwell on the commercial industry contexts of transmedia, smaller national communities and often far less commercial cultures around the world are now beginning to make very different … uses of transmedia, applying alternative modes of the transmedia phenomenon to the needs and structures of a nation or re-thinking this phenomenon by reapplying it to non-fictional, cultural, political, social or heritage based projects" (Freeman & Proctor, 2018).

The same sense of reinterpretation is also true for the use and role of transmedia in world of journalism, which as everyone is fully aware is now facing enormous challenges and constant changes. Ever since the rise and dominance of new digital technologies into our everyday media landscape, it has been assumed by many that journalism will need to adapt to survive; that developing alternative and more digitally specific strategies for reporting and relaying information to the public is necessary at a time when all sorts of information is freely and readily available to everyone. Thus, applying the underpinning principles of transmedia storytelling to journalism makes a great deal of sense, despite raising a number of industrial and ethical questions in the process. For instance, can journalism become transmedial without inheriting the latter's commercial practices and connotations? Can transmedia journalism retain the objective, public-service priorities of journalism? At what point does journalism become PR, especially in the context of industrially connected corporations and platforms? And, perhaps most pressingly of all, how much does journalism really *need* transmedia?

These, amongst many others, are the sorts of questions that will be addressed in this book—itself a hugely rich, diverse and much-needed collection of essays about the current face of transmedia journalism around the world. Gambarato and Alzamora have brought together a terrific range of scholars addressing topics as broad-ranging as narrative journalism, interactivity, social networks, media history, sport, fandom and participatory culture. In short, this collection is at the cutting-edge of transmedia studies right now, and the sheer breath and innovation at the heart of each chapter speaks of the way in which we have come full circle in terms of thinking about transmedia's potential. Back in the same magazine article from 2008, Kushner cited Tim Kring, creator of TV's *Heroes*, in saying: "We're the beta-testing ground. It's a Wild West: There are no rules. Just take something that sounds cool and go try it." Today's world of transmedia journalism, while not quite in the same Wild West territory, now has the opportunity to also try new ideas, and to adapt to new journalistic practices. Who knows where these transmedia practices will lead to next, but this book is a critical first step.

Matthew Freeman
Bath Spa University, UK

Matthew Freeman *is Reader in Transmedia Communication and Director of the Media Convergence Research Centre at Bath Spa University, UK. He is the author of Historicising Transmedia Storytelling: Earth Twentieth-Century Transmedia Story Worlds (Routledge, 2016), Industrial Approaches to Media: A Methodological Gateway to Industry Studies (Palgrave, 2016) and the co-author of Transmedia Archaeology: Storytelling in the Borderlines of Science Fiction, Comics and Pulp Magazines (Palgrave, 2014).*

REFERENCES

Freeman, M., & Proctor, W. (2018). *Global convergence cultures: Transmedia earth*. London: Routledge.

Kushner, D. (2008, May 1). Rebel alliance: How a small band of sci-fi geeks is leading Hollywood into a new era. *Fast Company*. Retrieved from http://www.fastcompany.com/798975/rebel-alliance

Preface

CHALLENGES AND OPPORTUNITIES OF TRANSMEDIA JOURNALISM

In order to reflect upon transmedia journalism in the digital age, the starting point could be addressing what the digital age entails. The digital age, or the Internet-driven era, dramatically changed the role of traditional media (television, print, and radio) by introducing new media (the Internet, social media, and mobile media). The 24-hour news cycle and the proliferation of social media networks are particularly relevant in the emergence of a distinct scenario in journalism, a hybrid of the mass media logic of transmission and the social media logic of sharing, a hybrid blurring of distinctions between professionals and amateurs, producers and users. The digital age has fomented two key developments: (1) The Internet facilitates publication of user-generated content, and (2) social media networks enable one-to-one communication, as opposed to the one-to-many structure of mass media. Consequently, the lines are blurred not only between professionals and amateurs but also between the message and the messenger, fiction and nonfiction, content and advertisement, facts and alternatives facts, truth and post-truth, and so forth. For instance, news feeds, such as Yahoo News, circulate sponsored stories that look like news, and ad placements in movies, on websites, on blogs, etc., are common practice. Furthermore, in the realm of breaking news, the dramatic changes are quite explicit: "The Associated Press was once the source for breaking news; when something happened in the world AP distributed the story over the wire to gain immediate attention. Now, when something happens, more often than not we learn about it on social media" (Benoit cited by Granados, 2016).

Discussing the role of journalism in the digital age, Bradshaw (2017) posits that the "online" in online journalism has become almost invisible—part of the fabric of all journalism, in the sense that broadcasters, reporters, and correspondents alike are all required to engage with audiences across multiple platforms, creating content for the Web and social media networks. This invisibility implies challenges and, at the same time, offers opportunities to further develop journalism in exciting and innovative ways, as is argued in this book.

With digitization, conceptual confusion surrounding the semantic galaxy around media and journalism universes has increased. Multimedia, crossmedia, intermedia, and transmedia storytelling are frequent terms aggregated in the media convergence process involving news in liquid, fluid, and participative environments (Bauman, 2000). Transmedia storytelling is one of the newest terms. Although it was coined by Henry Jenkins (2003) in the entertainment realm, transmedia storytelling has also been the focus of relevant academic studies connected to journalism (Alzamora & Tárcia, 2012; Ford, 2007; Gambarato, Alzamora, & Tárcia, 2016; Gambarato & Tárcia, 2017; Moloney, 2011, Renó & Flores, 2012).

However, Dominguez (2012) warns against the risk of putting new labels on old practices. Transmedia journalism is an elastic term with a wide variety of theoretical proposals that are explored in this book. Nonetheless, transmedia journalism is still a scarcely explored field with many possibilities to grow and develop into a contemporary approach to news media *prosumption* (a model of consumption based on production, or co-production of the consumed commodity). This book aims to fill an editorial gap related to the lack of titles that deal specifically with transmedia journalism theory and praxis. The book moves far beyond studies on multimedia journalism to explore how to tell pervasive news stories across multiple platforms and formats, using current digital technologies, expanding the content and engaging audiences. This publication offers a conceptualization of transmedia journalism, delving into theoretical and critical approaches to this new subject. Moreover, the book presents analytical views on transmedia journalism case studies and the applications and implications of technological advancements, such as virtual reality, hashtags, and podcasts in the journalism realm.

Challenges of Transmedia Journalism

As the first specific studies on transmedia journalism were conducted only in the late 2000s, difficulties and challenges are as vividly present as the potential to inform people in the best way possible, offering audiences a meaningful and enriching experience across multiple media platforms. Gambarato and Tárcia (2017) define transmedia journalism as follows:

In sum, we consider that transmedia journalism, as well as other applications of TS [transmedia storytelling] in fictional and nonfictional realms, is characterized by the involvement of (1) multiple media platforms, (2) content expansion, and (3) audience engagement. Transmedia journalism can take advantage of different media platforms such as television, radio, print media, and, above all, the internet and mobile media to tell deeper stories. Content expansion, as opposed to the repetition of the same message across multiple platforms, is the essence of TS and, therefore, should be the focal point of transmedia journalism as well. The enrichment of the narrative is facilitated by the extended content. Audience engagement involves mechanisms of interactivity, such as the selection of the elements to be explored, the option to read a text, watch a video, enlarge photographs, access maps, click on hyperlinks, and share information through social networks. Audience engagement deals with participation via, for instance, remixing content and creating original user-generated content. (p. 1386)

Sam Ford (2007), one of the pioneers in conducting such studies, describes transmedia journalism by highlighting that:

I'm not talking . . . about giving conglomerates the chance to squeeze more blood from the stone, to get three times as much work from half as many journalists, or else the myth of the uberjournalist, *where one person should be sent into the field to take the pictures, do the story, get video, and then come back to write the story, publish the photographs, put the video up on the Web, appear on the TV station, and so on. Instead, what I mean is finding the best platform possible to tell the story in, to use each medium to its strengths. (original emphasis)*

In this sense, probably the first challenge is to ensure that the news media industry understands what transmedia storytelling applied to journalism means and how this form of storytelling can be beneficial for media conglomerates, journalists, and audiences. One of the main concerns surrounding transmedia journalism is the time-constrained brevity characteristic of news media. Although every newsworthy event could have the potential to be transmediatic, transmedia journalism is optimized when it becomes a proactive planned process (Gambarato & Tárcia, 2017), including the content planning and the design of the audience experience. Moloney (2011) argues that "daily journalism, with its time-constrained brevity, is not a viable option. Transmedia must be designed carefully and developed with a lengthy lead time to be effective" (p. 12). Canavilhas (2014) suggests that the journalism styles more suitable and adaptable to transmedia strategies are reportage, newsgames, and interactive infographics.

In addition, difficulties regarding financing, technical skills, and the material resources necessary and limited staff, human resources, and a transmedia mind-set to produce transmedia news stories are common obstacles to overcome. Throughout the book, these and other challenges, such as incorporating the core principles of transmedia storytelling in journalistic productions, are presented, discussed, and reflected upon.

Opportunities for Transmedia Journalism

Journalism has been historically configured as the emergence of a professional identity with claims to an exclusive role and status in society. Deuze (2005) argues that although the conceptualization of journalism as a professional ideology can be traced throughout the literature on journalism studies, particularly in the second half of the 20th century, these values are challenged or changed in the context of current cultural and technological developments. How new media and multiculturalism intertwine with contemporary journalism in the context of fast-changing technology and society impact the perceptions of the roles and functions of journalism.

The changes in technology and society reflected in journalism practices also provoke changes in the roles performed by the media. Couldry and Curran (2003) argue that the power of the media functions in two ways. On the one hand, media power is a term that points out how other powerful forces use the media's middle mechanism (press reports, television coverage, websites, etc.) to wage their battles. On the other hand, "the power of the media is the emergent power of social power in complex societies whose basic infrastructure increasingly depends on the rapid circulation of information and images" (Couldry & Curran, 2003, p. 4). This scenario outlines challenges for contemporary journalism but also provides opportunities for its necessary transformation.

Newman (2009) argues that media coverage of news events is changing radically. He examined how journalists from top news organizations in the United Kingdom and the United States are increasingly involving the public in the way they search and tell stories and concluded the following: (1) There has been an explosion of social participation in the circulation of news; (2) journalists are increasingly embracing professional actions on social networking tools, such as Twitter and Facebook; (3) social media is not replacing journalism but is creating an important extra layer of diverse information and opinions; and (4) social recommendations have begun to play a significant role in driving traffic to traditional news content.

In this mediascape, transmedia journalism configures the possibility of new approaches and new empirical routes in the contemporary processes of production, distribution, and circulation of news. Although still incipient, the initiatives of transmedia journalism characterize important improvements in the realm of journalistic professional activity. For example, transmedia journalism configures the possibility of expanding the circulation of news in the connections of online social media, as well as favoring social engagement with the news in editorial initiatives of multiplatform distributions of journalistic content.

Scolari (2013) posits that transmedia journalism is still a relatively uncharted territory but argues that journalism is undergoing a profound transformation, in which the broadcasting model is giving way to emergent forms of bottom-up communication that, from his point of view, permeate transmedia journalism. As occurs with any type of transmedia storytelling, in transmedia journalism the story is told on various platforms and formats, and prosumers participate in constructing the narrative world.

The combination of the productive activity of the audience and the professional actions of journalists delineates varied possibilities for expanding the news in digital media connections. Transmedia journalism represents, therefore, an empirical and conceptual opportunity to expand news production and circulation of digital media based on multiplatform editorial planning.

According to Steensen and Ahva (2017), digitalization has brought a need to reassess the theories with which we make sense of journalism. Transmedia journalism subscribes to these transformations by providing theoretical and methodological subsidies to support the analytical exercise about professional practices more pertinent to the current technological and social context, as well as to support more sophisticated editorial projects. In this sense, this book portrays transmedia journalism practiced today on a global scale, presenting theoretical and methodological revisions of transmedia journalism, as well as case studies and comparative studies with various approaches.

Organization of the Book

This book addresses the current empirical-conceptual context of transmedia journalism in several theoretical-methodological approaches. These contributions, written by international experts in the field, delineate a global panorama of transmedia journalism by situating general features, empirical specificities, trajectories, and tendencies. The chapters put forward reflections based on case studies and thoughts involving virtual reality, algorithms, hashtags, and podcasts, among others. The book presents a logical chain of aspects that delineate transmedia journalism and its possible uses.

In the first chapter of *Exploring Transmedia Journalism in the Digital Age*, João Canavilhas (Universidade de Beira do Interior, Portugal) proposes a framework that can support journalists in producing transmedia contents that conveniently explore the characteristics of the media formats and languages involved, enabling the user to engage in the interpretation, change, and distribution of such contents.

Subsequently, in Chapter 2, Tobias Eberwein (Austrian Academy of Sciences, Austria) presents a reflection on transmedia journalism based on the following questions: How does journalistic storytelling evolve from analog to digital? What are the potentials of narrative journalism across multiple media types and platforms? And what effects do such transmedia narratives have on media users? These questions are answered based on a multi-method research design, which includes an explorative communicator study and an experiment with users.

In Chapter 3, Lila Luchessi (Universidad Nacional de Río Negro, Argentina) analyzes how instantaneity and viralization have affected not only journalistic activity but also information selection criteria and audiences' input on the Web. She based her research on the assessment that online osocial networks have modified the activities of the press, the actions of audiences, and the social perceptions.

In the view of André Fagundes Pase, Bruna Marcon Goss, and Roberto Tietzmann (Pontifical Catholic University of Rio Grande do Sul, Brazil), transmedia projects often need a longer time frame than usual news articles. In Chapter 4, these authors discuss how time plays an important role in transmedia journalism through an analysis of three cases: Blackhawk Down (published by the *Philadelphia Enquirer*, in 1997), Inside Disaster (released by PTV, in 2010), and Harvest of Change (published by the *Des Moines Register*, in 2014).

In Chapter 5, Nohemí Lugo Rodríguez (Tecnológico de Monterrey, Mexico) proposes a question-based model that focuses on transmedia design when an immersive journalism piece is integrated into a transmedia space. She reviews the narrative techniques and aesthetics of immersive experiences that may contribute to the design of the immersive piece and the transmedia space.

In Chapter 6, Kevin Moloney (Ball State University, United States), based on his current transmedia project, explores the design and execution of transmedia journalism projects to inform professional production and academic experimentation. He discusses how design thinking and audience targeting contribute to project success and presents the Refuge project as a design example of transmedia journalism.

In Chapter 7, Mariana Ciancia and Michele Mattei (Politecnico di Milano, Italy) explore journalism through the design lens. In the first part of the chapter, they describe the contemporary communication scenario, and in the second part, the authors suggest guidelines for applying a transmedia approach within the Italian news business in the form of a conceptual and operational tool.

In Chapter 8, Renira Rampazzo Gambarato (National Research University Higher School of Economics, Russia), Geane Carvalho Alzamora (Federal University of Minas Gerais, Brazil), and Lorena Peret Teixeira Tárcia (University Center of Belo Horizonte, Brazil) analyze how transmedia features are structured and implemented in the news coverage of the 2016 Summer Olympics in Rio de Janeiro, Brazil. The research findings indicate that the coverage presented systematic content expanded throughout various media platforms (a core characteristic of transmedia journalism) but involved limited mechanisms of audience engagement, particularly in terms of citizen participation.

In Chapter 9, Renira Rampazzo Gambarato (National Research University Higher School of Economics, Russia) discusses the participatory flair of transmedia journalism within the concreteness of urban spaces by examining The Great British Property Scandal, a transmedia experience designed to inform and engage the public and offer alternative solutions to the long-standing housing crisis in the United Kingdom.

In Chapter 10, Alexander Godulla and Cornelia Wolf (University of Leipzig, Germany) analyze the Future of Food, one of the largest transmedia projects in journalism. The authors consider that this case study provides insights into the modes and combinations of story elements and draws attention to challenges and opportunities for researchers, producers, and users.

In the view of Colin Porlezza (University of Zurich, Switzerland), Eleonora Benecchi (Università della Svizzera italiana, Switzerland), and Cinzia Colapinto (Ca' Foscari University of Venice, Italy), the analysis of the transmediality of the record-breaking podcast Serial can revitalize long-form journalism, particularly investigative journalism, and strengthen forms of slow and networked journalism. Chapter 11 looks at fan communities not only as an engaged audience, useful for commercial purposes, but also as a source for story development and production.

In Chapter 12, Luciana Andrade Gomes Bicalho (Federal University of Minas Gerais, Brazil) investigates how media activism movements appropriate hashtags to expand the narrative through social engagement. In this sense, hashtags appear as sign processes that perform a mediating function. The study analyzes the news production by the Brazilian media activism group Mídia Ninja [Ninja Media] based on the Peircean semiotic approach.

In Chapter 13, Geane Carvalho Alzamora (Federal University of Minas Gerais, Brazil) presents a case study of the transmedia dynamics of the multiplatform and participative journalistic program Especial

9-N [9-N Special], produced by channels TV3 and 3/24 in 2014, about the non-binding referendum on the sovereignty of Catalonia. The analysis was based on systematic observation of the program and its records on online social networks, seeking to gauge the nature and intensity of the transmedia circulation of the news based on the social engagement observed.

In Chapter 14, Anahí Lovato (National University of Rosario, Argentina) proposes a journey through an experience of transmedia journalism developed by the multimedia communication team at the National University of Rosario, Argentina. In this chapter, she analyzes Women for Sale, a transmedia documentary that addresses the trafficking of people for sexual exploitation purposes and reveals the creation of a complex narrative universe and the selection of stories, platforms, user experiences, and the execution of a transmedia project.

Last, in Chapter 15, Yvana Fechine and Sofia Costa Rêgo (Federal University of Pernambuco, Brazil) discuss how transmedia strategies are part of the construction of the ethos in television journalism, based on an analysis of Jornal da Record News, the first Brazilian newscast to be introduced as a transmedia production.

The chapters of *Exploring Transmedia Journalism in the Digital Age* jointly constitute a relevant contribution to academic research and to the professional practice of transmedia journalism. Although this subject is still rarely explored in the field of transmedia studies, the interest that transmedia journalism arouses around the world is undeniable, as attested by the studies integrated in this book.

Renira Rampazzo Gambarato
National Research University Higher School of Economics, Russia

Geane C. Alzamora
Federal University of Minas Gerais, Brazil

REFERENCES

Alzamora, G., & Tárcia, L. (2012). Convergence and transmedia: Semantic galaxies and emergent narratives in journalism. *Brazilian Journalism Research*, *8*, 22–34.

Bauman, Z. (2000). *Liquid modernity*. Cambridge, MA: Polity Press.

Bradshaw, P. (2017). *The online journalism handbook: Skills to survive and thrive in the digital age* (2nd ed.). London: Routledge.

Canavilhas, J. (2014). Jornalismo transmídia: Um desafio ao velho ecossistema midiático [Transmedia journalism: A challenge to old media ecosystem]. In D. Renó, C. Campalans, S. Ruiz, & V. Gosciola (Eds.), *Periodismo transmedia: Miradas múltiples* [Transmedia journalism: Multiple perspectives] (pp. 53–67). Barcelona, Spain: Editorial UOC.

Couldry, N., & Curran, J. (2003). *Contesting media power: Alternative media in a networked world*. Lanham, MD: Rowman and Littlefield.

Deuze, M. (2005). What is journalism? Professional identity and ideology of journalists reconsidered. *Journalism*, *6*(4), 442–464. doi:10.1177/1464884905056815

Dominguez, E. (2012). Periodismo transmedia, ¿nuevo o renovado? [Transmedia journalism, new or renewed?]. *Revista de los Estudios de Ciencias de la Informacion e Comunicacion*, 13. Retrieved from http://comein.uoc.edu/divulgacio/comein/es/numero13/articles/Article-Eva-Dominguez.html

Ford, S. (2007, April 5). Transmedia journalism: A story-based approach to convergence. *Futures of Entertainment*. Retrieved from http://www.convergenceculture.org/weblog/2007/04/transmedia_journalism_a_storyb.php

Gambarato, R. R., Alzamora, G., & Tárcia, L. (2016). Russian news coverage of the 2014 Sochi Winter Olympic Games: A transmedial analysis. *International Journal of Communication*, *10*, 1446–1469.

Gambarato, R. R., & Tárcia, L. (2017). Transmedia strategies in journalism. An analytical model for the news coverage of planned events. *Journalism Studies*, *18*(11), 1381–1399. doi:10.1080/1461670X.2015.1127769

Granados, N. (2016, October 3). What is media in the digital age? *Forbes*. Retrieved from https://www.forbes.com/sites/nelsongranados/2016/10/03/what-is-media-in-the-digital-age/#4989549a51ea

Jenkins, H. (2003). Transmedia storytelling. *MIT Technology Review*. Retrieved from https://www.technologyreview.com/s/401760/transmedia-storytelling

Moloney, K. T. (2011). *Porting transmedia storytelling to journalism* (Unpublished master's thesis). University of Denver, Denver, CO.

Newman, N. (2009, September 3). *The rise of social media and its impact on mainstream journalism*. Reuters Institute for the Study of Journalism, University of Oxford. Retrieved from: http://reutersinstitute.politics.ox.ac.uk/our-research/rise-social-media-and-its-impact-mainstream-journalism

Renó, D., & Flores, J. (2012). *Periodismo transmedia* [Transmedia journalism]. Madrid, Spain: Fragua Editorial.

Scolari, C. (2013). *Narrativas transmedia: Cuando todos los medios cuentan* [Transmedia narratives: When all the media count]. Barcelona, Spain: Deusto.

Steensen, S., & Ahva, L. (2017). *Theories of journalism in a digital age*. London: Routledge.

Acknowledgment

The editors would like to acknowledge with gratitude the involvement of all contributors in this project, especially each one of the 22 authors for their time and expertise dedicated to this book. Without their support, this book would not have become a reality. Our sincere gratitude goes also to Dr. Matthew Freeman for writing an inspiring foreword.

Renira Rampazzo Gambarato
National Research University Higher School of Economics, Russia

Geane C. Alzamora
Federal University of Minas Gerais, Brazil

Chapter 1
Journalism in the Twenty-First Century:
To Be or Not to Be Transmedia?

João Canavilhas
Universidade da Beira Interior, Portugal

ABSTRACT

Transmedia content has been the subject of several studies in the field of fiction, sustaining relative unanimity about the characteristics that this kind of content should have. In the field of journalism, the situation is fairly different due to its particular specificities. Multimedia, intermedia, or cross-media are often wrongly used as synonymous of transmedia, although there are important differences between all these concepts. In part, this misunderstanding is motivated by the fact that all of them relate to convergence processes in journalism, but a more detailed analysis allows us to find differences, highlighting transmedia as the most complete concept. This chapter proposes a framework that can support journalists in the production of transmedia contents that conveniently explore the characteristics of the involved media, using formats and languages that better fit the story, and enabling the user to engage in the interpretation, change, and distribution of these contents.

INTRODUCTION

The exhibition of highly successful series and movies has aroused the attention of the scientific community to transmedia contents and has contributed to an extensive discussion, which has helped to explain this concept when applied to fiction (Scolari, 2009, 2014; Gosciola, 2012; Bona & Souza, 2013). In journalism, the situation is quite different due to the field's specificities. Notions as intermedia (Rajewsky, 2002), multimedia (Salaverría, 2005) or cross-media (Veglis, 2012) are often confused with transmedia given their similarities, though they have important differences.

In the first part of this chapter, the author will present a detailed analysis to allow finding differences between diverse concepts about transmedia, emphasizing the difficulty to apply transmedia to journalism due to the complexity of its application in an activity where short-term periodicity is paramount. As a

DOI: 10.4018/978-1-5225-3781-6.ch001

starting point, the author uses the considerations about transmedia storytelling initially discussed by Jenkins (2003, 2006) because their simplicity help to transpose them into the field of journalism. To the author, a story can be considered transmedia when: 1) It is expanded through different media, formats and languages; 2) each of the story contents is autonomous, has a proper meaning and can be used as an entry point into the narrative; and 3) the audience participates in the story through the aggregation of elements and their sharing.

Jenkins compiled in his blog in 2009 what he has called the core principles of transmedia storytelling, which have been updated/improved over time. Those principles are: Spreadability vs. Drillability, Continuity vs. Multiplicity, Immersion vs. Extractability, World building, Seriality, Subjectivity and Performance. The simultaneous verification of all these conditions in a journalistic environment can be difficult due to their intrinsic characteristics, constraints related to production time, and a lack of human resources in the newsrooms. In the second part of the paper, the author explores those same principles in Moloney's (2011) perspective when applied to journalism.

In the third part, the chapter focuses on an example of a successful Portuguese transmedia journalism product called "E Se Fosse Consigo?" [What if it Were You?], a TV show expanded to a second TV channel, press, sites and social networks. Lastly, the paper delineates an indicative framework that can support the producers of transmedia contents in the elaboration of products that conveniently explore the characteristics of the involved media, using the formats and languages that better fit the story and enable the user to engage in the interpretation, change and distribution of these contents.

Having explained the approach to the concept of transmedia, and its transposition from fiction to the journalism field, the relation between journalism and the future remains to be understood, as mentioned in the title of this work. That is, why is there this link between transmedia journalism and journalism in the XXI century?

Recent studies show journalism trends for the next few years and among them are some that fit perfectly into transmedia journalism. The increasing consumption of online news has been reported every year by the Reuters Institute Digital News Report (Reuters Institute, 2017), which also confirms the increase in accesses to Internet through mobile devices (Rosenstiel & Mitchell, 2012). The use of these platforms facilitates the personalization of consumption (Lorenz, 2014) and the participation of users (Kammer, 2012), allowing the passage "from the monarchy of content to the republic of users" (Aguado & Güere, 2013, p.64). Other phenomena linked to transmedia journalism, such as the use of news gamification (Ferrer Conill & Karlsson, 2015), confirm that the future of journalism could undergo a transmedia process.

MANAGING CONCEPTS AROUND TRANSMEDIA

Updating a previous compilation (Canavilhas, 2013), it is worthwhile to approach the concept of transmedia to better isolate the characteristics that distinguish transmedia from other similar concepts, and try to integrate the discussion into the field of journalism.

The starting point is the concept of *multimedia* because it is the simplest and the most associated with journalism. According to Salaverría (2005), multimedia is "the ability, granted by the digital support, to combine in a single message at least two of the three following elements: text, image and sound" (p.32). In 2014, Salaverría simplified the definition, not because the previous one was too complex, but because he considered that the constituent elements of a multimedia product are now more than the ones initially enunciated (text, image and sound) and that in the future many more will appear, associating the concept of multimedia with human senses. Keeping in mind that the current elements of text, photography, graphics and videos appeal to vision, just as sound appeals to hearing and vibration appeals to the touch. In the future, it is predictable that temperature and shape may also rise associated with touch, and aromas associated with smell, and taste will be associated with the palate. In this sense, Salaverría (2014) proposes a simplified definition: To be multimedia, content must "combine at least two types of language into one message" (p. 39), but in this larger context of elements. The author stresses that, in fact, this simple combination is a very common feature, even in the pre-digital media, but it has become more visible with the emergence of the Internet because this is a medium clearly understood as the combination of contents previously distributed by massive mainstream media. It seems obvious that there is no possibility of confusing multimedia with transmedia.

The second concept analyzed is *cross-media*; which could be defined as "the production of any content (news, music, text, and images) for more than one media platform (for example print, web, and TV) within the same media organization" (Veglis, 2012, p.210). Salaverría (2014) calls that a kind of "multimedia as a platform" (p.27), referring to the logistic combination of several media. Boumans (2004) adds that the content must be delivered to a range of devices and "the use of more than one medium needs to support one theme/story/one purpose/one goal/one message" (p.4). Thus, a cross-media story uses several devices to deliver multimedia content that complement the purpose of empowering the story, but audiences do not necessarily participate in the spreading process, and that is why the concept cannot fit with the definition proposed by Jenkins.

Other possibility is the concept of *intermedia*, understood by Rajewsky (2005) in two dimensions: As a medial transposition, i.e. "the transformation of a given media product (a text, a film, etc.) or of its substratum into another medium" (p.52) or as a media combination, which is "the result or the very process of combining at least two conventionally distinct media or medial forms of articulation" (p. 52). The concept falls in line of previous ones, ignoring the audiences and the complementarity between elements of a certain story.

Finally, the concept of *transmedia* brings together some of the characteristics set out in a single formula: "stories that unfold across multiple media platforms, with each medium making distinctive contributions to our understanding of the world, a more integrated approach to franchise development than models based on urtexts and ancillary products" (Jenkins, 2006, p.334). As noted by Veglis (2012),

Transmedia is not just about multiple stories, but about creating a rich in-between space, an archive of shared meaning in-between different parts of the story. By using different media, it attempts to create "entry points" through which users can become immersed in a story world. (p.315)

Thus, adapting this concept to journalism becomes more complex than in cases of fiction, because the journalistic contents are always related to real events, which causes problems to create multiple entry points, but also because of the current reduced newsrooms and the fact that cycles of production in journalism are quite different from those in the fiction industry.

TRANSMEDIA JOURNALISM

The considerations about the transmedia phenomenon jumped from fiction to journalism, prompting several discussions due to the previously mentioned difficulty in adapting the concept to an activity marked by the periodicity of the publications, the short cycles of production, and to the use of a raw material difficult to handle: The unpredictability of society's daily reality.

As expected, in the early years, authors sought to label what defines transmedia journalism, focusing initially on two essential fields: 1) Narrative, namely the relation between content and media (Moloney, 2011; Renó & Flores, 2012; Alzamora & Tárcia, 2012), and 2) the user's participation in the contents (Davis, 2013). In addition to these fields, other authors have dealt with some particularities of transmedia journalism, such as the possible formats (Canavilhas, 2013), the factors that affect production (Hayes, 2011), and the design (Serrano Telleria, 2016), to name just a few examples, which will not be analyzed in this chapter.

Concerning the definition of transmedia journalism, Renó & Flores (2012) agree with Jenkin's definition, when they say that a narrative must use more than one medium and mention the obligation of the user's participation. The authors highlight the role of mobile devices in the process. Although they consider them a mere intervention by the users, it is enough to fulfill this requirement because it is not mandatory that their participation change the narrative. However, Scolari (2013), referring specifically to non-fictional transmedia, reinforces the significance of the user's interventions, which can change the narrative, to be considered as transmedia content: Therefore, this possibility must be considered in journalism. In fact, this is one of the greatest difficulties of journalistic content and the one that most divides researchers in the area: Whether the role of users can be limited to a low involvement participation (e.g. comment) or the participation must necessarily influence the development of the reported story. Livingstone (2004) notes that, the activity of viewing "is converging with reading, shopping, voting, playing, researching, writing, and chatting. Media are now used anyhow, anyplace, anytime" (p.76). This ubiquitous communication has created a media ecosystem where audiences are compelled to participate. The massification of smartphones with Internet connectivity, as well as the exponential growth of social networks, have created the conditions for the shift from a one-to-many system to a many-to-many system, requiring people's participation. That is why audience participation is crucial for the content to be considered transmedia, transforming the previous passive audience into a complex tangle of opinions and proposals that change and enrich the content.

If the issue of user's participation is important for the discussion, the relationship between media and content is equally fundamental. Keep in mind that news stories can be expanded through independent information nodes with their own meaning and that the nodes can be of three different types, each with its own significance. Therefore, according to Rost, Bernardi and Bergero (2017), "*expansion* is when each message adds inputs that expand and enrich the original story through information, opinions or inspiring ideas, ranging from the addition of sametime location data or space, into links, images, among others" (p.16). On the other hand, "*adaptation* is when you bring the same content to another medium or platform, adapting it to the narrative possibilities of the new support but without adding inputs. Story does not expand, it only adapts itself to another environment" (p.16). Lastly, "*tipped over* is when exactly the same content is replicated in another medium or platform, without respecting its own language" (p.16). This classification will be used in the analysis of the contents offered by the TV show "E Se Fosse Consigo."

One of the most comprehensive approaches to transmedia journalism, and the one that will be used here, emerges from a master thesis: Moloney (2011) revisits Jenkin's principles, adapting them to in-depth journalistic formats (features and documentary) because "daily journalism, with its time-constrained brevity, is not a viable option. Transmedia must be designed carefully and developed with a lengthy lead time to be effective" (p.12). Moloney (2011) "revisit[s] these principles, albeit in a new arrangement" (p.62):

Spreadability is about content dissemination. To be spreadable, the content must include the Internet in its dissemination strategy, whether in its own website, using aggregators, e-mail, newsletters or, the most popular way, through social networks. This feature is present today in almost all news, which facilitates its sharing by providing an icon of several social networks at the end of the content.

Drillability seems to be a strange concept to journalism because reporters aspire to tell the whole story. However, powered by the Internet, news is now faster, which forces journalists to leave reading tracks expanding the developments of the subject, linking to databases or more accurate information offered by other media. This is a very common feature in online news, which, in addition to the intext links, offers information related to the topic of the news, and background of the event itself, provided by the characteristic databases of this generation of journalism.

Continuity is something that, within journalism, may be visible in the editorial approach and in the style the media uses to address the issues. In a multiplatform story with different kinds of contents, and independently of the journalists that participate in it, the final work is cohesive and meets a set of common requirements.

Diverse and Personal in Viewpoint is a fundamental characteristic of journalism because objectivity depends on the selection of different voices in the story. In this case, it is about double diversity because it works on two levels: The different perspectives on the subject of the story but also the diversity in the authorship, i.e. the connection with other works that can add other points of view. In this case, user's participation can be seen as an important contribution to the diversity of views, since it introduces elements with the potential to open new paths to the news.

Immersion is another transmedia principle that challenges journalism. The author suggests the gamification as a way to reach the user's immersion in news contents. Another possibility is to be able to transport the reader to the place of the event, which can be done with multimedia contents and life stories with which people can identify themselves. This kind of "sense of being there" can still be achieved with the use of immersive technologies that explore virtual reality.

Extractability is about the things that users can do with the knowledge absorbed from the news. Contents must include enough information to help the users in their daily life and allow them to understand the world where they live. In fact, this is one of the principles of journalism, so it warrants to be enumerated to distinguish journalistic content from entertainment, something very important because transmedia initially ascended associated with this field.

Built in real worlds is one of the easiest principles to put into practice because the goal of a feature is exactly to transmit the local environment in the most helpful way and as close as possible to reality, which can be done using sound, for example.

The corollary of Jenkins' principles adapted by Moloney (2011) is *Inspiring to action*. "If journalists enter the profession hoping to inspire change and engage the public in democracy, facilitating a way for the public to act on information is a significant goal" (p.91). Combining this principle with extractability, it is possible to say that transmedia journalism keeps one of the essential journalism missions, even when using principles from fiction.

This is fundamental because one of the basic objectives of journalism, and especially long-form genres, is to inform users with accuracy. Helping citizens to perceive the world in which they live and, thus, help them to make decisions in electoral moments, is fundamental for the functioning of democracies. The recent phenomenon of fake news, and its possible influence in American elections, is a living example of what can happen in a context where information is insufficient or not diverse: The absence of a multitude of sources and the non-participation of users opens the field for phenomena, such as the so called "post-truth" with unforeseeable consequences.

The fulfillment of this objective—the provision of independent, varied, accurate, reliable information inserted in a meaningful context—depends on the proper function of the trilogy "media support » content architecture » user participation" in a media environment characterized by diversity and the emergence of bidirectional, interactive and personalized media that allows users to have a more effective role in the news process. Transmedia journalism could be one of the ways to offer this to the user, although only in long format contents due to the complexity of production, which includes eventual developments resulting from the participation of users.

E SE FOSSE CONSIGO? AN EXAMPLE OF TRANSMEDIA JOURNALISM IN PORTUGAL

Considering all that has been mentioned previously, for this research a Portuguese journalistic production that fulfills all the transmedia requirements was chosen, although one of the items only meets the minimum. To select an example was not a simple mission because of the demands it entailed. The TV show "E Se Fosse Consigo?" [What if it Were You?], broadcasted on the SIC channel in 2016, may be one of the few examples of transmedia content. Produced by Impresa, one of the largest Portuguese media groups, the program involved the national television channel SIC (Sociedade Independente de Televisão) [Television Independent Society] and the cable channel SIC Notícias as central elements. The narrative was complemented with the works published in the two most widely read press titles in its segments—Expresso (weekly newspaper) and Visão (news magazine) —and in online social networks.

The main show, broadcasted simultaneously by SIC (prime time) and SIC Notícias, was developed around situations in which actors staged cases of prejudice and social intolerance in public places. The reactions of anonymous citizens around the location where the staging took place were recorded through hidden cameras, seeking to analyze their ability to intervene in defense of fundamental values of society. This central element was contextualized with interviews conducted previously and interviews with the citizens recorded immediately after the staging had ended.

In the presentation of the show, Ricardo Costa, Impresa's general-director of information at the time, described it as a social experimentation program. SIC Notícias website stated that the show "tests the Portuguese's capacity of intervention in defense of others, departing from fictional situations" (SIC Notícias, 2016a) and asked: "To what extent do we say no to intolerance, prejudice, and violence?" (SIC Notícias, 2016a). Eight episodes have addressed topics such as racism, homophobia, domestic violence, dating violence, youth and alcohol, bullying, obesity, and elderly abuse.

The transmediality of the format occurs through developments on other platforms. At SIC Notícias, the show was followed by a studio debate led by the anchor, Conceição Lino, where experts and victims of the situations covered in the episodes participated. Issues and comments made by the audience on the show's Facebook page appeared on the ticker during the debate. Although the first television program was broadcasted on April 18, 2016, the show began its public debut on April 7, 2016, with the creation of the Facebook page and the publication of the first post on the 8th.

Welcome to the "E Se Fosse Consigo" page on Facebook. Here you can access more contents, besides those which you will see on SIC information program. I hope you enjoy the page, and join us and use your power to share it. This page was created to be even closer to our viewers. So please do not hesitate to send us comments, suggestions, criticisms or compliments. We value intelligent and well-informed contributions that can enrich our work and represent different points of view. We reserve the right not to accept inappropriate comments with offensive or commercial purposes. If you notice any of these situations, please be sure to let us know. (E Se Fosse Consigo?, 2016a)

In this first message, it is possible to find two features of transmediality: On the one hand, the use of a second platform; on the other, the opening of the show to the audience's participation. Moreover, on this day, the first promos of some themes to be addressed in the program were released as well as the show's jingle and the hashtag that was going to be used in various social networks: #esefossecontigo. The following day posts were dedicated to the introduction of the show to the press, to the video clip of the music used in the beginning and to the presence of the presenter in other information channels to talk about the program. Small reports about the first theme—racism—started to be published and will be analyzed. In parallel, two journalistic publications belonging to the same group—Visão and Expresso—published weekly pieces on the show's themes. Likewise, opinion polls and texts were published. In the online industry, "E Se Fosse Consigo" used the SIC Notícias website, the Expresso website and the Snapshat of this publication, and followed the Twitter publications that used the hashtag #esefossecon-sigo. In order to better understand the transmediality of the program, the first show will be analyzed: *Theme*: Racism; *Date of issue*: April 18, 2016; *SIC audience*: 1.2 million viewers.

Television

On April 16, 2016, two days before the show's debut, SIC and SIC Notícias news programs included a survey on racism, advertising that the subject would be the theme of "E Se Fosse Consigo?"

Most Portuguese do not consider themselves racist, however, as for accepting someone black in the family, the answer is different. These are the results of a Eurosondagem opinion study for SIC. Get to know the results of an opinion study on racism in Portugal. What do you have to say about these numbers? (SIC Notícias, 2016b)

The next day, April 17, 2016, the host of the show was interviewed during SIC's Evening News. On the 18th, after Jornal da Noite, the first program was shown on SIC, and this is the central element of the transmedia story. The content of this first program is summarized below.

After a small block of contextualization images, the first scene occurs: On a café's esplanade, a young woman presents her black boyfriend to her father. The father, surprised, does not greet the boy and tells his daughter that she has disappointed him by choosing a person of that color. He emphasizes that they have a different set of values and culture and, before leaving the place, tells her to find another boyfriend. From this moment on, the show continues with diverse contents on the subject, namely interviews (couples living in a similar situation, such as a member of Parliament (British)/a Representative (American), whose children felt victim of racism; a black judge who recounts some stories that happened in court; a businessman who talks about episodes that occurred in his business; social activists; and a musician). The program also included the repetition of an experience with black and white children where skin color preferences were analyzed, a video that explains how the scene used in this episode was rehearsed, and a fundamental part in the program—interviews with citizens who witnessed the staging and who had different reactions, ranging from complete ignorance in relation to the scene to those who directly intervened.

On the 19th, the day after the first episode was aired, the two channels broadcasted news about the program's premiere, using images and reactions on social media networks. SIC Notícias broadcasted, after the program, which was broadcasted simultaneously with SIC, a debate moderated by Conceição Lino, where a social psychologist, a writer, and a musician participated. In the opening of the debate, the journalist calls for the participation of viewers via Facebook. During the program, the phrases the viewers published on the social media network about the theme were presented on the ticker.

Printed Press

The weekly newspaper Expresso also participated in this transmedia content: In the paper edition of the 16th, a text entitled "More than 16% of the Portuguese say they are racist" (Expresso, 2016a) was published, using the poll results that were also broadcasted by SIC. Still in the group's written press, the news magazine Visão published a report named "Our subtle racism" (Carvalho 2016) on the 14th.

Online Media

The online versions of Expresso, Visão and SIC Notícias were also part of the transmedia process, disseminating some of the works published in traditional media, but also adding some personal contents. The first video on the theme of the first show—racism—was published on the Sic Notícias website on April 15, 2016, three days before the show's premiere on television. The text that accompanied the video was as follows:

The debate came in force on social media networks, opinions either overlap or are divided, as in all subjects not well studied and discussed. There is a belief that the Portuguese consider themselves tolerant and inclusive people. But is it really like that? In social relationships, when it comes to getting a job or making a list of deputies, does not the skin color weigh on criteria, choices, decisions? (Sic Notícias, 2016b)

In addition, on this day, a second video was published, this time with a group of 11th grade students discussing the theme in the classroom (SIC Notícias, 2016b). The next day, April 16, 2016, a video was published with the survey on racism, a content produced for the television channels and used on the program. On the 17th, a new video with testimonials that were to be used in the show the next day was published. Likewise, on the same day, they published the video with the children's experience, launched with the question: "To what extent are children influenced or aware of what racism is? See the responses of our respondents aged 6 to 8" (SIC Notícias, 2016c). On the 18th, before the program was broadcasted, excerpts of videos to be included in the program were published on the website. That same day, after the TV show aired, the program was fully available on the website. The debate was also made available.

In the following days, the website offered the expanded interviews of some statements that appeared in the program, prolonging the discussion on the subject.

The online version of Expresso presented two contents on the subject during this period. On April 18, 2016, the report "I am not racist, I even have a friend..." (Expresso, 2016b), which included text and video excerpts, was presented. In the following day, an opinion article by Henrique Monteiro (2016) named "The racism of soft Portuguese," was published.

Social Media

Facebook (E Se Fosse Consigo?, n.d.): On April 15, 2016, the video published on the SIC Notícias website was shared with the 11th grade student group, generating several comments. The next day, another video was published, reversing the order used on the Sic Notícias website. The previously mentioned survey was also published on Facebook and the post was highly commented and shared. On the 17th and 18th, several posts with videos that would later be broadcasted on the program and commenting on Expresso's article were published. Conceição Lino's interview with SIC's Jornal da Noite was published as well. On April 18, 2016, in an exclusive video for Facebook, Conceição Lino called for citizen participation on Facebook to express their opinion on the topic and intervene in the debate. A day after the show's premiere, the debate continued on social media networks, adding interviews with reactions and other contents that pursued to extend the media effect of the program.

Snapchat: Among other contents, there is a video made for Snap-Expresso (name of Snapchat's Expresso channel) by Iryna Shev (E Se Fosse Consigo?, 2016) in which the journalist begins by presenting the theme and interviews with the reactions of youngsters after watching a video of the program on their mobile phones.

Twitter: The program did not officially use this social media network, but the reactions that just used the hashtag #esefosseconsigo were followed and used in some content produced for the other media in the group.

In a first approach, all the principles enunciated by Moloney (2011) have been fulfilled in this program, although in some cases their presence is minimal. Studying the show, it is possible to confirm the *spreadability* because they used the websites of SIC Notícias, Facebook and Snapchat to engage people and spread the content on different platforms and attract users. Hence, the hybrid media strategy followed by Impresa resulted in thousands of content shares on Facebook and Twitter. *Drillability* is confirmed in the connection between online news and other media contents about the subject of the show that results from journalistic research. The connection between contents is quite visible and confirms a web of knowledge about racism and the way Portuguese society is dealing with this issue. The *Continuity* of the contents is easily achieved because this is a transmedia story from the same media group and the presence of an editorial orientation and cohesion of the whole content is clearly observed.

The *Diverse and Personal in Viewpoint* is partially guaranteed in the studio interviews and in the content, when the journalist talks with different people placed around the scene. However, this content would need to deepen the audience's point of view: Although the debate organized by SIC Notícias showed some user's opinions in the ticker, which allows it to meet the basic criteria, this participation did not change the content because the journalist did not introduce these questions or observations in the discussion between experts.

Immersion is another difficult characteristic to identify in this product. Nevertheless, it is in the personal stories about white/black couples, children, artists, activists, and a huge variety of actors with which audiences can identify themselves because of its diversity. The immersion can be inferred due to the use of the hidden camera during the filming of the scenes, since this transports the user to the situation. Another more effective way to create immersion would have been to develop an online game to measure participants' racism, something that would be closer to what is done in fiction.

The last three principles are in the matrix of the content: *Extractability* is one of the goals of the program because they want to sensitize people to a social problem called racism using a situation from the *real world* (racism) and *Inspiring to action*, i.e., encouraging people to react against all forms of racial discrimination.

Lastly, looking at the type of content used by the classification proposed by Rost, Bernardi and Bergero (2017), it can be concluded that all types were used. The "expansion" is materialized in the survey, articles published in the press (Expresso and Visão) and the work produced for Snapchat, since they are contents that add inputs that enrich and expand the story. In the case of "adaptation", its presence is mainly visible on the Internet, albeit on a reduced scale because it has been limited in some cases to the reduced edition of some content used in television: It is the same content, on another platform, but without adding information to the story. Finally, "tipped over" was the type of content most used, especially on social networks, which simply reproduced the videos and news received from the sites or the newspapers.

CONCLUSION

The transmedialization of journalistic content is not a simple process. The examples of transmedia journalism that fulfill all the core principles of transmedia storytelling are scarce and, as a rule, imply the existence of a set of human resources unusual in actual newsrooms, which are experiencing a time of crisis. Therefore, this research proposes a simplification of the above-mentioned principles, in a formulation close to that advanced by other authors (Renó & Flores, 2012; Rost, Bernardi & Bergero, 2017). Thus, to be considered transmedia, a journalistic content should meet three conditions: 1) Full integration between content and platforms. The content should be multiplatform, since the effectiveness of each type of content depends on its use in the specific platform for which it was initially created, i.e, using expansive or adapted contents, including immersive contents, ranging from the simplicity of 360º images to the use of augmented reality and virtual reality. The use of the Internet is mandatory. 2) Each story must be composed by independent chunks of information and they should be sufficiently meaningful to be used as an entry point into the narrative. These chunks should have links to more than one chunk of the same story, to allow multiple reading paths and, consequently, enable a personalized navigation for each user. 3) The user should be able to contribute to the story by adding elements that can change the content. This participation may vary between low complexity (comments in the news or posts) and high complexity (joining contents that change and/or expand the course of the narrative).

Taking into consideration the three rules previously mentioned, and in line with what was mentioned by Renó and Flores (2012), there is a media platform that can contribute strongly to improve a transmedia journalistic narrative: Mobile media. Being a stable and user-friendly technology, an object for personal use and having Internet connection, the smartphone can be exploited in two ways: As a consumption platform and as participation interface.

As a consumer platform, the smartphone is an everyday life object that accompanies its owner permanently. It became, therefore, an extension of the senses in a personal level. For these reasons, the smartphone allows the maximum degree of news personalization, which can happen by consumer drive (preferences declared voluntarily), by their habits of consumption (cookies in browsers) or by the location of the consumer powered by the Global Positioning System (GPS). As a platform for receiving content, smartphones have another important advantage in the context of transmedia journalism because they facilitate one of the most difficult strands to be achieved: Immersive contents. This occurs because these devices allow an easy adaptation to virtual reality glasses and because they are already a gaming platform (gamification of information). In terms of user participation interface, the smartphone facilitates the whole process of contributing to the story, since its multimedia recording capacity (photo, video, and sound) and its easiness to send content or comments is an incentive for a greater engagement of users in the expansion of transmedia products. By fulfilling the three conditions previously stated, and using smartphones as a fundamental part of the system, all the fundamental rules of transmedia journalism are fulfilled.

Applying the three rules to the content studied in this chapter, it can be said that "E Se Fosse Consigo?" is a transmedia production, although the perfect integration between content and platforms does not always occur. Actually, the shovelware occurs in many situations, with the replication of the same content in diverse platforms, but sometimes with small adaptations, such as reducing the duration of the videos. The connection between story chunks exists and the user could start reading from several contents and platforms without problems to understand the subject of the program. The contribution of the user can occur through the participation in the television show itself, but also via the websites and online social media network comments, which were referred by the newspapers, giving rise to new content about the subject. The role of smartphones was not measured in this chapter, but could be analyzed in the new season of the program scheduled for 2017.

REFERENCES

Aguado, J. M., & Güere, H. (2013). Comunicación móvil: Ecosistema digital e industrias culturales [Mobile communication: Digital ecosystem and cultural industries] In J. M. Aguado, C. Feijoó, C. Martínez, & I. Martínez (Eds.), *La comunicación móvil: Hacia un nuevo ecosistema digital* [Mobile communication: Towards a new digital ecosystem] (pp. 57–87). Barcelona: Editorial Gedisa.

Alzamora, G., & Tárcia, L. (2012). Convergence and transmedia: Semantic galaxies and emerging narratives in journalism. *Brazilian Journalism Research*, *8*(1), 23–34.

Bona, R. F., & Souza, M. P. (2013). A narrativa transmidia na era da convergência: Análise das transposições midiáticas de the Walking Dead [Transmedia narrative in the age of convergence: Analysis of the media transpositions in the Walking Dead]. *Razón y Palabra*, *82*, 1–16.

Boumans, J. (2004). *Cross-media: E-Content Report 8*. ACTeN—Anticipating Content Technology Needs. Retrieved from http://www.sociologia.unimib.it/DATA/Insegnamenti/13_3299/materiale/04%20-%20jak%20boumans%20cross-media%20acten%20aug%202004.pdf

Canavilhas, J. (2013). Jornalismo Transmedia: Um desafio ao velho ecossistema mediático [Transmedia journalism: A challenge to the old media ecosystem]. In D. Renó, C. Campalans, S. Ruiz, & V. Gosciola (Eds.), *Periodismo Transmedia: Miradas múltiples* [Transmedia journalism: Multiple views] (pp. 53–68). Bogotá: Editorial Universidad del Rosario.

Carvalho, A. M. (2016, April 13). O nosso racismo subtil [Our subtil racism]. *Visão*. Retrieved from http://visao.sapo.pt/actualidade/sociedade/2016-04-13-O-nosso-racismo-subtil

Davis, C. H. (2013). Audience value and transmedia products. In T. Storsul & A. Krumsvik (Eds.), *Media Innovations* (pp. 175–190). Goteborg: Nordicom.

Se Fosse Consigo, E. (2016a, April 8). Bem-vindo à página do E Se Fosse Consigo no Facebook [Welcome to the E Se Fosse Consigo Facebook page] [Facebook post]. Retrieved from https://www.facebook.com/esefosseconsigo/posts/983757405065882

Se Fosse Consigo, E. (2016b, April 19). O Snap-Expresso (nome do canal Snapchat do Expresso) foi para a rua perguntar aos jovens "E Se Fosse Con(s)tigo?" [The Snap-Expresso (name of the Snapchat channel of Expresso) went to the streets to ask youngsters "What if it Were You?"] [Facebook post]. Retrieved from https://www.facebook.com/esefosseconsigo/videos/990130521095237

Se Fosse Consigo, E. (n.d.). In *Facebook*. Retrieved August 03, 2017, from https://www.facebook.com/esefosseconsigo

Expresso. (2016a, April 16). *Mais de 16% dos portugueses dizem que são racistas* [More than 16% of Portugueses declare that they are racist]. Retrieved from http://expresso.sapo.pt/sociedade/2016-04-16-Mais-de-16-dos-portugueses-dizem-que-sao-racistas

Expresso. (2016b, April 16). *Não sou racista, até tenho um amigo….* [I am not racist, I even have a friend…]. Retrieved from http://expresso.sapo.pt/sociedade/2016-04-18-Nao-sou-racista-ate-tenho-um-amigo

Ferrer Conill, R., & Karlsson, M. (2015). The gamification of journalism. In H. Gangadharbatla & D. Z. Davis (Eds.), *Emerging research and trends in gamification* (pp. 356–383). Hershey, PA: IGI Global.

Gosciola, V. (2012). A máquina de narrativa transmídia: Transmidiação e literatura fantástica [The transmedia narrative machine: Transmission and fantastic literature]. *Revista Comunicación*, *10*(1), 131–139.

Hayes, G. P. (2011). *How to write a transmedia production bible*. Retrieved from http://videoturundus.ee/bible.pdf

Jenkins, H. (2003). *Transmedia storytelling: Moving characters from books to films to video-games can make them stronger and more compelling*. Retrieved from https://www.technologyreview.com/s/401760/transmedia-storytelling/

Jenkins, H. (2006). *Convergence Culture: Where old and new media collide*. New York: New York University Press.

Kammer, A. (2013). Audience participation in the production of online news: Towards a typology. *Nordicom Review*, *3*, 113–126.

Livingstone, S. (2004). The challenge of challenging audiences, or, what is the audience researcher to do in the age of the Internet? *European Journal of Communication*, *19*(1), 75–86. doi:10.1177/0267323104040695

Lorenz, M. (2014). Personalização: Análise aos 6 graus [Customization: 6 degrees analysis]. In J. Canavilhas (Ed.), *Webjornalismo: 7 caraterísticas que marcam a diferença* [Webjournalism: 7 characteristics that make a difference] (pp. 137–158). Covilhã: Livros Labcom.

Moloney, K. T. (2011). *Porting transmedia storytelling to journalism* (Unpublished master's thesis). University of Denver, Denver, CO.

Monteiro, H. (2016, April 19). O racismo do português suave [The racism of the soft Portuguese]. *Expresso Online*. Retrieved from http://expresso.sapo.pt/blogues/blogue_chamem_me_o_que_quiserem/2016-04-19-O-racismo-do-portugues-suave

Rajewski, I. O. (2005). Intermediality, intertextuality, and remediation: A literary perspective on intermediality. *Intermédialités*, *6*, 43–64.

Renó, D., & Flores, J. (2012). *Periodismo transmedia. Reflexiones y técnicas para el ciberperiodista desde los laboratorios de medios interactivos* [Transmedia journalism. Reflections and techniques for the cyberjournalist from the interactive media labs]. Madrid: Fragua.

Reuters Institute. (2017). *Digital news report*. Retrieved from http://www.digitalnewsreport.org/

Rosenstiel, T., & Mitchell, A. (2012). *Future of mobile news. The explosion in mobile audiences and a close look at what it means for news*. Retrieved from http://www.journalism.org/files/legacy/Futureofmobilenews%20_final1.pdf

Rost, A., Bernardi, M. T., & Bergero, I. (2017). *Transmedia: La narración distribuida de la noticia* [Transmedia: The distributed narration of the news]. Neuquén: PubliFadecs.

Salaverría, R. (2005). *Redacción periodística en Internet* [Newspaper writing techniques on the Internet]. Pamplona: EUNSA.

Salaverría, R. (2014). Multimedialidade: Informar para cinco sentidos [Multimediality: To inform to five senses] In J. Canavilhas (Ed.), *Webjornalismo: 7 caraterísticas que marcam a diferença* [Webjournalism: 7 characteristics that make a difference] (pp. 25–52). Covilhã: Livros Labcom.

Scolari, C. (2009). Transmedia storytelling. Implicit consumers, narrative worlds and branding in contemporary media production. *International Journal of Communication*, *3*, 586–606.

Scolari, C. (2013). *Narrativas transmedia. Cuando todos los medios cuentan* [Transmedia narratives. When all media count]. Barcelona: Deusto.

Scolari, C. (2014). Lostología: Narrativa transmediática, estrategias crossmedia e hipertelevisión [Lostology: Transmedia narrative, crossmedia strategies and hypertelevision]. In C. Campalans, D. Renó, & V. Gosciola (Eds.), *Narrativas transmedia: Entre teorías y prácticas* [Transmedia narratives: Between theory and praxis] (pp. 137–163). Bogotá: Editorial UOC.

Serrano Tellería, A. (2016). Transmedia journalism: Exploring genres and interface design. *Trípodos*, *38*, 67–85.

Notícias, S. I. C. (2016a, June 14). *E se fosse consigo?* [What if it were you?]. Retrieved from http://sicnoticias.sapo.pt/programas/e-se-fosse-consigo

Notícias, S. I. C. (2016b, April 15). *Há ou não racismo em Portugal?* [Is there or not racism in Portugal?]. Retrieved from http://sicnoticias.sapo.pt/programas/e-se-fosse-consigo/racismo/2016-04-15-Ha-ou-nao-racismo-em-Portugal--1

Notícias, S. I. C. (2016c, April 17). *O racismo explicado às crianças* [Racism explaned to children]. Retrieved from http://sicnoticias.sapo.pt/programas/e-se-fosse-consigo/racismo/2016-04-17-O-racismo-explicado-por-criancas

Veglis, A. (2012). From cross media to transmedia reporting in newspaper articles. *Publishing Research Quarterly*, *28*(4), 313–324. doi:10.1007/s12109-012-9294-z

KEY TERMS AND DEFINITIONS

Journalistic Convergence: A phenomenon characterized by the disappearance of frontiers and/or integration of different mass media that can occur in the fields of content, production processes, professional activities, and business models.

Journalistic Shovelware: Republication of journalistic contents without the necessary adaptation to the characteristics of the new media.

Long-Form Journalism Contents: Extensive digital journalistic formats that require an in-depth research and production process and should also include extensive multimedia resources.

Media Ecosystem: Set of different media and its relations with environments, structures, contents, and audiences.

Portable Devices: Portable and personal communication devices capable of receiving online news, such as smartphones and tablets.

Post-Truth: Related to circumstances in which objective facts are less influential in shaping public opinion than appeals to emotion and personal belief.

Ubiquitous Journalism: Journalism developed from anywhere and intended for users holding mobile reception devices.

Chapter 2
A Question of Trust:
Functions and Effects of Transmedia Journalism

Tobias Eberwein
Austrian Academy of Sciences, Austria

ABSTRACT

Narrative forms of journalistic reporting are traded as a sheet anchor in many newsrooms, as editors hope that they could brave the never-ending storm of the media crisis. But how does journalistic storytelling evolve from analog to digital? What are the potentials of narrative journalism across multiple media types and platforms? And what effects do such transmedia narratives have on media users? These questions are answered based on a multi-method research design, which includes both an explorative communicator study and an experiment with users. The investigation demonstrates that journalists expect narratives in digital media surroundings to invigorate the authenticity and comprehensibility of their coverage. This hope, however, only partly becomes a reality on the side of the recipients. Indeed, users judge multimedia online reportages to be more emotional than monomedia offline pieces, but as far as remembering and comprehending their contents is concerned, print texts are more effective.

INTRODUCTION: ACCELERATE, DECELERATE

In the digital age, journalistic production is influenced by manifold processes of uninhibited *acceleration*: Not only the time span between an event and its coverage becomes shorter and shorter, particularly in the new media; moreover, there is much evidence to indicate an increased density of journalists' working days (through an increased amount of tasks, both journalistic and non-journalistic) and, thereby, also a reduction in time per task, which results in a reduced length of the prevalent attention cycles and, in many cases, an increased publication frequency (see Krüger, 2014). The consequences are clearly perceptible in everyday news work: While it is often a matter of seconds which newsroom can boast to break a story first, pressure on journalistic actors is notably on the rise. At the same time, the quality of journalistic output appears to be at stake, in many instances: When speed becomes the paramount aim of editorial routines, other quality criteria—such as accuracy, truthfulness, comprehensibility, etc.—necessarily fall behind (see e.g. Eberwein, 2015a).

DOI: 10.4018/978-1-5225-3781-6.ch002

In reaction to this maladjustment, many media scholars—as well as practitioners—are calling for a fundamental redefinition of journalism's identity and its professional purpose (see e g. Lee, 2014). Rather than following the general obsession with speed, which has become characteristic for most online news platforms around the globe, they argue that *deceleration* is the key to help journalism (re)gain public trust and to fulfill its social function in the best possible way (see e.g. Greenberg, 2007). Particularly high hopes are nourished by the approach of a narrative journalism, which is often said to have multifaceted positive effects, e.g. for generating attention for certain topics and communicating them in a most comprehensible manner (see e.g. Boynton, 2005; Kramer & Call, 2007; Sims, 2007). Success proves them right: Apparently, narrative forms of journalistic reporting have recently been experiencing a proper upsurge in many newsrooms (see e.g. Eberwein, 2013). In fact, quite a few editors are trading storytelling techniques as a sheet anchor that could not only help them to sell their products, but also highlight the social significance of journalistic writing in general and, thus, brave the never-ending storm of the ongoing media crisis, which has irritated the profession to the core.

Indeed, various experimental studies have shown that narrative forms of journalistic reporting have many advantages when it comes to explaining an ever more complex social reality to readers and viewers, while the traditional news form often interferes with remembering and comprehending journalistic contents, among other things (for an overview see Frey, 2014). However, many questions are still unanswered in this context: What does this mean for the future of journalistic genres in the Internet age? How does journalistic storytelling evolve from analog to digital? What are the potentials of narrative journalism across multiple media types and platforms? And what effects do such transmedia narratives have on media users?

Up to now, questions like these have not been analyzed systematically—neither in communication and media studies, nor in adjacent academic disciplines. This paper is supposed to assemble some first answers based on an innovative multi-method design, which combines an explorative communicator study with a reception experiment.[1] Before the empirical studies are presented in detail, however, it is necessary to provide a brief sketch of the underlying theoretical concepts and the previous state of relevant research in this field.

JOURNALISTIC STORYTELLING: DEFINITIONS AND STATE OF RESEARCH

Scientific debates about storytelling have regularly been receiving high levels of attention in recent years (see e.g. Kleine Wieskamp, 2016). The cause for this concern can be seen in an increased interest among media practitioners in the various developments associated with this term: Not only in journalism, but also in other professional contexts—particularly in PR and marketing—the cultivation of well-told stories is considered to be a quality indicator (see Fog et al., 2010; Prinzing, 2015). However, it is striking to see that it remains unclear what this actually means, both in media practice and research. The heterogeneity of scientific definitions of terms like narration, story or narrativity is exemplified by a recent content analysis (Frey & Früh, 2014), for which a broad spectrum of different journal articles from this field of research has been evaluated. They allude to manifold sources from the most different scientific contexts, thereby referring to a multitude of possible key characteristics. So far, a consensus about a universally applicable definition is not in sight.

The study presented here follows an approach that originates from the narratological theories in literary studies and can, therefore, rely on a comparatively long tradition of academic inquiry (for an introduction see e.g. Fludernik, 2009; Schmid, 2010). In this sense, narrations can be defined as representations of real or fictitious events that are communicated by a *narrator* to one (or more) *narratee(s)* (see Prince, 1987, p. 58). They adhere to particular *structural* (e.g. orientation, complication, evaluation, resolution, coda; see Labov & Waletzky, 1967), *stylistic* (e.g. poetic language, detailedness/clearness, images/metaphors; see Lausberg, 1998) and *formal* (dissociation from description, argumentation or statistical representations; see for instance Brooks & Warren, 1979) attributes and are usually designed to create certain *effects* (such as suspense, empathy or entertainment; see Brewer & Lichtenstein, 1982).

By now, the notion seems to be generally accepted that the production of narrative texts is by no means restricted to the literary field, but can also result in non-literary publications (see Berning, 2010). Especially in journalism, narrative forms are usually associated with typical genres such as reportage, feature or profile (see Abrahamson, 1995; Hartsock, 2000), which are differentiated from other genres such as "inverted pyramid" news, commentary, interview, etc. (see e.g. Pöttker & Kornilov, 2010). In many journalistic cultures, narrative patterns of reporting have in fact turned into an explicit alternative to the mainstream of traditional news journalism—with the aim of counterbalancing its limitations and creating a more effective "third way" of describing social reality, in the territory between journalism and literature (see Connery, 1990; Eberwein, 2015c). By now, the historical development of this literary journalism has been described quite thoroughly by a large scope of individual studies (for a first overview see the *Selected bibliography of scholarship and criticism examining literary journalism* by the International Association for Literary Journalism Studies, 2011), even from a comparative perspective (see e.g. Bak & Reynolds, 2011; Keeble & Tulloch, 2012), although a contextualizing social history of the genre and its specific functions still remains a desideratum (see also Eberwein, 2013, p. 102).

Besides, the links between narratology and journalism studies have also been put to the test only insufficiently so far, although the reference to narratological theories would be exceedingly advantageous for journalism scholars, for several reasons: First of all, it is conducive to systematizing the basic definitions in this area of research, thus illustrating what journalistic storytelling actually is—or can be. At the same time, it provides a comprehensive analytical framework that allows for a structured approach to the investigation of journalistic (and other) narratives (see Andrews, Squire & Tamboukou, 2013).

Moreover, the historical development of relevant models in the field of narratology already points to an illuminating shift of the analytical perspective, which is also relevant for this study: While classical discriminations such as Stanzel's typology of "narrative situations" (see Stanzel, 1984) were primarily focusing on the relationship between the narrator of a text and the figures that he reports about, many younger theoretical approaches display an increasing interest in the role of the reader in the process of receiving narrative communication (for a general view see e.g. Suleiman & Crosman, 1980). Such a shift of focus seems to be even more obvious when—as in our case—a research project is supposed to reconstruct how journalistic storytelling advances from traditional print reportage to the innovative multimedia productions that are currently sprouting on various online news sites across all journalism cultures. In order to live up to the reality of narrative journalism in digital media surroundings and across multiple media types and platforms, conventional narrative theories need to be adapted—among other things to specify the changing relationship between author and reader. The necessity of such a theory modification becomes evident in the case of new multimedia and interactive forms of storytelling that go beyond traditional narrative techniques in journalism and literature (see Bull, 2010; Penn, 2013). Well-known international landmark productions such as *The New York Times*' "Snow fall" (Branch, 2012), *The Guardian*'s "Firestorm" (Henley, 2013) or "Killing Kennedy" by *National Geographic* (National Geographic Channel, 2013) may serve as interesting case studies in this context, as they exemplify different degrees of multimedia integration and user interaction and, thus, demonstrate how the reader can take over a more or a less active role in the process of absorbing and co-creating journalistic narratives online. They also offer meaningful examples of transmedia storytelling (Jenkins, 2003): By complementing the conventional offline coverage by the respective newsroom and moving the featured protagonists across different media platforms, they are expected to enhance the reception experience of their users and catapult narrative journalism to a new level (see e.g. Moloney, 2011; Schlichting 2015; Gambarato & Tárcia, 2017).

Empirical research has not yet tackled these developments in a satisfactory manner. Indeed, there is a large quantity of experimental studies that discuss cognitive, emotional, evaluative and motivational-conative effects of narrative forms of communication within and outside of journalism (besides Frey, 2014, see also Bilandzic & Kinnebrock, 2009; Echterhoff & Straub, 2003, 2004; Green, Strange & Brock, 2013; Hinyard & Kreuter, 2007; Ricketts, 2007). However, the specific case of journalistic transmedia storytelling is largely blanked out. After all, existing research indicates that narrative communication apparently has the ability to positively influence intended effects, such as remembering and comprehending specific contents (see Machill, Köhler & Waldhauser, 2006) or the emotional experience of a given text (see Adaval & Wyer Jr., 1998). The impact, however, can vary, depending on moderating influences such as gender, age, social status and previous knowledge (see Flath, 2013; Vanoost, 2017), but also due to different modes of representation, which may include or exclude the use of photos, sound effects, etc. (see Lee & Gretzel, 2012)—a first clue leading to the assumption that the effects of monomedia newspaper reportages and transmedia reportages can be expected to differ.

However, it remains unclear in previous studies how exactly these differences come to manifest themselves. Indeed, quite a few scholars have been ascribing clear advantages to online journalism in general, which they believe to be superior to traditional print coverage because of its hypertextuality, multimediality and interactivity (see e.g. Steensen, 2011). Nevertheless, several reception experiments were also able to detect counterproductive effects: Particularly among recipients without a discernible affinity to web applications, for instance, the use of hyperlinks, audio and video elements as well as the active inclusion of users often lead to a feeling of disorientation and cognitive overload (see e.g. Opgenhaffen & d'Haenens, 2011) with negative consequences for the overall impact of the particular coverage.

Investigations of the specific effects of web-based journalistic narratives in comparison to offline newspaper or magazine reportages do not exist so far. What is missing, therefore, is a combination of the two above-mentioned strands of research regarding the effects of narrative communication, on the one hand, and online communication, on the other hand. This desideratum is going to be amended by the multi-method study that is detailed in the following parts of this chapter. Accordingly, two central research questions need to be answered:

1. Which specific aims and effects do reporters in print and online newsrooms strive to reach with their narrative texts, and in how far do the two actor groups differ from each other?
2. Can these aims be adequately realized with the available narrative means offline and online, or in other words: Do the intended effects really impact on the side of the recipients?

JOURNALISTIC STORYTELLING IN TRANSITION: A MULTI-METHOD APPROACH

In order to probe into these questions, the research project presented in this chapter made sure to implement a two-step analytical design, which initially—on the basis of semi-structured interviews—highlighted the perspective of journalistic actors on the object of analysis. Subsequently, the focus was redirected to the perspective of the recipients, which was evaluated with the help of an experimental user survey. Thus, the superordinate aim of the study was to bridge the usual gap between communicator and reception research—a scientific strategy that has been postulated more and more vehemently in recent years, without having become a common practice up till today (see Dohle & Loosen, 2014).

The *communicator study* intended to retrace and comprehend current changes in the field of journalistic storytelling, in order to lay the foundation for a more systematic analysis of this widely neglected area of media research. Following an explorative approach, a total of 30 problem-centered interviews (see Witzel, 2000) with reporters from selected print and online newsrooms of German-language news media were conducted during Winter term 2012/2013. The interviewees were handpicked, in order to represent different types of print media (e.g. daily newspapers such as *Süddeutsche Zeitung* and *Frankfurter Allgemeine Zeitung*, weekly newspapers such as *Die Zeit*, or news magazines such as *Der Spiegel*) and their online counterparts as well as different positions in the newsroom hierarchy (e.g. freelancer, reporter, editor-in-chief). The interviews followed a half-standardized field manual that was supposed to help the interviewers to structure the relevant issues of the analysis and reflect them with the interviewees in a comprehensive manner. This manual comprised different thematic blocks, which focused, among other things, on the interviewees' professional self-concept, typical workflows in their newsroom, and the practical aims and objectives that they want to reach with their publications. The interviews were conducted face to face or via telephone and lasted up to 80 minutes. They were recorded, and afterwards, key passages were transcribed in full, before being evaluated with the help of a qualitative content analysis (see Mayring, 2014). By this means, it became possible to develop a set of assumptions that stressed the differences between printed and web-based reportages in convergent media spaces, particularly with regard to their specific benefits and intended effects.

These effects were subsequently analyzed in the context of a *reception experiment* (see e.g. Thorson, Wicks & Leshner, 2012) during Summer term 2013, for which exactly 100 probands were confronted with monomedia (print) and multimedia (online) versions of different journalistic narrations from the same news outlets as examples of transmedia journalism in practice. The members of two control groups each read a reportage that had been published in the German quality print media *Süddeutsche Zeitung*[2] and *Der Spiegel*[3] in a similar form. The test persons in the two treatment groups received the same articles on screen, with audio and video elements added to the original text, but otherwise congruent contents. Thus, the multimediality of the journalistic coverage, which was intentionally manipulated by the research team, served as the independent variable in the experimental research setting; the aim of the study was to measure its impact on the process of remembering and comprehending the presented topics as well as other qualities of the narrative approach offline and online (dependent variables). The probands were recruited with the help of a quota plan that was differentiated based on sociodemographic attributes (including gender, age and educational background); the allocation to the four test groups adhered to the principle of randomization. In order to avoid socially desirable behavior, the test persons were initially kept in the dark about the intention of the experiment: They were only instructed as vaguely as possible, by indicating that the research project was designed to evaluate "new trends in journalistic storytelling." In the test situation, under laboratory conditions, each proband first had time to read (and if necessary, re-read) one of the assigned reportages, which could take up to 20 minutes. Directly after the process of reception, the test persons completed a fully standardized (face-to-face) survey with 18 questions altogether, which, among other things, included an examination of how many basic facts they had remembered and if they had understood the article's central meaning. Additionally, it was also tested how the participants themselves would rate the quality of the different reportages.

The following passages of this chapter are going to document key findings from both steps of the analysis, which are juxtaposed afterwards in order to assess in how far the aims and intentions of journalistic storytellers, both offline and online, are actually realized on the side of the recipients.

RESULTS

From the Perspective of Professional Communicators...

The qualitative communicator study demonstrates that the self-concepts and professional aims of reporters in print and online media hardly differ: Both actor groups have in common that their narrative strategy of communication is understood as a purposeful opposition to conventional news work, which is still the dominant pattern of coverage, both in analog and in digital media surroundings. According to the interviewed reporters, traditional news journalism brings along various limitations, first and foremost because it claims to be detached and objective. However, as one of the interviewees put it: "Things that insinuate they are objectively true—they are exceedingly silly. [...] They are full of attitude—attitude by the people that carry them."[4] Objectivity, therefore, is considered to be an ideal which is impossible to reach. Consequently, journalists that intend to create a reliable understanding of social reality need to develop alternative strategies and vehicles to describe it.

Such a vehicle is spotted in the approach of narrative journalism, which diverges from the mainstream of news journalism in many respects. According to several interviewees, an important constraint of conventional journalism is the fact that is has to operate under severe time pressure: "It is a classic view that a journalist does not have time. That is a typical limit. [...] Quite a few rules in journalism are a result of a lack of time," one reporter explained—adding that he tries to escape this dilemma by deliberately "trying to have time, acting unjournalistically, in a way." Only with sufficient time resources, it becomes possible to realize a key condition of any reportage journalism that is to have a first-hand view on the issues and events that are supposed to be described. As another interviewee stated, it is of paramount importance "that we see with our own eyes what is really happening. Because I increasingly have the feeling that other forms of journalism—mostly news journalism—only create a kind of informational layer that is not accurate any more—that is simply not true."

But narrative journalists not only demand different research methods, they also distance themselves from conventional journalistic routines by generating their own modes of presentation: Instead of summarizing the mere facts of an event or topic, which is the common practice in most informatory journalistic genres, they want to capture and tell the story behind it. With narrative means, they want to make their readers "feel the facts," as one of the interviewees said, thus, enabling them to live through the covered events themselves. Reaching this aim is only thought possible with "a certain formation of language, [...] a certain style," another colleague added, claiming a substantial degree of narrative freedom, often inspired by the conventions of literary writing, that would be precluded by the strict standards of the "inverted pyramid" form. Through creating narrative forms of journalism instead, he strives for a transmission of social contexts that is "as vivid and authentic as possible"—a wording that resounded in many of the interviews in a similar way (see also Eberwein, 2013, pp. 162–215). As assessments like these seem to be typical both for print and web reporters, the conclusion that the self-concepts and professional aims of the two sub-groups are basically identical is relatively obvious.

At the same time, however, the qualitative investigation delivers various cues, which suggest that both actor groups also differ from each other. For instance, quite a few of the interviewed newspaper journalists made it clear that they tend to cultivate a critical view on current trends in the realm of digital journalism. While they themselves are evidently happy with the available forms of offline storytelling, they feel that online journalists should rather focus on non-narrative modes of high-speed news coverage "because the Internet is always quicker anyway," as one of the interviewees pointed out. In the eyes of many print reporters, the online media are the true driver of journalism's current obsession with speed, paving the way for a new kind of "fast food coverage" that merely consists of short and incoherent bits of information, while impeding longer narrative or analytical publications. Elaborating on this argument, another interviewee expressed hope that the Internet might one day even "depollute" printed newspapers and magazines from the daily news coverage altogether, thus, making room for more reportages and other forms of contextual journalism. In his view, print media are the ideal container for narrative reporting and he is convinced that they will continue to fulfill this function in the future, despite the current transformations of the media landscape. This view was seconded by a further colleague, who believes that the ongoing media transition

is paradoxically quite good for the literary reportage, because those forms that do not work out online are going to work out on paper in the long run. [...] I believe that reportage has a bright future in print media but rather not in the digital media.

This argument, however, was challenged by many web reporters, who retorted that the communicative potentials of online storytelling actually entail manifold chances, which could even help to renew and reinforce the narrative approach in journalism, in general, and in transmedia journalism, in particular. These chances are essentially accounted for by the ingredients of multimediality and interactivity, which lead some of the reporters to believe that they might enhance the authenticity and effectivity of their coverage. "Adding sound and images creates an atmosphere that would not be thinkable in traditional print reportage," one interviewee argued, adding that "it helps to activate the user and it draws him into the scene, until he becomes a part of the narration himself." From her point of view, digital storytelling can even be seen as the future of narrative journalism, which might eventually get ahead of conventional print reporting by strengthening its traditional aims and objectives. In order to underline this argument in the interview sessions, many of the online journalists referred to impressive examples of award-winning online projects, such as the aforementioned "Snow fall" by the *New York Times*, which seem to be expanding the territory of journalistic narration and serve as role models for many newsrooms in their attempts to redefine what storytelling journalism is all about. At any rate, web reporters refuse to accept the view by their print colleagues that online platforms should only serve the exchange of quick news coverage and be off-limits for long-form narrative pieces. Transmedia journalism examples, such as "The Sochi Project" (Hornstra & van Bruggen, 2013), help to support their refusal.

...And From the Perspective of the Recipients

These conflicting assumptions by print and online reporters needed to be tested in a second step of the investigation, after finishing the communicator study. However, the experimental survey demonstrates that the hopes fostered by the web journalists can only partly be substantiated.

On the one hand, it was evaluated whether online reportages—in contrast to their print counterparts—are in a better position to facilitate the process of *remembering* single facts and *comprehending* the larger context of the published contents. In order to approach these questions, the procedure of cued recall seemed to be the most valuable strategy, since it had been applied in a similar way in earlier experimental studies on the effects of narrative journalism (see e.g. Machill, Köhler & Waldhauser, 2006; Flath, 2013). In practice, after having received one of the stimuli, the probands were confronted with a set of test questions, which were designed to quantify how many details of the contents they were able to reproduce. Among them were several very simple open questions (e.g. "Which airport does the family live on?" and "How old is the boy?") as well as multiple factual statements that the survey participants could comment on with "true" or "false" (e.g. "The protagonist and the woman are married to each other" and "The family earns money by collecting empty bottles"). The succeeding questions for investigating the degree of comprehension were considerably more complex. Here, the test persons were deliberately taken to the task of reflecting on the causes and consequences of the problems being discussed in the articles (e.g. "South Africa is a very liberal country when it comes to rights for homosexuals. Which reasons for the hostile attitude of many persons does the text mention?"). Afterwards, the answers from both blocks of questions were evaluated with the help of a pre-defined marking grid, which made it possible to compare the effects of print and online reportages on the process of remembering and comprehending their contents.

As Table 1 shows, printed monomedia reportages are clearly more effective than multimedia online reportages with regard to remembering and comprehending essential journalistic contents. While the probands in the two control groups were able to reach 12.64 out of 16 maximally possible points on average for the test questions in the area of remembering (that equates a share of 79 percent), the two treatment groups only scored 10.21 out of 16 points (or 64 percent). In the context of the comprehension questions, the control groups—with 5.64 out of 12 points per proband (47 percent)—also scored higher than the treatment groups (4.98 out of 12 points or 42 percent). This result refutes the assumption that was expressed in the qualitative interviews, according to which narrative multimedia articles can communicate their contents in a more effective manner than monomedia print narratives—at least as far as remembering and comprehending is concerned.

However, small deviations from the average values are notable within the four test groups, when certain moderating influences are taken into account. For example, younger users (14 to 29 years) tend

Table 1. Remembering and comprehending print and online reportages

	Remembering		Comprehending	
	Points per Proband	Percentage	Points per Proband	Percentage
Print	12.64/16	79.0	5.64/12	47.0
Online	10.21/16	63.8	4.98/12	41.5

Source: own research project

to remember and comprehend the contents of online reportages more successfully than older users (50 or more years). Moreover, female recipients achieve considerably lower scores for the online stimuli as compared to the print versions in both the categories of remembering and comprehending, while the discrepancies among the male test persons are much smaller. Both age and gender are correlated with the average amount of time that the test persons usually spend online and their previous experience with mobile media (smartphones, tablets, etc.), which generally lead to higher scores in both categories too. Finally, previous knowledge about the topics of the reportages also has a positive effect on the average test scores. These moderating influences help to explain the specific impact of web-based multimedia storytelling, thus offering insights that may be valuable for newsrooms in the process of planning their editorial agendas.

On the other hand, the reception study was also a helpful instrument to test which other qualities the probands ascribe to the different narrative texts, for instance, with regard their *information value*, their *entertainment value* and their *emotional qualities*. Therefore, they were shown twelve further statements (e.g. "The presentation of the article is entertaining", "The article evokes my compassion", and "I consider the article to be trustworthy"), which they were supposed to rate on a scale from 1 ("I totally disagree") to 5 ("I fully agree").

Table 2 exemplifies that the overall interest in the chosen articles is slightly higher among the print readers as compared to the online readers. While the former assessed the respective statement with an average value of 3.62, the latter only reached a value of 3.44. A similar discrepancy resulted from the statement "The presentation of the article is informative"—here the control groups leave the treatment groups behind too (3.84 vs. 3.64). It may come as a surprise that the readers of the monomedia narratives (2.92) also judged their articles as more entertaining than the recipients of the multimedia pieces (2.82), since this result again stands in contrast to the assumptions derived from the qualitative study in which the web reporters insisted that their forms of reporting are a warranty for more authenticity and vividness. On the other hand, the experiment also makes it obvious that multimedia online reportages create a distinctly higher degree of compassion (4.02 vs. 3.42) and, furthermore, that they are considered to be more trustworthy (4.52 vs. 4.33), although the value of trust for the print articles also reaches a high level.

In analogy to the results for the test of remembering and comprehending, moderating influences such as age, gender, affinity to online and mobile media as well as previous knowledge about the reported topics may lead to small variations within the test groups. These moderating influences, however, do not change the overall tendencies indicated by Table 2 and are, therefore, negligible in this context.

Table 2. Other qualities of print and online reportages

	Print (Mean Value)	**Online (Mean Value)**
Article is interesting	3.62	3.44
Presentation is informative	3.84	3.64
Presentation is entertaining	2.92	2.82
Article evokes compassion	3.42	4.02
Article is trustworthy	4.33	4.52

Source: own research project

DISCUSSION: TRANSMEDIA STORYTELLING—BOOSTING TRUST IN JOURNALISM?

What can be learned from this multi-method study? In how far does it advance our previous knowledge about narrative journalistic concepts in the age of media convergence? And what are possible implications for the practice of transmedia journalism?

The qualitative communicator study demonstrates that journalistic storytellers ascribe extraordinary potentials to narrative forms of presentation such as reportages or profiles, particularly if they are looking for a lively and authentic strategy of communicating social reality. Many reporters explicitly describe their narrative modes of journalistic coverage as a countermovement to the dominant pattern of a seemingly objective news journalism, which is regarded as an insufficient means to describe the contemporary world. Oddly, while several print reporters blame the digitization of the media landscape to propel a hitherto unknown demand for speed in many newsrooms, it is generally agreed among their online colleagues that the special features of web-based communication (for instance, interactivity and multimediality) may even invigorate the impact of narrative journalistic genres.

This hope, however, only partly becomes a reality on the side of the recipients: Based on the user experiment, it can be shown that recipients indeed perceive multimedia and interactive reportages as more emotional than traditional narrative articles in newspapers and magazines. However, with regard to remembering and comprehending the communicated contents of the stories, the printed text forms are considerably more effective. Interestingly, multimedia online contents are also regarded to be more trustworthy than monomedia offline reporting, although the level of trust is remarkably high for the latter as well.

Certainly, the empirical research design developed for this study is by no means beyond doubt. The communicator study, for example, with its sample of 30 journalists, can merely claim to have an explorative character; a representative survey on the self-conception and professional aims of the specific groups of narrative journalists, both offline and online, is still missing—not only in the German-speaking world. Also, the narrow focus of the reception experiment, specifically pinpointing the issue of remembering and comprehending journalistic contents, is far too limited to allow for a universal judgment about the impact of storytelling practices on different media platforms. Here, more complex analytical designs, also with a more precise discrimination of varying degrees of multimedia integration and user interaction, could undoubtedly help to produce much more differentiated findings. Such a differentiation would also make it necessary to produce more complex stimuli, a requirement that was impossible to be addressed in this chapter, in view of the limited resources of the research seminar that realized the project presented here.

Nonetheless, the results of the study—even though only documented in an abbreviated version—provide various entry points for further discussion: Currently, media practitioners in many newsrooms around the world lament the fact that audiences do not seem to trust journalistic products any longer (see also Donsbach, Rentsch, Schielicke & Degen, 2009; Peters & Broersma, 2013). The reputation of journalistic actors is at the usual low level (see e.g. Institut für Demoskopie Allensbach, 2013) and recent discussions about media performance in a time of "post-truth" politics have done their share to discredit the profession even further (see Tanz, 2017; Eberwein, Fengler & Karmasin, in press). Surely, these are not the best of circumstances to justify why it is still important to invest in professional journalism in the middle of a media crisis. At the same time, the data which have been collected for this study illustrate quite impressively that a narrative presentation can clearly enhance the credibility of journalistic output. Apparently, this is even more so if a story is covered in different formats across different media types.

If this insight is thoroughly reconsidered, the concept of transmedia storytelling applied to journalism, which includes both on- and offline media outlets, functions not only as an instrument for communicating journalistic contents to media users, but also as a valuable strategy for newsrooms in their struggle for public trust, which the profession needs more than ever these days. Transmedia journalism can reconcile print and digital storytelling, extracting the best of both universes, as the empirical research highlighted. Such an interpretation may once more substantiate why journalistic storytelling is being traded since recently as a multifaceted concept with manifold potentials, not only in communication and media studies, but also in practical journalism. If journalism is to have a future, more deliberation on this topic will be inevitable.

REFERENCES

Abrahamson, D. (Ed.). (1995). *The American magazine. Research perspectives and prospects*. Ames, IA: Iowa State University Press.

Adaval, R., & Wyer, R. S. Jr. (1998). The role of narratives in consumer information processing. *Journal of Consumer Psychology*, *7*(3), 207–245. doi:10.1207/s15327663jcp0703_01

Andrews, M., Squire, C., & Tamboukou, M. (Eds.). (2013). *Doing narrative research* (2nd ed.). London: Sage. doi:10.4135/9781526402271

Bak, J. S., & Reynolds, B. (Eds.). (2011). *Literary journalism across the globe. Journalistic traditions and transnational influences*. Amherst, MA: University of Massachusetts Press.

Berning, N. (2010). *Narrative means to journalistic ends. A narratological analysis of selected journalistic reportages*. Wiesbaden: VS Research.

Bilandzic, H., & Kinnebrock, S. (2009). Narrative experiences and effects of media stories. *Communications*, *34*(4). doi:10.1515/COMM.2009.022

Boynton, R. S. (2005). *The New New Journalism. Conversations with America's best nonfiction writers on their craft*. New York: Vintage.

Branch, J. (2012, December 20). Snow fall. The avalanche at Tunnel Creek. *The New York Times*. Retrieved from http://www.nytimes.com/projects/2012/snow-fall/#/?part=tunnel-creek

Brewer, W. F., & Lichtenstein, E. H. (1982). Stories are to entertain. A structural-affect theory of stories. *Journal of Pragmatics*, *6*(5–6), 473–486. doi:10.1016/0378-2166(82)90021-2

Brooks, C., & Warren, R. P. (1979). *Modern rhetoric* (4th ed.). New York: Harcourt Brace Jovanovich.

Bull, A. (2010). *Multimedia journalism. A practical guide*. London: Routledge.

Connery, T. B. (1990). A third way to tell the story. American literary journalism at the turn of the century. In N. Sims (Ed.), *Literary journalism in the twentieth century* (pp. 3–20). New York: Oxford University Press.

Dohle, M., & Loosen, W. (2014). Journalismusforschung und Rezeptions- und Wirkungsforschung: Intradisziplinäre Trennung oder selbstverständliche Verbindung? [Journalism studies and research about media reception and effects: Intradisciplinary division or natural link?]. In W. Loosen & M. Dohle (Eds.), *Journalismus und (sein) Publikum. Schnittstellen zwischen Journalismusforschung und Rezeptions- und Wirkungsforschung* [Journalism and (its) audience. Gateways between journalism studies and research about media reception and effects] (pp. 1–13). Wiesbaden: Springer VS. doi:10.1007/978-3-531-19821-7_1

Donsbach, W., Rentsch, M., Schielicke, A.-M., & Degen, S. (2009). *Entzauberung eines Berufs. Was die Deutschen vom Journalismus erwarten und wie sie enttäuscht werden* [Disenchantment of a profession. What Germans expect from journalism and how they are disappointed]. Constance: UVK.

Eberwein, T. (2013). *Literarischer Journalismus. Theorie – Traditionen – Gegenwart* [Literary journalism. Theory – traditions – present]. Cologne: Halem.

Eberwein, T. (2015a). Der Widerspruch von Schnelligkeit und Aktualität. Medienethische Überlegungen zum gegenwärtigen Geschwindigkeitswahn im Journalismus [The contradiction between quickness and timeliness. Media-ethical reflections on the current obsession with speed in journalism]. *Communicatio Socialis*, *48*(4), 407–411. doi:10.5771/0010-3497-2015-4-407

Eberwein, T. (2015b). Journalistisches Erzählen im Wandel. Ergebnisse einer Mehrmethodenstudie [Journalistic storytelling in transition. Results from a multi-method study] In O. Hahn, R. Hohlfeld, & T. Knieper (Eds.), *Digitale Öffentlichkeit* (pp. 107–120). Constance: UVK.

Eberwein, T. (2015c). Der "andere" Journalismus. Verselbständigung und Differenzierung an der Grenze von Journalismus und Literatur [The "other" journalism. Autonomization and differentiation on the border between journalism and literature]. *medien & zeit*, *30*(1), 5–16.

Eberwein, T., Fengler, S., & Karmasin, M. (Eds.). (in press). *Media accountability in the era of post-truth politics: European challenges and perspectives*. London: Routledge.

Echterhoff, G., & Straub, J. (2003). Narrative Psychologie. Facetten eines Forschungsprogramms. Erster Teil [Narrative psychology. Facets of a research program. First part]. *Handlung Kultur Interpretation*, *12*(2), 317–346.

Echterhoff, G., & Straub, J. (2004). Narrative Psychologie. Facetten eines Forschungsprogramms. Zweiter Teil [Narrative psychology. Facets of a research program. Second part]. *Handlung Kultur Interpretation*, *13*(1), 151–186.

Flath, H. (2013). *Storytelling im Journalismus. Formen und Wirkungen narrativer Berichterstattung* [Storytelling in journalism. Forms and effects of narrative coverage]. (Diss.). TU Ilmenau.

Fludernik, M. (2009). *An introduction to narratology*. London: Routledge.

Fog, K., Budtz, C., Munch, P., & Blanchette, S. (2010). *Storytelling. Branding in practice* (2nd ed.). Berlin: Springer.

Frey, F. (2014). Wirkungen des Narrativen. Ein systematischer Forschungsüberblick zu Effekten narrativer Kommunikationsformen [Impacts of narrative. A systematic synopsis of research on effects of narrative forms of communication]. In W. Früh & F. Frey (Eds.), *Narration und Storytelling. Theorie und empirische Befunde* [Narration and storytelling. Theory and empirical findings] (pp. 120–192). Cologne: Halem.

Frey, F., & Früh, W. (2014). Die Vielfalt der Erzählung: Eine Inhaltsanalyse zur Definition von "Narration," "Geschichte" und "Narrativität" in wissenschaftlichen Fachzeitschriften [The diversity of story: A content analysis on the definition of "narration," "story" and "narrativity" in scientific journals]. In W. Früh & F. Frey (Eds.), *Narration und Storytelling. Theorie und empirische Befunde* [Narration and storytelling. Theory and empirical findings] (pp. 14–62). Cologne: Halem.

Gambarato, R. R., & Tárcia, L. P. T. (2017). Transmedia strategies in journalism. An analytical model for the news coverage of planned events. *Journalism Studies*, *18*(11), 1381–1399. doi:10.1080/1461670X.2015.1127769

Green, M. C., Strange, J. J., & Brock, T. C. (Eds.). (2013). *Narrative impact. Social and cognitive foundations*. New York: Psychology Press.

Greenberg, S. (2007). Slow journalism. *Prospect*, (2), 15–16.

Hartsock, J. C. (2000). *A history of American literary journalism. The emergence of a modern narrative form*. Amherst, MA: University of Massachusetts Press.

Henley, J. (2013, May 23). Firestorm. *The Guardian*. Retrieved from https://www.theguardian.com/world/interactive/2013/may/26/firestorm-bushfire-dunalley-holmes-family

Hinyard, L. J., & Kreuter, M. W. (2007). Using narrative communication as a tool for health behavior change. A conceptual, theoretical, and empirical overview. *Health Education & Behavior*, *34*(5), 777–792. doi:10.1177/1090198106291963 PMID:17200094

Hornstra, R., & van Bruggen, A. (2013). *The Sochi project*. Retrieved from http://www.thesochiproject.org/en/chapters/the-summer-capital/

Institut für Demoskopie Allensbach. (2013). Hohes Ansehen für Ärzte und Lehrer – Reputation von Hochschulprofessoren und Rechtsanwälten rückläufig [High esteem for doctors and teachers – Reputation of university professors and lawyers on the decline]. *Allensbacher Berufsprestige-Skala 2013*. Retrieved from http://www.ifd-allensbach.de/uploads/tx_reportsndocs/PD_2013_05.pdf

International Association for Literary Journalism Studies. (2011). Selected bibliography of scholarship and criticism examining literary journalism. *Literary Journalism Studies*, *3*(1), 123–141.

Jenkins, H. (2003). Transmedia storytelling. Moving characters from books to films to video games can make them stronger and more compelling. *Technology Review*, *15*(January). Retrieved from http://www.technologyreview.com/biotech/13052/

Keeble, R. L., & Tulloch, J. (Eds.). (2012). *Global literary journalism. Exploring the journalistic imagination*. New York: Lang.

Kleine Wieskamp, P. (Ed.). (2016). *Storytelling: Digital – Multimedial – Social. Formen und Praxis für PR, Marketing, TV, Game und Social Media* [Storytelling: Digital – multimedia – social. Forms and practice for PR, marketing, TV, game, and social media]. Munich: Hanser.

Kramer, M., & Call, W. (Eds.). (2007). *Telling true stories. A nonfiction writers' guide from the Nieman Foundation at Harvard University*. New York: Plume.

Krüger, U. (2014, March). *Acceleration in journalism: A theoretical approach to a complex phenomenon.* Paper presented at the conference "Journalism in Transition: Crisis or Opportunity?" of the Journalism Studies Section within the European Communication Research and Education Association (ECREA) in Thessaloniki.

Labov, W., & Waletzky, J. (1967). Narrative analysis. Oral versions of personal experience. In J. Helm (Ed.), *Essays on the verbal and visual arts* (pp. 12–44). Seattle, WA: University of Washington Press.

Lausberg, H. (1998). *Handbook of literary rhetoric. A foundation for literary study*. Leiden: Brill.

Lee, A. M.-C. (2014). *How fast is too fast? Examining the impact of speed-driven journalism on news production and audience reception* (PhD thesis). University of Texas, Austin, TX.

Lee, W., & Gretzel, U. (2012). Designing persuasive destination websites. A mental imagery processing perspective. *Tourism Management*, *33*(5), 1270–1280. doi:10.1016/j.tourman.2011.10.012

Machill, M., Köhler, S., & Waldhauser, M. (2006). Narrative Fernsehnachrichten. Ein Experiment zur Innovation journalistischer Darstellungsformen [Narrative television news. An experiment on the innovation of journalistic genres]. *Publizistik*, *51*(4), 479–497. doi:10.1007/s11616-006-0241-x

Mayring, P. (2014). *Qualitative content analysis: Theoretical foundation, basic procedures and software solution*. Klagenfurt: SSOAR.

Moloney, K. T. (2011). *Porting transmedia storytelling to journalism* (MA thesis). University of Denver.

National Geographic Channel. (2013). *Killing Kennedy*. Retrieved from http://kennedyandoswald.com

Opgenhaffen, M., & d'Haenens, L. (2011). The impact of online news features on learning from news. A knowledge experiment. *International Journal of Internet Science*, *6*(1), 8–28.

Penn, W. S. (2013). *Storytelling in the digital age*. New York: Palgrave Macmillan. doi:10.1057/9781137365293

Peters, C., & Broersma, M. (Eds.). (2013). *Rethinking journalism. Trust and participation in a transformed news landscape*. London: Routledge.

Pöttker, H., & Kornilov, E. A. (2010). Genre-Systematik [Taxonomy of genres]. In A. G. Bespalova, E. A. Kornilov, & H. Pöttker (Eds.), *Journalistische Genres in Deutschland und Russland. Handbuch* [Journalistic genres in Germany and Russia. Handbook] (pp. 46–52). Cologne: Halem.

Prince, G. (1987). *A dictionary of narratology*. Lincoln, NE: University of Nebraska Press.

Prinzing, M. (Ed.). (2015). *Die Kunst der Story* [The art of story]. Thun: Werd & Weber.

Ricketts, M. S. (2007). *The use of narratives in safety and health communication* (Diss.). Kansas State University, Manhattan, KS.

Schlichting, L. (2015). Transmedia storytelling and the challenge of knowledge transfer in contemporary digital journalism. A look at the interactive documentary *Hollow* (2012–). *Image*, *21*, 81–95.

Schmid, W. (2010). *Narratology. An introduction*. Berlin: De Gruyter.

Sims, N. (2007). *True stories. A century of literary journalism*. Evanston, IL: Northwestern University Press.

Stanzel, F. K. (1984). *A theory of narrative*. Cambridge, UK: Cambridge University Press.

Steensen, S. (2011). Online journalism and the promises of new technology. A critical review and look ahead. *Journalism Studies*, *12*(3), 311–327. doi:10.1080/1461670X.2010.501151

Suleiman, S. R., & Crosman, I. (Eds.). (1980). *The reader in the text*. Princeton, NJ: Princeton University Press. doi:10.1515/9781400857111

Tanz, J. (2017). Journalism fights for survival in the post-truth era. *Wired*. Retrieved from https://www.wired.com/2017/02/journalism-fights-survival-post-truth-era/

Thorson, E., Wicks, R., & Leshner, G. (2012). Experimental methodology in journalism and mass communication research. *Journalism & Mass Communication Quarterly*, *89*(1), 112–124. doi:10.1177/1077699011430066

Vanoost, M. (2017, May). *Reading news as narrative or as inverted pyramid: The role of gender on the reading experience*. Paper presented at the 12th annual conference of the International Association of Literary Journalism Studies (IALJS), Halifax, Nova Scotia, Canada.

Witzel, A. (2000). Das problemzentrierte Interview [The problem-centered interview]. *Forum Qualitative Social Research*, *1*(1), 22. Retrieved from http://www.qualitativeresearch.net/index.php/fqs/article/view/1132/2522

KEY TERMS AND DEFINITIONS

Hypertextuality: The extent to which online texts (or parts of them) are related to each other by internal or external hyperlinks.

Interactivity: The degree to which users are involved in the exchange of information with computers.

"Inverted Pyramid" News: A form of news story that communicates the basic facts in the initial sentences.

Multimediality: The extent to which different media channels (text, images, audio, and video elements) are combined and integrated in a common digital form.

Narratology: A branch of literary theory that focuses on the study of narrative structure.

Problem-Centered Interview: A theory-generating research method in qualitative social sciences that aims at combining the principles of induction and deduction.

Reportage: A journalistic form of storytelling that, first and foremost, intends to create an authentic account of the events it covers.

Storytelling: A method of communicating information in the form of stories that is applied in journalism and organizational communication as well as in fields such as knowledge management, education, psychotherapy, etc.

ENDNOTES

1 The point of origin for the thoughts presented in this paper was a project seminar in the MA program for Journalism at Technische Universität Dortmund, Germany, which the author supervised in Winter term 2012/2013 and Summer term 2013, together with Horst Pöttker (see Eberwein 2015b for further details). The participants of this seminar deserve recognition and gratitude for their contributions to the empirical parts of the study.

2 The text delineates the fate of a Bulgarian family of refugees that has been living at the airport in Munich, Germany, for several months. The original version is available online at: http://www.sueddeutsche.de/muenchen/krisenfluechtlinge-am-flughafen-muenchen-alles-ist-besser-als-zurueckgehen-1.1534989

3 The article broaches the issue of homosexual women and men in South Africa. Its original version is online as well: http://www.spiegel.de/spiegel/print/d-8515-7573.html.

4 All direct quotations that are not attributed to any particular source are taken from the problem-centered interviews which were conducted for this study. They were translated from German to English by the author.

Chapter 3
Viral News Content, Instantaneity, and Newsworthiness Criteria

Lila Luchessi
Universidad Nacional de Río Negro, Argentina

ABSTRACT

Social networks have modified the activities of the press, the actions of audiences, and the perceptions of societies. The strategies displayed to avoid losing consumers aim at fulfilling the audience's needs and the gap between the producers' and the consumers' interests tends to widen. This leads to a crisis point in news financing, affecting the traditional logic of the media industry; while advertisers are now able to reach their audiences without its mediation, viralization and instantaneity force the media to publish information incompatible with the public interest as considered by the press. In this way, traditional newsworthiness criteria are replaced by other criteria that redefine the concept of information. The aim of this chapter is to analyze the way in which instantaneity and viralization have affected not only the journalistic activity but also the information selection criteria and the audiences' input on the web.

INTRODUCTION

Digital tools have been used for the production of news since the eighties (Canavilhas, 2009). In the beginning, the editing of texts and images simplified the journalistic tasks and accelerated the speed of the construction of news. While technology progressed, the press began to publish news online. At first, they only posted the information that had been published on their print editions. In only twenty years, the possibility of combining print editions with information search and narrative experimentation tools grew in such a way that the digital media became independent of their print origins, while audiences gained ground through collaboration and participation. In the beginning of the 21st century, the gap between the producers of news and their audiences—that had relied on asymmetric knowledge, interests and information sources—started to narrow. At the same time, the thematic choices, coverages and information preferences began to diverge more and more (Boczkowski & Michelstein, 2013). The

DOI: 10.4018/978-1-5225-3781-6.ch003

reduction in the price of digital devices, the widespread use of mobile phones, and the lower costs of Internet brought about a rapid increase in the number of users and opened new business opportunities for the media and the press. And although the news companies insisted on thinking the business with the same logic of before, the new consumers' habits made that situation change.

In 1995, Randy Conrad created "Classmates," a social network to find old classmates. It is considered to be the main precursor of Facebook, since it was created with the same purpose (Ponce, 2012). With this project, the idea of "digital network" took root. However, it was not until the first decade of the 21st century—with the massive inclusion of users and the incorporation of networks based on general issues—that the ideas of participation, discussion, collaboration and agenda-setting became possible. In this scenario, the press is faced with two problems. On the one hand, the digital tools have become inputs for the construction of news. On the other hand, these very same tools have been used as platforms for the media to post material and interact with their audiences. Interactivity, which is inherent to the digital platforms, subverts the languages and structures of journalistic communication. Although news companies are present in all these platforms, they end up using them as ad-blackboards, coverage channels and transmission bands that almost in no case enable vertical interactions. While the news consumers throw themselves into the digital platforms, interaction between peers becomes more frequent: Discussion, collaboration, conversation and participation among users take place on a horizontal level. However, an analysis monitoring national, regional, local and Latin American press companies, which includes in-depth interviews with the editors of such companies (Luchessi, 2016a), shows that the news companies and the journalists working for them do not give answers, correct, acknowledge or argue with the public, and keep a distance from their audiences.

Since the beginning of Twitter, in 2006, and Facebook, in 2004, an extensive mass of consumers has begun to use the social networks for different purposes. Online entertainment, ideas spreading, interactions and the consolidation of networks and communities where people socialize, have been crossed by news inputs, which always fit the media logics. In some cases, the news media even question their audiences about the news material they cannot have access to. For example, a local editorial department has created a WhatsApp line to receive inputs from the audience and to cover some events without having to leave the newsroom; also, certain news materials they use have been published in other sites or emerge from the audiences' inputs within the social networks, especially in those cases in which the witnesses of relevant events transmit live or upload photos or videos of events, which are distant from the news professionals (Luchessi, 2016b). In this regard, YouTube channels, Facebook pages, Twitter, Snapchat and Instagram accounts combine with Telegram and WhatsApp. It is through all these platforms that the media receive reports, videos, data and other inputs to generate content. Nevertheless, there are very few records of acknowledgments, mention of the sources or answers to the demands made by the audiences through these channels. In this situation, users tend to assume an unexpected role and start to produce information, breaking the logics of the traditional construction of news. As social networks became massive, the audiences' subject matters and concerns began to circulate without the mediation of the press. Furthermore, with the use of segmentation and audience identification tools based on metrics that allow to see nodes contained inside them, advertisers may also have access to their consumers without having to resource to the media. Consequently, news companies are now faced with two problematic issues: On the one hand, the financing of the contents and, on the other hand, a drastic change in the idea of information (Aguado, 2013).

As advertisers are now able to hire hosting services and community managers that skip a step between them and their potential customers, communication budgets drop and advertising investment decreases. Although the case of The New York Times might have been an innovative way of financing contents via subscription instead of advertisement (Kafka & Molla, 2017), the experience of the media analyzed show that audiences are not particularly interested in paying for information and, in those cases in which they might be willing to, subscriptions result insufficient to finance the business (Boczkowski & Michelstein, 2017). With an advertising market that remains—at its very best—stable, the growth in the supply of traditional and digital contents makes the news market stumble. The traditional sections no longer take into account the current concerns, preferences, and habits of audiences. In some cases, modifications are made to sustain the tacit agreement with the public. Even so, the lower credibility ratings of the press and the possibility of posting information without its mediation allow Internet users to remove the media from the equation.

The aim of this chapter is to analyze the impact of viral news contents and instantaneity on information quality, the decentralization of the role of information professionals and the criteria for the production of news. Also, the impact of transmedia storytelling on news production, and the media strategies to reach the reticular and segmented audiences in a context of social and cultural reorganization, which affects the media business units.

JOURNALISM, NEWS AND TRANSMEDIA STORYTELLING

The organization of societies is based on relational networks (Barnes, 1954; Bott, 1957). Anthropology, as well as Sociology, have acknowledged the importance of studying the relationships that shape social structures (Waserman & Faust, 1994) and the linkages established inside them. Despite that, studies on virtual communities' relations (Ricaurte & Ramos-Vidal, 2015) do not acknowledge the research that has studied the ties, relations and structures of social practices in different territorial communities. In the last years, research has been made, taking some elements from the Graph Theory (Harary & Norman, 1953; Storkman & Srenger, 1989), to study the relationships built in the digital networks and the matrix structures related to journalism subjects and problems. In that sense, the research that compares the constitution of virtual communities, opinion groups, virtual leaderships and structural breakdowns with the conventions that were established before the upsurge of digital platforms, tends to reach findings which are more related to the social and cultural practices that already existed before the appearance of digital platforms and specific applications. It should be observed that digital platforms enable more dynamic and fluent communication between the participants of the virtual communities. In fact, the most distinctive feature of this interactivity is its high speed. Governed by a prevailing contemporaneity, users interact instantaneously on debating topics, ideological stances and common actions. Later in this chapter, the construction of the concepts of time and space will be elaborated. However, it is important to stress that the present chapter refers to "contemporaneity" as a synchronic process that places different situations, that occur in different places, as a unique present.

The modes of social functioning within the social networks are not new. When comparing the findings of the research on interactions on digital networks—and before, on the spaces opened for debate by the media and the publications of their audiences—with the interactions that took place before the existence of the platforms, it is possible to find that the relational ties and the hierarchical clustering inside them remained stable in relation to the ones that could be found in the communities established in different territories (Luchessi, 2016b). From this point of view, the fact that the forms of interaction remained stable is a significant contribution to think the differences between the traditional and the digital audiences. Besides, it enables the consideration of new ways for the information producers to relate to audiences. Apart from that, if Jenkins (2006) is right when he says that transmedia storytelling is necessarily interactive, the narrative breaking to be analyzed in the news context is the one that leaves aside the unidirectional view of the news companies, and adds to a digital palimpsest in which participants are able to dialogue, build relationships, displace the institutional hierarchies to create new ones, and mix subjects that juxtapose with each other at high speed, without establishing hierarchies. At the same time, it will be interesting to study the relationships built by the users among themselves. When examining media forums and networks, the interventions of the audiences are usually conversational and interactive, while the exchanges take place on a horizontal level only. In most cases, users question, provoke or discredit the press—as an institution—as well as its agreements, negotiations, stands, agenda-setting strategies and explanations of social events. In the last years, several traditional media, in particular those included in the corpus of the study abovementioned, made the mistake of publishing fake news for taking material posted on the networks. Especially in Argentina, these phenomena—added to the discussion over the regulation of audiovisual media that revealed the interests of the multimedia holdings in the eyes of society (Becerra & Mastrini, 2017)—affected the image of the news companies, their most visible journalists and the credibility of the information they publish (Blaustein, 2013). The press credibility ratings, on the very top in the nineties, decrease year after year (Amado, 2016a) as audiences participate massively and create a dialogue the journalists and the press companies exclude themselves from. At this point, it is possible to make two interpretations that will put into context the journalistic practices and their relations with users. First, it may be said that a research (Amado, 2016a) on the content of publications related to news of public interest has shown that the institution of journalism, as a central actor in the news process, is being questioned, that the credibility ratings of its publications have dropped and that the cohesion and credibility of the communities people belong to strengthens, while they are considered to be sources to be taken into account. Second, when analyzing the demonstrations in public places and the claims that spring from them, the questioning of the institutions of democracy, of the hierarchy of its representatives and of the credibility of the political leaders, it will be possible to draw a correlation between the strengthening of community participation and the reticular construction of leaderships.

Regarding journalism studies, certain topics have emerged since the analysis of the press began: Routine procedures (Gans, 1979), construction of news (Tuchman, 1978), and media influence on public opinion (Lippman, 1922; Habermas, 1981; Price, 1994). Using different tools and different platforms, current studies tend to focus on the same issues (Boczkowski, 2013). What does the public need to know to make political decisions? Who should select, frame and analyze the events? How are stereotypes built to simplify the message? And finally, are the traditional techniques efficient in the news production processes and analysis? Historically, there are three stages in the production process: (1) the selection of events, (2) the hierarchy of news values, and (3) the edition of the content that will later be published in media socially recognized by the audience (Martini, 2000). This process in which news inputs arrive to the newsroom to be processed and published by professionals is known as Newsmaking. The construction of news is founded on two pillars: (1) the systematization of events through planning, and (2) the monitoring of the breakings those events cause in the everyday life, which alter the productive routine and the work of the journalists for the construction of news. Those breakings are usually organized through different criteria, which allow to manage the production of news and organize the press agenda (McCombs, 2004), according to the dispute over meaning established in society. In fact, the traditional tensions over agenda-setting had, at least, three main actors: Politicians, press media, and society. These disputes and negotiations arise the subjects and framings over which audiences had to be informed to take a stance consistent with their social, ideological, political and cultural backgrounds. Up to this point, the scheme might be the same. However, the productive acceleration of the social system and the change in the perception of the concept of time, modify the roles, functions and interactions played by the press with their news sources, their financing sources and society as a whole.

Traditionally, time regulated the periodicity of news products and the temporal pace of organization of the press industry had a direct influence on the organization of the rest of the production activities of communities the press kept informed. The acceleration of the pace of news brought about higher production speed and, therefore, higher levels of consumption. The phenomenon above mentioned does not only apply to the press industry. In capitalist systems, acceleration and speed are key to generate competition and productivity (Gitlin, 2005). However, the acceleration resulting from the digitization of platforms completely changed the way time is assessed. Although the production techniques are not new, the possibility of synchronizing the occurrence of the event with its publication destroys the concept of periodicity (Luchessi, 2013). This process, which Paula Sibilia calls "detemporalization" (2012, p. 133) is one of the elements which constitute the *omnipresence of the present*. Despite the descriptive coincidence, this chapter will refer to "contemporaneity," since the term enables the study of this temporal synchronicity and, at the same time, the processes of spatial simultaneity. This temporal synchronicity does not only influence the historical contemporaneity process. The decontextualized idea of a permanent "here and now" has a direct impact on the cultural conceptions, social production assessments and news interests of the online communities.

Oscar Landi (1992) studied the cultural changes resulting from the consumption of audiovisual products at home and the spread of the pay-per-view system. To Landi' studies, it should be added that the use of digital platforms generates the possibility of interacting with others. The audiences Landi referred to still had an asymmetric relation with the information producers. However, in the era of technological platforms, leaderships and reputations are built by numbers of followers, amounts of clicks and digital omnipresence. Consequently, people who are unknown to the media and the non-virtual communities might be summoned by them because of the popularity of their posts, becoming instant celebrities or opinion leaders. In order to understand these changes, it will be necessary to take into account that nowadays there is direct access—through easily available technology—to events that occur in remote, unknown and culturally different places. Almost half of the world population uses smartphones; while in periphery countries the mobile phone market share represents around 30% of the population, in the central countries that share represents 75% (Infobae, 2015). This direct access breaks with the traditional idea of distance expressed in miles or kilometers, enabling a spatial synchronicity within an also synchronic time. It is in this scenario that periodicity, scoop and topicality lose their traditional places in the set of news values known up to date. The predominance of the producers, eroded by the strong participation of the online audiences, was characterized by stable newsworthiness criteria; when that asymmetry breaks down and the users leave their passive role to interact online, those criteria, as well as the methods of news production, are bound to change (Amado, 2016b).

The change in the habits of consumers and the direct marketing strategies carried out by the advertisers and the social actors, who had historically acted as sources of information, cause the news companies many problems. Asymmetry, which characterized the news tradition and placed journalism as a mediator between power and society, is broken down by the possibility of having direct contact with sources and advertisers in accordance with very specific interests. Thus, the users of platforms and news applications have access to direct sources that, in many cases, provide information before the media outlets. Politicians, social leaders, prominent figures new referents confront the concept of exclusive news and leave the media professionals on a situation of temporal delay when it comes to covering events. The users see instantaneity as a strong news selection criterion. Their eagerness to know the events on real time brings about an anxiety in the consumption of news that affect the newsmaking process, the routines known by the journalists and the news companies financing. In that sense, the time of news production shortens, with a direct impact on the quality of news. At the same time, society becomes immersed in an idea of constant contemporaneity in which the political, cultural and economic contexts are left behind in a career against time that, to be successful, must equal the moment of the event with the moment of its publication. Even so, there are old informational pieces circulating on the Web, which keep being updated for the number of interested users. In these cases, many members of a given community are interested in this kind of contents based on shared criteria, such as spectacularity, entertainment or ideological stance, and the moment of the occurrence of the event becomes less important. These consumption practices off-center the work of journalists (Luchessi, 2016b). Time is no longer a linear construction (Sibilia, 2012): Time is now the moment in which the event is published. News coverage, considered in traditional contexts as a professional way of managing and presenting information, is put at a disadvantage by the compulsive publication of erroneous, incomplete or utterly false data. Furthermore, the contents circulating online mix together relevant and irrelevant news, privacy and entertainment, rumor and information.

In this scenario, audiences tend to draw together in communities, which share their same interests (Calvo, 2015). Within them, prejudices, beliefs and stands become stronger. Thus, it is the stand that the media and the journalists might take on a certain subject that is being questioned, and not the truth of information. This reorganization of the way social events are published, which is managed directly by the communication teams of the sources, has direct consequences on the news production routines. Transformed into mere reproducers of the things *everybody knows*, journalists no longer tell the facts but hide behind their desks, stay online and do not have enough time to carry out a professional work that would allow them to check the information. The newsmaking process, which begins when data arrive to the newsroom, suffers modifications since the access of the journalists to those data usually coincides with the access of the audience. In relation to that, the difference between the two groups would lie on the organization into a hierarchy that characterizes the traditional news criteria. Even though some criteria remain stable, the new forms of consumption destroy others and create new conceptions when it comes to selecting news. As a matter of fact, some news values such as magnitude, topicality and level of impact on society are still operational to select news, but values such as proximity and relevance of the major figures should be revised (Luchessi, 2007). For instance, the value of proximity, linked to a strong territorial conception and the idea of a nation-state regulating social relations, has been affected by a community construction of a different kind: Now, the community does not necessarily identify itself with territorial borders or national mythologies. In the online social media networks, the community identity is built by cultural agreements linked to certain interests, expressions and reticular forms of consumption. However, the use of algorithms to organize the informational volume that circulates on the Web allows people to have access to certain subjects, sources and publications, which coincide with their own interests; a tighter sense of belonging and a common perception is developed, which closes the circle built around that information. There is an idea of "wholeness" generated around this knowledge, since the "everybody" of every community shows no cracks. Each community takes homogeneous stands which show no contradictions and that "everybody" seems to accept. Nevertheless, when analyzing the information flow and the interactions within it, it is possible to see that there are many "everybody."

Isolated by its own prejudices, each community strengthens its own convictions, undermining or demonizing the others. Therefore, interaction calls for uniformity, since it does not tolerate nuances.

When studying the value of celebrity as a newsworthiness rule, it may be seen that, despite the construction of alternative ways of becoming famous, the criterion remains relatively stable. The circle feeds itself with the traditionally famous people, who reinforce their public presence by participating on the online social media networks, and those who are not famous but achieve popularity through their digital activism. The relevance of the events and their assessment as information input are also subverted by the appearance of a gap (Boczkowski & Michelstein, 2013), showing that the editorial and personal interests of the journalists diverge from those constructed by audiences. In the midst of a constant information flow related to personal, sectorial and community interests, audiences move away from the concerns of bigger sectors of society. In that sense, the information supply, dealing with specific issues, works better than the traditional general press. Therefore, the balance of the negotiation needed to maintain the public's interest (Luchessi & Cetkovich, 2007) is tipped in the audience's favor, creating a newsworthiness criterion. In this way, the news companies make concessions with their audiences, as their customers, distorting and conditioning the role and the practice of those professionals, who are attached to their ethics, aesthetic and job methodology.

The concept of viral news, which is the kind of news that goes from the social networks to the newsroom and sets a disruptive agenda, is key to understand the industry and the social practices around it. Viralization, which seems to hold together the interests of different communities of users, ends up falling within the contents of the traditional press: The use of analytical tools enables an instantaneous quantification of consumption by numbering the amount of "clicks" of each content, and these data decide its inclusion (or exclusion). Then, the "when," the "where" or the "who" are no longer important, but how many clicks, shares and views support the popularity of a content; this is what decides whether an event is newsworthy. If the preferences of digital media audiences are followed (Boczkowski & Michelstein, 2013) and compared with the social networks posts, an unavoidable question arises that reorganizes the journalists' routines and the analysis related to the news industry: What do producers and consumers understand when talking about information?

For around twenty years, advertising campaigns, entertainment material, sports and "soft" sections have been the preferred contents of traditional press audiences (Luchessi, 2006). Boczkowski and Michelstein (2013) add that these preferences remain stable as long as there is no need for hard section information. The cases the authors take into account are electoral processes or crisis situations. In these circumstances, the gap tends to narrow. These consumption practices, that are common to different press media in Argentina, coexist, in the beginning of the 21st century, with a constant supply from the social networks. There, thousands of cybernauts share material consistent with their preferences. Public events mix with private life, shallowness mixes with deepness, and the common events mix with news. However, these mixtures, which become preferences, are not essentially thematic. The recurrence of certain contents is associated with stances related to ideological, religious, social or cultural tendencies.

Originality lies on the formation of nodes, mostly opposed to each other, in which a given stance totally excludes any other stance, regardless of whether the information pieces on circulation stem from truthfulness, professionalism and production rigor. It is also interesting to notice that audiences do not demand more precision in the news content. In fact, people want the media and the journalists to explicit their positioning in relation to the circulating topics. It is not important if they add information or show professional inadequacy. Then, people exhort the media and the journalists to openly approve or condemn specific matters. In this scenario, the production of information is focused on the third stage of the process. According to Omar Rincón (2013), the tasks of journalism in the digital platforms will slowly resemble those of a DJ: Cutting, linking and mixing other people's productions seems to be the more stable activity of the media professionals. In addition, in the case of the coverage of events on real time in which information professionals cannot possibly compete with people holding cellphones with cameras in the very scene of the events, editing dominates the rest of the stages of newsmaking.

The news selection and organization into a hierarchy emerge from algorithms expressed in metrics that measure the practices of audiences within the media. More and more the satisfaction of the demand moves away from the idea of information, the agenda-setting disputes and the predominance of the corporate positioning of the news companies. However, this is not the only way in which the subjects to be published are selected. Viralization, which will be discussed in following paragraphs, becomes key in the editorial decision-making process. The unidirectional idea of traditional information is challenged by a net, whose nodes are constituted by potential popularity and not by professional practices. From viralized interconnections emerge new criteria for news selection.

In the meantime, as images, gifs and micro-videos flood the social media networks, the textual weight of many of the news published in informative sites is swimming against the tide of transmedia storytelling. To discuss transmedia storytelling, it will be useful to return to Jenkins (2003). From his perspective, narrative experiences circulate fragmented through the different media and platforms, and the users are the ones who actively collaborate on the construction of a narrative universe. Furthermore, it is important to analyze the consumption practices of the new generations that, in their micro breaks, find the time to consume stories or video fragments, or write posts in blogs. These micro breaks or "Leisure Bubbles" (Igarza, 2009) are nurtured by the widespread use of smartphones, Internet connection (Liuzzi, 2014) and the ability of the new generations to adapt to the languages used.

The most interesting but also disruptive aspect of the notion of transmedia storytelling in relation to traditional storytelling is that, according to Gosciola, "transmedia storytelling unfolds a media convergent force while remaining open for audiences to collaborate, express questionings, and become a determining factor in the construction of storytelling" (2012, p. 9, own translation). The prominent role of audiences might seem auspicious, but it also contributes to the proliferation of fake news, climates of biased opinion isolated from the social nuances of everyday relationships, and exchanges between the networks and the real world, which distort perceptions and, in many cases, generate violence (Calvo, 2015). In this regard, different outlooks on a same issue stimulate irreconcilable positions over a specific event. In Argentina, the conflict over the export taxes imposed on the agricultural sector, which began on March 11, 2008, and lasted 127 days, ended up in a dispute between the opposition, which had links with the agricultural sector, and the followers of the government of Cristina Kirchner. The media took an explicit stance, while participation in social networks was high (Aruguete & Zunino, 2010). The agricultural corporations carried out protests—including verbal aggressions through the networks and forums of digital newspapers—which derived in incidents involving threats, punches and the destruction of vehicles in the country's roads as a consequence of clashes between the opposing parties (Infobae, 2012).

Allcott and Gentzkow define fake news as "news articles that are intentionally and verifiably false, and could mislead readers" (2017, p.3). Although the distortion of news is not always intentional, it is true that the lack of training, professionalism and informational inputs on certain subjects magnifies the impact of the content spread and viralized by the users. Despite the potential for narrative construction enabled by the platforms, which allow audiences to participate, collaborate and be part of subjects that might spread outside social media, there is also a need for news professional management and narrative adjustments in the supply of news. The decision of not exploiting to the full the narrative possibilities offered by the medium is based on conservative conceptions of the news business. The lack of investment on professional transdisciplinary teams, the journalists' work overload and the use of social media networks as content creators distort the news products. Furthermore, the fact that companies do not give enough training and pay low wages, force journalists to train on their own (Amado, 2016b), at the expense of their own incomes. The combination of complex languages with precarious working conditions, lack of trust from the public and contemporaneity of events puts strain on the news space. Therefore, viralization of contents, which will later become news, seems to be one of the stable tools of the news market, and of the logics of production.

GOING VIRAL

There are several contents, which are not mediatized through the press institutions. In some cases, this is decided by the traditional application of newsworthiness criteria. In other cases, by censorship. Finally, there are events which are not mediatized because they do not comply with the concept of news. To understand this decision-making process, it should be stressed that news is "the journalistic construction of an event whose novelty, unpredictability and future effects upon society are publicly displayed for recognition" (Martini, 2000, p. 33, own translation). However, ranging from the social networks to the traditional press contents, the common elements are the number of clicks, views and shares they receive, and also the fact that, when they gain ground in the press, the topics are already widespread known as a consequence of their high exposure in social networks. "Gone viral" is usually the band these contents carry when incorporated by the traditional press. In this sense, the decision to publish a topic, which interest derives from the high sensation it caused on the Internet, is made to the detriment of the news scoop.

The concept of "spreadable media" (Jenkins, Ford & Green, 2013) might be useful to understand the complexity of this phenomenon. The users' actions and participations go beyond the idea of contagion and strengthens the idea of performing a concrete action to encourage the circulation of content. Nevertheless, the tensions between the interests of the industry and those of the users, and those of the communities they belong to, should be part of the spreadable media context. According to Carlos Scolari (2008), the porosity of that border is sustained by negotiations and tensions that "might end in temporal cooperation agreements" (Scolari, 2013). In Latin America, the studies on the tensions between the borders and the center of the culture refer to certain concerns expressed not only in the literature of Borges (1974), but also in the scientific studies on the region's communication and culture. The works of Jesús Martín Barbero (1987), Aníbal Ford (1994) and Néstor García Canclini (1990) had already dealt with the disputes between cultural industries and collaborative culture, and the work of Scolari (2008) analyzes the negotiations, borrowings and tensions between the logic of the traditional industry and the participation of the users in the networks. Even so, the institutionalized press is modified by the very same elements it loathes. First, because its informative and commercial interests do not generally coincide with those proposed by the users. And second, because a break in the negotiations would leave them with no public.

To understand the way in which this news selection methodology works, this chapter will focus on three examples: (1) The Lioness with the Green Uniform. Estela Morandi, an Argentinian doctor, who directed the Disaster Response Team of the City of Buenos Aires emergency medical unit SAME, suddenly died on April 13, 2015. A photo of her was taken during her work in a railroad tragedy that took place on February 22, 2012, at the Once Station of the Sarmiento Line (Devana, 2015). The photo went viral and, four days later, the traditional press decided to cover the story. However, the Government of the City of Buenos Aires only held a small ceremony in her honor on May 1, 2015. (2) The revolts that broke out in Tunisia in 2010, and spread to the rest of the Arab countries. The events, known as the Arab Spring, allowed many youngsters to bypass the censorship of the ruling regime by resorting to the online social networks. Thanks to their posts, the world came to know events censored by their governments, triggering widespread political and social repercussions. (3) The chapter will refer to Chewbacca Mom, a video which first version reached 9,269,282 views on YouTube (Deak, 2016). Up to now, the video is the most viralized content in the history of Facebook, with 164 million reproductions (Payne, 2016). Furthermore, the appearance of the mom in "The Late Late Show with James Corden" reached 16,173,186 views on YouTube (The Late Late Show, 2016).

Anonymous Heroine

Estela Morandi devoted her life to Medicine. She always worked in the Public Healthcare System, with a high social commitment. Her relationship with the press media was not very good. Focused on her work in the emergency response team, she got mad when journalists, photographers and camera persons burst into the disasters zones, wanting to get a scoop, while she was saving lives. During her twenty years as head of the Disaster Response Team of the City of Buenos Aires emergency medical unit SAME, she organized the rescues of the victims of the attacks on the Embassy of Israel and the Argentine Jewish Mutual Aid Association; of the LAPA tragedy—the plane crash that took the lives of 62 passengers on August 31, 1999 (La Nación, 2014)— and of the Cromagnon club that caught fire on the night of December 30, 2004, leaving 194 teenagers killed (La Nación, 2012). The tragedy of Once took place when a brakeless train hit on the terminal station, leaving 51 persons killed (Sánchez, 2017).

Trained on emergency and health management, she was an outstanding professional. However, she did not feel comfortable when it came to public relations and preferred to establish personal relations. Her daughter, a young lawyer who works as a photojournalist, had taken a great picture of her mother working at the Once tragedy, in 2012. Dr. Morandi became known due to the visual impact of her expression, caught in all its essence by one of the persons who knew her most. Then, the photo went viral. Many interviews, prizes and a certain level of popularity, which she disliked, arose from that viralization. After that, she was always present in the different events of the busy life of the City of Buenos Aires. In the morning of April 13, 2015, she died unexpectedly at her house, assisted by her husband, Dr. Rafael Acunzo, and by an ambulance of the emergency team she had worked with.

Up to this point, many classical criteria for news selection were present: Unpredictability, proximity, and social relevance of the figure, even though she was not a widely known person. Few hours after her decease, social media was flooded with her photo, the one her own daughter had taken three years before. The photo shows her desperate and weeping face as she was carrying an injured man on a stretcher to the ambulance, in the middle of the train crash (Devana, 2015). The photographer's friends, young journalists who had known Dr. Morandi, discussed the publication of the event in their newsrooms. But, almost in every case, the news companies decided not to cover the story. Only the website of the National Supreme Court, Infojus, published an article on the very same day. Her death coincided with the deaths of two well-known writers: Eduardo Galeano, from Uruguay; and Günter Grass, from Germany. In the meantime, fragments of The Open Veins of Latin America, Galeano's pivotal work published in 1971, mixed with the photo of Dr. Morandi along with messages mourning her death. The overflowing number of shares, views, and comments made editors change their attitude and raise the topic. Once again, isolated from the audience's interest, they had to reconsider. Five days later, the news channel TN made an interview at her house. "A lioness with a green uniform" was the title chosen by journalist Julio Bazán (Telenoche, 2015). Her sons, nephews and husband were there. But they did not show the moving goodbye at the gates of the building where she had worked. The quality of the images captured by emotional non-professional cell phones users was not suitable for television. In any case, a story that had been analyzed as a topic of little interest found its way into the agenda, and broke yet another criterion related to periodicity. An event that had taken place five days before was updated by the force of viralization.

Broken Fences

There was a traditional conception of the regimes installed in the Arab countries: Authoritarian policies, censorship, and media control seemed to set a comfortable scenario to silence discontent. With the irruption of digital technology, the citizens began to have access to information forbidden to them. Moreover, they could start spreading unknown facts to other countries. Social media, along with its storytelling practices, interactions, collaborations, and participation, put the conflict on the social agenda, even though the local political leaders and media would not have included it. The revolts began in Tunisia. On September 17, 2010, Mohamed Bouazizi, a street vendor who had his wares confiscated by the police, set himself on fire in the middle of the street. He died on January, 2011 (Fisher, 2011). The protests, demonstrations and gatherings ended the ruling of Zin Abidile Ben Ali, who had been in power since 1987. The events known as the Jasmine Revolution were the first of a series of events that followed in other parts of the region. Protests broke out in Egypt, Libya, Algeria, Syria, and Yemen. Their governments had similar methodologies. All of them were presided by political leaders who had been in power for more than a decade, and who imposed censorship, isolated citizens and forbid the entry of foreign press (Soengas, 2013). In Egypt, Hosni Mubarak was overthrown on February 10, 2011, after 30 years in power (Lee, 2017). Social media and the collaborations of cybernautic activists from all over the world helped young people organize themselves, publish the information and circumvent the information fence imposed by the regime. Demonstrations spread all around the region. The conflict in Libya with Muammar Gaddafi was the first conflict to have major consequences. The opponents to the regime organized a Liberation Army that collided with the loyal forces resulting in a Civil War, spanning from January to October, 2011 (CNN, 2017). The intervention of the United States and the North Atlantic Treaty Organization (NATO), both acting on the rebels' side and throwing bombs over the country, ended with the execution of Gaddafi.

This topic was included in the agenda worldwide, although there are several reasons why it would supposedly not be included. Investing in the coverage of remote events does not imply that the return will match the expenditure of the news companies. Besides, the censorship and terror that characterize this type of regimes forbid the access of the foreign press. On the other hand, the local sources working on government propaganda do not add enough information to understand the conflict, and are not considered news input by the foreign press. The armed conflicts, the intervention of global forces, the famine deriving from them and, above all, the irruption of the publication of protests across social media add new elements in relation to the information flow and the forms of organization. The political impact of the events opens new forms of discontent, less bloody, but which also question the management of a society. The events, organized through digital tools, are now spread by news channels and imposed themselves on the global agendas by means of viralization.

The Laughter Mask

On May 20, 2016, Candace Payne posted a video wearing a mask of Chewbacca, the Star Wars character. Sitting insider her car, on the parking lot of a toy store in Texas, she was telling her Facebook followers that, although her son had asked her to buy him that toy, it was hers and only hers. In the meantime, she could not stop laughing. Only an hour after the posting, the video had 50,000 views. Later, it became the most seen viral video on the history of social media. Quickly, the traditional media covered it. The video was reproduced in the news around the world: Almost from one day to the next, Chewbacca Mom became a celebrity.

Which are the criteria used by the press to include in the news this kind of content? If we think of the traditional criteria, none of them applies. A woman has fun with a toy bought to her son and she says she is not giving it to him. What principles of the transmedia language become appealing and disruptive for the conventional storytelling practices? It is not possible to find other elements apart from instantaneity and the possibility of sharing content. There are no references to other contents because the material consists only on that: A lady laughs with a Chewbacca mask on. What are the elements that appear on this video and make it interesting for the global press? Analyzing the changes in information management, it is noticeable that the almost immediate huge number of shares and views guarantees the success of the product. Maybe the key of its success relies on the fact posed by Candace's words: "Laughter is a universal language. My video was just joyful and had nothing to do with any agenda" (Williams, 2016).

CONCLUSION

These are only few cases considered to analyze the new forms of assessing the contents published in news media. Although the chapter incorporates events with a local impact in Argentina, the analysis of the Arab Spring, as an event organized through social media that had political consequences, and the Chewbacca Mom video, that transforms an insignificant event into global news, enable us to think viralization as a newsworthiness criterion within networking contexts. Along with other examples, these cases present inadequacy to traditional criteria as a constant. When events are newsworthy, according to traditional journalistic criteria, issues like censorship or information fences imposed on societies with non-democratic institutions help the events impose themselves on the social agenda, with the help of the new technologies. These practices, which question the institutions of the political systems, also question the credibility of the press. Interested on information segments related to soft news, audiences seem to demand explicit positioning from the media in relation to the coverage of political topics. Another phenomenon to be taken into account is the violence these irruptions carry when going beyond the bounds of social media. Microblogging, as a tool for political organization, also irrupts in the news as well as in the democratic practices of the current societies. At the same time, there is a direct correlation between the immediate access to information, tactics and viewpoints, and the impatience seen in other processes. From this point of view, questioning the traditional institutions is beginning to be seen as a problem.

Another factor that emerges from this research is the two-way game played by the online social networks over the media: Viralization puts on the spot the demand for certain ignored topics, while the strength of viralization makes those topics newsworthy. On the other hand, censorship on the media forces the flow of information to find other channels that will prove the importance of the content published. It is also interesting to see that contemporaneity changes the perceptions and expressions of the social tissue, which is now characterized by constant, instantaneous and, in some cases, shallow, demands. Contemporaneity operates upon the press decision-making processes and changes the hierarchy of the published topics. The use of metrics in the analysis of the topics proposed mixes together important and insignificant subjects. The importance of the click, the share and the view as newsworthiness values transforms the consumption practices but also the methods of news production. The stability of these tendencies and their impact on the knowledge and participation practices of the society requires further analysis. In the meantime, viralization seems to consolidate as a newsworthiness criterion, even though the possibilities given by transmedia storytelling can be developed further. The implications of viralization in transmedia journalism are directly connected to the core aspects of transmedia storytelling, in general, and transmedia journalism, in particular: Multiple media platforms, content expansion, and audience engagement (Gambarato & Tárcia, 2017). As the examples discussed in this chapter highlight, multiple media platforms are involved when the news worthy content migrates from social media networks and invades several other outlets, such as television, radio, and the printed media. The migration of content creates the conditions for the news to be expanded and further explored in different media environments. The audience direct involvement occurs when creating the content as well as when sharing and disseminating it online. Therefore, journalism transforms the force of viralization into a newsworthy criterion.

REFERENCES

Aguado, J. (2013). La industria del contenido en la era Post-PC: Horizontes, amenazas y oportunidades [The industry of content in the post-PC era. Horizons, threats and opportunities]. In J. Canavilhas (Ed.), *Noticias e mobilidade: O jornalismo, na era dos dispositivos moveis* [News and mobility. Journalism in the era of mobile devices] (pp. 5–31). Covilha, Portugal: Livros Labcom.

Allcott, H., & Gentzkow, M. (2017). *Social media and fake news in the 2016 election*. Retrieved from https://web.stanford.edu/~gentzkow/research/fakenews.pdf

Amado, A. (2016a). *Periodismos argentinos. Modelos y tensiones del siglo XXI* [Argentine journalisms. Models and tensions in the 21st century]. Buenos Aires, Argentina: Infociudadana, KAS.

Amado, A. (2016b). Del newsroom al cloudsroom. El periodista y los productores de información [From the newsroom to the cloudsroom. Journalists and the information producers]. In L. Luchessi & L. Videla (Eds.), *Desafíos del periodismo en la sociedad del conocimiento. Discusiones a partir del tercer Seminario Brasil–Argentina de Pesquisa em jornalismo* [Challenges of journalism in the society of knowledge. Reflections from the 3rd Seminar Brazil-Argentina on Research in Journalism] (pp. 13–21). Viedma, Argentina: Editorial UNRN.

Bazán, C. (2015). Periodismo hiperlocal: El valor de contar lo que está cerca [Hyperlocal journalism. The value of telling stories from nearby] In G. Roitberg & F. Piccato (Eds.), *Periodismo disruptivo. Dilemas y estrategias para la innovación* [Disruptive journalism. Dilemmas and strategies for innovation] (pp. 53–60). Buenos Aires, Argentina: La Crujía.

Blaustein, E. (2013). *Años de rabia. El periodismo, los medios y las batallas del kirchnerismo* [Years of rage. Journalism, media and the battles of Kirchnerism]. Buenos Aires, Argentina: Ediciones B.

Boczkowski, P., & Michelstein, E. (2013). *The news gap. When the information preferences of the media and the public diverge*. London: MIT Press. doi:10.7551/mitpress/9780262019835.001.0001

Boczkowski, P., & Michelstein, E. (2017). Noticias fusión [Merging News]. *Anfibia*. Retrieved from http://www.revistaanfibia.com/ensayo/noticias-fusion/

Borges, J. L. (1974). *Evaristo Carriego. Obras Completas*. Buenos Aires, Argentina: Emecé. (Original work published 1930)

Calvo, E. (2015). *Anatomía política de twitter en Argentina. Tuiteando #Nisman* [Political anatomy of Twitter in Argentina. Twitting #Nisman]. Buenos Aires, Argentina: Capital Intelectual.

Canavihas, J. (2009). Ensino do jornalismo: O digital como oportunidade [Journalism: digitality as an opportunity]. In J. Fidalgo, & S. Marinho (Eds.), *Actas do Seminário Jornalismo, Mudanças na Profissão, Mudanças na Formação* [Proceedings of the seminar Journalism: changes in the profession and in the training] (pp. 49–56). Braga, Portugal: Universidade do Minho.

Carabajal, G. (2012, December 30). Cromagnon: El sufrimiento aún sigue [Cromagnon. The suffering still remains]. *La Nación*. Retrieved from http://www.lanacion.com.ar/1541601-cromagnon-el-sufrimiento-aun-sigue

CNN. (2017). *2011 Libya Civil War fast facts*. Retrieved from http://edition.cnn.com/2013/09/20/world/libya-civil-war-fast-facts/index.html

Deak, J. (2016, May 19). *Laughing Chewbacca Mask Lady* [Video file]. Retrieved from https://www.youtube.com/watch?v=y3yRv5Jg5TI

Devana, C. (2015, April 16). Adiós para una leona de ambo verde [Goodbye to a lioness with a green uniform]. *Infojus Noticias*. Retrieved from http://infojusnoticias.gov.ar/nacionales/adios-para-una-leona-de-ambo-verde-8195.html

Fisher, M. (2011, March 26). In Tunisia, act of one fruit vendor sparks wave of revolution through Arab world. *The Washington Post*. Retrieved from https://www.washingtonpost.com/world/in-tunisia-act-of-one-fruit-vendor-sparks-wave-of-revolution-through-arab-world/2011/03/16/AFjfsueB_story.html?utm_term=.582d6f8b9fd1

Ford, A. (1994). *Navegaciones. Comunicación, cultura y crisis* [Navigations. Communication, culture and crisis]. Buenos Aires, Argentina: Amorrortu.

Gambarato, R. R., & Tárcia, L. P. T. (2017). Transmedia strategies in journalism. An analytical model for the news coverage of planned events. *Journalism Studies*, *18*(11), 1381–1399. doi:10.1080/1461670X.2015.1127769

Gans, H. (1979). *Deciding What's News. A study of CBS Evening news, NBC Nightly news, Newsweek and Time*. New York, NY: Random House.

García, L. (2008). Distribución y promoción del producto informativo [Distribution and promotion of the news product]. In *Organización y gestión de la empresa informativa* [Organization and management of news companies] (pp. 129–141). Madrid, Spain: Síntesis.

García Canclini, N. (1990). *Culturas híbridas. Estrategias para entrar y salir de la Modernidad* [Hybrid cultures. Strategies to entering and leaving Modernity] Mexico City, Mexico: Grijalbo.

Gitlin, T. (2005). *Enfermos de información. De cómo el torrente mediático está saturando nuestras vidas* [Sick of news. How the torrent of images and sounds overwhelms our lives]. Barcelona, Spain: Paidós.

Gosciola, V. (2012). Narrativa transmedia: Concepto y orígenes [Transmedia Narrative. Concept and origins]. In C. Campalans, D. Renó, & V. Gosciola (Eds.), *Narrativas transmedia entre teorías y prácticas* [Transmedia narratives. Theories and practices] (pp. 7–14). Bogotá, Colombia: Editorial Universidad del Rosario.

Habermas, J. (1981). *Historia y crítica de la opinión pública* [History and criticism of public opinion]. Barcelona, Spain: Gustavo Gilli.

Harary, F., & Norman, R. (1953). *Graph Theory as a mathematical model in the social sciences*. Ann Arbor, MI: ISR.

Igarza, R. (2009). *Burbujas de ocio. Nuevas formas de consumo cultural* [Leisure Bubbles. New forms of cultural consumption]. Buenos Aires, Argentina: La Crujía.

Infobae. (2012, July 17). *Cronología del conflicto agropecuario por la resolución 125* [Cronology of the agricultural conflict over Resolution No. 125]. Retrieved from http://www.infobae.com/2012/07/17/659506-cronologia-del-conflicto-agropecuario-la-resolucion-125/

Infobae. (2015, May 21). *La Argentina, entre los 25 países con mayor cantidad de usuarios de smartphones* [Argentina, among the 25 countries with more smartphone users]. Retrieved from http://www.infobae.com/2015/05/21/1730171-la-argentina-los-25-paises-mayor-cantidad-usuarios-smartphones/

Izquierdo Labella, L. (2012). El nuevo periodismo de proximidad, una ventana abierta al mundo [The new proximity journalism. An open window to the world]. In J. Correia (Ed.), *Ágora, jornalismo de poximidade: Limites, desafios e oportunidades* [Journalism and proximity: Boundaries, challenges and opportunities] (pp. 87–98). Covilha, Portugal: Labcom Books.

Jenkins, H. (2003, January 15). Transmedia storytelling. *Technology Review*. Retrieved from http://www.technologyreview.com/news/401760/transmedia-storytelling/

Jenkins, H. (2006). *Convergence culture: Where old and new media collide*. New York, NY: New York University Press.

Jenkins, H., Ford, S., & Green, J. (2013). *Spreadable media: Creating value and meaning in a networked culture*. New York, NY: New York University Press.

Kafka, P., & Molla, R. (2017, May 4). How The New York Times saved itself. *Recode*. Retrieved from https://www.recode.net/2017/5/4/15550052/new-york-times-subscription-advertising-revenue-chart?curator=theedge

La Nación. (2014, September 15). *La tragedia de LAPA. Una causa judicial de la que fue absuelto por prescripción* [The LAPA tragedy. An action barred and an acquitted person]. Retrieved from http://www.lanacion.com.ar/1727346-la-tragedia-de-lapa-una-carga-judicial-de-la-que-fue-absuelto-por-prescripcion

Landi, O. (1992). *Devórame otra vez. Qué hizo la televisión con la gente. Qué hace la gente con la televisión* [Swallow me again. What did television do to people? What does people do with television?]. Buenos Aires, Argentina: Planeta.

Lee, I. (2017, March 24). Six years ago the Arab Spring came to Egypt -- and Hosni Mubarak fell. *CNN*. Retrieved from http://edition.cnn.com/2017/03/24/middleeast/egypt-six-years-after/index.html

Lippmann, W. (1965). *Public Opinion*. New York, NY: The Free Press. (Original work published 1922)

Liuzzi, A. (2014). Transmedia storytelling. De documentales interactivos y géneros híbridos. [Transmedia storytelling. Interactive documentaries and hybrid genres] In F. Irigaray & A. Lovato (Eds.), *Hacia una comunicación transmedia* [Toward a transmedia communication system]. (pp. 65–86). Rosario, Argentina: UNR.

Luchessi, L. (2006). *Informe final del Seminario de Política y Medios* [Final report of the Seminar on politics and media]. Buenos Aires, Argentina: Universidad de Buenos Aires.

Luchessi, L. (2013). *Calidad informativa. Escenarios de postcrisis* [Information quality. Post-crisis scenarios]. Buenos Aires, Argentina: La Crujía.

Luchessi, L. (2016a). Descentramientos, influencias y reacomodamientos en el ejercicio periodístico [Off-centerings, influencies and readaptations of the journalistic activity]. In A. Amado (Ed.), Periodismos argentinos. Modelos y tensiones del siglo XXI [Argentine journalisms. Models and tensions in the 21st century] (pp.37–49). Buenos Aires, Argentina: Infociudadana, KAS.

Luchessi, L. (2016b). *PI UNRN 40-C-153. Información y periodismo en contextos transmediáticos. Informe final* [Journalism and information in transmedia contexts. Final report]. Viedma, Argentina: UNRN.

Luchessi, L., & Cetkovich, G. (2007). Punto Ciego. [Blind spot] In L. Luchessi & M. Rodriguez (Eds.), *Fronteras globales. Cultura, política y medios de comunicación* [Global borders. Culture, politics and mass media]. Buenos Aires, Argentina: La Crujía.

Martín Barbero, J. (1987). *De los medios a las mediaciones. Comunicación, cultura y hegemonía* [From media to mediations. Communication, culture and hegemony]. Mexico City, Mexico: Gustavo Gili.

Martini, S. (2000). Periodismo, noticia y noticiabilidad [Journalism, news and newsworthiness]. Bogotá, Colombia: Norma.

Mastrini, G., & Becerra, M. (2017). *Medios en Guerra. Balance, crítica y desguace de las políticas de comunicación 2003-2016* [Media at war. Assessment, criticism and destruction of communication policies]. Buenos Aires, Argentina: Biblos.

McCombs, M. (2004). *Setting the agenda*. Cambridge, MA: Polity Press.

Payne, C. (2016, May 19). *It's the simple joys in life…* [Video file]. Retrieved from https://www.facebook.com/candaceSpayne/videos/10209653193067040/

Ponce, I. (2012). *Monográfico: Redes sociales. Historia de las redes sociales* [Monograph: Social networks. The history of social networks]. Retrieved from http://recursostic.educacion.es/observatorio/web/es/internet/web-20/1043-redes-sociales?start=2

Price, V. (1994). *La opinión pública. Esfera pública y comunicación* [Public opinion. Public sphere and communication]. Barcelona, Spain: Paidós.

Ricaurte, P., & Ramos-Vidal, I. (2015). Investigación en redes sociales digitales: Consideraciones metodológicas desde el paradigma estructural [Research on digital social networks. Methodological reflexions from the structural paradigm]. *Revista Virtualis, 11*(1), 165–194.

Rincón, O. (2013). El periodista DJ es el medio [The DJ journalist is the medium]. In L. Luchessi (Ed.), *Calidad informativa. Escenarios de postcrisis* [News quality. Post-crisis scenarios] (pp. 9–31). Buenos Aires, Argentina: La Crujía.

Sánchez, N. (2017, February 22). Tragedia de Once: Familiares y sobrevivientes pidieron cárcel común para los funcionarios [Once Station tragedy. Relatives and survivors demand for the public officers to be put in regular jails]. *Clarín.* Retrieved from https://www.clarin.com/ciudades/tragedia-once-familiares-sobrevivientes-pidieron-carcel-comun-funcionarios_0_rJl-v8sFl.html

Scolari, C. (2008). *Hipermediaciones. Elementos para una teoría de la comunicación digital interactiva* [Hypermediations. Elements for a theory on interactive digital communication]. Barcelona, Spain: Gedisa.

Scolari, C. (2013, June 27). Spreadable media. Entre la cultura de masas y la colaborativa (II) [Between the mass and the collaborative culture]. *Blog Hipermediaciones.* Retrieved from https://hipermediaciones.com/2013/06/27/spreadable-media-entre-la-cultura-de-masas-y-la-colaborativa-ii/

Sibilia, P. (2012). *La intimidad como espectáculo* [Intimacy as spectacle]. Buenos Aires, Argentina: FCE.

Soengas, X. (2013). El papel de Internet y de las redes sociales en las revueltas árabes: Una alternativa a la censura de la prensa oficial [The Role of the Internet and social networks in the Arab spring. An alternative to official press censorship]. *Comunicar, 41*(21), 147–155.

Storkman, F. N., & Sprenger, C. J. A. (1989). GRADAP. Graph definition and analysis package: User's manual. Groningen, The Netherlands: Iec ProGAMMA.

Telenoche. (2015, April 17). *Murió Estela Morandi, una heroína anónima* [Estela Morandi died, an anonimous hero] [Video file]. Retrieved from https://www.youtube.com/watch?v=sy1SiG6mfrk

The Late Show with James Corden. (2016, May 23). *Chewbacca mom takes James Corden to work* [Video file]. Retrieved from https://www.youtube.com/watch?v=uQereoIxioI

Tuchman, G. (1978). *Making news. A study in the construction of reality*. New York, NY: The Free Press.

Wasserman, S., & Faust, K. (1992). *Social network analysis: Methods and applications, structural analysis in the social sciences.* Cambridge, MA: Cambridge University Press.

Williams, N. (2016, December 27). "Chewbacca Mom" on winning Facebook in 2016. *BBC*. Retrieved from http://www.bbc.com/news/world-us-canada-38348401

KEY TERMS AND DEFINITIONS

Contemporaneity: Spatial and temporal symmetry in which time and space do not necessarily coincide.

Gap: Difference of informational interests between the producers of information and the public.

Juxtaposition: The cultural scenario is thought as a patchwork in which the traditional press and the contents emerged from the web coexist.

Market: System of rules for the production of news in which actors compete with one another to achieve profitability and influence the public opinion.

Newsmaking: The process of construction of news in which sources, professionals, companies, and public opinion are involved.

Press: The information industry developed in markets by news companies, which consider news as a consumption product; the activity performed by communication professionals specialized in information management.

Social Networks: Spaces for virtual community interactions, emerging from the interrelations that take place within society.

Viralization: Process of massive circulation of contents through online social media networks and communities with shared interests.

Chapter 4
A Matter of Time:
Transmedia Journalism Challenges

André Fagundes Pase
Pontifical Catholic University of Rio Grande do Sul, Brazil

Bruna Marcon Goss
Pontifical Catholic University of Rio Grande do Sul, Brazil

Roberto Tietzmann
Pontifical Catholic University of Rio Grande do Sul, Brazil

ABSTRACT

Among all factors that compose the journalistic routine, time plays an important role. It delimitates the period to produce content. Transmedia projects often need a faster pace than usual articles, mostly because the reporters need to plan before they leave newsrooms to capture content and, depending on the media used, work on different platforms to deliver the whole content. This chapter discusses the process behind three transmedia journalistic cases: Black Hawk Down (published by Philadelphia Enquirer, in 1997), Inside Disaster (released by PTV, in 2010), and Harvest of Change (published by Des Moines Register, in 2014). Using the case study method, they will be discussed, analyzing the process behind their publication. This reflection highlights how the adoption of tools and usage of paths to connect or publicize content on different media increased the relevance not only of time to create but the effort dedicated to plan the transmedia strategy.

INTRODUCTION

Breaking the narrative arc into various and interconnected stories is a strategy often used in the realm of entertainment, but transmedia narratives are used for journalistic purposes as well. Different from professionals from cinema or video games, journalists rarely have an extended time to think about the strategies and craft products before deadlines, mostly because stories are produced and published in minutes—except long pieces. As pointed by Jenkins (2011), to better understand these processes "we need to come back to the relations between media and not simply count the number of the media platforms."

DOI: 10.4018/978-1-5225-3781-6.ch004

Thinking about news, the "time to produce" factor shall be analyzed, observing how some products use the proper technical language and devices for transmedia content. It seems that these stories demand a new comprehension of time and technology, going from choosing texts and videos to connect paper and the Internet to immersive experiences in virtual reality that place the reader inside a scene.

Transmedia journalism is not just a collection of stories transposed from newspaper into one online homepage with a video published along the complete text transcribed. These are two examples of common routines for daily news with automatic actions defined by content-management systems (CMS). Frequently, these publications are not pieces that together form a bigger narrative that uses the best of its technology to communicate. To create a unified and cohesive narrative spread across multiple media platforms requires time to produce, even if they were not going to be "transmediated," therefore, this procedure is commonly applied just for special content. Special stories not only give time to craft content but to test and drive audiences to new grounds. Within the journalistic routines, this configures a movement of change, when creators change their mindset of producing one piece to craft a series distributed across different platforms. To better understand transmedia journalism, this chapter will study three transmedia stories from three different periods. This selection also helps to understand how transmedia journalism evolved along the past two decades.

The first case is Black Hawk Down (Bowden, 1997), a production published by Philadelphia Enquirer in 1997, that used the Internet as a living repository for a printed series about the "Battle of Mogadishu," with videos, audios, and sessions of "question and answers" with the lead reporter. It is relevant to map a transmedia initiative short after the term spread but before its massive adoption. The second one is Inside Disaster (PTV Productions, 2010a), a documentary by PTV Productions with extras and a game published online. Using short videos connected by a narrative tree, the viewer can experience through three different perspectives the aftermath of the huge earthquake that hit Haiti in 2010. The case is relevant to understand how content created for television can be edited again to produce a different experience in different platforms. Contemporary, the third case will be Harvest of Change (Des Moines Register, 2014). Published in 2014 by Gannett Media as a special section inside two newspapers, it was one of the first usages of virtual reality (using Oculus Rift) for daily news. The five-part series provided an in-depth view on how farming industries changed in the American state of Iowa, along with an online virtual experience. It immerses the audience in a farm, recreating an exploration of a three-dimensional rural environment.

To understand how time is a challenge to producers, this chapter uses the case study methodology (Yin, 2001) to observe how the content was produced and how professionals dealt with time, and discussing how the technologies used influenced the narrative.

The case study is preferred in examining contemporary events, but when the relevant behaviors cannot be manipulated. The case study relies on many of the same techniques as a history, but it adds two sources of evidence not usually included in the historian's repertoire: direct observation of the events being studied and interviews of the persons involved in the events. Again, although case studies and histories can overlap, the case study's unique strength is its ability to deal with a full variety of evidence—documents, artifacts, interviews, and observations—beyond what might be available in a conventional historical study. (Yin, 2009, p. 128)

This is helpful to understand each of the three projects and later discuss them, pointing at the time and technologies used. The main goal is to reconstruct their processes, using interviews about the projects, alongside press releases and other relevant information. With this mindset, it is possible to understand the time factor and how it influenced the production processes. The cases are relevant because connect transmedia with new technologies (Internet, newsgames and virtual reality) and demonstrate how time management and new platforms are combined to tell stories.

DEADLINES AS LIMITS FOR TRANSMEDIA EXPERIENCES

Besides special sections or stories that demand deep reporting, news professionals are constantly running against deadlines to publish and deliver information. Even with the possibility to correct and edit a story, one of the differentials of the content published in websites in relation to traditional media, is the pressure to act quickly and without errors.

News is both constituted by and constitutive of time. On the one hand, time is one of the major factors that shape and constrain the production of news. On the other hand, news narratives, in their representation and construction of societies' past, present, and future, contribute to the shaping of public time. (Tenenboim-Weinblatt & Neiger, 2017, p. 14)

The importance of time can is noticed when professionals "race" against rival companies to be the first ones that published an important story. The urgency of some pieces leads professionals to broadcast piece by piece of information concomitantly with the process of collecting new assets. Thus, deadline is an important word, with its own folklore, and designates the "time by which copy must be submitted for publication or broadcast" (Danesi, 2009, p. 88). It is the limit to finish the first version of the work—and without changing it too much afterwards.[1]

Transmedia projects enhance this problem because they are constituted not by one video or one report, but by a series of tied items. The newsroom staff compromised to finish a project should work on more than one platform and, sometimes, with colleagues from other departments, enhancing the need to plan for its proper development. Then comes the first dilemma: This kind of projects seems to work better when planned. It is not impossible, although it is hard, to create multiple outputs for a single theme after the fact happened. A series about an accident cannot be planned, but the following pieces about the same content and how it will be connected can be discussed after a story broke, like a deep reporting or a series discussing the fact on the following days.

Any thoughtful study of contemporary transmedia must start with the vital caveat that transmedia is not a new phenomenon, born of the digital age. Even if the term is new, the strategy of expanding a narrative into other media is as old as media themselves; think of paintings dramatizing biblical scenes or iconic nineteenth-century characters such as Frankenstein or Sherlock Holmes whose narrative scope transcends any single medium. (Mittell, 2014, p. 253)

Like other forms of storytelling, transmedia journalism is not new and did not originate from digital technologies. Nevertheless, Internet and other digital changed journalism and, in parallel, made easier to think about stories as series and with different approaches. The three projects later discussed in this chapter were produced in conditions that faced their own deadlines, but they were outside the traditional rush because they were developed as special projects. Even the Inside Disaster project, as it will be presented later, had a different news cycle. Notwithstanding, time is an important factor concerning news. As Tenenboim-Weinblatt and Neiger (2017, p. 4) proposes, there are temporal affordances related to journalistic content. They are related to the production, the reception and the permanence of stories and are defined as immediacy, liveness, preparation time, transience, fixation in time, and extended retrievability.

Drawing on affordances theory and scholarship on journalism and time, we define temporal affordances in the news as the potential ways in which the time-related possibilities and constraints associated with the material conditions and technological aspects of news production and dissemination are manifested in the temporal characteristics of news narratives. (Tenenboim-Weinblatt & Neiger, 2017, p. 3)

Special projects leverage this discussion to another level: Huge stories demand special teams to produce it (or help someone who is investigating a subject, as Mark Bowden during Black Hawk Down) and configure products with a different lifespan than a piece about a football team that won an important game or a daily routine of a president.

The preparation-time affordance refers to the amount of time journalists are able to invest in developing a news story, including the temporal extension of news narratives. This would include going backwards in time for contextual information and forward in time to evaluate possible implications of current events, or working on stories that go beyond the most recent events (e.g. investigative stories, analysis of social trends). (Tenenboim-Weinblatt & Neiger, 2017, p. 6)

Furthermore, the average amount of time dedicated to production varies by the type of story and media used. With transmedia projects, it is possible to state that this effort is multiplied by the number of platforms used, even when it is just an online version of a text previously edited to fit in a certain number of printed pages. Just the effort to read it all again, check spelling, copy from text processor to paste inside the content management system, pick a photo, place correctly inside text and publish it takes its own time.

Regarding the type of news media, preparation time is closely associated with the position of the various news outlets in the news cycle and the related affordance of immediacy. For instance, the 24/7 cycle of online news constrains the amount of time that can be invested in each story. (Tenenboim-Weinblatt & Neiger, 2017, p. 6–7)

Transmedia projects are outside these limits, but they have their schedules. The other factor can be noticed when a large amount of work that took so long to be produced often receive a special place over covers and inside broadcasted shows, along with headlines, when published for the first time. For online media, bottom areas of landing pages use to concentrate these features, sometimes even as placeholders. Another point is that online tools allow the reader to find the content later, using pages created by the journalistic companies with their legacy work or accessed through search engines (as long as the files are available). This factor is connected to the affordance of "Transience versus fixation in time" (Tenenboim-Weinblatt & Neiger, 2017, p. 7).

Journalistic use of transmedia storytelling (Jenkins, 2006; Gambarato, 2016; Gambarato & Tárcia, 2017) also reminds the slow journalism idea. It is not just a huge amount of content to read, but long pieces that require a different reading process, comparing it with traditional daily news. These pieces may be the result of a deep investigation but presented in a style that reminds literary journalism.

The journalistic equivalent of slow food keeps the reader informed about the provenance of the information and how it was gathered. More time is invested in both the production and consumption of the work, to discover things we would not otherwise know, or notice things that have been missed, and communicate that to the highest standards of storytelling craft. (Greenberg, 2012, p. 381–382)

Considering print media production cycles, long stories and slow ones often require more time to be published—and crafted—due to the high amount of effort and polish this kind of content demands. This is rewarded with a different degree of attention and may justify even the printing process and consequent acquisition by the readers, who prefer paper rather than digital screens. Transmedia stories borrow this combination of deep focus with strong products and try to bring this force to guide the reader through different platforms, also guiding audiences in a world of multiple possibilities.

At this point, we could generalise that slow journalism requires the time for deeper reflection and/or investigation about an original subject. It is not necessarily long form, but usually requires length. The stylistic focus tends to be narrative storytelling, in any medium, produced to high standards of the craft. This means telling stories using narrative techniques, not just the mechanistic expository style of hard news stories. (Le Masurier, 2014, p. 143)

Even with this resemblance with transmedia storytelling, slow news stories are different, among other factors, because they are produced by independent or alternative organizations, with the periodicity of its delivery in slow cycles, to increase the pleasures of production and consumption (Le Masurier, 2014, p. 143). On the other hand, Gambarato (2016) discusses how these two forms of journalism are alike, mainly due to the strong emphasis dedicated to the power of narrative.

The story is number one and works on multiple levels, or dimensions, creating a dynamic storytelling experience and leaving space for the content to expand across different media platforms. A storyworld is developed to support the expansion of content and multiplicity of media channels. Both TS [Transmedia Storytelling] and slow journalism embrace new technologies (mobile, locative media, for instance) and devices (smartphones, tablets, etc.) to tell compelling stories able to reach a diversified public. (Gambarato, 2016, p. 448)

The worldbuilding aspect of transmedia projects configures an important contribution of this kind of content for journalism. New technologies help storytellers to offer new perspectives to drive audiences to immersive fluxes, with new ways to experience a story. With new tools, such as computer-generated video in 360º or interactive virtual reality experiences, the journalistic ethics is recreated to not lead viewers to experiences that pervert the idea of a well-researched content and is took as novelty, with the information as just background.

Another important point of view about this relationship comes from the study of the convergence process saw inside some newsrooms, which started about a decade ago. Salaverría and Negredo (2008) propose the idea of integrated journalism, in which technology drives an important force orientating workflow, but the platforms and delivery constrain should guide the process of news creations. The authors also state that journalists live in a constant process of "professional convergence" (Salaverría & Negredo, 2008, p. 48). Each decade, one task made by a specific person is absorbed by the regular reporter. From reporting to editing to the designing of a page, these skills demand more effort but, on the other hand, help workers to understand better the whole chain of steps from writing to publishing. Regarding the creation of transmedia projects, it is easier for the staff to plan how one main theme will explore the properties from each platform involved in the project. It is important to notice that the newsroom rhythm and its dynamics (people available to work and budget dedicated to the project, as examples) influence the creation of this kind of products. The knowledge of the staff is important too because short time leads professionals to lean on ways they are confident to express their ideas, rarely relying on experimental techniques. Transmedia projects may be developed as the stories unfold, such as the Black Hawk Down case, but publish this way with contemporary tools and platforms may characterize a poor usage of actual possibilities to communicate. With the Internet and other digital paths that offer no limits of time and space, plan before creating content became an important step, if not the most important one, for these communicational strategies. However, the initial discussion shall think not only about the content but about the medium and tools that can be used as well.

EVOLUTION OF THE JOURNALISTIC TOOLS

Our three case studies follow a 17-year production span, during which the technologies of content production, delivery, and consumer habits have widely changed. We address these changes from two standpoints: (1) the improvement of broadband connectivity as an enabler of richer experiences, and (2) the progressive incorporation of video and other languages that blurred boundaries between print and electronic media. These two movements are important to understand how new technologies (multimedia authoring tools and displays, as examples) enabled content developers to create transmedia experiences. The connection between text and video experience, that in the past was seen as novelty (like in Black Hawk Down), seeded experiences such as Harvester of Change that combines words, images and virtual reality 16 years later.

Since the early 1960s, the production, circulation, and consumption of digital video underwent a continuous improvement of technical and technological features. As a starting point of digital imaging in those days—with uses directly linked to the United States government investments motivated by the Cold War and the space race—the National Aeronautics and Space Administration (NASA) implemented the digital transmission of image data for the mappings made on the lunar surface and in the reception of visual data from their spy satellites (Gaskell, 2003). At the time, the first experiences of computer-assisted animation (Youngblood, 1970) were marked by a non-figurative character of the images. The digital video came close to everyday life through television sports broadcasts of the CBS television network in 1965 (Owens, 2007, p.158). The disc video recorder provided a replay of a major move or the freezing of a frame for debate more swiftly than the use of tapes for the same purpose. The digitalization of the tools of television production had a new impulse in 1971, with the CMX-600 editing system. As a result of a joint effort of CBS and Memorex, it was able to record 27 ½ minutes of black and white video at low resolution on hard drives, allowing the editor to try out different editing solutions (Schneider, 1997). The innovative concept was well received by the television editors, but it was not an agile and economically viable system enough to become more widespread than the linear television edition, which would still be widely used for the years to come. Other expensive and proprietary solutions, as the EditDroid developed by Lucasfilm in the 1980s, implied that the use of digital tools in the production and circulation of video was still restricted to large companies. After Avid's first Macintosh-based video editing platforms in the late 1980s, the concept of making video playback and editing independent of hardware came to personal computers with the release of the QuickTime multimedia component for the Apple Macintosh platform in December 1991. It was followed by Adobe non-linear editing software Premiere in the same month. Revised and expanded versions of these products continue to exist for over two decades.

Operating with QuickTime and Premiere 1.0, a user would have an image resolution of only 160x120 pixels, approximately four times less than that available in Video Home System (VHS) —the *de facto* standard of home video format of the day—and eighteen times less than that of a Digital Versatile Disc (DVD). As much as the Compact Disc Read-Only Memory (CD-ROM), a disc based media, did promise "full-motion video" or other catchphrases to its potential buyers, it delivered most of the times a subpar experience when compared to domestic tape-based media. By the end of the 1990s, the production of video content in personal computers would reach broadcast quality and continue to pursue High Definition (HD) and beyond in the first decade of the 21st century.

In parallel to the enhancement of the video editing resolution on personal computers, the circulation of video content also saw dramatic improvements since the late 1980s. The aforementioned QuickTime technology, its Microsoft counterpart Video For Windows (or its further developments) and open source Moving Picture Experts Group (MPEG) standards grew in two directions: Catered to more robust professional needs on television and film production as well as sorted out ways to transmit video online.

Before broadband connections, CD-ROM became the ideal medium to offer multimedia journalism and infotainment content. Achieving a quality rich experience required data transmission capacity that was greater than that available to most Internet users at the time. A "simple speed" CD-ROM had a transfer rate of 150Kb/s between the drive and the computer, sufficient for audio and images, but limited for video. A 33.6Kb/s modem[2] did not exceed 4.5KB/s at best, resulting in a 33-fold difference. Disc-based magazines as Metatec's Nautilus, published first in 1990 under a subscription model, took advantage of the storage space and media versatility of the new medium and inspired other titles as Medio, Substance and Blender, among others. The utopia of home multimedia consumption was identified with the inclusion of CD-ROMs in all domestic computers and the existence of over 10,000 titles globally, as defined by Negroponte (1995). Although it is uncertain how many of these titles actually did reach a large audience and raw numbers always leave questions regarding how they came upon, these arguments operate as a token of the importance dedicated to the disc-based recording media. CD-ROMs had many issues regarding its use in news and journalism, mostly regarding its long production time. The authoring tools, as Macromedia Director, took advantage of the media and managed complex projects but required a set of specific skills, different from authoring to web-based contents. The industrial part of the process, the mastering, pressing and distribution of the discs, could take as long as three months. This made them suitable for databases, documentaries or long subjects, but not for hard news. Some discs had links to online features, but the message recorded could not be updated. On the other hand, they could deliver video content on home computers, and this feature was a huge selling point due to the perceived crossing of boundaries between print and electronic media and its creative possibilities.

However, digital media, different from analog ones, are fields with constant experimental research that just require the publication of a new codec or software for the world to test, provide feedback and later use it (Pase, 2008). Therefore, on online media, the competition was fierce with several companies with incompatible standards offering gradual advances, such as Progressive Networks (Real Player), Vivo Software (VivoActive), VXTreme (VivoActive), among others. In 1997, Real Player 4.0 was released, which included Real Video technology. Built on top of Real Audio, launched in 1995, it offered the possibility of watching audio and video in synchrony over the Internet with modems of 33.6Kbps or higher. Mirroring the first few days of the video on personal computers, the size of the windows was 160x120 pixels at most, with 10 frames per second as usual mark. This fact stresses the innovation of Black Hawk Down reporting, that inserted video clips throughout the available media, encoded in Real Player format. Although many of the files are still available two decades later, their playback is still restricted by the installation of a proprietary browser plug-in. The online video came to a new standard after the release of YouTube in 2005, in which the flexibility to post and watch contents became the feature to be expected and, thus, being mirrored by competing services, such as Vimeo or Dailymotion.

The broadband Internet diffusion pointed out by Gilder (2001) and Castells (2008) facilitated the circulation of the contents and ended up making largely obsolete disc-based media, as delivery medium for journalistic contents. Time and investment restraints that remain pervasive in the professional field also suggest that the development of a delivery method that adapts to various screens and circumstances (as a browser or app-based reader) from a single source is more cost-efficient than undertaking two production efforts with different tools and specificities. However, these tactics may face the obsolescence too, like the content created for Inside Disaster. The product is a child of the last years of Flash as dominant language to produce rich content for the Internet. An heir of Macromedia´s Director and formerly called Shockwave Flash was a tool to author rich content that could be displayed just with one plugin, without one for each specific language or data compression. In addition, it offered a kind of protection to avoid content being stolen and published out of its Small Web Format (SWF) file. Websites could offer interactive animated content with text, images, and video.

Issues with mobile devices and the rise of new tools to develop applications for these devices, along with the development of HyperText Markup Language version 5 (HTML5), ruined the market share of the multimedia authoring tool[3]. Even Adobe changed the creator software name to Adobe Animate in 2016 (Shankland, 2015). Shortly, when Flash Player will not be updated anymore (Bradley, 2017), a large part of rich content online will not be accessed anymore. Thinking about producers, the skill mastered during the last two decades will not be useful anymore, a fact that highlights that news producers must constantly learn—if possible even help to create—new programming languages[4]. As pointed earlier, transmedia storytelling demands the proper connection between the platforms that carry the multiple information. The short history digression above illustrates the constant evolution—from technological to commercial aspects—that requires frequent updates from professionals and audiences. Moreover, journalism, as it is discussed later, is an important path for new literacies, as the three cases illustrate.

BLACK HAWK DOWN

The first case discussed here is Black Hawk Down: A Story of Modern War (Bowden, 1997). The story developed as a series of 30 pieces published by Philadelphia Enquirer from November 16th to December 14th, in 1997, about an American military operation in Mogadishu, Somalia, in 1993, called "Battle of Mogadishu" or "Battle of the Black Sea". An American task force was designated to capture Mohamed Farrah Aidid, a leader of a Somali faction, but two UH-60 Black Hawk helicopters were hit during the operation and fell. Another group was quickly forged to rescue the crew but had to face a street-level combat to reach the soldiers and leave battleground.

The Battle of the Black Sea, as it is known, was the most serious firefight involving American troops since the Vietnam War. Eighteen American soldiers were killed, and more than 70 wounded, in 15 hours of ferocious fighting. More than 500 Somalis—not all of them, by any means, combatants—were killed, among more than a thousand casualties. (Finnegan, 1999)

Years later, the story became worldwide famous due to a movie with the same name directed by Ridley Scott, in 2002. The motion picture was nominated for four Academy Awards: Best Cinematography, Best Director, Best Film Editing, and Best Sound Mixing, winning the latter two.

Black Hawk Down: A Story of Modern War is characterized by: (1) year of release: 1997; (2) total time: 22 months, 21 months for reporting and one for publishing; (3) total crew: 16 professionals; and (4) media platforms involved: Print version of Philadelphia Enquirer, special website with extra features, CD-ROM, book by Penguin Press and a documentary. The effort by Philadelphia Enquirer was not framed originally as a transmedia project. It is a classic example of early adaptation of content from print media to the open space of the websites. The webpage reunites the options of the full content published in 1997 and links to buy the documentary and book. When the user enters "The Original Newspaper Series Online," finds a deep exploration of the subject, with the texts, photos, videos, audios, maps, glossary of terms, and even a "who´s who" list.

Those who arrived a day or two later were preoccupied with covering the ongoing story of Mike Durant, who was being held captive. Task Force Ranger was strictly off limits to the press, and reporting in Mogadishu is tough. Nevertheless, Rick Atkinson of The Washington Post wrote a remarkably accurate account of the battle for that newspaper soon after it happened. Events move swiftly in international news, and newspapers and TV stations tend to be far more interested in what's happening today than what happened last week, or last month. (Bowden, 1997)

The whole work took almost two years, led by the main author and photographer Peter Tobia with support from other colleagues for the website. During the spring of 1996, Bowden discovered the story while working on another one. "I worked on the project part time for about a year and full time since February" (Bowden, 1997). The turning point came when he interviewed the father of one of the dead Rangers and noticed that were few untold stories about this subject. Before the mass usage of digital social networks, the website also hosted regular sessions of "questions and answers" of the readers with the staff, a classic but nowadays forgotten kind of interactivity between newsroom and its audience. Bowden states that sessions helped even with the content, correcting eventual errors during the whole narrative. "One of the great advantages of online journalism is that I can reach back and correct anything that's wrong instantaneously" (Bowden, 1997). There were 16 people involved in the process: Two for the reporting process (Bowden and Tobia), other five for the print (and main) content, five dedicated to the documentary and other four for the website. Twenty years later, the website layout seems too simple, but it is efficient and clear, a mark of times when multimedia features had to use Flash and a bit of authoring process. During the series, about 70 people were interviewed, some of them to cross-check facts recollected by others.

I also have an official list of the injuries received, which serves as further hard evidence. Lastly, I have many of the accounts -- written either by soldiers in the fight or recorded after interviews with them in the days following the battle. Against that, I have several official Army accounts of the battle in varying degrees of detail, and of course, the transcript of the command net. All of these things together have created the body of this narrative. (Bowden, 1997)

In 1997, Bowden expected that the "multimedia approach" would become a new standard. Even with the development of new technologies, something like this project received attention of the audience only fifteen years later when "Snow Fall, The Avalanche at Tunnel Creek" was released in 2012 (Branch, 2012). Back to the case, one story was published every day during a month, with extra content online. Even with the new format for a series, this approach was also criticized by some readers.

A number of people have complained about the short chapters. You have to remember this is, first and foremost, a newspaper series. The series has been averaging 30 to 40 inches of copy in the paper every day. That's a long newspaper article. The Inquirer's editor, Max King, is rightly concerned about giving readers too long a story every day for 30 days. The Inquirer does often run much bigger pieces, and the Sunday stories in this series have been up to 100 inches or so, which is a huge newspaper article. (Bowden, 1997)

The book and video piece were released later. In the end, it is possible to state that Black Hawk Down pushed the boundaries of the web to host in-depth content with more content than the news that fit to print. The project shows the strength of the journalistic content, and that a simple structure with clear access to its features does the basic and necessary for the readers to dive into the story. While it is not a self-called transmedia project, probably because it was published years before the word got attention (as in Jenkins, 2006), it forms one of the earlier journalistic usages of this strategy of storytelling. The crew had a clear goal, short stories with online extras, and made it during the month of publication. This case reminds the ideas of Salaverría and Negredo (2008) about the importance of focus on delivery process over the technology used, something that could be easily reproduced nowadays.

INSIDE DISASTER

Inside Disaster (PTV Productions, 2010a) is a project developed in 2010 by PTV Productions and the Canadian government. The project shows how the Red Cross International works after huge tragedies and the case witnessed was the tragedy caused by an earthquake in Haiti, in January 2010. It is composed of three main features: (1) a documentary in three parts, (2) a website with news and other important data about the tragedy in Port-au-Prince, and (3) a newsgame, also published online. "Consistent with the characteristics compiled by Jenkins referring to transmedia, there is no doubt that Inside Disaster is a representative of transmedia journalism" (Pase, Nunes, & Fontoura, 2012, p. 71). Inside Disaster is characterized by: (1) year of release: 2010; (2) total time: 14 months; (3) total crew: 19 professionals; and (4) media platforms involved: Television documentary series, weblog, website with deep content, and an online newsgame.

Inside Disaster Haiti follows the disaster relief teams of the Red Cross as they mount the largest single-country response in their history. In Haiti, 600 trained humanitarians, from over 30 countries, are on the ground. Embedded in the Red Cross base camp, our cameras had unprecedented access to the gripping stories, compelling characters and intense drama that unfolded after Haiti's horrific quake on January

12th, 2010. This intense and compelling series takes us behind the headlines of a large-scale disaster to document the emergency relief operation from first response to recovery. (PTV Productions, 2010b)

The project received its approval in September 2009. Before January of the following year, the team prepared themselves without knowing which kind of story they would report.

We had two film crews on standby ready to deploy the moment the Red Cross mobilized its international disaster response teams. Because we had no way of knowing whether we would be filming in the aftermath of a cyclone, a tsunami or an earthquake, we had to be prepared for every situation. We packed military food rations, water filters, sleeping bags, mosquito nets, satellite phones, a generator... and then we waited. (Pequenza, 2010)

During this time, the crew tracked warning signs, such as tropical storms, earth tremors, and rumbling volcanoes. As the director states in the press release, "then, the most unexpected disaster struck... at 16:54 on January 12th, an earthquake in Haiti" (Pequenza, 2010). One hour after receiving the news, Pequenza contacted Red Cross and two days later she and her colleagues arrived at Port-au-Prince. There, two teams recorded content, one dedicated to tracking Red Cross workers, while the other registered stories of survivors. This was a process that took six more months because it had to track the rebuilding process of Haiti, not just the case of arriving there, produce factual stories and leave as soon as possible. Thus, it captured the moment Red Cross Field Assessment and Coordination Team (FACT) arrived there for long-term recovery. FACT is a "multi-disciplinary team, trained to assess need, call in help, and oversee a disaster response" (PTV Productions, 2010b), with experts in health, relief, logistics, water, and sanitation.

Back before the earthquake, during pre-production time, they already defined that the goal was to create an interactive experience with three points of view: (1) the FACT workers, (2) survivors, and (3) journalists. With this idea in mind, the script was created by Pequenza and Michael Gibson, a game developer with experience in serious games. Nicolas Jolliet, co-director and author of the interactive experience, also traveled to Haiti. Online content was published first. Hours after the arrival, Jolliet started a weblog with raw content. It became the channel to track the progress of the crew, mixing journalistic stories with backstage information. "Throughout the month following the quake, InsideDisaster.com featured daily blogging, photos and mini documentaries direct from the disaster zone, uploaded nightly via satellite modem" (PTV Productions, 2010b, p. 19). Away from a newsroom or proper space, Jolliet used a Canon 5D video camera, sound gear, and a MacBook Pro. During a month in the country, he filmed and edited twenty mini-documentaries, shot hundreds of photos, and wrote over 25 blog posts. The main documentary was edited later and not during the initial rush of the coverage. The first structure was roughly composed of sequences of images and videos, but in August 2010 they had to fly back to shoot more material. Months later, the website relaunched during Autumn.

The newsgame is a "simulator" consisted of interactive video snippets that create a story based on life decision scenarios. The player must pick one character after the question "What decisions would you make as an earthquake survivor, aid worker, or journalist in Haiti after the earthquake?" (PTV Productions, 2010a)

As a transmedia initiative, Inside Disaster is a puzzle with many, but still measurable, parts, grouped into three segments that compose the main narrative. The individual cognitive intersection between different segments of this story is a choice of each user, but the three parts are related to each other in a planned manner to form a cohesive and complete story. (Pase, Nunes, & Fontoura, 2012, p. 70)

The authors point that this project is based on the deconstruction of a linear reasoning and the classic production logic of traditional journalism. The attention given to content creation and the design of the experience, helped with the fact that the blog also produced content for the audience, the crew surpassed natural limits of time, even in a post-tragedy scenario. "There lies the challenge of the expansion of transmedia communication within the newsrooms of major media groups: the triad composed of time, market and cost" (Pase, Nunes, & Fontoura, 2012, p. 70). This is a strategy that can be deployed or used as inspiration by other teams.

The project also connects all content to build an immersive product. The user can play the game without watching the videos or read texts, but there will be some missed points. One of the purposes of the game is to test the audience, checking if the player got the message the journalists aimed to publish, and a game based on decisions can be seen as the perfect tool for this. As example, the track of the journalist is composed of moments when the player must define scenes, a form of checking if the audience has the comprehension of the fact desired by the crew.

Inside Disaster articulates this informational synergy in order to make the storyline immersive and critical. The simulator adds the perspective of several characters, and invites the audience to participate by making decisions. The background of this story depends on the path chosen by the interagent: for those who favor the articles of the site, the background becomes the simulator and the television documentary, but the reverse also applies. (Pase, Nunes, & Fontoura, 2012, p. 71)

The project took months to be created, even with initial planning. This shows that even emergency reporting needs its proper time to produce deep products. The multimedia authoring, in this case, use technologies more complex than the ones saw in Black Hawk Down, even with the fact that the videos used for the project were already digital. The newsgame and some parts of the content were authored in Flash.

In comparison to the other two cases discussed in this chapter, Inside Disaster involves a middle-point of complex skills. However, even with a transmedia mindset during the publication process, the act of coming back to shoot more images of Port-au-Prince months after the main quake highlights how content drives the whole process, a balance of the pendulum of content versus planning that regulates transmedia projects. The crew had a clear idea of what to shoot, a basic outline of the stories, and even though had to come back later to the scenario. This project shows how planning is important to avoid missing a key aspect that will not be possible to be captured later—luckily it was possible this time. It is impossible to plan everything that will be captured, and a keen journalistic eye will be necessary (more than during traditional reporting) to change the story, in case something important suddenly happens. This may be a small but important procedure to avoid the rush against time.

HARVEST OF CHANGE

The last project studied is Harvest of Change (Des Moines Register, 2014), an analysis of how farming culture changed in Iowa, United States, during the last decades. The project was published by Des

Moines Register, a newspaper owned by Gannett Company (owner of USA Today), and shows the life of the Dammann family, with a six-generation farming tradition. The project is characterized by: (1) year of release: 2014; (2) total time: 4 months; (3) total crew: 25 professionals; and (4) media platforms involved: A series of five-part stories on Des Moines Register, website with extras (such as 360º video) and an application for Oculus Rift.

At first sight, this case reminds Black Hawk Down: A series of stories printed on newspaper in five pieces during a week followed by online extras. The project discusses how aging of farmers, change of culture, immigration, new technologies, and globalization affects the traditional farming processes in Iowa. However, it became famous due to the usage of Oculus Rift to place the user inside the new scenario and compare with the previous one described in the stories. This was one of the first uses of virtual reality released as a journalistic piece and by a media outlet, using a product that was not sold to regular consumers (Oculus Rift Development Kits). Users without the gadget can experience it with versions for computers, playable online or offline (with the same version downloaded to use with Rift). Different from other stories, Harvester of Change experiments how an immersive new device could improve storytelling. Rift, the virtual reality headset, was first launched in 2012, in the crowdfunding platform Kickstarter with an initial price of $275 for the headset. By the time Harvest of Change was published, in 2014, 125,000 development kits had been sold, mostly to development companies and gamers (DeBarros, 2014). In the same year, Oculus was acquired by Facebook for $2 billion. The consumer edition was released only in 2016. Therefore, the option to do a virtual reality experience was a bet on a new medium, but with a familiar subject for the rural audience of the Des Moines Register. For most people, the experience can be downloaded as a desktop app for Windows and Mac. To produce it, the journalists had the help of Total Cinema 360, a New York City film company that shot the 360º videos.

In our project, viewers can take an immersive, self-guided tour of the farm, rendered in 3-D using the Unity video game engine. Along the way are a dozen 360-degree video segments in which the family and others in agriculture discuss their work and issues they face with technology, genetically modified crops, shifting culture and the future of farming in a time of rapid change. (DeBarros, 2014)

The interactive feature has the scheme of a game, created with Unity, a game creation language. The project allows the reader to see and explore a virtual version of the Dammann family farm. When interacting with several special locations, the story is expanded with more information about their lives and farm. Photos and infographics present extra information in a manner that resembles Role-Playing Games (RPG) with players interacting with objects to understand the scenario and advance on quests. Although today the Harvest of Change graphics may be seen as raw or unrealistic, they offer an interactive experience different from 360º videos that do not allow the user to explore the area like a "sandbox", with a high level of detail to recreate buildings and places. "Aerial imagery was used to accurately place and size objects. Everything in the environment was built to scale, and several objects, such as buildings, incorporate actual textures from photographs" (DeBarros, 2014).

The Harvest of Change project highlights how a scenario can be created to place the reader inside the story, and it is very successful when it is combined with 360º videos, focusing on the characters' stories. Even though it is called "explanatory journalism," the project can be viewed as a documentary with a nonlinear narrative (Gayomali, 2014), and the viewer is encouraged to explore the whole area to form a bigger picture. To create a three-dimensional experience like this to discuss farming may seem an odd idea, but the transition from past to present on the project helps the viewer to fill the gaps, compare and contrast the conditions in which the Dammann family is living and their challenges.

Among the three projects studied here, Harvest of Change is probably the most ambitious: It uses virtual reality, a headset that was not widely known at the time, a game engine and even 360º video. However, it was also the one with shorter time from planning to publish, only four months. To record the videos for Oculus Rift, a small crew followed the family for three months (Gayomali, 2014) to film and detail objects that were placed inside the virtual experience. There were more than 320 hours spent on the farms, 22 professionals involved, 17 hours of video transcribed and more than 16,000 words written. Even though it is one of the most ambitious projects, it is also the most aligned with current news—from the subject to the way of reporting—focused on the characters, with interviews and a more "traditional" approach. Like Philadelphia Enquirer before, this series was created by a company with the proper tools to present a different form of storytelling and eager to develop new experiences.

During its design and rendering time, Harvest of Change allowed the journalists to combine real video with virtual environments. The series indicates that these projects can reconstruct scenes, a good alternative to other journalism projects such as the ones based on historic events and education. Moreover, the idea of an immersive experience, even without image accuracy, can be used as a new form to present Hawk-Eye systems to the audience, offering a way to experience the vision a footballer had when he scored a goal, as example.

CONCLUSION

The three cases analyzed in this chapter help to understand the value—and therefore the function—of time within transmedia journalism. Transmedia projects offer an interesting path to test new ideas, borrow strategies from movie writers or game producers and introduce it into the realm of journalism. The mindset for creation is different, acting more like a "content designer" that thinks about the pieces of a puzzle of stories that will be published, expecting to catch audiences with one link or the full story. In a context that puts Journalism in a dangerous position, corroded by the torrent of content produced by reliable or non-reliable sources, transmedia configures a bet on time. More days to gather information or polish will not avoid errors, but bring different information that can influence the strategy of the whole experience. The challenge is to fit this content into regular editions and their cruel production cycles, combining fast and slow content. These stories may be produced by organizations with different goals than journalistic ones, but a careful process is a characteristic inherent to news producers.

If the main story is not a fact that is being developed as days pass by, like the earthquake in Haiti, a transmedia scheme can be designed with the proper time and without the rush to fulfill the deadline or publish before rivals. It is not a matter of time to be the first discussing a topic, but more time to build the scenario of the story, to build the world (Gambarato, 2016; Gambarato & Tárcia, 2017). With the diverse opportunities to discover new stories, from long video series published by Netflix to video games based on real cases, journalists face other rivals struggling for the attention of audiences. With ethical limits as basis and technological knowledge (or will to experiment), transmedia storytelling opens new paths to discuss the world. The technological development increased the importance of the time to craft, and planning is an act that may take its own time. Like in Inside Disaster, the team was preparing themselves while the perfect story was not available. When it happened, the team knew what to shoot and interview. Black Hawk Down and Harvester of Change had different calendars. While the first is a consequence of a team that captured everything possible and later spread it over print media and its website, the latter one is a symbol of actual tools that allows the newsroom to think about a theme and quickly present it differently. It is not just the case to be the first to publish using a new gadget, but try to place journalism as a source for rich experiences.

Another issue that can be noticed through the three cases is that all of them have a little bit of experimentation. While Black Hawk Down tried to push the limits of a large story inside the (almost) infinite space of the Internet, almost publishing every information acquired, Inside Disaster opted to test the connection of traditional experiences with one driven by the audience, a newsgame. Inside their limits, the path to watch and think was the result of choices by the persons that had the freedom to think about which platform would be chosen to discover content and now have to think about the stories to play a game and mount the big picture of transmedia journalism.

The scenario is different for Harvest of Change. The support of a large media company and the will to bring readers to new forms to browse content, also being one of the first ones to test virtual reality for journalistic purposes, allowed the team to produce a whole project in a short period, but with a clear strategy. In addition, an external team was hired to shoot some videos and help them to produce it. Outsourcing is a measure used inside entertainment industries, helping teams to gather quality assets and maybe overcome short deadlines. Moreover, two aspects that may cause fear in some journalists should not be neglected: Trial and error. New technologies or new forms to use cutting-edge tools may not result in successful projects when used for the first time. Furthermore, the newsroom should consider the feedback provided by the audience, paying attention to the ways the project was enjoyed. Looking back to the response of Black Hawk Down, as pointed by Bowden (1997), readers may not be treated as "lords of expression," and journalists have to walk the thin line between surprising the audience with interesting stories with forms that can be easily comprehended and, therefore, used.

The time factor is a byline for these projects. Transmedia requires deep planning and professionals should understand that time used to think about strategies is important. This may include even tests to check if something can be done, as checkpoints—another idea that comes from games. Above all, journalists must understand that the validation to apply transmedia strategies to journalism will come after a recurrent publication history of this kind of projects, and the constant process of improving the craft to tell stories.

REFERENCES

Bolter, J. D., & Grusin, R. (2000). *Remediation: Understanding new media*. Cambridge, MA: The MIT Press.

Bowden, M. (1997). *Black Hawk Down*. Retrieved from http://inquirer.philly.com/packages/somalia/

Bradley, T. (2017, July 29). *The death of Adobe Flash is long overdue*. Retrieved from https://www.forbes.com/sites/tonybradley/2017/07/29/the-death-of-adobe-flash-is-long-overdue/#7893ee536f8b

Castells, M. (2008). *A era da informação: Economia, sociedade e cultura* [The age of information: Economy, society and culture] (11th ed.). São Paulo: Paz e Terra.

Danesi, M. (2009). *Dictionary of media and communications*. New York: M. E. Sharpe.

DeBarros, A. (2014, September 17). *Harvest of Change: Virtual reality project is a journalism first*. Retrieved from http://www.desmoinesregister.com/story/money/agriculture/2014/09/17/harvest-of-change-virtual-farm-virtual-reality/15785377/

Des Moines Register. (2014). *Harvest of Change: Iowa farm families confront a nation in transition*. Retrieved from http://www.desmoinesregister.com/pages/interactives/harvest-of-change/

Finnegan, W. (1999, March 14). *A million enemies*. Retrieved from http://www.nytimes.com/books/99/03/14/reviews/990314.14finnegt.html

Gambarato, R. R. (2016). The Sochi Project: Slow Journalism within the transmedia space. *Digital Journalism*, *4*(4), 445–461. doi:10.1080/21670811.2015.1096746

Gambarato, R. R., & Tárcia, L. P. T. (2017). Transmedia strategies in journalism. An analytical model for the news coverage of planned events. *Journalism Studies*, *18*(11), 1381–1399. doi:10.1080/1461670X.2015.1127769

Gaskell, E. (2003). *The complete guide to digital video*. London: Cengage Learning.

Gayomali, C. (2014, September 22). *How an Iowa newspaper is using Oculus Rift for big, ambitious journalism*. Retrieved from https://www.fastcompany.com/3035851/world-changing-ideas/how-an-iowa-newspaper-is-using-oculus-rift-for-big-ambitious-journalism

Gilder, G. (2000). *Telecosm*. New York: Free Press.

Greenberg, S. (2012). Slow journalism in the digital fast lane. In R. Keeble & J. Tulloch (Eds.), *Global literary journalism: Exploring the journalistic imagination* (pp. 381–393). New York: Peter Lang.

Hochberg, A. (2014, November 04). *News for the Minecraft generation: Gannett experiments with virtual reality*. Retrieved from http://www.poynter.org/2014/news-for-the-minecraft-generation-gannett-experiments-with-virtual-reality/270633/

Jenkins, H. (2006). *Convergence culture: Where old and new media collide*. New York: New York University Press.

Le Masurier, M. (2015). What is slow journalism? *Journalism Practice*, *9*(2), 138–152. doi:10.1080/17512786.2014.916471

Mittell, J. (2014). Strategies of storytelling on transmedia television. In M.-L. Ryan & J.-N. Thon (Eds.), *Storyworlds across media: Toward a media-conscious narratology* (pp. 253–277). Lincoln, NE: University of Nebraska Press. doi:10.2307/j.ctt1d9nkdg.16

Negroponte, N. (1995). *Being digital*. New York: Alfred A. Knopf.

Owens, J. (2007). *Television sports production*. New York: Focal Press.

Pase, A. (2008). *Vídeo online, alternativa para as mudanças da TV na cultura digital* [Online video, alternative for the transformation of TV inside digital culture] (Unpublished doctoral dissertation). Pontifícia Universidade Católica do Rio Grande do Sul.

Pase, A., Nunes, A. C., & Fontoura, M. (2012). One subject, many paths: Transmedia communication in journalism. *Brazilian Journalism Research*, *8*(1), 63–76.

Pequenza, N. (2010). Production story. In PTV Productions. *Inside Disaster: Press Kit*. Retrieved from http://insidedisaster.com/outreach/IDH-PressKit_Dec2010.pdf

PTV Productions. (2010a). *Inside Disaster*. Retrieved from http://insidedisaster.com/haiti/

PTV Productions. (2010b). *Inside Disaster: Press Kit*. Retrieved from http://insidedisaster.com/outreach/IDH-PressKit_Dec2010.pdf

Salaverría, R., & Negredo, S. (2008). *Periodismo integrado: Convergencia de medios y reorganización de redacciones* [Integrated journalism: Media convergence and reorganization of newsrooms]. Barcelona: Sol90.

Schneider, A. (1997). Jump cut! Memoirs of a pioneer television editor. Jefferson: McFarland.

Shankland, S. (2015). *The death of Adobe's Flash is lingering, not sudden*. Retrieved from https://www.cnet.com/news/the-death-of-adobes-flash-is-lingering-not-sudden/

Tenenboim-Weinblatt, K., & Neiger, M. (2017). Temporal affordances in the news. *Journalism*, *1*(19), 1–19.

Yin, R. K. (2009). *Case study research: Design and methods* (4th ed.). London: Sage Publication.

Youngblood, G. (1970). *Expanded Cinema*. New York: P. Dutton & Co. Inc.

KEY TERMS AND DEFINITIONS

360º Video: Video recordings where a view in every direction is recorded simultaneously, using an omnidirectional camera or a collection of cameras.

Avid: A professional software-based non-linear editing system used in the television and video industry.

Codec: A portmanteau of *coder-decoder*. A computer program for encoding and decoding a digital data stream or signal.

EditDroid: A computerized non-linear editing system developed by Lucasfilms in the 1980s. It was later sold to Avid Technology.

Flash: A multimedia software platform used for production of animations, internet applications, desktop applications, mobile applications, mobile games, and embedded web browser video players.

Oculus Rift: A virtual reality headset that completely immerses users in virtual worlds.

Sandbox: A term for video games used to describe titles that offer freedom to explore scenarios and leave to the player the option to choose the order of the objectives or missions.

ENDNOTES

1 In 2016, the newspaper Washington Post created a bot using the communication service Slack to act as a virtual version of the Executive Editor Marty Baron. The tool could track how the newsroom was dealing with time and message reporters when their time was ending.

2 A modem with 33,6 Kb/s was the standard speed offered by Internet service providers in the middle of the nineties.

3 Apart from the debate Apple vs. Adobe about Flash and its problems, such as the high usage of the random-access memory (RAM) of the devices, HTML5 was an open-source standard and even Microsoft's NotePad could be used to edit these files, different from Adobe and its idea of freedom to use its codecs, but creating and editing content only with their tools.

4 The authors understand that journalists shall program, or at least develop basic notions of software programming. This shall happen not on a level of understanding how something can be made using Adobe Dreamweaver or Wordpress, as examples, but being able to read the code and comprehend how content display works.

Chapter 5
Immersive Journalism Design Within a Transmedia Space

Nohemí Lugo Rodríguez
Tecnológico de Monterrey, Mexico

ABSTRACT

The purpose of this chapter is to contribute to the theoretical frame of transmedia journalism by proposing a question-based model that focuses on transmedia design when an immersive journalism piece is integrated into a transmedia space. Immersive journalism is a new medium that could be effectively used to foster social empathy by means of virtual reality stories in journalism. The chapter is guided by the following ideas: (1) narrative strategies that may be useful in the design of immersive journalism experiences; (2) aesthetic principles of immersive experiences; and (3) inclusion of an immersive experience in a transmedia space. Thus, this chapter reviews the narrative techniques and aesthetics of immersive experiences that might contribute to the design of both the immersive piece and the transmedia space.

INTRODUCTION

Virtual Reality (VR) headsets such as Oculus Rift, Samsung Gear, HTC Vive, Google Daydream, Google Cardboard, and PlayStation VR are now cheaper and more portable than previous interfaces for experiencing virtual reality. Their presence makes the production and the consumption of immersive experiences for different purposes, including journalism, simultaneously easier and more widespread. VR has been used to produce immersive journalism: "the production of news in a form in which people can gain first-person experiences of the events or situations described in news stories" (De la Peña, Weil, Llobera, Giannopoulos, Pomés, Spanlang, & Slater, 2010, p. 291). In addition to these three-dimensional (3D) modeled environments, 360-degree video has been used to report in the field and to produce what could be called live action immersive chronicles and documentaries.

Immersive journalism has become a new asset of the transmedia journalism space. Transmedia space, according to Saldre and Torop (2012) "appears as a notion that integrates meta- and inter-communicative levels, presuming the interpretation of the same message as the sequence of proto- and meta-texts described in different discourses and fixed in different sign systems and media" (p. 41). An immersive

DOI: 10.4018/978-1-5225-3781-6.ch005

experience may function both as a *mothership*, that is, the main work from which other products derive (Jenkins, 2009), or it may function as an *extension*: Media products that have a complete meaning on their own but serve to enrich the main story (Scolari, 2013; Gambarato, 2013). When combining VR with other media in order to create a transmedia space, VR should have a clear, non-superfluous role in the whole user experience.

Since immersive journalism is a recent trend, it is necessary to develop a theoretical frame that assists in both the design and analysis of immersive journalism within a transmedia space. This chapter contributes as a theoretical-practical tool for journalists, researchers, and students of communication and journalism. Thus, this work includes a literature review from the fields of journalism, digital media aesthetics, virtual reality and transmedia storytelling. In order to write this chapter, the author explored different interfaces such as Oculus Rift, HTC VIVE, and Samsung Gear; downloaded different VR applications for general purposes; used different headsets such as Google Cardboard, Viewmaster, and VMAX; and downloaded different immersive journalism experiences on Android and IOS phones. The chapter is guided by the following ideas: (a) narrative strategies that may be useful in the design of immersive journalism experiences; (b) aesthetic principles of immersive experiences; and (c) inclusion of an immersive experience in a transmedia space.

JOURNALISM AND VIRTUAL REALITY

Journalism in this century has broadened its meaning. Van der Haak, Parks, and Castells (2012) argue that journalism is about telling meaningful stories on what is new or what is happening in the world, understanding it in context, explaining it to others, and making it available to the public so they can use it for their own needs. This demonstrates how journalism in this century is more contextual than it was in the past. Fink and Schudson (2014) explain how the rise and predominance of contextual journalism started in the 1960's. Furthermore, they clarify the difference between conventional stories and contextual stories: Conventional stories answer the "who-what-when-where" questions, usually ignoring or only implicitly addressing "why"; they describe activities that have occurred or will occur within 24 hours; and they focus on one-time activities or actions. In contrast, contextual stories vary formally, have a wider focus, and describe more complex issues.

According to Menke, Kinnebrock, Kretzschmar, Aichberger, Broersma, Hummel, and Salaverría (2016), contemporary journalism, has been influenced by convergence culture and has been evolving over the last two decades. Van der Haak et al. (2012) insist that "good" journalists in the 21st century tell fact-based stories about the real world through text, audio, and visual media which people can relate to, share, and appropriate. Through the transmedia nature of journalism, a journalist should consider how every medium is used for doing what it does best (Jenkins, 2006) and ideally, as with any social or cultural transmedia project, active user participation should be included in the design (Lugo, 2016).

What virtual reality does best as a medium is to offer users the opportunity to "see for yourself" and "be there." For Ryan (2015), virtual reality is the latest technology that attempts to erase the interface in favor of creating a believable experience. Wilson and Zoranzo (2015) declare that one of the main advantages of virtual reality is stereoscopic depth, which creates the illusion that the viewer is seeing objects in a virtual space. The advantage of VR is the ability to present stimuli in three dimensions. The power of virtual reality simulations is evident in fields as psychology and neuroscience studies because of the key feature of this medium that makes the user a participant: *Presence*. North and North (2016) relate *presence* with the awareness of being in a place, with the realness and vividness of the place and experience, and with the behavior of users. It is considered a good sign that users behave as if the virtual world portrayed is real. When used for social purposes, VR offers the opportunity to be in somebody else's shoes.

Through the use of VR, one may observe what it is like for a Syrian girl to live in the Za'atari refugee camp (*Clouds over Sidra,* Here Be Dragons, Arora & Milk, 2015); what it is like to be in the vicinity of a bombing in Aleppo (*Project Syria,* De La Peña et al., 2014); what it is like to live in a confinement cell (*6x9:A virtual experience of solitary confinement*, The Mill, The Guardian, Panetta, & Poulton, 2016); what it is like for a man to go into diabetic shock in a Los Angeles food bank (*Hunger in Los Angeles*, De la Peña & Virtual Pyedog, 2012); what it is like for three children in different locations around the world to see their houses destroyed and to be forced to leave their homes (*The Displaced*, Silverstein, 2015); what Fukushima is like years after a nuclear disaster (*Fukushima, contaminated lives*, Verdú, 2016). These are just a few examples of immersive experiences that try to connect average citizens with an unfamiliar situation experienced by others.

Chris Milk (TED, 2015), director of 360-degree VR documentaries, has claimed that VR technologies are "empathy machines." Empathy created through VR could be explained as feeling in a similar way to the way one would feel in real life; thus, the immersive experience represents a situation that in real life would make people feel empathy. Empathy is a complex psychological response. It is studied in fields such as neuroscience and psychology. Empathy is an oriented emotional response congruent with the perceived welfare of another person (see Batson, Batson, Slingsby, Harrell, Peekna, & Todd, 1991). Decety and Ickes (2009) emphasize that empathy is a process in which observation, memory, knowledge, and reasoning are combined; they add that it is essential to recognize the other person as like oneself, while maintaining a clear separation between self and other. However, the empathy of users cannot necessarily be predicted nor controlled. Keen (2006) points out that users' experiences differ from one another. In the VR realm, North and North (2016) consider that there are individual differences in the sense of *presence* when subjects are confronted with the same virtual environment. The individual's personal experiences contribute to this factor and this is very difficult to be controlled by designers. It is important to add that users may possibly also have physical reactions to VR experiences: "One problem associated with using VR is that it can cause nausea and dizziness, a phenomenon known as 'simulator sickness'" (Schuemie, Van Der Straaten, Krijn, & Van Der Mast, 2001, p. 188). However, there are high expectations that this new medium can foster empathy. In addition, empathy is not just seen as a reaction from the audience, but it is also viewed as a strategy in psychology and in narrative empathy studies. This chapter, therefore, explores the design of immersive journalism experiences, which in most cases up until now are stories. Theoretical explorations can be useful in inspiring designers to reflect on and analyze immersive journalism pieces from a storytelling and media aesthetics points of view.

IMMERSIVE JOURNALISM DESIGN

Empathy and Narratives

Batson, Lishner, Cook and Sayer (2005) state that humans can feel empathy for strangers in need and that these empathic feelings include sympathy, compassion, tenderness, sorrow, and grief, for instance. They add that "these feelings have been found to be a source of motivation to help relieve the empathy-inducing need" (Batson et al., 2005, p. 15). According to Sillesen, Ip, and Uberti (2015), empathic responses increase as we gather more information about others. Hence, knowledge and time are important factors in the generation of empathy: Human contact should continue for at least thirty minutes for a person to feel empathy for somebody he/she does not know. Interestingly, empathy can be induced. For more than 20 years, Batson has conducted diverse studies related to the relationship between empathy, altruism, and, the change in attitudes. Batson, Chang, Orr, and Rowland (2002) found that inducing empathy toward a member of a stigmatized group can improve attitudes toward the group as a whole. According to these authors, empathy inducement has been used to improve attitudes toward people with Acquired Immune Deficiency Syndrome (AIDS), toward the homeless, and toward racial and ethnic minorities. These authors, who propose an improved model based on Batson's et al. (1991) first model, add that their results provide reassurance about the practical value of using empathy as a technique for creating more positive responses to the plight of the stigmatized. Empathy changes not only attitudes, but also actions: "Those induce to feel empathy appear willing to put their money where their mouth is. And if they are, then there may be real reason for optimism" (Batson et al., 2002, p. 1666).

It is important to remember that immersive journalism productions are mediated experiences. The way in which designers decide to organize information may vary. *Form* is an essential aspect of empathy stimulation. In this sense, the power of narrative as a communicative form over other formats is clear. Oliver, Dillard, Bae, and Tamul (2012) highlight the power that narratives have to foster feelings of empathy and compare this to the power that narratives have to motivate actions and to alter beliefs and attitudes. In their study, they illustrate specifically how narratives help to reduce prejudices toward stigmatized groups (Oliver et al., 2012).

In the narratology field, Taylor, Hodges, and Kohányi (2003) discuss a concept they call *narrative empathy* and describe it as the sharing of feeling and perspective-taking induced by reading, viewing, hearing or imagining narratives of another's situation and condition. Specifically in the field of journalism, Fink and Schudson (2014) mention, among other types of journalistic contextual stories, *social empathy stories,* which encourage readers to "be interested in, have compassion for, or empathize with the experiences and problems of people who are largely unfamiliar to them" (p. 11). According to Fink and Schudson (2014), these *social empathy stories* have the following characteristics:

- Describe a person or group of people not often covered in news stories.
- May answer the question, "what does it feel like to be this person?"
- Use personal experiences to talk about larger social problems.
- Often begin with anecdotal leads, using many direct quotes from their main sources.
- Structure narratives around the observations of sources rather than those of a detached observer.

Social empathy stories appear to follow part of the empathy model proposed by Batson et al. (2005), since this model implies two of the following steps: (a) adopting the perspective of a needy individual leads to increased empathic feelings, then (b) these feelings lead to a perception of increased valuing of this individuals' welfare. *Social empathy stories* also appear to use what Keen (2006) calls *ambassadorial strategic empathy*, which refers to cultivating readers' empathy for an in-group, often for a specific purpose, such as an appeal for justice, for recognition, or for assistance.

Oliver et al. (2012) showed that when there is compassion for a specific individual, such as a character in the story, then a certain attitude toward the group represented by the character is generated. This study was based on the model proposed by Batson et al. (1991). Oliver et al. (2012) discuss the importance of taking the perspective of the other (e.g., the character represented) in the empathy process. However, from the storytelling point of view, the way that perspective-taking is induced in a narrative should be carefully crafted. Keen (2006) argues that the achievement of *narrative empathy* is frequently taken for granted via the use of a small set of narrative tropes, such as the use of first person narration and the interior representation of a character's consciousness and emotional states. The author points out that more empirical testing is needed to make sure that these and other strategies can effectively promote empathy in readers.

In addition to avoiding false generalizations about "narrative recipes" to foster empathy, producers should be careful to avoid over-stimulating audiences. Maier (2015) explains how mass media have contributed to what has been described as *compassion fatigue,* which is an indifferent or negative attitude toward the pain and suffering of others. Readers are tired of formulas that over-simplify complex challenges and that stereotype victims. These hero-victim portrayals are a failure in storytelling when trying to promote an important cause; other failures in storytelling are caused by psychic numbing, sensationalism, and lack of context. When journalists and VR designers work together to design an immersive experience, they need to explore the aesthetics of this medium to tell stories, and they need to be innovative. However, there are no specific formulas for achieving this.

Immersion and Narratives

Immersion is defined by Janet Murray (1997) as a sense of being contained within a space or state of mind that is separate from ordinary experience. Since immersion could be considered both a personal and a psychological state, different media offer different degrees and methods of immersion according to the language of each medium. This is not an exclusive affordance of digital media, as theater, novels, and films are immersive as well. Ryan (2015) proposes three forms of involvement in narratives that appear especially suited for virtual reality: Spatial immersion, temporal immersion, and emotional immersion.

Spatial Immersion (The Response to Setting)

Ryan (2015) asserts that there is a difference between space and place, since the second has an emotional meaning for users because they are somehow emotionally and cognitively related to that space. Murray (1997) adds that immersive experiences are disrupted by the inconsistency and incompleteness of an environment and yet are reinforced by encyclopedic detail and a sense of vast spaces within clearly marked boundaries. Moreover, Jenkins (2004) presents the concept of *environmental storytelling,* which creates the preconditions for an immersive narrative experience in four ways: (a) by evoking pre-existing narrative associations, (b) by providing a staging ground where narrative events are enacted, (c) by embedding narrative information within their *mise-en-scène*, and (d) by providing resources for emergent narratives.

Evoking Pre-Existing Narrative Associations

In this case, users recognize the place. This could be because it is a real place, like Paris; because it represents the conventions of a narrative genre, for instance a horror movie; or because the space refers to a specific fiction that users know, such as spaces in the Harry Potter saga. Recognizing Hogwarts in a movie after having read the novel or recognizing the objects placed in a thematic attraction park after having watched the movie are examples of this. Evidently, this also fosters emotional immersion.

Providing A Staging Ground Where Narrative Events Are Enacted

In this situation, users are playing roles. For instance, in the *Bioshock* saga video games, or *The Last of Us* video games, users play a first-person role. The player interacts with objects and non-player characters, and when the player arrives at a specific place, spends certain amount of time in a given zone, or uses certain objects, then pre-determined events occur.

Embedding Narrative Information Within Their Mise-En-Scène

The *Bioshock* saga is particularly good at this. Much of what players learn about the nature of the setting and its history comes not from text or character dialogue, but rather from forgotten objects on the street, plaques on walls or (sometimes defaced) statues, puddles of blood next to protest signs, government posters warning about certain groups or activities, locked doors, etc.

Providing Resources for Emergent Narratives

In video games like *The Sims* or *Minecraft*, users can create identities, stock and trade belongings, and have interactions with other characters, whose relationships are not predetermined. This also happens in massively multiplayer online role-playing games (MMORPG's) where the player can choose, form, and develop the identity of her character throughout the game.

These four strategies of *environmental storytelling* were proposed by Jenkins (2004) in reference to video games, but they can be applied to virtual reality in two ways: (a) determining how to use the space to tell a story and evoke memories, feelings and narrative genre conventions, what Jenkins calls creating *evocative spaces;* and (b) deciding how users are going to participate in the virtual space. Users can participate in a virtual space in the following three ways: (a) as witnesses observing what occurs around them; (b) as actors enacting a narrative in a first-person role; or (c) as explorers and builders, both exploring the space and building their own narrative.

Temporal Immersion (The Response to the Story)

The reader's involvement in the process of time progression within a story is referred to as *temporal immersion*. The passing of time matters to the reader because it is a process of disclosure. Ryan (2015) notes:

The art of creating interest in a story requires an efficient interweaving of two temporal dynamics: the dynamics inherent to the temporal unfolding of the told events, of the causal chain that constitutes story, and the dynamics inherent to the telling, to the revealing or withdrawing of the information that enables readers to apprehend the logic of the story. (location 31%)

Emotional Immersion (The Response to Characters)

According to Schuemie, Van Der Straaten, Krijn, and Van Der Mast (2001), "Perhaps one of the most important consequences of presence is that a virtual experience can evoke the same reactions and emotions as a real experience" (p. 187). While Ryan (2015) describes this kind of involvement in relation to identification with characters, which is essential, it could be said that emotional immersion is a consequence of all the strategies used for the user to be present: Identification with characters, spatial immersion, and temporal immersion. It is worthwhile to remember another affordance of digital media proposed by Murray (1997): *Agency*. *Agency* occurs when interactivity is meaningful and users directly see the power of their actions. Ryan (2015) proposes two criteria for classifying interactivity, according to the relationship between the user and the storyworld:

Membership of the User

The user's interaction with the storyworld can be *internal,* when the actions of the user correspond to events in the story of the world, or *external,* when the user controls the story from a godlike perspective or is simply not "inside" the story.

Creative Power of the User

In an *exploratory* interaction, the user might be able to observe what exists in the world but not be able to change anything. In an *ontological* interaction, "the storyworld evolves as a result of the interaction" (Ryan, 2015, location 50%). The observations of these two criteria can then be presented in four combinations. User interaction may thus be one of the following: (a) *internal-exploratory*, (b) *external-exploratory*, (c) *ontological-internal*, and (d) *ontological-external* (Ryan, 2015).

In many immersive journalism experiences, users can just select where to direct their line of vision, but they do not belong to the story in an explicit way. This is the case of *Clouds of Sidra* (Here Be Dragons et al., 2015), which is an example of *external-exploratory* interactivity. In some works, such as *Underworld* (The Guardian, 2016) and *6x9* (The Mill and The Guardian, 2016), users take the place of a character that enacts a narrative that they cannot change. These works are examples of *internal-exploratory* interactivity. However, immersive journalism has yet to present examples of *ontological interactivity, either internal or external*. Even so, there are instances of *ontological interactivity* in VR applications, but not in the field of journalism. One example is *Tilt Brush*, where users can draw the world around them, in a similar way to what happens in the videogame *Minecraft*, where users create and inhabit their own world.

The combination *internal-exploratory* interactivity might appear to be the best option for VR because it promotes more involvement inside the world as a character and provides a sense of wandering and exploring. However, this depends on the purpose: While many immersive journalism projects will be focused on creating a contemplative aesthetic, some others might be more focused on creating an active experience through agency. This would be more like what is done in video games, where actions of the user are a priority. In this sense, the concept of *game aesthetics* coming from the game design field could be useful for VR. "Aesthetics describes the desirable emotional responses evoked in the player, when interacting with the game system" (Hunicke, LeBlanc & Zubek, 2004, para. 11). Nevertheless, immersive journalists will need to develop their own set of aesthetics. For now, some of the aesthetics stated by these authors could work as a base to clarify the specific emotions that the immersive journalism experience is trying to foster. From the list that Hunicke et al. (2004) propose, the most appropriate aesthetics for immersive journalism are the following: (a) sensation—game as sense-pleasure, (b) fantasy—game as make-believe, (c) narrative—games as story, and (d) discovery—game as uncharted territory.

Some immersive journalism projects are already exploring different levels of agency as well as more specific aesthetics focused on evoking emotional responses. For instance, in "Arctic 360: A virtual experience of a disappearing landscape" (The Guardian, 2017a), spatial immersion is most important, since the objective is to contemplate how the arctic is being destroyed. The emotional reaction desired might be indignation. "See for yourself" and "contemplate" might be the main purposes to reach this emotion. In "First impressions: A virtual experience of the first year of life" (The Guardian, 2017b), users are placed in the perspective of an infant who is in her parents' living room. Here the most interesting activity is exploring the point of view of a baby. In this story, temporary immersion is more important than spatial immersion, since the user can hear and see how the baby changes his/her outlook over time; in this experience, "wonder" might be the main emotion fostered.

In "Underworld" (The Guardian, 2016), the user can travel through London's sewers. Here the user has a lamp, and by moving a joystick, he/she can explore the sewers guided by a narrator. Interaction goes beyond just directing the user's line of vision. It is still an exploratory interactivity but because of its internal nature, the user might feel more active than just looking around. The environment attempts to foster curiosity and fear, and its interface is similar to that of a video game. The aesthetic of the experience is "discovery." In "6×9: A virtual experience of solitary confinement" (The Mill & The Guardian, 2016), the user is invited to "hear the stories and experience the psychological damage that can happen during extreme isolation." This experience makes the user step into the shoes of a prisoner in a confinement cell. In this case, 3D modeling, 3D animation, two-dimensional (2D) animation, audio and video are used in a masterful way. The emotions fostered could be anxiety, frustration, and indignation. The aesthetic is "narrative."

Immersion Production Technologies and VR Media Language Exploration

The influence of immersive production technologies also impacts the affordances and constraints that filmmakers and VR designers have. 3D environments built into video game engines such as *Unity* and *Unreal* allow one to make up the story, as well as to design both the space and the interaction. 360-degree stereoscopic video cameras record live action, which helps to create immersion, especially in cases where settings are real world places and where it is very important that real characters are known by the user. However, due to their nature, 360-degree videos constrain the interaction of the user. In the following paragraphs, there is a brief comparison of how immersive journalism experiences, whose objective is to foster awareness and empathy, explore the aesthetics of the media used.

Clouds over Sidra (Here Be Dragons et al., 2015) is a mini documentary of a girl living in a refugee camp produced with a stereoscopic 360-degree camera. *Project Syria* (De la Peña et al., 2014) is a 3D-modeled environment based on real scenarios and contains real audio from bombings in Syria. *6x9* (The Mill & The Guardian, 2016) is a 3D modeled and animated immersive experience about being locked up in a confinement cell. These three immersive experiences have a linear temporal structure. Two of them include personal and real stories to connect to a bigger problem just as traditional social empathy journalistic stories do. In *Clouds over Sidra* and *6x9*, characters narrate their story. In all three of these stories it is important that the user approximates a sensation of authentically being in the space in order to be immersed in that world: A refugee camp, a street in Aleppo, a 6x9-foot confinement cell. However, the power of the media and the explorations that authors make with media language used is very different in these three stories. In *Clouds over Sidra* (Here Be Dragons et al., 2015), identification is reached through listening to Sidra's thoughts and observations about living in a refugee camp. Spectators can see her room, her school, the playground where children take turns playing. The user is an invisible witness, limited to only looking around. Sidra narrates her story as a first-person narrator but is not talking to the user. She is seen on the screen just three or four times; the rest is voice-over dubbed in English. She looks directly at the camera in only two shots. The camera movements are basic; there are no close-ups and few possibilities to vary the camera shot. Audiovisual language is very basic in comparison to regular 2D live action films. In this film, the camera is always at a considerable distance from Sidra. In regular videos, a close-up to see her expressions, the combination of subjective views, and a variation in angles and shots could tell the story in a different and certainly even better way. Nevertheless, an emotional impact, which is difficult to explain, remains. This might be due to the 3D stereoscopic vision. Seeing real people, in a real situation, is very powerful.

In *Project Syria* (De la Peña et al., 2014), based on a 3D-modeled environment, the intention is similar: Promoting awareness about the situation Syrians, especially children, are living in. There is a narrator telling the audience facts. The environment is very well modeled, based on a real street and real people, but the characters look fake, like robots. The user can move around the space but movement does little to substitute the connection obtained from live action.

6x9 (The Mill & The Guardian, 2016) appears to be the best experience in its immersive design and the exploration of media selection and media language. The purpose of this immersive experience, according to The Guardian (2016), is that it "aims to highlight the psychological toll on those subjected to such harsh incarceration for between 22 and 24 hours a day." It presents temporal, spatial, and emotional immersion strategies. Users are immersed in a virtual, but photorealistic 6x9-foot confinement cell that was modeled based on a real cell, and they hear real stories and see fragments of real footage. In nine minutes, users experience what it is like to be day and night in a confinement cell, since the piece has a temporal structure. Selective lighting is used to direct the user's attention to certain objects in the room. When users look at the illuminated objects, stories emerge. Users are supposed to go through the experience in first-person. The narrator invites the user to enter the cell and take part in the experience directly. At the same time, the user is a witness who hears and sees visualizations of the thoughts, visions, hallucinations and daydreaming of the incarcerated based on the testimonies of prisoners that have been in such confinement. This is done using 2D animation, simulating video projected on the wall of the cell, and motion graphics.

Immersive language is very young. As with any other media from the past, virtual reality may borrow resources from other media and develop its own. For now, producers are experimenting with the media and discovering how to use and how to extend it. Based on the concepts explained in this section and on the work from Fink & Schudson (2014), Ryan (2015), Murray (1997), Hunicke et al. (2004), and Jenkins (2004) —with original work from the author—some questions to be considered in the design or analysis of immersive journalism narratives are posed in Table 1.

IMMERSIVE JOURNALISM IN A TRANSMEDIA SPACE

Immersive journalism experiences, especially if focused on awaking emotions, might be consider a complete experience in the sense that new media easily promote wonder, surprise, and as producers claim, they have a great potential to promote empathy. Following the trend brought by VR, these immersive experiences appear to be a novelty, a new strategy to attract readers to online newspapers. Within just a few months during 2016 and 2017, The New York Times, The Guardian, CNN and El País each published their first immersive experiences. While VR is a unique medium through which one can experience stories, these stories are short experiences with a specific point of view and limited information. If used for journalism, activism, awareness-raising or any other purposes related to citizenship, they are not enough to increase knowledge or foster awareness alone. Maier (2015) claims that the news media can

Table 1. Immersive journalism narratives design

Criteria	Questions
Narrative and immersion design	• What is the intended purpose? Is it informative or persuasive? If persuasive, what should the user's expected reaction be? • What are the different emotions that the piece should invoke in order to promote empathy? (in the case that it is a social empathy story). • Are any stylistic devices used for persuasion (e.g., metaphor, analogy, symbolism)? • Are there any game aesthetics involved? (e.g., narrative, discovery). Is this a contemplative or an active experience? • Is this a story based on characters, conflicts and drama or world-building? Does the user experience a story, a specific situation or a place? • What strategies are used to promote involvement and immersion? Are they temporal, spatial, or emotional? • How is the user inserted into the story? Is he/she placed in the shoes of a character? Is he/she an invisible witness? Does he/she enact or build a narrative in the immersive environment? • Does the environment promote agency (i.e., actions that are related not just to interaction but to the story itself)? • Is the immersive experience multimedia in nature (i.e., several media are used within the given environment) or hypermedia in nature (i.e., several media are used and the user can choose the surrounding scenery)? How does this affect the experience?

influence people's charitable and emotional responses to humanitarian crises, particularly when people are given *mobilizing information*. Immersive experiences could be the point of entry to a transmedia story, a transmedia game, a transmedia world or to journalism in general which could be considered a complex transmedia space. According to Saldre and Torop (2012), "understanding transmedia projects in terms of worldmaking instead of storytelling is justified by the scope of its applicability to both artistic and non-artistic as well as to narrative and non-narrative texts" (p. 28). This is very important in the field of journalism where many texts are non-artistic, non-narrative and non-fiction. The concept of transmedia space is also more suitable for integrating other recent assets into the transmedia journalism design such as newsgames, persuasive games, and data visualization.

As seen in the different examples provided in the previous section, VR allows users to immerse themselves in the world which was constructed or portrayed. The constructed world can be a literal, realistic, surreal, fantastic or symbolic space. Thus, immersive experiences can be a valuable part of transmedia space, presenting a rich panorama of an issue, complete with different points of view, diverse characters, expert opinions, and testimonies. For this reason, the immersive experience could also function as a *mothership* (Jenkins, 2009) or a *nuclear text* (Zorrilla-Abascal, 2016) that expands through other different media that complement the piece. In this way, users could immerse themselves not just in the VR experience but, as Rose (interviewed by Jenkins, 2011) states when talking about deep media, readers can delve into a story at any level of depth they like. In every extension users could also play different roles: As readers of news extensions, spectators of video extensions; participants, moderators, commentators and distributors of social media extensions; players in game extensions; and content producers or collaborators in the production of extensions (Lugo, 2016).

Currently, a few *immersive journalism* productions exist which are integrated with other media. For instance, the first The New York Times documentary that used immersion, *The Displaced,* is "a feature story, interviews, three photo essays and, for the first time in the history of *The New York Times*, a virtual-reality film" (The New York Times, 2015). Frequently, journalism productions are *hypermedia* (i.e., different media which converge on the same platform and are connected through hyperlinks) instead of *transmedia* (i.e., different media which are dispersed across different platforms) because online newspapers are interested in attracting reader traffic and keeping the reader on their own website in order to promote the sustainability of the website. However, a hypermedia focus can constrain the ways in which readers can participate in the experience.

A particularly good example of how an immersive experience can be included within a transmedia space is *6x9* (The Mill & The Guardian, 2016), as it fits the definition for transmedia storytelling proposed by Jenkins (2009): Each medium should be used for what it does best. This documentary, which reports on seven people in confinement, is comprised of a VR experience, which functions as a mothership for the following media: Audio testimonies, a video testimony, a podcast dedicated to psychologists who are experts on the topic of discussion, an audio documentary, a written report, and a multimedia chronicle. All these texts were published throughout the week from April 27, 2016 to May 4, 2016 by The Guardian.

Using intertextuality, *6x9* offers transmedia extensions in an exemplary way by quoting segments of interviews made with people in confinement and with experts. Therefore, the user is introduced to the characters' more meaningful experiences in the immersive environment, but they can search for their complete testimonies separately. In fact, the immersive experience is partially a summary of the seven testimonies from people in confinement and from the expert testimonies. These complete interviews, available in podcasts, are much longer. Moreover, The Guardian dispersed some content on some other platforms. In addition to their website, audios were available on iTunes and on Soundcloud. Hyperlinks, interspersed throughout the written texts on the blogs, take the user to a whole other space, *Solitary Watch* (Casella & Ridgeway, 2013), a multimedia web-based project dedicated to the topic of solitary confinement in American prisons and jails.

Part of transmedia design is making sure that the content is not just a redundant offer for reader, but that the transmedia content is strategically dispersed, offering new and valuable content across different media platforms. Jenkins (2009), Scolari (2013), Pratten (2011), Gambarato (2013), and Zorrilla Abascal (2016) propose different transmedia design frames. Based on that—with original work from the author—Table 2 proposes key questions to be asked in the design of transmedia journalism spaces.

Table 2. Transmedia journalism design criteria questions

Criteria	Questions
Transmedia journalism design	• What are the properties of the constructed world? How does the concept of world building work for this transmedia piece? (In an abstract, literal or symbolic way). • What role is the immersive experience playing in the design of the whole piece in terms of transmedia design? Is the immersive experience supposed to work as a mothership or an extension? Does this depend on the user's point of entry? • How is the world building and immersion constructed? How is this achieved through the immersive experience and the extensions? • What are the expansions? Are the pieces distributed in sequential or parallel moments? • Are they distributed throughout the online newspaper website or what other platforms are used? • How is the whole transmedia discourse built in relation to the immersive journalism piece? Is there any kind of intertextuality between the immersive journalism pieces and other expansions and among expansions that assist in promoting a deeper experience for the reader? • How will the user have the opportunity to participate in some or all of the pieces comprising the transmedia work? (Roles: Commentator, distributor, moderator creator, player, etc.). • What are the functions of expansions in terms of storytelling? (e.g., backstory of the issue, knowing other stories, knowing more characters of the same story, knowing more related issues, knowing more locations where the issue takes place, knowing different points of view or different voices, predicting future consequences).

CONCLUSION

When discussing virtual reality in general, one may overlook the fact that there are at least two different media involved with different forms of logic: 360-degree stereoscopic videos and environments created in video game engines. Hence, the kinds of stories, the kinds of interactions, and the aesthetics of these two media are very different. To be immersed in a story, a user might be an onlooker or a main character who represents the group for which empathy is trying to be fostered. The point of view appears to be a complex matter when there is a camera that directs the user's point of view, which can be partially changed by user, but which is limited by the fact that the camera does not allow close-ups. Although VR uses certain visual language conventions common to other media such as photography and movies, there can be different narrators competing in the space.

In immersive journalism now, social empathy stories are the most popular. Therefore, it is important to measure, through quantitative and qualitative techniques, how effective these immersion experiences are in terms of promoting social empathy and fostering certain actions or attitudes in people, not just during the experience, but in the short and long term afterwards. Game design theory and serious game theory might be useful for promoting empathy and emotional immersion in immersive journalism experiences where the user plays an active role in changing reality. Role-playing games allow players to explore institutional, geographical, and temporal settings that would otherwise be inaccessible, allowing players to learn from the consequences of choices made in the game world that would be impractical or dangerous to experience directly (Raphael, Bachen, Lynn, Baldwin-Philippi, & McKee, 2010). There might be a crossover between immersive journalism, newsgames, and serious games. Transmedia artivism, for instance, works at exploring not just how to disseminate content and attitudes through art and media, but also how to promote these attitudes so that people apply them to their public life.

In immersion, it is also important to consider ethical aspects within the discourse of the virtual environment. This field of ethical discourse should be developed along within immersive experiences. The frame for video game discourse proposed by Pérez-Latorre (2015) could be a useful starting point. The author divides the discourse into the representation of the world, the representation of the gameplay, and the representation of the characters. Translated to VR environments, the representation of the world, the representation of the characters, the role of the user, and the actions of the user could be initial categories for ethical discourse in immersive experiences.

As pointed out in this chapter, immersive experiences have a great potential for promoting empathy, since virtual environments allow the user to be present in a place where he/she can experience moving/touching situations. However, it is important not to assume that an immersive experience inevitably fosters social empathy. In order to foster social empathy, it is necessary to have storytelling abilities, to wield new tools and conventions that are emerging, as part of virtual reality as a medium. It is essential to innovate, not only in technology, but also in discourse creation, in response to a compassion fatigue tendency that has been triggered by mass media.

It is best practice to implement immersive experiences as part of transmedia spaces and not on their own. This is due to the existing constraints on the media, which include costs, limited duration of experiences, the need to tell contextual stories in contemporary journalism, along with the commercial imperatives for online newspapers, such as generating more visitors or keeping visitors within the newspaper website. Thus, newspapers and news agencies need to consider other issues besides spreadability in order to get the audience to participate more actively in transmedia spaces, especially since journalism involves not only business but also social good. The theoretical review and the questions presented here intend to contribute to the academic toolbox for the analysis and design of transmedia journalism narratives and spaces, whenever they include immersive journalism experiences. Further studies should be made to broaden this frame.

REFERENCES

Batson, C. D., Batson, J. G., Slingsby, J. K., Harrell, K. L., Peekna, H. M., & Todd, R. M. (1991). Empathic joy and the empathy-altruism hypothesis. *Journal of Personality and Social Psychology*, *61*(3), 413–426. doi:10.1037/0022-3514.61.3.413 PMID:1941512

Batson, C. D., Chang, J., Orr, R., & Rowland, J. (2002). Empathy, attitudes, and action: Can feeling for a member of a stigmatized group motivate one to help the group? *Personality and Social Psychology Bulletin*, *28*(12), 1656–1666. doi:10.1177/014616702237647

Batson, C. D., Lishner, D. A., Cook, J., & Sawyer, S. (2005). Similarity and nurturance: Two possible sources of empathy for strangers. *Basic and Applied Social Psychology*, *27*(1), 15–25. doi:10.1207/s15324834basp2701_2

Casella, J., & Ridgeway, J. (2013, September 22). New project: Photo requests from solitary. *Solitary Watch*. Retrieved from http://solitarywatch.com/2013/09/22/new-project-photo-requests-solitary/

De la Peña, N. & Virtual Pyedog (Producers) & De la Peña (Director) (2012). *Hunger in Los Angeles* [VR Documentary]. USA: Sand Castle Studios.

De La Peña, N. (Author), Licht, M., MxR Studio, USC School of Cinematic Arts, Vangelis Lympouridis, World Economic Forum (Producers). (2014). *Project Syria* [VR Documentary]. USA: MxR Studio.

De la Peña, N., Weil, P., Llobera, J., Giannopoulos, E., Pomés, A., Spanlang, B., & Slater, M. (2010). Immersive journalism: Immersive virtual reality for the first-person experience of news. *Presence (Cambridge, Mass.)*, *19*(4), 291–301. doi:10.1162/PRES_a_00005

Decety, J., & Ickes, W. (2011). *The social neuroscience of empathy*. Cambridge, MA: The MIT Press.

Fink, K., & Schudson, M. (2014). The rise of contextual journalism, 1950s–2000s. *Journalism*, *15*(1), 3–20. doi:10.1177/1464884913479015

Gambarato, R. R. (2013). Transmedia project design: Theoretical and analytical considerations. *Baltic Screen Media Review*, (1), 80–100.

Hayes, G. P. (2011). How to write a transmedia production bible. *Screen Australia*. Retrieved from http://videoturundus.ee/bible.pdf

Here Be Dragons (Producer), Arora, G., & Milk, C. (Directors). (2015). *Clouds over Sidra* [VR Documentary]. USA: The United Nations.

Hunicke, R., LeBlanc, M., & Zubek, R. (2004, July). MDA: A formal approach to game design and game research. *Proceedings of the AAAI Workshop on Challenges in Game AI, 4*(1).

Jenkins, H. (2004). Game design as narrative architecture. In N. Wardrip-Fruin & P. Harrigan (Eds.), *First person: New media as story, performance and game* (pp. 118–130). Cambridge, MA: The MIT Press.

Jenkins, H. (2006). *Convergence culture. Where old and new media collide*. New York: New York University.

Jenkins, H. (2009, December 12). The revenge of the origami unicorn: Seven principles of transmedia storytelling (Well, two actually. Five more on Friday). *Blog Confessions of an aca-fan*. Retrieved from http://henryjenkins.org/2009/12/the_revenge_of_the_origami_uni.html

Jenkins, H. (2011, January 26). "Deep media," transmedia, what's the difference? An interview with Frank Rose (Part one). *Blog Confessions of an aca-fan*. Retrieved from http://henryjenkins.org/blog/2011/01/deep_media_transmedia_whats_th.html

Keen, S. (2006). A theory of narrative empathy. *Narrative, 14*(3), 207–236. doi:10.1353/nar.2006.0015

Lugo, N. (2016). *Diseño de narrativas transmedia para la transalfabetización* [Design of transmedia narratives for the transalphabetization] (Unpublished PhD dissertation). Universidad Pompeu Fabra, Barcelona, Spain.

Maier, S. R. (2015). Compassion fatigue and the elusive quest for journalistic impact: A content and reader-metrics analysis assessing audience response. *Journalism & Mass Communication Quarterly, 92*(3), 700–722. doi:10.1177/1077699015599660

Menke, M., Kinnebrock, S., Kretzschmar, S., Aichberger, I., Broersma, M., Hummel, R., & Salaverría, R. et al. (2016). Convergence culture in European newsrooms: Comparing editorial strategies for cross-media news production in six countries. *Journalism Studies*, 1–24. doi:10.1080/1461670X.2016.1232175

Murphy, T. (2014). Solitary confinement is cruel and all too usual. Why is it only getting worse? *The Guardian*. Retrieved from https://www.theguardian.com/commentisfree/2014/oct/13/solitary-confinement-us-prisoners-rehabilitation

Murray, J. H. (1997). *Hamlet on the holodeck: The future of narrative in cyberspace*. Cambridge, MA: The MIT Press.

North, M. M., & North, S. M. (2016). A comparative study of sense of presence of traditional virtual reality and immersive environments. *AJIS. Australasian Journal of Information Systems, 20*, 1–15. doi:10.3127/ajis.v20i0.1168

Oliver, M. B., Dillard, J. P., Bae, K., & Tamul, D. J. (2012). The effect of narrative news format on empathy for stigmatized groups. *Journalism & Mass Communication Quarterly, 89*(2), 205–224. doi:10.1177/1077699012439020

Pérez Latorre, Ó. (2015). The social discourse of video games analysis model and case study: GTA IV. *Games and Culture, 10*(5), 415–437. doi:10.1177/1555412014565639

Pratten, R. (2011). *Getting started in transmedia storytelling: A practical guide for beginners*. London: CreativeSpace. Retrieved from http://www.tstoryteller.com/getting-started-in-transmedia-storytelling

Raphael, C., Bachen, C., Lynn, K. M., Baldwin-Philippi, J., & McKee, K. A. (2010). Games for civic learning: A conceptual framework and agenda for research and design. *Games and Culture*, *5*(2), 199–235. doi:10.1177/1555412009354728

Ryan, M. L. (2015). *Narrative as virtual reality 2: Revisiting immersion and interactivity in literature and electronic media* [Kindle version]. Baltimore, MD: Johns Hopkins University Press.

Saldre, M., & Torop, P. (2012). Transmedia space. In I. Ibrus & C. A. Scolari (Eds.), *Crossmedia innovations: Texts, markets, institutions* (pp. 25–44). New York, NY: Peter Lang.

Schuemie, M. J., Van Der Straaten, P., Krijn, M., & Van Der Mast, C. A. (2001). Research on presence in virtual reality: A survey. *Cyberpsychology & Behavior*, *4*(2), 183–201. doi:10.1089/109493101300117884 PMID:11710246

Scolari, C. A. (2013). *Narrativas transmedia: Cuando todos los medios cuentan* [Transmedia narratives: When all media count]. Barcelona, Spain: Deusto-Planeta.

Sillesen, L. B., Ip, C., & Uberti, D. (2015). Journalism and the power of emotions. *Columbia Journalism Review*, *54*(1). Retrieved from https://www.cjr.org/analysis/journalism_and_the_power_of_emotions.php

Silverstein, J. (2015, November 5). The displaced. *The New York Times*. Retrieved from https://www.nytimes.com/2015/11/08/magazine/the-displaced-introduction.html?_r=0

Taylor, M., Hodges, S. D., & Kohányi, A. (2003). The illusion of independent agency: Do adult fiction writers experience their characters as having minds of their own? *Imagination, Cognition and Personality*, *22*(4), 361–380. doi:10.2190/FTG3-Q9T0-7U26-5Q5X

TED. (2015). *Chris Milk: How virtual reality can create the ultimate empathy machine* [Video file]. Retrieved from https://www.youtube.com/watch?v=iXHil1TPxvA

The Guardian. (2016, November 10). *Underworld: – Trailer for latest virtual reality experience from the Guardian* [Video file]. Retrieved from https://www.youtube.com/watch?v=rgQJH9_xgpo

The Guardian. (2017a, January 3). *Arctic 360: A virtual experience of a disappearing landscape* [Video file]. Retrieved from https://www.youtube.com/watch?v=ncEj8rZaQs8

The Guardian. (2017b, April 3). *First impressions: A virtual experience of the first year of life* [Video file]. Retrieved from https://www.youtube.com/watch?v=QKhZYZfq8Zk

The Mill. & The Guardian, (Producers), Panetta, F., & Poulton, L. (Directors). (2016). *6x9: A virtual experience of solitary confinement* [VR Documentary]. United Kingdom: *The Mill*.

Van der Haak, B., Parks, M., & Castells, M. (2012). The future of journalism: Networked journalism. *International Journal of Communication*, *6*(16), 2923–2938.

Verdú, D. (2016, May 1). *Fukushima, vidas contaminadas* [Fukushima, contaminated lives] [Video file]. Retrieved from http://elpaissemanal.elpais.com/documentos/fukushima-vidas-contaminadas/

Wilson, C. J., & Soranzo, A. (2015). The use of virtual reality in psychology: A case study in visual perception. *Computational and Mathematical Methods in Medicine*, *2015*, 1–7. doi:10.1155/2015/151702 PMID:26339281

Zorrilla Abascal, M. L. (2016). Transmedia intertextualities in educational media resources: The case of BBC Schools in the United Kingdom. *New Media & Society*, *18*(11), 2629–2648. doi:10.1177/1461444815590140

KEY TERMS AND DEFINITIONS

Agency: The power of the user to participate actively in virtual environments.

Compassion Fatigue: Newspapers readers' and spectators' unwillingness to get involved with social empathy stories as a result of mass media strategies that have desensitized them.

Contextual Journalism: Journalism that goes beyond informing news. It goes deeper, explores more complex social issues and contextualizes readers.

Immersion Aesthetics: Immersion media language and principles important to consider in immersion design.

Immersive Experience: Environment or film created in order to immerse the user in a situation. It can be created with different techniques such as 360° cameras or 3D video game engines.

Immersive Journalism: The use of immersion spaces usually through virtual reality environments so readers experience different kinds of journalistic stories.

Narrative Empathy: The narratology field of study that considers how empathy is fostered through authorial strategies and what happens with the aesthetics of reception in relation with empathy.

Presence: The subjective sense of users of virtual reality environments to react to virtual spaces as if they were a real space.

Social Empathy Stories: Contextual journalistic stories that promote empathy for a specific group or cause.

Chapter 6
Designing Transmedia Journalism Projects

Kevin Moloney
Ball State University, USA

ABSTRACT

This chapter explores the design and execution of transmedia journalism projects to inform professional production and academic experimentation. It draws on the author's current project to illustrate real-world production planning. The chapter opens with a discussion of how design thinking and audience targeting apply to this task and contribute to project success. The chapter then elaborates the flow of decisions required for a thorough transmedia plan and finally presents the Refuge project as a design example. This pilot transmedia story network focuses on the single issue of refugees: those who migrate by force, either to escape suffering and deprivation or to build new, more hopeful lives elsewhere. It is the first in a networked series of similar projects that will explore the issues that polarize the electorate in the American West, from economic stratification to religious identity, environment, and gun ownership rights.

INTRODUCTION

A transmedia project in any other industry must first build a storyworld, a superbly imagined, detailed space and culture the characters inhabit and in which the public may immerse, as described by Frank Rose (2011) and by others (Jenkins, 2006, 2009; Ryan, 2006, 2014). Journalism, however, works within the real universe (often as it is in the process of falling apart). For the transmedia journalism project creator or analyst, this refocuses the question: How does a transmedia journalist build a project that does not fall apart? For a transmedia story to function most effectively it should leave much less to chance than that to which journalists are accustomed. Thoughtful, comprehensive design is imperative.

Deep and pre-planned design is a relative rarity in journalism. The task of covering an ever-changing world and the role of check and balance on governmental and social structures leaves journalists reacting to news as it emerges. Other media industries, however, must design the production and delivery of all content they produce. In journalism, rarely enough thought is given to how that work may better reach critical publics across a complex mediascape—there just is not enough time in the news cycle. Though

DOI: 10.4018/978-1-5225-3781-6.ch006

not all stories should be given a transmedia structure, and though the news business will always be a heavily reactive one, journalism can certainly benefit from applying transmedia storytelling techniques to longer-term, investigative and socially concerned work.

This chapter will explore the broad idea of *design thinking* as well as audience targeting that is applicable to the design and execution of transmedia journalism projects, and it will draw from the author's own current project to inform academic experimentation and professional production. As discussed in the growing body of literature (Gambarato & Tárcia, 2017; Moloney, 2011, 2015; Ryan, 2013) and throughout this book, transmedia storytelling in journalism differs as much from its counterparts in other media industries as it is similar. To illustrate this, the chapter will elaborate the flow of decisions required for a thorough transmedia plan (Moloney, 2015, pp. 99–101) and will finally present as a design example the *Refuge* project, being launched by the author and a team of transmedia journalists as of this writing. For practicing journalists, this example could be used as a customizable template in the design of new projects. For academics, this example can help inform the study and critique of transmedia journalism production decisions.

DESIGN THINKING AND TRANSMEDIA STORYTELLING

There are many essentialist traps in the study and production of transmedia storytelling. Definitions of transmedia logic vary by media industry and by the researcher describing it. In journalism, understanding of the term and how to implement it differ between publisher and between editors or reporters. Similarly, as Johansson-Sköldberg, Woodilla and Çetinkaya (2013, p. 132) note, the concept of *design thinking* defies essentialist description as its character and use changes between academics and industry, and between analysts and designers. Despite this lack of codification, the common elements among these many views on design thinking are a valuable entry point to transmedia journalism project design. They can help journalists bring the care they put into the creation of traditional single stories into the planning of a complex project constructed of many interconnected parts.

Definitions

Johansson-Sköldberg et al. (2013), in their comprehensive examination of the history of the term, divide design thinking into two broad discourses. The first, *designerly thinking,* includes academic analysis along with the "creation of artefacts," a "reflexive practice" (the self-critique of cognitive perspective), a "problem-solving activity," and the "creation of meaning." The second discourse, *design thinking,* they largely attribute to management practice and a business manager's role in building and maintaining a creative environment of the creation and marketing of products. This discourse, they describe as including design thinking as "a way of working," as a "necessary skill for managers" and a "part of management theory." Their analysis is clearly an academic one, declaring the latter discourse to be "less thoughtful and robust than contributions to the designerly thinking discourse that have been argued and reflected on by scholars over several decades" (p. 127). In simpler, less taxonomic terms, the two discourses might be better discussed as practices of *creation* and *implementation.* These terms place the discourses they astutely identified at a more equal level of importance. Creativity without implementation (or public accessibility) is as low in ultimate value as is the implementation of uncreative work. Though their analysis of both discourses is thorough and complete, their greater valuation of the creative acts within designerly thinking appears biased toward the academic world.

Of most relevance to this chapter is the design thinking realm of implementation. Crafting a good individual story—using anything from tried-and-true legacy reporting methods to cutting-edge game forms—is universal to journalism and is of enormous value. The design of a more complex transmedia journalism project is an act of implementation and management. It coordinates the creative work of content production to build an effective storyworld. In industry, the powerhouses of design thinking include Stanford University's d.school and IDEO, a company founded by Stanford engineering professor David Kelley. In the Harvard Business Review, IDEO chief executive officer Tim Brown, described the company's design thinking process as "best described metaphorically as a system of spaces rather than a predefined series of orderly steps" (2008, p. 88). He continues:

Design projects must ultimately pass through three spaces. We label these "inspiration," for the circumstances (be they a problem, an opportunity, or both) that motivate the search for solutions; "ideation," for the process of generating, developing, and testing ideas that may lead to solutions; and "implementation," for the charting of a path to market. Projects will loop back through these spaces – particularly the first two – more than once as ideas are refined and new directions taken. (pp. 88-89)

These very broad spaces are certainly applicable to the design of transmedia journalism projects, and one could consider the *inspiration* space as where a project's story world is identified, *ideation* as where that storyworld is delimited and refined, and *implementation* as how both the individual stories and their wider network can reach the publics that can best use them. "Put simply," Brown writes, "it is a discipline that uses the designer's sensibility and methods to match people's needs with what is technologically feasible and what a viable business strategy can convert into customer value and market opportunity" (p. 86).

In *Design Thinking* (2010), editor Thomas Lockwood of the Design Management Institute collects articles on design thinking theory and practice from the organization's *Design Management Review*. The articles explore design thinking from a management perspective while acknowledging the broad scope of theory and practice that fall under the term. Despite that broad scope, Lockwood identifies five key tenets of design thinking that cross between these perspectives. The first is to engage observational and ethnographic research into consumer insights and unarticulated needs—to *understand the market* rather than to *market your understanding*. The second tenet he identifies is to collaborate, both with users and with multidisciplinary teams. "This helps to move a company toward radical innovation, rather than incremental improvement, and of course seeks added value" (p. xi). The third tenet is to learn through hands-on experimentation and rapid prototyping. Failing early and often fuels quick and comprehensive learning. The fourth tenet is to visualize key concepts through sketches, rough physical mockups, stories, role playing or storyboards. "The objective is to make the intangible become tangible, and visualization is the best way to do that" (p. xii). His final tenet is the use of concurrent business analysis through the duration of a project, rather than as a post-facto success measure or as a limit on extreme creative thinking. "This can be a tricky balance," he writes. "But the key is to enable integrative thinking by combining creative ideas with more traditional strategic aspects in order to learn from a more complete and diverse point of view" (p. xii).

Creation

Traditional business strategy concerns fueled the creativity of one of the world's best known (if accidental) transmedia stories. When Lucasfilm Ltd. negotiated for the *Empire Strikes Back* sequel they reclaimed all merchandising rights for the series, expanding not only transmedia engagement but the fiscal market that continues to fuel it today (Fleming, 2015). In *The Art of Immersion: How the Digital Generation is Remaking Hollywood, Madison Avenue, and the Way We Tell Stories*, Frank Rose (2011) breaks down how Lucasfilm was able to turn the chaotic spin-off and merchandising success that followed the original 1977 film into a cohesive transmedia storyworld:

Star Wars had its own, unique problem. The licenses turned out tons of stuff—novels, comics, lightsabers, action figures, video games, radio adaptations, what have you. Some of it was great—like Boba Fett, the bounty hunter who started life onscreen as an obscure character in a 1978 TV special and ended up, thanks to the fans' response to the action figure that came out afterward, a significant figure in the movies. But try to put it all together and you have a confused jumble. If it wasn't Marvel conjuring up a giant bunny[1], it was Luke Skywalker in the 1978 novel Splinter of the Mind's Eye (Foster, 1978) getting affectionate with Princess Leia—who five years later, in Return of the Jedi, would turn out to be his twin sister. (p. 71)

With these apocryphal story texts erupting without apparent control, Lucasfilm refocused on the comprehensive, long-term design of the *Star Wars* storyworld—an activity within Brown's *inspiration* and *ideation* spaces discussed above. At least until the Walt Disney Company's purchase of Lucasfilm in 2012, the design of the transmedia story and its characters would be guided by *The Holocron,* a database of characters, events, worlds, languages and other details of the *Star Wars* galaxy. The Lucasfilm *Holocron* illustrates a kind of "storyworld bible," described in 2009 by experience designer Lance Weiler as the important first step in transmedia experience design:

The process starts with the creation of a storyworld bible, a document that provides an overview of the experience that I wish to create. It shows the relationships between storylines, characters, locations and interactions online and in the real world. Media consumption habits of the audience are considered and there is focus placed on how to build story bridges that provide seamless flow across devices and screens. (2009)

In transmedia fiction, the storyworld bible helps define how the storyworld expands and where the characters might go over the timeline. Useful templates and examples of storyworld bible building for transmedia fiction projects are available (Hayes, 2011; Phillips, 2012) and their guidelines may act as conceptual starting points. In transmedia journalism, however, the storyworld bible must constrain the storyworld—defining the limits of topic coverage, who and what the subjects will be and where coverage will stop. As the real world is interconnected in an all-but-unlimited way, haphazard expansion of subjects and ideas resembling the early days of *Star Wars* is likely if clear borders are not drawn. The author saw this very problem when analyzing the 2014 *Future of Food* project produced by the National Geographic Society (Moloney, 2015). In the case of this mammoth early transmedia journalism project, one particular channel that developed impressive influence in the story network—*The Plate* blog series (Fulton, McKenna, McMillan, & Rupp, 2014)—clouded the definition of the storyworld through too little planning and relatively unsupervised production. This story channel had been an afterthought in the project's design but proved to have deep and wide connections to communities of interest that gave the project its greatest traction. As D.W. Harding (1963, p. 166) wrote, "The most important thing is not what the author, or any artist, had in mind to begin with but at what point he decided to stop." In transmedia journalism, delimitations on the issue, topic, characters and focus of the project—the storyworld—are critical. Later in this chapter a template list of questions illustrates how these delimitations may be drawn.

Brown's space of ideation and Lockwood's tenet of collaboration combine in the planning structure of transmedia entertainment powerhouse Pixar Animation Studios. Pixar president Ed Catmull (2014) describes the company's Braintrust, a flexible collective of writers and producers assembled for each film to "push us toward excellence and to root out mediocrity." He continues, "Its premise is simple: Put smart, passionate people in a room together, charge them with identifying and solving problems, and encourage them to be candid with one another." That candor, he writes, is the critical element in the process. "This isn't some pie-in-the-sky idea—without the critical ingredient that is candor, there can be no trust. And without trust creative collaboration is not possible" (pp. 86-87). Most journalists would argue that candor is never a scarcity in a working newsroom. The high-speed pressure of filling a news publication's content feed strips most interactions of delicacy. Conversations can be blunt, serious and often loud. However, Catmull is not describing this often-caustic candor that is thinly veiled in newsroom politics, status and personality. Effective collaboration, he argues, requires not only clear honesty, but "humility and ego, openness and generosity" (p. 87). These qualities also require maintenance, a role performed by Catmull and Pixar general manager Jim Morris:

The fear of saying something stupid and looking bad, of offending someone or being intimidated, of retaliating or being retaliated against—they all have ways of reasserting themselves, even once you think they've been vanquished. And when you do, you must address them squarely. (p. 87)

Transmedia journalism is, by necessity, a team effort. Building complex projects made of serialized, interrelated parts while reporting on timely and complex issues is beyond the scope of a single person. Collaboration in the transmedia planning process is critical, and Pixar's candid model is a great improvement over the hierarchical and tense decision-making structures of daily journalism. This candid and equal-status collaboration also fuels another philosophy that Pixar shares with other design innovators: to "fail early and fail fast." Innovation in design requires experimentation, and with it, risk of failure, as Lockwood also described in his third tenet above. "Mistakes aren't a necessary evil," Catmull writes. "They aren't evil at all. They are an inevitable consequence of doing something new (and, as such, should be seen as valuable; without them, we'd have no originality)." This, he argues, is not as simple as it sounds. People fear failure. It tends to spark personal feelings of shame and inadequacy developed in childhood by Western educational systems. The answer, he notes, is for its leaders to inspire a fearless culture. "Part of the answer is simple: If we as leaders can talk about our mistakes and our part in them, then we make it safe for others" (pp. 108-109).

Implementation

For most journalists, Brown's "space of implementation" is limited to simply publishing material. At legacy journalism organizations, Brown's "charting the path to the market" means that the content goes exclusively to the wholly-owned channels controlled by the organization. *New York Times* content is found first and often exclusively on its own printed pages, websites and mobile applications. This is fueled partly by the need to keep audience eyes on the advertising that funds these organizations, and partly by habitual practice. For two centuries prior to the Internet revolution, news organizations had captive audiences and could depend on the public to come to them for content. Now, however, readers across the globe have constant access to nearly every publication produced anywhere. The audience has scattered. Here, Brown's space of implementation is best seen through the eyes of other media industries where audiences are very specifically targeted. The entertainment and advertising media work not to appeal to mass audiences, but to talk directly to the most efficient publics.

Transmedia producers in all industries and the scholars who study their work describe the building of community and active engagement as key qualities. To accomplish this, the design of transmedia journalism projects should target publics as other media industries do. Most journalists conceive of their audience as they report, interview and craft their stories. In the end, they talk to those readers through their work. This is typically a "gut instinct" about who those readers are, built on assumption, knowing vaguely who makes up the audience, and the interactions a reporter has with the engaged readers with whom they come in contact. Though the organizations track demographic data and engagement, this data is generated mostly for the benefit of advertising sales teams and rarely do reporters seek it out. By contrast, story designers in other media industries rely on this and other data to model their audiences and determine where to most effectively find them. A well-targeted transmedia journalism project has a much better chance of succeeding in its communication goals.

The tools used by advertising media buyers are the most thorough and effective for both modeling the audience and knowing through what media channels it can be found. These tools—such as Simmons Research (2017) and Kantar's SRDS (2017) in the U.S., for example—are extremely expensive. They are a sizable investment for a large organization, and an impossibility for small groups of independents working together on a transmedia project. Other tools are available, however. Statista (2017) is an online statistics, market research and business intelligence aggregation and interpretation portal from Germany. The organization boasts 1.5 million statistics on 80,000 topics serving both industry and academia. Their regularly-produced infographics can be a valuable source for story topic insights, and their volume of data can help model the audiences for the individual stories in a transmedia project. The pricing ranges from limited free accounts, through affordable premium, corporate and university accounts. Though this quantitative resource is familiar to many researchers, it is less familiar to journalists. For the latter, it and others can assist in project design from the creation stage of designing interesting and relevant journalistic storyworlds to the first implementation design stage of understanding what publics can best use that transmedia reporting. If the demographics and psychographics—age, gender, brand preferences, political affiliations, activities, religions and more—of a target audience are modeled, they can be invaluable in selecting what media channels will reach that audience.

The tools used by advertising media buyers, such as SRDS in the U.S., are also expensive to access. The high price is due to the exclusive datasets built by media buying research organizations and the scale of the economics of the advertising and marketing industries. They are thorough and their data is specific. Often databases can be accessed through university libraries. SRDS and Simmons are available for free in many institutional libraries, but the data provided for library use is three or more years old. Though this is often adequate for journalistic purposes, other options can provide good data for Internet engagement—which evolves rapidly—and this can often be extrapolated to print and broadcast media as well. The most popular Web engagement data service is Google Analytics Solutions (2017). Though it is heavily used in tracking Web engagement, the statistics it generates are private, provided only to the owner of a URL. This does not render them completely out of reach, however. If negotiating for the publication of a transmedia project story, the channel a journalist wishes to use may provide demographic and psychographic data. Quantcast (2017), however, makes the tracking data it collects for online media that contract its services free and publicly accessible. This relative newcomer to the digital engagement data industry is now one of the world's most influential, and it provides a valuable way to select media channels for transmedia project implementation. By correlating the psychographics of target audience groups, media channels used by publics with that psychographics can be selected to deliver transmedia content.

The design of an effective transmedia journalism project is a complex process, beginning with the definition of a topical storyworld to be covered, through collaborative brainstorming, experimentation and creation of a series of stories designed for digital, analog and brick-and-mortar media channels. The richness of the creative design should fuel deep engagement from readers and move them through the story network to maintain that engagement over a longer period. That design then places those stories directly in front of the readers who can best use the information reported. By targeting media channels that reach critical publics, a transmedia journalism designer can make the project more efficient as a public good.

TRANSMEDIA JOURNALISM DESIGN DECISIONS

Collaborative design thinking is a post-structuralist act. By its nature, creativity is best accomplished in a uniquely balanced condition of freedom and constraint (Saleh, 2015) and within delimitations discussed in the previous section. When in a designing mode, however, one tends to minimize structure and often pays the price for that excessive freedom. The following decision flow is intended to help transmedia journalism designers achieve a more successful implementation of their creative work by posing questions that should be asked of most projects at the initial stages of the design process. This list of questions is meant as a starting point as each project requires a unique set of decisions specific to its goals. Each decision below inevitably leads to a new series of questions:

1. **What Is the Storyworld?** As discussed above, defining a real-world storyworld is an act of delimitation rather than expansion. As any subject taken from the real-world interconnects infinitely with every other, more than a broad subject identification is required here. In this initial design stage, you must decide on the timely issue or topic covered, what are the individual stories and characters that will put a face on that issue and how those stories interconnect with each other across a complex mediascape.
2. **What Are the Starting-Point Stories?** Like a good news *lede*, the initial stories set a tone or an operatic overture for what will come after. Here the scope of planned stories is examined to determine which story for each separate media channel will quickly engage the target public while also alluding to what more will come through subsequent stories the series. Though transmedia projects are inherently nonlinear in structure, story elements published early in a project timeline should still act as an overture for what is to come.

3. **What Are the Continuing Stories, and How Will They Unfold?** Continuing story elements should be planned to embrace this nonlinear nature. Though each must add new information, context and perspective, producers must assume that they will be engaged in random order as the public discovers them. Though producers may time the release of stories or explicitly direct their publics to read these individual pieces, it will be rare that such direction functions. As journalism, each story should be able to both stand alone as if it were the only story found, and add new value for readers who engage with more than one story.
4. **Who Are the Key Publics for Each Story?** Here one should think in great detail about who can best use the information from individual stories or their extensions. Are they young? Old? Rich? Poor? Do they play games? Liberal? Conservative? Are they policy makers or voters? Do they hunt or fish? Cook or play chess? One should "talk" to them through the stories. Most good journalists have a reader in mind as they write, photograph, produce or edit.
5. **What Media Channel Would Best Reach Those Publics?** This also requires specific and detailed research using, if possible, the demographic and audience research databases used in advertising. Identify in very specific detail, what media channels are most likely to reach the publics that can best use the information gathered. Partnerships will likely be necessary to get those stories published, and agreements that are beneficial to both transmedia producer and publisher are possible.
6. **What Media Forms Will Best Tell the Story?** One should think critically here about what works, not simply what one is most confident producing. Text is best for context. Video tells powerful stories that have a strong narrative arc and puts the flesh on characters better than almost any other form. Still photos isolate discrete moments. Audio engages the imagination. Games describe systems. Artifacts connect. Illustration accesses the camera-inaccessible. The channel necessary to reach one's public may create a limit on the possibilities here. If necessary, channel could be revisited in light of the best form for the story.
7. **What Genre, Length or Structure Will Best Serve a Story's Public?** Different channels encourage different levels of engagement. A *New Yorker* magazine reader flips open the cover expecting a 10,000-word story, but a *Vice* reader might expect a quick short-form video. One should provide content that appeals to attention spans that may vary from 30 seconds to two hours. Most journalists are comfortable selecting the appropriate genre for a story; however, much may be learned from the demographic study of the target public. Stories should be produced for the reader, not for the journalist him- or herself.
8. **How Should These Stories Interconnect?** The network one builds is the key to good transmedia storytelling. Carefully plan what stories will interlink. Are they hot-linked in digital spaces? Referred to in analog spaces? Are source materials and external content available with a click to provide transparency? This planning could extend to the design of a reader's investigative path through the project either as a trail of breadcrumbs or with a more gameful quality if desired. Whether the public follows that path or not, the design will only improve project structure. The project should allow the most engaged readers to build mastery of the subject, and by doing so, they will become the most powerful social advocates—both online and offline—for the project (Moloney, 2015, p. 54).
9. **How Can These Stories Be Conversations?** As all media become social, producers of transmedia journalism must engage the many-to-many cultural production ethos of the digital age (Lessig, 2009). A successful production will enable social commenting, sharing, remixing and amateur

production of the work produced. Though these varying forms of public engagement are often seen as separate phenomena, the author argues they should be seen collectively as different degrees of user contribution. In traditional journalism comment blocks on digital stories are common, they alone do not make for a conversational space. Engagement will increase if the reporters and producers of a transmedia journalism project enter that conversation with responses and updates. Public contribution should allow engaged readers to help build stories with the producers or contribute their own for consideration. This will increase their ownership in the story and their engagement, and it will enable more transparency and a multi-perspective view on the subject. These spaces cannot be left journalistically unattended, though. Public contribution should face the same editorial rigor as the contribution from contracted journalists, or the space should be clearly identified as amateur production.

10. **Who Is on the Team?** First, assemble a Pixar-inspired Braintrust (Catmull, 2014, pp. 108–109) as a check and balance on your thinking. Few brilliant ideas are generated in social isolation or free of candid critique. Select individual story producers who both understand the goals of the overall project and will produce content at the quality level expected of professional journalism. If you are assembling a production group of like-minded independents, seek out people with needed skillsets for business management and fundraising as well as good reporters.
11. **Where Does the Money Come From?** Complex, long-term projects are expensive. Your time is valuable. If you are producing a transmedia journalism project in a large media company with a sizable staff, be sure your budget calculations are thorough and accurate so you can maintain the support of the company for the project. Independents must decide from where their operational and reporting budget will come. Is it grant funded? Crowd funded? Private donor funded? Is time donated? After this can content created as part of the project be licensed to target media channels at rates high enough to pay for the reporting and producing time?
12. **What is the Timeline?** Decide how the project will launch, set target points for key elements of the project along the way, and define when and how the project ends. Though reporting and publishing may end, does the project remain on its publication channels as an archive? Which stories might be fleeting in accessibility and which should not?

Change is a constant, and though some answers to these decisions will necessarily change, likely multiple times, from concept to finish, a thorough and comprehensive plan will result in a more cohesive, fluid, engaging and successful project. Constant iteration from within the borders of the storyworld will inevitably improve the outcome.

UNDER CONSTRUCTION: THE REFUGE PROJECT STORYWORLD BIBLE

The storyworld bible need not be complex. The example that follows as a real-world illustration of these ideas is from a simple, shared Google Docs document that acts as a working outline for the author's current transmedia journalism project. Though it will continue to evolve and refine the subject delimitations and implementation plans of the project, it is frozen here as of this April 2017 writing. This is a transmedia journalism storyworld bible in the very early stages of project development.

REFUGE

What Is the Refuge Project?

Refuge is a pilot transmedia story network that will focus on the single issue of refugees: those who migrate by force, either to escape suffering and deprivation or to build new, more hopeful lives elsewhere. It is the first in a series of similar projects that will explore the issues that polarize the electorate in Colorado and the American West, from economic stratification to religious identity, environment and gun ownership rights.

The American West has always attracted dreamers, from 16th-century silver-hunting Spanish explorers, to gold rushers, homesteaders and entrepreneurs. But it has also been a magnet for those escaping social, political or economic oppression. Many of those same Spanish silver hunters that settled New Mexico (Chávez, 2012; Simmons, 1993) and southern Colorado as early as 1598 were Jews fleeing the Inquisition (Chávez, 1974; Orme, 2014). Former slaves, tenant farmers, Mormons and others preceded more recent resettlements of Japanese-Americans locked into camps for the duration of the Second World War, Holocaust survivors, former urban gang members and exhausted police officers, hippies and survivalists escaping the grid, property rights activists invading public lands, and, of course, migrant workers and war refugees.

Storyworld

Refuge will define its storyworld around the characters of contemporary westerners who have fled real or perceived oppression, from across the social spectrum and political divide, humanizing their stories. It will build a "sense of place" for their particular refuge and, when possible, the situation they escaped.

Why Does It Matter?

Why Now?

Immigration and refugee policies are perennial issues in American politics, dating all the way back to American founding father Benjamin Franklin's 18th-century disdain for low-class German immigrants (Franklin, 2006), through 19th-century refugees of the Irish potato famine, 20th-century fear of Mexican migrant farmworkers and, most recently, Syrian war refugees. The 2016 U.S. presidential election made more raw the ongoing rhetoric on immigration policy, refugee resettlement and border security. The current highly-polarized debate would benefit from a cross-political and cross-cultural look at refugees of all origins, from Syrian and Iraqi refugees to Holocaust and Japanese internment survivors, Soviet defectors and others.

Why Here?

As noted above, the West is perceived as a place of reinvention, boot-straps hope and possibility as open as its spaces. Whether this mythology actually holds true or not, the region provides a scope for this work and an emotional connection for readers.

Why Us?

Kevin Moloney is a transmedia designer and scholar, a veteran international journalist and descendent of the American West's first European refugees. He is one of the world's earliest researchers of transmedia journalism and an internationally recognized visual storyteller and teacher.

Matt Slaby is a polymath westerner with deep experience covering, engaging with and working toward solutions for marginalized communities. He and his company LUCEO are internationally recognized transmedia storytellers.

Who and What Are the Subjects?

With an eye on the liberal and conservative, expected and unexpected, subjects and characters will be researched and vetted from the realms of:

- Political refugees.
- Cultural refugees.
- Economic migrants and refugees.
- Environmental migrants and refugees.
- Urban "refugees."

Reporting will focus on the emotional experience of loss and relocation, and the hope of reinvention. Much has already been done on the horrors of war and imprisonment or the difficulties of starvation or discrimination. This will be covered enough for context, but the internal emotional life in this situation shows the universal in the experience. In addition to character-driven visual storytelling and interview, content that develops a sense of place for each character's story will be gathered—images, audio and other content that conveys either the place escaped and/or the refuge found.

Starting-Point Stories:

(These are not necessarily in order of publication. The first is under imminent threat of deportation. Another two, who are in their 80s-90s, should be interviewed and photographed soon.)

- *Ingrid Latorre* is in sanctuary at a Denver Mountain View Quaker Meeting House. The illegal Peruvian immigrant mother of two faces deportation and separation from her U.S. citizen children.
- *Bob Sakata* was interned by the U.S. government in the Tanforan Race Track (2017) and Topaz (2017) relocation camps in 1942. Later that year he was released to perform sponsored farm work in Colorado, a refuge for Japanese-Americans thanks to the foresight of level-headed republican governor Ralph Carr (2017). Carr's political career floundered after he opposed the internment of Japanese-American citizens. After the war Sakata, moved his father and siblings to Colorado and built one of the most productive large-scale vegetable farms in the region.
- *Walter Plywaski* survived multiple Nazi death camps during the Holocaust, systematically working to move from camp to camp to avoid death and cajoled his way into the U.S. "I like the idea of low population density," Plywaski said of his wish to move into the mountains above Boulder. "I don't like big crowds," he added about the concentration of the Nazi camps. He more recently had

to flee a wildfire that destroyed his home. Or Fanny Starr, who survived Auschwitz, and relocated to Denver after a long journey through displaced persons camps in Europe and new homes in the U.S.

- *Neal Schwieterman* was a first-responding sheriff's deputy at the Columbine high school shooting in 1999. The first-hand experience with the horrible event pushed Schweiterman and his wife to move to rural Paonia, Colo., where he became first a bicycle-bound police officer and later mayor of the quiet rural town.
- *The Lack of Legal Immigration Options* consistently foils those wishing to move to the U.S. legally. Though the political right often argues that immigrants should follow legal procedure, very few options for long-term or permanent immigration to the U.S. actually exist in 2017. Can a subject abroad with whom few Americans would have objections, and document their extreme struggle to follow federal immigration laws be found?
- *More to come.*

Secondary Stories

Multiple interesting support characters surround the main subjects—those who help, protect, teach, support or advocate for refugees and immigrants. Short interviews may be made for use on social media feeds as additive content or for use in external channels. Examples may include:

- **Dan Carr:** Attorney and grandson of 1940s-era Colorado governor Ralph Carr who risked his political career to support Japanese-American citizens during WWII internment.
- **Hans Meyer:** Denver-based immigration attorney, who represents illegal immigrant Jeanette Vizguerra—herself named one of *Time* Magazine's 100 Most Influential People in the World ("Time 100," 2017)—and fights to require Immigration and Customs Enforcement (ICE) to secure a warrant before arresting those appearing in Denver courts for immigration violations.
- Sanctuary Church Pastors.
- Sanctuary City Organizers.
- Refugee Relocation Workers.
- Friends and Family Members of Primary Subjects.
- More to come.

How Will It Look and Feel?

Sensitivity to Unequal Degrees of Suffering and Loss

This is a wide-ranging set of subjects, from those who simply up-and-left a situation that had become uncomfortable to those who survived the modern era's most horrific atrocities. The project producers must avoid any mistaken understanding that it puts these disparate experiences on equal footing. Consultation with relevant communities will help determine how material is published for pairing, interconnection and order.

Is the starting point going to be with subjects escaping situations that put their lives and families at very mild risk (like Neal Schwieterman, for example) and progress to Syrian atrocity refugees and Holocaust survivors? Or does the project limit subjects to those on the same scale—fewer subjects that include only atrocious events from the Holocaust to Stalin's gulags, Cambodia, the Balkans, Kurdistan, Syria and others on varying horrific scale?

The philosophy behind the wider perspective is to ease the reader ultimately into the horrific space. Kevin would like to use the closer-to-us-all ideas of escape to carry readers incrementally to the more hellish. This will hopefully make the atrocious more real and immediate than it might otherwise be, and to liberate it from political rhetoric, national origin or economic class.

What Media Forms Will Be Used and How?

This will be a largely visual storytelling project, making use of video, still photography, audio and artifact in early stages, and lecture as a final stage. For sake of scale the project uses a small set of the many possible media forms.

- **Video:** Extended 30-minute videos when justifiable for Web, cable or over-the-air use, to short 3- to 5-minute Web segments, to Instagram-length for social media use. Web-length videos will pair interview clips and moving portrait clips with archival images and clips of the story spaces (location left behind, and/or refuge found) in a randomized diptych and triptych screen format. Separate and exclusive video portrait clips will be held out along with short interview statements for social media use. Documentary-length television segments will be edited for the standards and aesthetics of the potential partner channel.
- **Stills:** At the time of interviews, intimate and highly-polished portraits of the subject for gallery or museum exhibition will be made. These can be created digitally, though Kevin envisions medium- or large-format black and white silver prints. This work can imply both permanence and scarcity to the images, and provide a way for those deeply engaged with a story to take it home into their lives through purchase of a portrait or landscape print. Behind-the-scene digital images for Instagram will also be made to give the community a peek into coming stories as the pace of the project accelerates.
- **Audio:** Interview audio can be edited for independence from the visual elements of the story, allowing for over-the-air radio, podcast and use by the visually impaired. For Web audio, stories read by voice actors could remove a layer of bias. Stories centered on the emotional stress of rebuilding a life in a new culture would be aimed at making these experiences universal and help listeners of all political or cultural backgrounds internalize the experience.
- **Text:** Though this is a visually-driven project, transcribed interview text should be provided for those engaging with the project in quiet spaces and for those who prefer to read rather than listen. Like all other forms in use here, additive information will be provided in all text, encouraging engagement with all media forms in use. It will not simply be a repurposing of interview audio.
- **Artifact:** When possible, physical objects related to each story's experience will be borrowed for careful and respectful display in exhibition spaces. Artifacts like this add direct physical presence with a story better than any other media form. Items will be insured, packaged and transported with extreme care and documentation and receipts provided in accordance with museum collection best practices.

- **Community-Generated Content:** The editorial system will allow for meaningful community-generated contribution to the project. Unsegregated space will be provided to contribute vetted comment and story. Though this material must meet project journalistic standards, the community will be able to add meaningfully to our work.

Options:

- **Game:** Simple gamefulness could be created with a minimum of design demand using the voice-acted audio described above. Deep engagement could be encouraged from listeners by asking them to identify when and/or from where a refuge seeker originated, but without the clue of accent. This form is best planned and created by experienced game designers.
- **Lecture:** A small series of lectures or forums may be produced late in the project publication process to foster community conversation over the issue, and to provide community members with the opportunity to hear from and meet project characters.

What Media Channels Will Be Used and How?

Our project will use digital, analog and brick-and-mortar channels to reach targeted publics. As rich and powerful as digital channels are, the rare, singular and physical of the analog world add invaluable depth to story. Our publication goal is to place our work in people's paths rather than hoping they will just happen upon us.

- **Web:** A story hub will be created interconnecting as many pieces of the larger story as possible. While much of the work will be available on the site, it will not be intended to be the project's final destination. Well-targeted external channels will be the final destination for the varying project elements. Its design will allow for as much nonlinear story interaction as possible. Off-the-shelf Web technologies will be used—content management and display through Wordpress, video hosting through Vimeo, audio through Soundcloud or similar systems—to pilot the easiest possible construction and to avoid the pitfalls of singular, personally-coded systems.
- **Mobile:** Wordpress (if used) content can easily be fed to app-like mobile templates providing deep access to the project to the fastest-growing media channel technology. As above, however, our aim is not to create a destination channel of our own, but to feed our content to targeted high-traffic external channels. Here digital social media is an important piece of our mobile strategy, with non-repetitive and targeted content distributed through *Instagram, Twitter, Facebook* and other online social spaces.
- **Digital Social Media**: Here exclusive and native content that adds to story depth is included rather than simply using social to link to full stories elsewhere. Content should be designed as if this will be the only place readers may find the story, but coax them into the wider digital and analog story network. In similar projects, *Instagram* has proven to be an excellent channel for behind-the-scenes looks into the project and *Twitter* as a discussion and dissent space. Facebook is now an excellent storytelling channel where new publics can be reached with greater depth.
- **Galleries:** Highly-polished portrait and landscape imagery and artifacts will be used to bring these stories into physical space. Each portrait will be paired with a scene-setting image of a space key to the story. For example, an intimate and provocative portrait or Bob Sakata could be paired with

an image of the Topaz Relocation Center today, or of his vast farming empire on Colorado's Platte River. Artifacts from his story would stand in a case near the images. Potential gallery spaces include the display space on the Concourse A bridge at Denver International Airport where an extremely broad population waits in security lines or passes transit time. More targeted options may include the Mizel Museum in Denver, a social justice organization centered around the Jewish experience, to local community centers in less urban areas of the state. In small scale spaces care will be taken to display work that conforms to local filter bubbles in pair with that which does not.

- **Links to Existing External Projects:** Following Google's Law of the Internet—the more you send people away, the more they keep coming back—other reporting and social engagement projects operating in the same spirit will be linked to *Refugee*. Links through which the public can act on the information produced will be also provided, allowing deeper investigation into topics or related organizations.

Options:

- **Lecture/Forum Spaces:** In a similar vein as the galleries, in-person interaction with willing story subjects, project producers, local issue activists and politicians will be coordinated to create analog social media spaces. These may be in pair with gallery openings, as part of larger community events or in collaboration with local educational institutions.
- **Legacy Media:** Content may be distributed through the online, print or broadcast channels of commercial and public media in the region capable of reaching new targeted publics (Figure 1). In order to break filter bubbles, broadcast or publication of stories that are more recognizable to their demographics could be paired with those that upend expectations.

Figure 1. The Refuge project storyworld visualized

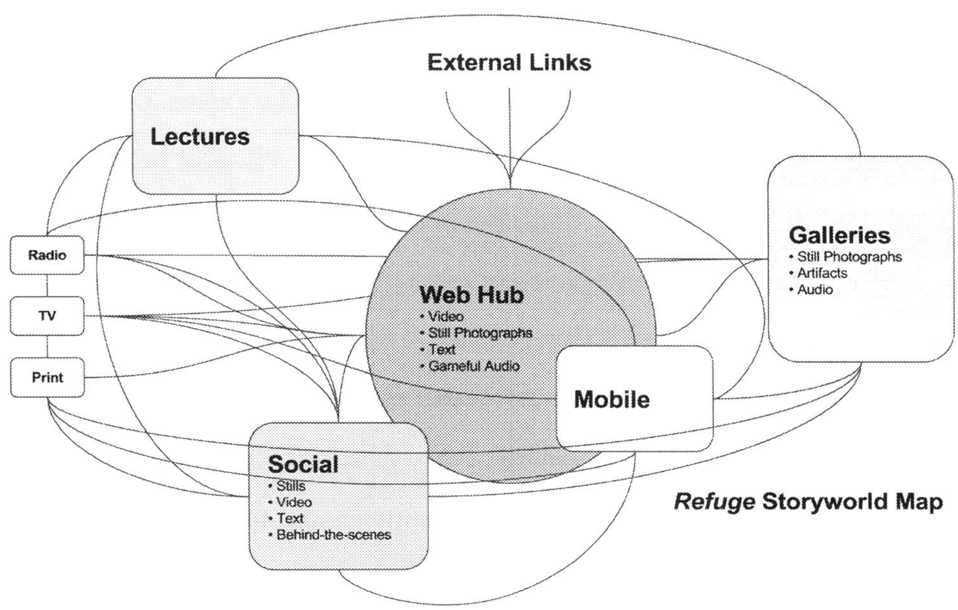

Who Should It Reach?

The goal is to reach more than the choir—those within various social or political bubbles—with this project. The work will be not only to reach the Trump voter with a compelling and relatable view on refugees, immigrants and others looking for sanctuary in the American West, but to reach refugee-supporting liberals with a broader view of refuge. For both poles, the hope is to convey that one person's refugee is another's threat.

To achieve these goals, first there will be exploration of published research and reporting into regional attitudes about refugees, immigrants and the concept of sanctuary to make sure gut-level understanding of these attitudes is supported and to expand that basic understanding. On more broadcast-oriented media content from both perspectives will be paired. Channels where more specific demographics could be most efficiently reached will be identified. The project will foster comparisons between situations with which a reader or viewer may agree and another with which he or she may not.

Targeting

Initial target media channels will be determined through research into the demographics of the users of these channels. The team currently has access through university libraries to databases like SRDS for legacy media, Quantcast for much online media, Simmons OneView for demographic cross-tabulation of interests and media consumption. For other channels, such as brick-and-mortar gallery spaces, demographic and traffic information is likely available from the source. This data will assist in determining which stories land in which channels, and how they are paired or arranged to most effectively engage each audience. *Refuge* should not rely on legacy journalism's simple "spray and pray" distribution model.

When Will It Happen?

Initial Launch Schedule for an 18-Month Production and Publication Timeline

- **April:** Moloney and Slaby continue to refine the project definition and map the storyworld limits and set storytelling and publication goals. Research into public attitudes about refugees and immigrants will be initiated.
- **May**: Production begins on four to six initial stories. The first one will be with Ingrid Latorre because of possibly short availability before deportation, and follow with nonagenarian subjects like Bob Sakata and Walter Plywaski. Work on defining target audiences and how to reach them will be initiated.
- **June**: Infrastructure building for Web, social channels, content management and backup archiving systems. Story production continues as subjects arise. Consider attending a Quaker retreat on the sanctuary movement to be held at Ghost Ranch, N.M. for background reporting.
- **July:** Begin feeding preliminary story elements to social media channels.
- **August:** Launch first full Web stories.
- **October:** Begin negotiation with external publication channels—regional legacy and online media, brick and mortar exhibition locations. Plan and book lecture series locations and schedule.

- **April:** Opening of exhibitions at brick-and-mortar locations such as Denver International Airport, public gallery spaces on the Western Slope and rural Colorado and other western states.
- **September:** Lecture series launch (Figure 2).

How Will It Be Funded?

Beyond initial investment in time and resources by the producers, a scale-up of the project would require funds for content gathering and distribution to venues that would not or could not pay to license the content. Though most producers named below would be likely to donate their work to the goal, this project hopes to pay market rates for content production and provide at least a modest stipend to administrators.

- Moloney and Slaby will work with the Colorado Nonprofit Development Center (CNDC) on a fiscal sponsorship to ease the workload in fundraising and accounting. This arrangement will last through the wider Divided Colorado series of transmedia projects.
- Initial needs could be met through a crowdfunding campaign to produce content.
- Ongoing needs may be met through topical grant funding sought with the aid of the CNDC. Funding will be sought from organizations that support refugee, immigration, journalism and documentary projects.

CONCLUSION

If implemented thoughtfully and carefully, transmedia storytelling shows promise for journalists as a possible answer to an ever-more complex mediascape. The required design and planning of transmedia projects can be a foreign idea for journalists accustomed to reacting to a rapid news cycle. This chapter described design thinking as a loose structure for effectively planning transmedia journalism projects and briefly examined cases where too little design planning led to complications of their storyworlds. In answer to those complications, the author proposed a decision flow to aid transmedia journalism design-

Figure 2. Refuge project tentative production and publication timeline

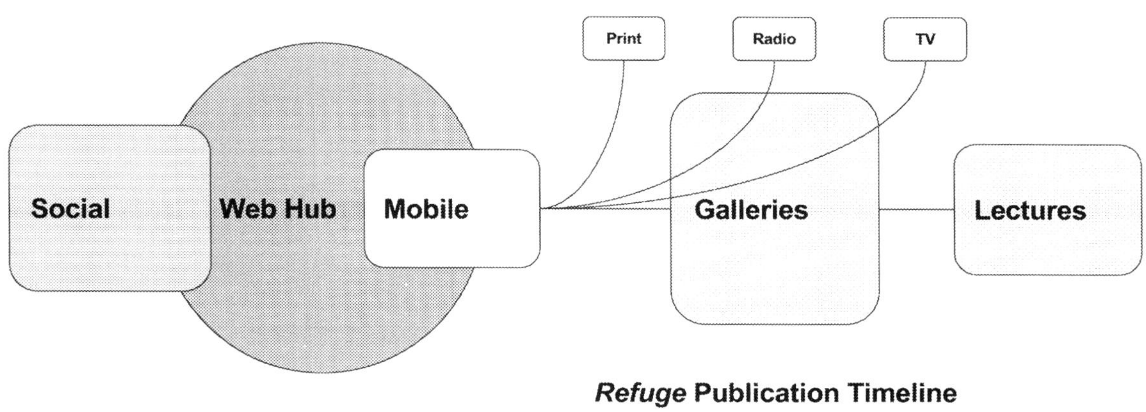

ers and analysts in understanding how to prioritize the needs of a project and iterate its design without losing sight of its purpose. This decision flow was demonstrated with an early-stage storyworld design document for a developing transmedia journalism project: *Refuge*.

For the bulk of traditional, day-to-day newsgathering, the classic design of journalism is usually enough: Report double-sourced, timely and relevant information; verify it; craft it into a compelling story; publish it to the appropriate section of a preexisting channel with social media links and start over again the next day. This cycle is a difficult one to escape because by the time one round is finished, new events and issues have arisen that demand a journalist's attention. This process also persists because it has worked for more than two centuries and still works adequately enough to keep most journalism organizations afloat for now. Because it is a fast-paced, stressful and important job performed largely in the public eye, journalists like this author must give it an almost religious purpose to endure it. Like all religions, dogma and tradition make it very slow to change.

Other media industries do not often see their work through such idealistic lenses. No matter the importance or social value of the product being created, all methods to reach an efficient public are explored and coordinated with other methods. This has led to the rise of transmedia storytelling there far sooner and more rapidly than it has in journalism. Their eyes-on-the-prize focus on measurable success also requires detailed start-to-finish planning of projects to achieve their goals. To be most effective, transmedia journalism must be thoughtfully designed to achieve its goals too. A careful user-centered design that is both constrained and liberated by a prioritized set of decisions is critical to ensure that the project does not fall apart.

REFERENCES

Brown, T. (2008). Design thinking. *Harvard Business Review*, *86*(6), 84–92. PMID:18605031

Catmull, E. (2014). *Creativity, Inc.: Overcoming the unseen forces that stand in the way of true inspiration*. New York, NY: Random House Publishing Group.

Chávez, F. A. (1974). *My penitente land: Reflections on Spanish New Mexico*. Santa Fe, NM: Museum of New Mexico Press.

Chávez, F. A. (2012). *Origins of New Mexico families: A genealogy of the Spanish colonial period*. Albuquerque, NM: University of New Mexico Press.

Fleming, M. J. (2015, December 18). *"Star Wars" legacy II: An architect of Hollywood's greatest deal recalls how George Lucas won sequel rights*. Retrieved April 27, 2017, from http://deadline.com/2015/12/star-wars-franchise-george-lucas-historic-rights-deal-tom-pollock-1201669419/

Foster, A. D. (1978). *Splinter of the mind's eye*. New York, NY: Warner Books.

Franklin, B. (2006). *Letter to Peter Collinson, the support of the poor, May 9, 1753*. Retrieved April 26, 2017, from http://teachingamericanhistory.org/library/document/letter-to-peter-collinson/

Fulton, A., McKenna, M., McMillan, T., & Rupp, R. (2014, April 1). The plate [blog]. Retrieved April 28, 2017, from http://www.nationalgeographic.com/people-and-culture/food/the-plate/

Gambarato, R. R., & Tárcia, L. P. T. (2017). Transmedia strategies in journalism. An analytical model for the news coverage of planned events. *Journalism Studies*, *18*(11), 1381–1399. doi:10.1080/1461670X.2015.1127769

Google Analytics Solutions. (2017). Retrieved April 28, 2017, from https://www.google.com/analytics/#?modal_active=none

Harding, D. C. W. (1963). *Experience into words*. CUP Archive.

Hayes, G. P. (2011). How to write a transmedia production bible. *Screen Australia*. Retrieved from https://www.screenaustralia.gov.au/getmedia/33694e05-95c2-4a05-8465-410fb8a224aa/Transmedia-production-bible-template.pdf

Jaxxon. (n.d.). [Fan Wiki]. Retrieved April 28, 2017, from http://starwars.wikia.com/wiki/Jaxxon

Jenkins, H. (2006). Searching for the origami unicorn. In *Convergence Culture: Where Old and New Media Collide* (pp. 93–130). New York, NY: NYU Press.

Jenkins, H. (2009, December 12). The revenge of the origami unicorn: Seven principles of transmedia storytelling (Well, two actually. Five more on Friday). *Confession of an Aca-fan Blog*. Retrieved October 10, 2010, from http://henryjenkins.org/2009/12/the_revenge_of_the_origami_uni.html

Johansson-Sköldberg, U., Woodilla, J., & Çetinkaya, M. (2013). Design thinking: Past, present and possible futures. *Creativity and Innovation Management*, *22*(2), 121–146. doi:10.1111/caim.12023

Lessig, L. (2009). *Remix: Making art and commerce thrive in the hybrid economy*. London: Penguin.

Lockwood, T. (2010). *Design thinking: Integrating innovation, customer experience, and brand value*. New York, NY: Skyhorse Publishing, Inc.

Moloney, K. (2011). *Porting transmedia storytelling to journalism (M.A. Thesis)*. Denver, CO: University of Denver. Retrieved from http://0-proquest.umi.com.bianca.penlib.du.edu/pqdlink?did=2510689501&Fmt=2&rqt=309

Moloney, K. (2015). *Future of story: Transmedia journalism and National Geographic's Future of Food Project* (dissertation). University of Colorado, Boulder, CO.

Orme, W. (2014, February 19). *"Crypto-Jews" in the Southwest find faith in a shrouded legacy*. Retrieved April 26, 2017, from http://www.npr.org/sections/codeswitch/2014/02/19/275862633/crypto-jews-in-the-southwest-find-faith-in-a-shrouded-legacy

Phillips, A. (2012). *A creator's guide to transmedia storytelling: How to captivate and engage audiences across multiple platforms*. New York, NY: McGraw Hill Professional.

Quantcast. (2017). Retrieved April 28, 2017, from https://www.quantcast.com/

Ralph Lawrence Carr. (2017, April 4). In *Wikipedia*. Retrieved from https://en.wikipedia.org/w/index.php?title=Ralph_Lawrence_Carr&oldid=773864607

Rose, F. (2011). *The art of immersion: How the digital generation is remaking Hollywood, Madison avenue, and the way we tell stories*. New York, NY: W. W. Norton & Company.

Ryan, M.-L. (2006). *Avatars of story* (Vol. 17). Minneapolis, MN: University of Minnesota Press.

Ryan, M.-L. (2013, October). *Transmedia storytelling: Myth or reality?* Keynote Speech (from author transcript) presented at the Rethinking Intermediality in the Digital Age, Cluj, Romania. Retrieved from http://www.youtube.com/watch?v=zqFsg8zqcLA&feature=youtube_gdata_player

Ryan, M.-L. (2014). Story/worlds/media: Tuning the instruments of a media-conscious narratology. In *Storyworlds across media: Toward a media-conscious narratology* (pp. 25–49). Lincoln, NE: University of Nebraska Press. doi:10.2307/j.ctt1d9nkdg.6

Saleh, S. H. (2015). Freedom from freedom: The beneficial role of constraints in collaborative creativity. *Dissertation Abstracts International.*

Simmons, M. (1993). *The last conquistador: Juan de Onate and the settling of the Far Southwest*. Norman, OK: University of Oklahoma Press.

Simmons Research. (2017). Retrieved April 28, 2017, from https://simmonsresearch.com/product-portfolio/

SRDS media planning platform. (2017). Retrieved April 28, 2017, from http://www.kantarmedia.com/us/our-solutions/media-planning-tools/srds-media-planning-platform

Statista. (2017). Retrieved April 28, 2017, from https://www.statista.com/

Tanforan Racetrack. (2017, February 13). In *Wikipedia*. Retrieved from https://en.wikipedia.org/w/index.php?title=Tanforan_Racetrack&oldid=765226913

Time 100. (2017). Retrieved from http://time.com/collection/2017-time-100/

Topaz War Relocation Center. (2017, April 26). In *Wikipedia*. Retrieved from https://en.wikipedia.org/w/index.php?title=Topaz_War_Relocation_Center&oldid=777385616

Weiler, L. (2009). Lance Weiler explains why filmmakers should expand their films into a "storyworld." *Filmmaker Magazine*. Retrieved April 27, 2017, from http://www.filmmakermagazine.com/archives/issues/summer2009/culture_hacker.php#.WQJzGcm1s3E

KEY TERMS AND DEFINITIONS

Audience Targeting: Strategic placement of advertising, entertainment, or news content in media channels to reach predetermined segments of the public.

Decision Flow: An ordered set of decisions in which the prior questions are ideally answered before the subsequent.

Demographics: The statistical characteristics of a population, including age, race, gender, income, and others.

Design Thinking: The problem-solving process of creating, marketing, and implementing products or services with a focus on end-user utility and satisfaction.

Essentialism: A view that every entity has an essential set of attributes that define it. The Linnean taxonomy of biological organisms is an example of an essentialist structure.

Lede: (/lid/) An American journalism spelling differentiation that clarifies it from the similar pronunciation of lead. A lede is the paragraph of a news story that introduces the subject. A lead (/lid/) is a clue to follow in reporting and well as the leader of a reporting team. Lead (/led/) is also the space between typeset lines of text, named for the heavy metal used in early letterpress typesetting.

Psychographics: Statistics that classify populations by psychological characteristics, such as preferences, affinities, fears, and social values.

ENDNOTE

1 Marvel released a series of apocryphal comics following the success of *Star Wars* that included Jaxxon, a giant rabbit-like alien as an Empire-battling character alongside Han Solo and Chewbacca. After a canonical absence of 20 years, he has since reappeared in games and Web comics ("Jaxxon," n.d.).

Chapter 7
Tell Me a Story, but It Should Be Real!
Design Practice in Transmedia Journalism

Mariana Ciancia
Politecnico di Milano, Italy

Michele Mattei
Politecnico di Milano, Italy

ABSTRACT

Multi-channel structures within the convergence era, both as crossmedia and transmedia phenomena, have become increasingly important, and have completely changed the role of the audience, undermining the notions of authority and authorship, shaping society, and influencing media habits. This has created a mediascape in which readers can vicariously enter fictional and non-fictional spaces that can be explored through multiple media windows. Starting from the assumption that transmedia design can address not only the entertainment market but also the non-fictional field, this chapter aims at exploring journalism through the design lens. The first part of the work is devoted to a description of the contemporary communication scenario, and the second part aims to suggest guidelines for the application of a transmedia approach within the Italian news business, in the form of a conceptual and operational tool.

INTRODUCTION

Along with the development of social interconnections through digital technologies, nowadays multi-channel structures, both as crossmedia and transmedia systems, have become increasingly important, undermining the notion of authority and authorship. While "crossmedia" are concerned with the process of adaptation (Long, 2007), "transmedia" are concerned with the building of a story world (Wolf, 2012) through different channels to enhance the role of the audience (Jenkins, 2006; Pratten, 2015). Therefore, *transmedia practice* (Dena, 2009) is a phenomenon that allows audiences to participate in the meaning-making process and change the relationship between the mainstream media and the participatory culture (Jenkins, Ford, & Green, 2013). This chapter starts from the assumption that, as a result of story-building

DOI: 10.4018/978-1-5225-3781-6.ch007

processes capable of fostering audience engagement, *transmedia design* can address not only the entertainment field, but also the issue of contemporary complexity, through a phenomenological approach to the coeval reality (Ciancia, 2016).

This chapter focuses on the non-fiction field of journalism, a domain in which transmedia storytelling can be "a method for journalists to target their work to an increasingly dispersed public across an unlimited array of both digital and analog media" (Moloney, 2012, p. 2). The work proposes an exploration of journalism through a transmedia approach, considering the following core points: How multichannel strategies are changing journalism practice; how aesthetic, technological and economic issues work together in the "news business;" and what are possible transmedia forms in the journalism field? Is *transmedia design* an approach able to support networks and broadcast opportunities?

The first part of this chapter (*Authors, Audiences and Media Texts: A Continuous Balance of Power*) is devoted to the description of the contemporary *mediascape* (Appadurai, 1990). Subsequently, the section focuses on the journalism field, presenting national and international case studies to illustrate some reflections on the ethical aspects of reporting versus telling a story within news media production. This section aims to also tackle issues related to the role of the audience within processes such as open publishing, in which the process of news creation is open to readers, and thus to a certain extent can impact on editorial decisions, and citizen journalism, described as "a citizen, or group of citizens, playing an active role in the process of collecting, reporting, analyzing and disseminating news and information" (Bowman & Willis, 2003, p. 9), bottom-up phenomena of the 21st century fostered by the spreading of social media and the consequent creation of social networks.

The second part of the work suggests a transmedia approach in the specific context of the Italian news business. The first part of this section gives a definition of the term "transmedia," and identifies three key features: 1) building of story worlds; 2) the distribution of these story worlds across multiple media channels; and 3) audience engagement. It also describes how, and to what extent, transmedia practice can be considered a design practice. Finally, a *design model* is proposed to explore 1) what are the possible transmedia forms of a news story; 2) what is the role of the designer in an Italian newsroom; 3) what are the distribution models of transmedia news; and 4) what all of this means in terms of audience engagement.

AUTHORS, AUDIENCES AND MEDIA TEXTS: A CONTINUOUS BALANCE OF POWER

The contemporary widespread use of digital videos, pictures, audio, and text and their distribution across social media has led to the rise of new consumption behaviors and the spread of new narrative forms that rely not only on technological developments, but also on the spontaneous practices of audience engagement (such as user-generated content). Moreover, people are surrounded by many forms of media, in which they can vicariously enter fictional and non-fictional spaces that can be explored through multiple media windows according to the multi-channel paradigm.

Today's societal context is one in which changes in the business and social environments have created a complex landscape where the relationship between the mainstream media (*top-down*) and participatory culture (*bottom-up*) have completely changed, undermining the notions of authority and authorship. As a result, now more than ever, fictional and non-fictional narratives are experienced on the small screens of our portable devices, such as laptops, tablets, and mobile phones, and the viewer/user/player (Dinehart, 2010) can choose how and when to interact with them: He/she "[...] transforms the story via his or her own natural cognitive psychological abilities, and enables the Artwork to surpass medium. It is in transmedial play that the ultimate story agency, and decentralized authorship can be realized. Thus, the VUP becomes the true producer of the Artwork" (Dinehart, 2008).

Currently, the contemporary mediascape is addressing three main issues: 1) audiences and their habits, 2) the technological developments that lead people to interact with a digital vision of reality, and 3) the participatory processes related to the socio-cultural dimension. This scenario is making audiences more and more knowledgeable and eager for information, which is now spread across several devices, platforms, and channels. Thanks also to technological innovation, which has become an important tool for how we envisage the future, people are putting together different messages stemming from everyday life to shape the collective imagination. Three fields—audience, technology, and engagement—exist in a situation of interchange, and have given rise to the following concepts that have shaped the media field: Textual poaching (de Certeau, 1980; Jenkins, 1992), remediation (Bolter & Grusin, 1999), convergence culture (Jenkins, 2006) and participatory culture (Delwiche & Henderson, 2013; Jenkins, 1992, 2006; Jenkins et al., 2013; Lessig, 2008; Miller, 2011).

The first concept—*textual poaching*—is strictly related to the audience field. Since the dawn of time, people have tended to individualize mass culture and media consumption (Bauman, 2000), looking for a personal meaning-making approach to media texts. Michel de Certeau was the first to identify such active reading, in *L'Invention du Quotidien. Vol. 1, Arts de Faire* (1980), and coined the term "*braconner*", "poacher" in English, to describe readers as travelers that "move across lands belonging to someone else, like nomads poaching their way across fields they did not write, despoiling the wealth of Egypt to enjoy it themselves" (de Certeau, 1984, p. 174). This concept taken up by Henry Jenkins in his seminal work *Textual Poachers: Television Fans and Participatory Culture* (1992), devoting to the description of the relation between industrial strategies and fannish tactics, an evolving tactical relationship between the audience, authors, and media texts, that faces a continuous balance of power.

Bolter and Grusin (1999) coined the concept of *remediation* in 1999. With this term, they expressed the idea that media are not isolated, and that technology is articulated through the relationships between infrastructure and social networks (in terms of social structures intended as social entities). This is a process that started far before the digital revolution, and that has existed through the centuries in Western visual culture (Bolter & Grusin, 1999, p. 11). Certainly, *digitization*; that is, the process of transforming analog information into digital bits of 1s and 0s, and *digitalization*, which shapes the social life around digital media infrastructure, fosters the spreading of new media. But according to Bolter and Grusin, "[w]hat is new about new media comes from the particular ways in which they refashion older media and the ways in which older media refashion themselves to answer the challenges of new media" (Bolter & Grusin, 1999, p. 15).

The third concept—*convergence culture*—is related to the emergence of a cultural change that led people to cross the boundaries of the single medium, looking for new information and connections. Convergence culture is a concept that overcomes the idea of access, moving toward a process of participation and engagement that connects technological issues and socio-cultural dimensions (Jenkins, 2006). Thus, the concept of convergent culture theorized by Jenkins (2006) highlights not only how media develop according to remediation theory (Bolter & Grusin, 1999), but also how they can interact with each other, creating a fertile communicative space.

According to Jenkins (Scott, 2013), if the focus of textual poaching was on reception and production, in talking about *participatory culture* the focus has moved toward the concept of circulation. "The reality is that the 'digital revolution' has resulted in real, demonstrable, shifts in media power, expanding the capacity of various subcultures and communities to access the means of media production and circulation" (Scott, 2013, p. xxiii). Based on the findings of Jenkins (Scott, 2013), it can be argued that the concept of participatory culture pushes the idea of participation further, going beyond not only spectatorship and consumption, but also the nomadic approach of poaching.

These concepts shape a networked society in which people are "no longer dependent upon the particular forms of dialog to which we have grown accustomed and new forms will have to be developed" (Burnett, 2011). The first two—textual poaching and remediation—refer to narrative structures that give people more tools for telling and listening to stories. Consequently, there are new generations of interactive narratives able to change the connection between the mass media and the participatory culture. Instead, the last two—convergence culture and participatory culture—are related to how people, thanks to developments in technology and media habits, can interact with each other, creating collaborative networks: a way that allows audiences to experience narratives spread by non-linear communication systems through collective intelligence (Lévy, 1997), and to participate in the meaning-making process. This is a change in the media structures that embraces not only the entertainment field, but also non-fictional areas, such as journalism, documentary making, and social innovation.

Crowd Intelligence: From Documentary Making to the Journalism Field

An illustration of the ways in which people can be engaged by content, thereby contributing to the spread of crowd intelligence—a notion strictly connected to Pierre Lévy's concept of collective intelligence (1997)—comes from Associate Professor Mandy Rose (2011), Director of the Digital Cultures Research Centre (University of West England) in Bristol. While Pierre Lévy conceptualized the idea of collective consumption, describing a knowledge-based culture sustained by the shift of knowledge among individual and collective, Mandy Rose provides a categorization of projects (specifically documentaries), according to the type of contribution made by the audience: The *Creative Crowd*, the *Participant Observer*, the *Community of Purpose*, and the *Traces of the Multitude*.

In the first model—the Creative Crowd—the participants contribute to the entire project with their fragments. The individual units may not be self-sufficient, but their value is increased when they contribute to the construction and the aesthetics of the main text as a whole. An example is the project *Evolution of Get Lucky* (PV Nova, 2013) in which the French author, composer, singer, videomaker, and blogger PV Nova proposed a cover of the famous song *Get Lucky* (Daft Punk, 2013), and then asked to the audience "to playfully build the pieces of a participatory music video" (San Cornelio & Roig Telo, 2015, p. 85). In the second model—the Participant Observers—people decide whether and to what extent they want to contribute. According to Mandy Rose (2011), a paradigmatic example is *Life in a Day* (Macdonald, 2011), a 94-minute documentary edited from the material filmed by people during a single day (24 July 2010), an experience that was repeated in Italy with *Italy in a Day* (Salvatores, 2014). On October 26, 2013, people were asked to use a camera or a mobile phone to record something about themselves. The final aim of the project was to describe one day in the life of Italian people. In the third model—the Community of Purpose—a group of people (the participants) take part in the production, sharing a specific aim related to social good. In this specific model, the collaborative process is more important than the final product. Again, the example is an interactive documentary from the National Film Board of Canada, *Out my Window* (Cizek, 2010). This was a collaborative project that involved over a hundred people, including photographers, journalists, architects, residents, activists, developers, and researchers, which aimed to collect and tell the stories of the suburbs of 13 cities: Chicago, Toronto, Montreal, Havana, Sao Paulo, Amsterdam, Prague, Istanbul, Beirut, Bangalore, Phnom Penh, Tainan, and Johannesburg. The fourth model—the Traces of the Multitude—introduces the idea of anonymous collaboration among contributors thanks to social media content. An example is *#18DaysInEgypt* (Elayat & Mehta, 2011), a crowd-sourced documentary that grows as a choral story of the Arab Spring, alive and constantly updated, constituted by the individual stories of people gathered through personal media.

Based on the findings of Mandy Rose (2011), it can be argued that the evolution of digital technologies, online networks, and distributed production tools have enabled participatory practices that are shaping the contemporary communication scenario in terms of production and consumption: "[...] a specific set of social practices that deal with the decision-making practices of actors situated in imbalanced power relations [...]" (Carpentier & Dahlgren, 2013, p. 309). This evolution has also affected the role of the audience within the news media production field.

Audience Participation in the Media Stream

This section does not aim to trace the history of the evolution of journalism practice, but it will be useful to identify the main processes and forms of the news business. Media scholars have observed emerging trends in the journalism field that merge the concept of multimodality (Kress & van Leeuwen, 2001), open publishing and multi-channel distribution. This led to the definition of new forms for the news business, such as citizen journalism (Bowman & Willis, 2003; Rodriguez, 2001), convergent journalism (Quinn & Filak, 2005), and transmedia journalism (Alzamora & Tárcia, 2012; Ford, 2007; Gambarato & Tárcia, 2017; Moloney, 2012; 2011; Renó, 2014).

In open publishing, the process of news creation is open to readers, who can affect editorial decisions to a certain extent. They can contribute with stories that are filtered as little as possible, usually uploading content directly. This scenario has witnessed the rise of sub-practices of content control, according to Linus's Law "[g]iven enough eyeballs, all bugs are shallow'' (Raymond, 1999, p. 30). Furthermore, people can become involved in editorial decisions and can redistribute news (always in an open publishing platform). It is possible to cite as an example *Wikipedia*, which began in 2000 as a complementary project to *Nupedia*, an online encyclopedia that, founded by Jimmy Wales and Larry Sanger, should be based on the peer review mechanism. Given the slow pace at which the entries were developed, they decided to launch a *wiki*, a platform that allows teams to work collaboratively on a project, then write and edit shared content. In a short period of time, these entries exceeded those on the original project, and *Wikipedia* was officially launched in 2002. According to Lessig (2008, pp. 156–162), *Wikipedia* establishes a set of rules and depends on contributions from a community whose reasons go beyond the economic reward. Another interesting project from the Wikimedia Foundation is *Wikinews*, a collaborative journalism program based on a neutral point of view policy that distinguishes it from other citizen journalism projects.

As anticipated in the Introduction, citizen journalism describes "how ordinary citizens, empowered by digital technologies that connect knowledge throughout the globe, are contributing to, and participating in, their own truths, their own kind of news" (Bowman & Willis, 2003, p. v). It is a form of journalism that merges citizen media, a term coined by Clemencia Rodriguez in 2001 to describe how audiences became participants in the media stream, using new digital technologies, devices, and platforms (such as blogs, vlogs, and podcasts that can be easily distributed online), and user-generated content. These technological developments not only allow people to access the news worldwide, but also to report news and events more quickly than broadcasters and official reporters. Renowned examples of citizen journalism projects in which the audience has played an important role in reporting major events by going beyond infrastructural and political problems are the aforementioned Arab Spring (*#18DaysInEgypt,* Elayat & Mehta, 2011), the Occupy Wall Street movement, which began on September 17, 2011, and the 2013 protest in Turkey.

According to Quinn and Filak (2005, p. 3), "convergence is a revolutionary and evolutionary form of journalism that is emerging in many parts of the world." As a result, journalists must understand the evolution of the contemporary mediascape in terms of fragmented audiences, availability of cheap technology, and changes in the balance of power between media companies and consumers in order to reach people across multiple media (Quinn & Filak, 2005, pp. 7–8). This situation led many scholars (Alzamora & Tárcia, 2012; Ford, 2007; Gambarato & Tárcia, 2017; Moloney, 2012; 2011; Renó, 2014) and also practitioners (Gomez, 2010) to connect the concept of transmedia storytelling (TS) to journalism because, according to Heinrich (2011, p. 2), the "number of producers and disseminators of news as well as the instantaneity of global news flows indicate that journalistic practice is changing." Since "[a] ctually, our brain is transmedia" (Renó, 2014, p. 8), and the multi-channel news distribution is already a reality, Kevin T. Moloney (2012) described journalism as a post-digital narrative, applying the Seven Core Concept of Transmedia Storytelling identified by Jenkins (2009a, 2009b) to the journalism field (Moloney, 2011).

DESIGN PRACTICE IN TRANSMEDIA JOURNALISM

The evolution of social interconnections through digital technologies has emerged from a phenomenological approach to the contemporary mediascape. Multi-channel structures within the convergence era, both as crossmedia and transmedia phenomena, have become increasingly important, and completely changed the role of the audience, fostering the sharing of meaning-making processes between producers and audiences, shaping society, and influencing media habits. This in turn has allowed for the development of widespread creativity through collaborative creation and the collective consumption of fictional and non-fictional narrative worlds.

According to Moloney (2012, p. 2), TS can be "a method for journalists to target their work to an increasingly dispersed public across an unlimited array of both digital and analog media." There have been many attempts to define the meaning of transmedia. In consequence, there is conceptual confusion regarding the term and misleading use of it. First, it is necessary to clarify the way in which the term is used in this research by describing the key features of the transmedia phenomenon in order to go beyond the buzzwords. TS was conceptualized by Henry Jenkins in 2003, starting from the work of Marsha Kinder (1991) that use the term "transmedia" in reference to the franchise entertainment super-system that works "to position consumers as powerful players while disavowing commercial manipulation" (Kinder 1991, pp. 119–120). In 2006 Jenkins went further, defined TS as "Stories that unfold across multiple media platforms, with each medium making distinctive contributions to our understanding of the world, a more integrated approach to franchise development than models based on urtexts and ancillary products" (Jenkins, 2006, p. 293). In this work "transmedia" is intended as the practice concerned with the building of a story universe through different channels in order to enhance the role of the audience.

Considering these premises, it can be concluded that a new discipline at the intersection of *media studies* and *design cultures* is about to arise. *Transmedia Design* is a field of research that allows researchers and practitioners to analyze, develop, and manage multi-channel narrative-based communication systems. The design lens allows researchers to consider transmedia as a practice that operates both as a *problem-solver* and a *sense-maker*, reflecting the roles of design as highlighted by Ezio Manzini (2015). Transmedia is therefore a discipline in which the *problem-solver* side has an impact on aspects of production, as well as on the development processes of multi-channel communication systems; while the *sense-maker* aspect links sense-making procedures and the development of narrative media texts capable of allowing people to become aware of their prominent role in the contemporary media scenario (Ciancia, 2016, pp. 162–163).

As a result of this digital shift and the growing emphasis on a storyteller's ability to support multiple points of view, journalists must become practitioners who possess several skills and competences in addition to their traditional ones. Thus, this work aims at exploring the role of a communication designer, or better, a transmedia designer, within an Italian newsroom, in accordance with the idea that nowadays designers are cast as mediators. Indeed, in the contemporary scenario, communication designers can play a dual role: As story listeners, they collect stories from real life, the audience, and their repertoires; and as storytellers, they organize these stories into news and experiences, according to the idea that narrative could be considered a *primary modeling system* (Scolari, 2009).

The Italian News Business: Four Main Obstacles to Face the Digital Shift

To address the need for professional figures suitable for a new kind of newsroom in the Italian context, this work adopts a design-based perspective. To examine transmedia practice as a design practice (Ciancia, 2016), the workflow of the publishing model must be rethought. In order to do this, this research began with the *Transmedia Design Framework* developed by Mariana Ciancia (2016) and was carried on by Michele Mattei (2016), employing a variety of integrated methods:

1. With the aim of approaching the world of journalism from a scientific point of view, the starting point has been the reading of journalism, media, and technology predictions 2016 (Newman, 2015), plus the analysis of quantitative data presented in several reports, such as the *Digital News Report* published by Reuters Institute in 2015, and in-depth study of the full *New York Times Innovation Report*, written by a team of journalists from the New York Times in 2015.
2. Seven in-depth qualitative interviews of chief editors and deputy directors, chosen from the most renowned Italian newsroom, with the aim of understanding how they manage the daily workflow and retracing the main issues, controversies, and biases related to the digital shift. The publishing models of the main Italian newspapers (Sole 24 Ore, Corriere della Sera, La Stampa, La Repubblica, Gazzetta dello Sport and Quotidiano Nazionale) have been further scrutinized through ethnography, spending a full day in their newsrooms and comparing that experience with the publishing models declared by the international newspapers.
3. In order to complete the analysis of the possible forms of news, the researchers have performed a stylistic analysis of some news content produced by the abovementioned Italian newspapers and other renowned international players (Buzzfeed, ESPN, First Look Media, The New York Times, The Huffington Post, Vice News, Medium, Quartz, Storify, Flipboard).

The interviewed Italian deputy directors and chief editors highlighted the four main obstacles that slow or block changes in their newspapers, which are described below.

Move Away From Competitors

As noted by some of the interviewees, generalist newspapers have to find a way to stand out among the large number of publishers offering the same content, the same comments, and the same points of view. MC, deputy editor at La Stampa, highlighted how readers pay gladly for high-quality premium contents if they understand the relevance, brilliance and uniqueness of this newspaper (personal communication, January 22, 2016). MM, Newsroom Managing Editor at Il Sole 24 Ore, went further, explaining that their advantage is that they add value to the content, while for other newspapers with general content it is difficult to make news attractive enough to overcome the subscription barrier (personal communication, October 28, 2015).

Optimize Newsrooms

The second issue is time. Indeed, the timing of the production of digital news is very tight, sometimes few hours, often minutes; but in the newsrooms, there is a kind of "reasoned mess" for years, with the days marked by fixed appointments, which are almost rituals, with the aim to make the newspapers for the following days. ADC, deputy manager at Gazzetta dello Sport and manager of Gazzetta.it, identified how they had to find the right balance between the journalists who write for the paper, and the people who deal with the digital area, without creating "elephants" on one side and "small Steve Jobs" on the other side (personal communication, January 28, 2016).

Maximize Revenue

Discussions of the business side of a newsroom led the interviewees to talk about return on investment. The production effort should always lead to an income maximized by spreading the product across as many platforms as possible, so as to achieve different audiences with different parts of the same product. MM pointed out that there is no perfect recipe, but only the quest for balance between high-quality news on one side, and focused attention to the unique visitors on the other side. This is a topic often discussed in the editorial offices, and one that strongly affects the business model of the newspaper (personal communication, October 28, 2015).

Retain Readers

Finally, it is necessary to enhance the brand awareness of the newspaper through the creation of a relevant audience. Hence, every newsroom should focus on building an audience, understanding people, their demands, and their needs as readers. The journalist and author Mario Calabresi, in his first speech as Director of the Italian newspaper La Repubblica, stated that what they need to do is to give interpretive keys and, as in the first issue of La Repubblica, they must have the patience to explain the facts and speak to their readers. While once they had to go and find readers, now the reader can easily come to them (Calabresi, 2016).

To address the research questions stated in the Introduction, the comments, feedback, and reflections from the interviewed practitioners were linked to an analysis of the news form and the publishing models. This lead the authors to propose the use of a transmedia approach to Italian newsrooms, addressing the issue of the digital shift.

A TRANSMEDIA APPROACH TO ITALIAN NEWSROOMS

Given the developments in the contemporary media scenario highlighted in the first part of this chapter, all the interviewees agreed in their identification of the main obstacles that Italian journalism faces. According to these practitioners, one of the main aspects is content quality, which should be high to engage and attract the reader. Mario Calabresi (2016) stated that years ago, when people bought a newspaper, the reading experience took place on that piece of paper, while now the world, photographs, travel, e-mails, and friends are just one click away. As researchers in the media field, it is reasonable to talk about possible and optimized ways to reach and engage readers, in order to achieve high levels of reliability while ensuring good income to justify investment.

The news field is characterized by different points of view, and it is not easy to find a publisher with clear ideas that is able to face cutting-edge projects, even though almost the entire news field agrees that it is not enough to work on repackaging the news (no matter how technologically advanced this is), and it is not enough to redesign platforms. ADC went further, saying that if the newsroom is well organized, pronouncing the sentence "the paper will die" would mean that only one of the outputs would be shut down, not the whole company. Therefore, starting from now it is necessary to change how newsrooms are organized and how news is handled and published (personal communication, January 28, 2016).

The evidence and the interviews suggest that it is necessary to rethink the workflow and reorganize the habits inside newsrooms, focusing on news gathering, the distribution process, and the economic issues according to specific aims (Figure 1).

Therefore, this work proposes the use of the transmedia approach to news in order to support networks and broadcast opportunities. Applying this approach to newsrooms means a complete redesign of workflow, inspired by the one used in the development of the content and production of movies, TV series, video games, and entertainment. The transmedia approach may allow publishers to distribute content able to engage and retain audiences, while at the same time moving away from competitors.

As stated before, the outcome of this work is a set of guidelines for the application of a transmedia approach within Italian newsrooms, in the form of a conceptual and operational tool. Specifically, the proposal suggests: 1) the concerted use of several media and devices; 2) changing the process schedule in terms of organization and timing, starting from the arrival of a breaking news item until its publication; and 3) a new project workflow, composed of two news management models and an operational tool that can help journalists to organize their work and their resources inside the newsroom.

Figure 1. Needs and strategic aims of a newsroom after the digital shift

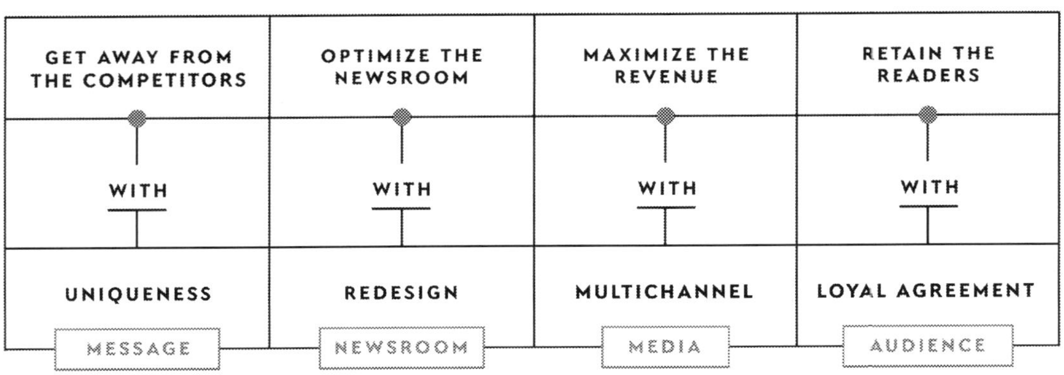

The first point of this proposal is a reflection strongly connected to the definition of TS proposed by Henry Jenkins (2006, p. 293): In the same way as in the entertainment market, it is possible to use several channels to convey news, according to the specific contribution that each medium can give. Since the outcomes of the second and the third points are two management models and a tool, they will be described in depth in the following sections.

Revising the Process Schedule

The second point of this proposal is related to the review of the process schedule inside newsrooms. Mario Calabresi (2016) explained the different habits of journalists within different newsrooms, such as traditional and digital ones. While journalists in the traditional field arrived at their offices late in the morning and finished work after dinner, usually during the night, in order to have their articles ready as close as possible to the newspaper's print time, their colleagues in digital news work in the early hours of the morning, according to their readers' habits. To stress this point, Mario Calabresi (2016) brought up the case of Luna Rossa, the Italian sailboat racing syndicate that raced in the America's Cup in the first decade of the 2000s. Calabresi (2006), in his first speech as Director of La Repubblica, posed the question "Do you remember when all the newspapers followed Luna Rossa and the newsrooms were open until 2.30 in the morning to know how it would end?" Then he explained that it was called "the battle of the night". However, now all is changing, and even if something happens at 4 am, 5 am, or 6 am, the "battle" should not be based on how fast the news is published, but on the publisher's intelligence in proposing a different point of view that allows them to move away from their competitors. He continued by explaining how today's battle is in the morning, in terms of telling immediately, at the first meeting, all that has happened. He stated that he did not know other people's habits, but the first thing he did in the morning was to read the news on his phone, while he was still in bed, and that he loved to read the newspaper during his breakfast to better understand something related to the happenings of the day before (Calabresi, 2016). Thus, if a newsroom no longer has to face the "battle of the night," it can think about print newspapers as one possible medium for conveying the news, possibly dedicated to an in-depth exploration of the previous day's news. This in turn could lead to a change in newsroom staff's working hours.

As a result, this work proposes a revision of the newsroom process schedule: Specifically, an increase in the number of editorial meetings, from two to three (Figure 2). The first should be early in the morning, followed by a second meeting late in the morning, and a third mid-afternoon. The final aim is the closure of the office before dinner. Under this new process schedule, the first morning meeting is devoted to the creation of the overall structure of the main daily news items and their digital forms and adaptation. The two other meetings are dedicated to taking stock of the relevant in-depth material, providing editorial guidelines, and the inclusion of breaking news into the news management cycle.

Revising the Project Workflow

The third point of this proposal has two components: Two news management models and an operational tool. Moloney (2011, p. 12) highlights that "[d]aily journalism, with its time-constrained brevity, is not a viable option. Transmedia must be designed carefully and developed with a lengthy lead time to be effective." Assuming the chance to manage the editorial line of a newspaper from the beginning, the possibility of choosing between two news management models emerges, each of which differs in terms of

Figure 2. Comparison between the traditional process schedule and the proposed schedule

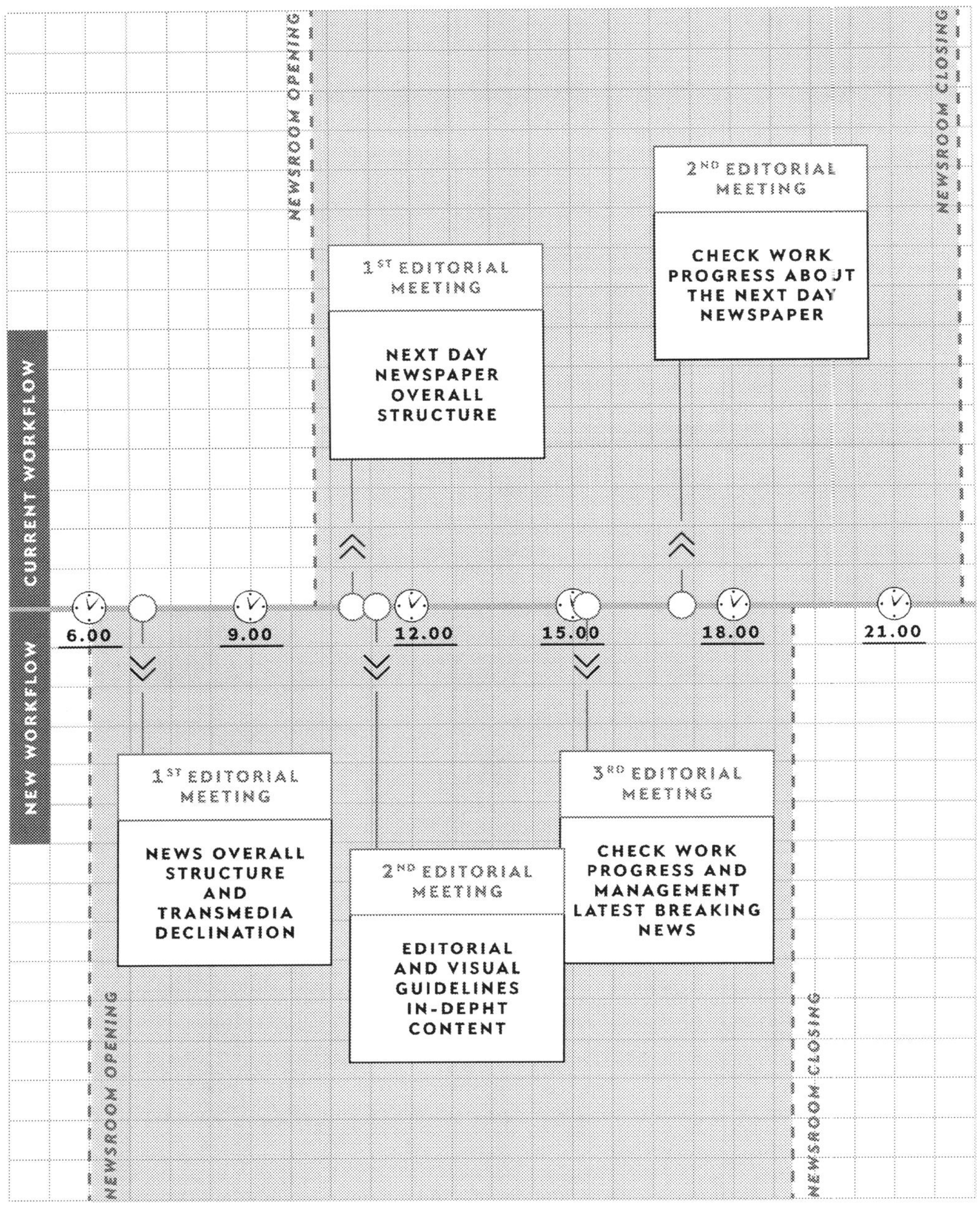

the design, construction, distribution, and archiving of news stories. These involve two different working methods, each with their own characteristics, which can meet different goals: Dealing with news with a high level of depth and offering a transmedia production and distribution, with the aim of satisfying different audiences and moving away from competitors; or conveying breaking news without any great depth, but in a manner designed to be visually and interactively engaging.

The first management model, the "low-rotation content model," is based on the idea of slow journalism (Gambarato, 2016; Le Masurier 2015) and is suitable for the production and consumption of low-turnover contents. However, it requires choosing only arguments with a high level of newsworthiness, which can be described through a transmedia storytelling system. Producing content with a high level of depth, newspapers managed under this model can move away from the breaking news as told by their competitors. To put the low-rotation model in action, content is published with distant pauses: For example, a main update during the early hours of the morning and a second one after lunch. Editors should not be afraid of the low rate of news updates, because this content needs that: In-depth stories, with several reading levels, and strong multimedia material distributed in a different manner across each channel. Certainly, this kind of wrap-up for a news item needs more time to be realized, but it provides great enjoyment to the readers. The news stories should be proposed through teaser activities (like trailers in the movie industry) right up to the time of publication, telling each content item like a news-event. The slow rotation of the new items gives time to the editors to design a complete and in-depth story, with the aim of retaining the public and differentiating themselves from their competitors, pushing the audience to contribute not only to the content creation, but also financially (such as crowdsourcing and crowdfunding practices). According to Gambarato (2016, pp. 448–449), "The audience engagement is a central point for both [TS and Slow Journalism] to involve the audience as collaborators and create a more valuable experience. In order to do so, more time is invested from the side of authors/producers as well as from the public." In addition, it may be possible to apply a business model with different subscription barriers designed for different audiences.

The low-rotation content model performs best if it is supported by the "high-rotation content model," which deals with breaking news designed for social networks and mobile sharing in order to keep the reader active throughout the day. The focus of the team managing this high-rotation model is to control the balance between reliability of the newspaper and the low-quality contents. With regard to this, it may be useful to openly separate the high-rotation model from the low-rotation one to avoid breaking loyalty agreements with the target audiences. The work during the production stage is optimized by moving most of the resources (which in the low-rotation model are focused on the production of in-depth quality contents) toward the search for different kinds of packaging or different interaction models, in order to be as fast as possible during the distribution phase. Accordingly, it is important to be constantly up to date with the ultimate technical and visual solutions, designing the news content to be shared on every social platform (such as Facebook, Twitter, Instagram, YouTube and other social networks) to maximize income with a relatively small effort during production. In terms of skills and knowledge, it will be sufficient to arrange small multidisciplinary teams able to distribute the same breaking news on different platforms in a short time span. Finally, the use of multiple channels allows the implementation of a business model with revenues from unique visitors, and income from publishing agreements with social networks. The revisions of the project workflow (Figure 3) also introduce the need for a person responsible for coordinating the two different production models, ensuring the continuity of the news life cycle.

Each news item is singular according to several factors, including its newsworthiness: The quality of how much of a news item can be told in depth, how easily it can reach different targets, and if it is easily expanded and extended on different devices and channels. When a new story arrives in the newsroom, it must be evaluated to determine the editorial guidelines, organize the work, and understand if it should be managed with the high-rotation model or the low-rotation one. For that reason, this study proposes the introduction of the "Switch," a small team composed of chief editors and communication design-

Figure 3. Difference between the "low-rotation" and "high-rotation" content models

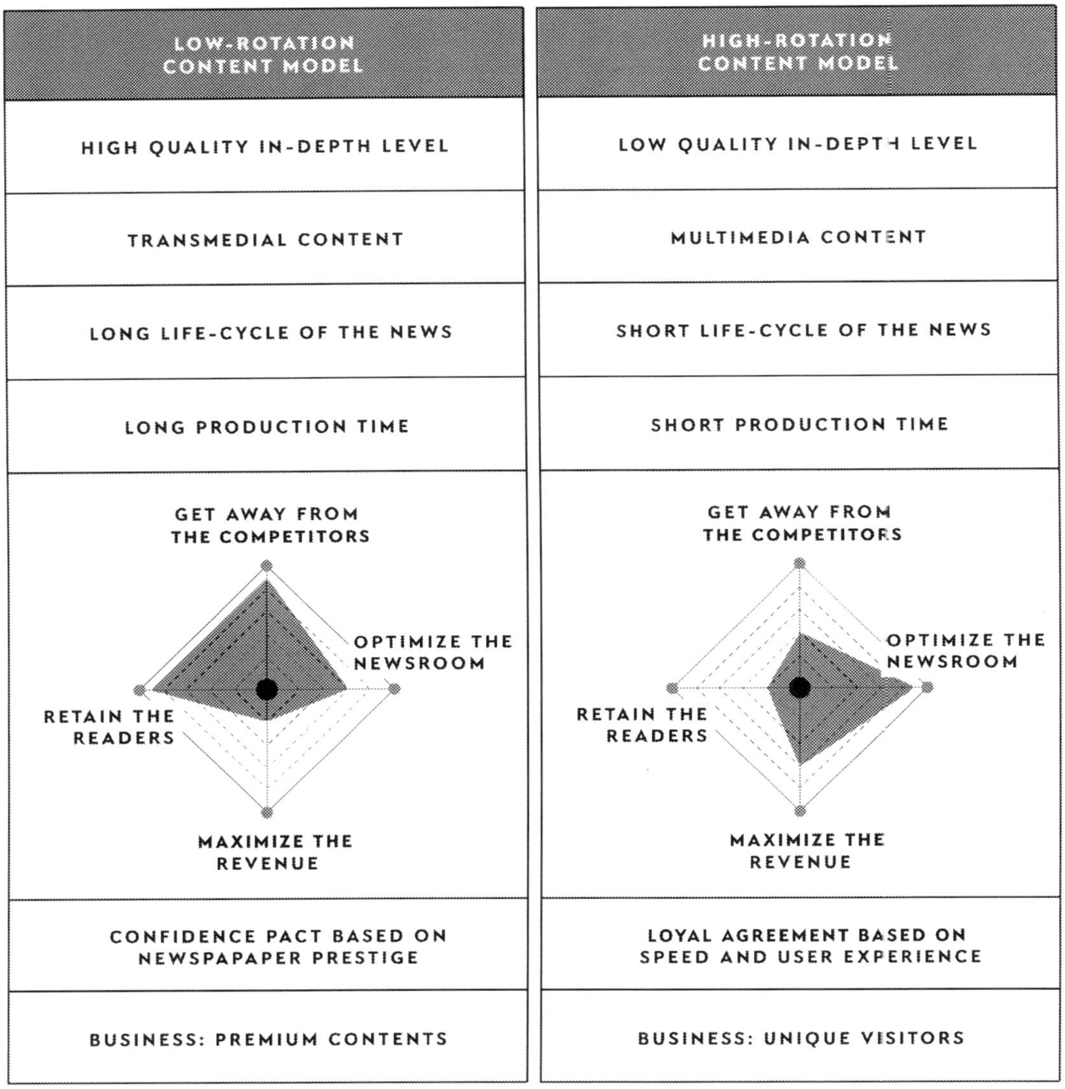

ers, which offers multidisciplinary skills including journalism, communication, and management. The Switch's first task is to lead the three editorial meetings and coordinate the newspaper staff throughout the day. This small team is known Switch as result of its second task: It must decide which management model should be used with each news item as it arrives in the newsroom. For example, breaking news must be produced in a way suitable for multimedia and published without waiting for the next editorial meetings. In contrast, if a news item is managed by the low-rotation model the process is longer and involves professionals with cross-disciplinary skills (visual designers, video-makers, illustrators). In this case, the Switch's task is to provide editorial guidelines, coordinate the timing and resources, and choose the appropriate expertise. As a result, this work also proposes an operational tool, the *Transmedia News Building Model*, with the purpose of supporting the Switch and defining a default process.

The Transmedia News Building Model

With the short timeframes and limited budgets available, the different personalities, backgrounds, skills, and approaches to work of the journalists and technical staff are the perfect ingredients to create chaos during the production stage. For that reason, the authors have developed a tool that aims to support the coordination work of the Switch. This shared management tool is intended to provide a useful guide to the designing, planning, and dissemination of news required when developing transmedia distribution of content (e.g., as suggested with the low-rotation content model). It is predominantly aimed at the Switch team, not only for those editors and collaborators who are experienced in designing multi-channel distribution of content, but also for those who are new to the field.

A working instrument was developed from the *Transmedia Building Model* (Ciancia, 2016) that suggested guidelines, tools, and existing online platforms for the development of a transmedia project within multidisciplinary teams. Specifically, the model comprises four main sections (storyworld, narrative context, functional specification, and production specification) for the activation of an iterative design process, each of which requires specific skills.

The application of this framework to the journalism field led the researchers to propose the *Transmedia News Building Model*: A list of questions related to these four main sections, with the aim of helping the chief editors to define what to tell, how to tell it, how to engage the audience, and how to organize the workflow. Each stage produces a visual artifact, a diagram that allows the understanding of the content in terms of storyline structure, and the specific roles of the people involved during the production phase. Although the *Transmedia News Building Model* is currently a simple paper sheet (Figure 4), the idea is that in the future it could become a project management software package: A comprehensive guide for editors and their collaborators involved in the creation of transmedia news.

FUTURE RESEARCH DIRECTIONS

Based on the need to understand how esthetic, technological, and economic issues work together in the news business, a conceptual and operational tool was developed according to expert reflections on the use of multi-channel strategies, revision of the process schedule and a new project workflow that combines two elements: Two news management models and an operational tool, the *Transmedia News Building Model*.

Thus far this research has focused on the design aspect. The next step in this work will be the application of the proposed models and tool, and the consequent assessment of readers' engagement. In terms of application, it may be interesting to apply the editorial models described to a zero-based design of an Italian newspaper; however, using this design approach in the redesign of a process beginning "[...] from scratch, without preconceptions or existing models to guide you, beginning with your goal in mind" (Polak & Warwick, 2013, pp. 400–401). For instance, the application of the proposed models and tool to a newspaper that wants to make small changes in order to survive is possible, but this could be more difficult and lead to poor quality results.

As stated previously, zero-based design involves the ability to create a new publishing model from scratch and it is a common situation for brand-new publishers, but that might also happen in traditional newspapers, such as the newsrooms in which is it possible to recognize "astral alignment," as MM stated

Figure 4. The Transmedia News Building Model

TRANSMEDIA NEWS BUILDING MODEL		
WORKFLOW STAGES		**STAGE DESCRIPTION**
WHAT I HAVE TO TELL?	WHAT IS THE MAIN THEME?	*I HAVE TO WRITE THE PLOT, THE NEWS BACKGROUND AND THE SKILL OF THE CHARACTERS.* *I HAVE TO FIND ALL THE STORY-LINES AND ORDER THEM BY PRIORITY.*
	WHO IS THE MAIN CHARACTER? AND THE OTHERS?	
	WHAT IS THE MAIN STORY-LINE?	
	ARE THERE SECONDARY STORY-LINES?	
TOOL:	PLOT POINT CHART	*A CHART TO VISUALIZE ALL THE STORY-LINES AND THE PLOT POINTS.*
HOW CAN I EXPLAIN THIS?	WHAT ARE THE CHANNELS?	*I HAVE TO UNDERSTAND THE BEST CHANNELS AND THE RIGHT DEVICES.*
	WHAT'S THE MAIN FUNCTION ABOUT EACH CHANNEL?	
	WHAT KIND OF CONTENT?	
	WHAT DEVICES ARE USED?	
HOW CAN I ENGAGE THE AUDIENCE?	WHAT IS THE RABBIT HOLE?	*I'VE TO THINK ABOUT THE WAY TO INTERACT AND TO ENGAGE THE AUDIENCE.*
	WHAT ARE THE POINTS OF ENTRY?	
	WHAT IS THE ENGAGEMENT STRATEGY?	
	HOW TO MANAGE THE AUDIENCE CONTENTS?	
TOOL:	PLATFORM ACTION CHART	*A CHART TO VISUALIZE ALL THE STORY-LINES, HOW THEY ARE PUBLISHED ON DIFFERENT CHANNELS AND WHAT ARE THE INTERACTION POINTS WITH THE AUDIENCE.*
HOW CAN I ORGANIZE THE WORKFLOW?	WHAT CONTENTS TO PRODUCE?	*I'VE TO FIND THE BEST SKILLS INSIDE (OR OUTSIDE) THE NEWSROOM.*
	WHAT CONTENTS ARE READY TO PUBLISH?	
	WHAT ABOUT THE VISUAL GUIDELINES?	
	WHAT KIND OF COMPETENCE I NEED?	
	WHAT IS THE DEADLINE?	
TOOL:	TRANSMEDIA ROLL OUT + TIME TABLE SCHEDULE	*A TIMELINE THAT SHOW HOW DIFFERENT CONTENTS ARE PUBLISHED ON DIFFERENT CHANNELS AND A TIME SCHEDULE WITH THE PRODUCTION DEADLINES.*

(personal communication, 2015). These are publishers where the business owner, the editorial director, the chief editors, and most of the journalists are moving in the same direction.

Starting from scratch, the two proposed models (the low-rotation and the high-rotation content models) should be designed at the same time. The former should not take priority over the latter, but at the same time, the second cannot exist without the first. Moreover, further steps in reflecting on contemporary journalism in Italy should relate to understanding the particularities of the Italian context and the analysis of the latest technological and social trends.

As researchers in the media field, it is necessary to take into account that in Italy the news field is mainly in the hands of non-specialist publishers. This means identifying the correct model to apply, according to the identity of the publisher and the newspaper, in order to retain the uniqueness of the message and to add value. In this sense, the chosen editorial and business model should be able to create a reference audience and a trusting relationship between readers and journalists, to face their fears of fake news, as stated by Nic Newman (2016, p. 2): "[K]ey developments will center on fears about how changing technology is affecting the quality of information and the state of our democracy."

Finally, publishers must study technological and social trends to keep pace with developments in the mediascape. For instance, it is only since 2016 that those inside the news industry in Italy have talked about new smartphone notification systems, new editorial and economic contracts with social networks, new ways to communicate with "dialog devices" (e.g., chat-bots) or through vocals system (e.g., Amazon Echo and Google Home), and new ways to use virtual and augmented reality systems for content consumption. Currently, it is uncertain which of these technological systems will be the most important for the news industry in future years. This is why it is very important to create a second "extremely fluid" and "light" editorial model, always up to date with technological changes and able to exploit their features to reach the highest number of people, while simultaneously maximizing revenue.

FINAL REMARKS

As stated at the beginning of the chapter, this work proposes an exploration of journalism through a transmedia approach, developing a conceptual and operational tool for the Italian news business. A further step in this research will be the application of the proposed framework within an Italian newsroom.

The first section of this chapter—*Authors, Audiences and Media Texts: A Continuous Balance of Power*—is devoted to describing how the development of the media scenario has been shaped by a networked society in which the relationships between authors and readers have completely changed. As a result, media scholars have been witnessing how multi-channel strategies are changing journalism practice and the role played by readers, leading to the spread of participatory forms that merge the concepts of multimodality, open publishing, multi-channel distribution, and circulation of the news. A transmedia mind-set emerges within the news media business, requiring journalist to be audience-centric, story-driven and tool-neutral (Kolodzy, 2012), in conveying stories across platforms (Gambarato & Tárcia, 2017).

Reflections on the "media ecology" of the information field and the emerging forms of news are tackled in the second part of this chapter—*Design Practice in Transmedia Journalism* and *A Transmedia Approach to Italian Newsrooms*. These sections propose guidelines for the application of a transmedia approach according to the design lens, considering transmedia as a practice that operates as problem-solver and sense-maker. The design perspective was applied because "[d]esign research creates a place to braid theory and practice to make the work stronger" (Lunenfeld 2003, p. 10). Therefore, a design-oriented approach can support research in fields characterized by the intersection of theory and practice, such as journalism.

This led the researchers to reply to the last question: Is *transmedia design* an approach able to support networks and broadcast opportunities? Considering the results presented, it can be concluded that transmedia systems, in which the creation of storyworlds leads to the enactment of social values, are able to sustain innovation, collaboration, and participation of the reader (now viewer/user/player, according to Dinehart, 2010). However, this opens up a whole set of reflections on the ethical aspects of *reporting* versus *telling a story*.

The use of stories and storytelling practice has been spreading in many areas over the last decade, not only related to the entertainment field, but also in "real life," such as in marketing, advertising, and political communication. The result has been the abuse and exploitation of these words, leading to conceptual confusion and fear of the storytelling practice itself. According to Christian Salmon (2010), the art of telling stories has been manipulated by politicians and marketers, becoming a scientific tool of persuasion and propaganda: A sort of shift from *telling stories* to *telling tales*. Therefore, talking about storytelling within the journalism field, an area whose main moral obligation is the faithful reconstruction of reality and facts, seems ambiguous. Over the years, two positions have emerged from the ongoing debate: On the one hand, those practitioners who promote the idea of journalism as narration; and on the other hand, reporters who do not share the tendency of Italian journalism to create stories.

Davide Pinardi (2011), writer, author, and lecturer, talked about the relationship between storytelling and journalism, saying that journalism is narration. Often, the problem is a misunderstanding. He criticizes the widespread misconception that makes a division between a journalism of facts and a journalism of opinions. He underlined that journalism IS narration. Making documentaries or taking pictures IS narration. This implies that the focus is different: Real-life stories should be honest, and should not invent anything. People live in a society in which images are powerful: Images can be shown and edited in many different ways, bringing the narratee, the one who receives the narration, to read different realities (Cracco, Galli, & Pinardi, 2011, pp. 26–27).

Luca Sofri, director of the digital publisher ilPost.it, went further in the ongoing debate regarding the use of storytelling within journalism. In a blog post released in August 2015 (Sofri, 2015), he shed lights on the ambiguous expression "tell a story," describing how there are different shades of gray between the act of telling and the act of building a story. According to him, the problem within Italian journalism is the disequilibrium that leads reporters too close to the "dark gray" area. The evidence suggests that two ways coexist: The *telling tales* way, to indicate who is lying or novelizing a news item, and the *storytelling* path.

AB, professional storyteller and author for *Nòva—Il Sole 24 Ore*, *Corriere Innovazione*, and *CheFuturo!*, declared that in his opinion storytelling is a technique, and not something that can shape good or bad news, or a true or false presentation of facts. He believes that in the journalistic field, storytelling allows both the author and the reader to reach aspects of the news that people cannot enjoy via traditional modes of consumption. Thus authors, and hence journalists, should never lose sight of the criteria and norms that outline their position toward an ethical discourse (Bettini, personal communication, January 20, 2016).

To conclude, storytelling has always been a powerful tool, not only in building relationships and mutual understanding, but also in manipulating a crowd in the search for consensus (Salmon, 2010). Since the transformative power of stories in shaping and sharing the imagination of many can be so powerful, journalists should not lose sight of the ethical aspects of narration in everyday practice. Indeed, in the development and distribution of news there can be no confusion between reality and fiction. Readers, now audiences, must always be informed about the nature of what they are enjoying, in order to respect them, thereby maintaining their loyalty.

REFERENCES

Alzamora, G., & Tárcia, L. (2012). Convergence and transmedia: Semantic galaxies and emerging narratives in journalism. *Brazilian Journalism Research*, *8*(1), 22–34.

Appadurai, A. (1990). Disjuncture and difference in the global cultural economy. *Theory, Culture & Society*, *7*(2), 295–310. doi:10.1177/026327690007002017

Bauman, Z. (2000). *Liquid modernity*. Cambridge, MA: Polity Press.

Bolter, D., & Grusin, R. (1999). *Remediation: Understanding new media*. Cambridge, MA: The MIT Press.

Bowman, S., & Willis, C. (2003). *We media: How audiences are shaping the future of news and information*. Reston, VA: The Media Center at the American Press Institute.

Calabresi, M. (2016). Il piano editoriale di Mario Calabresi: Un giornale trasparente, racconteremo l'Italia che si impegna [The editorial plan of Mario Calabresi: A transparent newspaper, we will tell the commitments undertaken by Italy]. *Repubblica TV*. Retrieved from http://video.repubblica.it/cronaca/il-piano-editoriale-di-mario-calabresi--un-giornale-trasparente-racconteremo-l-italia-che-si-impegna/225390/224653

Carpentier, N., & Dahlgren, P. (2013). The social relevance of participatory theory. *Comunicazioni Sociali*, *3*, 301–315.

Ciancia, M. (2016). *Transmedia Design Framework. Un approccio design-oriented alla transmedia practice* [Transmedia Design Framework. Design-oriented approach to transmedia practice]. Milan, Italy: FrancoAngeli.

Cizek, K. (Director). (2010). Out My Window [Web documentary]. Canada: National Film Board of Canada.

Cracco, G., Galli, G., & Pinardi, D. (2011). Narrare: Tra controinformazione, storia e rappresentazioni di realtà [Telling stories: Between counterinformation, history and representations of reality]. *Paginauno*, *22*, 26–27.

de Certeau, M. (1980). L'Invention du quotidien. Vol. 1, arts de faire [The practice of everyday life]. Paris, France: Union générale d'éditions.

de Certeau, M. (1984). *The practice of everyday life*. Berkeley, CA: University of California Press.

Delwiche, A. A., & Henderson, J. J. (2013). *The participatory cultures handbook*. London: Routledge.

Dena, C. (2009). *Transmedia Practice: Theorizing the practice of expressing a fictional world across distinct media and environments* (Doctoral dissertation). Retrieved from http://ciret-transdisciplinarity.org/biblio/biblio_pdf/Christy_DeanTransm.pdf

Dinehart, S. (2008). Transmedial play: Cognitive and cross-platform narrative. *The Narrative Design Explorer*. Retrieved from http://narrativedesign.org/2008/05/transmedial-play-cognitive-and-cross-platform-narrative/

Dinehart, S. (2010). DAREtoENGAGE. *TEDx Transmedia Talk*. Retrieved from https://www.youtube.com/watch?v=gz9fZJatIQw

Ford, S. (2007, April 5). Transmedia Journalism: A story-based approach to convergence. *MIT Convergence Culture Consortium*. Retrieved from http://www.convergenceculture.org/weblog/2007/04/transmedia_journalism_a_storyb.php

Gambarato, R. R. (2016). The Sochi Project: Slow journalism within transmedia space. *Digital Journalism*, *4*(4), 445–461. doi:10.1080/21670811.2015.1096746

Gambarato, R. R., & Tárcia, L. P. T. (2017). Transmedia strategies in journalism. An analytical model for the news coverage of planned events. *Journalism Studies*, *18*(11), 1381–1399. doi:10.1080/1461670X.2015.1127769

Gomez, J. (2010). Pergunta: Esse modelo de narrativa transmídia storytelling pode ser aplicado ao jornalismo? Você conhece algum caso? [Issue: Can transmedia storytelling be applied to journalism? Do you know of any cases?]. *Tá Rolando*. Retrieved from http://redeglobo.globo.com/platb/tarolando/category/workshop-transmedia-storytelling-jeff-gomez/

Heinrich, A. (2011). *Network Journalism: Journalistic practice in interactive spheres*. New York, NY: Routledge.

Jenkins, H. (1992). *Textual Poachers: Television fans and participatory culture*. New York: Routledge.

Jenkins, H. (2003). Transmedia Storytelling. *MIT Technology Review*. Retrieved from https://www.technologyreview.com/s/401760/transmedia-storytelling/

Jenkins, H. (2006). *Convergence Culture: Where old and new media collide*. New York: New York University Press.

Jenkins, H. (2009a, December 12). The revenge of the origami unicorn: Seven principles of transmedia storytelling (Well, two actually. Five more on Friday). *Confession of an Aca-Fan*. Retrieved from http://henryjenkins.org/blog/2009/12/the_revenge_of_the_origami_uni.html

Jenkins, H. (2009b December 12). The revenge of the origami unicorn: The remaining four principles of transmedia storytelling. *Confession of an Aca-Fan*. Retrieved from http://henryjenkins.org/blog/2009/12/revenge_of_the_origami_unicorn.html

Jenkins, H., Ford, S., & Green, J. (2013). *Spreadable Media: Creating value and meaning in a networked culture*. New York: New York University Press.

Kinder, M. (1991). *Playing with power in movies, television, and video games: From Muppet Babies to Teenage Mutant Ninja Turtles*. Berkeley, CA: University of California Press.

Kolodzy, J. (2012). *Convergence Journalism: Writing and reporting across the news media*. London: Routledge.

Kress, G., & van Leeuwen, T. (2001). *Multimodal discourse: the modes and media of contemporary communication*. London: Hodder Education.

Le Masurier, M. (2013). What is Slow Journalism? *Journalism Practice*, *9*(2), 138–152. doi:10.1080/17512786.2014.916471

Lessig, L. (2008). *Remix: Making art and commerce thrive in the hybrid economy*. New York, NY: Bloomsbury. doi:10.5040/9781849662505

Lévy, P. (1997). *Collective Intelligence: Mankind's emerging world in cyberspace*. Cambridge, MA: Perseus Books.

Long, G. (2007). *Transmedia Storytelling: Business, aesthetics and production at the Jim Henson Company* (Master of Science Degree thesis). Retrieved from http://cmsw.mit.edu/transmedia-storytelling-jim-henson-company/

Lunenfeld, P. (2003). The Design Cluster. In B. Laurel (Ed.), *Design Research. Methods and Perspectives* (pp. 10–15). Cambridge, MA: MIT Press.

Manzini, E. (2015). *Design, when everybody designs. An introduction to design for social innovation*. Cambridge, MA: The MIT Press.

Marshall, L. (Producer), & Macdonald, K. (Director). (2011). *Life in a Day* [Motion picture]. United Kingdom, United States: National Geographic Films.

Mattei, M. (2016). *Transmedia News. Un approccio alternativo per affrontare la svolta digitale del giornalismo* (Master of Science Degree thesis). Retrieved from POLITesi. (https://www.politesi.polimi.it/bitstream/10589/122020/3/Tesi.pdf)

Miller, V. (2011). *Understanding digital culture*. London: Sage.

Moloney, K. (2011). *Porting transmedia storytelling to journalism (Master of Arts Degree thesis)*. Denver, CO: University of Colorado. Retrieved from http://www.colorado.edu/journalism/photojournalism/Transmedia_Journalism.pdf

Moloney, K. (2012). *Transmedia Journalism as a post-digital narrative*. Denver, CO: University of Colorado Press.

Newman, N. (2015). *Journalism, media and technology predictions 2016*. Oxford, UK: University of Oxford, Reuters Institute.

Newman, N. (2016). *Journalism, media and technology predictions 2017*. Oxford, UK: University of Oxford, Reuters Institute.

Polak, P., & Warwick, M. (2013). *The business solution to poverty. Designing products and services for three billion new customers*. San Francisco, CA: Berrett-Koehler Publishers.

Pratten, R. (2015). *Getting started with Transmedia Storytelling: A practical guide for beginners* (2nd ed.). CreateSpace Independent Publishing Platform.

Renó, D. (2014). Transmedia Journalism and the new media ecology: Possible languages. In D. Renó, C. Campalans, S. Ruiz, & V. Gosciola (Eds.), *Periodismo Transmedia: Miradas Múltiples* [Transmedia journalism: Multiple perspectives] (pp. 3–19). Barcelona, Spain: Editorial UOC.

Reuters Institute. (2015). *Digital News Report 2015*. Retrieved from https://reutersinstitute.politics.ox.ac.uk/sites/default/files/Reuters%20Institute%20Digital%20News%20Report%202015_Full%20Report.pdf

Rodríguez, C. (2001). *Fissures in the mediascape: An international study of citizens' media*. New York, NY: Hampton Press.

Rose, M. (2011, November 30). *Four categories of collaborative documentary.* Retrieved from https://collabdocs.wordpress.com/2011/11/30/four-categories-of-collaborative-documentary/

Salmon, C. (2010). *Storytelling: Bewitching the modern mind*. New York, NY: Verso Books.

Salvatores, G. (Director). (2014). *Italy in a Day* [Motion picture]. Italy, United Kingdom: Indiana Production Company, Rai Cinema, Scott Free Production.

San Cornelio, G., & Roig Telo, A. (2015). Being Lucky. Transmedia and co-creation practices in music video-clips. *International Journal of Transmedia Literacy*, *1*(1), 131–145.

Scolari, C. A. (2009). Transmedia Storytelling: Implicit consumers, narrative worlds, and branding in contemporary media production. *International Journal of Communication*, *3*, 586–606. Retrieved from http://ijoc.org/index.php/ijoc/article/view/477

Scott, S. (2013). Textual poachers, twenty years later: A conversation between Henry Jenkins and Suzanne Scott. In H. Jenkins (Ed.), *Textual Poachers: Television fans and participatory culture* (pp. vii–I). New York, NY: Routledge.

Scruton, R. (1996). The eclipse of listening. *The New Criterion*, *15*(3), 5–13.

Sofri, L. (2015, August 20). *Il Fottuto Storytelling* [The fucking storytelling] [Blog Post]. Retrieved from http://www.wittgenstein.it/2015/08/20/storytelling-giornalismo

The New York Times. (2014, March 24). *The full New York Times innovation report.* Retrieved from http://mashable.com/2014/05/16/full-new-york-times-innovation-report/#SAhU_lDTkPqo

Wolf, M. J. P. (2012). *Building imaginary worlds. The theory and history of subcreation*. New York, NY: Routledge.

KEY TERMS AND DEFINITIONS

High-Rotation Content Model: News publishing model that aims to publish breaking news as soon as possible, taking full advantage of the technological and social tools currently available.

Low-Rotation Content Model: News publishing model that allows the creation of high-quality content conveyed across multiple channels with many depth levels.

Switch: A team that manages the daily workflow in the newsroom. Composed of chief editors and communication designers, it comes into action when a news item arrives in newsroom. The Switch must define the editorial guidelines and decide which of the two publishing models is the best to manage that item.

Transmedia Design: A field of research, at the intersection between *media studies* and *design cultures*, that allows researchers and practitioners to analyze, develop, and manage multi-channel narrative-based communication systems.

Transmedia News Building Models: An operational tool to support newsroom coordination. This shared management tool is intended to provide a useful guide to the design, planning, and dissemination of news required when developing transmedia distribution of content.

Transmedia Storytelling: A practice concerned with the building of a story universe through different channels to enhance the role of the audience.

Zero-Based Design: A design approach mainly used in redesigning process, workflows, and business plans. The primary approach is to begin from scratch, with the goal in mind, without preconceptions or existing models.

Chapter 8
2016 Rio Summer Olympics and the Transmedia Journalism of Planned Events

Renira Rampazzo Gambarato
National Research University Higher School of Economics, Russia

Geane C. Alzamora
Federal University of Minas Gerais, Brazil

Lorena Peret Teixeira Tárcia
University Center of Belo Horizonte, Brazil

ABSTRACT

The news coverage of the 2016 Rio Summer Olympics in Brazil encompassed multiple media platforms and the flow of information in the intersection between mass media (especially television) and social media (especially Snapchat and Instagram). The 2016 Rio Olympics was the Games of Snapchat stories and filters along with Instagram stories for news coverage. This chapter aims to investigate how transmedia features are structured and implemented in the news coverage of the 2016 Olympics by the official Brazilian broadcaster, Globo Network. The theoretical framework focuses on transmedia journalism of planned events, and the methodology is based on the analytical model for transmedia news coverage of planned events developed by Gambarato and Tárcia (2017). The research findings indicate that the coverage presented systematic content expanded throughout various media platforms (a core characteristic of transmedia journalism) but involved limited mechanisms of audience engagement, particularly in terms of citizen participation.

INTRODUCTION

This chapter aims to investigate how transmedia features are structured and implemented in the news coverage of the 2016 Rio Summer Olympics by the official Brazilian broadcaster, Globo Network. Globo Network (Rede Globo, in Portuguese), the largest Brazilian network, bought the broadcasting rights for the Olympic Games until 2032. The broadcaster has the non-exclusive right to transmit the Games on

DOI: 10.4018/978-1-5225-3781-6.ch008

television and has the exclusive rights for cable television, the Internet, and mobile phones (UOL, 2015). The International Olympic Committee (IOC) owns the global broadcast rights to the Olympics, including broadcasts on television, radio, mobile, and Internet platforms. The Brazilian broadcaster, which invested in important technological advancements (such as holographic projections and online live-streaming) for the transmedia coverage of the 2014 Fédération Internationale de Football Association (FIFA) World Cup, expanded its investment for the largest and most comprehensive sports coverage in the network's history (Rede Globo, 2016c). During the Rio Games, Globo Network (in partnership with the Japanese broadcasting organization NHK) broadcasted live in the ultra-high-definition 8K format, using dense wavelength division multiplexing (DWDM) technology (Lobo, 2016). Other innovations, as a strategic move to gain market share and boost Globo Network businesses domestically and internationally, included sports commentators' use of augmented reality and, especially, images in high-definition on the network's Internet streaming service, Globo Play.

It's not just Brazilian athletes who are under pressure to perform well at the first Olympic Games to be hosted by their country. Brazil's Grupo Globo, Latin America's biggest television network, will also be gunning for gold in Rio de Janeiro as its rolls out a battery of state-of-the-art TV technology. Relaying images of key Olympic moments in 8K and using virtual reality to spice up commentaries are among the novelties Globo plans to roll out. But more than just a special feature for the Games, the cutting-edge visuals are crucial components in Globo's longer-term strategy to retain and grow audiences and advertisers as the fight for them gets ever fiercer. (Hopewell, 2016, para. 2)

As a means of building this transmedia journalism case study, the theoretical framework of the chapter focuses on transmedia journalism (Moloney, 2011; Renó, 2014; Renó & Flores, 2012) of planned events (Dayan & Katz, 1992; Gambarato, Alzamora, & Tárcia, 2016; Gambarato & Tárcia, 2017; Getz, 2012; Hepp & Couldry, 2010). The methodology used in this research is based on the analytical model for transmedia news coverage of planned events developed by Gambarato and Tárcia (2017). The research findings indicate that the coverage presented systematic content expanded throughout various media platforms (a core characteristic of transmedia journalism) but involved limited mechanisms of audience engagement, particularly in terms of citizen participation. Interaction prevailed to the detriment of audience participation.

TRANSMEDIA JOURNALISM OF PLANNED EVENTS

Henry Jenkins' (2006) conceptualization of transmedia storytelling draws on Marsha Kinder's (1991) studies of "commercial supersystems of transmedia intertextuality" (p. 3), referring to robust franchises distributed across multiple media platforms. Transmedia storytelling involves the unfolding of storyworlds throughout diverse media outlets and embraces audience engagement as a core element of transmedia experiences. Although Kinder and Jenkins primarily considered the entertainment realm and Freeman (2016b) identifies the origins of transmedia phenomena with advertisement strategies, the transmedia storytelling principle has expanded to nonfictional spheres, such as activism, branding, politics, education, and journalism, among others. Kerrigan and Velikovsky (2016) argue that transmedia forms applied to nonfiction follow the same features and definitions of fiction transmedia, and the authors acknowledge that this phenomenon continues to increase. Thus, transmedia journalism presents dynamics similar to those of transmedia entertainment, expanding news narratives through distribution over platforms that include citizen participation. Audiences can be involved in adding, editing, and sharing news via digital media. Gambarato and Tárcia (2017) conclude:

In sum, we consider that transmedia journalism, as well as other applications of TS [transmedia storytelling] in fictional and nonfictional realms, is characterized by the involvement of (1) multiple media platforms, (2) content expansion, and (3) audience engagement. Transmedia journalism can take advantage of different media platforms such as television, radio, print media, and, above all, the internet and mobile media to tell deeper stories. Content expansion, as opposed to the repetition of the same message across multiple platforms, is the essence of TS [transmedia storytelling] and, therefore, should be the focal point of transmedia journalism as well. The enrichment of the narrative is facilitated by the extended content. Audience engagement involves mechanisms of interactivity, such as the selection of the elements to be explored, the option to read a text, watch a video, enlarge photographs, access maps, click on hyperlinks, and share information through social networks. Audience engagement deals with participation via, for instance, remixing content and creating original user-generated content. (p. 1386)

Another relevant characteristic of transmedia storytelling that has direct implications in transmedia journalism is the *ad hoc*/contingent and the planned/strategic aspects of transmedia creations. Fast and Örnebring (2015) discuss the *ad hoc*/emergent nature of transmedia storytelling, referring to the fact that transmedia worlds can evolve over time and be co-created by professionals and amateurs alike, and the planned/strategic essence of transmedia productions, considering the media companies careful structuring and portioning of narratives across multiple media platforms. Among these features, transmedia journalism combines the "carefully orchestrated company strategies" (Fast & Örnebring, 2015, p. 2) and the commodification of media texts (Bolin, 2007; Freeman, 2016b) with the *ad hoc* nature of audience engagement within transmedia experiences. Gambarato and Tárcia (2017) emphasize the planned aspect involved in the optimization of transmedia journalism because it becomes a proactive planned process with journalists assuming responsibility for structuring a storyworld in which the audience can be engaged. Although transmedia-breaking news journalism is possible, Moloney (2011) argues that "daily journalism, with its time-constrained brevity, is not a viable option. Transmedia must be designed carefully and developed with a lengthy lead time to be effective" (p. 12). In addition, Renó (2014) reinforces the need to design and plan not only the content to be produced but also how the audience will experience it. Per Renó (2014),

the construction of content must be developed from a transmedia script, which is programmed so that all the linked fragments relate cognitively to each other and, at the same time, does not assume the role of cross-media content, in other words, the same content in distinct platforms. (p. 11)

Planned events are temporal occurrences well schematized and publicized in advance. They are noteworthy occurrences within a special set of circumstances at a given place and time, with a detailed program and schedule known in advance (Getz, 2012). Getz (2012) proposes an experiential typology of planned events, embracing mega-events, media events, participant events, and so forth, which are organized consistent with their functions and meanings: (1) cultural celebrations (festivals, carnivals, heritage commemorations, religious rites, etc.), (2) business and trade (meetings, conventions, fairs, exhibitions, etc.), (3) arts and entertainment (concerts, shows, installations, award ceremonies), (4) political and state (summits, political congresses, military events, etc.), (5) private functions (rites of passage, weddings, funerals, etc.), and (6) sport and recreation (championships, tours, fun events, etc.). The term media event was introduced and gained visibility with Dayan and Katz's (1992) mass communication studies focused on live, real-time broadcasting of extraordinary, pre-planned public events. Hepp and Couldry (2010) extend the conceptualization of media events, discussing the globalization and multifaceted power structure of communication processes reinforced by the role of the Internet and multiplatform production in media cultures in the Digital Age. Likewise, recent publications about media events (Fox, 2016; Mitu & Poulakidakos, 2016) draw on Dayan and Katz's (1992) concepts and challenge the live broadcasting and printed media assumptions typical of mass communication, incorporating the social media reality into the debate. Thus, transmedia news coverage of planned events is comprehensive and encompasses much more than the sports sphere. The relevance of transmedia journalism of planned events relies on the fact that these events usually entail (1) *ad hoc*/emergent aspects, attracting large domestic and international audiences, potentially engaging and integrating them in the news-making process, and (2) planned/strategic aspects, involving a significant amount of human, technical, and financial resources, and providing numerous protagonists and primary and parallel stories (Gambarato & Tárcia, 2017).

As discussed by Gambarato et al. (2016), multiplatform news coverage of global planned events with citizens involved in producing and distributing content is a practice that gained traction especially during the 2012 London Summer Olympics. Due to the British Broadcasting Corporation (BBC) coverage of the 2012 Olympic Games, London Olympics is considered the "first truly digital Olympics" (O'Riordan, 2012, para. 3). The Olympic Games held in London in 2012 (with multiscreen production) and in Sochi in 2014 (with the addition of discreet hints of transmedia features in the coverage) confirmed the emergence of a distinct scenario in journalism, a hybrid of the mass media logic of transmission and the social media logic of sharing, a hybrid blurring of distinctions between professionals and amateurs, producers and users. This blend of production and consumption of information/content, or *produsage* (Bruns, 2008), and its subsequent engagement of audiences, creating communities around the storyworlds and user-generated content (UGC), is a core principle of transmedia experiences (Jenkins, 2006), in the fiction and nonfiction realms. UGC concerns media content freely created, circulated, and consumed by the public, including, for instance, "blogs, wikis, discussion forums, posts, chats, tweets, podcasts, and pins, delivered in text, image, video, or audio modes" (Smith, Stavro, & Westberg, 2017, p. 59). The ethics related to this type of unpaid user labor (Gambarato & Nanì, 2016) is a subject extensively explored by critical media studies scholars (Andrejevic, 2009; Fuchs, 2010, 2012; Hesmondhalgh, 2010; Terranova, 2000), who consider the dark and bright sides. On one hand, there is the discourse that the co-creation model encourages free-labor exploitation by generating surplus value that is extracted by media industries (Fuchs, 2010, 2012; Stanfill & Condis, 2014; Terranova, 2000). On the other, there is empirical evidence that this model produces enjoyment and collectivity, and users do not perceive co-creation as exploitation (Allan & Thorsen, 2009; Banks & Deuze, 2009; De Kosnik, 2012). The tension between the exciting opportunity for audiences to co-create and participate in fictional and nonfictional transmedia experiences and the commodification of users' creativity in favor of the commercial interests of media industries is part of the complex communication process behind transmedia storytelling (Gambarato & Nanì, 2016; Sokolova, 2012). The celebratory and critical approaches to UGC are not mutually exclusive (Gambarato & Nanì, 2016), and believing that audiences are exploited in the context of participatory culture ignores the joy of generating content and sharing experiences and most importantly, contradicts the capacity audiences have to simply stop doing what they do (Baym & Burnett, 2009).

Lewis (2012) suggests that "the struggle between the professional logic of control, embedded in journalism's ideology, and the participatory logic of free engagement, embedded in the substance and culture of digital media" (p. 850) is paving the way for the emergence of "a hybrid logic of adaptability and openness: a willingness to see audiences on a more peer level, to appreciate their contributions, and to find normative purpose in transparency and participation, *à la* open-source technology culture" (p. 851). Notwithstanding, in the case of the Olympics, the IOC imposes a strict set of rules and regulations on athletes, coaches, officials, and media organizations, among others, that can deliberately interfere in such a hybrid process (see International Olympic Committee, 2015, 2016). According to the Olympic historian David Wallechinsky (Barkho, 2016), over the years, the IOC has wanted to control the way the Olympics are perceived and therefore, has closely guarded content based on dated, conservative rules. The relevant role social media networks play today in the *produsage* of the Games is fairly new. "For instance, at the 2004 Athens Summer Games, Twitter (2006) did not exist, and at the 2008 Beijing Games, Instagram (2010) had not been released" (Gambarato & Tárcia, 2017, p. 1387). Although the hashtag #Rio2016 was an official Olympics trademark distributed across various social media platforms (such as Twitter, Instagram, and Facebook), only in 2008 was the first Olympics hashtag (#beijing2008) created by Twitter users, not the IOC (Barkho, 2016). The hashtag #Rio2016 was the most tweeted hashtag of 2016, followed by #Election2016, second, and #PokemonGo, third (Kottasova, 2016). The 2010 Winter Olympic Games in Vancouver, Canada, "solidified Facebook's role as the home of live updates for the official Olympics accounts" (Barkho, 2016, para. 6), and the 2012 London Olympics consolidated Instagram as the premier photo-sharing media platform online (Barkho, 2016). The 2016 Rio Olympics was the Games of Snapchat stories and filters along with Instagram stories for news coverage worldwide, including Brazil, the host of the Games (Barkho, 2016; Rede Globo, 2016a; Zirondi, 2016). "Snapchat, a direct messaging platform not designed to be a news source is trying to adjust its services to enable it to provide news services in an attractive form, such as live videos, to its audiences" (Bialy & Svetoka, 2016, pp. 28–30). Moreover, Snapchat is an emergent social media network with a strong appeal for younger audiences. First released in 2011, the platform gained more traction in 2015 with the "Live Stories" feature, which allows users to compile photos and videos into storylines. This feature became the platform's signature product. Globo Network established a partnership with Snapchat, and the public could follow live behind the scenes of the Olympics from various angles. In addition, the application included special content produced by Globo Network for the Olympics in the section devoted to publication in real time (Zirondi, 2016).

Live Stories draw 10 million to 20 million pairs of Millennial eyeballs every day. (…) The platform is compelling precisely because it is interactive, it is temporary, and it is a glimpse into another life—just like television was for previous generations. (Dodson, 2015, para. 5)

Social media as a source of news is a trend confirmed by recent studies conducted by renowned institutions, such as the North Atlantic Treaty Organization (NATO) Strategic Communications Center of Excellence (Bialy & Svetoka, 2016), the Pew Research Center (Gottfried & Shearer, 2016), and Reuters Institute for the Study of Journalism (Newman, Fletcher, Levy, & Nielsen, 2016). In addition to the current labels of being a tool for entertainment and engaging with others, social media has become a platform for gathering information, and the latest updates on domestic and international events (Bialy & Svetoka, 2016; Gottfried & Shearer, 2016; Newman et al., 2016). The 2016 study by the Pew Research Center claims that 62% of American adults get their news on social media (Gottfried & Shearer, 2016, p. 2). In agreement with these research findings, in January 2017 Facebook announced The Facebook

Journalism Project, whose focus is three dimensions: (1) collaborative development of new products (new storytelling formats, local news, emerging business models, and hackathons), (2) training and tools for journalists (e-learning courses, CrowdTangle, and help with eyewitness media), and (3) training and tools for everyone (promoting news literary and continuing efforts to curb news hoaxes; Simo, 2017). Fidji Simo, Facebook's director of product, states,

we're announcing a new program to establish stronger ties between Facebook and the news industry. We will be collaborating with news organizations to develop products, learning from journalists about ways we can be a better partner, and working with publishers and educators on how we can equip people with the knowledge they need to be informed readers in the digital age. (2017, para. 2)

The news coverage of the 2016 Rio Olympic Games reflects these communication trends, as depicted by the following transmedia analysis of Globo Network's coverage of the Games.

ANALYTICAL MODEL

The analysis of transmedia strategies for news coverage of planned events aims to contribute to a clearer understanding of transmedia news production and to boost and improve transmedia journalistic practices. The method chosen for the transmedia analysis of Globo Network news coverage of the 2016 Summer Olympics is the analytical model for planned events proposed by Gambarato and Tárcia (2017). The model addresses the specificities of such multiplatform news productions, clarifying how transmedia features are structured and implemented. Identifying transmedia strategies of journalistic coverage assists the analytical purposes of scholars and journalists in the interest of the contemporary news media industry. As proposed by Freeman (2016a), "our role as media industry studies scholars is perhaps to be brainstormers and analysts to help theoretically advance cutting-edge media industry workings" (p. 205). The method draws on the transmedia project design analytical model developed by Gambarato (2013) and establishes 10 main topics and subsequent practicable questions, regarding, for instance, news storytelling, media platforms, and audience engagement. The rationale behind this transmedia journalism model's incorporation of several characteristics commonly related to fictional transmedia is that nonfictional and fictional transmedia productions share the same core principles and features (Gambarato & Tárcia, 2017; Kerrigan & Velikovsky, 2016). A concise description of the model is provided in Table 1. In a similar milieu, this model has been applied to analyze the transmedia dynamics of Russian news coverage of the 2014 Sochi Winter Olympic Games (see Gambarato et al., 2016) and Brazilian news coverage of the 2014 FIFA World Cup (see Gambarato, Alzamora, Tárcia, & Jurno, 2017).

TRANSMEDIA ANALYSIS OF GLOBO NETWORK COVERAGE OF THE 2016 RIO SUMMER OLYMPICS

Premise and Purpose

The 2016 Summer Olympics, known as Rio 2016, took place from August 5 to August 21, 2016, in Brazil. More than 11,000 athletes represented 205 National Olympic Committees, including first-time entrants Kosovo, South Sudan, and the Refugee Olympic Team. Three hundred six events spanning 42 sports disciplines occurred across 32 competition venues over 16 days (Long, 2016). Rio de Janeiro became the first South American city to host the Summer Olympics. These were also the first Games held in a Portuguese-speaking country. The last Olympics held in the Southern Hemisphere was in 2000, in Australia.

Although the fundamental objects of the coverage were the competitions, the athletes, and their performances, the media also had to be aware of issues connected to the coverage. This scenario included the coverage of (1) social and political demonstrations and controversies, (2) an ongoing outbreak of the mosquito-borne Zika virus in Brazil, (3) the pollution of Guanabara Bay, whose waters were used for sailing and windsurfing competitions, (4) political instability and economic crises, (5) crime in Rio de Janeiro, and (6) the Russian doping scandal and participation restrictions, for instance.

Structure and Context

For the 2016 Summer Olympics in Rio, Brazilian television channels Globo Network, Record Network, and Bandeirantes Network were responsible for generating the international radio and TV signals. The accreditation of more than 25,100 official media professionals started three years before the event (Mioli, 2015). More than 7,000 hours of video and audio coverage were produced and distributed to an audience of six billion people in 220 countries (Long, 2016). Globo Network planned multiplatform coverage of the Games, including online streaming, social media networks, mobile applications, and websites. The websites remain live and are updated.

Globo Network's journey toward the 2016 Rio Olympics began in August 2009, shortly before the Games were awarded to Brazil for the first time. The company, which aired its first Olympics coverage in 1992, secured the domestic rights to the event as the head of the consortium that included the other two Brazilian media companies (Record Network and Bandeirantes Network). Under the terms of the contract with the IOC, Globo Network was obligated to broadcast a minimum of nine hours of free-to-air coverage per day. However, the network aired at least ten hours of programming each day, as well as a suite of comprehensive programming across cable, video-on-demand, and online services. The broadcaster's free-to-air offering included a total of 160 hours of content throughout the Games fortnight, more than 100 hours of which were broadcasted live and in prime time. SporTV, Globo Network's cable sports channel, provided high-definition transmission on television, the Internet, and mobile platforms (SporTV, 2016). The round-the-clock video-on-demand service, SporTV Play, and a dedicated mobile application, SporTV Rio 2016, rounded out the free coverage (Long, 2016).

During the Games, the company's technical workforce was increased by more than 2,000 individuals. The team was split into two groups: One group was positioned at Globo Network headquarters in Rio de Janeiro, and the other was based in a newsroom situated inside the International Broadcast Center (IBC). The broadcaster's public-facing operations took place inside the network's Olympic Studio facility located in the heart of the Olympic Park. Constructed almost entirely out of glass, the 500-square-meter, three-storey facility was the set for the many news shows and on-air interviews aired during the Games (Long, 2016). Anchoring the coverage was what the network called its "dream team," comprising a dozen former star athletes. Globo Network allegedly invested around US$250 million in this coverage (Feltrin, 2016). This structure and large investment corroborated to effectively execute the planned transmedia strategies of the news coverage.

Table 1. Concise description of the analytical model regarding transmedia news coverage of planned events (Gambarato & Tárcia, 2017, pp.1389–1391)

Topic	Practicable Questions
1. Premise and Purpose: The nature of the event, its magnitude, and comprehensiveness influence the journalistic coverage.	What is the planned event agenda? What is its core theme? What is the fundamental purpose of the event? What is the magnitude of the event? Is it a local, regional, or global event? Which areas are involved in the coverage (sports, culture, politics, economics, etc.)?
2. Structure and Context: The organization of the transmedia journalistic coverage, the professionals involved, and the infrastructure available depict how the operations were planned and executed.	Which media enterprise is covering the event? How big is it? What is the available coverage infrastructure offered by the event organizers? What is the media enterprise budget for the news coverage of the event? Is the journalistic coverage planned to be transmediatic? How does the coverage end? Do some extensions continue to be active after the event ends?
3. News Storytelling: The news coverage of the event involves primary and parallel stories.	Primary and Parallel News Stories: What elements of the news story (who, what, where, when, why, and how) of the event are involved in the coverage? What is the timeframe of the news story? Does the news coverage utilize gaming elements? Does it involve winning or losing? Is it possible to identify intermedial texts in the news stories?
4. Worldbuilding: The storyworld in which the news is placed should be robust enough to support multiplatform expansions.	Where is the event set? Does the storyworld involve any fictional characteristics? Are different time zones involved in the news coverage? If yes, what are the potential issues related to it and the alternative strategies for each platform? What are the regulations and policies related to the journalistic coverage? Is the event big enough to support expansions throughout multiplatform coverage?
5. Characters: The characters implicated in the coverage could be journalists, characters of the news stories *per se*, sources of information to be reported, and the audience as collaborators.	Who are the main characters presented by the coverage? How many? Are they aggregated to the coverage a posteriori? Who are the primary and secondary sources of information regarding the event? What is the approach of these sources? Are the sources official, nonofficial, or both? Can the audience be considered a character as well?
6. Extensions: News stories meant to spread throughout multiple media platforms should not simply transpose or repurpose the content from one medium to another but expand the news, taking advantage of the media platforms available.	How many extensions are included in the news coverage? Are the extensions mere reproductions of the same content or genuine expansions of the news stories across various media? Is there a plan to keep the content updated in each extension (for instance, on blogs and social media networks)? Do the extensions have the ability to spread the content and provide the possibility to explore the narrative in-depth? How long does the event last? If the event is overlong, how does the coverage proceed to maintain audience interest throughout the entire period?
7. Media Platforms and Genres: In addition to telling news stories with more than one medium, transmedia news coverage can embrace several journalism styles, such as news articles, reports, and opinions; a number of journalism genres; and different technological devices.	What kind of media platforms (television, radio, print media, Web, mobile) are involved in the news coverage? Which devices (computer, tablet, mobile phone, etc.) are required by the coverage? Is there a roll-out strategy for launching each coverage extension? If yes, what is the plan to release the platforms? Which journalism styles (news articles, reportages, opinions, etc.) are included in the coverage? Which journalistic genres (sports, celebrity, investigative journalism, etc.) are presented by the coverage?
8. Audience and Market: Scoping the audience is fundamental for a more appropriate delivery of the transmedia news coverage.	What is the target audience of the coverage? Who is the intended reader/user/viewer/listener? What kind of readers (methodical or scanner; intimate, or detached) does the project attract? Does other journalistic coverage like this exist? Do they succeed in achieving their purpose? What is the coverage business model? Does it involve open platforms, open television channels, cable TV, satellite, pay-per-view, monopoly, etc.? Is the event coverage successful revenue-wise?
9. Engagement: The relationship between the story and the people interested in it is an essential aspect of transmedia strategies.	What percentage of the public participates in the event *in loco*, and what percentage of the audience accesses the event via news coverage? What are the mechanisms of interaction in the transmedia strategy of coverage? Is participation involved in the coverage? If so, how can the *reader/user/viewer/listener* participate in the open system? Is there user-generated content (UGC) related to the event (parodies, recaps, mashups, fan communities, etc.)? Are there any policies restricting the disclosure of UGC? What activities are available to the audience within social media networks related to the event? Is there a system of rewards and penalties? For example, can the audience have its comments/photos published, can people get rewards for social media activities, and can they have comments blocked/removed?
10. Aesthetics: The visual and audio elements contribute to the news coverage and enhance the overall transmedia experience unfolded across multiple media platforms.	What kinds of visuals (video, photo, infographics, news games, animation, holography, etc.) are used in the coverage? Is the overall look of the coverage realistic or a composed environment (usage of graphism, holography, immersive journalism, augmented reality)? Is it possible to identify specific design styles in the coverage? How does audio work in the coverage? Is there ambient sound, sound effects, music, and so forth?

News Storytelling

The news coverage of the 2016 Rio Games involved different kinds of stories. In general, the primary stories broadcasted, especially on television, were directly related to the sports events, such as the Olympic competitions, games' results, and stories about the athletes being portrayed as heroes. However, parallel stories, especially when shared via social media in conjunction with mass media, were also diffused widely. Some of the highlighted parallel stories included (1) American Olympic swimmer Ryan Lochte fabricating a story of being robbed at gunpoint during the Games, (2) two boxers arrested and accused of trying to rape housekeepers, (3) Patrick Hickey, a top Olympic official, arrested after illegally selling tickets to the Games, and (4) an Olympic media bus attacked on a highway. The secondary stories, in conjunction with the primary ones, enriched the coverage and functioned as crucial elements of content expansion of the transmedia coverage.

World-Building

The event was set throughout Rio de Janeiro, which provided the opportunity to build worlds in different aspects. Numerous artistic demonstrations and shows were programmed during Olympic events. Although the storyworld did not involve fictional characteristics directly, two official mascots were named by the public after two of the most renowned artistic figures in the country: Vinicius de Moraes and Tom Jobim. Globo Network also had its own mascot named Globolinha (a diminutive form of Globo ball). The broadcaster built the concept "we are all Olympians," upon which the network based its actions to involve and engage the audience. The warm-up for the Games started in March 2016, and around 2,500 news pieces on the subject were aired before the Opening Ceremony.

The Olympics were big enough to support expansions throughout multiplatform coverage. Globo Group, comprising Globo Network (television), Globosat (cable television), Infoglobo (printed media), and Globo Radio System (radio), involved several of the group's content platforms in this coverage. This group coverage did not occur during the coverage of the 2014 FIFA World Cup (Gambarato et al., 2017). This time, Globo Group created different concepts for each media platform, a core characteristic of transmedia storytelling and consequently, of transmedia journalism. Cable television, with more than 1,000 professionals involved in the coverage, provided a broad experience of the Games. Printed media, under the premise of "digital first," delivered material to websites, mobile applications, and e-books, in addition to special magazines. Furthermore, a free printed tabloid paper was distributed, as well as a guide to the Olympics. A special digital environment was created that followed the competitions in real time and focused on interactivity with users. Infographics, photo galleries, videos, quizzes, mini-documentaries, etc., were also available. Specific actions were conducted on social networks to encourage users' involvement through posts and comments. The coverage also offered a competition-based game, divided into stages in which the player scored points by answering questions related to the Games. The mobile application was developed to provide information and news about competitions, as well as itineraries for the event's day-to-day schedule. For example, the application provided information about at which bars one could watch competitions, venues where fans from a certain country were getting together, as well as other services. The newspapers focused on stories about citizenship, optimism, overcoming difficulties, inclusion, and other Olympic values. With information about and services for how to make the most of their stay in the city, Infoglobo served as an alternative for brands wanting to play host to tourists and communicate directly with them. The radio operations concentrated on information, thrills, and humor throughout bulletins and programs, always striving to present Olympic sports in an easier and practical manner to the audience. Moreover, the Construindo Campeões [Building Champions] project visited schools in Rio de Janeiro and neighboring municipalities, offering students the opportunity to experience the role of radio reporters and commentators in broadcasting their schoolmates' games (Grupo Globo, 2016).

Characters

According to Jenkins (2007), "most often, transmedia stories are based not on individual characters or specific plots but rather complex [...] worlds which can sustain multiple interrelated characters and their stories" (para. 4). That is what happens during mega-events such as the Olympics, a complex storyworld with multiple characters highlighted by journalists and/or by the event organizers. Several characters, in addition to the array of international athletes, were the focus of the news coverage in 2016. Although the regulations imposed by the IOC are considered strict, especially regarding social media, the visibility of the Globo Network studio in the Olympic Park created a different phenomenon in these Olympics. During the main televised broadcasts, many people crowded in front of the building and ended up being incorporated into the show. At times, the broadcaster transferred its interviews to the outdoor environment, where invited athletes could be seen at the news desk. Even with this initiative, the excessive control, regulations, and economic interests restricted the audience's overall capability to actively participate in the news coverage. Therefore, the audience cannot be considered a leading character in the media coverage.

Data collected daily during the Olympics coverage highlighted numerous prominent athletes and non-athlete characters. For instance, despite Olympic officials' efforts to avoid an uncomfortable scenario, Brazilian residents loudly booed interim President Michel Temer as he opened the Games. He did not receive an introduction to the crowd, which is standard for the leaders of the host countries. The event was one of the first official gatherings that Michel Temer had attended since becoming the country's president on August 31, 2016, after President Dilma Rousseff was impeached and removed from office. Olympics fans, in general, and social media users, in particular, were neither necessarily aware of nor worried about the IOC restrictions. During the Games, spectators wearing T-shirts criticizing Michel Temer were expelled from Olympic venues. In addition, spectators were ordered by members of the security forces to put away signs with political messages. A Brazilian federal judge ruled in favor of allowing peaceful political protests at the Olympic Games in Rio. Globo Group covered this controversy on all platforms.

Another character highlighted by the media was Vanderlei Cordeiro de Lima, a former long-distance runner who specialized in marathons. He was internationally acclaimed after a spectator attacked him at the 2004 Summer Olympics marathon, while he was leading the race. Following the incident, he fell back from first to third place, winning the bronze medal. He was later awarded the Pierre de Coubertin medal for sportsmanship for that race. During the Opening Ceremony of the 2016 Summer Olympics, he carried the Olympic flame and lit the Olympic cauldron. Gisele Bundchen was also featured at the 2016 Olympics Opening Ceremony. The world's highest-paid supermodel walked the length of the Maracanã Stadium to the sound of "Girl from Ipanema." Spotify reported that the song was streamed more than 40,000 times the day after her appearance, representing an increase of 1,200% (Bromwich, 2016). The 2016 edition of the Games was also distinguished by the team of 10 refugee Olympic athletes. One of them, swimmer Yusra Mardini, had an extraordinary backstory explored by the media. She and her sister are responsible for helping to save the lives of 20 people, including their own, after they jumped off their sinking dinghy into the Aegean Sea and pushed their boat to land.

Extensions

Despite the restrictions imposed by the IOC, Globo Network planned the "biggest coverage in the broadcaster's history after the inauguration of its Olympic Studio" (Rede Globo, 2016c, para. 1). Primarily, the extended coverage involved all the Globo Group media platforms: television, printed media, Internet, and radio. For instance, Globo Group's cable sports channel SportTV broadcasted live 100% of the competitions, using 56 signals across television and the Internet. Subscribers could choose from among 56 broadcasting options available in applications for computers, tablets, and smartphones. The video-on-demand platform SportTV Play offered special programs and an interactive video player that displayed pause and rewind options, allowing users to choose events according to the date and the sport (Rede Globo, 2016a). Likewise, the SportTV Rio 2016 mobile application granted users exclusive access to the channel's schedule and medals table. In this application, which operated with augmented reality technology, the user could activate alerts to receive notifications about the events schedule and information about their favorite athletes, as well as access to a services guide to Rio de Janeiro that showed tourist attractions, means of transportation, bike rentals, police stations, hospitals, and health centers in three languages: Portuguese, Spanish, and English (Rede Globo, 2016b).

This distinctive coverage, although it still prioritized a mass media logic of transmission, included several multiplatform extensions based on the Olympic Studio. The content aired in the multiscreen environment enabled various possibilities of exploring journalistic content and interacting via social media networks. During the broadcasts, public participation in online social media, mediated by the hashtag #SomosTodosOlímpicos [#WeAreAllOlympians], was exhibited live on a large screen at the Olympic Studio. The aim was to update the content on the different media platforms used during the news coverage, while promoting audience engagement generated via social media interactions. Although feed updates on social media networks, such as Twitter, Facebook, and Instagram, prioritized the televised coverage, according to the linguistic particularities of each social media platform, a genuine extension was observed on Snapchat. In an unprecedented partnership (Rede Globo, 2016a), the profile "Snapredeglobo" offered specific content for the feature "Live Stories" on Snapchat, including photos and videos behind the scenes of the event recorded by journalists, commentators, and fans. Thus, a news coverage strategy based on multiplatform broadcasting was established, in which specific content was allotted to certain extensions to foster engagement.

Media Platforms and Genres

The multiplatform perspective that outlined the news coverage of the Olympic Games produced by Globo Network involved numerous journalistic styles, such as news stories, articles, interviews, and opinion pieces. Television broadcasts prevailed among the journalistic strategy adopted by the broadcaster, particularly in relation to national news programs and sports programs on its public access channel, such as Globo Esporte. Public access broadcasts favored the most popular sports in the country, such as football, volleyball, and gymnastics, as well as competitions in which Brazilian athletes participated. Broadcasts on cable channels favored specific sports. In both cases, there was a strong correlation with the Internet via websites, applications, and profiles on online social media networks.

The website globoesporte.com, for instance, broadcasted 100% of the Olympic Games events on two live streaming channels, and scores were updated in real time on the website's homepage. The video-on-demand platform *Globo Play* offered free content, complementing the public access channel on a 24-hour basis. Users could also access on-demand material from competitions that had already happened in a catalogue organized according to the athletes, sports, and participating nations. Among the exclusive content produced by globoesporte.com, a series of special narratives containing infographics, videos, and specific interactive spaces stands out. Among them are (1) Mapa das Medalhas [Medals Map], in which users were able to filter results by athlete, sport, and chronology of the medals since the beginning of the competitions; (2) Biotipo dos Atletas [Athletes' Biotype], for which 60 athletes, at least one from each sport, were photographed to display how the practice of sports influences body shape; (3) Baía de Guanabara [Guanabara Bay] with profiles of residents and workers of the region that sought to depict the area's safety and its urban features; (4) Medalhões Olímpicos [Olympic "Big Medals"], athletes' profiles in comics and animations; (5) Time de Ouro [Golden Team], a series of videos that profiled 11 Globo Network commentators, who had been acclaimed athletes during previous Olympic Games; (6) Meu Pódio Olímpico [My Olympic Podium], an application showcasing caricatures in which users could choose their favorite athletes, with the option to share the experience on Facebook; and (7) Mapa da Tocha [Torch Map], the Olympic Torch relay with data on dates, people, and places (Esporte e Mídia, 2016).

Although the multiplatform coverage of the event focused mainly on television and the Internet, radio and printed media were also included. Globo Group temporarily launched the CBN Globo Radio Station, aggregating Olympic content in a 24-hour schedule produced by Globo Radio and CBN Radio. The radio station was also available online and on mobile applications. The printed newspapers *O Globo* and *Extra* jointly launched the digital platform Infoglobo Rio 2016, providing exclusive services and highlights of the Games behind the scenes presented in real time. Furthermore, the editorial content prepared for Infoglobo included supplementary inserts in printed newspapers, such as (1) *Rio Olímpico, uma nova cidade* [Olympic Rio, a new city], regarding the transformations in the city for the Games; (2) *Guia dos Jogos Olímpicos Rio 2016* [Guide to the 2016 Rio Olympic Games], a complete guide of the Games; (3) *Cadernos de esporte especiais–Jogos Olímpicos Rio 2016* [Special sports supplement–2016 Rio Olympic Games], comprising daily special coverage; and (4) *Cadernos especiais gratuitos* [Free special supplements], a free bilingual publication distributed at the Olympic Park and its vicinity (Propmark, 2016).

In sum, the content produced by Globo Network in the scope of the broadcaster's multiplatform coverage of the Olympic Games was complementary and eventually redundant, favoring users' choices according to their mediatic consumption habits. In this sense, it was possible to identify the valorization of second screen applications and geolocation, as well as the interaction on online social media networks, stemming from journalistic content offered by the broadcaster.

Audience and Market

The multiplatform audience of Globo Network during its Olympic Games coverage registered an unparalleled growth rate. The cable channel SportTV, Globo's main channel for the coverage, reached 38 million people during 2,400 hours of broadcasting in 17 days. This number is 27% bigger than the sum of spectators of the broadcaster's three direct competitors (ESPN, Fox, and BandSports) and 29% bigger than the total number of spectators reached by SporTV during the 2012 London Olympics coverage. During the Rio Olympics, SportTV and SportTV2 took the lead in prime-time cable television (Stycer, 2016).

Regarding the impact made by the event on different media platforms involved in the network's news coverage strategy, televised broadcasting registered an increase of 40% of people reached compared to the 2012 London Olympics. Between August 3 and August 21, 2016, the free-to-air Globo Network channel reached 177 million people, a sum that represents 53.5 million people more than during the 2012 London Games, corresponding to a 43% increase. The group's digital platforms registered 6.5 million users, the audience peaks related to the transmissions of the Opening and Closing Ceremonies of the Games. The broadcast of the Closing Ceremony drew a 27 audience rating, the highest since the 1996 Atlanta Olympics. Furthermore, globoesporte.com reached a daily average of 15 million accesses during the Games, and a historical record was set during the women's football semi-final between Brazil and Sweden: 20.1 million views (Mermelstein, 2016). These numbers show that the multiplatform coverage strategy was successful: Globo Network beat audience records and became the leader of that segment, reaching a varied public with a robust and diversified editorial project. However, this does not mean that citizen participation widely permeated the editorial planning, even if participation was discernible in specific contexts, notably on the online social media networks.

Engagement

According to the study disclosed by the marketing company SocialBrain (Soutelo, 2016), Globo Network attained the most engagement of any brand on online social media during the 2016 Rio Olympic Games. Throughout the Games, Globo Network's profile on Twitter posted 1,800 tweets, generating around 180,000 shares. The hashtag #SomosTodosOlímpicos, created by the broadcaster, was mentioned 234,000 times on Twitter between August 3 and August 21, 2016, 10 times more than, for example, the hashtag #NBCOlympics of the American television network NBC, which registered 22,000 mentions on Twitter during the same period. Globo Network's coverage became a trending topic on Brazilian Twitter 509 times and on the global Trending Topics list 165 times. Facebook registered around 830 posts with the hashtag #SomosTodosOlímpicos, which generated around 6 million accesses. On Instagram, this hashtag was deployed for around 630 posts, with nearly 5.8 million likes. On Snapchat, the broadcaster's profile registered about 730,000 daily visits (Soutelo, 2016).

The engagement generated on online social media networks, especially when mediated by the hashtag put forward by Globo Network, indicates that the hashtag acted as a symbolic articulation of the broadcaster's posts on social media. This mechanism of interaction stimulates social involvement in news dissemination based on contemporary habits of information consumption. Therefore, social engagement around this hashtag boosted Globo Network's presence on online social media connections. This element is extremely important for the editorial strategy adopted by the company in its multiplatform coverage of the event, because it emphasizes the relevance of online social media networks in the diffusion of journalistic content.

In this sense, the Olympic Games became the most talked-about event ever on Instagram, with 916 million interactions between 131 million Instagram users (G1, 2016). For the event, Twitter Brazil organized the challenge #TweetCampeão [#ChampionTweet], which designated whoever achieved the highest number of views on their profile and mentions on social media the winner. Ana Paula Renault, a participant in the Globo Network Big Brother Brazil reality show, won the contest with a tweet that yielded 3.4 million views and 35,000 mentions. As a reward, her tweet was projected on Arcos da Lapa, one of the many tourist attractions in Rio de Janeiro. She celebrated her victory on Twitter by using, among others, the hashtag #SomosTodosOlímpicos (Joven Pan, 2016). This action demonstrates the social pervasiveness of the hashtag created by Globo Network for the Olympic Games, in the social interactions on Twitter during that period and in the online/offline connections. Overall, the broadcaster's audience engagement strategy privileged interaction to the detriment of participation. Interaction presupposes that the audience can "act/react/interact but cannot interfere with the narrative" in the sense that the "audience can decide the path to experiencing it, can click here or there, can react to social media entries, but it is not able to collaborate and co-create" (Gambarato, 2012, p. 76). Participation implies co-creation, engaging the audience "in a way that expresses their creativity in a unique, and surprising manner, allowing them to influence the final result" (Gambarato, 2012, p. 74). In this scenario, the IOC rules and regulations played a major role, decreasing the opportunities to foster participation during the Games.

Aesthetics

The aesthetic perspective of the Globo Network coverage of the Olympic Games excelled in journalistic accuracy, combined with technological innovation. On one hand, no language innovations were observed in relation to, for instance, initiatives of incorporating virtual reality narratives or newsgames in content expansion. On the other, editorial planning produced sophisticated strategies of broadcasting and information access, made available by the broadcaster throughout multiple media platforms. As an example, the use of augmented reality in mobile applications, such as Globo Rio 2016, allowed the audience to, for instance, point their smartphones at a competition venue and receive in real time information about what was happening at that specific location. Globolinha, the coverage's mascot, could be visualized by users when accessing data about ongoing matches based on geolocation, in a similar aesthetics as Pokémon Go. Thus, augmented reality added to the Games transmissions in real time and enriched the audience experience.

Technological advancements were highlighted by holographic projections and by the partnership established between Globo Network and the Japanese broadcasting organization NHK for live transmissions in the ultra-high-definition (UHD) 8K format during the Opening and Closing Ceremonies of the Games. The 8K technology defines a cutting-edge standard in image quality, offering a resolution 16 times better than the current high-definition (HD) used in digital television (Lobo, 2016). This noteworthy broadcasting, however, did not result directly in possibilities of transmedia expansion in the journalistic narrative.

The series of special narratives produced by globoesporte.com—which employed infographics, comics, and animations extensively—is another example of the preoccupations regarding the creation of a refined aesthetic, grounded in the production of autonomous and complementary narratives in the digital connections of Globo Network news coverage. However, as in other examples, this element presented limited possibilities for citizen participation, a crucial aspect for the development of transmedia narratives.

CONCLUSION

Transmedia journalism essentially implies (1) multiple media platforms, (2) content expansion, and (3) audience engagement. The Globo Network news coverage of the 2016 Rio Olympics embraced, to a certain extent, all three core dimensions of transmedia phenomena. In relation to diversified media platforms,

Globo Network took advantage of the consortium of subsidiary media outlets within the Globo Group, incorporating television, Internet, printed media, social media, and radio. The tentpole of the coverage was television and the second-screen experience offered to the audience. Notwithstanding, social media networks, such as Instagram and Snapchat, played a major role in the expansion of content and audience engagement. The 2016 Summer Olympics was the most "instagramed" event in history (G1, 2016), and this was the Games of Snapchat stories and filters (Barkho, 2016). Globo Network stablished an unprecedented partnership with Snapchat to offer live behind-the-scenes broadcasts of the event from various perspectives. Social media as a source of news is a global trend verified by multiple studies conducted by renowned institutions (see Bialy & Svetoka, 2016; Gottfried & Shearer, 2016; Newman et al., 2016), and the Olympics followed this trend. This occurrence is so prevalent in news that although the Snapchat platform is not designed to be a news source, the firm adjusted its services for insertion in transmedia journalism. A highlight of the Globo Network coverage of the Games was the carefully orchestrated strategy and proactive planned process with journalists that structured an up-front transmedia approach. This planned/strategic aspect (Fast & Örnebring, 2015) of the coverage, noticeable in 2016, is a step forward from what the broadcaster offered on the occasion of the 2014 FIFA World Cup. Two years later, Globo Network created distinctive concepts for each media platform involved, articulating content originated by various Globo Group media outlets. Differently from what occurred during the 2014 FIFA World Cup coverage (see Gambarato et al., 2017), during the 2016 Olympics, there was a more solid transmedia plan aimed at creating transmediality to build a storyworld designed for and with various integrated media platforms. The *ad hoc*/emergent aspect (Fast & Örnebring, 2015) of transmedia creations manifested in the audience engagement potential of the coverage. Globo Network focused on interactivity with users to the detriment of effective citizen participation. The opportunities for the public to interact involved infographics, quizzes, polls, posts, comments, and sharing, for instance. The mobile applications developed by Globo Network for the event contributed to audience interaction, for example, via the augmented reality tools and the geolocation systems incorporated into the applications. Few hints of participation appeared in specific situations, especially connected to the broadcasts direct from the Olympic Studio in the middle of the Olympic Park, where people crowded in front of the studio and were incorporated into the transmission. Nonetheless, the strict set of regulations foisted by the IOC on the public and the media organizations allegedly interfered in the hybrid logic of adaptability and openness (Lewis, 2012) inherent to audience participation in journalism.

In a nutshell, the Globo Network coverage is aligned with the essential features of transmedia storytelling, investing in content expansion across different media platforms within technological advancements, but the coverage presented limited mechanisms of audience participation. Technological innovations, such as holographic projections of virtual athletes, augmented reality, and 8K ultra-high-definition transmissions, contributed to offer the audience a kind of immersive experience, in which the public could feel absorbed in the coverage. The Brazilian coverage of the Rio Olympics represents an advance in the transmedia coverage of planned events in relation to what Globo Network had previously offered in news coverage of similar major events. The transmedia planning and integration of multiple media platforms disseminating content via mobile applications, live-streaming on the Internet and on social media networks, and an immersive experience based on technological innovations were the transmedia highlights of the Globo Network coverage. However, improvement in audience engagement, especially in terms of citizen participation, is still to be achieved.

REFERENCES

G1. (2016, August 28). Rio 2016 é evento mais "instagramado" da história [Rio 2016 is the most "instagramed" event in history]. *G1*. Retrieved from http://g1.globo.com/tecnologia/noticia/2016/08/rio-2016-e-evento-mais-instagramado-da-historia-foto-de-neymar-bomba.html

Allan, S., & Thorsen, E. (2009). *Citizen journalism: Global perspectives*. New York, NY: Peter Lang.

Andrejevic, M. (2009). Exploiting YouTube: Contradictions of user-generated labor. In P. Snickars & P. Vonderau (Eds.), *The YouTube reader* (pp. 406–423). Stockholm, Sweden: National Library of Sweden.

Banks, J., & Deuze, M. (2009). Co-creative labour. *International Journal of Cultural Studies*, *12*(5), 419–431. doi:10.1177/1367877909337862

Barkho, G. (2016, August 11). How social media changed the Olympics, and what it means for #Rio2016. *Later*. Retrieved from https://later.com/blog/how-social-media-changed-the-olympics-and-rio-2016/

Baym, N. K., & Burnett, R. (2009). Amateur experts: International fan labour in Swedish independent music. *International Journal of Cultural Studies*, *12*(5), 433–449. doi:10.1177/1367877909337857

Bialy, B., & Svetoka, S. (2016). *New trends in social media*. Riga, Latvia: NATO Strategic Communications Centre of Excellence. Retrieved from http://www.stratcomcoe.org/new-trends-social-media

Bolin, G. (2007). Media technologies, transmedia storytelling and commodification. In T. Storsul & D. Stuedahl (Eds.), *Ambivalence towards convergence: Digitalization and media change* (pp. 237–248). Gothenburg, Sweden: Nordicom.

Bromwich, J. E. (2016, August 9). "The girl from Ipanema" goes walking again, with Gisele Bundchen's help. *The New York Times*. Retrieved from https://www.nytimes.com/2016/08/10/arts/music/the-girl-from-ipanema-goes-walking-again-with-gisele-bundchens-help.html

Bruns, A. (2008). *Blogs, Wikipedia, Second Life, and beyond: From production to produsage*. New York, NY: Peter Lang.

Dayan, D., & Katz, E. (1992). *Media events: The live broadcasting of history*. Cambridge, MA: Harvard University Press.

De Kosnik, A. (2012). Fandom as free labor. In T. Scholz (Ed.), *Digital labor: The Internet as playground and factory* (pp. 98–111). New York, NY: Routledge.

Dodson, P. C. (2015, October 21). Why Snapchat's Live Stories are the most powerful new social media. *Fast Company*. Retrieved from https://www.fastcompany.com/3052322/why-snapchats-live-stories-are-the-most-powerful-new-social-media

Esporte e Mídia. (2016, July 13). Globoesporte.com detalha cobertura dos Jogos Olímpicos; saiba mais [Globoesporte.com presents the details of the Olympic Games coverage; learn more]. *Esporte e Mídia*. Retrieved from http://www.esporteemidia.com/2016/07/globoesportecom-detalha-cobertura-dos.html

Fast, K., & Örnebring, H. (2015). Transmedia world-building: The Shadow (1931–present) and Transformers (1984–present). *International Journal of Cultural Studies*. doi:10.1177/1367877915605887

Feltrin, R. (2016, August 21). Exclusivo: Globo investiu US$ 250 milhões na Rio 2016 [Exclusive: Globo invested US$250 million on Rio 2016]. *UOL*. Retrieved from https://tvefamosos.uol.com.br/noticias/ooops/2016/08/21/exclusivo-globo-investiu-us-250-mi-na-rio-2016-veja-gastos-de-outras-tvs.htm?cmpid=copiaecola

Fox, A. (Ed.). (2016). *Global perspectives on media events in contemporary society*. Hershey, PA: IGI Global. doi:10.4018/978-1-4666-9967-0

Freeman, M. (2016a). *Industrial approaches to media: A methodological gateway to industry studies*. London: Palgrave Macmillan. doi:10.1057/978-1-137-55176-4

Freeman, M. (2016b). *Historicising transmedia storytelling: Early twentieth-century transmedia story worlds*. New York, NY: Routledge.

Fuchs, C. (2010). Labor in informational capitalism and on the Internet. *The Information Society*, *26*(3), 179–196. doi:10.1080/01972241003712215

Fuchs, C. (2012). Class and exploitation on the Internet. In T. Scholz (Ed.), *Digital labor: The Internet as playground and factory* (pp. 211–224). New York, NY: Routledge.

Gambarato, R. R. (2012). Signs, systems and complexity of transmedia storytelling. *Communication Studies*, *12*, 69–83.

Gambarato, R. R. (2013). Transmedia project design: Theoretical and analytical considerations. *Baltic Screen Media Review*, *1*, 80–100.

Gambarato, R. R., Alzamora, G., & Tárcia, L. (2016). Russian news coverage of the 2014 Sochi Winter Olympic Games: A transmedial analysis. *International Journal of Communication*, *10*, 1446–1469.

Gambarato, R. R., Alzamora, G., Tárcia, L., & Jurno, A. (2017). 2014 FIFA World Cup on the Brazilian Globo Network: A transmedia dynamics? *Global Media and Communication*. doi:10.1177/1742766517734256

Gambarato, R. R., & Nanì, A. (2016). Blurring boundaries, transmedia storytelling and the ethics of C.S. Peirce. In S. Maras (Ed.), *Ethics in screenwriting: New perspective* (pp. 147–175). Melbourne, Australia: Palgrave Macmillan. doi:10.1057/978-1-137-54493-3_7

Gambarato, R. R., & Tárcia, L. (2017). Transmedia strategies in journalism. An analytical model for the news coverage of planned events. *Journalism Studies*, *18*(11), 1381–1399. doi:10.1080/1461670X.2015.1127769

Getz, D. (2012). *Event studies: Theory, research and policy for planned events*. New York, NY: Routledge.

Gottfried, J., & Shearer, E. (2016). *News use across social media platforms 2016*. Washington, DC: Pew Research Center. Retrieved from http://www.journalism.org/2016/05/26/news-use-across-social-media-platforms-2016/

Grupo Globo. (2016, June 22). Grupo Globo announces media sponsorship of the Rio 2016 Olympic Games. *Grupo Globo*. Retrieved from http://grupoglobo.globo.com/ingles/news/grupo_globo_sponsorship_olympic_games.php

Hepp, A., & Couldry, N. (2010). Introduction: Media events in globalized media cultures. In N. Couldry, A. Hepp, & F. Krotz (Eds.), *Media events in a global age* (pp. 1–20). London: Routledge.

Hesmondhalgh, D. (2010). User-generated content, free labour, and the cultural industries. *Ephemera: Theory and Politics in Organization, 10*(3/4), 267–284.

Hopewell, J. (2016, August 2). Brazil's Globo hopes to vault to future with Rio Games. *Variety*. Retrieved from http://variety.com/2016/tv/global/brazil-globo-network-rio-olympics-technology-1201828462/

International Olympic Committee. (2015). *IOC social and digital media guidelines for persons accredited to the Games of the XXXI Olympiad Rio 2016*. Retrieved from https://stillmed.olympic.org/media/Document%20Library/OlympicOrg/Games/Summer-Games/Games-Rio-2016-Olympic-Games/Social-Media-Blogging-Internet-Guidelines-and-News-Access-Rules/IOC-Social-and-Digital-Media-Guidelines-Rio-2016.pdf#_ga=1.124100364.74130809.1484839460

International Olympic Committee. (2016). *Editorial use of the Olympic properties by media organisations*. Retrieved from https://stillmed.olympic.org/Documents/THE%20IOC/IOC_guide_media_web%2029.11.13.pdf

Jenkins, H. (2006). *Convergence culture: Where old and new media collide*. New York: New York University Press.

Jenkins, H. (2007). Transmedia Storytelling 101. *Blog Confessions of an Aca-Fan*. Retrieved from http://henryjenkins.org/2007/03/transmedia_storytelling_101.html

Joven Pan. (2016, August 5). Rio 2016: Ex-BBB Ana Paula vence desafio e terá tweet projetado em monumento [Rio 2016: Ex-BBB Ana Paul won the challenge and her tweet will be projected onto monument]. *Joven Pan*. Retrieved from https://beta.jovempan.uol.com.br/esportes/rio-2016-ex-bbb-ana-paula-vence-desafio-e-tera-tweet-projetado-em-monumento.html

Kerrigan, S., & Velikovsky, J. T. (2016). Examining documentary transmedia narratives through The Living History of Fort Scratchley Project. *Convergence (London), 22*(3), 250–268. doi:10.1177/1354856514567053

Kinder, M. (1991). *Playing with power in movies, television, and video games: From Muppet Babies to Teenage Mutant Ninja Turtles*. Berkeley, CA: University of California Press.

Kottasova, I. (2016, December 6). The top hashtag of the year had nothing to do with Donald Trump. *CNN*. Retrieved from http://money.cnn.com/2016/12/06/technology/twitter-top-events-hashtags-2016/

Lewis, S. (2012). The tension between professional control and open participation. *Information Communication and Society, 15*(6), 836–866. doi:10.1080/1369118X.2012.674150

Lobo, A. P. (2016, August 8). Globo usa DWDM nacional para transmitir em 8K na Rio 2016 [Globo uses national DWDM to broadcast in 8K in Rio 2016]. *Convergência Digital*. Retrieved from http://www.convergenciadigital.com.br/cgi/cgilua.exe/sys/start.htm?UserActiveTemplate=site&%25252525253Butm%252525252525252525255Fmedium=&UserActiveTemplate=site%252Csite&infoid=43182&sid=4

Long, M. (2016, August 4). Globo gathering: How Brazil's biggest broadcaster is tackling Rio 2016. *SportsPro*. Retrieved from http://www.sportspromedia.com/magazine_features/globo_gathering_how_brazils_biggest_broadcaster_is_gearing_up_for_rio_2016

Mermelstein, A. (2016, August 26). Olimpíada impulsionou Globo em diversas plataformas [Olympics boosted Globo Network in various platforms]. *Converge Comunicações*. Retrieved from http://converge-com.com.br/telaviva/paytv/26/08/2016/olimpiadas-impulsionaram-globo-em-diversas-plataformas/

Mioli, T. (2015, October 26). Rio 2016 Olympic Games communications director explains how the city is getting ready for 30,000 journalists. *Journalism in the Americas*. Retrieved from https://knightcenter.utexas.edu/blog/00-16397-rio2016-olympic-games-communications-director-explains-how-city-getting-ready-30000-jo

Mitu, B., & Poulakidakos, S. (Eds.). (2016). *Media events: A critical contemporary approach*. Basingstoke, UK: Palgrave Macmillan. doi:10.1057/9781137574282

Moloney, K. T. (2011). *Porting transmedia storytelling to journalism* (Unpublished master's thesis). University of Denver, Denver, CO.

Newman, N., Fletcher, R., Levy, D. A. L., & Nielsen, R. K. (2016). *Reuters Institute digital news report 2016*. Oxford, UK: Reuters Institute for the Study of Journalism. Retrieved from http://reutersinstitute.politics.ox.ac.uk/sites/default/files/Digital-News-Report-2016.pdf

O'Riordan, C. (2012, August 13). The story of the digital Olympics: Streams, browsers, most watched, four screens. *BBC*. Retrieved from http://www.bbc.co.uk/blogs/bbcinternet/2012/08/digital_olympics_reach_stream_stats.html

Propmark. (2016, June 28). Infoglobo prepara ambiente digital para cobertura da Rio 2016 [Infoglobo prepares digital environment for the coverage of the Rio 2016]. *Propmark*. Retrieved from http://propmark.com.br/midia/infoglobo-prepara-ambiente-digital-para-cobertura-da-rio-2016

Rede Globo. (2016a, August 3). Rio 2016: Globo e Snapchat fecham parceria para produção de conteúdo [Rio 2016: Globo and Snapchat agree on partnership for content production]. *Rede Globo*. Retrieved from http://redeglobo.globo.com/novidades/noticia/2016/08/rio-2016-globo-e-snapchat-fecham-parceria-para-producao-de-conteudo.html

Rede Globo. (2016b, July 29). Aplicativo Globo Rio 2016: Guia de serviços e realidade aumentada; baixe [Rio 2016 Globo Application: Service guide and augmented reality; download it]. *Rede Globo*. Retrieved from http://redeglobo.globo.com/novidades/noticia/2016/07/aplicativo-globo-rio-2016-guia-de-servicos-e-realidade-aumentada-baixe.html

Rede Globo. (2016c, July 29). Globo estreia estúdio no coração dos Jogos Olímpicos no domingo, dia 31 [Globo launches studio in the heart of the Olympic Games on Sunday, 31]. *Rede Globo*. Retrieved from http://redeglobo.globo.com/novidades/noticia/2016/07/globo-estreia-estudio-no-coracao-dos-jogos-olimpicos-no-domingo-dia-31.html

Renó, D. (2014). Transmedia journalism and the new media ecology: Possible languages. In D. Renó, C. Campalans, S. Ruiz, & V. Gosciola (Eds.), *Periodismo transmedia: Miradas múltiples* [Transmedia journalism: Multiple perspectives] (pp. 3–19). Barcelona, Spain: Editorial UOC.

Renó, D., & Flores, J. (2012). *Periodismo transmedia* [Transmedia journalism]. Madrid, Spain: Fragua Editorial.

Simo, F. (2017, January 11). Introducing: The Facebook Journalism Project. *Media*. Retrieved from https://media.fb.com/2017/01/11/facebook-journalism-project/

Smith, A., Stavros, C., & Westberg, K. (2017). *Brand fans: Lessons from the world's greatest sporting brands*. Melbourne, Australia: Palgrave Macmillan. doi:10.1007/978-3-319-48854-7

Sokolova, N. (2012). Co-opting transmedia consumers: User content as entertainment or free labour? The cases of S.T.A.L.K.E.R. and Metro 2033. *Europe-Asia Studies*, *64*(8), 1565–1583. doi:10.1080/09668136.2012.712253

Soutelo, N. (2016, August 26). O que as redes sociais fizeram pelas Olimpíadas e o que também podem fazer pela sua marca [What have social media networks done for the Olympics and what they can also do for your brand]. *SocialBrain*. Retrieved from http://www.socialbrain.com.br/inbound-marketing/o-que-as-redes-sociais-fizeram-pelas-olimpiadas-e-que-tambem-podem-fazer-pela-sua-marca/

Spor, T. V. (2016, July 8). SporTV entrega a maior cobertura dos Jogos Olímpicos Rio 2016 [SporTV delivers the biggest coverage of the 2016 Rio Olympic Games]. *SporTV.* Retrieved from http://sportv.globo.com/site/programas/rio-2016/noticia/2016/07/sportv-entrega-maior-cobertura-dos-jogos-olimpicos-rio-2016.html

Stanfill, M., & Condis, M. (2014). Fandom and/as labor. *Transformative Works and Cultures*, *15*. doi:10.3983/twc.2014.0593

Stycer, M. (2016, August 25). Audiência do SporTV na Rio-2016 foi maior que a soma de todos os concorrentes [SporTV's audience during the 2016 Rio Olympics was bigger than the sum of all other concurrents]. *Blog do Mauricio Stycer*. Retrieved from https://mauriciostycer.blogosfera.uol.com.br/2016/08/25/audiencia-do-sportv-na-rio-2016-foi-maior-que-a-soma-de-todos-concorrentes/

Terranova, T. (2000). Free labor: Producing culture for the digital economy. *Social Text*, *18*(2), 33–58. doi:10.1215/01642472-18-2_63-33

UOL. (2015, December 10). *Globo assegura direitos de transmissão das Olimpíadas até 2032* [Globo ensures the Olympic broadcast rights until 2032]. Retrieved from https://olimpiadas.uol.com.br/noticias/2015/12/10/globo-assegura-direitos-de-transmissao-das-olimpiadas-ate-2032.htm

Zirondi, M. (2016, August 11). Snapchat se destaca na Olimpíada com transmissões ao vivo [Snapchat excels in the Olympics with live broadcasts]. *Propmark*. Retrieved from http://propmark.com.br/rio-2016/snapchat-se-destaca-na-olimpiada-com-transmissoes-ao-vivo

KEY TERMS AND DEFINITIONS

8K: Refers to the horizontal resolution of 7,680 pixels, forming the total image dimensions of 7680 × 4320 pixels.

***Ad hoc*:** A Latin phrase meaning "made for this specific purpose or need, not planned before it happens."

Augmented Reality: Technology that superimposes computer-generated images on the user's view of the real world.

CrowdTangle: A tool for surfacing stories, measuring their social performance, and identifying influencers.

FIFA: *Fédération Internationale de Football Association* is the international football association responsible for organizing major football tournaments, notably the World Cup and the Women's World Cup.

Newsgames: Games that apply journalistic content to their creation, aiming at providing context for complex situations.

Pokémon Go**:** A location-based augmented reality game for mobile devices.

Chapter 9
Transmedia Journalism and the City:
Participation, Information, and Storytelling Within the Urban Fabric

Renira Rampazzo Gambarato
National Research University Higher School of Economics, Russia

ABSTRACT

This chapter discusses the participatory flair of transmedia journalism within the concreteness of urban spaces by examining The Great British Property Scandal (TGBPS), a transmedia experience designed to inform and engage the public and offer alternative solutions to the long-standing housing crisis in the United Kingdom. The theoretical framework is centered on transmedia storytelling applied to journalism in the scope of urban spaces and participatory culture. The methodological approach of the case study is based on Gambarato's (2013) transmedia analytical model and applied to TGBPS to depict how transmedia strategies within urban spaces collaborated to influence social change. TGBPS is a pertinent example of transmedia journalism within the liquid society, integrating mobile technologies into daily processes with the potential for enhanced localness, customization, and mobility within the urban fabric.

INTRODUCTION

The ever-changing waters in Heraclitus' river appropriately illustrate the fluidity issues well considered by Bauman (2000) in his liquid society. A liquid society in which changeability, flow, uncertainty, and conflict are constant. Deuze (2008) relates journalism to Bauman's liquidity, reflecting upon the fact that "Media as social institutions do not escape the sense of accelerated, unsettling change permeating liquid modern life, and it is exactly this notion of volatile, uncertain (global and local) flux that professional journalism fails to come to terms with" (p. 856). Furthermore, Deuze advocates that the involvement of audiences in rich forms of transmedia storytelling paves the way for the so-called "liquid journalism" (ibid., p. 859), in which news industry tries to integrate "disruptive technologies" (ibid., p. 856), such as the Internet. Transmedia journalism absorbers Bauman's fluidity combined with Deuze's conception of

DOI: 10.4018/978-1-5225-3781-6.ch009

liquid journalism, encompassing multiple media outlets and narrative expansion with integrated actions between journalists and citizens. Transmedia journalism ought to be participatory, broadly exchangeable, and essentially expandable (Alzamora & Tárcia, 2012).

In this scenario, the aim of the chapter is to discuss the participatory flair of transmedia journalism within the concreteness of urban spaces by examining The Great British Property Scandal (TGBPS), a transmedia experience designed to inform and engage the public and offer alternative solutions to the long-standing housing-crisis in the United Kingdom (UK). The journalistic project was created by Channel 4, one of the largest British television broadcasters. Architect George Clarke, the project's host, started a personal crusade against the British housing problem after discovering how many livable homes were empty or being demolished, while a significant number of families needed a home. The project appeals to audiences' civic and social sense for not wasting empty properties as a result of the difficulties faced by private owners to bring them back into use. Therefore, the core goal of TGBPS was to report the issue and force it on the government agenda, seeking for actual policy amendment and, consequently, social change within the urban fabric. The main proposition of TGBPS was the creation of a low-cost loan fund established to support empty property owners, who would like to refurbish their properties and put them back into the market.

TGBPS, a transmedia experience that weaves people, participation, information, and storytelling in the city space, collaborates to a new perception of the context, in which cities achieve an enhanced hybrid function. Moreover, "It is likely that urban media content will gradually develop into content that can provide storytelling, not just information, to receivers" (Kim & Hong, 2013, p. 9). Thus, this chapter focuses on the analysis of the transmedia strategies of TGBPS to demonstrate how this production contributed (1) to make the public aware of the senseless waste of a million empty homes in the UK (Syndicut, n.d.); and (2) to offer opportunities for the audience to take action and change government policies in order to promote the revitalization of abandoned properties in the cityscape. "Inspiration to action" (pursue intervention by the public in real actions seeking solutions to problems) is one of the core features of transmedia journalism proposed by Moloney (2011) and the highlight of TGBPS.

The theoretical framework of this chapter is centered on transmedia storytelling applied to journalism (Alzamora & Tárcia, 2012; Gambarato & Tárcia, 2017; Moloney, 2011) in the scope of urban spaces (Bachelard, 1997; Calvino, 1974; De Certeau, 1984) and participatory culture (Carpentier & Dahlgren, 2014; Jenkins et al., 2013). The methodological approach of the case study is based on Gambarato's (2013) transmedia analytical model and applied to TGBPS to depict how transmedia strategies within urban spaces collaborated to report an issue and influence social change. The research findings point to the transformative potential of TGBPS, which is increased by the participatory nature of the project. Concrete tools for taking action and fostering social change are offered to the audience. TGBPS is a pertinent example of transmedia journalism within the liquid society (Bauman, 2000), integrating mobile technologies into daily processes with the potential for enhanced localness, customization, and mobility within the urban fabric.

TRANSMEDIA PRODUCTIONS AND URBAN SPACES

Transmedia storytelling involves the unfolding of a storyworld (Jenkins, 2006) in which installments of the narrative are distributed across multiple media platforms to engage the audience and offer a more meaningful experience. Transmedia storytelling "is clearly premised on a macro-story that weaves itself throughout the various story pieces" (Kim & Hong, 2013, p. 7). Bernardo (2014) emphasizes that "In the past decade, transmedia has proved invaluable as a communication strategy. Its real value lies in its prioritization of a dynamic storytelling experience as opposed to a more or less static broadcast" (p. 125). The classic examples of transmedia storytelling are often related to entertainment, as the case of *The Matrix* (1999) by the Wachowskis: In between each feature film, additional content (including graphic novels, animations, video games and memorabilia, for instance) were launched, offering the audience a richer understanding of the storyworld and the opportunity to keep engaged (Gambarato, 2013, p. 85). Nevertheless, transmedia storytelling goes beyond fiction, encompassing journalism, as the project TGBPS demonstrates.

Gambarato and Tárcia (2017) consider that transmedia journalism, as well as other applications of transmedia storytelling, basically involves (1) multiple media platforms, (2) content expansion, and (3) audience engagement. The challenge of transmedia journalism is to build a participatory environment in which journalism turns into a conversation, as regarded by Anderson, Dardenne, and Killenberg (1994). In addition, Moloney (2011) stresses that the relevance of transmedia journalism relies on telling compelling stories and allowing them to be a conversation that "draws people deeper by giving them a sense of ownership in that story. Through transmedia journalism we can, as public journalism hoped, build relevance to the public and engage in a conversation about what news matters" (pp. 58–59).

In the midst of new trends in current media, which involve narrative, participation and experience, space acquires an active role in communication processes, in general, and in the transmedia realm, in particular. Narrative space (Cooper, 2002), which also includes the unseen, engages audiences in collective experiences. Participatory space, anchored in the technological developments, enable innovative ways to tell, to listen and to experience stories. Experiential space, connected to the collective process described by Lévy (1997), amplifies the complexity of transmedia storytelling distributed across multiple media platforms. In this context, the urban fabric becomes a space of possibilities for fiction and nonfiction transmedia productions; the city-text proposed by De Certeau (1984) and discussed by Collie (2013) indicates that "Pedestrians, in effect, tell urban stories through their movements" (p. 11).

Michel de Certeau (1984) differentiates the concept of place from space. According to the author, "A place (*lieu*) is the order (of whatever kind) in accord with which elements are distributed in relationships of coexistence. (…) A place is thus an instantaneous configuration of positions. It implies an indication of stability" (ibid., p. 117). Space, on the other hand, embraces vectors of directions, velocities and time variables.

In short, space is a practiced place. Thus, the street geometrically defined by urban planning is transformed into a space by walkers. In the same way, an act of reading is the space produced by the practice of a particular place: a written text, i.e., a place constituted by a system of signs. (ibid.)

De Certeau's city-text (1984) is in consonance with Calvino's imaginable cities (1974). Italo Calvino, in his acclaimed *Invisible Cities*, describes the imaginary city of Tamara, which belongs to the group *City and Signs* in the book, as a space where:

Your gaze scans the streets as if they were written pages: the city says everything you must think, makes you repeat her discourse, and while you believe you are visiting Tamara you are only recording the names with which she defines herself and all her parts. (Calvino, 1974, p. 14)

Describing the group *City and Memory*, Calvino (ibid., p. 10) states that the city consists of the "relationships between the measurements of its space and the events of its past," however, the city "does not tell its past, but contains it" (ibid., p. 11). In addition, Gaston Bachelard, in *The Poetics of Space*, introduces the concept of "topoanalysis" as "the systematic psychological study of the sites of our intimate lives" (1997, p. 8). Bachelard advocates the idea that it is space, not time, which invokes memories:

Of course, thanks to the house, a great many of our memories are housed, and if the house is a bit elaborate, if it has a cellar and a garret, nooks and corridors, our memories have refuges that are all the more clearly delineated. All our lives we come back to them in our daydreams. A psychoanalyst should, therefore, turn his attention to this simple localization of our memories. I should like to give the name of topoanalysis to this auxiliary of psychoanalysis. (ibid.)

Bachelard, therefore, emphasizes the experience behind our relationship with space and time. In the interplay between narrative and experience, Jenkins (2002) highlights the role of spatial stories and environmental storytelling. Environmental storytelling intertwines story elements and the physical space in which the story is experienced. Jenkins (ibid.) describes four ways environmental storytelling creates the conditions for immersive narrative experiences: (1) evoked narratives (spatial stories evoke pre-exiting stories or draw upon well-known genre traditions); (2) enacted narratives (spatial stories can provide a staging ground where the narrative is enacted); (3) embedded narratives (spatial stories may embed narrative information within the *mise-en-scène*); and (4) emergent narratives (spatial stories provide resources for narratives to emerge). TGBPS, which has characteristics of emergent narrative, creates conditions for nonfictional stories to emerge from the cityscape by means of audience participation, as the comprehensive analysis of the project depicts.

In the transmedia realm, environmental storytelling is, not only, but specially connected to the portmanteau transmedia. Pratten (2015) describes three types of transmedia stories: Franchise, portmanteau, and complex transmedia experience. Franchise includes a series of individual and independent media outlets, such as films, video games, and comic books that cover different narrative spaces, such as prequels, sequels, and spin-offs (ibid., p. 15). *The Matrix* is an example of franchise. Portmanteau is a kind of puzzle in which multiple interdependent platforms contribute to a single experience (ibid., p. 16). This is the case of Alternate Reality Games (ARGs). An ARG is "an interactive narrative that blends real life treasure hunting, interactive storytelling, and online community" (Gambarato, 2013, p. 86). A prominent example of ARG is *Why So Serious?*, produced in 2007, which played out for 15 months before the release of Christopher Nolan's film *The Dark Knight* (2008), and involved phone calls, coded websites, printed posters, newspaper ads, and live events, for instance. Complex transmedia experience (Pratten, 2015, p. 16), combines franchise and portmanteau, offering the audience a broader experience. The TV series *Lost* (ABC, 2004–2010) is an example of this type of transmedia production because it incorporates traces of franchise (TV series, mobisodes, books, and more) and an ARG called the *Lost Experience*, produced in 2006.

ARGs involve a recurring shift between the real and fictional realities offered by the experience, drawing participants into both online and offline activities. In this sense, the urban space plays a key role in ARGs. "The capacity of lived environments to be repurposed and to acquire new meanings is what makes environmental games and alternate reality games (ARGs) possible—and, perhaps, necessary" (Ruiz, Stokes & Watson, 2012, p. 7).

TRANSMEDIA JOURNALISM AND PARTICIPATORY CULTURE

TGBPS incorporates the urban space into the journalistic storytelling but, moreover, engages the public into a participatory experience for social change. This topic of "inspiration to action" (Moloney, 2011) could cause controversy in the sense since some may question whether the role of journalism is to lead the public to take meaningful action (Gambarato & Tárcia, 2017). However, contemporary journalism is currently moving toward user-generated content and concrete action. Moloney's proposition to pursue audience intervention in real actions for problem solving, reinforces audience engagement and content expansion, which are fundamental characteristics of transmedia journalism.

According to Carpentier and Dahlgren (2014), "participation captures a specific set of social practices that deal with the decision-making practices of actors" (p. 45). Participatory transmedia projects invite audiences to engage in a way that expresses their creativity, allowing them to influence the final result. Participation occurs when audiences can, with respect at least to a certain aspect of the project, influence on the set of components, such as the story and change the outcome of the project (Gambarato, 2013, p. 87).

TGBPS exemplifies grassroots circulation practices in which "a media text becomes material that drives active community discussion and debate at the intersection between popular culture and civic discourse—conversations that might lead to community activism or social change" (Jenkins et al., 2013, p. 168). However, what motivated people to participate and take action, and embrace TGBPS? Drawing on Bradham's (2013, p. 122) list of motivations, individuals, in this case, would like (1) to challenge themselves to solve a tough problem; (2) to contribute to a large project of common interest; (3) to share with others; (4) to collaborate on housing issues; (5) to protect house safety and household welfare; and (6) to make a difference in society. Nanì (2013) adds "publics participate and get engaged because of the rise of a new culture that enhances the co-creation of 'spreadable' texts" (p. 20). Among the series of models of engagement, such as the *dragonfly effect* by Aaker and Smith (2010), the equation proposed by Nanì (2013) seems to clearly describe the major focuses that should be involved in the development of transmedia projects for social change in the scope of participatory culture: "civic engagement = specific proposition + design to call attention + publics' empowerment" (p. 36).

Following the equation, *a specific proposition* refers to offering the public concrete goals. "Goals that are not specific are usually vague, risking, therefore, not being meaningful … and most likely unclear, ergo lacking engaging power" (ibid.). *Design to call attention* concerns the use of text and audiovisual features across multiple media platforms to attract people's attention to the project and, consequently, to the cause behind it. *Publics' empowerment* is about "the synergy between producers and publics in the co-production of meaningful texts" (ibid., p. 37). TGBPS has as its specific propositions the goal to report empty homes to the authorities and establish a low-cost loan fund to support empty homes owners, who want to refurbish their properties and put them back into use. The design of the Channel 4 project calls attention with a contemporary layout, the good technical quality of the audiovisual content, and the leadership of a well-known host. The publics' empowerment of TGBPS gives people the opportunity to demonstrate their support by reporting empty homes via mobile application and by signing an online petition to pressure the government to launch a low-cost loan fund in favor of the renovation of empty properties. Around 10,000 empty homes were reported, over 118,200 petition signatures were gathered within the project and, as a result, £17 million were allocated for the new low-cost loan fund in the UK (Channel 4, n.d.b).

METHODOLOGY OF ANALYSIS

The analytical model developed by Gambarato (2013) is the method chosen to examine the case study of TGBPS because this model contributes to a qualitative understanding of the design process of transmedia projects. The model was elaborated in 2013 as a tool to facilitate the analysis of transmedia projects in the fictional and nonfictional realms. Therefore, it is appropriate for transmedia journalism analysis. For other analyses applying this model see Gambarato (2014, 2016) and Gambarato and Medvedev (2015a, 2015b, 2017). The structure of the model involves ten specific topics that are guided by a series of practicable questions. A brief description is presented in Table 1.

THE GREAT BRITISH PROPERTY SCANDAL ANALYSIS

Premise and Purpose

TGBPS reports the housing-crisis affecting England, Scotland, and Wales. Moreover, this transmedia project proposes alternative solutions for the fact that there are two million families in need of a home and one million empty houses in the UK (Syndicut, n.d.). The aim of the journalistic project is to raise awareness about the housing issue and take action, through audience engagement, to change government policies in order to promote the revitalization of abandoned properties. The proposal is to achieve this goal by means of the establishment of a low-cost loan fund designed to support empty property owners, who are willing to refurbish their properties and put them back into the market.

According to the housing and homeless charity Shelter (n.d.), in England alone there are 1.7 million households enrolled in housing waiting lists, while living in temporary accommodations. TGBPS emphasizes that this situation is unacceptable when considering that more than a million homes currently lie empty in the UK (Owen, 2014).

Narrative

The storyline of TGBPS revolves around the fight against the senseless waste of a million empty houses, which are being preferably demolished instead of being renovated and put back into use. Architect George Clarke, together with non-governmental organizations such as Shelter (http://england.shelter.org.uk) and Empty Homes (http://www.emptyhomes.com), wrestled with the general unwillingness of government officials to create the low-cost loan fund and seriously lobbied for this alternative strategy to deal with the housing-crisis. After a year, they succeeded.

Clarke begins the Channel 4 journalistic TV series with interviews in which people are complaining about the housing issue. This is the starting point for presenting the facts and, consequently, raising awareness about the real extent of the problem in the UK. In his journey looking for supporters, Clarke portraits the struggles, failures, emotional experiences, and wins of TGBPS. On the one hand, the storytelling focuses on Clarke's crusade to change state policies and, on the other hand, showcases the real cases of families in need of a home. Negative capability, which leaves gaps into the story in order to generate tension and interest in continuing to follow the narrative, is specially used to maintain the suspense if the families are going to receive the help they need.

Table 1. Concise description of the transmedia project design analytical model

Topic	Practicable Questions
1. Premise and purpose State clearly what the project is about and why it exists.	What is the project about? Is it a fiction, nonfiction, or mixed project? What is its fundamental purpose? Is it to entertain, to teach, or to inform? Is it to market a product?
2. Narrative It is the structure that storyworlds evoke in the transmedia milieu.	What are the narrative elements of the project? What is the summary of its storyline? What is the time frame of the story? What are the strategies for expanding the narrative? Are negative capability and migratory cues included? Is it possible to identify intermedial texts in the story?
3. Worldbuilding A storyworld or story universe should be robust enough to support expansions, going beyond a single story.	When does the story occur? Which is the central world where the project is set? Is it a fictional world, the real world, or a mixture of both? How is it presented geographically? Is the storyworld large enough to support expansions?
4. Characters The features of the characters and how they appear across all the platforms should be consistent.	Who are the primary and secondary characters of the story? Does the project have any spinoffs? Can the storyworld be considered a primary character on its own? Can the audience be considered a character as well?
5. Extensions Transmedia storytelling involves multiple media in which the storyworld will unfold and be experienced.	How many extensions does the project have? Are the extensions adaptations or expansions of the narrative through various media? Is each extension canonical? Does it enrich the story? Are the extensions able to spread the content and provide the possibility to explore the narrative in-depth?
6. Media platforms and genres A transmedia project necessarily involves more than one medium and can also embrace more than one genre (science fiction, action, comedy, etc.).	What kind of media platforms (film, book, comics, games, etc.) are involved in the project? Which devices (computer, game console, tablet, mobile phone, etc.) are required by the project? How does each platform participate and contribute to the whole project? What are their functions in the project? Is each medium really relevant to the project? What is the rollout strategy to release the platforms? Which genres (action, adventure, detective, science fiction, fantasy, etc.) are present in the project?
7. Audience and market Scoping the audience is fundamental for a more appropriate delivery of the transmedia experience. The TS involves some level of audience engagement.	Who is the target audience of the project? What kind of "viewers" (real-time, reflective, and navigational) does the project attract? Do similar projects exist? Do they succeed in achieving their purpose? What is the project's business model? Was the project successful revenue-wise? Why?
8. Engagement All the dimensions of a transmedia project, at a lower or higher level, are drawn into the experience of people when engaging with the story.	Through what point of view (PoV) does the audience experience this world: first person, second person, third person, or a mixture of them? What role does the audience play in this project? What are the mechanisms of interaction in this project? Is there any participation involved in the project? Does the project work as a cultural attractor/activator? Is there UGC related to the story (parodies, recaps, mash-ups, fan communities, etc.)? Does the project offer the audience the possibility of immersion into the storyworld? Does the project offer the audience the possibility to take elements of the story and incorporate them into everyday life? Is there a system of rewards and penalties?
9. Structure The organization of a transmedia project, the arrangement of its constituent elements, and how they interrelate can offer concrete elements for analysis.	When did the transmediation begin? Is it a proactive or retroactive project? Is this project closer to a transmedia franchise, a portmanteau transmedia story, or a complex transmedia experience? Can each extension work as an independent entry point to the story? What are/were possible endpoints of the project? How is the project structured?
10. Aesthetics The visual and audio elements of a transmedia project should also contribute to the overall atmosphere and enhance the experience spread throughout multiple media platforms.	What kinds of visuals are used (animation, video, graphics, a mix) in the project? Is the overall appearance realistic or a fantasy environment? Is it possible to identify specific design styles in the project? How does audio work in this project? Are there ambient sounds (rain, wind, traffic noises, etc.), sound effects, music, and so forth?

The TV series is the introductory and inspirational part of the narrative. The storyworld is extended across social media networks (Facebook, Twitter, YouTube), website, mobile application, where the supportive audience can gather more information and take action, for instance, by signing a petition to pressure the government and reporting empty homes they are aware of, which is an activity developed across urban spaces. All the project's extensions have rather clear migratory cues, such as hyperlinks and direct speech of the host, motivating the audience to access the other extensions of TGBPS.

Worldbuilding

Geographically, TGBPS is located in the UK. The project's host itinerary includes a wide range of destinations, such as London, Manchester, Newcastle, and Leeds. The development of the project occurred between the end of 2011 and the end of 2012. Throughout the TV series episodes, references to war zones arise: From the portrait of depopulated and dilapidated areas in the cityscape to the frequent use of war metaphors such as "crusade." This scenario emphasizes the dramatic situation of the housing-crisis and contributes to motivate both politicians and citizens to take action and ignite social change. Since this problematic issue is wide spread in the UK, the world built by TGBPS is robust and rich enough to be unfolded across multiple media platforms in a transmedial way.

Characters

The protagonist of TGBPS is its creator, George Clarke. Clarke is a British architect, television presenter, lecturer, and writer, who hosts the project. After the successful achievements of TGBPS, he became Independent Empty Home Advisor to the government. As the main "hero" of the story, Clarke confronts a series of antagonists, such as local council's representatives, politicians, and red tape, who represent obstacles in his journey. However, Clarke is not alone. He counts on the support of celebrities such as the popular singer Will Young and the British designer Kevin McCloud, for instance, who help to call attention to the transmedia project. Moreover, Clarke is supported by an "army of online heroes" (Channel 4, n.d.a): ordinary citizens who experience the urban spaces and report empty homes and sign the petition to pressure the government to act to solve the housing-crisis. The audience, in this case, has an effective role in building the narrative within the urban fabric and specially in helping the project to achieve its main goal of changing policies and implementing the low-cost loan fund for the refurbishment of empty houses. They write their own chapter in the history of British housing. Notwithstanding, there are as well numerous secondary characters, such as the families in need of a home and voluntaries who help them to accomplish their objective.

Extensions

TGBPS has multiple extensions throughout different media platforms. Distinctive and valuable installments of content are distributed to provide the audience with the opportunity to explore the narrative in-depth and change government policy. The extensions are presented as following (see Table 2):

In addition to the TV series (two seasons, three episodes in total), which is the mothership of the project, Channel 4 broadcasted simultaneously two other TV programs integrated into TGBPS storyworld: *Phil's Empty Homes Giveaway* and *Kevin's Grand Design*. The single episode of *Phil's Empty Homes Giveaway*, presented by journalist Phil Spencer, was totally dedicated to the homeless issue. The

Table 2. The Great British Property Scandal extensions

Extension	Media Platform	Date of Launch	Commentary
The Great British Property Scandal TV series season 1	Television Channel 4	December 5, 2011 December 6, 2011	2 episodes
The Great British Property Scandal: Every Empty Counts TV series season 2	Television Channel 4	November 7, 2012	1 episode
Phil's Empty Homes Giveaway	Television Channel 4	December 7, 2011	1 episode
Kevin's Grand Design	Television Channel 4	December 8, 2011 December 15, 2011	2 episodes
The Great British Property Scandal website	Internet http://www.channel4.com/programmes/the-great-british-property-scandal	December, 2011	The petition was available in the website
Facebook page	Internet [Social Media] https://www.facebook.com/propertyscandal		Not available anymore
Twitter account	Internet [Social Media] @emptyhomes *#propertyscandal* #emptyhomes	October, 2011	9,691 followers 2,263 tweets
YouTube Channel 4	Internet [Social Media] https://youtu.be/N3OPfTlEEsw	November, 2011	TV series trailer has 199,667 views
Empty Homes Spotter iOS mobile application	Mobile	December, 2011	Free app 10,000 empty homes reported

two episodes of *Kevin's Grand Design*, presented by designer Kevin McCloud, discussed the building of affordable and sustainable homes.

The website serves as a hub to redirect the audience to the other extensions and, above all, is the platform for the online petition. Facebook and Twitter accounts promote the project and become an important source of information about other initiatives related to the housing-crisis, such as the ones offered by organizations like Shelter and Empty Homes. The YouTube account spread, for instance, the trailer of the project that went viral and helped to call people's attention to the project and to the housing-crisis. The iOS mobile application Empty Homes Spotter enable the audience, while experiencing the city, to make photos of empty properties and report them to the authorities. Overall, the set of extensions contribute to expand the content and, considering the general success of TGBPS, all of them consolidate the effectiveness of the project.

Media Platforms and Genres

A transmedia project is characterized by the expansion of content across diverse media platforms, fostering audience engagement. Each medium shapes the audience experience based on its own inherent characteristics. TGBPS combine television, Internet (website and social media networks) and mobile media. The devices necessary to access all the nuances of the project are a TV set, a computer or tablet, and a smartphone. In this case, one restriction of the project is related to the fact that the mobile application *Empty Homes Spotters*, a key extension within TGBPS, was available exclusively for iOS mobile operating system devices (iPhone, iPad, and iPod Touch). *Empty Homes Spotters* was considered among the best iPhones applications (Skinner, 2012) and, most importantly, enabled 10,000 homes to be reported via the app (The Project Factory, n.d.).

The Empty Homes Spotter app gave them the tools to make an impact. Using their smartphones, viewers could upload basic details about empty properties they'd spotted in their community, also supplying a photo with the app submitting these details automatically to the Empty Homes Officer responsible, using GPS to identify the correct local council. (ibid.)

Documentary/journalism is the predominant genre throughout all media platforms of the project, incorporating user-generated content. The diversity of TGBPS media platforms has an impact on attracting different audiences, for instance, a less active and mobile group of people mainly interested in TV broadcasting and a more active portion of the audience ready to not only access information about the project online but to get engaged in the participatory opportunities TGBPS offers.

Audience and Market

The primary target audience comprehends the residents of the areas covered by the project: England, Wales, and Scotland. They could be citizens directly affected by the housing-crisis or conscious sympathizers of this very important cause. Channel 4 has an international penetration; therefore, a larger audience contingent could be reached abroad as well. TGBPS engages different types of viewers, comprising real-time and navigational ones. According to Murray (1997), stories will have to work for two or three kinds of viewers in parallel. The real-time viewers are the ones who enjoy each single episode and the navigational viewers appreciate the connections between different installments of the story and the multiple arrangements of content (Murray, 1997, p. 257; Jenkins, 2006, p. 119). The navigational viewers are most likely the ones who effectively participated into the project and took action towards policy and social change.

Channel 4 already had previous experience with transmedia projects dedicated to policy and social change. In 2010, the public service broadcaster initiated *Fish Fight*, a transmedia project designed to "draw the public's attention to the reckless discarding of caught fish because of the quota system intended to conserve fish stocks in the domain of the European Union (EU)" and, consequently, to "pressure the authorities to change the EU Common Fisheries Policy" (Gambarato & Medvedev, 2015b, p. 43). TGBPS, produced by a public service broadcaster, was not planned for profit. All the platforms involved in the storytelling are offered totally free of charge, which contribute to the spreadability of the content and, consequently, massive response from audiences.

Engagement

The opportunities of audience engagement offered by TGBPS are key for the successful achievements of the project. Besides interaction with other members of the audience and the producers, TGBPS presents participatory contexts in which audiences could actively be part of the story and, moreover, influence on the results of the project. The audience is encouraged to participate by: (1) signing the petition on the website, (2) reporting empty homes they are aware of via the mobile application, and (3) being a volunteer able to help with the renovations needed to put back into use empty properties. During the first season, the emphasis relied on the petition and the reporting. More than 10,000 homes were reported and the greatest *Empty Home Spotter* of them all was John Fraser, who lives in Hartlepool, UK, and alone reported 612 homes (The Project Factory, n.d.). The mobile app allows and incorporates in the storyworld user-generated content. The audience could easily take pictures of the properties they want to report and the GPS (Global Positioning System) built into the app facilitates the precise identification of the location and automatically submits the details to the Empty Homes Officer of the correct local council (ibid.). In the second season, people were inspired to be immersed into the story and get physically involved to help rebuilding and restoring empty properties.

The audience experience the story in second-person, when they are directly invited to get involved in the project and in third-person, when the audience follows Clarke's narrative. Some of the "online heroes" can be seen experiencing the story in first-person, when presenting themselves in a series of videos available online (see Channel 4, n.d.a).

Structure

TGBPS was designed since the beginning to be transmediatic. "Pro-active transmedia projects are considered up front, full of tie-ins planned from the beginning" (Gambarato, 2013, p. 87). Audiences have access to independent entry points into the story universe. TGBPS is structurally organized with the TV series taking center stage and having two other TV programs being aired simultaneously on Channel 4. Gravitating around the television, there are the Internet extensions (with extra content and the petition) and the mobile application (directly related to the urban space with the reporting of empty homes). Although most of the content related to TGBPS can still be accessed online, the project ended with the second season of the TV series in 2012, which portrayed the achievements of the process of pressuring the government and raising public awareness about the senseless waste of empty properties.

Aesthetics

The main visuals presented by TGBPS are video (for TV and Internet), Web and mobile application design. The design elements are relatively simple, with emphasis on the typical black & yellow safety stripe, characterizing the hazards that could surround depopulated and dilapidated properties as well as under construction sites. This kind of tape is a symbol of risk and work in progress, a warning to not cross the line. The project's message is clearly communicated: There are several empty houses around and the community should force the government agenda to refurbish these places. The visual communication is quite straightforward and the eye-catching contrast between black and yellow corroborates for the clearness of the message.

The TV and Internet videos take advantage of animated texts that pop up in the middle of the screen with facts and figures about the housing-crisis, highlighting and reinforcing the gravity of the problem in the UK. The soundtrack of the project is dynamic and dramatic, presenting rhythmic elements such as basic pop beats to create an intriguing atmosphere.

RESEARCH FINDINGS AND FINAL REMARKS

The achievements of TGBPS demonstrate that the project connected to the community and the cityscape and was able to inspire audiences to take action regarding the deep-rooted housing issue in the UK.

According to Channel 4 (n.d.b), TGBPS succeeded in the following ways: (1) over 118,200 petition signatures (100,000 within a week of launching TGBPS), (2) 10,000 empty homes were reported, (3) £17 million allocated for the new low-cost loan fund in the UK, and (4) George Clarke was appointed Independent Empty Home Advisor to the Government.

The traditional role of producers and consumers was blurred and the *prosumers* (Toffler, 1980) effectively shaped the spatial story and influenced on the project's outcomes. Organized via social media networks, prosumers followed the flow of information across multiple media platforms and contributed generating content, sharing the experience, supporting the cause and, ultimately, promoting social change, especially with the government approval for the low-cost loan funds.

TGBPS's transformative potential increased with the participatory nature of the project and the transmedia approach empowered audiences with concrete tools for taking action and fostering social change. Transmedia journalism is inserted into the media convergence process involving society in fluid, participative environments. TGBPS is a relevant example of Bauman's (2000) liquid society, incorporating mobile technologies into everyday life processes with the potential for enhanced localness, customization, and mobility within the urban fabric.

Despite all the initiatives connected to TGBPS, the endemic housing-crisis in the UK is far from a resolution. Another core dimension of the problem is the fact that "by some measures British property is now the most expensive in the world, save in Monaco" (The Economist, 2015). The highlight of the 2015 New Ideas for Housing Competition in London is floating homes as a sustainable alternative to the housing shortage (Dowdy, 2015). Other alternative currently being discussed in the UK is the fact that, for instance, "more than 2.5m homes could be released on to the property market if older owners were given better incentives and information on downsizing, the Royal Institution of Chartered Surveyors (Rics) has claimed" (Osborne, 2015). These homes "could be released if homeowners received greater support to move into specialist retirement or smaller properties" (ibid.). However, this is a controversial move because there is an especially strong emotional dimension to people's homes, as emphasized by Bachelard (1997). Rics is another organization fighting for the government to be more effective in bringing empty properties back into use, suggesting that the local authorities should make available the details of their empty houses stock and publish a measurable timeline for getting them into the market (Osborne, 2015).

In a nut shell, TGBPS is a genuine example of transmedia storytelling applied to journalism, aiming at promoting social good. Anita Ondine, creative director of Transmedia Next (transmedia production and training company in London), discusses the overall pertinence of transmedia storytelling:

Will we still be talking about transmedia a few years from now? Well, maybe the word itself will go away, but we certainly will be doing transmedia. To me, I like to think about it sort of in the way that we used to talk about e-commerce a few years ago, when we were referring to buy books or booking flights online. Now, that is just how we do business, it is how we get stuff done. In the same way, we call it transmedia now but in a few years from now, it is just the way we will be telling stories. (Ondine, 2012)

Transmedia storytelling will be simply the way to tell stories, including news stories. TGBPS already take advantage of transmedia features and strategies to tell a compelling story within urban spaces able to inform the public and motivate audience engagement for social change.

REFERENCES

Aaker, J., & Smith, A. (2010). *The dragonfly effect: Quick, effective, and powerful ways to use social media to drive social change*. San Francisco, CA: Jossey-Bass.

Alzamora, G., & Tárcia, L. (2012). Convergence and transmedia: Semantic galaxies and emergent narratives in journalism. *Brazilian Journalism Research*, *8*, 22–34.

Anderson, R., Dardenne, R., & Killenberg, G. (1994). *The conversation of journalism: Communication, community, and news*. Westport, CT: Praeger.

Bachelard, G. (1997). *The poetics of space*. Boston, MA: Beacon Press.

Bauman, Z. (2000). *Liquid modernity*. Cambridge, UK: Polity Press.

Bernardo, N. (2014). *Transmedia 2.0 – How to create an entertainment brand using a transmedial approach to storytelling* [Kindle version]. Lisbon, Portugal: BeActive Books.

Bradham, D. (2013). Crowdsourcing: A model for leveraging online communities. In A. Delwiche & J. Henderson (Eds.), *The participatory culture handbook* (pp. 120–129). New York, NY: Routledge.

Calvino, I. (1974). *Invisible cities*. New York, NY: Harcourt Brace & Company.

Carpentier, N., & Dahlgren, P. (2014). The social relevance of participatory theory. In G. Patriarche, H. Bilandzic, N. Carpentier, C. Ponte, K. C. Schrøder, & F. Zeller (Eds.), *Building bridges: Pathways to a greater societal significance for audience research* (pp. 37–52). Brussels, Belgium: COST Action ISO906.

Channel 4. (n.d.a). *The Great British Property Scandal*. Retrieved from http://www.channel4.com/programmes/the-great-british-property-scandal/videos

Channel 4. (n.d.b). *Campaign results*. Retrieved from http://www.channel4.com/programmes/the-great-british-property-scandal/articles/all/campaign-results

Collie, N. (2013). Walking in the city: Urban space, stories, and gender. *Gender Forum: An Internet Platform for Gender and Women's Studies*, *42*, 1–5.

Cooper, M. (2002). Narrative spaces. *Screen*, *43*(2), 139–157. doi:10.1093/screen/43.2.139

De Certeau, M. (1984). *The practices of everyday life*. Berkeley, CA: University of California Press.

Deuze, M. (2008). The changing context of news work: Liquid journalism and monitorial citizenship. *International Journal of Communication*, *2*, 848–865.

Dowdy, C. (2015, October 14). A new NLA project proposes solutions for London's housing problems. *Wallpaper*. Retrieved from http://www.wallpaper.com/architecture/a-new-nla-project-proposes-solutions-for-londons-housing-problems#md2tCYfCPqVcmmw0.99

Gambarato, R. R. (2013). Transmedia project design: Theoretical and analytical considerations. *Baltic Screen Media Review*, *1*, 80–100.

Gambarato, R. R. (2014). Transmedia storytelling in analysis: The case of Final Punishment. *Journal of Print and Media Technology Research*, *3*(2), 95–106.

Gambarato, R. R. (2016). The Sochi Project: Slow journalism within transmedia space. *Digital Journalism*, *4*(4), 445–461. doi:10.1080/21670811.2015.1096746

Gambarato, R. R., & Medvedev, S. (2015a). Grassroots political campaign in Russia: Alexei Navalny and transmedia strategies for democratic development. In J. Svensson & V. Kumar (Eds.), *Promoting social change and democracy through information technology* (pp. 165–192). Hershey, PA: IGI Global. doi:10.4018/978-1-4666-8502-4.ch008

Gambarato, R. R., & Medvedev, S. (2015b). Fish Fight: Transmedia storytelling strategies for food policy change. *International Journal of E-Politics*, *6*(3), 43–59. doi:10.4018/IJEP.2015070104

Gambarato, R. R., & Medvedev, S. (2017). Transmedia storytelling impact on government policy change. In Y. Ibrahim (Ed.), *Politics, protest, and empowerment in digital spaces* (pp. 31–51). Hershey, PA: IGI Global. doi:10.4018/978-1-5225-1862-4.ch003

Gambarato, R. R., & Tárcia, L. (2017). Transmedia strategies in journalism. An analytical model for the news coverage of planned events. *Journalism Studies*, *18*(11), 1381–1399. doi:10.1080/1461670X.2015.1127769

Jenkins, H. (2002). Game design as narrative architecture. *MIT*. Retrieved from http://web.mit.edu/21fms/People/henry3/games&narrative.html

Jenkins, H. (2006). *Convergence culture: Where old and new media collide*. New York, NY: New York University Press.

Jenkins, H., Ford, S., & Green, J. (2013). *Spreadable media: Creating value and meaning in a networked culture*. New York, NY: New York University Press.

Kim, J., & Hong, J. (2013). Analysis of trans-media storytelling strategies. *International Journal of Multimedia and Ubiquitous Engineering*, *8*(3), 1–10.

Lévy, P. (1997). *Collective intelligence: Mankind's emerging world in cyberspace*. Cambridge, MA: Perseus Books.

Moloney, K. T. (2011). *Porting transmedia storytelling to journalism* (Unpublished master's thesis). University of Denver, Denver, CO.

Murray, J. (1997). *Hamlet on the holodeck: The future of narrative in cyberspace*. Cambridge, MA: MIT Press.

Nanì, A. (2013). *Crossmedia practices for the enhancement of civic engagement* (Unpublished master's thesis). Tallinn University Baltic Film and Media School, Tallinn, Estonia.

Ondine, A. (2012, September 3). *What is transmedia?* [Video file]. Retrieved from https://vimeo.com/48763753

Osborne, H. (2015, September 23). Downsizing could free up to 2.5m home. *The Guardian*. Retrieved from http://www.theguardian.com/money/2015/sep/23/downsizing-could-free-up-25m-homes?CMP=fb_gu

Owen, J. (2014, May 29). More than a million homes currently lie empty in Britain. *Independent*. Retrieved from http://www.independent.co.uk/news/uk/politics/more-than-a-million-homes-currently-lie-empty-in-britain-9456263.html

Pratten, R. (2015). *Getting Started in Transmedia Storytelling: A Practical Guide for Beginners* (2nd ed.). London: CreateSpace.

Ruiz, S., Stokes, B., & Watson, J. (2012). Mobile and Locative Games in the "Civic Tripod:" Activism, Art and Learning. *International Journal of Learning and Media*, *3*(3). doi:10.1162/IJLM_a_00078

Shelter. (n.d.). *The shortage of affordable homes*. Retrieved from http://england.shelter.org.uk/campaigns/why_we_campaign/the_housing_crisis

Skinner, C. (2012, January 10). Best iPhone app: Five property-related apps. *PC Advisor*. Retrieved from http://www.pcadvisor.co.uk/feature/software/best-iphone-apps-five-property-related-apps-3328918/

Syndicut. (n.d.). *The Great British Property Scandal*. Retrieved from http://www.syndicut.com/Posts/Channel-4/Great-British-Property-Scandal

The Economist. (2015, September 26). *Through the Roof*. Retrieved from http://www.economist.com/news/britain/21667973-britain-has-one-booming-market-could-do-crash-through-roof

The Project Factory. (n.d.). *The Great British Property Scandal*. Retrieved from http://www.theproject-factory.com/great-british-property-scandal

Toffler, A. (1980). *The third wave*. London, UK: Pan Books.

KEY TERMS AND DEFINITIONS

Cityscape: The urban equivalent of a landscape.

Crusade: A vigorous campaign for political, social, or religious change.

Customization: The process of modifying or creating according to individual or personal specifications or preferences.

Grassroot Movement: A bottom-up structure to foster community participation in politics.

Liquid Society: The reality in which society considers highly what is transitory rather than permanent, the immediate rather than long term.

Migratory Cues: Signals towards another medium—the means through which multiple narrative paths are marked by authors and located by users.

Mise-En-Scène: The settings or surroundings of an event.

Chapter 10
Future of Food:
Transmedia Strategies of National Geographic

Alexander Godulla
University of Leipzig, Germany

Cornelia Wolf
University of Leipzig, Germany

ABSTRACT

The National Geographic Society (NGS) has always sought to incorporate new ways of media production into its working routine, thus defining standards of journalism both in technical and narrative terms. As a logical result, the NGS also relies on cross media strategies, focusing on transmedia storytelling in order to connect its audience. The "Future of Food" project is one of the largest transmedia projects in journalism. The chapter first outlines the concept of transmedia storytelling and discusses 10 qualities in the context of journalism. Secondly, the authors systematically discuss the case study "Future of Food" by applying the transmedia qualities to the project. This provides insights into the modes and combinations of story elements and allows to draw attention to challenges and opportunities for researchers, producers, and users.

INTRODUCTION

The National Geographic Society (NGS) is regarded as one of the most influential organizations for the development of international photojournalism (Godulla & Wolf, 2016). In the past decades, the foundation has always sought to incorporate new ways of media production into its working routine, thus defining standards of journalism both in technical and narrative terms. According to its own mission statement, the global nonprofit membership organization is driven "by a passionate belief in the power of science, exploration and storytelling" (National Geographic Society, 2016). However, the

DOI: 10.4018/978-1-5225-3781-6.ch010

days of doorstep newspaper delivery, listening to a live radio show or being part of a national audience watching the debut of a hit TV show are mostly over. Instead, today's audiences enjoy reaching for content when, where and how they want it. (Clendenin & Stuckey, 2016)

Therefore, for the NGS extending its media brand to the digital world is a wise move as "we have entered an era of media convergence that makes the flow of content across multiple media channels almost inevitable" (Jenkins, 2013). Furthermore, the relevance of online and mobile platforms to access media brands for both news journalism and longform journalism has increased (Wolf & Godulla, 2016; Wolf & Schnauber, 2015).

As a logical result, the NGS also relies on strategies of transmedia storytelling in order to connect its audience "of more than 700 million people a month through its media platforms, products, events and experiences" (National Geographic Society, 2016).

The concept of transmedia storytelling has been applied in various contexts to date, including its integration into journalism (Gambarato & Tárcia, 2017). In this context, transmedia journalism is defined as projects that allow "a story to unfold across multiple media—analog, digital and even brick-and-mortar—in an expansive rather than repetitive way" (Moloney, 2014).

In 2014, the NGS launched its most ambitious transmedia project so far. "The Future of Food" was launched in May 2014, involving 823 stories and 472 social media posts on 41 different digital and analog channels, including three magazines, a cable TV series, museum exhibits and organized travel experiences (Clendenin & Stuckey, 2016). True to the motto "The new food revolution. Serving more than 7 billion every day" (National Geographic Society, 2014b), National Geographic reached out to its audience, asking people to collaborate by discussing global food trends or co-create by sending pictures of places connected with the production and consumption of food, calling these places "Foodscapes." By creating several cover stories, National Geographic Magazine attracted enormous attention to the topic, accompanying the discussion on social media using the hashtag #FutureOfFood. Being able to use a huge variety of media platforms, the foundation is able to react to an ongoing trend. Following Pratten (2015), it is important to integrate communications and customer feedback mechanisms

into the storytelling and experience design because the audience avoids and mistrusts advertising. By adopting this entertainment-marketing duality, the audience will advocate on your behalf and share content because it meets their personal and social needs, not because you have bribed them with promised rewards. (Pratten, 2015, p. 5)

Therefore, the authors consider this project to be an ideal example of transmedia storytelling in journalism. The paper will first outline the concept of transmedia storytelling and draw on ten qualities in the context of journalism. Based on Jenkins (2009a, 2009b) and Moloney (2015) this chapter focuses on Spreadability, Drillability, Immersion, Extractability, Worldbuilding, Seriality, Subjectivity, Continuity, Multiplicity, and Performance. Secondly, the authors will systematically discuss the case study "Future of Food" to provide insights into the modes and combinations of story elements and to draw attention to challenges and opportunities of transmedia storytelling in journalism for researchers, producers, and users.

TRANSMEDIA STORYTELLING IN JOURNALISM

Due to the long period of parallel existence of different media such as newspapers, magazines, radio, and television, one could argue that "journalism itself was born transmediatic" (Gambarato & Tárcia, 2017, p. 1382). Even user interaction and participation are not a new phenomenon created by Internet media, considering for instance phone calls to television shows and letters to the newsrooms. Due to the lack of a congruent usage of the term "transmedia storytelling" in journalism both on a practical level and in the research literature, this section begins by clarifying different terms like cross media, transmedia, digital, and multimedia storytelling.

After elaborating on a clear hierarchy and structure of these four different phenomena, attention is drawn to the fundamental qualities of transmedia storytelling. Following Jenkins (2009a, 2009b) and Moloney (2015), these qualities allow to refer to a set of categories which can be applied to journalism and later used to systematically analyze the "Future of Food" case study. Furthermore, this chapter also focuses on a core element of transmedia storytelling: Audience participation. In recent times, there has been much discussion about user participation under the heading of catchwords such as open journalism and co-creation. This marks a fundamental turning away from closed production processes in journalism where editorial offices controlled all parts of a story toward a more open approach that allows users to get involved in the media product itself by creating and contributing parts of the storyworld themselves.

Defining Transmedia Storytelling

Considering transmedia storytelling in general as well as in journalism in particular, there is a large variety of definitions and terms which are actually not identical. For example, in journalism, cross media storytelling, transmedia storytelling, digital storytelling, and multimedia storytelling are often used synonymously. However, some authors already claimed differences and discussed them. These differences will be referred to in the following section.

From the authors' perspective, cross media storytelling describes different editorial strategies. One of these can be transmedia storytelling. While both terms can—but do not necessarily have to—relate to digital media, multimedia storytelling solely exists as part of digital storytelling. The latter term, however, refers to an established narrative principle which is transferred to Internet media: To tell stories (see Figure 1).

In this paper, cross media storytelling is considered to be the widest term. Since the adoption of Internet media as a new means to publish journalistic content, there has been an inflationary usage of "cross media" (Wolf, 2014, p. 105). Moreover, it can be observed that different disciplines such as media management, advertising, strategic communication, and journalism all seem to have a different understanding of the term and its characteristics (Vogelsberg, 2006). As a minimal consensus, many authors agree that cross media refers to a combination of different institutionalized media platforms (e.g. Erdal, 2011; Gambarato, 2016).

Focusing on journalism, these media sets will most of the time focus on print media (book, newspaper, magazine), broadcasting media (radio and television), as well as online and mobile media (websites, apps, social networks). Nevertheless, depending on the diversification of the media organization, there might be other media integrated as well (Godulla & Wolf, 2017, p. 47). Different authors also agree on the fact that cross media strategies in general are implemented to increase the media company's (potential) audience (Gambarato & Tárcia, 2017, p. 1384; Moloney, 2015, p. 39; Wenzlaff, 2013).

Figure 1. Forms of cross media storytelling

In order to maintain a central position in this extended media network encompassing internet platforms, and to transform the tensions between old and new media, between payment markets and free product markets and between producers and users, the main solution chosen by the old media companies has been to deliver content across media platforms. (Bechmann, 2012, p. 889)

Therefore, since the rise of Internet media as a core part of journalism business, these cross media strategies are of constant interest in journalism research. However, different levels of cross media strategies must be considered. Firstly, a diversification on the organizational level, focusing on the media brand, which publishes for different markets. Secondly, a diversification on the content level which includes different strategies of cross media storytelling (Godulla & Wolf, 2017, p. 47; Panis, van den Bulck, Verschraegen, van der Burg, & Paulussen, 2014; Westlund, 2011).

The former is applied, if a television program and a printed magazine are published under the same media brand, but there is no exchange of ideas and content nor any relevant linking among the different media formats. Hence, this can also be described as a strategy of autonomy (e.g. Brüggemann, 2002). Furthermore, existing research also indicates that many media organizations rely on a strategy of repurposing content for different media that belong to their brand family. This allows synergies on the production level (e.g. Erdal, 2009; Quandt, 2008). Another possible cross media strategy focuses on references linking different media platforms. This strategy offers a clear added value for the users because it allows them to receive complementary content by shifting from one media platform to another (e.g. Brüggemann, 2002; Grüner, Kretschmer, & Täubig, 2010). However, if the reason for referring to other media platforms owned by the same media organizations is simply used to advertise for other media outlets, this should correctly be addressed as cross (media) promotion (Panis et al., 2014; Zacher, 2010).

Following this line of argument, online and mobile media may be part of cross media storytelling, but they do not necessarily have to be included. A cross media strategy on the content level might as well only link a printed newspaper and a television magazine produced by the same media brand. However, it has been the institutionalization of Internet journalism which has led to fundamental changes in editorial organization and acquired professional competencies: Newsdesk and newsroom models and convergent editorial offices producing for several media platforms have become widespread in many countries (Avilés, Meier, Kaltenbrunner, Carvajal, & Kraus, 2009; Wolf, 2010, 2014; Zhang, 2012).

Besides the two forms of cross media storytelling mentioned earlier, repurposing content and referring to other platforms, the authors suggest considering transmedia storytelling as a third strategy. The connection of platforms and content in this case reaches far beyond the two other strategies, because the different platforms are all used to contribute to the development of the story. Hence, transmedia storytelling is one possible outcome of cross media strategies (Gambarato, 2013). It can be described by three basic characteristics which are: The usage of multiple media platforms, content expansion, and audience engagement (Gambarato & Tárcia, 2017).

In the ideal form of transmedia storytelling, each medium does what it does best—so that a story might be introduced in a film, expanded through television, novels, and comics; its world might be explored through game play or experienced as an amusement park attraction. (Jenkins, 2008, pp. 95–96)

The main distinguishing element from repurposing content and referring to other platforms is that via transmedia storytelling all parts of the story published on different media platforms contribute to the development of a narrative "with new and relevant content in each and every media platform involved" (Serious Science, 2016). Hence, this draws on the second characteristic, that is content expansion (Gambarato & Tárcia, 2017, p. 1386). Like already known from fictional storytelling, a coherent storyworld is an important factor for transmedia stories in journalism as well:

A transmedia narrative tells altogether one big pervasive story, attracting audience engagement. It is not about offering the same content in different media platforms, but it is the worldbuilding experience, unfolding content and generating the possibilities for the story to evolve with new and pertinent content. (Gambarato, 2013, p. 82)

Although many media organizations have established cross media strategies, the majority still does not take advantage of the potentials of connecting all their media brands and platforms to create a coherent storyworld. As Moloney (2015) states, one reason might be seen in the established barrier between journalism and other media branches such as the film or advertising industries. Both journalists and journalism researchers consider their discipline as "work of a higher order" (Moloney, 2015, p. 63). This makes them blind to recognizing "how similar their economic models, story structure and position in the mediascape are to fellow media producers" (Moloney, 2015, p. 63). Considering this lack of openness in journalism, Moloney (2011) has published a miniature manifesto for transmedia journalism:

We journalists need to find the public across a very diverse mediascape rather than expecting them to come to us. The days of the captive journalism audience are over, and if we hope to serve our ideals of democracy, human rights, environment and positive social change, we need to find a broad public. To make our stories salient we need to engage the public in ways that fit those particular media. We lose an opportunity to reach new publics and engage them in different ways when we simply repurpose the same exact story for different (multi) media. Why not use those varying media and their individual advantages to tell different parts of very complex stories? And why not design a story to spread across media as a single, cohesive effort? (Moloney, 2011)

Because digital media today constitute an inherent part in the user's media repertoire (for news, see for example Newman, Fletcher, Levy, & Nielsen, 2016; Wolf & Schnauber, 2015, for longform journalism see Wolf & Godulla, 2016) many transmedia stories include digital and multimedia storytelling. Therefore, these two last terms connected with the phenomenon will be explained as well.

Following Alexander (2011), the authors define digital storytelling as "telling stories with digital technologies" (Alexander, 2011, p. 3). Hence, it is related to an ancient human tradition which can be observed from cave paintings to Aristoteles, and from the bible to fairies, up to contemporary literature (Godulla & Wolf, 2017, p. 51).

While other media industries like film, games or advertising primarily use storytelling to transport messages, journalism has always tried to avoid the impression of inventing stories, as opposed to reporting facts. Established journalistic genres only include certain narrative elements. However, due to the permanent access to information from manifold sources it has become even more challenging to create uniqueness and added value. Therefore, a kind of narrative turn can be observed in journalism toward transporting information in a more personal, emotional and immersive way (Godulla & Wolf, 2017, p. 51). This, however, has been made easier by combining different media elements in online and mobile media platforms. This makes multimedia storytelling a potential form of digital storytelling (see Figure 1): "[D]igital storytelling using multiple media can be seen as a potential but not a necessary element of added value to an online journalistic presentation [...] In other words: online journalism is not synonymous with multimedia journalism" (Deuze, 2003, p. 141).

Following Deuze, the authors can state that multimedia storytelling is often used as a synonym for digital storytelling although the latter does not necessarily have to include different media elements. On the other hand, the usage of different media elements alone does not turn the content into a multimedia story if the elements do not add relevant aspects to the story. The goal of multimedia storytelling is to build a complementary story by telling different aspects with different media elements. Digital longforms like The News York Times' Snow Fall can be seen as "a clear example of multimedia storytelling at an advanced state. They use text, photographs, video, maps and interaction to tell that story" (Moloney, 2014). In this case, multimedia storytelling is "the heart of its narrative structure" (Hiippala, 2016, p. 2).

Open Journalism and Co-Creation in Transmedia Storytelling

A further relevant component of transmedia storytelling is the role of the user: Interaction and participation can be seen as "crucial component[s]" (Gambarato, 2013, p. 87). If transmedia storytelling only allows users to select from different pre-produced options or to choose from various paths through the story the audience remains excluded from the process of storytelling (Gambarato, 2013, p. 87). This relates to the principle of closed journalism in a more general way which can be considered as having been the main mode of journalistic content production and publishing for many decades. From this perspective, the "conception and production of media content is a creative process that lies at the very heart of media companies" (Malmelin & Villi, 2015, p. 182).

Since several years, however, a new paradigm of open journalism and co-creation can be observed in different genres of journalism, for instance inviting users to report news, integrating crowdsourcing processes in investigative reporting or financing certain projects via crowdfunding (Aitamurto, 2015; Howe, 2008). Hence, for transmedia storytelling a second category of projects can be observed which "invites the audience to engage in a way that expresses their creativity in a unique, and surprising manner, allowing them to influence the final result" (Gambarato, 2013, p. 87). This process of co-creation is not limited to journalism:

Co-creation is based on a wider trend in society whereby consumers are no longer content with their traditional end-user role, and want to be involved in creating and developing products and services, and share their thoughts and experiences with other consumers. (Malmelin & Villi, 2015, p. 184)

Most of the time initiated by Internet media, the recipient changes his or her passive role into a prosuming one where he or she is actively involved in the development of the narrative (Malmelin & Villi, 2015, p. 184; Moloney, n. d.). This can be seen as an instrument that can be used to grow the user's involvement and his brand loyalty. As an unplanned but very successful example Star Wars can be cited: "Unintentionally, Lucasfilm set the stage for a highly successful transmedia franchise. Only reluctantly have they let some of the reins of storytelling pass out of their direct control" (Moloney, n. d.).

The main principle of this new form of co-creation in journalism can be summarized as "many stories rather than one, [...] expansively rather than redundantly" (Moloney, 2015, p. 39). Hence, the former closed universe of producing journalistic content has been opened for a participatory co-creation process where the audience is able to add aspects of the story themselves: "Participation occurs when the audience can, with respect at least to a certain aspect of the project, exert influence on the set of components, such as the story" (Gambarato, 2013, p. 87). This openness also means that media organizations are no longer the one and only authority that creates the story. The single narrator in this case is replaced by many narrators including both professionals and amateurs.

Qualities of Transmedia Storytelling

After defining the concept of transmedia storytelling, it is possible to focus on the question which qualities this specific form of cross media storytelling offers for journalism. Following other authors like Jenkins (2009a, 2009b) and Moloney (2015), transmedia storytelling can be categorized and described by specific qualities: Spreadability, Drillability, Immersion, Extractability, Worldbuilding, Seriality, Subjectivity, Continuity, Multiplicity, and Performance.

Although originally applied in fictional transmedia projects, these core principles developed by Jenkins and later referred to as qualities by himself offer a systematic tool to analyze transmedia storytelling projects in journalism. Due to the fact that all dimensions will later on be applied to the case study of the National Geographic Magazine, "Future of Food," each term will be discussed in this section.

Spreadability

As already explained, digital media are often an inherent part of and a main motor for transmedia stories. Social media are an important platform both to reach a broad audience in a short period of time and to create interaction and participation. Hence, the spreadability of a transmedia project means its quality to "move and evolve through fan interaction" (Moloney, 2015, p. 49). This includes the important characteristic of transmedia stories to "expand its economic value and cultural worth" (Jenkins, 2009a) through and during that process of viral success. Besides spreading the content through social media platforms owned by new Internet intermediaries, media organizations have the opportunity to create and include their own social hubs that offer users options for personalized interaction and participation.

Drillability

By creating a narrative complexity that is beyond stories published only on a single platform, transmedia stories offer the possibility to trigger a certain curiosity in its users and fans to dig deeper and deeper into the topic. In contrast to the short-term engagement for large numbers of people created by spreadable stories, drillable media content focuses on long-term engagement for people really interest in the story and its details (Jenkins, 2009a). While the first quality allows to enlarge the audience, drillability allows to keep the audience's attention in the long run. Journalism even benefits from the complexity of the real world in creating drillability: "In fictional storyworlds drillability must be created along with the core content. In dealing with real worlds, however, journalism has the advantage of only needing to engage the public's natural curiosity and enable its sleuthing" (Moloney, 2015, p. 50).

Immersion

Known especially from games or movies, immersion describes the state of letting fans dive deeply into the storyworld, forgetting about the real world around them. By integrating different media into a transmedia story journalism also has the chance to create immersive transmedia projects that allow first-person exploration of certain events or allow to see stories through different eyes (Jenkins, 2009b; Moloney, 2015, pp. 51–52). Moreover, with the rise of virtual reality (VR) technology and its adoption into journalistic storytelling, journalism has gathered a powerful immersive tool. Some media organizations like The Guardian have already experimented with VR. For example, the project "6x9: A virtual experience of solitary confinement" (The Guardian, 2016) allows the user to have a realistic experience of the life in a prison's cell using a 360° video application.

Extractability

Compared to immersion, extractability offers the audience an opposite direction of interaction with the transmedia story and its elements: "In immersion, then, the consumer enters into the world of the story, while in extractability, the fan takes aspects of the story away with them as resources they deploy in the spaces of their everyday life" (Jenkins, 2009b). These "aspects" of the story might appear in different forms, for instance physical as merchandising products referring to core characters, elements or content of the story. Moreover, they could also be philosophical or behavioral, which draws on normative aspects or facts included into the transmedia story that might have impact on the users' thoughts and actions (Moloney, 2015, p. 52).

Worldbuilding

Worldbuilding is a quality which has a long history in the genre of science fiction and fantasy where often many different stories are connected and intertwined. Applied to the nonfictional world, users might also become interested in getting to know other stories which are also taking place in the same setting. By creating interrelations of different parts of the story in a storyworld the complexity of certain aspects can be illustrated more efficiently. The challenge for worldbuilding in journalism will always be its limitation, as the real world already offers a highly complex storyworld that fictional storywriters first have to create. Therefore, in the context of journalism, transmedia storyworlds should still be masterable (Moloney, 2015, p. 53). Nevertheless, when "we enter a nonfiction storyworld our cognitive effort is certainly lower as we have our individual lives to help understand and contextualize the story" (Moloney, 2015, p. 53).

Seriality

A transmedia story which is published regularly in small parts can be mastered by its users although the whole storyworld might be huge. Although within transmedia storytelling the different parts of the story might be consumed in any order, journalistic transmedia stories also might follow a certain seriality (Jenkins, 2009b).

We can think of transmedia storytelling then as a hyperbolic version of the serial, where the chunks of meaningful and engaging story information have been dispersed not simply across multiple segments within the same medium, but rather across multiple media systems. (Jenkins, 2009b)

Subjectivity

Transferred to journalistic transmedia storytelling, subjectivity can be interpreted as the opportunity to get to know different perspectives and opinions on a complex subject. In doing so, each piece of the story might focus on another point of view (Jenkins, 2009b).

Journalists routinely bring the voices of both supporters and detractors into a story. However, in a transmedia storyworld these voices would more likely stand apart as singular stories alongside other reporting, offering personal viewpoints on a subject or issue. They provide an opportunity to express the complexity of views of the same world. (Moloney, 2015, p. 56)

Continuity

Well known from fictional stories, for fans of complex storyworlds continuity in every detail is very important to experience the transmedia story as a plausible and coherent combination of "the scattered bits" (Jenkins, 2009a). For journalism, this is always the case, if the transmedia story is based on real world facts. However, it might become difficult for the users to identify continuity if the transmedia project is presented in too many unconnected episodes that do not indicate a certain direction of the story.

Multiplicity

On the contrary, multiplicity offers the same aspects of a story from different perspectives with alternative outcomes. "Like its oppositional pair continuity, multiplicity is valuable if well organized and presented as an alternative to a clearly continuous storyworld" (Moloney, 2015, p. 51).

Performance

Performance refers to the possibility of "fans telling bits of the story" (Moloney, 2015, p. 56). Hence, this quality applies to the (new) realm of open journalism and user co-creation mentioned earlier where users may be actively encouraged by media organizations to directly contribute to the storyworld.

TRANSMEDIA STORYTELLING AT NATIONAL GEOGRAPHIC

National Geographic Society: From Foundations to Future of Food

The NGS is headquartered in Washington, D.C. (United States). It is among the 50 most influential non-profit organizations on the Internet (Top Nonprofits, 2017). Its work is focused on science and education alike, including topics such as natural science, geography, archeology, culture and history. According to its self-characterization, the NGS aims to gather knowledge on a scientific base, putting this information to good use for humanity: "The National Geographic Society is a global nonprofit organization committed to exploring and protecting our planet. We fund hundreds of research and conservation projects around the world each year and inspire new generations through our education initiatives and resources" (National Geographic Society, 2017b).

Today, the NGS is a joint venture with 21st Century Fox, reinvesting "27% of proceeds to help fund the conservation and education efforts of the National Geographic Society" (National Geographic Society, 2017b). Since 1896, periodical journalistic photographs have been regularly published in the National Geographic Magazine, the monthly publication has become one of the central publication bodies of international press photography (Godulla & Wolf, 2016). Many of the photos published in the flagship magazine with the iconic yellow portrait frame have won several awards and have gained global recognition (National Geographic Society, 1987, 2013a, 2013b). On that basis, the NGS has become an innovation leader in contemporary journalism. Thanks to its cross media diversification strategy, the NGS is linked to its line extensions, its books, its mobile applications, its websites, its own television stations (with different branches) and even its own museum. In scientific journalism, no other provider has such a major influence on the setting and design of topics.

The idea behind the transmedia project "Future of Food" is to use this unique position in order to include the audience into telling the complex story of modern production and consumption of food. Chris Johns, editor in chief of National Geographic Magazine, describes the core idea of the whole project: "Food, like water and air, is life. Starting this month and continuing through the end of the year, we will focus on food and the challenge of feeding the global population of nine billion projected by 2050" (Johns, 2014). A pending process of organizational restructuring created the necessary environment for a new transmedia philosophy:

It moved its editorial staff from compartmentalized offices to a new collaboration-encouraging open floor plan, welcomed a new chief executive officer and faced persistent struggles to maintain its prominence in a competitive industry that had already seen the loss of venerable publication titles. In the middle of all this, the NGS was actively rethinking how it tells stories. (Moloney, 2015, p. 59)

This process of "rapidly adopting home-grown transmedia techniques as a method to increase engagement in a complex mediascape" (Moloney, 2015, p. 59) laid the foundation for a storyworld of tremendous scale. It is not only one of the biggest projects in transmedia journalism ever, but also one of the best documented ones (Moloney, 2015).

Transmedia Qualities in the Context of Future of Food

Based on the transmedia qualities already discussed and defined, this chapter offers a systematic overview of their usage in the context of "Future of Food." Spreadability, Drillability, Immersion, Extractability, Worldbuilding, Seriality, Subjectivity, Continuity, Multiplicity, and Performance are connected to specific aspects of the project. Although there is no single core element for the story, this chapter repeatedly focuses on the NGS flagship magazine in this part of the discussion. This makes it possible for further research to relate to this still available material.

Spreadability

Fan interaction is a very important aspect for the success of "Future of Food." As Moloney (2015, p. 87) counted, social interactions on 26 enabled channels reached a total of around 1.7 million likes, nearly 100,000 shares and more than 6000 comments. Summed up, the average story was the trigger for a total of 1149 social interactions. Instead of giving away the lion's share of traffic to intermediaries like social networking sites, the NGS managed to place its own platforms at the heart of the project. Nearly half of all social interactions happened on their own news page (NEWS.nationalgeographic.com), directly followed by their nutrition centered website "The Plate" (THEPLATE.nationalgeographic.com), where another quarter came up. Claiming to serve "daily discussions on food," this platform sparked discussions on a variety of aspects. Instead of focusing the discussion on health aspects only, the journalists gave their audience the chance to interact on almost anything related to food. The NGS (2017a) explained "The Plate" to be "at the intersection of science, technology, history, culture and the environment" created in order to explore "the global relationship between what we eat and why." Even though more than a third of Americans under thirty used to consume news primarily through social networking sites (Pariser, 2011, p. 8) when "Future of Food" was created, the journalists chose to avoid especially Facebook when promoting their stories. According to Multimedia director Mike Schmidt, there was a strong preference for YouTube instead:

We need to go where the audience is, and YouTube is where the audience is. The traffic that we get on our site is great, but it is a small fraction of the traffic that we get from the exact same video asset on YouTube. (Moloney, 2015, p. 65, emphasis in original)

Facebook was considered by Schmidt to be a less attractive platform because of its asymmetric interpretation of media partnerships: "We can't monetize that, we can't get the metrics off of it, so, I'd rather just put it on *YouTube* where we can do those things… They're a terrible partner" (Moloney, 2015, p. 65, emphasis in original). As a direct result, the ten most shared stories related to the transmedia world of "Future of Food" appeared on NGS own platforms. Instead of focusing on engaging readers in distributing content through social networks, the foundation preferred to expand activity on its own webpages.

Drillability

Obviously, the NGS is in a unique position in the contemporary media landscape. There is an enormous variety of horizontal, integrated cross media places where content can be distributed, including magazines, websites, social media and TV channels, books and even museums. Therefore, the foundation is able to reach its audience almost everywhere. Although the storytelling was not focused on the flagship magazine with the famous yellow border, it could still be used as a kind of narrative backbone for the whole project. From 2014/05 to 2014/12, the journalists would use the flagship magazine in a strong cross media connection with the related tablet magazine app in order to place multifaceted stories of high complexity. These stories show the depth of nutrition related issues, inviting the audience to gather more information on the other platforms and to interact there. There was a big story in all eight issues, connected with a rather broad question. This question cannot be answered in a simple way, making it necessary and interesting for the audience to investigate certain details, related issues and the context of the stories.

NG 2014/05 (Foley, 2014): "A five step plan to feed the world. It doesn't have to be industrial farms versus small, organic ones. There's another way." Question: "Where will we find enough food for 9 billion?"

NG 2014/06 (Bourne, 2014a): "How to farm a better fish. The world now produces more farmed fish than beef–and that's just the beginning." Question: "Can the 'blue revolution' solve the world's food puzzle?"

NG 2014/07 (Bourne, 2014b): "The next breadbasket. Why big companies are grabbing up land on the planet's hungriest continent." Question: "Can Africa's fertile farmland feed the world?"

NG 2014/08 (McMillan, 2014): "The new face of hunger. Millions of working Americans don't know where their next meal is coming from." Question: "Why are people malnourished in the richest country on Earth?"

NG 2014/09 (Gibbons, 2014): "The evolution of diet. Some experts say modern humans should eat from a Stone Age menu. What's on it may surprise you." Question: "Could eating like our ancestors make us healthier?"

NG 2014/10 (Folger, 2014): "The next green revolution. Modern supercrops will be a big help. But agriculture can't be fixed by biotechnology alone." Question: "Science prevented the last food crisis. Can it save us again?"

NG 2014/11 (Kunzig, 2014): "Carnivore's dilemma. Unhealthy. Nutritious. Cruel. Delicious. Unsustainable. All-American. In the beef debate there are so many sides." Question: "Is America's appetite for meat bad for the planet?"

NG 2014/12 (Pope, 2014): "The joy of food. Food is more than survival. With it we make friends, court lovers, and count our blessings." Question: "What is it about eating that brings us closer?"

By giving the audience a reason to feel curiosity and activate its sleuthing instinct, the whole project inspires deeper drilling. Far beyond simple letters to the editor, the audience is given this opportunity not only in social interaction, but also in multimedia storytelling. On the periphery of the main stories discussed, especially the app contains selective content where the audience can choose to change the shape of data visualizations or access additional videos and animations not visible in the print product.

Immersion

At first sight, immersion does not seem to play a strong role in journalism. Its focus on the presentation of nonfictional information seems to contradict the idea of creating an autonomous world that pushes aside the daily life of the reader. In addition to the use of visual communication and its ability to reach the audience in a very direct and immediate way, the editorial staff decided to break the boundaries of print and online communication when choreographing this transmedia project. To do so, the position of a project manager was created to coordinate the 823 stories told in the context of "Future of Food." This position can be approximately compared to the position of a showrunner in modern quality TV, observing all the storylines and pulling the strings for the good of the project. Based on this coordination activity, unconventional aspects like a hackathon or an ice cream truck became part of the storyworld, making it possible to break into ordinary life in a very unspent way (Moloney, 2015, p. 67). NGS even seized the opportunity to open a food related exhibition at National Geographic Museum in Washington: "FOOD: Our Global Kitchen" invited the audience to "take a journey from farm to fork" and opened on World Food Day in 2014. According to the official press release, the program strived to activate a variety of cognitive and sensual experiences:

The National Geographic Museum will join the "farm-to-fork" process through an 18-foot-tall, hydroponic vertical growing system in the exhibition that will grow a variety of herbs to showcase sustainable food-growing techniques and agricultural biodiversity in increasingly urban habitats. Other highlights of "FOOD" include a life-size re-creation of a 16th-century Aztec marketplace, ingredient smelling stations, an interactive cooking table and a look at plates of food enjoyed by famous historical figures including Mahatma Gandhi, Jane Austen and Kublai Khan. (National Geographic Society, 2014a)

Another part of the exhibition included a test kitchen where professional cooks would prepare different kinds of food for the visitors. In order to spread awareness for the project even further, NGS also organized forums and lectures.

Extractability

Extractability is another quality that rarely occurs in contemporary journalism. Other than fictional stories, professional coverage of real life events does not depend on merchandising to gain credibility. Therefore, there has not been a focus in the NGS plans on becoming a player in the food industry to supply its audience with natural products related to stories. But there are other subtler aspects of extractability that have been transported through "Future of Food." Above all, there was a lot of information provided related to the preparation of food—something that can be implemented into the daily lifestyle of the audience. "As the NGS's project unfolds extractability reveals itself not only with that cake recipe, but also with clear sustainable food consumption and production practices" (Moloney, 2015, p. 52).

Worldbuilding

Surely, "Future of Food" was not created to build its own world, but to represent a true portrait of a certain part of reality. Apart from the aspects of journalistic qualities, the whole storyworld can be interpreted as an embodiment of the NGS mission statement, claiming to "believe in the power of science, exploration and storytelling to change the world" (National Geographic Society, 2017b). Therefore, the foundation's official self-characterization is especially true for this transmedia project:

Through the world's best scientists, photographers, journalists, and filmmakers, National Geographic captivates and entertains a global community through television channels, magazines, children's media, travel expeditions, books, maps, consumer products, location-based entertainment and experiences, and some of the most engaging digital and social media platforms in the world. (National Geographic Society, 2017b)

On this foundation, "Future of Food" created not a completely autonomous, but very consistent and prominent part of the NGS media activities. For example, the project gained a high recognition value by using recurring claims, layout designs and logos.

Seriality

"The analytical or investigative series is an old journalism form, with stories unfolding in chapters in newspapers, magazines, television and radio. This principle acknowledges the lengthened engagement provided by the serial, keeping a subject on the mind of the public longer" (Moloney, 2015, p. 55). This principle is also true to "Future of Food," where different media were used to continuously raise awareness for the issues covered. Other than in a storyworld that would consist of only one media channel, this project followed very different rhythms within its own time frame. While the flagship magazine would appear every month, especially social interactions on topics covered would follow a comparably swift change of information and opinions.

Subjectivity

This quality played a strong role for the whole project in one of the most classic ways known to journalism: By telling stories from different perspectives, a principle very popular in the flagship magazine, subjectivity was embodied in the biographies, viewpoints and actions of the persons involved. For example, the kick-off story "A five step plan to feed the world" (NG 2014/05) contained more than a dozen portraits of farmers (in that order) from Mali, Peru, The United States, Ethiopia, Ukraine, Bangladesh, Indonesia and The United Kingdom. Three issues later, "The new face of hunger" (NG 2014/08) gave glimpses into the daily life of US-citizens who cannot afford to eat on a regular or healthy basis. The app enriched these stories by showing videos of the daily struggle of these people. The final issue "The joy of food" (NG 2014/12) dealt with food rituals all over the world, portraying people during the preparation or consumption of food. By combining all these very individual situations, the flagship magazine made it possible to reflect on food and the results of its production as a global phenomenon.

Continuity

The term continuity is strongly linked to the idea of preserving the coherence and plausibility of a storyworld. In fictional storytelling, it is crucial to avoid the creation of inconsistent fictional events that destroy the logic of the whole cosmos. Certainly, this problem is very unlikely to occur as long as the journalists in charge stick to the facts. The presentation of different positions, for example in a sub story covering a controversial issue, is also not a contradiction to this principle, but a proof of journalistic diligence. Because of the sheer abundance of aspects covered, it is rather difficult to create continuity for the whole storyline of "Future of Food."

Multiplicity

Although the parts do not stand in disagreement, the ordinary recipient will not always be able to identify a dominating direction for the project. According to Multimedia director Mike Schmidt, this phenomenon is part of the strategy to relate to different audiences: "No one is going to see all of your content. And if they do, that's not so bad because the overlap is small. The people that read our magazine are not the same people that look at our *YouTube* channel. They're just not" (Moloney, 2015, p. 66). In this context, multiplicity may weaken the continuity of the whole project by blurring the visibility of the main storyline. In the case of "Future of Food," this problem is accepted in favor of the opportunity to stretch out for further audiences.

Performance

By promoting the hashtag #FutureOfFood, National Geographic offered audiences a variety of options to contribute their own bits to the whole story. The hashtag is usable in any kind of social network, making it almost impossible to predict every possible outcome of this creative process. A higher level of control was established by using the very popular user-contributed photo site "Your Shot" in the context of "Future of Food." Readers were asked to contribute food-related photographs, offering their personal approach as an inspiration to fellow recipients.

CONCLUSION

As a conclusion to his monograph dealing with "Future of Food," Moloney (2015, pp. 99–101) formulated questions, such as how the stories interconnect or how can these stories be conversations, that could serve as a starting point to build a transmedia project in journalism. These questions are valuable to anyone who strives to create a transmedia project. For practitioners, not only these though-provoking impulses are relevant, but also the project itself. Even though the borders of "Future of Food" are blurry sometimes and its direction not always clear, it is a relevant best practice example for transmedia journalism. But journalists are not the only professionals who can learn from reviewing this project. It is also relevant to scientists and lectures alike, showing contemporary problems in apparent resilient approaches to gathering and sharing knowledge. Apart from these occupational groups, the audience itself is also challenged to develop new strategies of media consumption leading to the greatest possible benefit. In order to give more food for thought for all of these groups, these statements shall be worked out now.

Media researchers should accept the fact that single method designs are not fit to grasp the complexity of an elaborated transmedia design. The reception of a project like "Future of Food" goes along with social interactions on different scales. Apart from liking, sharing and discussing content in the digital world, recipients talk face-to-face about the stories or are even inspired to take actions. On a small scale, they may simply decide to bake a banana cake. On a larger one, they may decide to completely change their lifestyle. Life plans affected cannot be grasped by simple content analyses or surveys. Instead, it is important to understand that transmedia journalism shares many qualities with concept art: Once the performance is over, the remnants cannot do the relationship between story and audience real justice. Scientists are well-advised to accompany projects like that in the making, because many aspects of transmedia stories are volatile and will not come back for further investigation. The remains of "Future of Food" have already started to disappear: Some links on webpages are broken, some comments have been deleted by users on social networks. Without the flanking measures on the digital channels, the stories of the flagship magazine do not stretch out to a living media environment any more. When trying to observe the production, reception and impact of a transmedia story, scientists should ideally prepare their instruments long before the real show starts to run.

The impact on media education is also enormous. Back in the days before cross media, the clear majority of journalists would more or less deal with one medium in his or her daily working routine. Cross media has changed that. Contemporary media companies expect journalists to be able to know at least the foundations of almost every medium. Transmedia journalism takes these expectations even further. Although journalism is based on facts instead of fiction, media lectures should reflect on the principles of fictional storytelling. When contemplating on "Future of Food," it becomes clear that—from time to time—modern journalism might even benefit from a basic knowledge in event management, making it possible to plan the appearance of a story-related ice cream truck or the promotion of a public lecture. The NGS invested not only resources, but also fantasy and imagination into this project. This does not point to a lack of interest in well investigated facts, but to a will to engage and activate the audience. By embracing this chance and following the example of "Future of Food," media education may open up new career prospects for their students, not only in the realm of money and safety, but also in terms like creativity and self-actualization.

Finally, it is important to mention the problem of media competence. Vast parts of the audience are still used to the idea of being part of the environment of journalism. Apart from commenting on social networking sites, there is not much to do. Transmedia journalism is radically changing that. "Future of Food" could not have worked without the active participation of the audience, making it possible to include user-generated content, such as the upload of photographs into media environments managed by professional journalists. It is vital for the active participation of the audience to understand and use these chances in order to expand them. Because of the vastness of this and other storyworlds, one must also understand that the complete reception of a whole story with all its subtleties could become impossible.

REFERENCES

Aitamurto, T. (2015). Crowdsourcing as a knowledge-search method in digital journalism. *Digital Journalism*, *4*(2), 280–297. doi:10.1080/21670811.2015.1034807

Alexander, B. (2011). *The new digital storytelling: Creating narratives with new media*. Santa Barbara, CA: Praeger.

Avilés, J. A. G., Meier, K., Kaltenbrunner, A., Carvajal, M., & Kraus, D. (2009). Newsroom integration in Austria, Spain and Germany: Models of media convergence. *Journalism Practice*, (3): 1–19.

Bechmann, A. (2012). Towards cross-platform value creation. *Information Communication and Society*, *15*(6), 888–908. doi:10.1080/1369118X.2012.680483

Bourne, J.K. (2014a). How to farm a better fish. The world now produces more farmed fish than beef–and that's just the beginning. *National Geographic Tablet Magazine, 225*(6).

Bourne, J.K. (2014b). The next breadbasket. Why big companies are grabbing up land on the planet's hungriest continent. *National Geographic Tablet Magazine, 226*(1).

Brüggemann, M. (2002). *The missing link: Crossmediale Vernetzung von Print und Online; Fallstudien führender Print-Medien in Deutschland und den USA* [The missing link: Cross media linking in print and online; Case studies of leading print media in Germany and the USA]. Munich, Germany: Fischer.

Clendenin, L., & Stuckey, D. (2016). *Transmedia journalism expands storytelling for deeper impact*. Retrieved from http://current.org/2016/10/transmedia-journalism-expands-storytelling-for-deeper-impact/

Deuze, M. (2003). The Web and its journalisms: Considering the consequences of different types of newsmedia online. *New Media & Society*, *5*(2), 203–230. doi:10.1177/1461444803005002004

Erdal, I. J. (2009). Repurposing of content in multi-platform news production. *Journalism Practice*, *3*(2), 178–195. doi:10.1080/17512780802681223

Erdal, I. J. (2011). Coming to terms with convergence journalism: Cross-media as a theoretical and analytical concept. *Convergence (London)*, *17*(2), 213–223. doi:10.1177/1354856510397109

Foley, J. (2014). A five step plan to feed the world. It doesn't have to be industrial farms versus small, organic ones. There's another way. *National Geographic Tablet Magazine, 225*(5).

Folger, T. (2014). The next green revolution. Modern supercrops will be a big help. But agriculture can't be fixed by biotechnology alone. *National Geographic Tablet Magazine, 226*(4).

Gambarato, R. R. (2013). Transmedia project design: Theoretical and analytical considerations. *Baltic Screen Media Review*, *1*, 80–100.

Gambarato, R. R. (2016). The Sochi Project: Slow journalism within transmedia space. *Digital Journalism*, *4*(4), 445–461. doi:10.1080/21670811.2015.1096746

Gambarato, R. R., & Tárcia, L. P. T. (2017). Transmedia strategies in journalism. An analytical model for the news coverage of planned events. *Journalism Studies*, *18*(11), 1381–1399. doi:10.1080/1461670X.2015.1127769

Gibbons, A. (2014). The evolution of diet. Some experts say modern humans should eat from a Stone Age menu. What's on it may surprise you. *National Geographic Tablet Magazine, 226*(3).

Godulla, A., & Wolf, C. (2016). Visuelle Grammatik im Fotojournalismus: Eine Untersuchung der Bildsprache von Pressefotos am Beispiel des National Geographic Magazins [Visual grammar in photojournalism: An examination of the imagery of press photos using the example of the National Geographic magazine]. In K. Arnold, T. Birkner, S. Geise, K. Lobinger, & M. Löblich (Eds.), *Historische Perspektiven auf den Iconic Turn. Die Entwicklung der öffentlichen visuellen Kommunikation* [Historic perspectives on the iconic turn. The development of public visual communication] (pp. 166–183). Cologne, Germany: Herbert von Halem Verlag.

Godulla, A., & Wolf, C. (2017). *Digitale Langformen in Journalismus und Corporate Publishing: Scrollytelling – Webdokumentationen – Multimediastorys* [Digital longforms in journalism and corporate media: Scrollytelling—Web documentations—multimedia stories]. Wiesbaden, Germany: Springer VS. doi:10.1007/978-3-658-17556-6

Grüner, U., Kretschmer, B., & Täubig, K. (2010). *Praxisbuch Crossmedia: Das Arbeitsbuch für Konzeption, Produktion und Evaluation* [Cross media practice book: The work book for concepts, production, and evaluation]. Norderstedt, Germany: Books on Demand.

Hiippala, T. (2016). The multimodality of digital longform journalism. *Digital Journalism*, 1–23. doi: 10.1080/21670811.2016.1169197

Howe, J. (2008). *Crowdsourcing: How the power of the crowd is driving the future of business*. New York, NY: Crown Business.

Jenkins, H. (2008). *Convergence culture: Where old and new media collide (Updated and with a new afterword)*. New York, NY: New York Univ. Press.

Jenkins, H. (2009a, December 12). The revenge of the origami unicorn: Seven principles of transmedia storytelling (Well, two actually. Five more on Friday). *Confessions of an Aca-fan Blog*. Retrieved from http://henryjenkins.org/2009/12/the_revenge_of_the_origami_uni.html

Jenkins, H. (2009b, December 12). The revenge of the origami unicorn: The remaining four principles of transmedia storytelling. *Confessions of an Aca-fan Blog*. Retrieved from http://henryjenkins.org/2009/12/revenge_of_the_origami_unicorn.html

Jenkins, H. (2013). *Transmedia storytelling: Moving characters from books to films to video-games can make them stronger and more compelling*. Retrieved from http://www.technologyreview.com/biotech/13052

Johns, C. (2014). Editor's note: Food for thought. *National Geographic Tablet Magazine*, (5).

Kunzig, R. (2014). Carnivore's dilemma. Unhealthy. Nutritious. Cruel. Delicious. Unsustainable. All-American. In the beef debate there are so many sides. *National Geographic Tablet Magazine, 226*(5).

Malmelin, N., & Villi, M. (2015). Co-creation of what? Modes of audience community collaboration in media work. *Convergence (London)*. doi:10.1177/1354856515592511

McMillan, T. (2014). The new face of hunger. Millions of working Americans don't know where their next meal is coming from. *National Geographic Tablet Magazine, 226*(2).

Moloney, K. (2011). *Transmedia journalism in principle*. Retrieved from https://transmediajournalism.org/2011/11/23/transmedia-journalism-in-principle/

Moloney, K. (2014). *Multimedia, crossmedia, transmedia... What's in a name?* Retrieved from https://transmediajournalism.org/2014/04/21/multimedia-crossmedia-transmedia-whats-in-a-name/

Moloney, K. (2015). *Future of story: Transmedia journalism and National Geographic's Future of Food project* (Unpublished doctoral dissertation). University of Colorado Boulder, Boulder, CO.

Moloney, K. (n.d.). *What is transmedia storytelling?* Retrieved from https://transmediajournalism.org/contexts/what-is-transmedia-storytelling/

National Geographic Society. (1987). *The National Geographic Society—100 Years of adventure and discovery*. Washington, DC: National Geographic Society.

National Geographic Society. (2013a). *National Geographic 125 Years: Legendary photographs, adventures and discoveries that changed the world*. Washington, DC: National Geographic Society.

National Geographic Society. (2013b). *The photography issue. 125th anniversary collector's edition*. Washington, DC: National Geographic Society.

National Geographic Society. (2014a). *'FOOD: Our global kitchen' Exhibition to Open at National Geographic Museum Oct. 16*. Retrieved from http://press.nationalgeographic.com/2014/10/02/food-our-global-kitchen-exhibition-to-open-at-national-geographic-museum-oct-16/

National Geographic Society. (2014b). Eat. The new food revolution: Serving more than 7 billion every day. *National Geographic Tablet Magazine, 225*(5).

National Geographic Society. (2016). *About the National Geographic Society*. Retrieved from http://press.nationalgeographic.com/about-national-geographic/

National Geographic Society. (2017a). *About The Plate*. Retrieved from http://www.theplate.nationalgeographic.com/

National Geographic Society. (2017b). *About us*. Retrieved from http://www.nationalgeographic.com/about/

Newman, N., Fletcher, R., Levy, D. A. L., & Nielsen, R. K. (2016). *Reuters Institute digital news report 2016*. Oxford, UK: Reuters Institute for the Study of Journalism.

Panis, K., van den Bulck, H., Verschraegen, B., van der Burg, M., & Paulussen, S. (2014). Does media cross-ownership translate into cross-promotion? *Journalism Studies, 16*(6), 868–886. doi:10.1080/1461670X.2014.953780

Pariser, E. (2011). *The filter bubble: What the Internet is hiding from you*. New York, NY: Penguin Press.

Pope, V. (2014). The joy of food. Food is more than survival. With it we make friends, court lovers, and count our blessings. *National Geographic Tablet Magazine, 226*(6).

Pratten, R. (2015). *Getting started with transmedia storytelling: A practical guide for beginners* (2nd ed.). CreateSpace Independent Publishing Platform.

Quandt, T. (2008). (No) news on the world wide web? *Journalism Studies, 9*(5), 717–738. doi:10.1080/14616700802207664

Serious Science. (2016, October 28). *Transmedia storytelling: Media scientist Renira Rampazzo Gambarato on multiplatform production, crossmedia and the world of Harry Potter* [video file]. Retrieved from http://serious-science.org/transmedia-storytelling-7392

The Guardian. (2016). *6x9: A virtual experience of solitary confinement*. Retrieved from https://www.theguardian.com/world/ng-interactive/2016/apr/27/6x9-a-virtual-experience-of-solitary-confinement

Top Nonprofits, L. (2017). *Top 100 nonprofits on the web*. Retrieved from https://topnonprofits.com/lists/best-nonprofits-on-the-web/

Vogelsberg, D. (2006). Crossmedia. In O. Altendorfer & L. Hilmer (Eds.), *Medienbetriebswirtschaftslehre - Marketing* [Media business management—marketing]. Opladen, Germany: Westdt. Verlag.

Wenzlaff, K. (2013). Bezahlbarer Journalismus in der digitalen Moderne [Affordable journalism in the modern digital]. In L. Kramp, L. Novy, D. Ballwieser, & K. Wenzlaff (Eds.), *Journalismus in der digitalen Moderne. Einsichten – Ansichten – Aussichten* [Journalism in the modern digital. Insights—viewpoints—perspectives] (pp. 147–158). Wiesbaden, Germany: Springer VS. doi:10.1007/978-3-658-01144-4_12

Westlund, O. (2011). *Cross-media news work*. Gothenburg, Sweden: JMG.

Wolf, C. (2010). Drehscheibe (mobiles) Internet: Integration mobiler Dienste in online basierte Crossmedia-Umwelten [Hub (mobile) Internet: Integration of mobile services into online based cross media environments]. In R. Hohlfeld, P. Müller, A. Richter, & F. Zacher (Eds.), Passauer Schriften zur Kommunikationswissenschaft. Crossmedia - Wer bleibt auf der Strecke? Beiträge aus Wissenschaft und Praxis [Cross media—Who is going to lose? Contributions from science and the practical field] (pp. 111–122). Berlin, Germany: Lit.

Wolf, C. (2014). *Mobiler Journalismus. Angebote, Produktionsroutinen und redaktionelle Strategien deutscher Print- und Rundfunkredaktionen. Aktuell. Studien zum Journalismus* [Mobile journalism. Content, production routines, and editorial strategies of German print and broadcasting editorial offices] (Vol. 8). Baden-Baden, Germany: Nomos.

Wolf, C., & Godulla, A. (2016). Potentials of digital longforms in journalism. A survey among mobile Internet users about the relevance of online devices, Internet-specific qualities, and modes of payment. *Journal of Media Business Studies*, 1–23. 10.1080/16522354.2016.1184922

Wolf, C., & Schnauber, A. (2015). News consumption in the mobile era: The role of mobile devices and traditional journalism's content within the user's information repertoire. *Digital Journalism*, *3*(5), 759–776. doi:10.1080/21670811.2014.942497

Zacher, F. (2010). Die normative Bewertung von Cross-Promotion: Eine akzeptable Marketing-Strategie für crossmedial aufgestellte Medienkonzerne? [The normative assessment of cross-promotion: an acceptable marketing strategy for cross media media groups?]. In R. Hohlfeld, P. Müller, A. Richter, & F. Zacher (Eds.), Passauer Schriften zur Kommunikationswissenschaft. Crossmedia - Wer bleibt auf der Strecke? Beiträge aus Wissenschaft und Praxis [Cross media—Who is going to lose? Contributions from science and the practical field] (pp. 210–227). Berlin, Germany: Lit.

Zhang, S. I. (2012). The newsroom of the future. *Journalism Practice*, *6*(5-6), 776–787. doi:10.1080/17512786.2012.667281

KEY TERMS AND DEFINITIONS

Co-Creation: Co-creation marks a fundamental turning away from closed production processes in journalism where editorial offices controlled all parts of a story toward a more open approach that allows users to get involved in the media product itself by creating and contributing parts of the storyworld themselves. The contribution may vary from inviting users to report news, integrating crowdsourcing processes in investigative reporting or financing certain projects via crowdfunding.

Cross Media Storytelling: Cross media storytelling describes three different editorial strategies which all refer to a combination of different institutionalized media platforms. Focusing on journalism, these media sets will most of the time focus on print media (book, newspaper, magazine), broadcasting media (radio and television), as well as online and mobile media (websites, apps, social networks). Nevertheless, depending on the diversification of the media organization, there might be other media integrated as well. Firstly, cross media strategies include a diversification on the organizational level, focusing on the media brand, which publishes for different markets. Secondly, a diversification on the content level which includes different strategies of cross media storytelling. Thirdly, transmedia storytelling where the connection of platforms and content reaches far beyond the two other strategies, because the different platforms are all used to contribute to the development of the story.

Digital Longform Journalism: Digital longforms are a specific form of digital storytelling where journalistic narrative content is especially produced for online and mobile devices. Digital longforms combine established journalistic content qualities with Internet specific qualities like multimedia, selectivity, interactivity, participation, and linking combined with adapted utility and usability. Digital longform journalism can be part of cross media and transmedia storytelling projects.

Digital Storytelling: Digital storytelling in journalism refers to telling stories with digital media technologies, such as online and mobile media devices. While other media industries like film, games or advertising primarily use storytelling to transport messages, journalism has always tried to avoid the impression of inventing stories, as opposed to reporting facts. Established journalistic genres only include certain narrative elements. However, due to the permanent access to information from manifold sources it has become even more challenging to create uniqueness and added value. Therefore, a kind of narrative turn can be observed in journalism toward transporting information in a more personal, emotional and immersive way. This, however, has been made easier by combining different media elements in online and mobile media platforms.

Multimedia Storytelling: Multimedia storytelling is a potential form of digital storytelling. In this case, different media elements like text, photo, audio, video, graphics and/or animation are combined to tell a journalistic story. Each element adds relevant aspects to the story. Hence, the goal of multimedia storytelling is to build a complementary story by telling different aspects with different media elements.

Transmedia Qualities: Transmedia stories in journalism can be categorized by referring to ten specific transmedia qualities. These qualities are: Spreadability, Drillability, Immersion, Extractability, Worldbuilding, Seriality, Subjectivity, Continuity, Multiplicity, and Performance.

Transmedia Storytelling: Transmedia storytelling is one possible cross media strategy which can be described by three basic characteristics which are: the usage of multiple media platforms, content expansion, and audience engagement. The different platforms (and authors) are all used to contribute to the development of the story by adding new and relevant aspects of a narrative.

Chapter 11
The Transmedia Revitalization of Investigative Journalism:
Opportunities and Challenges of the Serial Podcast

Colin Porlezza
University of Zurich, Switzerland

Eleonora Benecchi
Università della Svizzera Italiana, Switzerland

Cinzia Colapinto
Ca' Foscari University of Venice, Italy

ABSTRACT

This chapter analyzes the transmediality of the record-breaking podcast Serial with regard to three specific contexts: organizational structures and innovation, journalistic production, and user engagement. This case study shows that the transmedia approach of Serial cannot only revitalize long-form journalism, particularly in the case of investigative journalism, but it can also strengthen forms of slow and networked journalism. This case allows us to look at fan communities not only as an engaged audience, useful for commercial purposes, but also as a source for story development and production—even if both the journalistic production and the user engagement are confronted with specific ethical issues with regard to selective transparency and participation.

INTRODUCTION

Transmedia storytelling, coined by Henry Jenkins (2003) with regard to fictional content, has recently become a buzzword within journalism practice as well (Maloney, 2011; Serrano Tellería, 2016). The concept of transmedia storytelling involves the idea and the strategy of creating content across multiple platforms, genres and formats, that adds up to a unique story world with a cohesive narrative. In addition, it also includes activities that engage the audience by offering content that permeates the user's life (Jen-

DOI: 10.4018/978-1-5225-3781-6.ch011

kins, 2009). The advantage of transmedia journalism, in the context of the new journalism ecosystem, is that it allows news organizations to take advantage of the increased communicative possibilities, where interactivity, participation as well as engagement are playing a central role—what Lewis, Holton and Coddington (2017) may call reciprocity in the journalism-audience relationship. However, transferring the concept of transmedia storytelling to journalism requires some amendments to Jenkins' original concept, as will be possible to see further down the road of this chapter.

Until today, research dealt with transmedia journalism mainly in relation to current and planned events (Gambarato & Tárcia, 2017; Gambarato, Alzamora, & Tárcia, 2016). This chapter takes a different approach by looking at a specific phenomenon that evolved over time. The object of study is the podcast Serial, a spin-off of a radio program called This American Life, hosted by the journalist and producer Sarah Koenig and aired on the network WBEZ. The podcast, realized in collaboration with WBEZ, "tells one story—a true story—over the course of a season. Each season, we follow a plot and characters wherever they take us" (About Serial, n.d.). What made Serial so special was that the weekly episodes a) were not based on current and ongoing events, but rather on an old (crime) story revitalized through an investigative approach; and b) became a true transmedia product thanks to the continuous interaction between the journalist and the followers, who were so deeply engaged with the story that they became in fact fans.

Notwithstanding the fact that Serial season one was an international hit, being one of the podcasts most listened to in the world (Crook, 2014), scientific research that looks into the transmedia journalism side of the case is lacking. Hence, this chapter analyzes the case of Serial from three different angles: First, it examines structural aspects like organizational and economic strategies. Second, the chapter investigates the journalistic practice by looking at the use of different platforms as well as journalistic formats in order to build a cohesive "storyworld." Third, it studies the user engagement, looking at the materials that were produced around the story by fans and spread through different platforms. In addition, it analyzes how the author of Serial, the journalist Sarah Koenig, interacted with users.

This Serial case study may well demonstrate that transmedia journalism can actually revitalize long-form journalism, particularly in the case of investigative journalism. In other words, it can stimulate the collaborative "search for clues," a property inherent to every good transmedia story (Phillips, 2012). Therefore, producers of the podcast take advantage of the contemporary participatory culture (Jenkins, 2006) and capitalize on it by building a transmedia narrative model—even if the starting point of the success story is an "old" media such as the radio. The case study also shows how (journalistic) archives can be put to a good use, allowing journalists to build new stories on past and already published news or even on "cold-cases." Finally, the case of Serial allows to look at fan communities spontaneously built around the story not only as an engaged audience, useful for commercial purposes, but also as a source for story development and production.

Serial is an excellent starting point to study how transmedia journalism could look like in the digital age for several reasons. Firstly, its large popularity makes it an interesting case not only in the realm of transmedia journalism but also in the more general realm of transmedia productions. Secondly, it started a trend and became an object of imitation and transformation within the journalistic podcast realm. It provides a unique take on transmediality by embracing both traditional and transmedial storytelling techniques and by offering also a contemporary example of slow journalism. In addition, Serial experiments a new and interesting model of monetary success for podcasts. Lastly, Serial is also a cautionary tale in terms of engagement: It shows that there are also risks for journalism when it becomes truly transmedial, especially with regard to journalism ethics and the complex relationship between journalists and their publics (Goldstein, 2014). Therefore, the paper also sheds light on issues like withholding facts for the purpose of storytelling and drama, ultimately challenging ethical principles like transparency or the truth. Based on the empirical analysis, the chapter shows how transmedia storytelling is a promising but complex activity, which is, however, still confronted with practical and ethical problems when applied to journalism.

BACKGROUND

Media and communications industries have changed dramatically over the past decade, from a technological and a social point of view. Digitalization and convergence pose many challenges and redefine the news ecosystem within which content is created and disseminated—reshuffling the networks between individual actors, institutions and information markets as well. According to Normann (2001), the consonance between the firm and the business environment is a central issue and essential for success. He maintained that the systemic nature of the business idea requires coherence: The relation to the external environment depends on the services a firm can offer, which in turn depend on the organizational components such as structure and capabilities. This is the starting point for the analysis of the structural aspects of Serial's success.

Serial arrived during the golden age of podcasting, at the tipping point in maturity, with over 350,000 podcasts listed on iTunes (Berry, 2015a, 2015b): Technology made the experience of podcasting simpler, moving it from a niche to a mainstream media platform. Nowadays, podcasting is more accessible, requiring fewer skills from the users in terms of usability and less time to get used to the interfaces. It is in this context that the Serial podcasts, freely available on the Internet, either by streaming from the Serial website or downloading from a platform like iTunes, became a cultural phenomenon. The audience data for Serial demonstrates its popular impact: According to the numbers released by the producers (Binge-worthy journalism—Backstage with the creators of Serial, n.d.), the podcast reached 175 million cumulative downloads. Apple data also revealed that Serial was the fastest podcast to reach 5 million downloads and streams in iTunes' history.

From an economic point of view, while advertising constitutes the dominant revenue stream for podcasts, producers are experimenting with a wide range of revenue streams (Quirk, 2015). Serial is no exception to this phenomenon: During the first season, all staffers were funded by This American Life (all Serial staffers are employees of WBEZ Chicago Public Media, as are all This American Life employees). Some ad slots were available in 15-second segments at the beginning and end of the show while Koenig voiced the post-roll ads, and the email-marketing service MailChimp, a frequent podcast advertiser, was the main sponsor. The second season was made possible by donations: Towards the end of the twelve-week run the producers appealed for listeners to donate money for a second series, and for additional sponsorships. However, since the industry is still in its infancy, a business model for podcasting has yet to be established. Once again, technology gives flexibility to podcasting, which requires a smaller budget and a smaller staff.

From a narrative point of view, Serial is a non-fiction weekly podcast. The podcast's name refers to the story format and intends to provide the same experience of a TV series drawing out a single story for an entire season. The focus of the first and most popular season is the case against Adnan Syed, a Baltimore high school student who had been convicted of murdering his ex-girlfriend, Hae Min Lee, in 1999. The focus of the second season is on Bowe Bergdahl, an American army soldier who left his base and was captured by the Taliban. He was later exchanged for five Guantanamo Bay detainees. This type of offering fits the listener's taste. Over the last three decades, a massive growth of crime programming in television schedules occurred, ranging from crime dramas (such as Law & Order or CSI) to real crime programs. Reality crime programs present true stories about crime, criminals and victims, and are a hybrid form of programming merging aspects of news and entertainment programs (Fishman & Cavender, 1998, p. 3). The appeal of these programs relies on the general feeling that crime is a serious social problem attracting people's attention.

Considering the internal factors, a significant role has been played by the production team, made by expert and skilled people. The producers of the show, Sarah Koenig and Julie Snyder, are also producers of the popular radio show This American Life. Koenig, originally an investigative journalist, acts as the narrator. Serial was overseen by executive producer Ira Glass, whose storytelling (as well as ad) techniques were used to full effect (Berry, 2015b). Today, the team counts more than 21 members, among producers, researchers, sound designers, and other staff members. This group of professionals was able to lift the quality of the show in a way to become the first podcast to win a Peabody Award for public service achievement in the media.

By taking both the successful narrative structure as well as the structure of the team into account, a high consonance between the firm and the economic environment can be observed. This fit leads to the concept of value constellation or what in this chapter is defined as a particular setup of actors, who perform social transactions to extract value from existing and emerging business. In Serial's value constellation, listeners are expected to play an important role in creating this value and success. As will be explained in detail below, Serial fans took to the Internet to share their opinions on their favorite podcast. On Reddit's r/serialpodcast thread, hundreds of listeners went from merely debating the podcast to attempting to solve the crime themselves. During the season, more and more listeners supplemented their experience of the podcast with the additional investigation provided by these so-called "keyboard sleuths" (Dickson, 2014). This activity can be categorized as a hybridization between traditional fandom practices and citizen journalism, "a range of web-based practices whereby 'ordinary' users engage in journalistic practices" (Goode, 2009, p. 1288), another aspect that will be thoroughly analyzed in a specific section later in the chapter.

Previous researchers studied Serial from different perspectives. Economic theory backs Siegelman's (2016) work, which focuses on the central question of the series—the guilt or innocence of Adnan Syed—dealing with asymmetries of information. Durrani et al. (2015) assume an anthropological perspective to talk about why Serial was so popular. They consider Serial as a great example of how a podcast medium could be a robust site for new multivocal experiments in ethnographic representation. Closer to our approach, Berry (2015a) considers the show within a context of technical change and podcast histories and denotes it as a cultural object. He suggests that Serial occurred at the intersection of technical and social change and, therefore, may serve as a gateway through which new listeners (re) discover the medium. Buozis (2017) examines the way Serial used the accused's voice to challenge institutional truth claims from within the textual space of crime journalism. He interrogates modes of truth production and representation. Cramer (2014) explains Serial's success in terms of high quality content able to keep the targeted audience interested. Podcast networks and other miniature videos are playing a key role in declining interest in longer television shows and programs.

WHY IS SERIAL INNOVATIVE?

Serial was meant to be experimental and innovative, and many traced its newness to its serialized format and specifically to the very long form reporting of a complicated case in both seasons. It must be remarked, though, that this form of storytelling is not something new in itself. In fact, Serial revitalizes a popular genre of radio of the 1930s: Many radio crime programs (such as "True Detective Mysteries" or "Treasury Agent") dramatized real police cases as radio crime entertainment. This genre have repeatedly appeared in many movies and TV crime shows since the 1940s. The overlapping among journalism and (crime) entertainment goes back to the mid-1970s: Journalists and police worked together to produce the "Crime of the Week" for creating the American "Crime Stoppers" series (Carriere & Richard, 1989). As Goldstein (2014) points out: "By employing a multitude of tactics typically utilized in fiction—cliff-hangers, hunches, personal asides—Koenig's narration lands somewhere between straight reporting and something more personal." In the 2000s, a diverse range of series, podcasts, and documentaries share common concerns around the law and how it can be represented, particularly with regard to central concepts such as truth, evidence and miscarriage of justice. These true crime documentaries are hugely popular (Bruzzi, 2016).

Moreover, serialized forms of entertainment have been growing in popularity in recent years, leading to the widespread impression that "serialized products are more sophisticated, more complex and just plain better than other forms of mass-produced entertainment" (Denson, 2011). Jenkins (2009) himself (re-)introduced the concept of seriality into his writings, defining it one of the seven core principles of transmedia storytelling: Splitting a story into different chunks, connecting the different installments for instance through cliffhangers on different platforms, represents a meaningful way to offer a compelling experience. In this perspective, Serial is part of a trend and can be considered one of the most successful examples rather than its initiator. Concerning the technological aspect, which is undoubtedly another part of Serial's success, it must be remarked how radio is a medium that is growing in confidence and relevance thanks to the liberation afforded by digital technology and online and mobile delivery systems. Indeed, a relevant element for Serial success was the flexibility given by the digital only approach: Listeners can either go along (every Thursday) or can binge-listen all episodes have been released at once (Lurie, 2014). On the production side, podcasting allows some flexibility as well, as it unshackles the producers from broadcast conventions and schedules, as personal and subjective approaches to storytelling become possible. A very long-form storytelling was chosen. Serial stretches out one story during an entire season, asking listeners to take the time to listen and wait an entire week to find out what happens next. For podcasts, this is darn near revolutionary (Cramer, 2014). Moreover, each episode can be as long or short as it needs to be—another great advantage of podcasting. Being backed by WBEZ is a significant advantage, particularly with regard to the positioning of the product in the market. The association with This American Life reinforces not only Serial's innovative character (Edmond, 2015), but it exerts a positive effect on its positioning as well: The original radio show already had a huge public in terms of listeners (Desta, 2016). But what makes Serial even more innovative is the mix of established journalistic practices with new forms of expression and participation, as will be shown in the following lines.

FROM TRADITIONAL TO TRANSMEDIA JOURNALISM

What makes Serial so peculiar is the combination of traditional, hands-on investigative practices grounded on truth and facts, with innovative approaches in the use of different platforms, the participatory and networked approach to journalism and by strictly abiding to the principle of transparency. Bringing together different practices in relation to the editorial production largely defined the podcast's success. Right from the beginning, this strategy was carefully planned and implemented as can be seen in the publicity material for one of Koenig's public talks, where she describes how,

[a]t a time when being first and being fast dominates the media, and quick sound bites are offered at every turn, Serial did exactly the opposite [...] taking its time and proving that slow-motion journalism could captivate and sustain its vast podcast listenership. (Koenig cited in O'Meara, 2017)

Koenig specifically refers to the slow-motion characteristic of Serial, what somehow reflects the concept of slow journalism: This understanding of journalism tries to counterbalance the "fast news culture"—similarly to the slow food philosophy that evolved out of a protest against the fast-food culture—by using an approach to journalism grounded on narrative storytelling techniques, thorough research, non-sensationalistic and community oriented reporting, transparency and, last but not least, an ethical treatment of subjects and of producers (Le Masurier, 2015; see also Greenberg, 2012 and Gambarato, 2016).

Koenig's podcast is apparently part of the tradition of investigative journalism, particularly in its liberal understanding as watchdog journalism covering the role of a fourth estate. The investigative characteristic of the podcast is also reflected by the number of episodes dedicated to each of the cases analyzed. The dedication to and extensive coverage of a single case is what differentiates investigative reporting from daily news coverage, as Ettema and Glasser (1984, p. 6) described in their study on the epistemology of investigative journalism:

Because the hard news produced by investigative reporters tends to by less timely than the hard news produced by daily reporters, and because investigative reporters are able to utilize more and better resources than their daily counterparts, the hard news of the investigative reporter can be distinguished not only on the basis of its scheduling characteristics but on the rigors of inquiry to which it is likely to be subjected.

The thorough investigations into the different cases chosen by Koenig have shown their ability to revitalize long-form journalism, particularly in the case of investigative journalism, even if "old" media such as the radio are the starting point. Mainly because they can stimulate the "search for clues," which is a property inherent to every good transmedia story (Phillips, 2012).

However, although Koenig repeatedly insisted that her investigative approach to the cases was grounded on what Zelizer (2004, p. 103) described as "the originary status of fact, truth, and reality," her representation of the main characters such as Syed were unique in the sense that she focused primarily on the biography of the indicted. It is the focus on the prisoner's biography that challenges not only the way established crime journalism and court reporting is carried out, but also how evidence is taken into account:

This interrogation of biography as a way to arrive at objective truth, which Koenig facilitates and participates in, hints at the epistemological weakness of other forms of knowledge in criminal justice contexts, such as forensic science, eyewitness testimony, and psychological profiling, and offers an example of how journalistic practice, which tends to reinforce the epistemic strength of these knowledges, can also be turned into a critical tool for questioning them. (Buozis, 2017, p. 13)

The representation of Adnan Syed's case through his own voice, accompanied and commented by the show's host, becomes therefore not only a critique of the judicial system and its procedures in itself, but it challenges also established forms of journalism practice. The fact that Adnan Syed has been granted a new trial proves that this specific editorial strategy works, although—as can be seen in the subsequent section on the involvement of fans—the narrative structure alone is not enough.

Although Koenig follows an investigative approach when it comes to her thorough analysis of Adnan Syed's case, she also applies a principle that entails several issues in relation to investigative journalism:

What Koenig does that we don't normally do share our thoughts and views as we research a story. Normally we do all that work before publishing. We give our audience the most intelligent assessment we can. We go through the same hard work of interviewing and researching as Koenig – and we suffer through the same anxieties and soul searching. The difference is, we never make that work public. She breaks new ground because she makes journalism more transparent – and in my view, adds tremendous credibility to our field. (Barnathan, 2014)

Yet, transparency is a delicate issue when it comes to investigative reporting: In many cases it is vital to protect sources from being prosecuted, for instance, if they act as whistleblowers. Nevertheless, transparency is a central ethical norm and Houston (2010, p. 45) explicitly quotes it as a principle that will be vital for the future of investigative journalism. In addition, transparency is also relevant with regard to the concept of slow journalism: According to Le Masurier (2015, p. 143), a slow approach to journalism includes not only being factual and accurate, but the editorial output needs to be verifiable and traceable in terms of the sources—as long as they are not endangered. From this perspective, transparency plays also a central role when it comes to holding journalists accountable for what they produce (Eberwein & Porlezza, 2017).

Transparency is not only important when it comes to Serial as source transparency, but also as a normative guideline. It can be understood, following Karlsson's (2010; 2011) reflections, in two different ways: First of all, transparency means *openness*. Koenig radically respects this notion by discussing cases where her investigations were falling down a rabbit hole, situations in which she was not able to find relevant information or to interview people she would have liked to have on the show. She also talks about her doubts and her anxieties in relation to Syed's case, but even more remarkable, she communicates her worries with regard to the podcast itself, to the format that she is using to tell Syed's story. This kind of radical transparency brought fellow journalists to define her approach as "show-your-work journalism" (Haglund, 2014).

In journalism, transparency has also been related to *participation*, as it allows the audience not only to understand how the podcast has been produced and what kind of problems it encountered during the production, but it gives the audience also the opportunity "to monitor, check, criticize and even intervene in the journalistic process" (Deuze, 2005, p. 455). Serial's popularity was also due to the listener's opportunity to participate—not so much directly in the news production process of Serial, but in the form of user engagement, letting people feel as if they were part of the investigation. In fact, discussion forums about the podcast mushroomed, which eventually led to a networked community of engaged publics and to what Beckett (2008) defines networked journalism—a phenomenon that perfectly embodies the digital culture of participation (Jenkins, Ito, & boyd, 2015).

This networked form of journalism is essential in order to build a transmedia journalism experience, not only to foster user engagement, but also—as it can be seen in the next section—in terms of content expansion, as users started to investigate Syed's on their own, and the involvement of multiple media platforms by the provision of additional material and imaginary on their webpage. This triptych that characterizes transmedia journalism (Gambarato & Tárcia, 2017) demonstrates at the same time how Serial can illustrate the potential of journalism to become part of the convergence culture (Jenkins, 2006): "(…) cinema, radio journalism, television and digital content can influence and interact with one another, as can the producers and consumers of this intermedia" (O'Meara, 2017).

Ultimately, the traditional investigative journalism approach, combined with the notion of transparency—not only in terms of openness, but also in terms of participation (Eberwein & Porlezza, 2016)—and the captivating storytelling that, altogether, challenged current journalism practices, allowed Serial to become a huge success and one of the few phenomena of transmedia journalism not related to a planned event.

AUDIENCE ENGAGEMENT AND CO-CREATION

The main way a podcast's audience is generally measured is through downloads. Download data, however, is limited: The statistics do not identify if the downloaded podcast was actually listened to, how long, and by how many different people (Resler, 2015). But most of all, the available metrics do not take into account fan engagement, which is crucial to establish the popularity of Serial.

In Serial's value constellation, listeners were expected to play a crucial role in creating the value and success of the podcast. Based on this, Serial was conceived, since its launch, as an interactive experience, especially in regard to its online extensions. Producers' direct acknowledgement and questioning of their audience, their effort to complement audio storytelling with visual digital materials such as supplementary images and interactive maps, the constant dialogue unrolling between them and fans through social media platforms, are all traits that made Serial a unique interactive experience. Despite all of that, it was all but obvious that the crime podcast would become a participatory experience.

Something must be made clear at this point: Interactivity is not the same as participation. While interactivity refers to properties of the technologies which are designed to enable users to make meaningful choices that personalize the experience (Jensen, 1998), participation refers to properties of the culture where groups collectively or individually make decisions that have an impact on their shared experiences (Jenkins, 1992). So one interacts *with* something, while one participates *in* something. In other words: Technologies are not participatory, while cultures definitely are. Moreover, participatory culture is related to a community built around content. As soon as a fan community developed around the weekly crime podcast, Serial stopped being simply interactive and started to become fully participative. According to Jenkins' seminal work Textual Poachers (1992), fandom has in fact been a crucial element in shaping the contemporary participatory culture. Historically, fans were often early adopters of new media platforms and practices and experimenters with new modes of media-making. They were also among the first to interact within geographically dispersed communities of interest.

When fandom massively migrated online, a new cultural shift took place: The collective intelligence between media producers and consumers (Jenkins, 2006). Serial was able to capitalize on the traditional experimental and collaborative attitude informing fan communities and on the so-called "collective intelligence shift" by building a transmedia narrative model which "encouraged forensic fandom with the promise of eventual revelations once all the pieces are put together" (Mittell, 2015, p. 314). The main revelation promised for devoted fans was the answer to the classical crime question "did he do it?" Sarah

Koenig explicitly asked Serial's fans to help her solve the puzzle and to collaborate with her (episode 4). Supplementary "evidence" was strategically posted on Serial's website in order to encourage listeners to join forces and to engage with the series more deeply.

Another aspect that was crucial in fostering this "forensic fandom" was the choice to produce Serial as a single story told from a number of different angles: This opened up different entry points to dig into the crime story. It was in consequence of this stimulating technological and narrative environment that a sub-Reddit community emerged with the specific aim to "find information about the podcast and to discuss your theories, predictions and other aspects of the show and case" (r/serialpodcast introductory statement). The community on the sub-Reddit, with more than 51.584 "listeners" as of March 2017 and an average of 95 comments per post, was by far the most important online community devoted to Serial. It was this unofficial platform that contributed to develop a constant and interactive dialogue between the different subjects involved in the podcast. Nevertheless, the analysis of the r/serialpodcast community allows to observe that it was not only the "whodunnit" element to the story that kept people engaged. Indeed, the majority of Reddit users declared themselves unsure about Syed's innocence or guilt, even after the end of season one. What the ongoing discussion inside the community and with the producers of the podcast lead to was the belief that, regardless of his innocence or guilt, the justice system did not have enough to convict Syed.

Serial then turned into a holistic and immersive meditation on American justice, journalism, and the notion of "truth." This becomes clear if one looks at the high number of posts about the American justice system that the series provoked: Syed's case was compared to similar ones, particularly to those where evidence was, supposedly, wrongly discarded. Within the community, there is also a group of fans that shows more interest in the "making of" of Serial, and in questioning Koenig's take on the case. There is a specific section called "meta," devoted to reflections on the editorial construction of the podcast and Koenig's style of reporting. Serial producers nurtured this type of meta-discussions in turn by incorporating details concerning the construction of the podcast into the show. For instance, during some of the episodes, an automated voice from the prison phone introducing the calls between Koenig and Syed can be heard. The cutting and mixing of different tapes is evident and Koenig often talked about the construction of the podcast. In this way, Serial invites its most passionate listeners to look at the backstage of the investigation and ultimately to become part of it.

This type of meta-reflection both on the justice system and on the podcast format could also be a consequence of the mature age of the participants in the sub-reddit community, which different surveys revealed to be mostly between 40 and 59 (DRNC, 2015). To explain this age range, which seems unusual for an online community, it is necessary to take into account that the development of the Serial fan community profited from its producers' network of already existing fans, who were following the previous works on This American Life. As a storytelling gambit, This American Life had been proved a success long before Serial came along. Indeed, many users of r/serialpodcast declared in their initial posts their previous experience as listeners of Koenig's main program. The age range is therefore not surprising: According to radio ratings provider Arbitron, the median age of NPR radio listeners is 55. According to the Audience insight and research group internal to NPR, however, the median age drops to 48 among NPR.org users, while users of the NPR News iPhone app have a median age of 38. Podcast listeners, however, are the youngest with 33 years, a full 22 years younger than the general radio audience (Gallivan, 2010).

As stated by Jenkins (1992), a key trait of participatory culture is the adaptation of content produced by others and building upon their work. Similar to many other fan-beloved media products discussed on Reddit, Serial spawned parodies and meme within the community, with specific sections devoted to the sharing of such materials. The r/serialpodcast community is also a testament to the addictive nature of Serial documenting the obsessive and heated activities sprouting from the podcast such as googling names and locations, searching for and reading additional texts and documents, and discussing theories. It must be noted, though, that in this specific case, users generally focused on sharing information about the case or about the podcast itself. One of the main traits of the r/serialpodcast community was in fact its ability to reuse the information given by Koenig during the podcast, or the materials shared by the producers on the official website to build a parallel narrative universe with regard to the Syed case.

The Reddit community expanded Sarah Koenig's investigation in uncharted territories. Examples are the posts adding graphic visualization to help listeners better understand the information given by Koenig during the podcast such as the one titled "Visual Timeline" offering three different versions of the events of October 23, 2014. This post generated a discussion of the events narrated within the podcast that produced 66 comments and provided visual support to the so-called "investigative fans." Among the comments, many declared the importance of this kind of post in order to support listeners' independent investigation of the case, which was developing in parallel with the one by Sarah Koenig. To use their words: "This is exactly what we need to help sort this out" (Visual Timeline, n.d.). Those type of posts illuminate the fact that fans played, or rather felt that they played an active role in the construction of the podcast.

Remarkably, Serial also applied the concept of participatory culture by incorporating its most active investigative fans' efforts into some of the official episodes of the podcast. In doing so, the producers of Serial acknowledged that within a participatory culture perspective no story is ever complete. This concept of process journalism, coined by Jarvis (2009), is equally true for digital journalism: "We really are about process. Journalism and news is a process that doesn't begin and that doesn't end. When you think like that, I think you open up your world to collaboration."

But what was the specific value of this fan community to the producers of Serial? When it comes to a media product created and spread within a participatory cultural context, the content itself moves between commercial and non-commercial economies, creating possible dilemmas. For the producers of the show, the podcast represented a commodity. For the fan community, Serial was perceived as a resource or a gift (Benecchi, 2014). This means that Serial fans made the decision to pass the content along and to participate in the community connected to it, based on the social or sentimental value of the content itself. In this perspective, Koenig's openness to the listeners included her constant sharing of self-doubts and speculations about the cases such as in episode 2, when she asks

See what I mean? All this information, every scrap, it is currency for whatever side you're on. Spin. And the trouble with spin is that you can't totally disregard it, be cause swirling around somewhere inside, some tendril of it, is true. (Serial podcast, Episode 2).

Additionally, the form of the show as well as her own narrative style are instilled with what radio scholars (MacLuhan, 1994) call "the illusion of intimacy," which is part an affordance of the technology itself and part of a deliberate creation: From the earliest days of broadcasting, radio practitioners have actively sought to cultivate "a sense of spontaneity and sincerity, enabling listeners to enjoy the illusion of a direct and intimate conversation" (VanCour, 2008, p. 383). Following in the footsteps of the most successful radio speakers, Sarah Koenig sought to sound familiar and intimate in order to reach people at a remarkably personal level, thus fostering the construction of an active and pro-active fan community around Serial.

Serial's success was partly due to the way it motivated listeners to discuss the show's content (O'Meara, 2015). There are many examples of how fan labor activities can add to and affect media product development, marketing, distribution (Benecchi & Colapinto, 2011; 2010). Not surprisingly, Serial producers have turned directly to their fanbase to fund the second season of the podcast.

DISCUSSION AND CONCLUSION

The show smashed all previous podcasting records upon its release in 2014, and helped to introduce a broad audience to the new and unexpected possibilities of a rather classic (radio) format. However, the ease of access and the simple ways the audience could follow as well as participate in the show made the podcast a unique experience. As suggested by Berry (2015a, 2015b), the combination of story, technology and skill helped to ensure Serial a place in podcast history. In addition, the perfect consonance between Serial, the existing market in that particular moment in time, the technological environment, and the eagerness to experiment with a new format by implementing innovative processes fostered its success. Regardless of their achievements, it has to be taken into account that being a spin-off of This American Life helped Serial both in terms of its positioning and financing. Nevertheless, it must also be remarked that Serial reached one million unique listens per episode, the same as This American Life, which averaged one million podcast downloads an episode.

The success can be explained by the characteristics of the product itself. The team was able to find dramatic, underreported stories in season one, and to report chops and mine for subtle emotions in season two. Particularly when it comes to the journalistic practice, Serial shows its innovativeness as they apply new approaches in terms of production, distribution and style. The journalistic production differs from the one of a traditional newsroom, shifting from a linear and top-down production to a more collaborative and networked form of journalism. This involves the fact that Koenig and her team of journalists transcended the boundaries of their newsroom and included materials of their most active fans in several episodes, but established a collaborative nature—and mentality—in order to unfold all possible details of the cases treated in their shows. This means that (certain) newsrooms stop being the closed fortresses they were in the past decades. And it also means to acknowledge that the contributions of their publics can be fruitful and that the materials generated by fans are worth being included in the editorial content.

Moreover, what distinguishes Serial from its traditional radio counterparts is its radical transparency when it comes to the actual journalistic production. This not only refers to problems and issues the team, and Sarah Koenig in particular, encountered during the collection and the analysis of the material and the interviews. It applies especially to the voiced doubts about the presented format and whether and to what extent such a podcast could, ultimately, lead to a potential re-opening of the process about Adnan Syed. However, this transparency might also cause issues when it comes to a program with such a high participation of the audience, particularly of high engaged fans. The case study clearly showed that fans were not amused when it became known that Sarah Koenig withheld information for dramatic purposes. Once you have established an apparent full transparency, you have to stick to it.

On the other hand, the radical transparency both in terms of the published photo materials on the website as well as the missing information represents an invitation for the audience to engage with the show. In this sense, the show clearly builds on the concept of what game designer Neil Young called "additive comprehension" (Jenkins, 2009). As stated by Moloney, "we can carry those techniques to predesigned transmedia narratives so that, once engaged, the public has somewhere to find more. Through transmedia implementation we also open many more access points for the public to find our story" (Moloney, 2013).

The uniqueness of Serial in terms of its journalistic style is, however, not limited to the implementation of a networked form of journalism or the radical transparency. It is also related to Koenig's particular vision of audio journalism, applying a narrative approach to storytelling (and combining thus slow and transmedia journalism) that unfolds a (real story)-universe across multiple media channels. By seizing successful principles such as serialization from TV shows, she was able to revolutionize investigative radio journalism, by blending techniques used in fictionalized content with traditional reporting techniques—even if serialization is nothing new to radio journalism either, given that already in the 1940s *fictional* content was often serialized.

From our case analysis, it is clear that even in an on-demand world, shared experiences remain important. Serial applied participatory culture to perfection: A classic journalistic format that implements transmedia storytelling techniques to reap the benefits of a loyal fan base (Moloney, 2010). In this perspective, the producers of Serial did not wait for the public to come to them, but they reached out to the public wherever it was, connecting with it on its own terms. Serial also showed that the widespread circulation of media content through the conscious actions of dispersed networks of participants "tends to create greater visibility and awareness as the content travels in unpredicted directions and encounters people who are potentially interested in further engagements with the people who produced it" (Usher, 2010). In fact, media conglomerates have become aware of this in recent years, increasingly adopting forms of networked journalism and collaboration, fostering—as shown above in the section on the journalistic implications—"more relational forms of exchange among users in the network" (Lewis, Holton, & Coddington, 2017, p. 169).

In this sense, the distribution strategy of Serial is radically different from those of traditional news outlets: It is not limited to the distribution of the product across different channels and platforms such as webpages or social media, but it actively encourages and includes the fans' activities and their use and sharing of the published materials. The fact that these contributions are also included in certain episodes shows that the distribution strategy is closely related to the editorial production as it goes beyond the placement of the product on different platforms. Nurturing user engagement, participation, and using the fans' contributions pushes the boundaries of transmedia journalism even further, as transmedia storytelling becomes truly implemented in Jenkins' (1992) vision of shared experiences that culminate, eventually, in a *co-creation* where the content produced by Koenig and her team served, for the fans, as material to build upon. Thanks to this so called forensic fandom, the user generated materials, in turn, found their way back into the editorial product, resulting effectively in a collective intelligence between media producers and consumers (Jenkins, 2006)—a new trait to transmedia journalism.

However, this kind of open and interactive relationship, so crucial to determine Serial's success and to transform this podcast into a transmedia experience, did not come "free of charge." Listeners were repeatedly asked and encouraged to switch from observer to participant—and the Reddit community in particular was obsessed with the quest to solve the murder case. However, the participation required to connect with and enjoy the transmedia narrative format raises an ethical conundrum: The kind of engagement and participation necessitated from the Serial fan community matches those related to fictional products (Benecchi, 2014), but Serial is no fictional product. The podcast involves real people and a real murder case. This contrast is inscribed within the nature of Serial, a hybrid product between a journalistic and an entertainment product that raises ethical dilemmas.

If one considers Sarah Koenig a journalist in the context of Serial's production, one would also expect her to take journalism ethics and editorial standards into account. Koenig repeatedly puts some aspects of traditional journalism ethics such as objectivity and independency into question: She often speculates, although she admits that she is aware of doing so. In one occasion, she even confesses that she does not consider herself a proper crime reporter. Nevertheless, Koenig, who was in fact a reporter for the Baltimore Sun in her early years, explicitly calls herself "the reporter" in more than one occasion throughout Serial's first season. In addition, she also refers to a code of conduct and professional ethics she reckons must be respected when reporting about the people involved in the story and the materials collected during her research. Thus, by her own standards she plays the role of a journalist in Serial, which is why Serial should be judged by the ethical standards applying to journalism.

In this perspective, the first ethical dilemma raised by Serial is the decision to accept tips, calls and information provided by listeners and to integrate them within the transmedia narrative. It might occur that people who contacted Koenig and her team after the beginning of the podcast, especially the ones personally connected to the case, changed their story to reshaped their own role to look better to the audience. This could happen consciously or unconsciously, but in the end, the divulged story might not longer be accurate. It is also possible that the witnesses who came forward after the first episodes where influenced by Koenig's version of the "facts," or just wanted to be part of what was clearly becoming a popular product. In particular, the Reddit community developed into an important source of crowdsourced information based on the leads offered within the podcast. The question remains: How reliable can this type of information be, particularly in a format where editorial and entertaining aspects cohabit? And how could it harm the real people involved?

This leads to the second ethical dilemma raised by Serial: Even if one expects Koenig to respect the ethical norms connected to her profession (such as respecting the privacy of the people involved in the story), the same does not apply to the listeners and fans. People engaging with this transmedia product were able to discover personal information and intimate details concerning real individuals, even the ones not mentioned inside the podcast. This was possible by simply using the materials shared by the producers on the Serial website. In particular, the r/serialpodcast community collected and shared a high amount of information about the people involved in the case, although the group abided to the general rule that doxing was inadmissible. Even if not shared explicitly, there were numerous hints to the materials in different threads and a list of people involved in the story was eventually made available.

This connects to the third ethical dilemma raised by Serial: If online fans (such as Redditors) start to play the role of amateur detectives, they can threaten the reputation and life of people wrongly accused or identified as possible suspects. This is exactly what happened in the days after the Boston Marathon bombings when Reddit became a source of false accusations, causing a debate about the responsibilities of digital media platforms. At the time, Reddit's general manager Erik Martin (2013), recognized that "activity on Reddit fueled online witch hunts and dangerous speculation which spiraled into very negative consequences for innocent parties." This also demonstrates how Reddit is a sort of attention aggregator, but no replacement for news reporting.

There is also an ethical concern when it comes to publishing (new) information about people linked to a specific case without knowing how the case is going to end or what kind of effects the publications might entail. Even if you declare the relativity of the published information, it could end up in a defamatory cause or influence the witnesses' opinions and memories (see Goldstein, 2014). Even if the apparent application of transparency can be regarded as an asset, it remains a selective—and unethical—process if it is sometimes sacrificed for dramatic purposes. One must keep in mind that Serial gave its listeners a lot of information about the case, but applied a journalistic selection to the contents shared and the people included as "voices" of the program. Many theories discussed among Redditors were therefore influenced by the selections, the perspectives as well as the style used by Sarah Koenig, a white woman investigating a community of immigrants and minorities.

To conclude, Serial's practices are not unethical per se, but they put the show in a complex position: To what extent should journalistic podcasts involve fans and more generally listeners into the process of building and expanding the story they tell? Ultimately, this leads to the central question of how far one can develop a transmedia approach in investigative journalism before a product becomes a means to entertain rather than to inform?

Serial raises questions about the real-life consequences of this innovative form of reporting and its popularity encourages to reflect not only on the cultural significance of such a product but also on its responsibilities.

FUTURE RESEARCH DIRECTIONS

Certainly, this explorative study into the transmedia strategies of Serial presents some limitations. First of all, a single case study is limited in terms of its scope of analysis and qualitative approach. However, given that it is the first investigation into the transmedia strategy of Serial, the exploratory nature of the study is justified and allows for other follow-up studies to build on this research findings. A follow up study on similar podcasts could shed light on whether the strategies implemented by the team around Sarah Koenig have been adopted by other actors as well. It would be interesting, in the future, to compare different podcasts, maybe even in different countries, and to establish whether the innovations brought to both the podcast and the radio format have been a game changing and thus structural improvement for the specific media sector, or whether it was a unique phenomenon limited to Serial. In addition, it would also be useful to know more about the economic grounds on which such podcast would be based: What business models work best for transmedia products, particularly if they are carried out by small organizations or, another area to study, journalism startups. In any case, the Serial case study is useful to push forward the research in the area of transmedia journalism, particularly because it is not specifically related to either a planned event and because it had the potential to revitalize long-form investigative (radio) journalism. However, it would be relevant to check, whether this promise can actually be kept or not.

REFERENCES

About Serial. (n.d.). Retrieved from https://serialpodcast.org/about

Barnathan, J. (2014). *Why Serial is important for journalism.* Retrieved March 17, 2017, from http://archives.cjr.org/the_kicker/serial_sarah_koenig_journalism.php

Beckett, C. (2008). *SuperMedia: Saving journalism so it can save the world.* Chichester, UK: Wiley-Blackwell.

Benecchi, E. (2014). L'economia del Fandom [The Economy of Fandom]. In M. Cucco (Ed.), *La trama dei media* (pp. 75–96). Milan, Italy: Carocci.

Benecchi, E., & Colapinto, C. (2010). Engaging with Glee! Transmedia storytelling for a television in transition. In *Business models for a digital economy: The Value of Content* (pp. 201–218). Navarra, Spain: University Press of Navarra.

Benecchi, E., & Colapinto, C. (2011). Television and social media in the era of convergence and participation. In P. Faustino & Z. Vukanovic (Eds.), *Managing media economy, Media content and technology in the age of digital convergence* (pp. 321–344). Lisbon, Portugal: Media XXL.

Berry, R. (2015a). A golden age of podcasting? Evaluating Serial in the context of podcast histories. *Journal of Radio & Audio Media*, *22*(2), 170–178. doi:10.1080/19376529.2015.1083363

Berry, R. (2015b). Serial and ten years of podcasting: has the medium grown up? In M. Oliveira & F. Ribeiro (Eds.), *Radio, sound and Internet Proceedings of Net Station International Conference* (pp. 299–309). Braga: CECS - Universidade do Minho.

Binge-worthy journalism – Backstage with the creators of Serial. (n.d.). Retrieved from https://www.ctforum.org/binge-worthy-journalism

Bruzzi, S. (2016). Making a genre: The case of the contemporary true crime documentary. *Law and Humanities*, *10*(2), 249–280. doi:10.1080/17521483.2016.1233741

Buozis, M. (2017). Giving voice to the accused: Serial and the critical potential of true crime. *Communication and Critical/Cultural Studies*, *14*(3), 254–270. doi:10.1080/14791420.2017.1287410

Carriere, K., & Richard, E. (1989). Crime stoppers: A study in the organization of community policing. Research Report of the Centre of Criminology, University of Toronto.

Colapinto, C., & Benecchi, E. (2012). Movie industry goes viral. In I. Ibrus & C. Scolari (Eds.), *Cross media innovation* (pp. 161–178). Berlin: Peter Lang.

Cramer, T. (2014). Lessons from serial: The myth of the shrinking attention span. *EContent (Wilton, Conn.)*, *37*(10). Retrieved from http://www.econtentmag.com/Articles/Column/T.0/Lessons-from-Serial-The-Myth-of-the-Shrinking-Attention-Span-100832.htm

Crook, T. (2014). *Serial breaks iTunes records – and it's easy to see why*. Retrieved from https://theconversation.com/serial-breaks-itunes-records-and-its-easy-to-see-why-34388

Denson, S. (2011). To be continued…: Seriality and serialization in interdisciplinary perspective. *Conference Proceedings of: What Happens Next: The Mechanics of Serialization. Graduate Conference at the University of Amsterdam*. Retrieved March 1, 2017, from http://www.jltonline.de/index.php/conferences/article/view/346/1004

Desta, Y. (2016). *Ira Glass on 'Serial' and the 'secret sauce' that makes 'This American Life' so special.* Retrieved March 20, 2017, from http://mashable.com/2016/04/26/ira-glass-pandora/#VkTREMWWzgqD

Deuze, M. (2005). What is journalism? Professional identity and ideology of journalists reconsidered. *Journalism*, *6*(4), 442–464. doi:10.1177/1464884905056815

Dickson, E. J. (2014). How reddit ruined 'Serial' - and journalism. *The Daily Dot*. Retrieved February 22, 2017, from http://www.dailydot.com/opinion/serial-podcast-reddit-media/

DRNC. (2015, December 16). *State of the Subreddit survey results.* Retrieved from: https://www.reddit.com/r/serialpodcast/comments/3x333w/state_of_the_subreddit_survey_results/

Durrani, M., Gotkin, K., & Laughlin, C. (2015). Serial, seriality, and the possibilities for the podcast format. *American Anthropologist, 117*(3), 593–596. doi:10.1111/aman.12302

Eberwein, T., & Porlezza, C. (2016). Both sides of the story. *Journal of Communication, 66*(2), 328–342. doi:10.1111/jcom.12216

Edmond, M. (2015). All platforms considered: Contemporary radio and transmedia engagement. *New Media & Society, 17*(9), 1566–1582. doi:10.1177/1461444814530245

Ettema, J. S., & Glasser, T. L. (1984). *On the epistemology of investigative journalism.* Paper presented at the annual meeting of the AEJMC, Gainesville, FL.

Fishman, M., & Cavender, G. (Eds.). (1998). *Entertaining crime. Television reality programs.* New York: Aldine De Gruyter.

Gallivan, M. (2010). *Median ages across NPR Platforms.* Retrieved March 3, 2017, from: http://www.npr.org/sections/gofigure/2010/04/05/125578017/median-ages-across-npr-platforms

Gambarato, R. R. (2016). The Sochi Project: Slow journalism within transmedia space. *Digital Journalism, 4*(4), 445–461. doi:10.1080/21670811.2015.1096746

Gambarato, R. R., Alzamora, G. C., & Tàrcia, L. P. T. (2016). Russian news coverage of 2014 Sochi Winter Olympic Games: A transmedia analysis. *International Journal of Communication, 10*, 1446–1469.

Gambarato, R. R., & Tárcia, L. P. T. (2017). Transmedia strategies in journalism. An analytical model for the news coverage of planned events. *Journalism Studies, 18*(11), 1381–1399. doi:10.1080/1461670X.2015.1127769

Goldstein, J. (2014). *The Complicated Ethics Of 'Serial,' The Most Popular Podcast of All Time.* Retrieved February 22, 2017, from https://thinkprogress.org/the-complicated-ethics-of-serial-the-most-popular-podcast-of-all-time-6f84043de9a9#.yfkebqnk8

Goode, L. (2009). Social news, citizen journalism and democracy. *New Media & Society, 11*(8), 1287–1305. doi:10.1177/1461444809341393

Greenberg, S. (2012). Slow journalism in the digital fast lane. In R. L. Keeble & J. Tulloch (Eds.), *Global literaly journalism: Exploring the journalistic imagination* (pp. 381–393). New York: Peter Lang.

Haglund, D. (2014). *Was there an ending? We discuss the final episode of Serial.* Retrieved March 17, 2017, from http://www.slate.com/blogs/browbeat/2014/12/18/serial_podcast_last_episode_what_we_know_was_a_worthy_finale_slate_discuses.html

Houston, B. (2010). The future of investigative journalism. *Daedalus, 139*(2), 45–56. doi:10.1162/daed.2010.139.2.45

Jarvis, J. (2009). *The future of journalism is an entrepreneurial, collaborative process.* Keynote given at the Medientage München. Retrieved March 4, 2017, from: http://www.carta.info/17734/jarvis-keynote-medientage/

Jenkins, H. (1992). *Textual pochers: Television fans & participatory culture*. New York: Routledge.

Jenkins, H. (2003). *Transmedia storytelling*. Retrieved from MIT Technology Review: https://www.technologyreview.com/s/401760/transmedia-storytelling/

Jenkins, H. (2006). *Convergence culture: Where old and new media collide*. New York: NYU Press.

Jenkins, H. (2009, December 12). The revenge of the origami unicorn: Seven principles of transmedia storytelling. *Blog Confessions of an Aca-Fan*. Retrieved from: http://henryjenkins.org/blog/2009/12/the_revenge_of_the_origami_uni.html

Jenkins, H., Ito, M., & boyd, d. (2015). *Participatory culture in a networked era: A conversation on youth, learning, commerce, and politics*. Cambridge, UK: Polity Press.

Jensen, J. F. (1998). *Interactivity, tracking a new concept in Media and Communication Studies*. Retrieved March 3, 2017, from http://www.nordicom.gu.se/en/tidskrifter/nordicom-review-11998/interactivity-tracking-new-concept-media-and-communication-studies

Karlsson, M. (2010). Rituals of transparency. *Journalism Studies*, *11*(4), 535–545. doi:10.1080/14616701003638400

Karlsson, M. (2011). The immediacy of online news, the visibility of journalistic processes and a re-structuring of journalistic authority. *Journalism*, *12*(3), 279–295. doi:10.1177/1464884910388223

Le Masurier, M. (2015). What is slow journalism? *Journalism Practice*, *9*(2), 138–152. doi:10.1080/17512786.2014.916471

Lewis, S. C., Holton, A. E., & Coddington, M. (2017). From participation to reciprocity in the journalist-audience relationship. In C. Peters & M. Broersma (Eds.), *Rethinking journalism again* (pp. 161–174). London: Routledge.

Lurie, J. (2014). *"This American Life" channels "True Detective" in a new podcast*. Retrieved February 20, 2017, from http://www.motherjones.com/media/2014/09/ira-glass-sarah-koenig-julie-snyder-serial-podcast-this-american-life

MacLuhan, M. (1994). *Understanding media: The extensions of Man*. Cambridge, MA: MIT Press.

Martin, E. (2013). *Reflections on the recent Boston crisis*. Retrieved from https://redditblog.com/2013/04/22/reflections-on-the-recent-boston-crisis/

Mittell, J. (2015). *Complex TV: The poetics of contemporary television storytelling*. London: NYU Press.

Moloney, K. (2010). *Building transmedia journalism*. Retrieved February 20, 2017, from http://transmediajournalism.org/contexts/building-transmedia-journalism/

Moloney, K. (2013). *Breaking news as native transmedia journalism*. Retrieved July 1, 2017, from https://transmediajournalism.org/2013/10/

Normann, R. (2001). *Reframing business: When the map changes the landscape*. New York: John Wiley & Sons.

O'Meara, J. (2017). *"Like movies for radio": Media convergence and the Serial podcast sensation.* Retrieved March 17, 2017, from http://framescinemajournal.com/article/like-movies-for-radio-media-convergence-and-the-serial-podcast-sensation/#_edn3

Phillips, A. (2012). *A creator's guide to transmedia storytelling*. New York: McGraw-Hill.

Quirk, V. (2015). *Guide to podcasting. Report from the Tow Center for digital journalism.* Retrieved March 3, 2017, from http://towcenter.org/research/guide-to-podcasting/

Resler, R. (2015). The race to dominate the world of podcasting. *Jacobs Media Strategy*. Retrieved March 3, 2017, from http://jacobsmedia.com/the-race-to-dominate-the-world-of-podcasting/

Roberts, A. (2014). *The Serial podcast: By the numbers*. Retrieved March 3, 2017, from http://edition.cnn.com/2014/12/18/showbiz/feat-serial-podcast-btn

Serrano Tellería, A. S. (2016). Transmedia journalism: Exploring genres and interface design. *Trípodos, 38*, 67–85.

Siegelman, P. (2016). *An economist listens to serial*. Retrieved February 20, 2017, from http://works.bepress.com/peter_siegelman/43/

Usher, N. (2010). *Why spreadable doesn't equal viral: A conversation with Henry Jenkins.* Retrieved from http://www.niemanlab.org/2010/11/why-spreadable-doesnt-equal-viral-a-conversation-with-henry-jenkins/

VanCour, S. G. (2008). *The sounds of Radio*. Wisconsin, MA: ProQuest.

Visual Timeline. (n.d.). Retrieved February 20, 2016 from https://www.reddit.com/r/serialpodcast/comments/2k3o0h/visual_timeline/

Zelizer, B. (2004). When facts, truth, and reality are God-terms: On journalism's uneasy place in cultural studies. *Communication and Critical/Cultural Studies, 1*(1), 100–119. doi:10.1080/1479142042000180953

KEY TERMS AND DEFINITIONS

Doxing: Involves the publication of personal information about people without their consent. Personal documentation posted online with malicious intent may include a physical residential address, or information protected by law (social security numbers, medical records, and so forth).

Forensic Fandom: A type of fandom encouraged by transmedia narrative and its promise of eventual revelations once all the pieces are put together. Within this mode of fandom, people are invited to dig beneath the surface to understand the complexity of a story and its telling.

Hybrid Business Model: It is a model that combines the conventional ways of doing business with the technical means made possible by the Internet. Media hybrids can also combine some elements of private market support (e.g., advertising revenues) with some elements of public or philanthropic support (e.g., tax-deductible donations from individuals, or grants made by foundations).

Media Accountability: The media's obligations for the quality of their contents and performances towards their stakeholders and, specifically, to their publics. It transcends therefore the narrow focus on the media's responsibility, but focuses on the practices and instruments through which the publics can hold the media to account for their conduct.

Networked Journalism: A collaborative form of news production, where professional journalists and amateurs work together across brands and newsroom boundaries.

Slow Journalism: A specific type of journalism that does not follow the hasty production cycles of breaking news and that applies thorough research, narrative storytelling techniques, a non-sensationalistic reporting style based on clear ethical standards.

Transmedia Journalism: It is a form of transmedia storytelling applied to the journalistic field. The concept of transmedia storytelling involves the idea and the strategy of creating content across multiple platforms, genres and formats, that add up to a unique story world with a cohesive narrative. In addition, it includes activities that engage the audience by offering content that permeates the user's life.

Value Constellation: Nowadays, the competitive advantage relies on the capability of reconfiguring roles and relationships among a constellation of actors—suppliers, partners, customers—in order to mobilize the creation of value by new combinations of players.

Chapter 12
Potential Mediations of Hashtags Within Transmedia Journalism

Luciana Andrade Gomes Bicalho
Federal University of Minas Gerais, Brazil

ABSTRACT

In the last few years, sociopolitical events have been marked by the presence of hashtags on social networks, creating a direct dialogue with street protests. This chapter aims to investigate how media activism movements appropriate hashtags to expand the narrative through social engagement. In this sense, hashtags appear as signic processes that perform a mediating function. They articulate common positioning that creates hybrid and transmedia storytelling using online and offline dynamics. From the theoretical-methodological support of semiotics by Charles Sanders Peirce and the principles of transmedia, this study analyzes the news production by the Brazilian media activism group Mídia Ninja [Ninja Media]. The results point to a transmedia journalism anchored to the social use of hashtags by the association of new signs to semiosis, generating provisional action habits from collateral experience.

INTRODUCTION

In the communication processes related to the convergence culture (Jenkins, 2006), located in the connection between the transmissive dynamics of the mass media and the associative dynamics of social networks (Castells, 2012), it is possible to perceive an accumulation of records that leave various traces. With the increase in access to mobile devices, the production and sharing of contents have become a common practice by individuals. Sociopolitical events, which once gained visibility only through the traditional media agenda, are now also recorded and mainly disseminated by ordinary citizens. Records are organized in large files in programmable environments, under the influence of algorithms that design the network dynamics. This means a decentralization of communication tools, raising a controversial debate about journalistic practices.

DOI: 10.4018/978-1-5225-3781-6.ch012

This new media ecosystem (Canavilhas, 2014; Scolari, 2013), which incorporates collaborative production, has offered visibility to manifestations and protests around the world (Castells, 2012). Although they are born in the streets, they find a fertile and promising soil for the expansion of the stories on the Internet, shaping an organic network of content production. There is an occupation of the public space that gains notoriety and legitimacy through the shared narratives on social networks. This scenario is also marked by the distrust of corporate media, which leads to the strengthening of the free media format. After the appropriation of cyberspace by movements that began in the Arab world and then expanded through Iceland, Spain and the United States, it is possible to notice the emergence of sociopolitically organized groups that seek the apparent democratization of information, instigating the participation of the common citizen in the processes of verification, selection and production of news (Bentes, 2015).

This propagation of sociopolitical events has used hashtags to gain engagement in social networks. It favors the emergence of a new media agenda, which passes through the Trending Topics of the digital platforms, showing the relevance of certain subjects from the volume generated by the conversation on the network within a short period of time (Groshek & Groshek, 2013). However, although hashtags were created to group and monitor content on the Internet, with Twitter as their primary platform, they have played a major role in setting boundaries in common positioning inside and outside the digital environment. Their function extrapolates the physical condition of their trail to become an important agent in the production of meaning.

Thus, in this work, hashtags are understood as signic processes that fulfill a mediating function in the creation of new meanings. For Peirce (CP 2.308), the notion of mediation is tied to the idea of semiosis, containing three elements: Sign (representamen), object and interpretant. Semiosis is a reticular process involving the determination of a preceding sign (object) and the representation of a posterior sign (interpretant). What mediates the object and the interpretant is the sign (representamen) in order to produce another triad sign and so forth. The interpretant is the formation of a new sign that guarantees the vitality of semiosis.

This happens in the hashtags case because, in social networks, they are initially linked by the sociotechnical action of their index trail. In addition, through repetition and intermedia behavior (Müller, 2010) and by expanding content across multiplatforms, they also assume a normative function that indicates the construction of the thought. The same happens when hashtags are used on T-shirts and posters in street protests. Hashtags become signs that seek the determination and representation of an object (Alzamora & Andrade, 2016), which turns to be a complex semiosis (signification) process with infinite possibilities. For this reason, hashtags are used repeatedly in news production by media activism groups, as a feature that points to transmedia storytelling (Jenkins, 2006; Scolari, 2013).

The concept of transmedia journalism still generates many inconsistencies, especially in relation to professional practices. The exercise proposed in this chapter is to find new ways to elucidate this concept from the structuration of media activism groups, which seek narrative expansion through the integration between multiplatforms and the heterogeneity of points of view (Bentes, 2015). In this sense, the object used for the discussions is the Brazilian group Mídia Ninja [Ninja Media], which gained relevance after the manifestations of the 2013 June Journeys, an important Brazilian social movement that began with students' request for a reduction in the public transportation fare and then progressed to police violence and political corruption. The event was fundamental for the strengthening of new channels of information production and distribution in the country (Malini & Antoun, 2013). The group emerged as an alternative to the coverage of established media outlets, named "coup media" by the protesters. This scenario has established a new journalistic dynamic, producing and sharing content in a reticular way.

The narrative constructed by Mídia Ninja uses hashtags as a strategy for propagating a sociopolitical positioning, becoming a reference in the public debate. Hashtags are often created by the protesters themselves and then incorporated into journalistic content. In other cases, the group creates and shares its own hashtags, which also take effect in street protests. It is an organic process of creating news that gains vitality through social engagement. By showing a predilection for left-wing sociopolitical movements, the Mídia Ninja wishes to present itself as a transparent and partial vehicle, different from the dynamics of the traditional media. During the President Dilma Rousseff impeachment process, in 2016, the group became a benchmark in the sharing of several hashtags against the president's impeachment on various digital platforms, as well as a major influencer of the hashtag #nãovaitergolpe (written with the accent signal, because the spelling makes a difference to the Twitter algorithm in the grouping of content) [#therewillbenocoup], which has become a symbol widely used in discussions generated on the Internet and on the streets (Alzamora & Andrade, 2016).

In addition to having a hypertextual nature, which groups related content, hashtags today operate in the intermedia dynamics (Müller, 2010), extrapolating to Twitter and in force on other media platforms. With this, hashtags come to encompass the peculiar characteristics of each environment, impacting the formation of new meanings. For Elleström (2010), intermedia behavior indicates the forms of production, circulation and media consumption, configuring its interpretative capacity. In this sense, the news production by Mídia Ninja takes place in the intermedia and transmedia domains. In addition to being valid in several media environments, it is a narrative that arises from the social use of hashtags and gains visibility only through collective intervention in multiplatforms, in the interface between the networks and the streets. They are stories that complement each other and gain meaning through the mediating function of hashtags. Through the collateral experience and the incompleteness of the interpretant (Colapietro, 2011), a network of mobile meanings is created from the new associations, which guarantees the transmedia character of these semiosis.

This happens because the representative capacity of the sign is limited by its impossibility of covering the whole object that determined the sign, which demands the association of other signs (collateral experience) in the formation of the interpretant. The collateral experience concerns the prior familiarity with the object denoting the sign, a necessary condition for semiosis, operating by proximity and alterity with the object. According to Bergman (2010), the Peircean notion of collateral experience describes the impossibility of any contact with the objects of representation, or references, except through signic mediations. And since this process depends on social engagement, as in the case of hashtags, the creation of the interpretants is incomplete because it always points to new signs. Semiosis is a series of successive interpretants that prevent its closure. Thus, transmedia journalism reflects this plurality of possibilities of representation contained in the semiosis of hashtags, presenting a rich variation of mediatic arrangements through intermedia dynamics.

In order to understand these relations, this study has as a theoretical-methodological contribution the Semiotics by Charles Sanders Peirce and principles of transmedia storytelling (Gambarato & Tárcia, 2017; Jenkins, 2009; Scolari, 2013). An overview of the journalism productions by Mídia Ninja in 2016 is presented through investigation of the trajectories generated by the semiosis of the hashtag #foratemer [#outtemer], used in reference to the current president of Brazil during the narrative creation by the group. Subsequently, an analysis ensues in order to identify the potential of the mediations generated by this hashtag in the composition of transmedia journalism.

NON-FICTION TRANSMEDIA

Applying the specificities of transmedia storytelling has been a complex work for journalism. Jenkins (2006) consolidated the concept around fictional narratives, which are better suited and have more freedom to work with the characteristics of transmedia storytelling. Because journalism was born in the context of transmissive dynamics, it has experienced difficulties in adapting to the dynamics of social network sharing. This difficulty is attributed to the convergence scenario (Jenkins, 2006), which brings new paradigms for the production and distribution of information. There is integration between vertical (media corporations) and horizontal (individuals and groups) communication processes in digital connections. Convergence provides for a cultural transformation that encourages consumers to search for new information and make connections from scattered media content. This determines the migratory behavior of media audiences (Jenkins, 2006).

With the expansion of the media ecosystem (Canavilhas, 2014; Scolari, 2013), the circulation of content has become reticular, comprising the use of different media systems and seeking the active participation of consumers in the production and distribution of information, mainly through the mobility and connectivity offered by mobile devices. In Jenkins's (2006) view, this means that consumption has become a collective process, which increases the degree of complexity of the relationships between old and new media. This process of convergence is a central theme for journalism at the beginning of the 21st century, which calls into question the business model of corporate media (Moloney, 2015). However, as Alzamora and Tárcia (2012) demonstrate, the concept of convergence offers multiple paths, being too comprehensive to refer to such diverse phenomena.

In this context, Jenkins (2006) uses the term transmedia storytelling to indicate the processes of language and media expansion in the narrative production. Every text that unfolds in media environments needs to contribute in a distinctive and valuable way to the whole. As Scolari (2013) states, this is not an adaptation process that happens on multiple platforms but a complementary creation that integrates communication in several environments by overlapping mediations. Each generated text becomes a fundamental piece for the construction of narrative sense. However, it is important that each text also makes sense alone. Transmedia storytelling is the sum of independent texts that refer to a determining narrative, but which also construct meanings alone. Thus, according to Alzamora and Gambarato (2014), transmedia dynamics can be taken as a pragmatic branch of semiosis in the media, as will be shown below.

This idea means rethinking the whole path already taken by traditional journalism. Transmedia storytelling is important movement, according to Scolari (2013), because although the concept of transmedia was born in the field of entertainment, the use of transmedia in a non-fiction narrative has a latent potentiality. According to Canavilhas (2014), the difficulties of translating the concept into the field of journalism lie in the complexity of professional activity and in the multiplicity of concepts that already exist, such as multimedia, cross-media, intermediality and hybrid media, among others. For Scolari (2013), all these terms are part of the same semantic galaxy, and each contributes to the illumination of specific points of transmedia storytelling.

From this, Canavilhas (2014) tries to demonstrate that Web journalism has been working with several characteristics close to the universe of these concepts, mainly for acting with multiple platforms and languages (text, image, audio, video and infographic). Similar to Scolari (2013), Canavilhas believes that the concept of transmedia absorbs all others, its distinction being the convergence of content to a single end. Alzamora and Tárcia (2012) complement this understanding by stating that the focus is not only on the use of various platforms and languages but also on content production. It is "an effort to not lose focus of what is important in this discussion, placing excessive emphasis on technology (technocentrism) or on the media" (Alzamora & Tárcia, 2012, p. 28).

Alzamora and Tárcia's (2012) dialogue with Scolari (2011) explores the necessary resources for the sharing dynamics of transmedia storytelling. For Scolari (2011), stories need to seek the best of each medium to expand themselves. For this, they need to rely on prosumer collaboration in the development of the narrative world. This prosumer is a mix of a consumer and a producer, who take an active role in the process of expanding the narrative. "This is one of the points necessary to observe a transmedia structure: the expansion of the storytelling from the interactivity" (Renó, 2014, p. 7). In the field of journalism, this means an amalgamation of genres and formats through the integration of the communicational dynamics of transmission and sharing (Alzamora & Tárcia, 2012).

In this case, for Canavilhas (2014), the media have always stimulated social interaction, promoting discussions around themes essential to society. This participation could become strong fuel for news development, especially in a confluence with social networks. However, he asserts that not all journalistic genres are conducive to absorbing transmedia storytelling. The genres truly adapted to this dynamic are those natives of the Web and the great news stories, which present themselves as a transversal genre to all the media. In the second case, the possibility of deepening the narrative and the maturation time of the news are the factors that allow the transmediation of content.

Alzamora and Tárcia (2014) affirm that intermediality is an essential characteristic for the creation of transmedia storytelling, as the intersection between platforms favors the propagation of contents by the component of complementarity characteristic of these systems. Intermediality is the process of interweaving between different genres and media formats, resulting in differentiated aesthetic experiences (Müller, 2010). From this point of view, Alzamora and Tárcia (2014) present some types of narratives that can be configured today as transmedia journalism. The first is immersion journalism, which can put the public as the protagonist in the situations or events described in a news report. With the new media platforms, lived experience becomes more intense and can stimulate effective participation by the user. The other possibility is newsgames, experimental projects with public participation. Within this area, there are the current games, which are inspired by the daily repertoire to produce information quickly and with easy distribution. There are also interactive infographics, which allow users to change data and results in the system, proposing a collective way to update news. Finally, there are documentary genres, which facilitate the interaction and performance of the users, contributing to the construction of the narrative universe.

At the confluence of this notion, Canavilhas (2014) proposes four characteristics that must be present in the qualification of transmedia journalism. The first is interactivity, encouraging the relationship between content and between users. The second is hypertextuality, which allows linking content blocks by means of a link. This feature denotes a strong connection with the traces left during navigation, to be explained later. The third is integrated multimedia, as the organization of content seeks a specific goal in the use of multiplatforms. The last characteristic is contextualization, marking the antecedents and the conditions in which the event occurred. This characteristic facilitates the understanding of the narrative within the migratory behavior of the public. The degrees between contextualization and interactivity differentiate transmedia storytelling.

Narrative Expansion and Social Engagement

According to Canavilhas (2014), journalism's main challenge is to work with variations of time and space to encourage and deepen public participation. In this case, intermediality is fundamental for enriching the story being told. It is necessary to offer new entrances and itineraries to stimulate public interest. For Gosciola (2014), a narrative game promoted by intermediality contributes to the increase in public understanding, encouraging the public's curiosity and interest in the story narrated. This is because there is a significant change in content consumption due to increasing mobility and consequently, changes in the media textures (Jansson, 2013), that is, in the creation of communicative tissues. "Texture refers to the symbolic-material processes and arrangements through which communication and space co-constitute one another" (Jansson & Lindell, 2015, p. 81). From the transmedia dynamics, these textures become more integrated and flexible, revealing new consumption habits from certain spatiotemporal arrangements. "This is in regard to both how individuals navigate and orient themselves through representational spaces and flows, and how their media practices amalgamate with other activities in everyday life" (Jansson & Lindell, 2015, p. 79).

In Madianou and Miller's (2013) view, this scenario presupposes the concept of polymedia, articulating a complex media ecosystem that influences everyday life. In addition, it offers additional layers of meaning, creating a dynamic of overlapping mediations. This is because, for the authors, the media environment is similar to an integrated structure of possibilities. In the case of the transmedia texture, this is enhanced by the course of individual choices. This condition is decisive for news consumption, for, despite the intermedia power of multiple platforms, they are not always adapted to personal preferences. There are a variety of entry points, forming liquid consumption patterns. "These processes not only give rise to new compositions and experiences of news materials, but are also part of the ongoing texture of everyday life" (Jansson & Lindell, 2015, p. 82).

This transmedia texture is at the heart of participatory culture. For Shirky (2010), the way consumers are articulated today in media environments, especially online, presupposes a collaborative style of content production. This collaboration is a result of the desire for constant connectivity, which shapes the social use of technologies. In the field of entertainment, this participation is visible through fan culture, in which fans show interest and persistence in participating and updating content (Jenkins, 2006). However, Scolari (2013) states that it is possible to stimulate this participation in non-fiction narratives. However, it is necessary to horizontalize the creative control so that prosumers can contribute to the expansion of the narrative.

In this case, if consumption patterns are liquid, the focus may not be on the technical condition of the platform but on how the story is narrated (Scolari, 2013). This is what Scolari (2013) calls "journalism 3.0," which brings the citizen to the center of the news. If this transmedia texture also corroborates a texturing of daily life, the organic experiences on social networks are fundamental for understanding these processes. This even changes the media agenda, as it places peer-to-peer conversation at the center of social discussions. Proof of this is the constant updating of the Trending Topics on digital platforms, which show the intense flow of key terms and hashtags over a short period of time (Groshek & Groshek, 2013). These realized operations place hashtags as fundamental elements in the construction of meaning of the narratives, exploring the creative capacity of semiosis.

Groshek and Groshek (2013) note the emergence of Agenda Trending, which provides a rich scenario for thinking about the intermedia dynamics between traditional media and network conversations. Through an empirical analysis, the authors demonstrate a possible crossing between traditional and social media agendas. Despite the differences between the two, there is promising ground for thinking about how one influences the other. On one hand, this can increase the critical aspect of news production, broadening the spaces of debate. On the other, however, the authors warn that the expansion of monitoring and collective production tools can also end up homogenizing the public agendas. This homogenization reveals a decline in content diversity in news production. Thus, it is believed that a more in-depth discussion about transmedia dynamics and its potential in journalistic narrative expansion is essential, about the mediating function of hashtags.

THE MEDIATING FUNCTION OF HASHTAGS IN MEDIA ACTIVISM

At the intersection of media agendas are the guidelines for activist demonstrations, which have gained new formats through the integration of online and offline environments. If there was tension before between social manifestations and traditional media coverage, now the visibility of these events is also at the heart of the creation and production of collective information (Castells, 2012). In this way, Srivastava (2009) rethinks activism in the current media system based on participatory culture. According to the author, the transmedia dynamic offers new possibilities for movements with social change initiatives. There are decentralized actors who create entry points for issues and solutions linked to the topic across multiple platforms and languages. This favors the creation of strategies to generate social impact, influencing the perception and construction of communities.

As stated by Srivastava (2009), it is possible to notice the configuration of a "transmedia activism," which happens through the process of generating awareness, engagement, action and structuring change. For this to be achieved, a narrative goes through and encompasses the central theme. The shared contents trigger small fragments of this story from collective and collaborative work. The focus is to connect audiences and change agents with a particular worldview or specific action through local stories. This type of activism has as its main point the use of the local voice, aiming at community-centered participation. Through digital projection, these narratives gain visibility and can be expanded to a global level. Thus, activists use multiple platforms to achieve cultural appropriation in order to cross borders to promote transformation.

One of the ways to spread content quickly on social networks is through the use of hashtags. During protests, one can see the strong use of this tool. Yang (2016) signals the growth of "hashtag activism," which sets itself up as a discursive protest by the use of hashtags on social networks, carrying a social or political claim as content. This hashtag is a creative and communal narrative agency. The author argues that in the study of digital activism is neglectful of its narrative form. One way of thinking about this narrative structure is through the social use of hashtags. "I consider narrative agency in hashtag activism as the capacity to create stories on social media by using hashtags in a way that is collective and recognized by the public" (Yang, 2016, p. 14).

According to Bruns and Burgess (2015), the use of Twitter to coordinate social and political discussion has grown significantly in recent years, especially in electoral processes, activist movements and cultural, sports and television events. In this sense, hashtags have always been at the heart of the organization of these issues on the platform, operating in contexts ranging from general discussion about a topic to discussions that take place at local, state and national levels. The discussions may come as a reflection of a well-planned movement, created for a specific event, but may also be born from the spontaneity of networked conversations. For the authors, the most important thing is that hashtags are not static, as social use often changes their meaning by connecting them to other hashtags and platforms.

Although hashtags initially have the sole function of tagging and classifying tweets that are related to a specific topic through the hash (#), hashtags also enable communication between people and communities of interest. The use of hashtags was proposed in 2007 by Chris Messina, a Web developer, and was intended to gather content on Twitter to facilitate monitoring of the platform. His idea was to improve the listening experience, so that users could have more selective attention (Bruns & Burgess, 2015). At first, there was resistance to using hashtags because they were not part of the users' media habits. However, for Bruns and Burgess (2015), space for hashtags was won because it is an indexing system that imposes no rules or limits on users. They can create and share new hashtags whenever and however they want. In the view of the authors, this creates a process of "cultural generativity," since it intensifies and transforms public communication.

In this work, hashtags' capacity for connection is understood as a mediating function, capable of connecting one instance of meaning to another by sociotechnical linkage and social use outside the media environments (Alzamora & Andrade, 2016). In the first case, it has been observed that hashtags have not only permeated conversations on Twitter but have also appeared on Facebook, Instagram, YouTube, blogs and other digital platforms, even without performing the role of aggregating content in some instances. For Bruns and Burgess (2015), this is the result of improving the communicational use of hashtags, which are now at the heart of social and political discussions. This sets up intermedia behavior (Müller, 2010) that influences the construction of the meaning of hashtags. In the second case, the appropriation of hashtags by street protests shows the improvement in communication by the construction of ideas and thoughts. Outside usability as a content indexing monitoring tool, hashtags become effective on signs, t-shirts and printed materials as symbols of a common positioning (Alzamora & Andrade, 2016). This creates a transmedia dynamic, as we shall see later, as the hashtag spans several platforms and environments to construct new semiosis.

Therefore, a hashtag can be seen as a sign capable of representing a positioning, creating an interface between the online dynamics of programmable environments and the offline dynamics of the streets. This is because, for Peirce (CP 2.230), a sign is, in a way, something that represents something to someone, understanding semiosis as a process of interpretation *ad infinitum*, because the meaning of a sign is always another sign, over and over again. Thus, it is possible to affirm that the process of semiosis is also a process of mediation (Peirce, CP 2.308), because a sign always produces an effect in a mind, human or not, in order to represent the object that determined the sign:

A sign, or representamen, is something which stands to somebody for something in some respect or capacity. It addresses somebody, that is, creates in the mind of that person an equivalent sign, or perhaps a more developed sign. That sign which it creates I call the interpretant of the first sign. The sign stands for something, its object. It stands for that object, not in all respects, but in reference to a sort of idea, which I have sometimes called the ground of the representamen. (Peirce, CP 2.228)

This relationship arises from the logical engendering that exists among the sign (representamen), the object, and the interpretant (Peirce, CP 2.230). In later writings, Peirce (CP 2.308) defines media as the mediating function of the sign through which the sign produces communication and cognition. However, dependent on the collateral experience to form the interpretant, a sign can only partially reveal the object. This experience anchored in the baggage and in the accumulation of knowledge of each interpreter (agent), associates new signs with semiosis, creating connection dynamics through signic approximations (Colapietro, 2011). This sets up a network that is constantly expanding, ensuring that the reference to the object is maintained without compromising the creative ability of semiosis.

For Colapietro (2011), a sign is a place that a particle occupies within a short period of time. Thus, when hashtags are considered signs, within the sharing dynamics on social networks and the interactive dynamics of the streets, it is possible to realize that they relate to the objects that determine them in different and provisional domains of representation. In the category of firstness, the sign presents itself as an icon in relation to the object, referring to a mere quality (feeling), which cannot be apprehended or described. At the level of secondness, the sign is an index that establishes a physical connection, leaving a trail that points directly to the sign's object. Finally, thirdness perceives that the sign operates by the force of a law, of a convention, becoming a symbol by indicial repetition (Peirce, CP 2.230).

Thirdness provides the mediation between firstness and secondness, establishing a purpose for action (Colapietro, 2011; Peirce, CP 2.230). This shows that one category dispenses with the other, forming Peirce's concept of mediation, which is empirically linked to his notion of sign. These processes culminate in the network of meanings of a hashtag as a sign. It presents a feeling (firstness) that determines its physical inscription through the hash # (secondness), making the production of thought (thirdness) possible. This thought constitutes an action habit, as the outcome of the mediation between the feeling and the physical inscription of the hashtag. This happens because when the hashtag is understood as a sign, its action rarely happens alone, temporally or spatially, promoting a strong connection with other hashtags. This feature summons the audience to conversations on social networks connections at the interface with offline environments. Recursively, hashtags are updated by sharing, generating a network of logical connections. This creative dynamic offered by collateral experience articulates the chain of hashtags, enhancing the process of semiosis, which lies alongside the creation of transmedia storytelling.

In this sense, it is pertinent to understand the mediating function of hashtags in two complementary ways. On the one hand, hashtags promote the mediation between a common sociopolitical positioning, which is the sign's object, and a socio-technical link effect that triggers a new communicational context, the sign's interpretant. On the other, hashtags connect one instance of meaning to another by linking hashtags, creating a dynamic that can legitimize or reconfigure the initial sense of a hashtag. This space-time trajectory, shaped by mediation processes, imposes new challenges for the creation of transmedia storytelling on social networks, in a continuous flow with offline environments.

In this logic of connections, activism media groups consolidate in Brazil. They approach the narratives generated by protesters to create a news production different from those produced by major corporate media. For Malini and Antoun (2013), the heterogeneous voices of the crowd shape the processes of self-organization (*autopoiesis*) of networks with hashtags. Without the monopoly of speech, instituted by the large media groups, new forms of narrative experience emerge in the media ecosystem. In Bentes' (2015) view, this is a kind of "multitude-media," which is strictly linked to this mass media consumption. The author points to the emergence of post-journalism, which does not rule out professional techniques and practices but opens up to an experience of collective subjectivities within a transmedia scenario.

However, as Poell and van Dijck (2015) argue, a critical look at new forms of content production on social networks is needed. Despite the characteristics of customization and instantaneous circulation of information, a power war still prevails in this scenario. Although activism is less dependent on traditional media, it does not mean that activists have more control over the media ecosystem. On social networks, technological mechanisms and algorithmic selections of new social media corporations (such as Twitter, Facebook and YouTube, among others) guide the connections between users. This can significantly alter the path traced by narrative strategies:

As social media penetrate deeply into day-to-day personal communication in ways alternative media have never been able to do, activists can reach categories of people who would otherwise not be reached by activist communication. At the same time, the interactions and interests that tie dispersed social media users together to form protest movements, generating instant moments of togetherness, inevitably dissolve when social platforms algorithmically connect users to the next wave of trending topics. (Poell & van Dijck, 2015, p. 534)

Thus, because temporal and spatial dynamics are multiple, it is possible to visualize hashtags' semiosis networks only at the moment that new interpretants are formed (sign association by collateral experience). Therefore, considering the fluidity and dynamism of the analyzed objects, the theoretical-methodological procedures of Peircean semiotics serve as an aid to verify the trajectories created by hashtags at the moment of action of human and nonhuman agents. Certeau (2004) mentions the trajectory category as a procedure capable of transmuting the temporal articulation of places into a spatial sequence of points. This means creating a rigid structure in place of a performance, which is an operation. Thus, it is a fluid and unfinished trajectory of hashtags due to the interpreter's incompleteness, which is always triggering new networks and producing new narrative entries.

NEWS PRODUCTION BY MÍDIA NINJA IN BRAZIL

The dynamics of post-journalism, as demonstrated by Bentes (2015), live at the threshold of the relationships established between human and nonhuman agents in digital environments. For the author, the prefix "post" signals the problematization of journalism as a discursive regime. It is an open field that points to heterogeneous and disparate experiences of the media activism that emerges on social networks. Bentes (2015) uses Michael Hardt and Antonio Negri's (2004) concept of multitude to discuss this "multitude-media" that builds on the synergy and cooperation between singularities and differentiations. The crowd is not an amorphous and domesticated mass but is always in motion. The free media journalist can be any subject who, unlike the professionals who live in the corporatist sphere, participates in demonstrations and protests not only to register and report. He presents himself as a body of the crowd, and communication becomes an important tool in the mobilization and expression of this crowd (Bentes, 2015).

In this scenario of activism media productions, the Brazilian group Mídia Ninja (Narrative Independent, Journalism and Action) has stood out, mainly for structuring its narrative by taking into account human (public) and nonhuman (algorithms) action, with journalistic production as one of the spheres of communication. On the group's official website, the group presents itself as a specific type of journalism on the Web, which prioritizes partiality based on the sum and accumulation of all lived experiences. "Journalism is one of the tools and languages we use to raise themes and debates, strengthening narratives that have no visibility in conventional means of communication. But in addition to journalism we do midiativism" (Mídia Ninja Site, n.d.; *translation by the author*). The group absorbs activist practices to propose a social transformation through free and distributed media. Structured in a network, Mídia Ninja is maintained by the support of employees and partner institutions. However, anyone can contribute to the creation of new narratives, becoming a "Ninja." The objective is to discuss the national political agenda while giving voice to the common citizen.

Mídia Ninja's news production began in 2013, as a result of the cultural collective Fora do Eixo [Off-Axis network]. Because the group was born in the dynamics of social network sharing and its main focus is the coverage of street protests, the group configures what Malini and Antoun (2013) refer to as cyber-mediation or cyber-activism. This type of action, according to the authors, can be seen as the hacker of narratives, disregarding the visions edited by the great media conglomerates. Furthermore, despite maintaining an online news archive, the group uses social networks as its main platform to publicize its narrative, employing hashtags as mediators.

Thus, Mídia Ninja goes beyond and reinvents the notion of breaking news by using hashtags, as the group uses the instantaneity of the media to disseminate information in real time (Malini & Antoun, 2013). This is not a journalism structured in the order determined by the academy and with regular practices but an independent news production that draws a parallel with journalistic productions, mainly in the task of verifying events that often generate videos by streaming. "This hacked narrative, when subjected to the sharing of the many-many, generates a noise whose main value is to have a multiple, conflicting, subjective, and perspective view of the past event and of the future unfolding of a fact" (Malini & Antoun, 2013, p. 23; *translation by the author*).

For this reason, in this work, the dynamics of post-journalism, as described by Bentes (2015), becomes the ideal scenario for transmedia production. It is an active audience that interacts, comments, informs, analyzes and dialogues with journalists in various media environments, mainly through hashtags. This demonstrates a collective subjective experience that opens up a particular context of meaning in an interface with street protests and social networks. As Bentes (2015) states, Mídia Ninja narratives carry possible worlds within each statement. Each "matter" brings a cause, affection, a horizon of worlds around the news. This gives vitality to the creative production of semiosis.

ANALYSIS OF MÍDIA NINJA'S TRANSMEDIA JOURNALISM

Analysis Methodology

Based on the organization of transmedia activism proposed by Srivastava (2009), it has become fundamental to create a proper methodology of analysis to understand the movement of this free journalism, which not only participates in coverage and registration but also subscribes to the internal articulation of demonstrations. Thus, this research aimed to find ways to understand the semiosis created by the hashtag #foratemer [#outtemer] within the transmedia context of Mídia Ninja's journalism. Since it is not possible to cover all the extensions generated by semiosis, the intention is to look at the trajectories that point to the formation of new interpretants. This incompleteness, which is present in the determination of new habits of action by collateral experience, is analyzed from the principles of transmedia storytelling (Gambarato & Tárcia, 2017; Jenkins, 2009; Scolari, 2013).

As Srivastava (2009) argues, the intention of transmedia activism is to follow its purposes to generate awareness, engagement, action and effective change from distribution on several platforms. This is what motivates the existence of post-journalism (Bentes, 2015). In this context, the three categories of analysis proposed by Scolari (2013)—multiplatform, engagement and narrative expansion—are used to determine the strategies performed by Mídia Ninja in the use of hashtags. From this, the principles of transmedia are used, from the vision of Jenkins (2009) and Moloney (2015), to qualify each category. As methodological procedures of analysis, the characteristics listed by Gambarato and Tárcia (2017) are appropriated. The goal is to understand the course taken in the narrative construction of Mídia Ninja based on the mediation of the hashtag #foratemer [#outtemer] during the sociopolitical main events of 2016. Therefore, the three categories of analysis contemplate the following structure:

1. Multiplatform strategy.
    a. **Guiding Principles**: Spreadable and drillable.
    b. **Methodological Procedures**: Analyze objectives and premises, structure and context, platforms and genres.
2. Narrative expansion strategy.
    a. **Guiding Principles**: Continuity and seriality, worldbuilding immersion and extractability.
    b. **Methodological Procedures:** Analyze the construction of the universe, the development of new stories, characters involved and extensions.
3. Social engagement strategy.
    a. **Guiding Principles**: Diversity of points of view and inspiration to action.
    b. **Methodological Procedure**: Analyze the engagement.

Analyzing the Strategies of Mídia Ninja Journalism

Multiplatform Strategy

Multiplicity refers to the importance of narrative enrichment through the use of multiple platforms. The stories oscillate within a single coherent narrative realm (Moloney, 2015). This principle is directly related to the concepts of spreadability and drillability. Spreadability is the ability to "viralize" content through the mediascape. However, it is not just a strategy to make something visible without planning or direction. Spreadability "encourages the movement of the media itself, for personalized engagement, remix and reuse - all ideas that send shifts to the spines of intellectual property owners, but signal very deep and long-lasting engagement for compelling media" (Moloney, 2015, p. 49).

Another principle that points to the use of multiple platforms is drillability, which refers to the deepening of content to encourage public participation. This can be stimulated from the hypertextual construction of the narrative structure (Canavilhas, 2014), which always leads to denser unfolding, encouraging the public to create its own trajectory. "In dealing with real worlds, however, journalism has the advantage of only engaging the public's natural curiosity and enabling its sleuthing" (Moloney, 2015, p. 50). In order to understand how these principles operate in Mídia Ninja's production, it is fundamental to use the context and structure of the group to determine the objectives and premises of communication planning in order to verify the use of platforms and genres in the spreadability and drillability of the narrative (Gambarato & Tárcia, 2017).

Mídia Ninja was born in the transmedia perspective of the cultural collective Fora do Eixo. Before Mídia Ninja defined itself as activist media, the group was a branch of a complex chain aimed at establishing a free communication agency. Fora do Eixo was structured on six platforms with different approaches. There was a site called "Overmundo" [Overworld], with a focus on collaborative journalism, which spelled out the roots of Mídia Ninja. Moreover, it was comprised of Post TV, a streaming channel; Meme, the front responsible for the photographic production and graphic pieces; DF5, the audiovisual content; TNB, a site that connected independent artists in the country; and social networks, the distribution system for online content.

This happened before the outbreak of the June Journeys in favor of the "Passe Livre [Free Pass] Movement," due to the problems of students' urban mobility and later, the repercussion of corruption schemes in the country (Malini & Antoun, 2013). In March 2013, Mídia Ninja began its activities in the journalistic field, becoming a partner of Fora do Eixo. By already understanding the narrative structure in the order of multiplicity, the group stood out for its coverage and effective participation in social movements. From 2014 onward, with the protests due to the FIFA World Cup held in Brazil and the dissatisfaction with the government (D'Andrea, Alzamora, & Ziller, 2015), Mídia Ninja became a reference in the production and distribution of activist information. In 2016, the group invested in an organized structure to produce spreadable and drillable content. The purpose is to stimulate the visibility of sociopolitical causes on social networks (Facebook, Twitter, Tumblr, Instagram and YouTube), using the spreadability feature through hashtags. This is due to space-time appropriation of these environments, in which communication is fast and instantaneous. To create depth, the group has a collaborative site for news exploration (http://midianinja.org/) and a profile on Medium (https://medium.com/@MidiaNINJA). Additionally, through partners, the group offers other narrative lines that complement the central one, bringing in-depth information.

Narrative Expansion Strategy

For Jenkins (2009), the creation of worlds is fundamental to the process of public immersion and engagement. There is a desire of the audience to map and dominate all the content about the narrative that was created, which would indicate an "encyclopedic impulse." Therefore, the author delineates the importance of building complex worlds using various languages and media. However, Moloney (2015) states that this creation is limited in non-fiction narratives, for they deal with real worlds. The challenge is not to expand this world but to systematize it to facilitate public understanding. This does not leave out the wealth of narrative ramifications. "This provides a rich enough tapestry on which the main story can unfold, allowing alternate stories based on different characters and circumstances" (Moloney, 2015, p. 52).

In the case of the hashtag #foratemer [#outtemer], the constructed world concerns the period of the impeachment process of ex-president Dilma Rousseff. In 2015, dissatisfaction with the government triggered the impeachment process in 2016. During this process, there was political polarization between two distinct groups: One in favor and the other against the president's removal from office. To dialogue and show their position on social networks and street protests, users created and shared several hashtags that marked the Brazilian political scene. The main ones were #foradilma [#outdilma), to express support in favor of impeachment, and #naovaitergolpe [#therewillbenocoup], created to denounce impeachment as a coup against democracy (Alzamora & Andrade, 2016). On May 11 and 12, 2016, the Senate voted to abide by the protocol for opening the impeachment process. The president was removed from office, and Vice-president Michel Temer took up the position on an interim basis until the final trial in August, when he officially became president. This generated a great uprising and intensified the protests among those who were against the process.

In this scenario, Mídia Ninja stood out by taking a position against the impeachment demand. The group was one of the main influencers of the hashtag #nãovaitergolpe (with the accent signal). In addition, the group triggered a network of mobile meanings, working with the presence of several related hashtags (Alzamora & Andrade, 2016). After this period, the hashtag #foratemer [#outtemer] became a symbol of demonstrations against the new government. On August 31, 2016, the final vote of the impeachment process, monitoring was executed with the use of the Hashtagify.me tool, which elucidates the relationship between hashtags used on Twitter, to verify the semiosis formed by #foratemer [#outtemer] (Figure 1). The tool tracks the connections that had been generated, showing which other hashtags had been triggered by it at the time. What differentiates the process of semiosis is the degree of proximity between them, marked in the tool by the line that relates to each other. The closer to the analyzed hashtag, the newer the association. The thicker the line, the greater the intensity of the connection in the context of connectivity. In this way, the only trace that can be understood of these distinct temporalities is the formation of interpretants (new signs), materialized in the form of related hashtags.

Semiosis generated dialogues directly with other activism hashtags, mainly oriented toward the request for the return of ex-president Rousseff. However, it also evokes a crossroads with other stories, highlighting the relationship of media activism with the corporate media Rede Globo [Globo Network], through the hashtag #globogolpista [#coupplotterglobe], and with the 2016 Olympic Games, which took place in Brazil during the same period, through the hashtags #rio2016 and #cerimoniadeabertura [#openingceremony]. This scenario generated reflexes in the mediation of the Olympics from the political crossings. During mega-sports events, the hashtag #foratemerRio2016 [#outtemerRio2016] was created as a semantic variation to engender an intersection between the two narrative universes. This strategy was adopted by the demonstrators themselves and incorporated into the news production of the group Mídia

Figure 1. Relationships established by the hashtag #foratemer [#outtemer] on 08/31/2016. Source: Print screen of the analysis performed by the tool Hashtagify.me

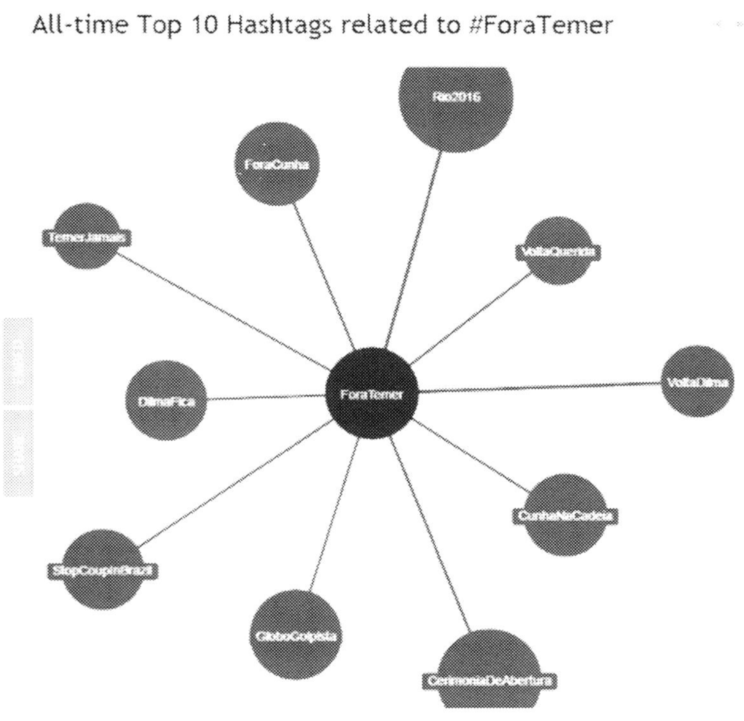

Ninja. Therefore, during this period, the group appears in second place on the list of influencers of the hashtag #foratemer [#outtemer] (Figure 2), first place having been conquered by the official profile of the former president (@dilmabr).

The principle of seriality (Jenkins, 2009; Moloney, 2015) aims to transform the narrative into scattered historical fragments in various media systems, which is assembled and reassembled only with the help of the public. This concerns the non-linear nature of the transmedia concept, which coincides with the behavior of hashtags that develop in a reticular way in the formation of new interpretants. Therefore, it would be impracticable to conceive the chronological trajectory of a hashtag. Serially, languages and media behaviors are mixed in meaning processes, as in the case of the hashtag #foratemer [#outtemer] during the Olympic Games. This dimension of continuity and seriality is also visible when the hashtag is transposed into the offline environment, appearing on signs and t-shirts during the Olympic Games events. Jenkins (2006) warns that it is necessary to master communication practices and to understand well the environments to be explored. In the streets, hashtags become slogans through social use. This transition between the indicial trail of online social networks and the presence of symbols in street manifestations determines the degree of detail and exploration of the world, guaranteeing the immersion of the public (Moloney, 2015). For this reason, it is also possible to understand the principle of extractability indicated by Jenkins (2009) as the ability of the public to take aspects of the storyworld into their daily lives. When hashtags are incorporated into the offline universe as a symbol, they gain new connotations in ordinary life.

Figure 2. Main influencers of the hashtag #foratemer [#outtemer] on 08/31/2016. Source: Print screen of the analysis performed by the tool Hashtagify.me

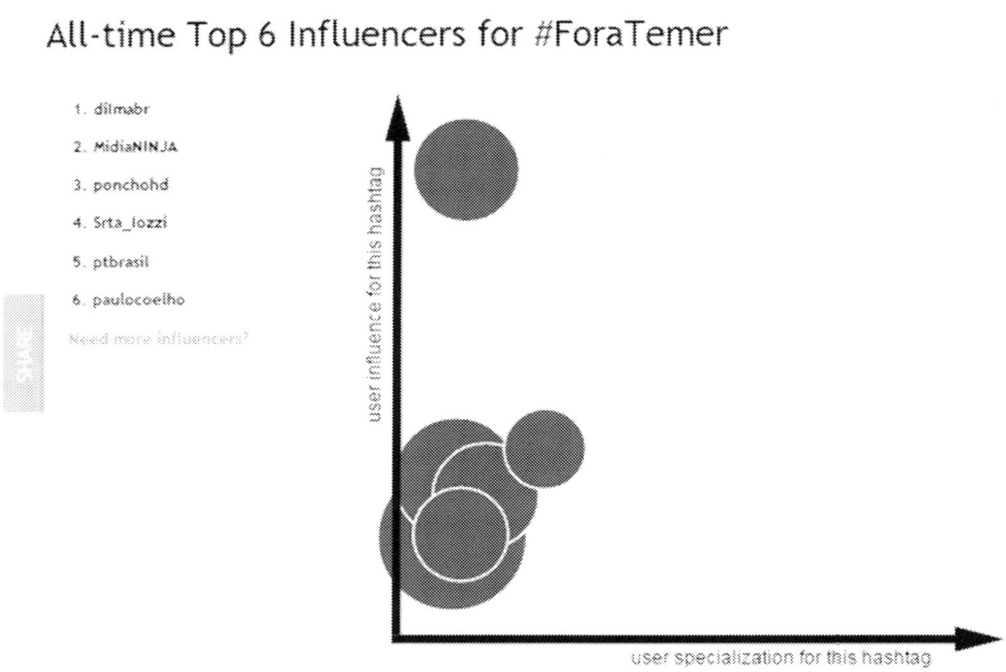

From this perspective, it is possible to understand that the mediation potential of hashtags delineates a transmedia dynamic through collateral experience. There is a dynamic purpose of action that is formed by the process of signic association between hashtags. Each line displayed in semiosis networks represents a new sign, that is, a new interpretant in the construction of meaning of the studied hashtag. These new interpreters may be seen as provisional unfoldings of the narrative of the demonstration against the government of President Michel Temer. They are ramifications that complement the meaning of semiosis but also construct parallel narratives.

Alzamora and Gambarato (2014) argue that the creative dimension offered by collateral experience denotes vitality for the narrative. It is precisely the domain of representation of the sign that leads to the productive incompleteness of the interpretant, since it is never possible to obtain the primary meaning of the object. As semiosis does not close and the final interpretant is not reached, this incompleteness is taken as a conceptual parameter to understand how media consumption regulates habits and models the transmedia dynamics in process of sign association (Alzamora & Gambarato, 2014). This is visible in the #foratemer [#outtemer] case, because it connects instances of distinct meanings and traverses narrative paths in a serial and hypertextual way (Canavilhas, 2014).

Thus, the use of hashtags demarcates demonstrators and users of social networks as important characters for the construction of the meanings of semiosis. Another form of narrative extension is the use of columnists for content creation and sharing. In 2016, the group invited teachers, politicians, members of religious organizations, minority leaders and students to compose the front line of news production. These characters also appropriate hashtags for narrative threads that intersect with the main one, resulting in a dimension in which the content is significantly deepened.

Social Engagement Strategy

As hashtags are the fruit of social engagement, the principles of subjectivity and performance (Jenkins, 2009) are essential for analyzing their mediation processes. According to Moloney (2015), subjectivity refers to the multiple voices and dimensions that permeate the narrative. The subjective perceptions of characters within the story are used to add to the narrative complexity. "They provide an opportunity to express the complexity of views of the same world" (Moloney, 2015, p 56). For hashtags, this creative and heterogeneous dimension configures what has been defined as collateral experience. Mídia Ninja stimulates these multiple voices as it opens its production space to the audience. Moreover, incorporating protest hashtags in the group's narrative generates visibility for local and global causes through interactivity (Canavilhas, 2014).

This interactivity is critical to the principle of performance, which gives the public the freedom to tell their bits of the story. In Moloney's (2015) view, it is an inspiration for action, that is, the creation of strategies to achieve effective transformation. This is the last stage of the narrative purpose of activist manifestations (Srivastava, 2009). This established relationship with the public is a partnership, fueling engagement. Mídia Ninja usually does some actions on social networks to encourage the use of specific hashtags. One is a "Twittaço," a call for a collective action to stimulate the use of a specific hashtag on Twitter with the intention of putting a hashtag among the Trending Topics, influencing the public agenda. The group seeks to use the algorithms in favor of engagement, always proposing actions to integrate humans and nonhumans. This creates an intermedia dimension between the platforms, since the dissemination of these events happens outside Twitter as well and brings about the transmedia dimension, connecting media platforms and the street environment.

CONCLUSION

This chapter aimed to discuss the relationship between transmedia and journalism from the perspective of the experiences of the Brazilian media activism group Mídia Ninja. The group is qualified as a type of immersive journalism, which promotes the participation of ordinary citizens in the investigation and creation of news. Through the intermedia behavior of hashtags, which link social networking platforms, and opening up to the transmedia dynamic in relation to street protests, Mídia Ninja stands as an alternative to corporate media, forming a kind of post-journalism. The group uses hashtags to create narratives anchored in the construction of a real world. This enhances audience participation and inspires action through the use of multiple platforms.

Because this, it was then necessary to develop a specific analysis methodology, seeking to crisscross the aspects of Peirce's semiotics and the principles of the transmedia storytelling, in order to intensify the observation of new habits of action by the interpretant's incompleteness. Peircean semiotics presumes the continuous improvement of the process of signic mediation, also called semiosis, which establishes provisional habits of action. Hashtags can operate in the mediation of a common positioning, triggering other hashtags in the creation of a complex and provisional network of meanings. Starting from this thought, the intention of this work was to understand hashtags as signic processes capable of generating symbolic dimensions from social use.

The interface between online and offline environments defines a serial and hypertextual communicative process, so that new media habits emerge from the use of hashtags. Street protests and online communication vehicles now appropriate hashtags to create an intersection with the digital environment. This mixture reinforces the expansion of the semiotic results generated by these hashtags. Because they are the product of online multiplicity, they are signs that establish new connections through the principles of transmedia storytelling. This defines the integration between vertical (media corporations) and horizontal (individuals and groups) communication processes in digital connections. Thus, this mediating process integrates differentiated communication dynamics that are part of the emergence of a transmedia journalism that is born from the provisional habits of action from the collateral experience.

ACKNOWLEDGMENT

This research was supported by Coordination for the Improvement of Higher Level Personnel (CAPES), Brazil.

REFERENCES

Alzamora, G., & Andrade, L. (2016). A representação do Impeachment Day mediada por hashtags no Twitter e no Facebook: semiose em redes híbridas [The representation of Impeachment Day mediated by hashtags on Twitter and Facebook: Semiosis on hybrid networks]. *Revista Interin, 21*(2), 100–121. Retrieved January 20, 2017, from http://interin.utp.br/index.php/vol11/article/view/478/pdf

Alzamora, G., & Gambarato, R. (2014). Peircean semiotics and transmedia dynamics. Communicational potentiality of the model of semiosis. *Ocula - Occhio semiotico sui medi, 15*(1), 1–13.

Alzamora, G., & Tárcia, L. (2012). Convergence and transmedia: Semantic galaxies and emerging narratives in journalism. *Brazilian Journalism Research*, *8*(1), 23–34.

Bentes, I. (2015). *Mídia-Multidão. Estéticas da comunicação e biopolíticas* [Multitude-media. Aesthetics of communication and biopolitics]. Rio de Janeiro, Brazil: Mauad.

Bergman, M. (2010). C. S. Peirce on interpretation and collateral experience. *Signs (Chicago, Ill.)*, *4*, 134–161.

Bruns, A., & Burgess, J. (2015). Twitter hashtags from ad hoc to calculated publics. In N. Rambukkana (Ed.), *Hashtag publics: The power and politics of discursive networks* (pp. 13–27). New York, NY: Peter Lang.

Canavilhas, J. (2014). Jornalismo transmídia: Um desafio ao velho ecossistema midiático [Transmedia journalism: A challenge to old media ecosystem]. In D. Renó, C. Campalans, S. Ruiz, & V. Gosciola (Eds.), *Periodismo transmedia: Miradas múltiples* [Transmedia journalism: Multiple perspectives] (pp. 53–67). Barcelona, Spain: Editorial UOC.

Castells, M. (2012). *Networks of outrage and hope. Social movements in the Internet age*. Cambridge, UK: Polity.

Certeau, M. (1984). *The practice of everyday life*. Berkeley, CA: University of California Press.

Colapietro, V. (2011). Ubiquitous mediation and critical interventions: Reflections on the function of signs and purposes of Peirce's semiotic. *International Journal of Signs and Semiotic Systems*, *2*(1), 1–27. doi:10.4018/ijsss.2011070101

D'Andréa, C., Alzamora, G., & Ziller, J. (2015). Hashtags as intermedia agency resources before FIFA World Cup 2014 in Brazil. In N. Rambukkana (Ed.), *Hashtag publics: The power and politics of discursive networks* (pp. 115–125). New York, NY: Peter Lang.

Elleström, L. (2010). The modalities of media: A model for understanding intermedial relations. In L. Elleström (Ed.), *Media borders, multimodality and intermediality* (pp. 11–50). New York, NY: Palgrave Macmillian. doi:10.1057/9780230275201_2

Gambarato, R. R., & Tárcia, L. (2017). Transmedia strategies in journalism. An analytical model for the news coverage of planned events. *Journalism Studies*, *18*(11), 1381–1399. doi:10.1080/1461670X.2015.1127769

Gosciola, V. (2014). Narrativa transmídia: conceituação e origens [Transmedia Storytelling: conceptualization and origins]. In C. Campalans, D. Renó, & V. Gosciola (Eds.), *Narrativas transmedia: entre teorías y prácticas* [Transmedia storytelling: Between theories and practices] (pp. 7–14). Barcelona, Spain: Editorial UOC.

Groshek, J., & Groshek, M. C. (2013). Agenda trending: Reciprocity and the predictive capacity of social network sites in intermedia agenda setting across issues over time. *Media and Communication*, *1*(1), 15–27. doi:10.2139/ssrn.2199144

Hardt, M., & Negri, A. (2004). *Multitude: War and democracy in the age of empire*. New York, NY: Penguin.

Jansson, A. (2013). Mediatization and social space: Reconstructing mediatization for the transmedia age. *Communication Theory, 23*(3), 279–296. doi:10.1111/comt.12015

Jansson, A., & Lindell, J. (2015). News media consumption in the transmedia age. Amalgamations, orientations and geo-social structuration. *Journalism Studies, 16*(1), 79–96. doi:10.1080/1461670X.2014.890337

Jenkins, H. (2006). *Convergence culture: Where old and new media collide*. New York: New York University Press.

Jenkins, H. (2009, December 21). *The revenge of the origami unicorn: The remaining seven principles of transmedia storytelling*. Retrieved December 12, 2017, from http://www.convergenceculture.org/weblog/2009/12/the_revenge_of_the_origami_uni.php

Madianou, M., & Miller, D. (2013). Polymedia: Towards a new theory of digital media in interpersonal communication. *International Journal of Cultural Studies, 16*(2), 169–187. doi:10.1177/1367877912452486

Malini, F., & Antoun, H. (2013). *A internet e as ruas: Ciberativismo e mobilização nas redes sociais* [The Internet and the streets: Cyber-mobilization and mobilization on social networks]. Porto Alegre, Brazil: Editora Sulina.

Mídia Ninja Site. (n.d.). Retrieved March, 30, 2017 from https://ninja.oximity.com/

Moloney, K. (2015). *Future of story: Transmedia journalism and National Geographic's future of food project.* ATLAS Institute Graduate Theses & Dissertations, University of Colorado Boulder. Retrieved December 20, 2017, from http://scholar.colorado.edu/atlas_gradetds/6

Müller, J. (2010). Intermediality revisited: Some reflections about basic principles of this axe de pertinence. In L. Elleström (Ed.), *Media borders, multimodality and intermediality* (pp. 237–252). London: Palgrave Macmillan. doi:10.1057/9780230275201_17

Peirce, C. S. (1932). Collected Papers of Charles Sanders Peirce (Vol. 2; C. Hartshorne & P. Weiss, Eds.). Cambridge, MA: Harvard University Press.

Poell, T., & van Dijck, J. (2015). Social media and activist communication. In C. Atton (Ed.), *The Routledge companion to alternative and community media* (pp. 527–537). London: Routledge.

Renó, D. (2014). Transmedia journalism and the new media ecology: Possible languages. In D. Renó, C. Campalans, S. Ruiz, & V. Gosciola (Eds.), *Periodismo transmedia: Miradas múltiples* [Transmedia journalism: Multiple perspectives] (pp. 3–19). Barcelona, Spain: Editorial UOC.

Scolari, C. (2011). *Narrativas Transmidiáticas: mundos de ficción y prosumidores en la ecología de los médios* [Transmedia storytelling: fiction worlds and prosumers in the ecology of the middle]. Retrieved December 20, 2017, from http://www.slideshare.net/cscolari/02-transmedia

Scolari, C. (2013). *Narrativa transmedia – cuando todos los medios cuentan* [Transmedia narrative - when all the media count]. Bilbao, Spain: Deustos.

Shirky, C. (2010). *Cognitive surplus: Creativity and generosity in a connected age*. New York, NY: Penguin.

Srivastava, L. (2009). *Transmedia activism: Telling your story across media platforms to create effective social change.* Retrieved March 30, 2017, from http://www.mediarights.org/news/Transmedia_Activism_Telling_Your_Story_Across_Media_Platforms_to_Create_Eff

Yang, G. (2016). Narrative agency in hashtag activism: The case of #BlackLivesMatter. *Media and Communication*, *4*(4), 13–17. doi:10.17645/mac.v4i4.692

KEY TERMS AND DEFINITIONS

Algorithm: Mathematical formula, code, or software that recognizes and generates information, the input/output.

Collateral Experience: Familiarity with the object in the construction of meanings.

Engagement: Participation in the production and sharing of contents.

Hashtag Activism: Persistent use of some hashtag that has for an objective an activist cause.

Media Activism: Independent media movement that uses social networks as the main platform for narrative production of activism.

Semiosis: Term used by Peirce to refer to the process of signification.

Sociopolitical Positioning: Process of manifestation in relation to some cause of a social and/or political nature.

Trending Topics: System offered by digital platforms to give visibility to hashtags and the most frequently commented terms for a short period of time.

Twittaço: Call for a collective action to stimulate the use of some specific hashtag on Twitter to reach the Trending Topics.

Chapter 13
The Transmedia Dynamics of TV3:
Newscast "Especial 9-N" on Connections of Online Social Media

Geane C. Alzamora
Federal University of Minas Gerais, Brazil

ABSTRACT

The newscast "Especial 9-N," produced by TV3 (Catalonia) in association with TV3's news channel 3/24, presents transmediatic components by combining multiplatform journalistic coverage and citizen participation in online social media. The program aired on November 9, 2014, the date of the non-binding referendum on the sovereignty of Catalonia, held by Generalitat, the regional government. This chapter discusses in what measure the editorial strategy adopted optimized social engagement with the news and favored the circulation of broadcast journalism on online social media. The analysis was based on the systematic observation of the program and its records on online social media, to assess the nature and the intensity of the communicational activity. It was concluded that TV3's institutional identification with aspects related to the region's sovereignty, in the context of significant social mobilization around the theme, fostered transmedia circulation and social engagement with the news story.

INTRODUCTION

Multiplatform distribution and citizen participation in online social media characterize most contemporary television programs, be they journalistic or not. The dissemination of television content on online social media integrates the joint action of producers and consumers through the recognition of a certain televisual syntax scattered across the networks. According to Jost (2010), televisual syntax involves aspects such as broadcasts defined by immediacy, the broadcaster's institutional identification, and references to the program schedule, the latter constituted of content related to news, entertainment, and education. Therefore, televisual syntax is a relevant parameter for the transmediatic configuration of television, for it enables its recognition on several digital connections, as will be discussed here within the scope of

DOI: 10.4018/978-1-5225-3781-6.ch013

the newscast "Especial 9-N" [9-N Special], produced by TV3 in association with TV3's news channel 3/24. Both channels were owned by group TVC in Catalonia, Spain.

Televisó de Catalunya [Catalonia Television] (or TVC)—the first television network to broadcast exclusively in Catalan—is a public communication company created in 1983 to disseminate Catalan language and culture. This institutional perspective guides the network's six television channels, one radio station, one news website, and an online video-on-demand service, all associated with *Televisò de Catalunya*. TV3 is the company's main news channel, as well as the oldest. TV3 broadcast for the first time on September 10, 1983, one day before the celebrations of *Diada*, the National Day of Catalonia. Since the network's first transmission, therefore, TV3 has publicly presented itself in favor of sovereignty for the region.

Acting from this institutional standpoint, TV3 proposed differentiated programming for coverage of the public consultation process and non-binding referendum that took place on November 9, 2014, about the sovereignty of Catalonia. The consultation process, which became known by the social designation "9-N," was convened by *Generalitat de Catalunya*, the regional government that functions locally, without the agreement of the central Spanish government. This situation caused significant social mobilization in Catalonia, with an impact on social engagement with the journalistic coverage of 9-N, as will be presented below.

Among the journalistic coverage of the event, the news program "Especial 9-N," broadcast on November 9, 2014, by TV3 in association with TV3's news channel 3/24, received special emphasis. Created in 2003, news channel 3/24 inaugurated its news portal in 2007. According to Micó and Barbosa (2009), the idea was to adapt to new consumption habits, related to the transition from a massive public to a fragmented audience. Therefore, the coverage presented by 9-N, born of cooperation between TV3 (broadcasting) and 3/24 (narrowcasting), was based on the experience with multiplatform production the news channel had accumulated and on the identification of TV3's institutional profile with matters pertaining to the sovereignty of the region.

The "Especial 9-N" program assumes transmediatic characteristics when it integrates multiplatform journalistic production and citizen participation in online social media networks. The program's production combined efforts from television, radio, news portals, and online social media, such as Facebook, Twitter, Instagram, and YouTube. Among the editorial measures which sought to stimulate the expansion of the journalistic narrative through social participation, we emphasize the invitation to use the hashtag #9NTV3 in contributions that would feed the collaborative experiment "El Mapa del 9-N" [The 9-N Map].

This chapter discusses in what measure the editorial strategy adopted optimized social engagement with the news and favored the dissemination of broadcast journalism on online social media. The analysis was based on systematic observation of the program and its records on online social media networks, to assess the nature and the intensity of the communicational activity.

TRANSMEDIA TELEJOURNALISM

Transmedia storytelling, as defined by Jenkins (2003), is characterized by spreading in the intersection of several communication mediums through the integrated action of producers and consumers. According to Jenkins (2003), the reading across the media sustains a depth of experience that motivates more consumption. Although fragmented and dispersed on varied mediatic connections, the transmedia audience tends to be dense, engaged, and organized around communities of interest, thus favoring a deeper and more immersive consumption experience. As a co-producer of the information the audience consumes, the transmedia audience is responsible for a considerable share of the expansion of the narrative universe on digital connections. Jenkins (2003) argues that we need a new model for co-creation, rather than adaptation of content across media, because the current structure is hierarchical. Transmedia dynamics, therefore, permeates forms of information production, circulation, and consumption consolidated in the context of Mass Culture. As a consequence, transmedia dynamics interfered with the nature and the density of the communicational activity generated around mediatic products and processes.

In this seminal text, Jenkins (2003) considers that films and television probably have the most diverse audiences and states that a good transmedia franchise attracts a wider audience by pitching the content differently in different media. Although in this publication Jenkins was not talking about television in general but about an audiovisual franchise in particular, such as films or TV series, his argument suggests the possibility of thinking about transmedia television in a broader manner. The theme has been developed by several researchers, such as Evans (2011), ever since.

Based on Jenkins' concept of transmedia storytelling, Evans (2011), for example, distinguishes transmedia storytelling distribution from transmedia storytelling engagement. "Transmedia engagement involves two interrelated processes, one that concerns the television industry and one that concerns the actual behavior of audiences" (p. 40). However, she considers that "transmedia distribution has resulted in an expansion of the spaces in which television is made accessible and the borders of the television industry becoming blurred" (p. 63). According to Jenkins, transmediality involves production, distribution, and reception practices that move away from the television set. The productive activity of the audience is highlighted in this scenario.

The transmediatic relation between the productive actions of the connected audience and the multiplatform distribution of television content (Evans, 2011) is discussed in this chapter in light of the notion of televisual syntax (Jost, 2010). Television audiences on online social media establish themselves according to the program schedule and the channel's institutional profile, which is still distinguishable on digital connections. Connected audiences (D'Andrea, 2014) usually engage with television content on online social media according to the conceptual perspective of the second screen, in broadcasts that are characterized by immediacy. That is also a typical case of spreadable media, the continuous process of repurposing and recirculation by individuals, communities, and corporations (Jenkins, Ford, & Green, 2013)

The use of a second screen while watching TV results in different modes of interaction, such as social sharing contents, additional content, or recommendations to the viewer, and a control device for enhancing content viewing (Doughty, Rowland, & Lawson, 2012). Therefore, using a second screen is a communicational experience that acts transmediatically because it combines the strategy of multiplatform distribution and the audience's productive activity in the form of sharing or complementarily expanding television content. The second screen experience occurs through the identification of televisual syntax on online social networks, in transmissions characterized by immediacy that emphasizes references to the program schedule and the institutional identification of the channel. However, the temporality of television dynamics is dilated and not restricted to the present, although the references to the program schedule and the channel's identification as a brand remain relevant aspects of the television syntax in transmedia dynamics.

The channel's identification on online social media is optimized by the notion of transmedia branding, a variation of transmedia storytelling. According to Tenderic and Williams (2015), transmedia branding emphasizes engaging audiences in compelling conversations and implies that information about a brand is being transformed into a story. They posit that participation can be a direct interaction with the brand or with audience members, content creation, or even becoming part of the story themselves.

The brand of a certain television channel operates as a mediating body of social conversation in the connections of online social media. This process occurs when the public identifies with the company's institutional profile and program schedule. Transmedia circulation of a television program, such as a newscast, may draw upon, for example, the collective use of hashtags related to the channel's brand to mediate a topic of social conversation. Many second screen experiences use this procedure to instigate online conversation during live broadcasts or to stimulate audience engagement on online social media connections before, during, and after a television program has aired. This engagement was observed with the newscast "Especial 9-N," which invited the audience to contribute on online social networks with the collective use of the hashtag #9NTV3.

The mediating function of this hashtag is to associate publications of journalists and citizens, coordinating interactions related to the theme of this newscast. Because of this, the connections outlined by hashtag tend to form reticular zones for mixing genres and formats among digital media connections. Genre and format miscegenation is one of the main elements of transmedia dynamics (Alzamora & Tárcia, 2012), which does not mean an erasure of the original mediatic references. In the case of "Especial 9-N," televisual syntax, in a broader sense, and the linguistic references of telejournalism more specifically, limit the possibilities of miscegenation.

The historical development of broadcast journalism emphasizes the perspective of speed and a preference for "live" (Marcondes Filho, 2000). On online social media connections, these elements specify the syntax of telejournalism, configuring a normative parameter for transmedia dynamics in broadcast journalism. According to Scolari (2013), transmedia journalism develops through expanding, exploring, and diversifying points of view. Based on this perspective, transmedia telejournalism configures a multiplatform and participative process characterized by expanding, exploring, and diversifying points of view on online social media, through the recognition of elements stemming from televisual syntax, in a broader manner, and more specifically, from broadcast journalism. The productive actions of a connected audience eventually result in formats and genres that are distinct from those historically consolidated by telejournalism, thus characterizing this activity as a transmediatic form of expression of the news. The historical references of telejournalism, however, act as a possible parameter for expansion.

The impact caused by the audience's productive activity on configuring television was discussed by Bruns (2008) in what he calls a *produsage* context, in which the consumer becomes a co-producer of the information he or she consumes. According to Bruns (2008), a strategy available for television in a produsage context is to engage more directly with users as producers themselves. This strategy, he states, operationalizes the weakening of the boundaries between professional and amateur content, by issuing a direct invitation for users to become content producers and to contribute to that content. The situation described by Bruns (2008) characterizes the transmedia dynamics of television when, for instance, the audience is invited to interact on online social media connections by collectively using an institutional hashtag, as has been argued.

Hashtags were created on Twitter, where they connect posts under the same theme and are automatically measured by Trending Topics, a tool that daily monitors the hashtags most frequently used on Twitter. However, their use has expanded through other mediatic contexts, in which they are not always automatically monitored. In these environments, hashtags operate as a symbolic expression that delineates topics of interest and of social positioning (Alzamora & Bicalho, 2016).

Highfield, Harrington, and Bruns (2013) present a study about tweets as TV audience research. They conclude that Twitter does not necessarily replace existing media channels but often complements them. "Not only do audiences tweet about what they see, but television programs themselves can be integrated partly or fully around the input provided by the viewers via social media" (p. 406).

This perspective refers to the idea of the second screen as one of the delineating aspects of televisual syntax in transmedia dynamics, for the second screen operates by expansion and not merely as an adaptation of television content. Jenkins (2009) argues that adaptation must not be seen as a transmediatic procedure, because adaptation does not introduce significantly different elements in the narrative from the original that serves as the reference. He proposes seven principles of transmedia storytelling: Spreadability vs. Drillability, Continuity vs. Multiplicity, Immersion vs. Extractability, Worldbuilding, Seriality, Subjectivity, and Performance. These principles emphasize the ability of the transmedia strategy to encourage and incorporate the productive action of the audience as part of the transmedia narrative itself.

Transmedia telejournalism unfolds in online social media connections in sync with the principles proposed by Jenkins (2009). Spreadability vs. Drillability, for example, describes how content is shared on a social network and the factors that motivate a person to share and explore that content. According to Jenkins (2009), Spreadability refers to the capacity of the public to engage actively in circulating media content through social networks, while Drillability is related to the depth and complexity of social engagement with the narrative. He (2009) argues that both potentials may be built into the same transmedia franchise but represent different dimensions of the experience. This chapter argues that both also represent different dimensions of the experience of engagement in transmedia journalism, especially in the context of great social mobilization, as is the case of 9-N in Catalonia in 2014.

ESPECIAL 9-N

The multiplatform and participative news program "Especial 9-N," produced by TV3 and its news channel 3/24, was broadcast on November 9, 2014, between 8 a.m. and midnight. Production encompassed all regions of Catalonia, Madrid, and global capital cities. TV3 and 3/24 transmitted live during the day, and from 7 p.m., "Especial 9-N" was aired on two occasions: "Especial 9-N, la votació" [Special 9-N, the Vote] from 7 p.m. to 9 p.m. and "Especial 9-N, l'anàlisi" [Special 9-N, the Analysis] from 10 p.m. until midnight. During the day, the audience was encouraged to participate by sending commentaries, videos, photos, and tweets geolocated through institutional hashtags, such as #9NTV3 and #9NCATRÀDIO, which resulted in the collaborative experiment "El Mapa del 9-N,"[1] produced in association with Catalunya Ràdio. Also available in apps for mobile communication devices, "El Mapa del 9-N" was updated in real time and presented geolocated results by election region, district, shift, and polling station.

Social engagement with this editorial proposal was predictable because it was a topic of great interest in the region. The social mobilization process that culminated in the 9-N was in motion at least since November 25, 2012, the date of the elections for *Parlament de Catalunya*, when a commitment was established by part of the majority in Congress to undertake a public consultation process about the population's right to decide on the political future of Catalonia. On September 11, 2013, the day of the *Diada* celebrations, or the National Day of Catalonia, separatism gathered massive support, expressed by a human chain spread over 400 kilometers, starting in the capital of Catalonia, Barcelona. According to information from the Guardia Urbana de Barcelona published in the newspaper *La Vanguardia* (2014a), on September 11, 2014, the *Diada* celebrations attracted 1.8 million people. Therefore, the theme generated significant social mobilization in the region, the reason the editorial planning for the "Especial 9-N" program was so rigorous.

The television broadcast of "Especial 9-N" was associated with the daily editions of "Telenotícies," a TV3 newscast which is, according to Herms (2003), the key element of TV3 journalism. The multiplatform and participative perspective of this journalistic coverage was thus based on the audience's identification with the channel's institutional profile, as well as in reference to the program schedule and to the transmissions defined by immediacy. The recognition of the televisual syntax of TV3 favored the establishment of a multiplatform and participative audience on that day, and the association with *Telenotìcies* strengthened the audience's identification with the editorial profile of the newscast.

According to Focus Media (Pastor, 2014), a company specialized in audience measurements, TV3 was the most-watched channel in Catalonia on November 9, 2014, and news channel 3/24, TV3's partner in producing "Especial 9-N," was the third most-watched of the day. TV3 celebrated these numbers, announcing them as an audience record (TV3, 2014). According to *La Vanguardia* (2014b), joint broadcasts of TV3 and 3/24 about 9-N favorably influenced the TV3 audience on that day. *Telenotìcies* reached 30.4% of the audience (1.1 million viewers on average), while the broadcast of "Especial 9-N, la Votació" reached 32.6% of the audience (950 thousand viewers on average), and that of "Especial 9-N, l'anàlisi," reached 31.1% of the audience (690 thousand viewers on average).

Data reveal that the connected audience, while fragmented and dispersed throughout the network, engages coherently with broadcasts that reflected themes in which the audience is interested. The editorial strategy adopted by TV3, therefore, resulted in a concentration of the audience and a strengthening of TV3's institutional profile with its public on online social media. According to data from the *Informe Reuters Institute Digital News Report 2014: España* (2014), those under the age of 35 in Spain seek information in a balanced manner between online social media and television, which legitimizes the editorial strategy adopted and incorporates it into the spectrum of transmedia journalism.

Joint broadcasts, however, are not new in TV3's history. In 1992, during the Summer Olympics in Barcelona, TV3 and TVE (*Televisión Española*) created the *Canal Olímpic* to broadcast the Games conjointly. According to Herms (2003), this deal between TV3 and TVE was especially important because it allowed the Games to be broadcast in Catalan to a large audience—this was one of the institutional cornerstones of TV3, the first television channel to broadcast solely in Catalan. In 1992, the joint broadcast was only on television, which clearly characterizes it as an intermedia dynamic. However, the multiplatform and participative coverage of 9-N in 2014 combined television, radio, and the Internet, as well as journalists and citizens, in the collective production of information through contributions published on online social media networks under institutional hashtags, such as #9NTV3. This journalistic coverage thus shaped a more sophisticated intermedia dynamic, permeated by typical elements of transmedia dynamics.

Intermedia dynamics is characterized by a mutual effect between the media involved and the subsequent exchange of meaning among them (Wenz, 2008), because the means of communication are porous, malleable, and absorbing. According to Herkman (2012), the intermedia flux is intertextual and founded on continuity and on the variation of mediatic arrangements in a particular context of meaning. As the Herkman (2012) states, each mediatic environment differs from another due to historical, social, cultural, aesthetic and institutional aspects. Such aspects persist, to a greater or lesser degree, in the dynamics of intermedia.

The *Canal Olímpic* is an example of intermedia dynamics because it is a result of mutual effect between TV3 and TVE, and is based on continuity and on the variation of the channel's mediatic arrangements in a particular context of meaning, that is, the Barcelona Summer Olympics in 1992. The same can be said of the editorial strategies adopted by TV3 for its multiplatform and participative journalistic coverage of 9-N. The institutional partnership established with 3/24 around the "Especial 9-N" favored the intermedia circulation of journalistic information on television, resulting in the strengthening of the individual brands on online social media and an intermedia concentration of the individual audiences. It was observed the exchange of meanings between transmissive communication process (typical of television) and collaborative communication processes (typical of interactions on online social media) was observed. However, in addition to intermedia, this television dynamic is transmedia, for it is characterized by a multiplatform distribution of television content combined to the productive action of the connected audience (Evans, 2011) through the recognition of televisual syntax (Jost, 2010) on online social media.

ESPECIAL 9-N AND TRANSMEDIA DYNAMICS

"Especial 9-N" was aired immediately after *Telenotícies*, the newscast with the largest audience on TV3. However, TV3 and 3/24 announced the program beforehand on their many online social media profiles, for instance, on Facebook, Twitter, Instagram, YouTube and Tumblr. Thus, the channels sought to instigate communicational activity in the form of visualizations, commentary, and sharing before, during, and after the television program was broadcast.

This is a typical procedure of transmedia journalism because it expands the temporality of social interactions regarding a newscast, thus favoring a careful exploration of the information published in each mediatic environment. Diverse points of view are encouraged, for example, by appealing to the audience to publish posts with the hashtag #9NTV3, with sights set on the collaborative production of "El Mapa del 9-N." Although hashtags can be used in an intermediatic way (D'Andrea, Alzamora, & Ziller, 2015), this is a typical transmedia use.

The program's temporality was expanded by the productive action of the audience with the social use of the hashtag #9NTV3, whose contributions in the form of geolocated tweets would be incorporated in the collaborative experiment "Mapa del 9-N," and by the institutional actions of the channel, which sought to amplify the communicational activity generated around the "Especial 9-N." As an example, we mention the institutional publication "El 9-N a TV3—Televisió de Catalunya" [The 9-N on TV3—Television of Catalonia], registered on Twitter at 3:22 p.m. on November 9, 2014. This publication, which announced the following broadcast on television of the program on that day, was associated with a similar post on Facebook and on TV3's news site, where the post was linked to another post, entitled "programación especial TV3, 324 y 324.cat del 9-N" [Special programming TV3, 342 and 34.cat of 9-N]. The text explained that throughout the day, Telenotícies, 3/24 and "Especial 9-N" would act in an integrated fashion on the coverage of 9-N and encouraged citizens to contribute under the hashtag #9NTV3 to build "El Mapa del 9-N." The relationship of mutual effect between communication vehicles linked to TV3 with the goal of generating a particular context of meaning—"Especial 9-N"—is distinctly intermedia. This perspective combined with that of the expansion of the journalistic narrative through the productive actions of the audience in, for example, the production of the collaborative experiment "El Mapa del 9-N," shapes an intermedia dynamic with a transmedia editorial purpose.

The singular temporality of transmedia journalism is underscored in this institutional publication. On the one hand, it disseminates information on intermedia dynamics with the goal of converging the audience dispersed on connections of online social media, in reference to the television's program schedule and to the immediacy of the television program's time of transmission. On the other hand, it stimulates the transmedia expansion of information, according to the temporality delimited by the audience's social engagement. Thus, transmedia dynamics unfolds in the intersection of these dissonant, albeit converging temporalities, and is characterized less by the linearity of a program schedule than by the deferred logics of data banks (Weissberg, 2004), which conducts digital connections.

This perspective is also made evident in 3/24's post on October 15, 2014, on Facebook and Twitter, about the campaign organized by *Generalitat* to urge volunteers to present themselves to act on 9-N. The post, which led to a news story published by 3/24 on its news site, returned to Facebook's timeline on November 9, 2014, due to the audience sharing comments. It is an example of the temporality characteristic of transmedia dynamics, because its visibility derives from the productive actions of the audience that acts on online social media in accord with the deferred logics of data banks.

The transformation of telejournalism's intermedia dynamics into transmedia dynamics depends, to a greater extent, on social participation and its impact on journalistic information on television. The hashtag #9NTV3 is an example of this process. It is in the nature of hashtags to act in varied temporalities because they operate as hyperlinks, which consist of a term indexed on search mechanisms on certain online social networks, such as Twitter—the mediatic environment where hashtags first appeared. Hashtags thus form hyperlinks through which it is possible to aggregate various posts on distinct mediatic contexts and with varied temporalities from a common significant form.

The productive actions of the audience mediated by the hashtag #9NTV3 expand the broadcast's real-time temporality but do not distance themselves from the references to the program schedule, characterized by the television broadcast of "Especial 9-N." Televisual syntax, thus, is updated according to the conceptual perspective of the second screen and transmedia branding. In this context, the audience tends to act in accordance with produsage logics (Bruns, 2008), which makes the separation between production and consumption opaque and circumstantial, because audiences participate, to a greater or lesser extent, in producing the information they consume.

The hashtag #9NTV3 reached 4.7 million tweets, boosting TV3's audience during the channel's coverage of 9-N on online social media. In November 2014, #9NTV3 reached the worldwide Trending Topics, became a vector of social participation for TV3 posts on online social media, and consequently, contributed to boost the audience of TV3's multiplatform and participative coverage of 9-N. On November 9, 2014, the date of the non-binding referendum, the hashtag #9NTV3 was mentioned 3,764 times on Twitter. During the day, 3/24 released partial results of the referendum results with this hashtag, and the results were widely retweeted, also using this hashtag. While posts made by citizens with this hashtag on November 9, 2014, received between 0 and 30 shares, 3/24 posts with the hashtag on the same day received from 17 to 462 shares (Alzamora, 2016). Data reveal that although citizen contributions prevailed on the network formed by this hashtag, journalistic posts deflagrated a more significant communicational activity. However, delimiting the extension of citizen interference in the journalistic dynamics observed is an unfeasible task, for this is a network in constant expansion, characterized by a diversity of points of view, in accordance with aspects of transmedia journalism as outlined by Scolari (2013).

Among the nine citizen posts recorded on Facebook on November 9, 2014, with the hashtag #9NTV3, five reproduced posts from Twitter. Among these posts, the post that received the most shares, 14 in total, is associated with other 41 posts on Twitter with the same hashtag, of which five are from 3/24, four from 324.cat, and three from TV3 (Alzamora, 2017). These data demonstrate that the process of transmedia expansion, which connects journalistic and citizen publications on social media networks, occurs on various temporalities.

The intermedia dynamics of TV3 and 3/24 regarding the joint production of "Especial 9-N" became predominantly transmedia insofar as the connected audience began to post about the 9-N using the hashtag #9NTV3. This hashtag associates the TV3 brand (transmedia branding) with the hashtag #9N, which was already being used on online social media as a reference to the social designation of the non-binding referendum on November 9, 2014. The hashtag #9NTV3 was employed as an effort to attach numerous citizen accounts about the theme to the journalistic narrative on online social media. Thus, transmedia dynamics is implemented through the collective use of the hashtag, which aggregated similar viewpoints in the context of social mobilization that characterized the non-binding referendum of November 9, 2014.

It is a communicational process based on identity connections, albeit they are fragmented and dispersed on the online networks. According to Bauman (2004), identity is not fixed but is negotiable throughout the paths taken by each individual. Social adhesion to the hashtag #9NTV3 denotes this malleable and individual trajectory that defines identification processes on connections of online social media. Therefore, it is a reflection of identification with the theme of the region's sovereignty and with the institutional commitment of TV3, a locally based channel, on this matter.

According to Muntsant (2014), local television performs an important role in preserving local identities by strengthening links between citizens who seek cultural proximity. The hashtag #9NTV3 aimed to assemble similar viewpoints, aligned to the perspective of identity historically built by TV3 in the Catalonia region. More than an occasional engagement with the news, the transmedia dynamics outlined by this hashtag sought to temporally expand the narrative in accordance with the capacity of the public to actively engage in the circulation of media content through social networks, in a deep and complex process of social engagement with the narrative (Jenkins, 2009). It is noteworthy that posts with this hashtag on Twitter recurrently brought hyperlinks that led to other mediatic environments, such as YouTube and Facebook, thus building an informational mosaic delineated on connections of online social media.

Although most of videos available on YouTube about the newscast "Especial 9-N" were posted by TV3 and 3/24, it was observed that fragments of these videos circulated on online social media, such as Twitter and Facebook, due to the productive actions of the connected audience. This process reveals the transmedia dynamics that is formed, to a greater extent, by digital texts, and they can be adjusted according to the editorial intentions of who manipulates them. An illustrative example is that of a citizen's post on Facebook, on November 10, 2014, which shared an interview with Arthur Mas, the then-president of *Generalitat de Catalunya*, aired by TV3 on the previous day on its "Especial 9-N: La Votació" program. This example demonstrates the compatibility between television and online social media in the task of providing information about daily facts, thus favoring the transmedia dynamics as observed on the newscast "Especial 9-N."

If broadcast journalism has historically developed by giving priority to speed and having a preference for live transmissions (Marcondes Filho, 2000), online social media narrate the story live and directly (García, 2013). On online social media, according to García (2013), television audiences become intermediaries of television broadcasts, interfering in the meanings that emanate from them by modifying, commenting on, and sharing them. Therefore, the transmediatic relationship between television and online social media is established through the combined action of journalists and citizens.

Although it was impossible to observe a differentiated journalistic offer, one adapted to each mediatic surrounding, which Sánchez, Rodriguez-Vásquez, and García (2015) identify as a fundamental condition for the configuration of a transmedia journalistic narrative, the "Especial 9-N" newscast expanded on online social media through collective citizen action, albeit dispersed. These actions were associated with posts by TV3 and 3/24 to a large degree due to the mediation of hashtag #9NTV3. Thus, a fragmented, flexible, and variable narrative was configured, spreading on online social media in various temporalities, although delineated by a temporality characterized by the immediacy of the television broadcast.

CONCLUSION

The newscast "Especial 9-N," produced by TV3 and its news channel 3/24 in the context of the non-binding referendum about the sovereignty of Catalonia, held on November 9, 2014, acquires transmedia outlines as it combines multiplatform journalistic production and citizen participation on online social media networks. This chapter sought to ascertain to what extent the editorial strategy adopted optimized social engagement with the news and favored the circulation of broadcast television on online social media. The analysis was based on the systematic observation of the program and its records on online social media, aiming to assert the nature and the intensity of the communicative activity generated.

The broadcaster's institutional identification with aspects pertaining to the sovereignty of the region instigated transmedia circulation of the program in a context of significant social mobilization around the issue. It also favored social engagement with the news, for the latter was produced to permeate television, radio, news sites and online social media. In this scenario, the editorial strategy of encouraging the audience to post on online social media with the hashtag #9NTV3 is emphasized. This hashtag fulfilled the communicative function of mediating connections between journalistic and citizen posts on online social media, just as it mediated (in the form of geolocated tweets, photos, videos, and comments) the production of the collaborative and multiplatform experiment "El Mapa del 9-N."

The productive activities of the audience, mediated by the hashtag #9NTV3, expanded the temporality of a broadcast otherwise characterized by immediacy, but they did not distance themselves from the program schedule that marked the television broadcast of "Especial 9-N." The televisual syntax of reference, thus, is updated, according to the perspectives of second screen and transmedia branding. In this context, the audience acts in accordance with produsage logics, which makes the separation between production and consumption opaque and circumstantial.

Although an offer of journalistic coverage specific to each mediatic environment was not identified (and which is a fundamental condition for the configuration of a transmedia journalistic narrative), the newscast "Especial 9-N" expanded on online social media through collective and dispersed citizen action, linked to posts by TV3 and 3/24 through the mediation of the hashtag #9NTV3. A fragmented, flexible, and variable narrative was thus configured, which was expanded through online social media in various temporalities. It is, therefore, a typically transmedia dynamic.

REFERENCES

Alzamora, G. (2016). A dinâmica transmidiática de #9NTV3 [The transmedia dynamics of #9NTV3]. In A. Angeluci (Ed.), *Comunicação Transmídia* [Transmedia communication] (pp. 112–149). Porto Alegre, Brazil: Editora Universitária da PUCRS. Retrieved from http://www3.pucrs.br/portal/page/portal/edipucrs/Capa/PubEletrEbook

Alzamora, G. (2017). El periodismo multiplataforma de TV3 en Facebook sobre el 9-N: Prácticas intermedia o transmedia? [TV3's multiplatform journalism on Facebook over 9-N—intermedia or transmedia practices?]. *Comunicació: Revista de Recerca i d'Anàlisi, 34,* 83–115. Retrieved from http://www.raco.cat/index.php/Comunicacio/article/view/326128

Alzamora, G., & Bicalho, L. (2016). A representação do Impeachment Day mediada por hashtags no Twitter e no Facebook: Semiose em redes híbridas [The representation of Impeachment Day mediated by hashtags on Twitter and Facebook: Semiosis in hybrid networks]. *Revista Ínterin, 21*(2), 100–121. Retrieved from http://interin.utp.br/index.php/vol11/article/view/478/pdf

Alzamora, G., & Tárcia, L. (2012). Convergence and transmedia: Semantic galaxies and emergent narratives in journalism. *Brazilian Journalism Research, 8*, 22–34.

Bauman, Z. (2004). *Identity: Conversations with Benedectto Vecchi*. Cambridge, UK: Polity Press.

Bruns, A. (2008). Reconfiguring television for a networked, produsage context. *Media International Australia Incorporation*. Retrieved from https://eprints.qut.edu.au/

D'Andrea, C. (2014, May). Conexões intermidiáticas entre transmissões audiovisuais e redes sociais online: Possibilidades e tensionamentos [Intermedia connections between live audiovisual transmissions and online social networks: Possibilities and challenges]. *Anais do XXIII Encontro Anual da Compós—Associação Nacional de Programas de Pós-Graduação em Comunicação Social*. Universidade Federal do Pará. Retrieved from http://www.compos.org.br/biblioteca/_artigodandreacompos2014_2130.pdf

D'Andrea, C., Alzamora, G., & Ziller, J. (2015). Hashtags as intermedia agency resources before FIFA World Cup 2014 in Brazil. In N. Rambukkana (Ed.), *Hashtag publics—The power and politics of discursive networks* (pp. 115–125). New York, NY: Lang.

Doughty, M., Rowland, D., & Lawson, S. (2012). *Who is on your sofa?: TV audience communities and second screening social networks. In Proceedings of the 10th European conference on interactive TV and video—EuroiTV 2012* (pp. 79–86). New York, NY: Association for Computing Machinery. doi:10.1145/2325616.2325635

Evans, E. (2011). *Transmedia television: Audiences, new media, and daily life*. New York, NY: Routledge.

García, J. S. (2013). Nuevas exigencias para el periodismo: gobiernos en la calle y ciudadanos en las redes sociales [New demands for journalism: Governments on the street and citizens in social networks]. *Telos: Cuadernos de Comunicación e Innovación*, 58–67. Retrieved from https://dialnet.unirioja.es/servlet/articulo?codigo=4255542

Herkman, J. (2012). Convergence or intermediality? Finnish political communication in the New Media. *Convergence (London), 18*(4), 369–384. doi:10.1177/1354856512448727

Herms, J. M. (2003). *"La Nostra": Vint anys de TV3* ["Ours": Twenty years of TV3]. Barcelona: Proa.

Highfield, T., Harrington, S., & Bruns, A. (2013). Twitter as a technology for audiencing and fandom: The #Eurovision phenomenon. *Information Communication and Society, 16*(3), 315–339. doi:10.1080/1369118X.2012.756053

Jenkins, H. (2003). Transmedia storytelling—moving characters from books to films to video games can make them stronger and more compelling. *MIT Technology Review*. Retrieved from https://www.technologyreview.com/s/401760/transmedia-storytelling/

Jenkins, H. (2009, December 12). *The revenge of the origami unicorn: Seven principles of transmedia storytelling*. Retrieved from http://henryjenkins.org/2009/12/the_revenge_of_the_origami_uni.html

Jenkins, H., Ford, S., & Green, J. (2013). *Spreadable media: Creating value and meaning in a networked culture*. New York: New York University Press.

Jost, F. (2010). *Compreender a televisão* [Understanding television]. Porto Alegre, Brazil: Sulina.

La Vanguardia. (2014a, September 11). *Las cifras de la Via Catalana 2014: 1,8 millones—La marcha ha tenido su vértice en la plaza de las Glòries, ha cubierto 11 kilómetros y ha contado también con 54 "colles" de "castellers"* [The figures of the Catalan Road 2014: 1.8 million—The march has had its vertex in the Plaza de las Glòries, has covered 11 kilometers and has also had 54 "colles" of "castellers"]. Retrieved from http://www.lavanguardia.com/politica/20140911/54414923722/cifras-via-catalana.html

La Vanguardia. (2014b, November 10). *TV3, referente informativo en la jornada del 9N—Más de un millón de personas vieron el "Telenoticies' cap de setmana vesper" que se emitía de forma conjunta por TV3 y el 3/24* [TV3, informative reference in the day of 9N—More than one million people saw the "Telenoticies" main of week evening, that was emitted jointly by TV3 and 3/24]. Retrieved from http://www.lavanguardia.com/television/audiencias/20141110/54419751982/audiencia-tv3-9n.html#ixzz3buH0nioP

Marcondes Filho, C. (2000). *A saga dos cães perdidos* [The long history of lost dogs]. São Paulo, Brazil: Hacker Editores.

Micó, J., & Barbosa, S. (2009). Models of business convergence in the information industry: A mapping of cases in Brazil and Spain. *Brazilian Journalism Research*, *2*(1), 1–18. doi:10.25200/BJR.v.5n1.2009.198

Muntsand, A. (2014). Televisión pública y era digital: las emisoras de proximidad en Cataluña como caso paradigmático en su adaptación a Internet [Public television and the digital age: The proximity stations in Catalonia as a paradigmatic case in its adaptation to the Internet]. *Obra digital – Revista de Comunicación*, *7*, 9–26. Retrieved from http://www.raco.cat/index.php/ObraDigital/article/view/283078

Pastor, D. (2014, November 10). Datos Audiencia 09 de noviembre de 2014 [Audience data on November 9, 2014]. *Focus Media*. Retrieved from http://www.focusmedia.es/datos-audiencia-09-de-noviembre-de-2014/

Reuters Institute digital news report 2014: España. (2014). Navarra, Spain: Universidad de Navarra. Retrieved from https://www.unav.edu/documents/3786985/0/Reuters-Institute-Digital-News-Report-2014-Espana.pdf

Sánchez, C., Rodríguez-Vásquez, A., & López-García, X. (2015). Del periodismo transmedia al replicante. Cobertura informativa del contagion del ébola en España por Elpais.com [From journalism transmedia to the replicant. Ebola contagion information coverage in Spain by Elpais.com]. *El Profesional de la Información*, *24*(3), 2820290. Retrieved from https://www.academia.edu/12777757/Del_periodismo_transmedia_al_replicante._Cobertura_informativa_del_contagio_de_%C3%89bola_en_Espa%C3%B1a_por_Elpais.com

Scolari, C. (2013). *Narrativas transmedia: Cuando todos los medios cuentan* [Transmedia narratives: When all the media count]. Barcelona, Spain: Deusto.

TV3. (2014, November 10). *TV3 i el 3/24, líders el 9-N un 24,3%* d'audiència [TV3 and 3/24, leading the 9-N 24.3% audience]. Retrieved from http://www.ccma.cat/tv3/TV3-i-el-324-liders-el-9-N-amb-un-243-daudiencia/noticia-arxiu/659460/

Tenderic, B., & Williams, J. (2015). *Transmedia branding—Engage your audience*. Los Angeles, CA: USC Annenberg Press.

Weissberg, J. L. (2004). Paradoxos da teleinformática [Paradoxes of teleinformatics]. In A. Parente (Ed.), *Tramas da Rede* [Network frames] (pp. 113–141). Porto Alegre, Brazil: Sulina.

Wenz, K. (2004). As formas intermidiáticas em textos [The intermedia forms in texts]. In L. Santaella & W. Nöth (Eds.), *Palavra e imagem nas mídias: Um estudo intercultural* [Word and image in the media: An intercultural study] (pp. 251–269). Belém, Brazil: Editora Universitária UFPA.

KEY TERMS AND DEFINITIONS

Hashtags: They connect posts under the same theme and are automatically measured by the Trending Topics, a tool that monitors the daily most used hashtags on Twitter.

Intermedia Dynamics: It is characterized by a mutual effect between the media involved and the subsequent exchange of meaning among them.

Produsage: The communicational context in which the consumer becomes a co-producer of the information he or she consumes.

Second Screen: The audience tweet about what they see on television.

Televisual Syntax: The process involves aspects such as broadcasts defined by immediacy, institutional identification of the broadcaster, and references to the program schedule.

Transmedia Storytelling: It is characterized by spreading in the intersection of several communication media through the integrated action of producers and consumers.

Transmedia Television: The process of integrating multiplatform journalistic production and citizen participation on online social media networks.

ENDNOTE

1 The map can be visualized here: http://www.ccma.cat/324/9-n/mapa-del-9-n/seccio-especial/590/1114/. Accessed September 20, 2017.

Chapter 14
The Transmedia Script for Nonfictional Narratives

Anahí Lovato
National University of Rosario, Argentina

ABSTRACT

This chapter proposes a journey through an experience of transmedia journalism developed by the multimedia communication team at the National University of Rosario, Argentina, focusing on the transformation of the current media ecosystem, the characteristics assumed by transmedia storytelling in a nonfictional field, and the development of the transmedia script for the project Women for Sale, a transmedia documentary that addresses the trafficking of people for the purposes of sexual exploitation. The creation of a complex narrative universe and the definitions of stories, platforms, user experiences, and the execution of a transmedia project are analyzed in light of what has been learned in this experience of journalistic production.

INTRODUCTION

In the last few decades, multiple processes of convergence have enabled the emergence of a techno-communicational scenario where digital narratives began a process of transmediation. Digital technologies and telecommunications accelerated media ecosystem mutations. In particular, the development and popularization of communication technologies, better connectivity conditions and data transfer speed have transformed the methods of media production, distribution and consumption. In the first decade of the 21st century, companies and media producers were surprised in the transition paradigm (Igarza, 2010) trying to move in a scenario marked by the absence of certainty, far from the shelter of stable models of the broadcast and monomediatic paradigm, seeking to create digital media and business models capable of adapting to mobile, hyperconnected and multiplatform audiences (Lovato, 2016).

Citizens inhabit a world where media and formats are reconfigured daily. This complex multi-platform ecosystem has become propitious for transmedia forms of storytelling, which have appeared in fictional and nonfictional projects, reaching even documentary and journalistic discourses. Talking about transmedia storytelling today involves referring to stories developed through multiple media platforms. In

DOI: 10.4018/978-1-5225-3781-6.ch014

these stories, each new element in the narrative structure makes a specific and valuable contribution to the whole. Transmedia narratives do not adapt or repeat content: They create complex and consistent universes whose referrals can be freely traveled by users, integrating digital media and traditional media, on- and off-line. Users also take an active role in the expansion of the plot, acting as disseminators but, moreover, participating and generating content for the story.

The project analyzed in this chapter falls within the field of transmedia nonfiction. The field of nonfiction includes a set of stories that seek to represent and interpret reality. Nonfiction discourses establish a pact of veridiction with their audience (Chillón, 1999): Their stories are truthful, verifiable and therefore credible. In particular, this chapter refers to the design and production of the transmedia documentary Women for Sale: Human Trafficking for Sexual Exploitation in Argentina, developed between 2015 and 2017 by the Department of Multimedia Communication team (#DCMteam) at the National University of Rosario, Argentina. The author of this chapter participated in the development of the project as the transmedia scriptwriter. Therefore, much of the text constitutes a review of this experience of production in the field of transmedia journalism in Argentina.

TRANSMEDIA STORYTELLING: A BRIEF GENEALOGY

Although a very popular term in contemporary communication studies, the term transmedia was not born in this century, and did not even come from the field of communication. In fact, the term transmedia can be traced back to the 1970s, when journalist Bernard Levin (1970) used it to title one of the chapters of his book *The Pendulum Years: Britain and the Sixties*. However, Matthew Freeman has identified narrative strategies developed even earlier, in the early 20th century, that today could be considered as belonging to the field of transmedia storytelling. Freeman took Frank Baum's *Land of Oz* storyworld and its multiple texts and promotional tie-ins as a case study. This storyworld developed between 1900 and 1907 included the publication of a series of novels, plays, comics and mock newspapers (Freeman, 2014). In 1975, Stuart Saunders Smith, an American composer and instrumentalist, used the term transmedia to refer to a consensus-building methodology (Humphries, 1991). The transmedia works of Saunders Smith functioned as a set of notations arranged for the artists to become co-composers of the work. The open and collaborative spirit of transmedia was present in its original genetics (Lovato, 2016). In 1991, transmedia was applied to the study of social communication by Marsha Kinder (1991) to explain complex intertextuality phenomena in the media industry of children's entertainment (Gosciola, 2012). These early conceptualizations paved the way for the development of transmedia storytelling, an area afterward profited by producers and experts, such as Brenda Laurel (2000), Henry Jenkins (2003), Jack Boumans (2004), Jeff Gomez (2012) and Carlos Scolari (2013), among others.

From academic studies of communication, Jenkins (2009) proposed a series of basic principles that describe the forms of production, circulation and consumption of transmedia stories. These principles include the expansion/depth pair (in reference to the public's ability to actively engage in circulating media content, expanding the commercial and cultural value of the proposals, but encouraging the investment of time and energy in exploring them beyond the surface, with a forensic spirit), the continuity/multiplicity pair (transmedia stories build a strong sense of coherence between pieces while encouraging audiences to dig between multiple frame connections and narrative subplots) and the immersion/extraction pair (the ability to create transmedia environments that are exploitable but are populated with transportable contents: A set of pieces and data that users can carry). Among the principles proposed by Jenkins, the construction of worlds deserves special attention. This principle is central in transmedia production: It is necessary to create three-dimensional maps of narrative universes, with their own logics and rules, with spaces, time periods, characters, relationships, transformations, causes and consequences. These worlds often go outside to the streets, squares and urban centers, becoming environments that users can explore off the screen. According to Jenkins (2009), transmedia storytelling uses seriality to create sequences and guarantee temporal continuity of the stories. These proposals also provide subjective perspectives so users can look at the story through the eyes of their characters, assuming multiple narrative points of view. Finally, the notion of performance suggests the participation of users, enabled to include their own content in the story. In transmedia storytelling, the world of fandom (fans' kingdom) joins the canon proposed by the narrators. Certainly, in the narrative plots of a transmedia story, fans always find potential spaces of participation, with or without invitation (Jenkins, 2009).

From a different perspective, Jeff Gomez (founder and chief executive officer of Starlight Runner Entertainment) created a series of commandments or rules to maximize the potential success of a transmedia story. Gomez is a media producer who thinks and works at the entertainment industry's core. The first of his commandments forces producers to deeply comprehend the essence of the brand they are creating and to never distance themselves from it. The transmedia brand includes the name of the product, its design and symbology: Everything that distinguishes it, in the eyes of its users, from any other production. This brand can be developed through a franchise where the intellectual property of the work is licensed so that other associated parts can produce derivative works and commercially exploit it. As he established, the world of the story in transmedia is unstoppable and rules above all: It is necessary to care for the integrity of the universe by developing a long-term plan. This allows the franchise to expand through the correct implementation of the world of the story. In addition, Gomez determines that the best creative talents from different professional areas should get engaged with the storyworld. To do so, he suggests creating highly organized resources for the canon and the assets of the story: Producing comprehensive documents about the characters, locations, conflicts and distinctive elements, where the essence of the brand is clear to all interested audiences. All the areas involved in the transmedia franchise must also hold regular meetings to coordinate production and preserve the transmedia world's coherence. According to Gomez, the implementation of the storyworld must validate and encourage audience participation. From the beginning of the project, it is necessary to design an architecture open to the dialogue between the interested parties and the target public. Licensing, merchandising and marketing franchises must feed and expand the storyworld. In this sense, licensees cannot build their share of the franchise in isolation: All content must celebrate the narrative. In line with Jenkins' (2009) proposals, it is necessary to create an accessible storyworld through a matrix that combines digital and traditional media, where each piece can contribute to the narrative structure (Gomez, 2012).

NONFICTIONAL PROJECTS IN THE TRANSMEDIA CONTEXT

The Women for Sale project is a transmedia documentary from a journalistic perspective. Throughout history, journalism has found in the documentary genre the opportunity to tell stories of long breath, with more depth, duration and time of investigation and production than the speed required by the daily production of content for newspapers, radio or TV, for example. From productions for traditional screens to early experimentations with new interactive formats, the intersection between documentary techniques and journalistic research has generated interesting and fruitful works everywhere.

As a record of reality, the documentary genre was born with the cinema. The origin of the documentary goes back to the technical experiments of Edison and the first records of the Lumière brothers, with the rudimentary cinematograph. The first images portrayed by this lens and the first publicly projected films documented places and people's actions in their daily lives through the intervention of a camera. Surely, over a hundred years of history, documentaries have been transformed, problematized, made complex and adapted to the technical, epistemic and narrative possibilities of each era. As defended before, the hybridizations of the current media ecosystem gave rise to the emergence of new narrative formats.

Interactive documentaries (i-docs), also called webdocs (web documentaries), are examples of these new formats. They arise in the convergence between the documentary genre and digital media, in an increasingly social and mobile ecosystem. According to Arnau Gifreu (2011), the fusion process operates through mutual attraction: The documentary genre contributes with its varied modalities of reality representation; digital media provide new modalities of navigation and interaction. As inheritors of film and television documentary tradition, i-docs preserve—and probably enhance—the intrinsic immersive capacity of the documentary, allowing users to dig into stories and contexts.

Digital media and their language characteristics provide new reading grammars for these stories: They are hypertextual stories, which can be experienced through multiple paths, integrating different media and allowing interactivity. As "frontier works," i-docs allow users to resignify their place and acquire a fundamental role in the narrative plot (Gifreu, 2014). Thinking about i-docs' characteristics supposes to establish, first, some of their differences from documentary films. Perhaps the most obvious difference is presented with the linearity dimension: The audiovisual documentary is a journey from a starting point to an end (A to B), following a route pre-established by the author. In this type of work, the limits of authorship and control over discourse are perfectly delimited, Gifreu (2012) has stated.

Interactive documentaries, however, give users more freedom to choose possible routes: Users can find a starting point and follow alternative bifurcations and paths. In this case, the director does not maintain control over the final consumption decisions. As Gifreu stated, the key element of differentiation is evident: A traditional narrative has a linearity and cannot alter the order of speech, while an interactive documentary can affect this order and modify it. In nonlinear formats, the coherence and continuity of the stories are finally supported by their users. Meaning is given by the relations between the informative nodes.

This loss of control by the author causes his or her own figure to become blurred, questioned or even eliminated in cases of horizontal, open and collaborative communication proposals. The interactive nature of i-docs requires active involvement by users, who become actants rather than spectators or observers (Gaudenzi, 2013). To make a story go, the user needs to act and interact physically with the interfaces. The user and the i-doc thus become interdependent: Interactive processes of action and reaction transform them equally. Analyzing in detail the interactive condition of i-docs, Gaudenzi (2013) proposes the following classification categories:

- **Documentaries With Semi-Closed Interactivity:** When the user can navigate but not change the content.
- **Documentaries With Semi-Open Interactivity:** When the user can participate but not change the structure of the interactive documentary.
- **Documentaries With Completely Open Interactivity:** When the documentary and the user change constantly to adapt to each other.

The first form of interactivity corresponds to a hypertextual documentary, the second to a participatory documentary and the third to an experimental documentary. However, the reality constructed by any type of documentary is still a discourse, involving the author's subjectivity. A documentary, like other discourses of the real, retains a residual responsibility for describing and interpreting the world of collective experience, a responsibility that is by no means a minor matter (Nichols, 1997). In the case of interactive documentaries, the author's responsibility is also multimedia. An i-doc takes advantage of the codes of text, video, photography, animation, computer graphics, audio and game, among others, to tell a story (an interpretation of reality) on a digital platform.

In a post-convergent world, the monomediatic models of production were overwhelmed. Nonfiction stories have been able to expand their stories through multiple media, generating transmedia environments where audience participation becomes a fundamental attribute of the narrative plot. Interactive and transmedia narratives are positioned as a type of textual construction that allows users to interpret information, navigate and play with the interface, learn and share in real time, as we advance in each project. In fact, they already offer highly immersive experiences in the new narratives, according to Gifreu (2016).

Transmedia storytelling has the ability to integrate geographic navigation as a way to involve participants "in environments not only virtual but also territorial" (Reno, 2014, p. 143). This storytelling can offer ways of navigation that do not depend exclusively on the digital space but also incorporate the territorial dimension as a narrative platform. Fernando Irigaray underlined this idea in his concepts of transmedia production. In this sense, transmedia can be considered a dimension that crosses different products on different screens, on traditional media and on territorial actions, thinking about audiences and users from the playful perspective of searching, discovering and playing (Irigaray, 2014).

This definition of transmedia, which incorporates territorial storytelling as a real possibility of expansion of the stories, forces transmutations of the traditional representations of the city and re-imagines it as a great organic hypertext where multiple devices, genres, languages and platforms coexist. According to Irigaray (2014), a city always has multiple narrative plots that can guide the development of convergent stories. Such stories are encouraged by urban practices of multitasking prosumers who can interact with the stories permanently. In urban spaces, real, complex and enveloping scenarios can contain and combine (new) digital media and (old) analogical media. Connectivity, mobility and ubiquity multiply these possibilities. Among them, story creators can add layers of virtual reality to the physical world that support people's daily lives.

The analogy that best fits transmedia storytelling is the symphony orchestra. In it, each instrument can be classified as a medium that develops a fragment of the work, a melody that can be appreciated individually with all logic but becomes meaningful when listened to in the coordination of the instrumental composition, according to Liuzzi (2014). The orchestral model of transmedia storytelling reorganizes the stage of nonfiction productions, enabling new spaces for experimentation and narrative innovation. These transformations have a correlate in the writer's practices, now concerned with the development of multilayer writing techniques (the musical score) that allow the orchestra to harmonically unfurl the musical beauty of their art.

WRITING NONFICTIONAL TRANSMEDIA SCRIPTS

Thinking about the experiences of transmedia production created by the team at the National University of Rosario, Argentina, this group of professionals is convinced that the core of transmedia storytelling resides in the storyworld (or the narrative universe). The elements of the story and their implications are the first steps that must be solved by a transmedia producer. In a logical and temporal order, this first task must be executed long before thinking, imagining and designing the platforms, technologies and possible user experiences to tell each story. The work of elucidating the theme of a story, its protagonists, in which scenarios it occurs, the actions and conflicts that are developed and, finally, how the elements of that story will be structured to become a good story is the challenge of every scriptwriter (Lovato, 2016).

In the field of nonfiction, "documentary and journalism largely share the same ethos and commitments to truth-telling, sense-making, and explaining (Urrichio et al., 2015, p. 10). It must be remembered here that journalistic work has always been narrative. Using investigative techniques, data collection, checking of sources and organization of the information, journalists are responsible for telling relevant stories to a community, in a specific spatial and temporal context. In this sense, journalistic stories have also tried to take advantage of digital narrative possibilities to experiment with the publication of innovative formats based on data and facts extracted from the reality that surrounds us. This exploration has resulted in immersive, visual and experimental journalistic proposals, seeking to reach new audiences and to make better use of the current interactive and collaborative technologies (Uricchio et al., 2015).

The episodes of DocuMedia: Multimedia Social Journalism, a project born in 2008 as a series of interactive documentaries created by the Department of Multimedia Communication team at the National University of Rosario were developed for such purposes. The series deals with journalistic issues that are not usually found in local media. These productions established links between documentary techniques, investigative journalism, data journalism and participation by fundamental users.

The four previous productions of DocuMedia were i-docs that addressed the following themes: The experience of the Barrio Ludueña Orchestra School (DocuMedia "Vibrato, Barrio Ludueña Orchestra School," New Latin American Journalism Prize finalist, awarded by Gabriel García Márquez), the problems generated by the construction boom in Rosario (DocuMedia "Danger, Construction Works"), the Paraná river wetlands opposite the city (DocuMedia "Migrations") and the illegal drug business and its mafia (DocuMedia "Lost Streets: The Advance of Drug Trafficking in Rosario," winner of the 2013 King of Spain International Journalism Prize in the Digital Journalism category).

However, Women for Sale: Human Trafficking for Sexual Exploitation in Argentina, the fifth episode, assumes the challenge of leaping from multimedia to transmedia journalism. Certainly, this narrative decision based on the complexity of the storyworld that Women for Sale sought to investigate meant a rethinking of the team's workflow, as well as the script formats required by the project.

Traditional formats for screens such as TV or cinema are characterized by the writing of linear stories where the significant matter are the images and the sounds. Instead, the content designed for connected screens, such as computers, tablets and mobile devices demands multimedia scripts for the development of non-linear, interactive proposals for active and participative users. Far from the protection of monomediatic thinking, transmedia narratives demand the design of a complex and coherent narrative universe where each piece can contribute to the totality of the story, generating connections and deepening the narrative lines without forgetting the specific format characteristics of each chosen medium.

The work of the scriptwriters, who were accustomed to unique platform productions, has been deeply modified and transformed as a result of the requirement to think and to write in transmedia forms. As Carlos Scolari (2017) stated, if in the old media ecology audiences were media-centered, in the new ecology they are narrative-centered. The skills and dexterity of scriptwriters who were experts in designing stories for traditional screens are now challenged by the emergence of hypermedia audiences that show non-linear consumption habits. Transmedia storyworlds must be designed for transreaders (Scolari, 2017): Multimodal users who dominate different languages and semiotic systems, who are capable of moving in complex textual networks. Against this reality, traditional scriptwriting—characterized by being unidirectional, two-dimensional and monomedia—has been clearly altered (Lovato, 2016).

The challenge of writing a transmedia story and designing a narrative universe for multiple platforms had already been assumed in 2013 by the National University of Rosario team, when the project Following the Footsteps of the Beast Man was developed. This first transmedia experience was directly recorded in the documentary field. The case of Women for Sale, however, involved the arrival of the Department of Multimedia Communication in transmedia journalism. The next sections of this chapter delve into the details of that process.

THE IMPORTANCE OF THE STORY AND USER EXPERIENCES: TRANSMEDIA UNIVERSE IN WOMEN FOR SALE

Every day in Argentina, trafficking networks capture women, deceive women, restrain women, exploit women, sell women and disappear women. Every day in Argentina, someone pays for them, and the cycle starts over. Based on this premise, in 2015 the National University of Rosario team launched a transmedia journalistic documentary, Women for Sale: Human Trafficking for Sexual Exploitation in Argentina. The story builds a complex network that includes pieces such as an i-doc, a comics series, posters on public roads with augmented reality interaction, content for LED screens on streets and in shopping malls, TV spots, a collaborative map, a TV documentary, a series of mobisodes, social media content and a multiplatform book.

The project allows users to immerse themselves in a story that examines recruitment, trafficking routes, sexual exploitation and the rescue of victims, exposing stories narrated by the protagonists themselves and offering a vivid experience tinged with the crudeness of the facts. Throughout different pieces, women victims, relatives, members of organizations that fight against sexual exploitation, judicial officers, legislators, members of the security forces and trafficking specialists address various aspects of one of the most serious crimes in Argentina.

Women for Sale was not the team's first transmedia production experience. The predecessor project Following the Footsteps of the Beast Man was developed in 2013 as a retroactive transmedia project. It was a narrative universe constructed from an earlier homonymous work: A documentary for TV released in 2011. In contrast, Women for Sale is a pro-active transmedia project: It was designed from a transmedia perspective from the beginning. Methodologically speaking, from the point of view of the script, this condition modifies the forms of construction of the narrative world. The project is presented as a blank canvas on which to draw the narrative lines, determine the set of experiences that will be offered to users, select the platforms that will tell the story and organize the tasks and deadlines necessary for the story's execution and launch.

The boundaries are arranged by the external reality on which the transmedia scriptwriter works: People, stories, conflicts, relationships, places, times, actions. The script that is generated starts on the creative and subjective treatment of that reality: There are appropriations, selections, transactions and resignifications. As in every narrative, the script of a transmedia journalistic project is a process of constructing meaning. Nevertheless, just as the reality is unpredictable, a nonfiction script should be plastic and flexible enough to accommodate events that cannot be planned.

The university team's previous experience in interactive and transmedia documentary made it clear that the starting point of any project is the narrative world. Even before thinking about platforms, technologies and formats, it is necessary to clarify the narrative elements of the storyworld. As Brenda Laurel (2000) stated, the key is to think in transmedia terms from the beginning. Traditional authorship is formal: The scriptwriter thinks first of the form (drama or novel or game, for example) and that form guides the selection and arrangement of materials. The new authorship is material: The emphasis is placed on the development of materials that could later be selected and arranged to produce many different forms (Laurel, 2000).

Certainly, the concern for the storyworld was the engine that started the production of Women for Sale. The team began deep research on the established subject: The trafficking of persons for the purposes of sexual exploitation in Argentina. The preliminary collection of information led to the revision of Argentine Law 26.364 on Prevention and Punishment of Human Trafficking and Victims Assistance, approved in the country in 2008 and reformed in 2012. This law recognizes typical stages in the criminal procedures of trafficking. Capture through mechanisms of deception, transfer to dissociate them from their social circles and sexual exploitation are inescapable instances in this process. The legislation also recognizes the rescue of and assistance to victims to reintegrate them in their previous work and social lives.

The structural approach of the law allowed the transmedia writers to organize, in advance, a possible narrative route. However, that structure was not enough to build the storyworld required. The journalistic work demanded an inescapable condition: The direct testimony of the victims. That meant finding women who had been trafficked and in one way or another, escaped the horror, as well as relatives of missing women captured by sexual exploitation networks. Only when it was possible to find these stories and to carry out in-depth reports with the protagonists did the elements to write the transmedia script and to design the narrative universe emerge. The stories of Vanessa, Zulma, Elizabeth, Natalia and Sofia, reconstructed from testimony, court records and archival material, constitute the core of this journalistic transmedia story.

From these stories, the transmedia script was taking shape, filling with content and structuring different phases. The first phase sought to arouse interest in the story and to prepare the stage for the i-doc release, the main piece (mothership) of the transmedia project. For that purpose, brief pieces were planned, in audiovisual formats, on paper and including messages in augmented reality, under the premise of occupying the street and urban spaces to summon audiences. In addition, the publication of content and the generation of conversations in social networks began. These first pieces underscored the idea that criminal networks were active in Argentina, operating daily in the recruitment and exploitation of victims and supported by clients: the consumers of sexual services.

The second phase focused on stories to show crudely the methods implemented by trafficking networks. Therefore, the contents were organized around five nodal points: Recruitment of women (through deception), transfer to places of submission, sexual exploitation, rescue (and social reintegration) of victims and finally, the role of the community, specifically calling on users to engage in anti-trafficking actions. Next, a set of pieces were designed to ask users to denounce facts related to sexual exploitation, to say no to trafficking and to spread the stories to prevent crime. Finally, social and government anti-trafficking organizations were asked to produce specific content about their experience of working with victims, trying to answer the question what happens next with women who were rescued from exploitation hell.

It is important to note here that the Department of Multimedia Communication usually works with online collaborative documents, which can be accessed by area heads such as the visual designer, the web developer, the audiovisual producer, journalists and the social media manager. This work methodology continued during the development of the Women for Sale project. Throughout the process, all members of the team had access to the overall narrative design of the transmedia project, as well as the individual scripts for each piece.

In conjunction with the narrative universe, it was also necessary to think about the experiences, forms and spaces of participation that a transmedia storyworld can offer to users. Experience design can be understood as a bridge that links a story with its technical elements (Hayes, 2011) and includes a clear sense of engagement: What users can do and what they can expect from the narrative, as well as a definition of the platforms and channels in which that experience will be developed. Surely, this includes a proposal of possible routes of circulation: Entrance doors to the story, user journeys between platforms and specific calls to action.

After the team defined the components of the global narrative structure (characters, thematic lines, narrative nodes, user experiences and platforms to develop the story), it was necessary to write particular scripts for each medium, adapted to the characteristics of their respective formats.

The narrative experience of Women for Sale combined online and offline platforms, including the following pieces:

- **Interactive Documentary:** Organized into five chapters (Capture, Trafficking Routes, Exploitation, Rescue, Get Involved), through which users can follow the stories of Vanessa, Zulma, Elizabeth and Natalia, all victims of trafficking, along with testimonies of specialists, militants, officers and members of organizations that are fighting to eradicate crime. The i-doc (Women for Sale, 2015a) also invites people to report facts that may be linked to human trafficking for sexual exploitation and to help with the task of disseminating information. For the development of the i-doc, a scroll-down navigation was chosen, with the assembly of multimedia elements through the parallax scrolling technique. Different layers of elements (short video pills, photographs, texts, graphics, images and icons) were designed to move at different rates during navigation, organizing the story. The consumption of all the information contained in this centerpiece of the transmedia universe has an estimated duration of 83 minutes. Although it is presented a priori as a linear project based on scrolling, the fragmentation of the content in different thematic nodes allows non-sequential access: Users can manage the rhythm of their journey through the story and make decisions about how much to explore. All the expansions of the transmedia project, even those that were not intended for digital platforms, were also digitized and accessible from the centerpiece. The last node, "Get Involved," invites the audience to share content with friends and distribute media through Facebook and Twitter, placing users as co-responsible in the fight against the sexual exploitation of women, reinforcing the message of denunciation and trying to stop the consumption. For this piece, the script took the form of the vertical path proposed by scroll-down navigation, describing neatly each of the elements that intervened in the construction of each narrative node and identifying its location as a background layer or a front layer. A code was also defined to identify types of elements and narrative function, discriminating, for example, testimony videos, transition videos and microstories. Information on how to play the content was included: Some pieces work in a loop, others in autoplay and others must be activated by the user.
- **Comic Series (Printed and Digital):** Women for Sale | Journalism in vignettes is a comic series with five chapters. It tells the story of Sofia, a teenage girl who escapes from a human trafficking network that brought her from Paraguay through deceptive practices to work in a brothel in the province of Buenos Aires. The script retrieves information about the judicial sentence of a case

tried in Rosario in 2012. The series Women for Sale | Journalism in vignettes was published with the edition of the Argentinean weekly El Eslabón. Comic episodes are also available in digital format for online reading and/or downloading (Women for Sale, 2015b). In this piece, it becomes evident how the story demands the narrative format. Sofia is not the real name of the victim, the protagonist of this comic series. This story was enclosed in a court file of hundreds of pages. The victim is now under witness protection; therefore, some sensitive data (such as her name) was changed in the script. However, the journalistic value of this story, which contains all the stages involved in the crime of human trafficking, was fundamental to this transmedia project. Thus, it was decided to transform the contents of the file into a script for cartoons, describing actions and dialogues in vignettes that were then interpreted by the cartoonist to launch the chapters.

- **Posters on Public Roads With Augmented Reality:** A street campaign that included 75 posters distributed throughout the city of Rosario, hiding a message in augmented reality that passersby could discover through a free mobile app (Women for Sale, 2015b). In terms of the script, the challenge was to think of two pieces (the paper poster plus the video reproduced through the application of augmented reality) that would work together and independently. In that sense, the message achieved worked perfectly for passersby who only read the poster, for whom the objective was to raise awareness about the problem of trafficking. Those who discovered the hidden piece in augmented reality also took a new message and an enriched experience, aiming to involve them in the denunciation and dissemination of information.
- **Light-Emitting Diodes (LEDs) in Public Locations:** Short videos designed to be projected on indoor and outdoor LED screens, on the street and in shopping centers. Here, the script was created with the premise of generating pills of a few seconds adapted to the consumption context. One was located in a traffic-centric downtown corner of the city where motorists and walkers stop at the traffic light. The short message called for help to eradicate trafficking and invited the audience to explore the interactive documentary. The second piece was displayed on an advertising screen inside a very popular shopping mall. In that case, the message followed the logic and aesthetics of advertising, aiming to deconstruct sexual consumption as a method of buying and subjugating women (Women for Sale, 2015b).
- **TV spots:** Micro-media designed to raise awareness of the problem of human trafficking and to encourage people to contribute to preventing and reporting crimes related to sexual exploitation (Women for Sale, 2015b). The television spots were broadcasted by Channel 3 in Rosario.
- **Collaborative Map:** An open map in permanent update to which all users can freely add data regarding human trafficking crimes for sexual exploitation (Women for Sale, 2015b). The map displays information about missing women, rescued women and places where brothels and exploitation networks operate.
- **TV Documentary:** 26 minutes long. The documentary focuses on the stories of three women who were exploited by trafficking networks in Buenos Aires, Córdoba and Santa Cruz. The women's testimony exposes the mafias' sexual exploitation operations and the police's complicity (Women for Sale, 2015b). Although an independent piece, coherent in its entirety, which can be consumed as the sole medium of the story, this piece also works perfectly as a complement to the i-doc since it focuses exclusively on stories of victims narrated in depth, in first person.
- **Mobisodes:** Short video pills, up to 3 minutes long, designed to be consumed from a mobile device, anytime, anywhere (Women for Sale, 2015b). The Women for Sale's mobisode series

contains five videos addressing topics such as deception and recruitment of victims, the case of Marita Verón, the repercussions of her trial and the struggle undertaken by her mother Susana Trimarco against the Tucumán mafias, discussions and points of view in abolitionist and regulatory positions regarding prostitution, the problem of social reintegration of rescued women and the relevance of sex education in the national fight against trafficking. These issues have remained outside the thematic development of the i-doc and can form small unit pieces that expand the transmedia universe.

- **Social Media:** The social media strategy was created to establish links between narrative media, call the community to action, share information about trafficking in Argentina and distribute content specifically designed for Twitter (Documedia Mujeres, n.d.) and Facebook (DocuMedia, n.d.). It began before the most important pieces were launched, at the zero point of the narrative, and lasted throughout the entire transmedia strategy.
- **E-Book:** The last piece of the transmedia storytelling. Based on a collective work, this publication brings together voices from different actors who provide assistance to victims of human trafficking. Texts and ideas come from specialized officers from different national agencies, professionals and members of non-government organizations, and political and judicial actors. The multiplicity of voices and their heterogeneity make valuable contributions to this book based on concrete trajectories in the reconstruction of rights violated by human trafficking mafias. The book also focuses on the challenges that Argentinean society must assume to build new horizons of life and hope for rescued victims. The book, *What Happens Next? Contributions and Challenges for the Reconstruction of Rights of Trafficking and Sexual Exploitation Victims,* was compiled by Matías Loja and Patricio Irisarri and published by UNR Editorial. This compilation includes texts by Fernando Irigaray, Viviana Caminos, Maria Rosa Ponce, Gloria Bonatto, Elisa Alarcón Izquierdo, Conrado Izura, María Eugenia Schmuck, Norma López, Fernanda Medina, Alicia Gutíerrez, Horacio Andrés Coutaz, Ale Rodenas and ONG (Mujeres tras las rejas), with illustrations by Cris Rosenberg and editorial design by Joaquin Paronzini (Women for Sale, 2015b).

NEXT STEPS IN TRANSMEDIA STORYTELLING: DESIGN AND IMPLEMENTATION

Once the transmedia universe is organized with the respective stories, experiences and platforms, the implementation must be synchronized, and the release dates for each component of the plot defined. The Women for Sale schedule was chosen to expand throughout 2015 and to continue during 2016 and 2017. Social media were used to sustain the whole narrative process.

The transmedia documentary script (and the specific script for each medium) traces a basic structure to guide the filming, production and design of the contents, but with sufficient plasticity to adapt to the unforeseen. However, the benchmarks planted at the beginning of the project will always serve as a guide for the progression and evolution of the storyworld. The pretension of flexibility and openness of the documentary script cannot ignore Gomez's mandate as an essential condition of transmedia production: To create highly organized resources for the canon and the assets of the story. Designing transmedia documentaries implies producing comprehensive documents of characters, locations, stories and distinctive elements of the story.

According to Gomez (2012), the essence of the transmedia brand must be clear to all interested audiences. Canon documents contain the mythology of a storyworld and must be accompanied by a centralized system of information that allows specific access to the key actors of the project. This is how the integrity of the franchise is promoted. As is evident, these definitions emphasize the importance of having a transmedia script to organize the production. This centralized system of information was possible, in the case of Women for Sale, from the development of collaborative documents, permanently accessible to the entire production team. The global matrix of the project, visible for each work area, ordered the production flow, the references between narrative pieces and the synchronized launch of each medium.

The transmedia script for Women for Sale also required the development of a specific script for each synchronized medium. In every instance, it was necessary to think about images, sounds, dialogues, infographics, cartoons, animations and transitions. This is why a transmedia script is a basic document made up of texts with specific languages for the Web, TV, radio, comics, mobile applications and social media. In these scripts, the narrative map is accomplished and three-dimensionally visualized (Lovato, 2015). That set of scripts held, at a micro level, the full global project.

The work of archiving and retrieving the particular scripts that were developed for each piece of Women for Sale shows a very clear graphic panorama: A constellation of textual scripts, sketches and storyboards that marked the production method. This production experience coincides with the point of view of Vicente Gosciola (2012), who stated that the story parts of a project based on a transmissible narrative are intricately linked because they originally belong to a single story. However, this does not guarantee that the audience will understand that they are pieces of a whole. In transmedia projects, every story must be perceived by the audience as a careful and properly separate part and not as a piece randomly cut from the whole.

That was one of the premises that supported the design of the pieces to ensure their operation independently and together, even in different reception contexts. In Women for Sale, the main piece of the storyworld (the i-doc) contains information and actions that allow the audience to understand it, but it does not tell everything. To learn more details of the main story, users are encouraged to consume other contents of the transmedia universe. In order to establish such narrative referrals and to invite audiences to follow the proposed routes, all Women for Sale pieces included cross references: From the i-doc to the transmedia universe, from the exterior pieces (posters and LEDs) to the web, from the TV pieces to social networks and more. These calls were overprinted in each format. This is basically the main difference between transmedia storytelling and any other way of telling stories (Gosciola, 2012).

However, the elements of the visual design of the project also collaborate to ensure the identity of the narrative as a whole. Images, fonts and color palettes are among the most important assets of a transmedia project. This is understood by Hayes (2011), who dedicates a complete chapter of the transmedia bible to design specifications, including guidelines that determine the overall look and feel of the proposal. This work on aesthetic design is also evident in Women for Sale, where a number of elements are constant and invariable in all media formats and constitute the identity mark of the transmedia experience.

The implementation of the set of pieces designed for this transmedia universe required an interdisciplinary team composed of twelve professionals, who were responsible for the direction, production, script, audiovisual realization, journalistic research, web development, visual design and social media management. For this edition of DocuMedia, the #DCMteam added a professional guest: Daniel González, the cartoonist responsible for the drawings of the five chapters of Women for Sale | Journalism in vignettes.

CONCLUSION

A transmedia production seeks to create a storyworld accessible through a matrix that combines digital and traditional media. In these stories, each piece is added to the main narrative. According to Jeff Gomez (2012), there is a multitude of entry points to the storyworld of a transmedia franchise. The relationship with the public is always reinforced by the creation of a consistent canon that maintains the integrity of a complex world.

In the case of Women for Sale, from the production point of view, the storyworld was distributed on various platforms and resulted in a very complex narrative map. These sets of pieces created for the transmedia story were designed with one premise: The users' participation constitutes the transmedia experience core. Throughout the plot, the users have an active role: From selective interactivity forms to communicative forms of expansion and transformation of the narrative universe.

It must be underlined that the National University of Rosario production team has its own way of understanding transmedia narratives. This conception includes the effective participation of users in virtual and real worlds, a form typified by Renó (2014) as a territorial navigation form. In terms of Fernando Irigaray (2015), transmedia storytelling requires citizens who inhabit and go across stories that develop not only through virtual scenarios but also in the urban territory of their cities. In this context, each component of the transmedia universe of Women for Sale generates different experiences and interaction forms. It is a project in which the story represents a central component, operating in virtuality but also taking advantage of real-world spaces as narrative platforms and including collaborative instances.

Women for Sale is an integral experience of transmedia journalism. According to Renó and Flores' (2012) definitions, transmedia journalism can be considered a form of journalistic language that contemplates, at the same time, different media, with several narratives forms to an infinity of users. Audiovisual media, mobile communication and interactivity are incorporated in the dissemination of content, which considerably increases the media circulation. According to Ford (2007), the use of transmedia storytelling in journalism has the purpose of informing readers in the best way possible, using a combination of media forms to make sense across platforms. The Internet provides the support to put together a package of text, audio, video and pictures in an overarching coverage package.

The production experience developed by #DCMteam of the National University of Rosario combines new and old media, constructing a transmedia script based on a journalistic investigation of human trafficking for sexual exploitation in Argentina. Data, sources and stories collected in this research have allowed journalists to give shape to a narrative universe where user experiences were especially considered in the content design for different platforms, adapting formats to specific contexts of media reception and consumption. News media must be inventive to compete for attention in a scattered landscape in the same ways entertainment media must.

A new style of storytelling has emerged there that, if combined with the goals and ethics of journalism, could create a new genre of documentary storytelling that would attract readers to a deep and compelling story with more context and complexity. The socially or politically important reportage might better engage the public. (Moloney, 2011, p. 7)

In the same sense, Renó and Flores (2012) added that transmedia storytelling makes it possible to take advantage of the communication possibilities that exist in postmodern society. In the context of digital convergence, content and practices diverge; the transmedia canon becomes permeable and receptive, including co-creation, collaboration and fandom contents as central components of the narrative. Reconsidering Stuart Saunders Smith's original idea (Humphries, 1991), transmedia producers are now software creators, developing narrative scores for others to collaboratively execute the stories.

It is clear that fiction and nonfiction constitute different forms of enunciation, with different degrees of referentiality to the existing world outside the discourse, and therefore different relations of veracity with their audiences (Chillón, 2009). Nonetheless, transmedia fiction and nonfiction have things in common, especially in their production modalities.

Daily journalism, with its time-constrained brevity, is not a viable option. Transmedia must be designed carefully and developed with a lengthy lead time to be effective. From conception to delivery, a Hollywood franchise takes years to launch. But also deeply embedded in the journalism tradition is the long-term investigation or the extended documentary. Coverage of a complex and ongoing issue — immigration, the aftermath of war, social struggle—lends itself perfectly to a considered approach and complex delivery. (Moloney, 2011, p. 12)

Even if these are journalistic genres, documentaries, testimonials or stories imagined by an author, from the transmedia script point of view, there are no substantial differences: These are narrative worlds to be constructed. In stories of fiction and nonfiction, a myth is always proposed: An order and an explanation of the world. An argument is also proposed: A thesis that is demonstrated throughout the story, even it is simple or complex (Lovato, 2016).

Nevertheless, the starting points of transmedia productions of fiction and nonfiction differ. At the beginning of a fiction project, everything is yet to be created. However, in nonfiction, everything is about to be found, to be discovered. Documentalists and journalists deal with people, testimonies, documents, real scenarios that will progressively be transformed into characters, actions, dialogues, conflicts, the turning points of our transmedia stories. Moreover, the protagonists of a transmedia nonfictional project may intervene, actively participate and modify the planned plot from the story canon. Based on this participatory condition, transmedia documentaries have a great capacity to become tools of social empowerment.

First, a transmedia approach to journalism would require that it be designed as transmedia from the start. Editors must consider what media are available to them and how the individual strengths of those media can be used to the story's advantage. (Moloney, 2011, p. 95)

To create a transmedia nonfictional project, every piece investigated, recorded, designed, written and produced must be thought of as multiplatform from its conception, with attention to a basic condition: The requirement to construct open and permeable frames that can be always modified. Surely, journalistic and documentary work stays open to record events, actions and testimonies that cannot be scripted in advance (Puccini, 2015). Therefore, it should be emphasized that a transmedia nonfictional script allows changes through the process. The script is created in pre-production, sustained in the production phase and modified, revitalized and resignified in the postproduction. The work of scriptwriting also includes editing, and vice versa. During the transmedia edition, the script is reorganized and rewritten to incorporate and contain the events of a dynamic and living narrative world.

The transmedia nonfictional script begins to be written from the first team meeting. It must be kept open and flexible to permanently adapt to environmental changes (Lovato, 2016). Nevertheless, the creation of a transmedia story—with its complexities and narrative references—always demands the development of a script for supporting production. This statement holds true for fictional and nonfictional transmedia storytelling: The production experience of Women for Sale, made by the team of the National University of Rosario (Argentina) and reviewed in this chapter, constitutes a complete sample of this.

REFERENCES

Boumans, J. (2004). *Cross-media, e-content report 8, ACTeN — Anticipating content technology needs*. Retrieved from http://www.sociologia.unimib.it/DATA/Insegnamenti/13_3299/materiale/04%20-%20jak%20boumans%20cross-media%20acten%20aug%202004.pdf

Chillón, A. (1999). *Literatura y periodismo. Una tradición de relaciones promiscuas* [Literature and journalism. A tradition of promiscuous relationships]. Barcelona, Spain: Universitat Autónoma de Barcelona.

DocuMedia. (n.d.). In *Facebook*. Retrieved August 15, 2017, from https://www.facebook.com/documedia.unr

Documedia Mujeres. (n.d.) In *Twitter*. Retrieved August 15, 2017, from https://twitter.com/mujeresenventa

Ford, S. (2007, April 7). *Transmedia journalism: A story-based approach to convergence*. MIT Convergence Culture Consortium. Retrieved from http://www.convergenceculture.org/weblog/2007/04/transmedia_journalism_a_storyb.php

Freeman, M. (2014). Advertising the Yellow Brick Road: Historicizing the industrial emergence of transmedia storytelling. *International Journal of Communication*, *8*, 2362–2381.

Gaudenzi, S. (2013). *The living documentary: From representing reality to co-creating reality in digital interactive documentary* (Unpublished doctoral thesis). University of London.

Gifreu, A. (2011). El documental multimedia interactivo como discurso de la no ficción interactiva. Por una propuesta de definición y categorización del nuevo género emergente [The interactive multimedia documentary as a discourse of interactive nonfiction. For a proposal of definition and categorization of the new emerging genre]. *Hipertext, 9*. Retrieved from http://www.upf.edu/hipertextnet/numero-9/documental-multimedia.html

Gifreu, A. (2012). Nuevo Modelo de No Ficción interactiva Móvil. Caracterización del reportaje y el documental Interactivo [New model of mobile non-fiction. Characterization of the report and the interactive documentary]. *Tendencias y Oportunidades de la Movilidad Digital*, 59–66. Retrieved from http://dialnet.unirioja.es/servlet/articulo;jsessionid=51B9CB65639F1302FE2A8CB2B38B28A4.dialnet01?codigo=4555307

Gifreu, A. (2014). El documental interactivo en la estrategia de la multidifusión digital. Evaluación del estado del arte en relación con la temática, las plataformas y la experiencia del usuario [The interactive documentary in the strategy of the digital multicast. Assessment of the state of the art in relation to the theme, platforms and user experience]. *Revista,* 96. Retrieved from http://telos.fundaciontelefonica.com/seccion=1268&idioma=es_ES&id=2013102313510003&activo=6.do

Gifreu, A. (2016). Inmersión en narrativas inmersivas y transmedia [Immersion in immersive and transmedia narratives]. In F. Irigaray & D. Renó (Eds.), *Transmediaciones. Creatividad, innovación y estrategias en nuevas narrativas* [Transmediations. Creativity, innovation and strategies in new narratives] (pp. 55–69). Buenos Aires, Argentina: Editorial La Crujía.

Gomez, J. (2012). The 10 commandments of 21st century franchise production. *Business Insider.* Retrieved from http://www.businessinsider.com/10-commandments-of-21st-century-franchise-production-2012-10

Gosciola, V. (2012). Narrativa transmídia: conceituação e origens [Transmedia narrative: conception and origins English translation of the title]. In C. Campalans, D. Renó, & V. Gosciola (Eds.), *Narrativa transmedia: entre teorías y practices* [Transmedia narrative: Between theories and practices] (pp. 7–14). Bogotá, Colombia: Editorial Universidad del Rosario.

Hayes, G. (2011). *How to write a transmedia production bible*. Retrieved from https://speakerdeck.com/jodieinblack/how-to-write-a-transmedia-production-bible

Humphries, C. (1991). On Quakerism, trans-media and democracy: Thoughts of Stuart Saunders Smith. *Ex-tempore*. Retrieved from http://www.ex-tempore.org/Humphrie.htm

Igarza, R. (2010). *Burbujas de Ocio. Nuevas formas de consumo cultural* [Bubbles of leisure. New forms of cultural consumption]. Buenos Aires, Argentina: La Crujía Ediciones. Col. Futuribles.

Irigaray, F. (2014). La ciudad como plataforma narrativa: El Documental Transmedia Tras los pasos de El Hombre Bestia [The city as a narrative platform: The transmedia documentary Following the footsteps of The Beast Man]. In F. Irigaray & A. Lovato (Eds.), *Hacia una comunicación transmedia* [Towards a transmedia communication] (pp. 113–131). Rosario, Argentina: UNR Editora. Retrieved from http://hdl.handle.net/2133/3610

Irigaray, F. (2015). Navegación territorial. Entramado narrativo urbano [Territorial navigation. Urban narrative lattice]. In F. Irigaray & A. Lovato (Eds.), *Producciones transmedia de no ficción. Análisis, experiencias y tecnologías* [Transmedia non-fiction productions. Analysis, experiences and technologies] (pp. 115–126). Rosario, Argentina: UNR Editora. Retrieved from http://hdl.handle.net/2133/5666

Irigaray, F. (2016). Documental transmedia: narrativas espaciales y relatos expandidos [Transmedia documentary: Spatial narratives and expanded stories]. In F. Irigaray & D. Renó (Eds.), *Transmediaciones. Creatividad, innovación y estrategias en nuevas narrativas* [Transmediations. Creativity, innovation and strategies in new narratives] (pp. 39–53). Buenos Aires, Argentina: Editorial La Crujía.

Irisarri, P., & Loja, M. (2017). *¿Qué pasa después? Aportes y desafíos para la construcción de derechos de víctimas de trata y explotación sexual* [What happens next? Contributions and challenges for the construction of rights of victims of trafficking and sexual exploitation]. Rosario, Argentina: UNR Editora. Retrieved from https://www.academia.edu/31773338/_Qu%C3%A9_pasa_despu%C3%A9s_Aportes_y_desaf%C3%ADos_para_la_construcci%C3%B3n_de_derechos_de_v%C3%ADctimas_de_trata_y_explotaci%C3%B3n_sexual

Jenkins, H. (2003). Transmedia storytelling: Moving characters from books to films to video games can make them stronger and more compelling. *MIT Technology Review*. Retrieved from http://www.technologyreview.com/news/401760/transmedia-storytelling/

Jenkins, H. (2009). The revenge of the origami unicorn: Seven principles of transmedia storytelling. *Blog Confessions of an Aca-Fan*. Retrieved from http://henryjenkins.org/2009/12/the_revenge_of_the_origami_uni.html

Kinder, M. (1991). *Playing with power in movies, television, and video games: From Muppet Babies to Teenage Mutant Ninja Turtles*. Berkley, CA: University of California Press.

Laurel, B. (2000). *Creating core content in a post-convergence world*. New York, NY: Tauzero.

Levin, B. (1970). *The pendulum years: Britain and the sixties*. London: Jonathan Cape.

Liuzzi, A. (2014). Transmedia "historytelling." De Documentales Interactivos y Géneros Híbridos [Transmedia "historytelling." From interactive documentaries and hybrid genres]. In F. Irigaray & A. Lovato (Eds.), *Hacia una comunicación transmedia* [Towards a transmedia communication] (pp. 65–86). Rosario, Argentina: UNR Editora. Retrieved from http://hdl.handle.net/2133/3610

Lovato, A. (2015). Del periodismo multimedia al periodismo transmedia. Guiones para pensar nuevas narrativas [From multimedia journalism to transmedia journalism. Scripts for thinking about new narratives]. In F. Irigaray & A. Lovato (Eds.), *Producciones transmedia de no ficción. Análisis, experiencias y tecnologías* [Transmedia non-fiction productions. Analysis, experiences and technologies] (pp. 33–52). Rosario, Argentina: UNR Editora.

Lovato, A. (2016). Guión transmedia en narrativas de no ficción [Transmedia script in nonfiction narratives]. In F. Irigaray & D. Renó (Eds.), *Transmediaciones. Creatividad, innovación y estrategias en nuevas narrativas* [Transmediations. Creativity, innovation and strategies in new narratives] (pp. 23–37). Buenos Aires, Argentina: Editorial La Crujía.

Moloney, K. (2011). *Porting transmedia storytelling to journalism* (Unpublished master's thesis). University of Denver, Denver, CO.

Nichols, B. (1997). *La representación de la realidad. Cuestiones y conceptos del documental* [The representation of reality. Issues and concepts of the documentary]. Barcelona, Spain: Paidos.

Puccini, S. (2015). *Guión de documentales: De la preproducción a la posproducción* [Documentary script: From pre-production to post-production]. Buenos Aires, Argentina: La marca editora.

Reno, D. (2014). Diversidade de modelos narrativos para documentários transmedia [Diversity of narrative models for transmedia documentaries]. *Revista, 14,* 93–112. Retrieved from http://www.doc.ubi.pt/14/dossier_denis_reno.pdf

Reno, D. (2014). Formatos y técnicas para la producción de documentales transmedia [Formats and techniques for the production of transmedia documentaries]. In *Hacia una comunicación transmedia* [Towards a transmedia communication]. Rosario: UNR Editora. Retrieved from https://es.scribd.com/doc/244926680/Hacia-una-Comunicacion-Transmedia

Renó, D., & Flores, J. (2012). *Periodismo transmedia* [Transmedia journalism]. Madrid, Spain: Fragua.

Scolari, C. (2013). *Narrativas transmedia. Cuando todos los medios cuentan* [Transmedia storytelling. When all media count]. Barcelona, Spain: Deusto.

Scolari, C. (2017). El translector. Lectura y narrativas transmedia en la nueva ecología de la comunicación [The transreader. Reading and transmedia storytelling in the new ecology of communication]. *Hipermediaciones*. Retrieved from https://hipermediaciones.com/2017/03/02/el-translector-lectura-y-narrativas-transmedia-en-la-nueva-ecologia-de-la-comunicacion/

Uricchio, W., Wolozin, S., Bui, L., Flynn, S., & Tortum, D. (2015). *Mapping the intersection of two cultures: Interactive documentary and digital journalism*. Cambridge, MA: MIT Open Documentary Lab and MacArthur Foundation.

Women for Sale. (2015a). Retrieved from http://www.documedia.com.ar/mujeres/index-en.html

Women for Sale. (2015b). *Transmedia tour*. Retrieved from http://www.documedia.com.ar/mujeres/universotransmedia-en.html

KEY TERMS AND DEFINITIONS

Collaborative Media: Productions that involve contributions of contents and information generated by the users in an open and horizontal communication proposal.

I-Doc: Multimedia documentary that mixes grammars of the traditional documentary and own dimensions of the digital media, producing nonlinear, hypertextual, and interactive narratives.

Media Platform: Set of digital and analog media that allow to create content, in multiple formats, to be consumed by different audiences, for example, a book, movie, video game, mobile application, or soap opera.

Nonfiction: Narrative field that contains productions that attempt to represent reality, applying techniques to register and treat it creatively in the context of a story. Included in this field are genres such as documentary film, essay, chronicle, and journalistic formats, among others.

Storyworld: Narrative canon defined by the producers, including a set of characters, scenarios, objects, times, actions, conflicts, and dialogues that make sense and are credible within the narrative.

Territorial Navigation: Concept used to analyze transmedia works that use physical, urban spaces (streets, squares, walls, buildings, etc.) as a narrative platform to involve citizens in the storyworld.

Transmedia Script: Set of documents that guide the production of a transmedia narrative. It includes details of the world of the story, definitions of the implemented platforms, narrative routes for the users, references between narrative pieces, and synchronization of the media launch.

User Experience: Perceptions and physical and emotional implications of the people generated during the interaction with technological and communicational environments, interfaces, or devices.

Chapter 15
Transmedia Television Journalism in Brazil:
Jornal da Record News as Reference

Yvana Fechine
Federal University of Pernambuco, Brazil

Sofia Costa Rêgo
Federal University of Pernambuco, Brazil

ABSTRACT

One of the main features of television is its appeal to transmediation—a production model oriented for the distribution of additional and/or associated content of a specific production in different media and technology platforms. In each field of television production (entertainment, journalism, advertising, etc.), transmediation takes various demonstrations and functions. The interest of the authors here is to show how transmedia strategies are part of the construction of the éthos in TV journalism, based on the analysis of Jornal da Record News, the first Brazilian newscast to be introduced as a transmedia production.

INTRODUCTION: TRANSMEDIATION AND JOURNALISM

Television cannot be limited just to television anymore. Media convergence supported the incorporation of other media and digital platforms, especially the Internet, in its creative and productive chain. Especially after Henry Jenkins' (2006, 2010) works on transmedia storytelling, the adjective "transmedia" widely spread, meaning a vast range of media integration phenomena stimulated by digitalization. However, the terms "transmedia" and "transmediation" acquired such a generalization in communication studies that, in some approaches, they convey the way content circulates within media convergence. In a more specific light, the term transmedia, as in the case of transmedia storytelling, is used to refer to a particular type of narrative, whose actions, situations and secondary characters can be deployed in an interdependent way in other media platforms (Scolari, 2013). In this chapter, the authors use the broader concept of transmediation.

DOI: 10.4018/978-1-5225-3781-6.ch015

Due to an excessively broad treatment, on one hand, and a much more restrictive understanding of the phenomenon, on the other hand, the first challenge for those who decide to observe transmediation in journalism is to specify the concept. Transmediation is understood here as a production model oriented by the distribution of content associated with each other in different media and technology platforms. In the same vein, the articulation of the model is docked in interactional strategies. Furthermore, it includes the practices offered by participatory culture, stimulated by digitalization and media convergence.

This approach is based on the assumptions of Fechine (2012, 2013, 2014), Fechine, Gouveia, Almeida, Costa, & Estevão (2013) and Fechine et al. (2015), who state that transmedia strategies are proposed by a communication producer (usually a media corporation) without which it would not be possible to think of transmediation as a production model. These transmedia strategies do not necessarily involve the participation of audiences. Even when producers appeal and allow a freer intervention from the public *over* or *through* the content, these actions do not cease to be, in a way, addressed or guided by a corporate intention, a "corporate authorship," as proposed by Evans (2011).

According to Jenkins (2006), audiences are creative agents, essential in the formation of transmedia strategies. They establish the relationships between the additional content and the television show to which the content refers to. However, public intervention is not only expected on what is offered (sharing, recommendations, comments, etc.), but their performance can be as content producers (uploading videos, photos, texts, etc.) as well. Even though the public participation is a component of the phenomenon, transmediation is foremost a set of strategic communication actions taken by media corporations to attract, retain, and engage the public on their own platforms (websites, television channels, profiles on social networks, etc.). Among these strategies, there is the articulation and integration of transmedia contents across multiple media platforms.

It is possible to consider that there is one specific medium responsible for leading this articulation. In this medium, a base text, which Jenkins (2006) called mothership, is developed (shows, movies, etc.) and the further articulations are created around it. In this chapter, they are respectively referred as reference medium and reference text. In the case of television journalism, the reference medium is television and the reference text is the newscast, around which transmedia contents are developed. The transmedia strategy is achieved when viewers assume the management of content, i.e. by performing necessary actions to the text construction (accessing and correlating these texts or producing new ones in response to the summons and instructions of the producers).

Despite the centrality that the viewer management has in the transmediation process, transmedia journalism is not the same as citizen journalism. Citizen journalism (Oliveira, 2010; Renó & Ruiz, 2012; Targino, 2009) describes the communication processes that occur in the publication of news *by* the citizen and *for* the citizens on digital platforms, by collaborating with journalists or ensuring that these themes and approaches are in the interest of Internet users, who have public visibility. Renó and Ruiz (2012) consider that transmediation has strengthened citizen journalism; while Scolari (2013, 2014) and Alzamora, Barros and Malta (2015) do not make a distinct differentiation between the types of information the Internet users have in circulation. Alzamora et al. (2015) consider transmedia as actions in journalism, which take place "both vertically, in private actions by media corporations, and horizontally, in collective attitudes of sharing and citizen participation" (p. 212). In this chapter, however, the authors argue that not all types of public collaboration on digital platforms, generically called citizen journalism, can be treated interchangeably as transmedia actions. In the perspective adopted here, transmedia manifestations are considered as the public collaborations proposed *as* part of or *from* production strategies.[1]

Although being initially described and identified in entertainment—especially TV series, reality shows and soap operas—transmedia strategies in the Brazilian mediascape are increasingly being adopted in journalism, including television journalism. It is not only about producing informational content and making them available on multiple platforms, a procedure generally observed in journalism within media convergence. It is about implementing a multi-platform production, guided by the complementarity between the various contents distributed in different media platforms, and by the strategic seek of public participation; two essential conditions to transmedia productions. In the Ibero-American context, recent studies about transmedia television (Cavalcanti, 2016; Fechine, 2012, 2013, 2014; Fechine et al., 2013; Fechine et al., 2015; Gouveia, 2015; Pereira, 2014; Sousa, 2015) demonstrate that these strategies can, in general, be used to spread or expand the narrative universe, whether in journalistic or entertainment shows.

In the entertainment realm, television shows, such as TV series or soap operas, the expansion strategies promote "spillovers" or unfolding of the narrative universe through the offering of elements that are endowed with a playful, but also narrative, function. In more complex actions, transmedia complements correspond to auxiliary or secondary narratives; contributing, from its articulation with the main (or reference) narrative, to the construction of transmedia stories, as proposed by Jenkins (2006). When the transmedia expansions have a playful function, they stimulate the viewer in fibbing, experiencing and coming into a game of make-believe, using their own involvement with the plot and the characters through games and jokes (memes, funny rearranged scenes, etc.), for instance.

In the analysis of soap operas, it was found that the transmedia strategies of propagation emphasize the feedback of the content (Fechine et al., 2013). When echoing a given narrative universe on social networks or beyond it, those strategies collaborate in maintaining the interest and involvement of the viewers with the reference show, appealing to the remissibility between the content offered on TV and those offered through digital platforms (websites and profiles on social networks, for example). Thus, content echoes or reverberates other transmedia contents, arousing the interest of the viewers for knowing more about what they see on TV, for sharing and for exchanging ideas on multiple contents. Therefore, a synergic cycle is formed.

An exploratory research on the news broadcasted by the main Brazilian television networks (Abreu e Lima, 2016; Pereira, 2014), such as Globo Network and Record TV, showed that most of them already adopts transmedia strategies of propagation and/or expansion (the difference between them will be discussed later). For a systemized analysis, the chosen case study is *Jornal da Record News* (JR News), presented by the journalist Heródoto Barbeiro. It airs Monday to Friday at 9 pm local time by the free-to-air news channel Record News, created in 2007 as part of the Record TV network. Founded in 1953, Record TV is the oldest active network in the country. After significant administrative changes occurred in 1991, Record TV currently has 108 TV stations spread over the whole Brazilian territory. Created in 2009, http://www.r7.com/ features news and entertainment content and is another important operational component of Record TV. JR News is the leading newscast from Record News and is one of the most important broadcasted by Record TV.

In addition to television, JR News has an online streaming at http://www.r7.com/, on their YouTube Channel (Jornal da Record News, n.d.), and on the network's Facebook page (Record News, n.d.). It was released in May 2011, being introduced as the country's first transmedia newscast (Notícia R7, 2015). To build the case study, JR News was systematically observed for five weeks, from July 11 to August 12, 2016, amounting to 25 editions. In addition, the website and both the show's and the host's profiles on two social networks (Facebook and Twitter) were checked on a daily basis in order to identify the transmedia strategies adopted by them. Another objective was to assess the strategies' role in the construction of the newscast's *éthos* (Fechine, 2008a).

THE *ÉTHOS* ON TELEVISION NEWS

The study of the *éthos* dates back to the Aristotelian tradition. For Aristotle, truth was built in speech. Therefore, the central concern of his rhetoric is to the persuasion procedures in public use of a speech. Rhetoric provides tools for the make-believe of the speaker. It can be considered, thus, an authentic "manual" of procedures used to convince the public in every situation. Consequently, rhetoric's concern is not only over the argumentative construction, but also over the emotions, passions, habits, and beliefs of the hearing. It is not focused on the construction of the truth, but on everything that may seem true to the listener (Cruz Junior, 2006). For this reason, there is a great concern in rhetoric over how the *éthos* of the public speaker appears to the audience. In other words, the concept refers to the configuration of character whereby the speaker conquers the confidence of the audience to persuade them.

In the Greco-Roman philosophical tradition, *éthos* was conceived in two distinct ways. For Isocrates or Quintilian, *éthos* was the result of the speaker's public image, built by factors that are exterior to the speech, especially his moral attributes (courage, integrity, etc.). It would refer, in short, to the reputation or the fame of the speaker. That way, it is understandable to some extent the collusion of television networks with the glamorization of its journalists, on the condition that this image, constructed by additional means other than the newscast, is favorable to them. Nowadays, the way the anchors build their reputation with the public depends, on one hand, on what is published about them in other media platforms, or even on their appearances in other TV shows (giving interviews, for example) and, on the other hand, on what they publish on their social network's profiles, for instance. Cruz Junior (2006) reinforces the importance of exogenous factors in the construction of credibility when he emphasizes that the effectiveness of the speech is determined by the institution that authorizes it, as well as by the social position of the person who gave it.

However, according to Aristotle and Cicero, the *éthos* did not depend so much on the speaker's social qualifications or his moral attributes. It was, above all, a construction of the speech itself (Cruz Junior, 2006). In the study of television news, nevertheless, the emphasis given to the construction of credibility can be more empirical (personal) or institutional, and at other times, linguistic. In the case of the *éthos* in the perspective of the French semiotics, Fiorin (2004) points out that the *éthos* corresponds to the image of the discursive author, an implicit author in the statement, and not the real author. In this perspective, the study of the *éthos* is part of the "position in speech" or enunciation. According to Fiorin (2004), the *éthos* is shown in "the marks of the enunciation left in the discourse. Therefore, the analysis of the enunciator's *éthos* has nothing of the psychologism that often seeks to infiltrate in the discursive studies" (p. 120). According to Fiorin (2004), when looking at a singular work, one can define only the narrator's traits. For this reason, it is only when the whole work of an author is studied that the *éthos* of the enunciator can be grasped. Thus, in the case study of JR News, the five-week period of observation contributed to a deeper understanding of the newscast's *éthos*. In this scenario, to better understand the *éthos*, a closer look at its enunciation and the roles involved in its discursive construction should be regarded.

In the theory of enunciation, the traditional roles of enunciator and enunciatte cannot be mistaken for the empirical author and reader. In the field of enunciation, empirical author and reader can only be considered when they are representations of concrete individuals who participate in the communicative circuit. As opposed to these empirical subjects ("flesh and blood" subjects), enunciator and enunciatte are defined as "semiotic subjects" ("speech subjects") that correspond to positions in textual functions, occupied respectively by who speaks (a "me") and for whom he/she speaks (a "you"). If enunciation itself is understood as some kind of simulacrum of communication built *in* and *through* the very speech—discourse, enunciator, and enunciatte can be defined, ultimately, as roles that symbolically replace in the text (in this case, television news) its real author and reader, according to the following schema (Fechine, 2008a):

Enunciator [**narrator** SPEECH **narratary**] Enunciatte

When thinking about actantial positions in the specific case of television news, it is possible to assume that the most immediate empirical communicative representation of the newscast seems to be every member of the production (reporters, anchors, commentators, cameramen, technicians, managers, etc.), called generically here as broadcaster. At the level of the speech itself (what is seen on the screen), the narrator of television news corresponds to the very figure of the anchor (or anchors). As it occurs in other television shows, newscasts can also represent its audience, in such a way that the receiver here is generally identified with the viewers' figurativization in the discourse. For that, newscasts frequently turn to interpellative speech, through which the anchors and reporters head directly to the viewer; whether by looking into the camera while talking, or by the use of vocatives or personal pronouns ("have you seen...," "you can...," "you know..."). However, it is possible to find some newscasts in which there is a recorded public participation (with polls, for example) or "live" (the Internet, for example). Although harder to find, there are also shows in which the viewers are invited to be in the studio during the filming, giving opinions or participating in the interviews with the guests. Therefore, the roles in newscasts could be seen as in the schema below (Fechine, 2008a). In this proposal, the expression "projected viewer" designates its different forms of figurativization.

Broadcaster [**Anchor** NEWSCAST **Projected viewer**] Viewer

However, due to the recursive structure of the newscast, the anchor is not the only actant (person) of the television newscast. The narrator-anchor organizes the entire show when he/she gives the floor to other auxiliary narrators (reporters, commentators, interviewees, etc.). Upon receiving the floor from the narrator-anchor, the reporter introduces himself/herself as another "me," setting those with whom he/she talks to as the "you." In this process of floor giving, oriented by an interchangeability of positions, the anchor defines his enunciative role: He/she acts as an instance of actantial anchorage, articulating the different actors of the enunciation. When he/she does that, he/she takes over the role of a broader narrator (the main narrator), and for this reason, he/she acquires a centrality in the building of the *éthos* of the newscast. However, the *éthos* is not defined merely by the image of the anchor perceived in the enunciation. Every anchor constructs an *éthos* in his/her own way based on his/her performance and characteristics, but this image plays a fundamental role in the construction of the *éthos* of the newscast. For this reason, it is common to observe anchors behaving differently when they replace others in their own newscasts.

Considering that the enunciator's *éthos* is defined in the very enunciation, the influence exerted by a given enunciator on an enunciatte does not depend solely on the content put into use: "The enunciatte does not accept a speech just because it is presented as a set of ideas that express potential interests; rather, he accepts it because he identifies with a given subject of enunciation, with a character, with a body, with a tone" (Fiorin, 2004, p. 134). Furthermore, the *éthos* could be considered as a connotation and consisted in the property that the enunciator had when delivering information (the *said*) to also state something about himself/herself (by the means of *saying*).

Although the building of the newscast's image depends on the *éthos* of the anchor himself/herself, the show "talks about itself" in many other ways. The participants in the construction of the *éthos* of the newscast are not only the editorial line: The scenery, the vignettes, the costumes, the technological resources that were used, the designs, etc., for instance, play significant roles in the construction of the *éthos* as well. With the increasing importance of the relationship between television and Internet, transmedia strategies—especially those which explore the anchor's and the newscast's profiles on social networks—acquired a very important role in the construction of the newscast's *éthos*, as it was found in the analysis of JR News.

TRANSMEDIA STRATEGIES AND THE *ÉTHOS* OF JORNAL DA RECORD NEWS

JR News adopts different strategies of articulation between media daily. At the beginning of the show, the anchor Heródoto Barbeiro warns that JR News is on a double platform: On television and on the channel's website. In addition, the anchor verbally summons the viewers to interact through the social networks. During the broadcast, tickers (crawlers) continuously invite the public to "like" anchor Heródoto Barbeiro's Facebook page, to follow him on Twitter and to send questions via WhatsApp. The anchor usually reads during the newscast at least one question submitted by the public to be answered by interviewees and/or commentators. Such interactions contribute to the construction of a proximity effect between the newscast and the public, stimulating interest and involvement. This constant invitation to the audience is a typical feature of transmedia projects, although they are not exclusive to them.

Since its release, JR News presents itself as the country's first transmedia newscast because of the extension of the TV interviews offered on the Internet—which falls into the already mentioned expansion strategy. The content expansion, instead of repetition, is another core principle of transmedia storytelling. At the beginning, JR News started the online streaming 15 minutes before the TV broadcast, showing the team's preparation for the official transmission, and ended 15 minutes after, extending the conversation from the studio. Currently, this procedure is no longer adopted. Nowadays, the online transmission takes place during the commercial breaks of the TV broadcast, giving rise to additional comments of the interviewees on the news.[2] When the streaming becomes strictly online[3], the guests receive a little more time to discuss politics, economics, and other topics, resuming the discussions started during the TV broadcast. However, this unfolding of the interviews contributes much more to reinforce the image of JR News as a newscast with a more in-depth approach than to the diversification of information.

Among the propagation strategies adopted by JR News, the most relevant to the construction of the newscast's *éthos* is airing backstage videos. A good example of this was Record News's Facebook post on July 20, 2016, about a video that shows the preparation of Heródoto Barbeiro before going on air (Record News, 2016c). The footage shows the anchor being made up, air-drying his hair, tidying up his shirt in front of the mirror in the dressing room, putting on the jacket, walking through the studio, talking to the cameraman, etc. Meanwhile, in some moments, he talks about his everyday life on Record News. This strategy promotes a greater "humanization" of the anchor and seems clearly directed not only to build a close relationship between the anchor and the audience, but to give a transparency effect to the extent that the enunciate exposes the very mechanism of the enunciation.

As part of this effort to increase its credibility, showing the news "from the inside," JR News innovated with the procedure of publishing videos of the backstage every day and adopting a transmedia strategy that the authors have not seen in no other Brazilian newscast during the period of observation. Moreover, since April 2016, staged editorial meetings via Live Facebook Mentions (Notícia R7, 2016a), Facebook's live video streaming technology, similar to Periscope (Twitter's streaming app), are broadcasted.

During the systematic observation, the streaming of the meetings was held by Record News's and Barbeiro's Facebook pages, with a link posted on the Twitter profiles of the network and the host, during the afternoons of Monday to Friday, at around 4 pm local time. On these occasions, it was announced informally for the Internet users what would be the highlights of the newscast, the guests, and the commentators. As the authors could apprehend in a further exploratory observation done in 2017, the staged editorial meetings began to be streamed most of the time only on Record News's Facebook page. In the period of systematic observation, the meetings lasted about ten minutes. In 2017, the streaming transmissions would last less than five minutes in order to hold the audience's attention even more.

During the period of systematic observation, the videos were made with Barbeiro's mobile phone, to his Facebook page, and by other journalists to Record News's Facebook page (they would film the meeting from different angles). As of 2017, the anchor stopped doing these footages, since the meetings ceased to be streamed on his Facebook page. In the newscast, Heródoto Barbeiro is the responsible for giving the floor to reporters and guests, while other journalists shoot the video, lead the conversation and give the floor to the other members of the team in the editorial meetings streamed online. In these transmissions, the anchor, the producers, and the editors talk about the news and exchange some ideas on how to approach the stories. They also make jokes with each other, laugh, show what they are eating and other private moments.

Through these streamings, Heródoto Barbeiro and his team get more space to reveal their personal and humorous side. On July 13, 2016, for example, editor José Simão started the editorial meeting saying he was rethinking his career (Record News, 2016b). He joked that he was going to become a hairdresser because he discovered that the French president pays around R$36,000 a month for his haircuts.

During these transmissions, they also have the opportunity to interact more informally and directly with the public; they read not only the Internet users' questions and opinions on the topics they are discussing, but also the more informal comments with hug requests published on Heródoto Barbeiro's Facebook page and Record News's as well. Whatever is mentioned on the posts of the editorial meetings is usually read and answered in the video itself during the live broadcast, in a direct conversation with the Internet user, who is given a voice at the meeting.

In this kind of transmedia content, the authors could see that, beyond Barbeiro, the other journalists of the team also become freer to give their opinion or make tougher and more personal comments or judgements, such as when executive editor Maria das Neves commented that a German who died in the explosion of an apartment in Rio de Janeiro "was way too bad news" (Record New, 2016a).

Notwithstanding, Heródoto Barbeiro is the protagonist and his ironic behavior is a striking feature in Barbeiro's *éthos* and the newscast's as well. On July 13, 2016, the anchor made a post on his blog, joked at the editorial meeting and spoke, at the beginning of the newscast, about the pilgrimage the former governor of Brasilia, José Roberto Arruda, was doing. Barbeiro said that the politician was doing a walk of atonement in Santiago de Compostela. He reminded that Arruda had already been arrested on corruption charges and wondered about what would the politician be making redemption for. On his blog, Barbeiro (2016) finished the post by asking ironically if Arruda was regretful or if he was simply showing off. During the editorial meeting, he joked even more pointedly suggesting that other politicians should also do pilgrimages, but crossing the North Pole or the Sahara Desert on foot.

Every content resulting from the transmedia strategies described above—posts on social networks, additional content giving and behind-the-scenes videos—promote varied effects and, consequently, participate in the construction of the *éthos* of the newscast: they promote the image of a critical, but fun, show (the irony fulfills an important role in this intersection); of a newscast that values professionalism, transparency (otherwise they would not show their backstage) and journalistic rigor, but without formality and without neglecting the proximity with their public. Moreover, it builds the image of a team who is forceful in addressing the facts (otherwise they would not make harsh comments on social networks) and who values public participation (by joking, interacting, answering to the questions, replying to the messages). Most of those traits associated with JR News collaborate, directly or indirectly, on the construction of a promise of authenticity, which is the basis of the *éthos* of a reliable newscast. Nevertheless, none of these transmedia actions seems to be as efficient and original in the construction of this critical and trustworthy, transparent and participatory newscast as the streaming of their staged editorial meeting.

In this specific transmedia action, the promise of authenticity results from the possibility offered to the viewer and Internet users to follow, and to some extent, participate in the *mise en scène* of the newscast's production process. The streaming of the editorial meeting has a key role to the extent that it gives JR News's viewers the feeling of witnessing online the information that they will see afterward live on television. Through this online transmission on Facebook, the audience have the feeling that everything they see on JR News is more real and honest because the newscast makes a deal with the public of presenting whatever was agreed by allowing them to witness the team discussing and making decisions. In this case, the main promise is the authenticity of the enunciation, which seems to make everything less manipulative *a posteriori*.

Just as television direct broadcasting, online live streaming produces a sense of presence (Fechine, 2008b) by placing senders and receivers of the communication in the same temporality (a shared duration). Due to this presence effect, it is possible to build a close proximity that involves the audience and allows them to feel part of the communicative process; whether by being able to communicate with journalists via social networks (as the authors have seen, JR News's team insists on reading the comments received during the streaming of the editorial meeting to produce this exact effect) or by witnessing what is presented as a critical step in the production of the newscast (the editorial meeting). While audiences have access to the off-air jokes, opinions, and discussions, and accompany the journalists during their snack time, they build on their sense of belonging, closeness, and empathy, increasing the reliability of the newscast.

CONCLUSION: THE EFFECTIVENESS OF THE STRATEGIES

Although the analysis of JR News does not represent, by any means, a comprehensive study on the effectiveness of transmedia strategies applied to journalism, the exploratory observation of the Internet user's comments offers useful clues on the efficiency of the strategies. In most cases, the comments evidence the construction of the intended *éthos*, through complimentary posts such as: "Definitely, the best anchor in Brazilian journalism... Nowadays, Jornal da Record News is by far the best in the country!!! Congratulations to Heródoto Barbeiro and the entire team of JR. News, I am a regular viewer" (Notícia R7, 2016b) and "Now that is what I call an informative newscast. I do not know if the others can ever reach it, but that is what they should do: elucidate, show the source materials of the facts, the various sides, consequences… anyhow, excellent" (Notícia R7, 2016b).

Since the *éthos*, in the perspective adopted here, is analyzed according to its discursive construction, the newscast is an expanded one that incorporates the Internet and digital platforms in its productive chain to encourage above all audience participation and the promotion of the general effect of proximity. Therefore, transmedia strategies should be considered as an integral part of the global enunciation process of the newscast. JR News is already taking good advantage of it, and not only to promote greater audience involvement and engagement but, foremost, to promote and advance its own image. This case study draws attention to a function of transmedia strategies that is frequently neglected by transmedia studies, i.e. its important role in the construction of the *éthos* of television shows and, especially, of its anchors.

This case study evidenced that the transmedia strategies used on JR News do not collaborate much in the journalistic qualification. This qualification is understood as a bigger diversity in source and approaches concerning a given fact or phenomenon. As shown in the study, these strategies are more used for the building of the newscast's *éthos* by reinforcing its communicative contracts with the audience. These contracts, which now have the Internet as a big ally, consist of the promises that the information is current, that the enunciation is authentic, and that the audience feels closer to the newscast.

However, transmedia strategies in television journalism do not collaborate merely for the building of the *éthos*. They also contribute for adding information and further explanations over the facts, and for helping in topic contextualization, accountability, and in publicizing the newscast. Nevertheless, they also explore the phatic function of communication by offering a more direct contact with the viewers through the Internet and through interactive online tools that promote a contact effect: On social networks, it is not always important *what* is said, or *how* it is said, but the possibility to say and have access to the content produced. This is explored by some transmedia strategies of JR News, such as the streaming of staged editorial meetings. JR News can be considered a good example of how Brazilian television journalism has been taking advantage of the transmediation because it explores a wide variety of effects produced by the strategic articulation between TV and Internet[4].

REFERENCES

Abreu e Lima, L. (2016). *A linguagem do telejornal. Um estudo sobre os modos de organização a partir dos principais telejornais da Rede Globo* [The language of newscast. A study on the modes of organization based on Rede Globo's main newscasts] (Unpublished doctoral dissertation). Federal University of Pernambuco, Recife.

Alzamora, G., Barros, V., & Malta, J. (2015). A narrativa transmídia de iReporter for CNN acerca dos protestos brasileiros de 2013 [iReporter for CNN's transmedia narrative about the 2013 Brazilian protests]. *Brazilian Journalism Research*, *11*(2), 204–221. Retrieved from https://bjr.sbpjor.org.br/bjr/article/view/710

Barbeiro, H. (2016, July 13). A estrada da salvação [The road to salvation]. *Notícias R7*. Retrieved from http://noticias.r7.com/blogs/herodoto-barbeiro/2016/07/13/a-estrada-da-salvacao/

Cavalcanti, G. (2016). *Televisão e redes sociais: Configurações de TV Social em Malhação* [Television and social networks: Social TV configurations in Malhação] (Unpublished master's thesis). Federal University of Pernambuco, Recife.

Cruz, D. F., Junior. (2006). *O Éthos do enunciador nos romances de Machado de Assis: Uma abordagem semiótica* [The enunciator's Éthos in Machado de Assis' novels: A semiotic approach] (Unpublished doctoral's dissertation). São Paulo University. Retrieved from www.teses.usp.br/teses/disponiveis/8/.../TESE_DILSON_FEREIRA_CRUZ_JUNIOR.pdf

Evans, E. (2011). *Transmedia television. Audiences, new media, and Daily Life*. New York: Routledge.

Fechine, Y. (2008a). Performance dos apresentadores dos telejornais: A construção do *éthos* [The performance of the presenters of a newscast: The building of the *éthos*]. *Famecos, 1*(36), 69–76. Retrieved from http://revistaseletronicas.pucrs.br/ojs/index.php/revistafamecos/article/view/4417/3317

Fechine, Y. (2008b). *Televisão e presença: Uma abordagem semiótica da transmissão direta* [Television and presence: A semiotic approach about direct transmission]. São Paulo: Estação das Letras e Cores/Centro de Pesquisas Sociossemióticas.

Fechine, Y. (2012). Transmidiação, entre o lúdico e o narrativo [Transmediation, between the ludic and the narrative]. In C. Campalans, D. Renó, & V. Gosciola (Eds.), *Narrativas Transmedia. Entre Teorías y Prácticas* [Transmedia narratives. Between Theories and Practices] (pp. 69–84). Bogotá, Colombia: Editoral Universidad de Rosario.

Fechine, Y. (2013). *Televisão transmídia: conceituações em torno de novas estratégias e práticas interacionais da TV* [Television transmedia: conceptualizations centered on the new interactional strategies and practices of TV]. Paper presented at Anais do XXIII Encontro Anual da Compós (Associação Nacional dos Programas de Pós-graduação em Comunicação). Universidade Federal da Bahia (UFBA), Salvador. Retrieved from http://compos.org.br/data/biblioteca_2109.pdf

Fechine, Y. (2014). Transmidiação e cultura participativa: Pensando as práticas textuais de agenciamento dos fãs de telenovelas brasileiras [Transmediation and participatory culture: Thinking about the textual practices of mediation from Brazilian soap operas fans]. *Revista Contracampo, 31*(1), 5–22. Retrieved from www.contracampo.uff.br/index.php/revista/article/viewFile/694/430

Fechine, Y., Gouveia, D., Almeida, C., Costa, M., & Estevão, F. (2013). Como pensar os conteúdos transmídias na teledramaturgia brasileira? Uma proposta de abordagem a partir das telenovelas da Globo [How transmedia contents in Brazilian soap operas should be thought? A proposal of approach based on Globo's productions]. In M. I. V. Lopes (Ed.), *Estratégias de Transmidiação na Ficção Televisiva Brasileira* [Transmediation Strategies in Brazilian Fiction Television] (pp. 19–60). Porto Alegre: Sulina. Retrieved from http://obitelbrasil.blogspot.com.br/p/publicacoes.html

Fechine, Y., Gouveia, D., Teixeira, C., Almeida, C., Costa, M., & Cavalcanti, G. (2015). Governo da participação: Uma discussão sobre processos interacionais em ações transmídias [Participation management: A discussion over the interactional procedures in transmedia actions]. In M. I. V. Lopes (Ed.), *Por uma teoria de fãs da ficção televisiva brasileira* [On a theory of the fans of Brazilian fiction television] (pp. 321–355). Porto Alegre: Sulina. Retrieved from http://obitelbrasil.blogspot.com.br/p/publicacoes.html

Fiorin, J. L. (2004). O *Éthos* do enunciador [The enunciator's *éthos*]. In A. Cortina & R. Marchezan (Eds.), *Razões e sensibilidades: a semiótica em foco* [Senses and sensibilities: Semiotic at issue] (pp. 117–138). Araraquara: Laboratório Editorial FLC/UNESP/Cultura Acadêmica Editora.

Gouveia, D. (2015). *Cultura participativa na TV Globo: Governo da audiência a partir de dispositivos midiáticos de participação* [Participatory culture on Globo Network: Audience management based on participation media devices] (Unpublished doctoral dissertation). Federal University of Pernambuco, Recife.

Jenkins, H. (2006). *Convergence culture: Where old and new media collide.* New York: New York University Press.

Jenkins, H. (2010). Transmedia storytelling 101. In *Cross-media communications. An introduction of creating integrated media experiences* (pp. 188–193). Lexington: ETC Press.

Jornal da Record News. (n.d.). *Home* [YouTube Channel]. Retrieved August 5, 2017, from https://www.youtube.com/playlist?list=PLt5YPA-Y-vppPke8WsreLH6DuVz7FPTQc

Notícia R7. (2015, October 20). *Jornal da Record News será o primeiro telejornal transmídia da TV brasileira* [Jornal da Record News will be first transmedia news show on Brazilian TV]. Retrieved from http://noticias.r7.com/record-news/jornal-da-record-news/videos/jornal-da-record-news-sera-o-primeiro-telejornal-transmidia-da-tv-brasileira-20102015

Notícia R7. (2016a, April 13). *JR News transmite reunião de pauta ao vivo pelo Facebook* [JR News transmits live on Facebook the editorial meeting]. Retrieved from http://noticias.r7.com/blogs/herodoto-barbeiro/2016/04/13/jr-news-transmite-reuniao-de-pauta-ao-vivo-pelo-facebook/

Notícia R7. (2016b, August 1). *Mais de meio milhão de pessoas conectadas no JR News* [More than a half million people connected to JR News]. Retrieved from http://noticias.r7.com/blogs/herodoto-barbeiro/2016/08/01/mais-de-meio-milhao-de-pessoas-conectadas-no-jr-news/

Record New. (2016a, July 11). Pauta JR News [JR News editorial meeting] [Facebook post]. Retrieved from https://www.facebook.com/recordnews/videos/1035902746457964/

Record New. (2016b, July 13). Pauta JR News [JR News editorial meeting] [Facebook post]. Retrieved from https://www.facebook.com/recordnews/videos/1037194792995426

Record News. (2016c, July 20). Como será que o Heródoto Barbeiro se prepara antes do JR News ir ao ar? Nós mostramos para você. [How Heródoto Barbeiro prepares himself before going on air on JR News? We show you] [Facebook post]. Retrieved from https://www.facebook.com/recordnews/videos/1040753445972894

Record News. (n.d.). In *Facebook*. Retrieved August 5, 2017, from https://www.facebook.com/recordnews

Renó, D., & Ruiz, S. (2012). Reflexiones sobre periodismo ciudadano y narrativa transmedia [Reflections over citizen journalism and transmedia narrative]. In C. Campalans, D. Renó, & V. Gosciola (Eds.), *Narrativas Transmedia. Entre Teorías y Prácticas* [Transmedia Narratives. Between Theories and Practices] (pp. 49–67). Bogotá: Editoral Universidad de Rosario.

Scolari, C. A. (2013). *Narrativas transmedia. Cuando todos los medios cuentan* [Transmedia narratives. When every medium counts]. Barcelona: Deusto.

Scolari, C. A. (2014). Transmedia storytelling: New ways of communicating in the digital age. *ACE digital culture annual report 2014*. Madri: Acción Cultural Espanhóla. Retrieved from https://www.accioncultural.es/media/Default%20Files/activ/2014/Adj/Anuario_ACE_2014/EN/6Storytelling_CScolari.pdf

Sousa, R. B. F. (2015). *As estratégias transmídias em Big Brother Brasil* [Transmedia strategies in Big Brother Brazil] (Unpublished master's thesis). Federal University of Pernambuco, Recife.

Targino, M. G. (2009). *Jornalismo cidadão: informa ou deforma?* [Citizen journalism: it informs or it deforms?]. Brasília: Ibict/UNESCO. Retrieved from http://unesdoc.unesco.org/images/0018/001823/182399por.pdf

KEY TERMS AND DEFINITIONS

Actant: In semiotic metalanguage, this term is used to describe any acting position in the enunciative process. In order to designate this acting, one can also talk about actanctial position. Enunciator and enunciatte are the enunciation's actants of the enunciation.

Actor of the Enunciation: This expression is used to designate an actantial position figurativized in the discourse, i.e., a "covered" or "incarnated" actantial position occupied by a character, for example (or by an anchor or commentator, in the case of newscast).

Enunciation: This term designates the "placing in speech." Enunciation is the act of production and enunciate is its product.

Enunciation Authenticity: This expression refers to the moments when mediation mechanisms, involved in the enunciative situation, produce an "unmasking" effect.

Phatic Function: The function of language dedicated to ensuring the effectiveness of the communication by asserting that the sender has access to the receiver through a given channel. When applied to a broader sense, the phatic function addresses the procedures in which being in touch through the use of a channel is an end in itself.

Recursive Structure: A structure is recursive when the most general configuration can also be observed in their parts (repetition of the whole in the parts).

Transmediation: The phenomenon from which transmedia contents are developed.

ENDNOTES

1 When Scolari (2013, p. 180–183) discusses journalism in the book *Narrativas Transmedias*, he highlights as an example of transmediation the case of Osama Bin Laden's death, which was disclosed by a tweet from the Pakistani Soahaib Athar almost an hour before the announcement of the White House. This can certainly be considered a manifestation of these new practices of dissemination of the news. In his argument, it is not clear, however, what makes this fact a transmedia manifestation. Throughout the development of his argument in this and in other works, the author ends up reinforcing the same idea we hold here: Transmediation as a corporate action, because he highlights, above all, the way the means of communication currently invite the public to send information in order to expand the news (Scolari, 2013, 2014).

2 Every day, the anchor interviews three guests among the network's commentators and journalists and other professionals that work outside Record TV. Usually, each one speaks in a block of the newscast. The person who spoke in a block resumes the talk with Heródoto Barbeiro in the next commercial break.

3 The summoning of the viewers for the continuation of the interview on the Internet is usually made by Heródoto Barbeiro indirectly, when he warns the interviewee on air that he will continue talking to him "in a minute." He rarely mentions explicitly that the conversation will be extended on the website. Usually, the continuity of the interviews online is not mentioned during the seconds before the commercial break. This is probably because the information that there is extra content during the commercial breaks is already comprehended in the "implied contract" of the newscast with the public and has already been announced by Barbeiro, in general, at the beginning of each program. When the exclusive interview to the website begins, the production puts a warning on the video: "R7 exclusive."

4 English translation by Renato Delgado.

Related References

To continue our tradition of advancing media and communications research, we have compiled a list of recommended IGI Global readings. These references will provide additional information and guidance to further enrich your knowledge and assist you with your own research and future publications.

Aas, B. G. (2012). What's real? Presence, personality and identity in the real and online virtual world. In N. Zagalo, L. Morgado, & A. Boa-Ventura (Eds.), *Virtual worlds and metaverse platforms: New communication and identity paradigms* (pp. 88–99). Hershey, PA: IGI Global. doi:10.4018/978-1-60960-854-5.ch006

Aceti, V., & Luppicini, R. (2013). Exploring the effect of mhealth technologies on communication and information sharing in a pediatric critical care unit: A case study. In J. Tan (Ed.), *Healthcare information technology innovation and sustainability: Frontiers and adoption* (pp. 88–108). Hershey, PA: IGI Global. doi:10.4018/978-1-4666-2797-0.ch006

Acilar, A. (2013). Factors affecting mobile phone use among undergraduate students in Turkey: An exploratory analysis. In I. Lee (Ed.), *Strategy, adoption, and competitive advantage of mobile services in the global economy* (pp. 234–246). Hershey, PA: IGI Global. doi:10.4018/978-1-4666-1939-5.ch013

Adams, A. (2013). Situated e-learning: Empowerment and barriers to identity changes. In S. Warburton & S. Hatzipanagos (Eds.), *Digital identity and social media* (pp. 159–175). Hershey, PA: IGI Global. doi:10.4018/978-1-4666-1915-9.ch012

Adeoye, B. F. (2013). Culturally different learning styles in online learning environments: A case of Nigerian university students. In L. Tomei (Ed.), *Learning tools and teaching approaches through ICT advancements* (pp. 228–240). Hershey, PA: IGI Global. doi:10.4018/978-1-4666-2017-9.ch020

Agarwal, N., & Mahata, D. (2013). Grouping the similar among the disconnected bloggers. In G. Xu & L. Li (Eds.), *Social media mining and social network analysis: Emerging research* (pp. 54–71). Hershey, PA: IGI Global. doi:10.4018/978-1-4666-2806-9.ch004

Aiken, M., Wang, J., Gu, L., & Paolillo, J. (2013). An exploratory study of how technology supports communication in multilingual groups. In N. Kock (Ed.), *Interdisciplinary applications of electronic collaboration approaches and technologies* (pp. 17–29). Hershey, PA: IGI Global. doi:10.4018/978-1-4666-2020-9.ch002

Aikins, S. K., & Chary, M. (2013). Online participation and digital divide: An empirical evaluation of U.S. midwestern municipalities. In *Digital literacy: Concepts, methodologies, tools, and applications* (pp. 63–85). Hershey, PA: IGI Global. doi:10.4018/978-1-4666-1852-7.ch004

Al Disi, Z. A., & Albadri, F. (2013). Arab youth and the internet: Educational perspective. In F. Albadri (Ed.), *Information systems applications in the Arab education sector* (pp. 163–178). Hershey, PA: IGI Global. doi:10.4018/978-1-4666-1984-5.ch012

Al-Dossary, S., Al-Dulaijan, N., Al-Mansour, S., Al-Zahrani, S., Al-Fridan, M., & Househ, M. (2013). Organ donation and transplantation: Processes, registries, consent, and restrictions in Saudi Arabia. In M. Cruz-Cunha, I. Miranda, & P. Gonçalves (Eds.), *Handbook of research on ICTs for human-centered healthcare and social care services* (pp. 511–528). Hershey, PA: IGI Global. doi:10.4018/978-1-4666-3986-7.ch027

Al-Khaffaf, M. M., & Abdellatif, H. J. (2013). The effect of information and communication technology on customer relationship management: Jordan public shareholding companies. In R. Eid (Ed.), *Managing customer trust, satisfaction, and loyalty through information communication technologies* (pp. 342–350). Hershey, PA: IGI Global. doi:10.4018/978-1-4666-3631-6.ch020

Al-Nuaim, H. A. (2012). Evaluation of Arab municipal websites. In *Wireless technologies: Concepts, methodologies, tools and applications* (pp. 1170–1185). Hershey, PA: IGI Global. doi:10.4018/978-1-61350-101-6.ch505

Al-Nuaim, H. A. (2013). Developing user profiles for interactive online products in practice. In M. Garcia-Ruiz (Ed.), *Cases on usability engineering: Design and development of digital products* (pp. 57–79). Hershey, PA: IGI Global. doi:10.4018/978-1-4666-4046-7.ch003

Al Omoush, K. S., Alqirem, R. M., & Shaqrah, A. A. (2013). The driving internal beliefs of household internet adoption among Jordanians and the role of cultural values. In A. Zolait (Ed.), *Technology diffusion and adoption: global complexity, global innovation* (pp. 130–151). Hershey, PA: IGI Global. doi:10.4018/978-1-4666-2791-8.ch009

Al-Shqairat, Z. I., & Altarawneh, I. I. (2013). The role of partnership in e-government readiness: The knowledge stations (KSs) initiative in Jordan. In A. Mesquita (Ed.), *User perception and influencing factors of technology in everyday life* (pp. 192–210). Hershey, PA: IGI Global. doi:10.4018/978-1-4666-1954-8.ch014

AlBalawi, M. S. (2013). Web-based instructions: An assessment of preparedness of conventional universities in Saudi Arabia. In M. Khosrow-Pour (Ed.), *Cases on assessment and evaluation in education* (pp. 417–451). Hershey, PA: IGI Global. doi:10.4018/978-1-4666-2621-8.ch018

Alejos, A. V., Cuiñas, I., Expósito, I., & Sánchez, M. G. (2013). From the farm to fork: Information security accomplishment in a RFID based tracking chain for food sector. In P. Lopez, J. Hernandez-Castro, & T. Li (Eds.), *Security and trends in wireless identification and sensing platform tags: Advancements in RFID* (pp. 237–270). Hershey, PA: IGI Global. doi:10.4018/978-1-4666-1990-6.ch010

Alkazemi, M. F., Bowe, B. J., & Blom, R. (2013). Facilitating the Egyptian uprising: A case study of Facebook and Egypt's April 6th youth movement. In N. Azab (Ed.), *Cases on web 2.0 in developing countries: Studies on implementation, application, and use* (pp. 256–282). Hershey, PA: IGI Global. doi:10.4018/978-1-4666-2515-0.ch010

Almutairi, M. S. (2012). M-government: Challenges and key success factors – Saudi Arabia case study. In Wireless technologies: Concepts, methodologies, tools and applications (pp. 1698-1717). Hershey, PA: IGI Global. doi:10.4018/978-1-61350-101-6.ch611

Alyagout, F., & Siti-Nabiha, A. K. (2013). Public sector transformation: Privatization in Saudi Arabia. In N. Pomazalová (Ed.), *Public sector transformation processes and internet public procurement: Decision support systems* (pp. 17–31). Hershey, PA: IGI Global. doi:10.4018/978-1-4666-2665-2.ch002

Amirante, A., Castaldi, T., Miniero, L., & Romano, S. P. (2013). Protocol interactions among user agents, application servers, and media servers: Standardization efforts and open issues. In D. Kanellopoulos (Ed.), *Intelligent multimedia technologies for networking applications: Techniques and tools* (pp. 48–63). Hershey, PA: IGI Global. doi:10.4018/978-1-4666-2833-5.ch003

Andres, H. P. (2013). Shared mental model development during technology-mediated collaboration. In N. Kock (Ed.), *Interdisciplinary applications of electronic collaboration approaches and technologies* (pp. 125–142). Hershey, PA: IGI Global. doi:10.4018/978-1-4666-2020-9.ch009

Andrus, C. H., & Gaynor, M. (2013). Good IT requires good communication. In S. Sarnikar, D. Bennett, & M. Gaynor (Eds.), *Cases on healthcare information technology for patient care management* (pp. 122–125). Hershey, PA: IGI Global. doi:10.4018/978-1-4666-2671-3.ch007

Annafari, M. T., & Bohlin, E. (2013). Why is the diffusion of mobile service not an evolutionary process? In I. Lee (Ed.), *Mobile services industries, technologies, and applications in the global economy* (pp. 25–38). Hershey, PA: IGI Global. doi:10.4018/978-1-4666-1981-4.ch002

Anupama, S. (2013). Gender evaluation of rural e-governance in India: A case study of E-Gram Suraj (e-rural good governance) scheme1. In *Digital literacy: Concepts, methodologies, tools, and applications* (pp. 1059–1074). Hershey, PA: IGI Global. doi:10.4018/978-1-4666-1852-7.ch055

Ariely, G. (2013). Boundaries of socio-technical systems and IT for knowledge development in military environments. In J. Abdelnour-Nocera (Ed.), *Knowledge and technological development effects on organizational and social structures* (pp. 224–238). Hershey, PA: IGI Global. doi:10.4018/978-1-4666-2151-0.ch014

Arsenio, A. M. (2013). Intelligent approaches for adaptation and distribution of personalized multimedia content. In D. Kanellopoulos (Ed.), *Intelligent multimedia technologies for networking applications: Techniques and tools* (pp. 197–224). Hershey, PA: IGI Global. doi:10.4018/978-1-4666-2833-5.ch008

Artail, H., & Tarhini, T. (2013). Runtime discovery and access of web services in mobile environments. In I. Lee (Ed.), *Mobile services industries, technologies, and applications in the global economy* (pp. 193–213). Hershey, PA: IGI Global. doi:10.4018/978-1-4666-1981-4.ch012

Asino, T. I., Wilder, H., & Ferris, S. P. (2013). Innovative use of ICT in Namibia for nationhood: Special emphasis on the Namibian newspaper. In H. Rahman (Ed.), *Cases on progressions and challenges in ICT utilization for citizen-centric governance* (pp. 205–216). Hershey, PA: IGI Global. doi:10.4018/978-1-4666-2071-1.ch009

Atici, B., & Bati, U. (2013). Identity of virtual supporters: Constructing identity of Turkish football fans on digital media. In S. Warburton & S. Hatzipanagos (Eds.), *Digital identity and social media* (pp. 256–274). Hershey, PA: IGI Global. doi:10.4018/978-1-4666-1915-9.ch018

Azab, N., & Khalifa, N. (2013). Web 2.0 and opportunities for entrepreneurs: How Egyptian entrepreneurs perceive and exploit web 2.0 technologies. In N. Azab (Ed.), *Cases on web 2.0 in developing countries: Studies on implementation, application, and use* (pp. 1–32). Hershey, PA: IGI Global. doi:10.4018/978-1-4666-2515-0.ch001

Bainbridge, W. S. (2013). Ancestor veneration avatars. In R. Luppicini (Ed.), *Handbook of research on technoself: Identity in a technological society* (pp. 308–321). Hershey, PA: IGI Global. doi:10.4018/978-1-4666-2211-1.ch017

Baporikar, N. (2013). Critical review of academic entrepreneurship in India. In A. Szopa, W. Karwowski, & P. Ordóñez de Pablos (Eds.), *Academic entrepreneurship and technological innovation: A business management perspective* (pp. 29–52). Hershey, PA: IGI Global. doi:10.4018/978-1-4666-2116-9.ch002

Barroca, L., & Gimenes, I. M. (2013). Computing postgraduate programmes in the UK and Brazil: Learning from experience in distance education with web 2.0 support. In N. Azab (Ed.), *Cases on web 2.0 in developing countries: Studies on implementation, application, and use* (pp. 147–171). Hershey, PA: IGI Global. doi:10.4018/978-1-4666-2515-0.ch006

Barton, S. M. (2013). Facilitating learning by going online: Modernising Islamic teaching and learning in Indonesia. In E. McKay (Ed.), *ePedagogy in online learning: New developments in web mediated human computer interaction* (pp. 74–92). Hershey, PA: IGI Global. doi:10.4018/978-1-4666-3649-1.ch005

Barzilai-Nahon, K., Gomez, R., & Ambikar, R. (2013). Conceptualizing a contextual measurement for digital divide/s: Using an integrated narrative. In *Digital literacy: Concepts, methodologies, tools, and applications* (pp. 279–293). Hershey, PA: IGI Global. doi:10.4018/978-1-4666-1852-7.ch015

Bénel, A., & Lacour, P. (2012). Towards a participative platform for cultural texts translators. In C. El Morr & P. Maret (Eds.), *Virtual community building and the information society: Current and future directions* (pp. 153–162). Hershey, PA: IGI Global. doi:10.4018/978-1-60960-869-9.ch008

Bentley, C. M. (2013). Designing and implementing online collaboration tools in West Africa. In N. Azab (Ed.), *Cases on web 2.0 in developing countries: Studies on implementation, application, and use* (pp. 33–60). Hershey, PA: IGI Global. doi:10.4018/978-1-4666-2515-0.ch002

Berg, M. (2012). Checking in at the urban playground: Digital geographies and electronic flâneurs. In F. Comunello (Ed.), *Networked sociability and individualism: Technology for personal and professional relationships* (pp. 169–194). Hershey, PA: IGI Global. doi:10.4018/978-1-61350-338-6.ch009

Bers, M. U., & Ettinger, A. B. (2013). Programming robots in kindergarten to express identity: An ethnographic analysis. In *Industrial engineering: Concepts, methodologies, tools, and applications* (pp. 1952–1968). Hershey, PA: IGI Global. doi:10.4018/978-1-4666-1945-6.ch105

Binsaleh, M., & Hassan, S. (2013). Systems development methodology for mobile commerce applications. In I. Khalil & E. Weippl (Eds.), *Contemporary challenges and solutions for mobile and multimedia technologies* (pp. 146–162). Hershey, PA: IGI Global. doi:10.4018/978-1-4666-2163-3.ch009

Bishop, J. (2013). Cooperative e-learning in the multilingual and multicultural school: The role of "classroom 2.0" for increasing participation in education. In P. Pumilia-Gnarini, E. Favaron, E. Pacetti, J. Bishop, & L. Guerra (Eds.), *Handbook of research on didactic strategies and technologies for education: Incorporating advancements* (pp. 137–150). Hershey, PA: IGI Global. doi:10.4018/978-1-4666-2122-0.ch013

Bishop, J. (2013). Increasing capital revenue in social networking communities: Building social and economic relationships through avatars and characters. In J. Bishop (Ed.), *Examining the concepts, issues, and implications of internet trolling* (pp. 44–61). Hershey, PA: IGI Global. doi:10.4018/978-1-4666-2803-8.ch005

Bishop, J. (2013). Lessons from the emotivate project for increasing take-up of big society and responsible capitalism initiatives. In P. Pumilia-Gnarini, E. Favaron, E. Pacetti, J. Bishop, & L. Guerra (Eds.), *Handbook of research on didactic strategies and technologies for education: Incorporating advancements* (pp. 208–217). Hershey, PA: IGI Global. doi:10.4018/978-1-4666-2122-0.ch019

Blau, I. (2013). E-collaboration within, between, and without institutions: Towards better functioning of online groups through networks. In N. Kock (Ed.), *Interdisciplinary applications of electronic collaboration approaches and technologies* (pp. 188–203). Hershey, PA: IGI Global. doi:10.4018/978-1-4666-2020-9.ch013

Boskic, N., & Hu, S. (2013). Blended learning: The road to inclusive and global education. In E. Jean Francois (Ed.), *Transcultural blended learning and teaching in postsecondary education* (pp. 283–301). Hershey, PA: IGI Global. doi:10.4018/978-1-4666-2014-8.ch015

Botero, A., Karhu, K., & Vihavainen, S. (2012). Exploring the ecosystems and principles of community innovation. In A. Lugmayr, H. Franssila, P. Näränen, O. Sotamaa, J. Vanhala, & Z. Yu (Eds.), *Media in the ubiquitous era: Ambient, social and gaming media* (pp. 216–234). Hershey, PA: IGI Global. doi:10.4018/978-1-60960-774-6.ch012

Bowe, B. J., Blom, R., & Freedman, E. (2013). Negotiating boundaries between control and dissent: Free speech, business, and repressitarian governments. In J. Lannon & E. Halpin (Eds.), *Human rights and information communication technologies: Trends and consequences of use* (pp. 36–55). Hershey, PA: IGI Global. doi:10.4018/978-1-4666-1918-0.ch003

Brandão, J., Ferreira, T., & Carvalho, V. (2012). An overview on the use of serious games in the military industry and health. In M. Cruz-Cunha (Ed.), *Handbook of research on serious games as educational, business and research tools* (pp. 182–201). Hershey, PA: IGI Global. doi:10.4018/978-1-4666-0149-9.ch009

Brost, L. F., & McGinnis, C. (2012). The status of blogging in the republic of Ireland: A case study. In T. Dumova & R. Fiordo (Eds.), *Blogging in the global society: Cultural, political and geographical aspects* (pp. 128–147). Hershey, PA: IGI Global. doi:10.4018/978-1-60960-744-9.ch008

Burns, J., Blanchard, M., & Metcalf, A. (2013). Bridging the digital divide in Australia: The potential implications for the mental health of young people experiencing marginalisation. In *Digital literacy: Concepts, methodologies, tools, and applications* (pp. 772–793). Hershey, PA: IGI Global. doi:10.4018/978-1-4666-1852-7.ch040

Cagliero, L., & Fiori, A. (2013). News document summarization driven by user-generated content. In G. Xu & L. Li (Eds.), *Social media mining and social network analysis: Emerging research* (pp. 105–126). Hershey, PA: IGI Global. doi:10.4018/978-1-4666-2806-9.ch007

Camillo, A., & Di Pietro, L. (2013). Managerial communication in the global cross-cultural context. In B. Christiansen, E. Turkina, & N. Williams (Eds.), *Cultural and technological influences on global business* (pp. 397–419). Hershey, PA: IGI Global. doi:10.4018/978-1-4666-3966-9.ch021

Canazza, S., De Poli, G., Rodà, A., & Vidolin, A. (2013). Expressiveness in music performance: Analysis, models, mapping, encoding. In J. Steyn (Ed.), *Structuring music through markup language: Designs and architectures* (pp. 156–186). Hershey, PA: IGI Global. doi:10.4018/978-1-4666-2497-9.ch008

Carrasco, J. G., Ovide, E., & Puyal, M. B. (2013). Closing and opening of cultures. In F. García-Peñalvo (Ed.), *Multiculturalism in technology-based education: Case studies on ICT-supported approaches* (pp. 125–142). Hershey, PA: IGI Global. doi:10.4018/978-1-4666-2101-5.ch008

Carreras, I., Zanardi, A., Salvadori, E., & Miorandi, D. (2013). A distributed monitoring framework for opportunistic communication systems: An experimental approach. In V. De Florio (Ed.), *Innovations and approaches for resilient and adaptive systems* (pp. 220–236). Hershey, PA: IGI Global. doi:10.4018/978-1-4666-2056-8.ch013

Carter, M., Grover, V., & Thatcher, J. B. (2013). Mobile devices and the self: developing the concept of mobile phone identity. In I. Lee (Ed.), *Strategy, adoption, and competitive advantage of mobile services in the global economy* (pp. 150–164). Hershey, PA: IGI Global. doi:10.4018/978-1-4666-1939-5.ch008

Caruso, F., Giuffrida, G., Reforgiato, D., & Zarba, C. (2013). Recommendation systems for mobile devices. In I. Lee (Ed.), *Mobile services industries, technologies, and applications in the global economy* (pp. 221–242). Hershey, PA: IGI Global. doi:10.4018/978-1-4666-1981-4.ch014

Casamassima, L. (2013). eTwinning project: A virtual orchestra. In P. Pumilia-Gnarini, E. Favaron, E. Pacetti, J. Bishop, & L. Guerra (Eds.) Handbook of research on didactic strategies and technologies for education: Incorporating advancements (pp. 703-709). Hershey, PA: IGI Global. doi:10.4018/978-1-4666-2122-0.ch061

Caschera, M. C., D'Ulizia, A., Ferri, F., & Grifoni, P. (2012). Multiculturality and multimodal languages. In G. Ghinea, F. Andres, & S. Gulliver (Eds.), *Multiple sensorial media advances and applications: New developments in MulSeMedia* (pp. 99–114). Hershey, PA: IGI Global. doi:10.4018/978-1-60960-821-7.ch005

Catagnus, R. M., & Hantula, D. A. (2013). The virtual individual education plan (IEP) team: Using online collaboration to develop a behavior intervention plan. In N. Kock (Ed.), *Interdisciplinary applications of electronic collaboration approaches and technologies* (pp. 30–45). Hershey, PA: IGI Global. doi:10.4018/978-1-4666-2020-9.ch003

Ch'ng, E. (2013). The mirror between two worlds: 3D surface computing for objects and environments. In D. Harrison (Ed.), *Digital media and technologies for virtual artistic spaces* (pp. 166–185). Hershey, PA: IGI Global. doi:10.4018/978-1-4666-2961-5.ch013

Chand, A. (2013). Reducing digital divide: The case of the 'people first network' (PFNet) in the Solomon Islands. In *Digital literacy: Concepts, methodologies, tools, and applications* (pp. 1571–1605). Hershey, PA: IGI Global. doi:10.4018/978-1-4666-1852-7.ch083

Chatterjee, S. (2013). Ethical behaviour in technology-mediated communication. In J. Bishop (Ed.), *Examining the concepts, issues, and implications of internet trolling* (pp. 1–9). Hershey, PA: IGI Global. doi:10.4018/978-1-4666-2803-8.ch001

Chen, C., Chao, H., Wu, T., Fan, C., Chen, J., Chen, Y., & Hsu, J. (2013). IoT-IMS communication platform for future internet. In V. De Florio (Ed.), *Innovations and approaches for resilient and adaptive systems* (pp. 68–86). Hershey, PA: IGI Global. doi:10.4018/978-1-4666-2056-8.ch004

Chen, J., & Hu, X. (2013). Smartphone market in China: Challenges, opportunities, and promises. In I. Lee (Ed.), *Mobile services industries, technologies, and applications in the global economy* (pp. 120–132). Hershey, PA: IGI Global. doi:10.4018/978-1-4666-1981-4.ch008

Chen, Y., Lee, B., & Kirk, R. M. (2013). Internet use among older adults: Constraints and opportunities. In R. Zheng, R. Hill, & M. Gardner (Eds.), *Engaging older adults with modern technology: Internet use and information access needs* (pp. 124–141). Hershey, PA: IGI Global. doi:10.4018/978-1-4666-1966-1.ch007

Cheong, P. H., & Martin, J. N. (2013). Cultural implications of e-learning access (and divides): Teaching an intercultural communication course online. In A. Edmundson (Ed.), *Cases on cultural implications and considerations in online learning* (pp. 82–100). Hershey, PA: IGI Global. doi:10.4018/978-1-4666-1885-5.ch005

Chhanabhai, P., & Holt, A. (2013). The changing world of ICT and health: Crossing the digital divide. In *Digital literacy: Concepts, methodologies, tools, and applications* (pp. 794–811). Hershey, PA: IGI Global. doi:10.4018/978-1-4666-1852-7.ch041

Chuling, W., Hua, C. M., & Chee, C. J. (2012). Investigating the demise of radio and television broadcasting. In R. Sharma, M. Tan, & F. Pereira (Eds.), *Understanding the interactive digital media marketplace: Frameworks, platforms, communities and issues* (pp. 392–405). Hershey, PA: IGI Global. doi:10.4018/978-1-61350-147-4.ch031

Ciaramitaro, B. L. (2012). Introduction to mobile technologies. In B. Ciaramitaro (Ed.), *Mobile technology consumption: Opportunities and challenges* (pp. 1–15). Hershey, PA: IGI Global. doi:10.4018/978-1-61350-150-4.ch001

Cicconetti, C., Mambrini, R., & Rossi, A. (2013). A survey of wireless backhauling solutions for ITS. In R. Daher & A. Vinel (Eds.), *Roadside networks for vehicular communications: Architectures, applications, and test fields* (pp. 57–70). Hershey, PA: IGI Global. doi:10.4018/978-1-4666-2223-4.ch003

Ciptasari, R. W., & Sakurai, K. (2013). Multimedia copyright protection scheme based on the direct feature-based method. In K. Kondo (Ed.), *Multimedia information hiding technologies and methodologies for controlling data* (pp. 412–439). Hershey, PA: IGI Global. doi:10.4018/978-1-4666-2217-3.ch019

Code, J. (2013). Agency and identity in social media. In S. Warburton & S. Hatzipanagos (Eds.), *Digital identity and social media* (pp. 37–57). Hershey, PA: IGI Global. doi:10.4018/978-1-4666-1915-9.ch004

Comunello, F. (2013). From the digital divide to multiple divides: Technology, society, and new media skills. In *Digital literacy: Concepts, methodologies, tools, and applications* (pp. 1622–1639). Hershey, PA: IGI Global. doi:10.4018/978-1-4666-1852-7.ch085

Consonni, A. (2013). About the use of the DMs in CLIL classes. In F. García-Peñalvo (Ed.), *Multiculturalism in technology-based education: Case studies on ICT-supported approaches* (pp. 9–27). Hershey, PA: IGI Global. doi:10.4018/978-1-4666-2101-5.ch002

Constant, J. (2012). Digital approaches to visualization of geometric problems in wooden sangaku tablets. In A. Ursyn (Ed.), *Biologically-inspired computing for the arts: Scientific data through graphics* (pp. 240–253). Hershey, PA: IGI Global. doi:10.4018/978-1-4666-0942-6.ch013

Cossiavelou, V., Bantimaroudis, P., Kavakli, E., & Illia, L. (2013). The media gatekeeping model updated by R and I in ICTs: The case of wireless communications in media coverage of the olympic games. In M. Bartolacci & S. Powell (Eds.), *Advancements and innovations in wireless communications and network technologies* (pp. 262–288). Hershey, PA: IGI Global. doi:10.4018/978-1-4666-2154-1.ch019

Cropf, R. A., Benmamoun, M., & Kalliny, M. (2013). The role of web 2.0 in the Arab Spring. In N. Azab (Ed.), *Cases on web 2.0 in developing countries: Studies on implementation, application, and use* (pp. 76–108). Hershey, PA: IGI Global. doi:10.4018/978-1-4666-2515-0.ch004

Cucinotta, A., Minnolo, A. L., & Puliafito, A. (2013). Design and implementation of an event-based RFID middleware. In N. Karmakar (Ed.), *Advanced RFID systems, security, and applications* (pp. 110–131). Hershey, PA: IGI Global. doi:10.4018/978-1-4666-2080-3.ch006

D'Andrea, A., Ferri, F., & Grifoni, P. (2013). Assessing e-health in Africa: Web 2.0 applications. In N. Azab (Ed.), *Cases on web 2.0 in developing countries: Studies on implementation, application, and use* (pp. 442–467). Hershey, PA: IGI Global. doi:10.4018/978-1-4666-2515-0.ch016

de Guinea, A. O. (2013). The level paradox of e-collaboration: Dangers and solutions. In N. Kock (Ed.), *Interdisciplinary applications of electronic collaboration approaches and technologies* (pp. 166–187). Hershey, PA: IGI Global. doi:10.4018/978-1-4666-2020-9.ch012

Dhar-Bhattacharjee, S., & Takruri-Rizk, H. (2012). An Indo-British comparison. In C. Romm Livermore (Ed.), *Gender and social computing: Interactions, differences and relationships* (pp. 50–71). Hershey, PA: IGI Global. doi:10.4018/978-1-60960-759-3.ch004

Díaz-Foncea, M., & Marcuello, C. (2013). ANOBIUM, SL: The use of the ICT as niche of employment and as tool for developing the social market. In T. Torres-Coronas & M. Vidal-Blasco (Eds.), *Social e-enterprise: Value creation through ICT* (pp. 221–242). Hershey, PA: IGI Global. doi:10.4018/978-1-4666-2667-6.ch013

Díaz-González, M., Froufe, N. Q., Brena, A. G., & Pumarola, F. (2013). Uses and implementation of social media at university: The case of schools of communication in Spain. In B. Pătruţ, M. Pătruţ, & C. Cmeciu (Eds.), *Social media and the new academic environment: Pedagogical challenges* (pp. 204–222). Hershey, PA: IGI Global. doi:10.4018/978-1-4666-2851-9.ch010

Ditsa, G., Alwahaishi, S., Al-Kobaisi, S., & Snášel, V. (2013). A comparative study of the effects of culture on the deployment of information technology. In A. Zolait (Ed.), *Technology diffusion and adoption: Global complexity, global innovation* (pp. 77–90). Hershey, PA: IGI Global. doi:10.4018/978-1-4666-2791-8.ch006

Donaldson, O., & Duggan, E. W. (2013). Assessing mobile value-added preference structures: The case of a developing country. In I. Lee (Ed.), *Strategy, adoption, and competitive advantage of mobile services in the global economy* (pp. 349–370). Hershey, PA: IGI Global. doi:10.4018/978-1-4666-1939-5.ch019

Douai, A. (2013). "In YouTube we trust": Video exchange and Arab human rights. In J. Lannon & E. Halpin (Eds.), *Human rights and information communication technologies: Trends and consequences of use* (pp. 57–71). Hershey, PA: IGI Global. doi:10.4018/978-1-4666-1918-0.ch004

Dromzée, C., Laborie, S., & Roose, P. (2013). A semantic generic profile for multimedia document adaptation. In D. Kanellopoulos (Ed.), *Intelligent multimedia technologies for networking applications: Techniques and tools* (pp. 225–246). Hershey, PA: IGI Global. doi:10.4018/978-1-4666-2833-5.ch009

Drucker, S., & Gumpert, G. (2012). The urban communication infrastructure: Global connection and local detachment. In *Wireless technologies: Concepts, methodologies, tools and applications* (pp. 1150–1169). Hershey, PA: IGI Global. doi:10.4018/978-1-61350-101-6.ch504

Drula, G. (2013). Media and communication research facing social media. In M. Pătruţ & B. Pătruţ (Eds.), *Social media in higher education: Teaching in web 2.0* (pp. 371–392). Hershey, PA: IGI Global. doi:10.4018/978-1-4666-2970-7.ch019

Dueck, J., & Rempel, M. (2013). Human rights and technology: Lessons from Alice in Wonderland. In J. Lannon & E. Halpin (Eds.), *Human rights and information communication technologies: Trends and consequences of use* (pp. 1–20). Hershey, PA: IGI Global. doi:10.4018/978-1-4666-1918-0.ch001

Dumova, T. (2012). Social interaction technologies and the future of blogging. In T. Dumova & R. Fiordo (Eds.), *Blogging in the global society: Cultural, political and geographical aspects* (pp. 249–274). Hershey, PA: IGI Global. doi:10.4018/978-1-60960-744-9.ch015

Dunn, H. S. (2013). Information literacy and the digital divide: Challenging e-exclusion in the global south. In *Digital literacy: Concepts, methodologies, tools, and applications* (pp. 20–38). Hershey, PA: IGI Global. doi:10.4018/978-1-4666-1852-7.ch002

Elias, N. (2013). Immigrants' internet use and identity from an intergenerational perspective: Immigrant senior citizens and youngsters from the former Soviet Union in Israel. In R. Luppicini (Ed.), *Handbook of research on technoself: Identity in a technological society* (pp. 293–307). Hershey, PA: IGI Global. doi:10.4018/978-1-4666-2211-1.ch016

Elizabeth, L. S., Ismail, N., & Tun, M. S. (2012). The future of the printed book. In R. Sharma, M. Tan, & F. Pereira (Eds.), *Understanding the interactive digital media marketplace: Frameworks, platforms, communities and issues* (pp. 416–429). Hershey, PA: IGI Global. doi:10.4018/978-1-61350-147-4.ch033

Erne, R. (2012). Knowledge worker performance in a cross-industrial perspective. In S. Brüggemann & C. d'Amato (Eds.), *Collaboration and the semantic web: Social networks, knowledge networks, and knowledge resources* (pp. 297–321). Hershey, PA: IGI Global. doi:10.4018/978-1-4666-0894-8.ch015

Ertl, B., Helling, K., & Kikis-Papadakis, K. (2012). The impact of gender in ICT usage, education and career: Comparisons between Greece and Germany. In C. Romm Livermore (Ed.), *Gender and social computing: Interactions, differences and relationships* (pp. 98–119). Hershey, PA: IGI Global. doi:10.4018/978-1-60960-759-3.ch007

Estapé-Dubreuil, G., & Torreguitart-Mirada, C. (2013). ICT adoption in the small and medium-size social enterprises in Spain: Opportunity or priority? In T. Torres-Coronas & M. Vidal-Blasco (Eds.), *Social e-enterprise: Value creation through ICT* (pp. 200–220). Hershey, PA: IGI Global. doi:10.4018/978-1-4666-2667-6.ch012

Eze, U. C., & Poong, Y. S. (2013). Consumers' intention to use mobile commerce and the moderating roles of gender and income. In I. Lee (Ed.), *Strategy, adoption, and competitive advantage of mobile services in the global economy* (pp. 127–148). Hershey, PA: IGI Global. doi:10.4018/978-1-4666-1939-5.ch007

Farrell, R., Danis, C., Erickson, T., Ellis, J., Christensen, J., Bailey, M., & Kellogg, W. A. (2012). A picture and a thousand words: Visual scaffolding for mobile communication in developing regions. In W. Hu (Ed.), *Emergent trends in personal, mobile, and handheld computing technologies* (pp. 341–354). Hershey, PA: IGI Global. doi:10.4018/978-1-4666-0921-1.ch020

Fidler, C. S., Kanaan, R. K., & Rogerson, S. (2013). Barriers to e-government implementation in Jordan: The role of wasta. In A. Mesquita (Ed.), *User perception and influencing factors of technology in everyday life* (pp. 179–191). Hershey, PA: IGI Global. doi:10.4018/978-1-4666-1954-8.ch013

Filho, J. R. (2013). ICT and human rights in Brazil: From military to digital dictatorship. In J. Lannon & E. Halpin (Eds.), *Human rights and information communication technologies: Trends and consequences of use* (pp. 86–99). Hershey, PA: IGI Global. doi:10.4018/978-1-4666-1918-0.ch006

Fiordo, R. (2012). Analyzing blogs: A hermeneutic perspective. In T. Dumova & R. Fiordo (Eds.), *Blogging in the global society: Cultural, political and geographical aspects* (pp. 231–248). Hershey, PA: IGI Global. doi:10.4018/978-1-60960-744-9.ch014

Fischer, G., & Herrmann, T. (2013). Socio-technical systems: A meta-design perspective. In J. Abdelnour-Nocera (Ed.), *Knowledge and technological development effects on organizational and social structures* (pp. 1–36). Hershey, PA: IGI Global. doi:10.4018/978-1-4666-2151-0.ch001

Fleury, M., & Al-Jobouri, L. (2013). Techniques and tools for adaptive video streaming. In D. Kanellopoulos (Ed.), *Intelligent multimedia technologies for networking applications: Techniques and tools* (pp. 65–101). Hershey, PA: IGI Global. doi:10.4018/978-1-4666-2833-5.ch004

Freeman, I., & Freeman, A. (2013). Capacity building for different abilities using ICT. In T. Torres-Coronas & M. Vidal-Blasco (Eds.), *Social e-enterprise: Value creation through ICT* (pp. 67–82). Hershey, PA: IGI Global. doi:10.4018/978-1-4666-2667-6.ch004

Gallon, R. (2013). Communication, culture, and technology: Learning strategies for the unteachable. In R. Lansiquot (Ed.), *Cases on interdisciplinary research trends in science, technology, engineering, and mathematics: Studies on urban classrooms* (pp. 91–106). Hershey, PA: IGI Global. doi:10.4018/978-1-4666-2214-2.ch005

García, M., Lloret, J., Bellver, I., & Tomás, J. (2013). Intelligent IPTV distribution for smart phones. In D. Kanellopoulos (Ed.), *Intelligent multimedia technologies for networking applications: Techniques and tools* (pp. 318–347). Hershey, PA: IGI Global. doi:10.4018/978-1-4666-2833-5.ch013

García-Plaza, A. P., Zubiaga, A., Fresno, V., & Martínez, R. (2013). Tag cloud reorganization: Finding groups of related tags on delicious. In G. Xu & L. Li (Eds.), *Social media mining and social network analysis: Emerging research* (pp. 140–155). Hershey, PA: IGI Global. doi:10.4018/978-1-4666-2806-9.ch009

Gerpott, T. J. (2013). Attribute perceptions as factors explaining mobile internet acceptance of cellular customers in Germany: An empirical study comparing actual and potential adopters with distinct categories of access appliances. In I. Lee (Ed.), *Strategy, adoption, and competitive advantage of mobile services in the global economy* (pp. 19–48). Hershey, PA: IGI Global. doi:10.4018/978-1-4666-1939-5.ch002

Giambona, G. J., & Birchall, D. W. (2012). Collaborative e-learning and ICT tools to develop SME managers: An Italian case. In *Wireless technologies: Concepts, methodologies, tools and applications* (pp. 1606–1617). Hershey, PA: IGI Global. doi:10.4018/978-1-61350-101-6.ch605

Giannakos, M. N., Pateli, A. G., & Pappas, I. O. (2013). Identifying the direct effect of experience and the moderating effect of satisfaction in the Greek online market. In A. Scupola (Ed.), *Mobile opportunities and applications for e-service innovations* (pp. 77–97). Hershey, PA: IGI Global. doi:10.4018/978-1-4666-2654-6.ch005

Giorda, M., & Guerrisi, M. (2013). Educating to democracy and social participation through a "history of religion" course. In P. Pumilia-Gnarini, E. Favaron, E. Pacetti, J. Bishop, & L. Guerra (Eds.), *Handbook of research on didactic strategies and technologies for education: Incorporating advancements* (pp. 152–161). Hershey, PA: IGI Global. doi:10.4018/978-1-4666-2122-0.ch014

Goggins, S., Schmidt, M., Guajardo, J., & Moore, J. L. (2013). 3D virtual worlds: Assessing the experience and informing design. In B. Medlin (Ed.), *Integrations of technology utilization and social dynamics in organizations* (pp. 194–213). Hershey, PA: IGI Global. doi:10.4018/978-1-4666-1948-7.ch012

Gold, N. (2012). Rebels, heretics, and exiles: Blogging among estranged and questioning American Hasidim. In T. Dumova & R. Fiordo (Eds.), *Blogging in the global society: Cultural, political and geographical aspects* (pp. 108–127). Hershey, PA: IGI Global. doi:10.4018/978-1-60960-744-9.ch007

Görgü, L., Wan, J., O'Hare, G. M., & O'Grady, M. J. (2013). Enabling mobile service provision with sensor networks. In I. Lee (Ed.), *Mobile services industries, technologies, and applications in the global economy* (pp. 175–192). Hershey, PA: IGI Global. doi:10.4018/978-1-4666-1981-4.ch011

Gregory, S. J. (2013). Evolution of mobile services: An analysis. In I. Lee (Ed.), *Mobile services industries, technologies, and applications in the global economy* (pp. 104–119). Hershey, PA: IGI Global. doi:10.4018/978-1-4666-1981-4.ch007

Grieve, G. P., & Heston, K. (2012). Finding liquid salvation: Using the Cardean ethnographic method to document second life residents and religious cloud communities. In N. Zagalo, L. Morgado, & A. Boa-Ventura (Eds.), *Virtual worlds and metaverse platforms: New communication and identity paradigms* (pp. 288–305). Hershey, PA: IGI Global. doi:10.4018/978-1-60960-854-5.ch019

Guha, S., Thakur, B., Konar, T. S., & Chakrabarty, S. (2013). Web enabled design collaboration in India. In N. Kock (Ed.), *Interdisciplinary applications of electronic collaboration approaches and technologies* (pp. 96–111). Hershey, PA: IGI Global. doi:10.4018/978-1-4666-2020-9.ch007

Gulati, G. J., Yates, D. J., & Tawileh, A. (2013). Explaining the global digital divide: The impact of public policy initiatives on e-government capacity and reach worldwide. In *Digital literacy: Concepts, methodologies, tools, and applications* (pp. 39–62). Hershey, PA: IGI Global. doi:10.4018/978-1-4666-1852-7.ch003

Gupta, J. (2013). Digital library initiatives in India. In T. Ashraf & P. Gulati (Eds.), *Design, development, and management of resources for digital library services* (pp. 80–93). Hershey, PA: IGI Global. doi:10.4018/978-1-4666-2500-6.ch008

Gururajan, R., Hafeez-Baig, A., Danaher, P. A., & De George-Walker, L. (2012). Student perceptions and uses of wireless handheld devices: Implications for implementing blended and mobile learning in an Australian university. In *Wireless technologies: Concepts, methodologies, tools and applications* (pp. 1323–1338). Hershey, PA: IGI Global. doi:10.4018/978-1-61350-101-6.ch512

Gwilt, I. (2013). Data-objects: Sharing the attributes and properties of digital and material culture to creatively interpret complex information. In D. Harrison (Ed.), *Digital media and technologies for virtual artistic spaces* (pp. 14–26). Hershey, PA: IGI Global. doi:10.4018/978-1-4666-2961-5.ch002

Hackley, D. C., & Leidman, M. B. (2013). Integrating learning management systems in K-12 supplemental religious education. In A. Ritzhaupt & S. Kumar (Eds.), *Cases on educational technology implementation for facilitating learning* (pp. 1–22). Hershey, PA: IGI Global. doi:10.4018/978-1-4666-3676-7.ch001

Hale, J. R., & Fields, D. (2013). A cross-cultural measure of servant leadership behaviors. In M. Bocarnea, R. Reynolds, & J. Baker (Eds.), *Online instruments, data collection, and electronic measurements: Organizational advancements* (pp. 152–163). Hershey, PA: IGI Global. doi:10.4018/978-1-4666-2172-5.ch009

Hanewald, R. (2012). Using mobile technologies as research tools: Pragmatics, possibilities and problems. In *Wireless technologies: Concepts, methodologies, tools and applications* (pp. 130–150). Hershey, PA: IGI Global. doi:10.4018/978-1-61350-101-6.ch108

Hanewald, R. (2013). Professional development with and for emerging technologies: A case study with Asian languages and cultural studies teachers in Australia. In J. Keengwe (Ed.), *Pedagogical applications and social effects of mobile technology integration* (pp. 175–192). Hershey, PA: IGI Global. doi:10.4018/978-1-4666-2985-1.ch010

Hayhoe, S. (2012). Non-visual programming, perceptual culture and mulsemedia: Case studies of five blind computer programmers. In G. Ghinea, F. Andres, & S. Gulliver (Eds.), *Multiple sensorial media advances and applications: New developments in MulSeMedia* (pp. 80–98). Hershey, PA: IGI Global. doi:10.4018/978-1-60960-821-7.ch004

Henschke, J. A. (2013). Nation building through andragogy and lifelong learning: On the cutting edge educationally, economically, and governmentally. In V. Wang (Ed.), *Handbook of research on technologies for improving the 21st century workforce: Tools for lifelong learning* (pp. 480–506). Hershey, PA: IGI Global. doi:10.4018/978-1-4666-2181-7.ch030

Hermida, J. M., Meliá, S., Montoyo, A., & Gómez, J. (2013). Developing rich internet applications as social sites on the semantic web: A model-driven approach. In D. Chiu (Ed.), *Mobile and web innovations in systems and service-oriented engineering* (pp. 134–155). Hershey, PA: IGI Global. doi:10.4018/978-1-4666-2470-2.ch008

Hernández-García, Á., Agudo-Peregrina, Á. F., & Iglesias-Pradas, S. (2013). Adoption of mobile video-call service: An exploratory study. In I. Lee (Ed.), *Strategy, adoption, and competitive advantage of mobile services in the global economy* (pp. 49–72). Hershey, PA: IGI Global. doi:10.4018/978-1-4666-1939-5.ch003

Hesapci-Sanaktekin, O., & Somer, I. (2013). Mobile communication: A study on smart phone and mobile application use. In I. Lee (Ed.), *Strategy, adoption, and competitive advantage of mobile services in the global economy* (pp. 217–233). Hershey, PA: IGI Global. doi:10.4018/978-1-4666-1939-5.ch012

Hill, S. R., Troshani, I., & Freeman, S. (2013). An eclectic perspective on the internationalization of Australian mobile services SMEs. In I. Lee (Ed.), *Mobile services industries, technologies, and applications in the global economy* (pp. 55–73). Hershey, PA: IGI Global. doi:10.4018/978-1-4666-1981-4.ch004

Ho, V. (2013). The need for identity construction in computer-mediated professional communication: A Community of practice perspective. In R. Luppicini (Ed.), *Handbook of research on technoself: Identity in a technological society* (pp. 502–530). Hershey, PA: IGI Global. doi:10.4018/978-1-4666-2211-1.ch027

Hudson, H. E. (2013). Challenges facing municipal wireless: Case studies from San Francisco and Silicon Valley. In A. Abdelaal (Ed.), *Social and economic effects of community wireless networks and infrastructures* (pp. 12–26). Hershey, PA: IGI Global. doi:10.4018/978-1-4666-2997-4.ch002

Humphreys, S. (2012). Unravelling intellectual property in a specialist social networking site. In A. Lugmayr, H. Franssila, P. Näränen, O. Sotamaa, J. Vanhala, & Z. Yu (Eds.), *Media in the ubiquitous era: Ambient, social and gaming media* (pp. 248–266). Hershey, PA: IGI Global. doi:10.4018/978-1-60960-774-6.ch015

Iglesias, A., Ruiz-Mezcua, B., López, J. F., & Figueroa, D. C. (2013). New communication technologies for inclusive education in and outside the classroom. In D. Griol Barres, Z. Callejas Carrión, & R. Delgado (Eds.), *Technologies for inclusive education: Beyond traditional integration approaches* (pp. 271–284). Hershey, PA: IGI Global. doi:10.4018/978-1-4666-2530-3.ch013

Igun, S. E. (2013). Gender and national information and communication technology (ICT) policies in Africa. In B. Maumbe & J. Okello (Eds.), *Technology, sustainability, and rural development in Africa* (pp. 284–297). Hershey, PA: IGI Global. doi:10.4018/978-1-4666-3607-1.ch018

Ikolo, V. E. (2013). Gender digital divide and national ICT policies in Africa. In *Digital literacy: Concepts, methodologies, tools, and applications* (pp. 812–832). Hershey, PA: IGI Global. doi:10.4018/978-1-4666-1852-7.ch042

Imran, A., & Gregor, S. (2013). A process model for successful e-government adoption in the least developed countries: A case of Bangladesh. In *Digital literacy: Concepts, methodologies, tools, and applications* (pp. 213–241). Hershey, PA: IGI Global. doi:10.4018/978-1-4666-1852-7.ch012

Ionescu, A. (2013). ICTs and gender-based rights. In J. Lannon & E. Halpin (Eds.), *Human rights and information communication technologies: Trends and consequences of use* (pp. 214–234). Hershey, PA: IGI Global. doi:10.4018/978-1-4666-1918-0.ch013

Iyamu, T. (2013). The impact of organisational politics on the implementation of IT strategy: South African case in context. In J. Abdelnour-Nocera (Ed.), *Knowledge and technological development effects on organizational and social structures* (pp. 167–193). Hershey, PA: IGI Global. doi:10.4018/978-1-4666-2151-0.ch011

Jadhav, V. G. (2013). Integration of digital reference service for scholarly communication in digital libraries. In T. Ashraf & P. Gulati (Eds.), *Design, development, and management of resources for digital library services* (pp. 13–20). Hershey, PA: IGI Global. doi:10.4018/978-1-4666-2500-6.ch002

Jäkälä, M., & Berki, E. (2013). Communities, communication, and online identities. In S. Warburton & S. Hatzipanagos (Eds.), *Digital identity and social media* (pp. 1–13). Hershey, PA: IGI Global. doi:10.4018/978-1-4666-1915-9.ch001

Janneck, M., & Staar, H. (2013). Playing virtual power games: Micro-political processes in inter-organizational networks. In B. Medlin (Ed.), *Integrations of technology utilization and social dynamics in organizations* (pp. 171–192). Hershey, PA: IGI Global. doi:10.4018/978-1-4666-1948-7.ch011

Januska, I. M. (2013). Communication as a key factor in cooperation success and virtual enterprise paradigm support. In P. Renna (Ed.), *Production and manufacturing system management: Coordination approaches and multi-site planning* (pp. 145–161). Hershey, PA: IGI Global. doi:10.4018/978-1-4666-2098-8.ch008

Jayasingh, S., & Eze, U. C. (2013). Consumers' adoption of mobile coupons in Malaysia. In I. Lee (Ed.), *Strategy, adoption, and competitive advantage of mobile services in the global economy* (pp. 90–111). Hershey, PA: IGI Global. doi:10.4018/978-1-4666-1939-5.ch005

Jean Francois, E. (2013). Transculturality. In E. Jean Francois (Ed.), *Transcultural blended learning and teaching in postsecondary education* (pp. 1–14). Hershey, PA: IGI Global. doi:10.4018/978-1-4666-2014-8.ch001

Jensen, S. S. (2012). User-driven content creation in second life a source of innovation? Three case studies of business and public service. In N. Zagalo, L. Morgado, & A. Boa-Ventura (Eds.), *Virtual worlds and metaverse platforms: New communication and identity paradigms* (pp. 1–15). Hershey, PA: IGI Global. doi:10.4018/978-1-60960-854-5.ch001

Johnston, W. J., Komulainen, H., Ristola, A., & Ulkuniemi, P. (2013). Mobile advertising in small retailer firms: How to make the most of it. In I. Lee (Ed.), *Strategy, adoption, and competitive advantage of mobile services in the global economy* (pp. 283–298). Hershey, PA: IGI Global. doi:10.4018/978-1-4666-1939-5.ch016

Kadas, G., & Chatzimisios, P. (2013). The role of roadside assistance in vehicular communication networks: Security, quality of service, and routing issues. In R. Daher & A. Vinel (Eds.), *Roadside networks for vehicular communications: Architectures, applications, and test fields* (pp. 1–37). Hershey, PA: IGI Global. doi:10.4018/978-1-4666-2223-4.ch001

Kale, S. H., & Spence, M. T. (2012). A trination analysis of social exchange relationships in e-dating. In C. Romm Livermore (Ed.), *Gender and social computing: Interactions, differences and relationships* (pp. 257–271). Hershey, PA: IGI Global. doi:10.4018/978-1-60960-759-3.ch015

Kamoun, F. (2013). Mobile NFC services: Adoption factors and a typology of business models. In I. Lee (Ed.), *Mobile services industries, technologies, and applications in the global economy* (pp. 254–272). Hershey, PA: IGI Global. doi:10.4018/978-1-4666-1981-4.ch016

Kaneda, K., & Iwamura, K. (2013). New proposals for data hiding in paper media. In K. Kondo (Ed.), *Multimedia information hiding technologies and methodologies for controlling data* (pp. 258–285). Hershey, PA: IGI Global. doi:10.4018/978-1-4666-2217-3.ch012

Kastell, K. (2013). Seamless communication to mobile devices in vehicular wireless networks. In O. Strobel (Ed.), *Communication in transportation systems* (pp. 324–342). Hershey, PA: IGI Global. doi:10.4018/978-1-4666-2976-9.ch012

Kaye, B. K., & Johnson, T. J. (2012). Net gain? Selective exposure and selective avoidance of social network sites. In F. Comunello (Ed.), *Networked sociability and individualism: Technology for personal and professional relationships* (pp. 218–237). Hershey, PA: IGI Global. doi:10.4018/978-1-61350-338-6.ch011

Kaye, B. K., Johnson, T. J., & Muhlberger, P. (2012). Blogs as a source of democratic deliberation. In T. Dumova & R. Fiordo (Eds.), *Blogging in the global society: Cultural, political and geographical aspects* (pp. 1–18). Hershey, PA: IGI Global. doi:10.4018/978-1-60960-744-9.ch001

Kefi, H., Mlaiki, A., & Peterson, R. L. (2013). IT offshoring: Trust views from client and vendor perspectives. In J. Wang (Ed.), *Perspectives and techniques for improving information technology project management* (pp. 113–130). Hershey, PA: IGI Global. doi:10.4018/978-1-4666-2800-7.ch009

Khan, N. A., & Batoo, M. F. (2013). Stone inscriptions of Srinagar: A digital panorama. In T. Ashraf & P. Gulati (Eds.), *Design, development, and management of resources for digital library services* (pp. 58–79). Hershey, PA: IGI Global. doi:10.4018/978-1-4666-2500-6.ch007

Kim, P. (2012). "Stay out of the way! My kid is video blogging through a phone!": A lesson learned from math tutoring social media for children in underserved communities. In *Wireless technologies: Concepts, methodologies, tools and applications* (pp. 1415–1428). Hershey, PA: IGI Global. doi:10.4018/978-1-61350-101-6.ch517

Kisubi, A. T. (2013). A critical perspective on the challenges for blended learning and teaching in Africa's higher education. In E. Jean Francois (Ed.), *Transcultural blended learning and teaching in postsecondary education* (pp. 145–168). Hershey, PA: IGI Global. doi:10.4018/978-1-4666-2014-8.ch009

Koole, M., & Parchoma, G. (2013). The web of identity: A model of digital identity formation in networked learning environments. In S. Warburton & S. Hatzipanagos (Eds.), *Digital identity and social media* (pp. 14–28). Hershey, PA: IGI Global. doi:10.4018/978-1-4666-1915-9.ch002

Kordaki, M., Gorghiu, G., Bîzoi, M., & Glava, A. (2012). Collaboration within multinational learning communities: The case of the virtual community collaborative space for sciences education European project. In A. Juan, T. Daradoumis, M. Roca, S. Grasman, & J. Faulin (Eds.), *Collaborative and distributed e-research: Innovations in technologies, strategies and applications* (pp. 206–226). Hershey, PA: IGI Global. doi:10.4018/978-1-4666-0125-3.ch010

Kovács, J., Bokor, L., Kanizsai, Z., & Imre, S. (2013). Review of advanced mobility solutions for multimedia networking in IPv6. In D. Kanellopoulos (Ed.), *Intelligent multimedia technologies for networking applications: Techniques and tools* (pp. 25–47). Hershey, PA: IGI Global. doi:10.4018/978-1-4666-2833-5.ch002

Kreps, D. (2013). Performing the discourse of sexuality online. In S. Warburton & S. Hatzipanagos (Eds.), *Digital identity and social media* (pp. 118–132). Hershey, PA: IGI Global. doi:10.4018/978-1-4666-1915-9.ch009

Ktoridou, D., Kaufmann, H., & Liassides, C. (2012). Factors affecting WiFi use intention: The context of Cyprus. In *Wireless technologies: Concepts, methodologies, tools and applications* (pp. 1760–1781). Hershey, PA: IGI Global. doi:10.4018/978-1-61350-101-6.ch703

Kumar, N., Nero Alves, L., & Aguiar, R. L. (2013). Employing traffic lights as road side units for road safety information broadcast. In R. Daher & A. Vinel (Eds.), *Roadside networks for vehicular communications: Architectures, applications, and test fields* (pp. 118–135). Hershey, PA: IGI Global. doi:10.4018/978-1-4666-2223-4.ch006

Kvasny, L., & Hales, K. D. (2013). The evolving discourse of the digital divide: The internet, black identity, and the evolving discourse of the digital divide. In *Digital literacy: Concepts, methodologies, tools, and applications* (pp. 1350–1366). Hershey, PA: IGI Global. doi:10.4018/978-1-4666-1852-7.ch071

L'Abate, L. (2013). Of paradigms, theories, and models: A conceptual hierarchical structure for communication science and technoself. In R. Luppicini (Ed.), *Handbook of research on technoself: Identity in a technological society* (pp. 84–104). Hershey, PA: IGI Global. doi:10.4018/978-1-4666-2211-1.ch005

Laghos, A. (2013). Multimedia social networks and e-learning. In D. Kanellopoulos (Ed.), *Intelligent multimedia technologies for networking applications: Techniques and tools* (pp. 365–379). Hershey, PA: IGI Global. doi:10.4018/978-1-4666-2833-5.ch015

Lappas, G. (2012). Social multimedia mining: Trends and opportunities in areas of social and communication studies. In I. Ting, T. Hong, & L. Wang (Eds.), *Social network mining, analysis, and research trends: Techniques and applications* (pp. 1–16). Hershey, PA: IGI Global. doi:10.4018/978-1-61350-513-7.ch001

Lawrence, J. E. (2013). Barriers hindering ecommerce adoption: A case study of Kurdistan region of Iraq. In A. Zolait (Ed.), *Technology diffusion and adoption: Global complexity, global innovation* (pp. 152–165). Hershey, PA: IGI Global. doi:10.4018/978-1-4666-2791-8.ch010

Lawrence, K. F. (2013). Identity and the online media fan community. In S. Warburton & S. Hatzipanagos (Eds.), *Digital identity and social media* (pp. 233–255). Hershey, PA: IGI Global. doi:10.4018/978-1-4666-1915-9.ch017

Lee, M. J., Dalgarno, B., Gregory, S., Carlson, L., & Tynan, B. (2013). How are Australian and New Zealand higher educators using 3D immersive virtual worlds in their teaching? In B. Tynan, J. Willems, & R. James (Eds.), *Outlooks and opportunities in blended and distance learning* (pp. 169–188). Hershey, PA: IGI Global. doi:10.4018/978-1-4666-4205-8.ch013

Lee, S., Alfano, C., & Carpenter, R. G. (2013). Invention in two parts: Multimodal communication and space design in the writing center. In R. Carpenter (Ed.), *Cases on higher education spaces: Innovation, collaboration, and technology* (pp. 41–63). Hershey, PA: IGI Global. doi:10.4018/978-1-4666-2673-7.ch003

Leichsenring, C., Tünnermann, R., & Hermann, T. (2013). Feelabuzz: Direct tactile communication with mobile phones. In J. Lumsden (Ed.), *Developments in technologies for human-centric mobile computing and applications* (pp. 145–154). Hershey, PA: IGI Global. doi:10.4018/978-1-4666-2068-1.ch009

Lemos, A., & Marques, F. P. (2013). A critical analysis of the limitations and effects of the Brazilian national broadband plan. In A. Abdelaal (Ed.), *Social and economic effects of community wireless networks and infrastructures* (pp. 255–274). Hershey, PA: IGI Global. doi:10.4018/978-1-4666-2997-4.ch014

Leung, C. K., Medina, I. J., & Tanbeer, S. K. (2013). Analyzing social networks to mine important friends. In G. Xu & L. Li (Eds.), *Social media mining and social network analysis: Emerging research* (pp. 90–104). Hershey, PA: IGI Global. doi:10.4018/978-1-4666-2806-9.ch006

Li, B. (2012). Toward an infrastructural approach to understanding participation in virtual communities. In H. Li (Ed.), *Virtual community participation and motivation: Cross-disciplinary theories* (pp. 103–123). Hershey, PA: IGI Global. doi:10.4018/978-1-4666-0312-7.ch007

Li, L., Xiao, H., & Xu, G. (2013). Recommending related microblogs. In G. Xu & L. Li (Eds.), *Social media mining and social network analysis: Emerging research* (pp. 202–210). Hershey, PA: IGI Global. doi:10.4018/978-1-4666-2806-9.ch013

Liddell, T. (2013). Historical evolution of adult education in America: The impact of institutions, change, and acculturation. In V. Wang (Ed.), *Handbook of research on technologies for improving the 21st century workforce: Tools for lifelong learning* (pp. 257–271). Hershey, PA: IGI Global. doi:10.4018/978-1-4666-2181-7.ch017

Liljander, V., Gummerus, J., Pihlström, M., & Kiehelä, H. (2013). Mobile services as resources for consumer integration of value in a multi-channel environment. In I. Lee (Ed.), *Strategy, adoption, and competitive advantage of mobile services in the global economy* (pp. 259–282). Hershey, PA: IGI Global. doi:10.4018/978-1-4666-1939-5.ch015

Litaay, T., Prananingrum, D. H., & Krisanto, Y. A. (2013). Indonesian legal perspectives on biotechnology and intellectual property rights. In *Digital rights management: Concepts, methodologies, tools, and applications* (pp. 834–845). Hershey, PA: IGI Global. doi:10.4018/978-1-4666-2136-7.ch039

Little, G. (2013). Collection development for theological education. In S. Holder (Ed.), *Library collection development for professional programs: Trends and best practices* (pp. 112–127). Hershey, PA: IGI Global. doi:10.4018/978-1-4666-1897-8.ch007

Losh, S. C. (2013). American digital divides: Generation, education, gender, and ethnicity in American digital divides. In *Digital literacy: Concepts, methodologies, tools, and applications* (pp. 932–958). Hershey, PA: IGI Global. doi:10.4018/978-1-4666-1852-7.ch048

Lovari, A., & Parisi, L. (2012). Public administrations and citizens 2.0: Exploring digital public communication strategies and civic interaction within Italian municipality pages on Facebook. In F. Comunello (Ed.), *Networked sociability and individualism: Technology for personal and professional relationships* (pp. 238–263). Hershey, PA: IGI Global. doi:10.4018/978-1-61350-338-6.ch012

Maamar, Z., Faci, N., Mostéfaoui, S. K., & Akhter, F. (2013). Towards a framework for weaving social networks into mobile commerce. In D. Chiu (Ed.), *Mobile and web innovations in systems and service-oriented engineering* (pp. 333–347). Hershey, PA: IGI Global. doi:10.4018/978-1-4666-2470-2.ch018

Maia, I. F., & Valente, J. A. (2013). Digital identity built on a cooperative relationship. In S. Warburton & S. Hatzipanagos (Eds.), *Digital identity and social media* (pp. 58–73). Hershey, PA: IGI Global. doi:10.4018/978-1-4666-1915-9.ch005

Maity, M. (2013). Consumer information search and decision-making on m-commerce: The role of product type. In I. Lee (Ed.), *Strategy, adoption, and competitive advantage of mobile services in the global economy* (pp. 73–89). Hershey, PA: IGI Global. doi:10.4018/978-1-4666-1939-5.ch004

Malinen, S., Virjo, T., & Kujala, S. (2012). Supporting local connections with online communities. In A. Lugmayr, H. Franssila, P. Näränen, O. Sotamaa, J. Vanhala, & Z. Yu (Eds.), *Media in the ubiquitous era: Ambient, social and gaming media* (pp. 235–250). Hershey, PA: IGI Global. doi:10.4018/978-1-60960-774-6.ch013

Mantoro, T., Milišic, A., & Ayu, M. (2013). Online authentication using smart card technology in mobile phone infrastructure. In I. Khalil & E. Weippl (Eds.), *Contemporary challenges and solutions for mobile and multimedia technologies* (pp. 127–144). Hershey, PA: IGI Global. doi:10.4018/978-1-4666-2163-3.ch008

Marcato, E., & Scala, E. (2013). Moodle: A platform for a school. In P. Pumilia-Gnarini, E. Favaron, E. Pacetti, J. Bishop, & L. Guerra (Eds.), *Handbook of research on didactic strategies and technologies for education: Incorporating advancements* (pp. 107–116). Hershey, PA: IGI Global. doi:10.4018/978-1-4666-2122-0.ch010

Markaki, O. I., Charalabidis, Y., & Askounis, D. (2013). Measuring interoperability readiness in south eastern Europe and the Mediterranean: The interoperability observatory. In A. Scupola (Ed.), *Mobile opportunities and applications for e-service innovations* (pp. 210–230). Hershey, PA: IGI Global. doi:10.4018/978-1-4666-2654-6.ch012

Martin, J. D., & El-Toukhy, S. (2012). Blogging for sovereignty: An analysis of Palestinian blogs. In T. Dumova & R. Fiordo (Eds.), *Blogging in the global society: Cultural, political and geographical aspects* (pp. 148–160). Hershey, PA: IGI Global. doi:10.4018/978-1-60960-744-9.ch009

Matei, S. A., & Bruno, R. J. (2012). Individualist motivators and community functional constraints in social media: The case of Wikis and Wikipedia. In F. Comunello (Ed.), *Networked sociability and individualism: Technology for personal and professional relationships* (pp. 1–23). Hershey, PA: IGI Global. doi:10.4018/978-1-61350-338-6.ch001

Matsuoka, H. (2013). Acoustic OFDM technology and system. In K. Kondo (Ed.), *Multimedia information hiding technologies and methodologies for controlling data* (pp. 90–103). Hershey, PA: IGI Global. doi:10.4018/978-1-4666-2217-3.ch005

McCarthy, J. (2013). Online networking: Integrating international students into first year university through the strategic use of participatory media. In F. García-Peñalvo (Ed.), *Multiculturalism in technology-based education: Case studies on ICT-supported approaches* (pp. 189–210). Hershey, PA: IGI Global. doi:10.4018/978-1-4666-2101-5.ch012

McDonald, A., & Helmer, S. (2013). A comparative case study of Indonesian and UK organisational culture differences in IS project management. In A. Mesquita (Ed.), *User perception and influencing factors of technology in everyday life* (pp. 46–55). Hershey, PA: IGI Global. doi:10.4018/978-1-4666-1954-8.ch005

McDonough, C. (2013). Mobile broadband: Substituting for fixed broadband or providing value-added. In I. Lee (Ed.), *Mobile services industries, technologies, and applications in the global economy* (pp. 74–86). Hershey, PA: IGI Global. doi:10.4018/978-1-4666-1981-4.ch005

McKeown, A. (2013). Virtual communitas, "digital place-making," and the process of "becoming". In D. Harrison (Ed.), *Digital media and technologies for virtual artistic spaces* (pp. 218–236). Hershey, PA: IGI Global. doi:10.4018/978-1-4666-2961-5.ch016

Medeni, T. D., Medeni, I. T., & Balci, A. (2013). Proposing a knowledge amphora model for transition towards mobile government. In A. Scupola (Ed.), *Mobile opportunities and applications for e-service innovations* (pp. 170–192). Hershey, PA: IGI Global. doi:10.4018/978-1-4666-2654-6.ch010

Melo, A., Bezerra, P., Abelém, A. J., Neto, A., & Cerqueira, E. (2013). PriorityQoE: A tool for improving the QoE in video streaming. In D. Kanellopoulos (Ed.), *Intelligent multimedia technologies for networking applications: Techniques and tools* (pp. 270–290). Hershey, PA: IGI Global. doi:10.4018/978-1-4666-2833-5.ch011

Mendoza-González, R., Rodríguez, F. Á., & Arteaga, J. M. (2013). A usability study of mobile text based social applications: Towards a reliable strategy for design evaluation. In M. Garcia-Ruiz (Ed.), *Cases on usability engineering: Design and development of digital products* (pp. 195–219). Hershey, PA: IGI Global. doi:10.4018/978-1-4666-4046-7.ch009

Metzger, M. J., Wilson, C., Pure, R. A., & Zhao, B. Y. (2012). Invisible interactions: What latent social interaction can tell us about social relationships in social network sites. In F. Comunello (Ed.), *Networked sociability and individualism: Technology for personal and professional relationships* (pp. 79–102). Hershey, PA: IGI Global. doi:10.4018/978-1-61350-338-6.ch005

Millo, G., & Carmeci, G. (2013). Insurance in Italy: A spatial perspective. In G. Borruso, S. Bertazzon, A. Favretto, B. Murgante, & C. Torre (Eds.), *Geographic information analysis for sustainable development and economic planning: New technologies* (pp. 158–178). Hershey, PA: IGI Global. doi:10.4018/978-1-4666-1924-1.ch011

Mingqing, X., Wenjing, X., & Junming, Z. (2012). The future of television. In R. Sharma, M. Tan, & F. Pereira (Eds.), *Understanding the interactive digital media marketplace: Frameworks, platforms, communities and issues* (pp. 406–415). Hershey, PA: IGI Global. doi:10.4018/978-1-61350-147-4.ch032

Miscione, G. (2013). Telemedicine and development: Situating information technologies in the Amazon. In J. Abdelnour-Nocera (Ed.), *Knowledge and technological development effects on organizational and social structures* (pp. 132–145). Hershey, PA: IGI Global. doi:10.4018/978-1-4666-2151-0.ch009

Modegi, T. (2013). Spatial and temporal position information delivery to mobile terminals using audio watermarking techniques. In K. Kondo (Ed.), *Multimedia information hiding technologies and methodologies for controlling data* (pp. 182–207). Hershey, PA: IGI Global. doi:10.4018/978-1-4666-2217-3.ch009

Montes, J. A., Gutiérrez, A. C., Fernández, E. M., & Romeo, A. (2012). Reality mining, location based services and e-business opportunities: The case of city analytics. In *Wireless technologies: Concepts, methodologies, tools and applications* (pp. 1520–1532). Hershey, PA: IGI Global. doi:10.4018/978-1-61350-101-6.ch601

Moreno, A. (2012). The social construction of new cultural models through information and communication technologies. In M. Safar & K. Mahdi (Eds.), *Social networking and community behavior modeling: Qualitative and quantitative measures* (pp. 68–84). Hershey, PA: IGI Global. doi:10.4018/978-1-61350-444-4.ch004

Morris, J. Z., & Thomas, K. D. (2013). Implementing BioSand filters in rural Honduras: A case study of his hands mission international in Copán, Honduras. In H. Muga & K. Thomas (Eds.), *Cases on the diffusion and adoption of sustainable development practices* (pp. 468–496). Hershey, PA: IGI Global. doi:10.4018/978-1-4666-2842-7.ch017

Mura, G. (2012). The MultiPlasticity of new media. In G. Ghinea, F. Andres, & S. Gulliver (Eds.), *Multiple sensorial media advances and applications: New developments in MulSeMedia* (pp. 258–271). Hershey, PA: IGI Global. doi:10.4018/978-1-60960-821-7.ch013

Murray, C. (2012). Imagine mobile learning in your pocket. In *Wireless technologies: Concepts, methodologies, tools and applications* (pp. 2060–2088). Hershey, PA: IGI Global. doi:10.4018/978-1-61350-101-6.ch807

Mutohar, A., & Hughes, J. E. (2013). Toward web 2.0 integration in Indonesian education: Challenges and planning strategies. In N. Azab (Ed.), *Cases on web 2.0 in developing countries: Studies on implementation, application, and use* (pp. 198–221). Hershey, PA: IGI Global. doi:10.4018/978-1-4666-2515-0.ch008

Nandi, B., & Subramaniam, G. (2012). Evolution in broadband technology and future of wireless broadband. In *Wireless technologies: Concepts, methodologies, tools and applications* (pp. 1928–1957). Hershey, PA: IGI Global. doi:10.4018/978-1-61350-101-6.ch801

Naser, A., Jaber, I., Jaber, R., & Saeed, K. (2013). Information systems in UAE education sector: Security, cultural, and ethical issues. In F. Albadri (Ed.), *Information systems applications in the Arab education sector* (pp. 148–162). Hershey, PA: IGI Global. doi:10.4018/978-1-4666-1984-5.ch011

Nemoianu, I., & Pesquet-Popescu, B. (2013). Network coding for multimedia communications. In D. Kanellopoulos (Ed.), *Intelligent multimedia technologies for networking applications: Techniques and tools* (pp. 1–24). Hershey, PA: IGI Global. doi:10.4018/978-1-4666-2833-5.ch001

Nezlek, G., & DeHondt, G. (2013). Gender wage differentials in information systems: 1991 – 2008 a quantitative analysis. In B. Medlin (Ed.), *Integrations of technology utilization and social dynamics in organizations* (pp. 31–47). Hershey, PA: IGI Global. doi:10.4018/978-1-4666-1948-7.ch003

Nishimura, A., & Kondo, K. (2013). Information hiding for audio signals. In K. Kondo (Ed.), *Multimedia information hiding technologies and methodologies for controlling data* (pp. 1–18). Hershey, PA: IGI Global. doi:10.4018/978-1-4666-2217-3.ch001

Norder, J. W., & Carroll, J. W. (2013). Applied geospatial perspectives on the rock art of the lake of the woods region of Ontario, Canada. In D. Albert & G. Dobbs (Eds.), *Emerging methods and multidisciplinary applications in geospatial research* (pp. 77–93). Hershey, PA: IGI Global. doi:10.4018/978-1-4666-1951-7.ch005

O'Brien, M. A., & Rogers, W. A. (2013). Design for aging: Enhancing everyday technology use. In R. Zheng, R. Hill, & M. Gardner (Eds.), *Engaging older adults with modern technology: Internet use and information access needs* (pp. 105–123). Hershey, PA: IGI Global. doi:10.4018/978-1-4666-1966-1.ch006

O'Hanlon, S. (2013). Health information technology and human rights. In J. Lannon & E. Halpin (Eds.), *Human rights and information communication technologies: Trends and consequences of use* (pp. 235–246). Hershey, PA: IGI Global. doi:10.4018/978-1-4666-1918-0.ch014

Odella, F. (2012). Social networks and communities: From traditional society to the virtual sphere. In M. Safar & K. Mahdi (Eds.), *Social networking and community behavior modeling: Qualitative and quantitative measures* (pp. 1–25). Hershey, PA: IGI Global. doi:10.4018/978-1-61350-444-4.ch001

Okazaki, S., Romero, J., & Campo, S. (2012). Capturing market mavens among advergamers: A case of mobile-based social networking site in Japan. In I. Ting, T. Hong, & L. Wang (Eds.), *Social network mining, analysis, and research trends: Techniques and applications* (pp. 291–305). Hershey, PA: IGI Global. doi:10.4018/978-1-61350-513-7.ch017

Omojola, O. (2012). Exploring the impact of Google Igbo in South East Nigeria. In R. Lekoko & L. Semali (Eds.), *Cases on developing countries and ICT integration: Rural community development* (pp. 62–73). Hershey, PA: IGI Global. doi:10.4018/978-1-60960-117-1.ch007

Ovide, E. (2013). Intercultural education with indigenous peoples and the potential of digital technologies to make it happen. In F. García-Peñalvo (Ed.), *Multiculturalism in technology-based education: Case studies on ICT-supported approaches* (pp. 59–78). Hershey, PA: IGI Global. doi:10.4018/978-1-4666-2101-5.ch005

Owusu-Ansah, A. (2013). Exploring Hofstede's cultural dimension using Hollins' structured dialogue to attain a conduit for effective intercultural experiences. In E. Jean Francois (Ed.), *Transcultural blended learning and teaching in postsecondary education* (pp. 52–74). Hershey, PA: IGI Global. doi:10.4018/978-1-4666-2014-8.ch004

Özdemir, E. (2012). Gender and e-marketing: The role of gender differences in online purchasing behaviors. In C. Romm Livermore (Ed.), *Gender and social computing: Interactions, differences and relationships* (pp. 72–86). Hershey, PA: IGI Global. doi:10.4018/978-1-60960-759-3.ch005

Palmer, M. H., & Hanney, J. (2012). Geographic information networks in American Indian governments and communities. In S. Dasgupta (Ed.), *Technical, social, and legal issues in virtual communities: Emerging environments: Emerging environments* (pp. 52–62). Hershey, PA: IGI Global. doi:10.4018/978-1-4666-1553-3.ch004

Pande, R. (2013). Gender gaps and information and communication technology: A case study of India. In *Digital literacy: Concepts, methodologies, tools, and applications* (pp. 1425–1439). Hershey, PA: IGI Global. doi:10.4018/978-1-4666-1852-7.ch075

Park, J., Chung, T., & Hur, W. (2013). The role of consumer innovativeness and trust for adopting internet phone services. In A. Scupola (Ed.), *Mobile opportunities and applications for e-service innovations* (pp. 22–36). Hershey, PA: IGI Global. doi:10.4018/978-1-4666-2654-6.ch002

Parke, A., & Griffiths, M. (2013). Poker gambling virtual communities: The use of computer-mediated communication to develop cognitive poker gambling skills. In R. Zheng (Ed.), *Evolving psychological and educational perspectives on cyber behavior* (pp. 190–204). Hershey, PA: IGI Global. doi:10.4018/978-1-4666-1858-9.ch012

Paschou, M., Sakkopoulos, E., Tsakalidis, A., Tzimas, G., & Viennas, E. (2013). An XML-based customizable model for multimedia applications for museums and exhibitions. In D. Kanellopoulos (Ed.), *Intelligent multimedia technologies for networking applications: Techniques and tools* (pp. 348–363). Hershey, PA: IGI Global. doi:10.4018/978-1-4666-2833-5.ch014

Pauwels, L. (2013). Images, self-images, and idealized identities in the digital networked world: Reconfigurations of family photography in a web-based mode. In S. Warburton & S. Hatzipanagos (Eds.), *Digital identity and social media* (pp. 133–147). Hershey, PA: IGI Global. doi:10.4018/978-1-4666-1915-9.ch010

Peachey, A., & Withnail, G. (2013). A sociocultural perspective on negotiating digital identities in a community of learners. In S. Warburton & S. Hatzipanagos (Eds.), *Digital identity and social media* (pp. 210–224). Hershey, PA: IGI Global. doi:10.4018/978-1-4666-1915-9.ch015

Peixoto, E., Martins, E., Anjo, A. B., & Silva, A. (2012). Geo@NET in the context of the platform of assisted learning from Aveiro University, Portugal. In M. Cruz-Cunha (Ed.), *Handbook of research on serious games as educational, business and research tools* (pp. 648–667). Hershey, PA: IGI Global. doi:10.4018/978-1-4666-0149-9.ch033

Pillay, N. (2013). The use of web 2.0 technologies by students from developed and developing countries: A New Zealand case study. In N. Azab (Ed.), *Cases on web 2.0 in developing countries: Studies on implementation, application, and use* (pp. 411–441). Hershey, PA: IGI Global. doi:10.4018/978-1-4666-2515-0.ch015

Pimenta, M. S., Miletto, E. M., Keller, D., Flores, L. V., & Testa, G. G. (2013). Technological support for online communities focusing on music creation: Adopting collaboration, flexibility, and multiculturality from Brazilian creativity styles. In N. Azab (Ed.), *Cases on web 2.0 in developing countries: Studies on implementation, application, and use* (pp. 283–312). Hershey, PA: IGI Global. doi:10.4018/978-1-4666-2515-0.ch011

Pina, P. (2013). Between scylla and charybdis: The balance between copyright, digital rights management and freedom of expression. In *Digital rights management: Concepts, methodologies, tools, and applications* (pp. 1355–1367). Hershey, PA: IGI Global. doi:10.4018/978-1-4666-2136-7.ch067

Pitsillides, S., Waller, M., & Fairfax, D. (2013). Digital death: What role does digital information play in the way we are (re)membered? In S. Warburton & S. Hatzipanagos (Eds.), *Digital identity and social media* (pp. 75–90). Hershey, PA: IGI Global. doi:10.4018/978-1-4666-1915-9.ch006

Polacek, P., & Huang, C. (2013). QoS scheduling with opportunistic spectrum access for multimedia. In M. Ku & J. Lin (Eds.), *Cognitive radio and interference management: Technology and strategy* (pp. 162–178). Hershey, PA: IGI Global. doi:10.4018/978-1-4666-2005-6.ch009

Potts, L. (2013). Balancing McLuhan with Williams: A sociotechnical view of technological determinism. In J. Abdelnour-Nocera (Ed.), *Knowledge and technological development effects on organizational and social structures* (pp. 109–114). Hershey, PA: IGI Global. doi:10.4018/978-1-4666-2151-0.ch007

Prescott, J., & Bogg, J. (2013). Stereotype, attitudes, and identity: Gendered expectations and behaviors. In *Gendered occupational differences in science, engineering, and technology careers* (pp. 112–135). Hershey, PA: IGI Global. doi:10.4018/978-1-4666-2107-7.ch005

Preussler, A., & Kerres, M. (2013). Managing social reputation in Twitter. In S. Warburton & S. Hatzipanagos (Eds.), *Digital identity and social media* (pp. 91–103). Hershey, PA: IGI Global. doi:10.4018/978-1-4666-1915-9.ch007

Prieger, J. E., & Church, T. V. (2013). Deployment of mobile broadband service in the United States. In I. Lee (Ed.), *Mobile services industries, technologies, and applications in the global economy* (pp. 1–24). Hershey, PA: IGI Global. doi:10.4018/978-1-4666-1981-4.ch001

Puumalainen, K., Frank, L., Sundqvist, S., & Tuppura, A. (2012). The critical mass of wireless communications: Differences between developing and developed economies. In *Wireless technologies: Concepts, methodologies, tools and applications* (pp. 1719–1736). Hershey, PA: IGI Global. doi:10.4018/978-1-61350-101-6.ch701

Rabino, S., Rafiee, D., Onufrey, S., & Moskowitz, H. (2013). Retention and customer share building: Formulating a communication strategy for a sports club. In H. Kaufmann & M. Panni (Eds.), *Customer-centric marketing strategies: Tools for building organizational performance* (pp. 511–529). Hershey, PA: IGI Global. doi:10.4018/978-1-4666-2524-2.ch025

Rahman, H., & Kumar, S. (2012). Mobile computing: An emerging issue in the digitized world. In A. Kumar & H. Rahman (Eds.), *Mobile computing techniques in emerging markets: Systems, applications and services* (pp. 1–22). Hershey, PA: IGI Global. doi:10.4018/978-1-4666-0080-5.ch001

Ratten, V. (2013). Adoption of mobile reading devices in the book industry. In I. Lee (Ed.), *Strategy, adoption, and competitive advantage of mobile services in the global economy* (pp. 203–216). Hershey, PA: IGI Global. doi:10.4018/978-1-4666-1939-5.ch011

Ratten, V. (2013). Mobile banking in the youth market: Implications from an entrepreneurial and learning perspective. In I. Lee (Ed.), *Strategy, adoption, and competitive advantage of mobile services in the global economy* (pp. 112–126). Hershey, PA: IGI Global. doi:10.4018/978-1-4666-1939-5.ch006

Ratten, V. (2013). Social e-enterprise through technological innovations and mobile social networks. In T. Torres-Coronas & M. Vidal-Blasco (Eds.), *Social e-enterprise: Value creation through ICT* (pp. 96–109). Hershey, PA: IGI Global. doi:10.4018/978-1-4666-2667-6.ch006

Rego, P. A., Moreira, P. M., & Reis, L. P. (2012). New forms of interaction in serious games for rehabilitation. In M. Cruz-Cunha (Ed.), *Handbook of research on serious games as educational, business and research tools* (pp. 1188–1211). Hershey, PA: IGI Global. doi:10.4018/978-1-4666-0149-9.ch062

Reinhard, C. D. (2012). Virtual worlds and reception studies: Comparing engagings. In N. Zagalo, L. Morgado, & A. Boa-Ventura (Eds.), *Virtual worlds and metaverse platforms: New communication and identity paradigms* (pp. 117–136). Hershey, PA: IGI Global. doi:10.4018/978-1-60960-854-5.ch008

Rieser, M. (2013). Mobility, liminality, and digital materiality. In D. Harrison (Ed.), *Digital media and technologies for virtual artistic spaces* (pp. 27–45). Hershey, PA: IGI Global. doi:10.4018/978-1-4666-2961-5.ch003

Rodrigues, R. G., Pinheiro, P. G., & Barbosa, J. (2012). Online playability: The social dimension to the virtual world. In M. Cruz-Cunha (Ed.), *Handbook of research on serious games as educational, business and research tools* (pp. 391–421). Hershey, PA: IGI Global. doi:10.4018/978-1-4666-0149-9.ch021

Romm-Livermore, C., Somers, T. M., Setzekorn, K., & King, A. L. (2012). How e-daters behave online: Theory and empirical observations. In C. Romm Livermore (Ed.), *Gender and social computing: Interactions, differences and relationships* (pp. 236–256). Hershey, PA: IGI Global. doi:10.4018/978-1-60960-759-3.ch014

Rosaci, D., & Sarnè, G. M. (2012). An agent-based approach to adapt multimedia web content in ubiquitous environment. In S. Bagchi (Ed.), *Ubiquitous multimedia and mobile agents: Models and implementations* (pp. 60–84). Hershey, PA: IGI Global. doi:10.4018/978-1-61350-107-8.ch003

Rosas, O. V., & Dhen, G. (2012). One self to rule them all: A critical discourse analysis of French-speaking players' identity construction in World of Warcraft. In N. Zagalo, L. Morgado, & A. Boa-Ventura (Eds.), *Virtual worlds and metaverse platforms: New communication and identity paradigms* (pp. 337–366). Hershey, PA: IGI Global. doi:10.4018/978-1-60960-854-5.ch022

Rouibah, K., & Abbas, H. A. (2012). Effect of personal innovativeness, attachment motivation and social norms on the acceptance of camera mobile phones: An empirical study in an Arab country. In W. Hu (Ed.), *Emergent trends in personal, mobile, and handheld computing technologies* (pp. 302–323). Hershey, PA: IGI Global. doi:10.4018/978-1-4666-0921-1.ch018

Ruiz-Mafé, C., Sanz-Blas, S., & Martí-Parreño, J. (2013). Web 2.0 goes mobile: Motivations and barriers of mobile social networks use in Spain. In N. Azab (Ed.), *Cases on web 2.0 in developing countries: Studies on implementation, application, and use* (pp. 109–146). Hershey, PA: IGI Global. doi:10.4018/978-1-4666-2515-0.ch005

Rybas, S. (2012). Community embodied: Validating the subjective performance of an online class. In H. Li (Ed.), *Virtual community participation and motivation: Cross-disciplinary theories* (pp. 124–141). Hershey, PA: IGI Global. doi:10.4018/978-1-4666-0312-7.ch008

Sabelkin, M., & Gagnon, F. (2013). Data transmission oriented on the object, communication media, application, and state of communication systems. In M. Bartolacci & S. Powell (Eds.), *Advancements and innovations in wireless communications and network technologies* (pp. 117–132). Hershey, PA: IGI Global. doi:10.4018/978-1-4666-2154-1.ch009

Sajeva, S. (2013). Towards a conceptual knowledge management system based on systems thinking and sociotechnical thinking. In J. Abdelnour-Nocera (Ed.), *Knowledge and technological development effects on organizational and social structures* (pp. 115–130). Hershey, PA: IGI Global. doi:10.4018/978-1-4666-2151-0.ch008

Salo, M., Olsson, T., Makkonen, M., & Frank, L. (2013). User perspective on the adoption of mobile augmented reality based applications. In I. Lee (Ed.), *Strategy, adoption, and competitive advantage of mobile services in the global economy* (pp. 165–188). Hershey, PA: IGI Global. doi:10.4018/978-1-4666-1939-5.ch009

Samanta, S. K., Woods, J., & Ghanbari, M. (2013). Automatic language translation: An enhancement to the mobile messaging services. In A. Mesquita (Ed.), *User perception and influencing factors of technology in everyday life* (pp. 57–75). Hershey, PA: IGI Global. doi:10.4018/978-1-4666-1954-8.ch006

Santo, A. E., Rijo, R., Monteiro, J., Henriques, I., Matos, A., Rito, C., & Marcelino, L. et al. (2012). Games improving disorders of attention deficit and hyperactivity. In M. Cruz-Cunha (Ed.), *Handbook of research on serious games as educational, business and research tools* (pp. 1160–1174). Hershey, PA: IGI Global. doi:10.4018/978-1-4666-0149-9.ch060

Sarker, S., Campbell, D. E., Ondrus, J., & Valacich, J. S. (2012). Mapping the need for mobile collaboration technologies: A fit perspective. In N. Kock (Ed.), *Advancing collaborative knowledge environments: New trends in e-collaboration* (pp. 211–233). Hershey, PA: IGI Global. doi:10.4018/978-1-61350-459-8.ch013

Sasajima, M., Kitamura, Y., & Mizoguchi, R. (2013). Method for modeling user semantics and its application to service navigation on the web. In G. Xu & L. Li (Eds.), *Social media mining and social network analysis: Emerging research* (pp. 127–139). Hershey, PA: IGI Global. doi:10.4018/978-1-4666-2806-9.ch008

Scheel, C., & Pineda, L. (2013). Building industrial clusters in Latin America: Paddling upstream. In J. Abdelnour-Nocera (Ed.), *Knowledge and technological development effects on organizational and social structures* (pp. 146–166). Hershey, PA: IGI Global. doi:10.4018/978-1-4666-2151-0.ch010

Sell, A., Walden, P., & Carlsson, C. (2013). Segmentation matters: An exploratory study of mobile service users. In D. Chiu (Ed.), *Mobile and web innovations in systems and service-oriented engineering* (pp. 301–317). Hershey, PA: IGI Global. doi:10.4018/978-1-4666-2470-2.ch016

Sermon, P., & Gould, C. (2013). Site-specific performance, narrative, and social presence in multi-user virtual environments and the urban landscape. In D. Harrison (Ed.), *Digital media and technologies for virtual artistic spaces* (pp. 46–58). Hershey, PA: IGI Global. doi:10.4018/978-1-4666-2961-5.ch004

Servaes, J. (2012). The role of information communication technologies within the field of communication for social change. In *Wireless technologies: Concepts, methodologies, tools and applications* (pp. 1117–1135). Hershey, PA: IGI Global. doi:10.4018/978-1-61350-101-6.ch502

Seth, N., & Patnayakuni, R. (2012). Online matrimonial sites and the transformation of arranged marriage in India. In C. Romm Livermore (Ed.), *Gender and social computing: Interactions, differences and relationships* (pp. 272–295). Hershey, PA: IGI Global. doi:10.4018/978-1-60960-759-3.ch016

Shaffer, G. (2013). Lessons learned from grassroots wireless networks in Europe. In A. Abdelaal (Ed.), *Social and economic effects of community wireless networks and infrastructures* (pp. 236–254). Hershey, PA: IGI Global. doi:10.4018/978-1-4666-2997-4.ch013

Shen, J., & Eder, L. B. (2013). An examination of factors associated with user acceptance of social shopping websites. In A. Mesquita (Ed.), *User perception and influencing factors of technology in everyday life* (pp. 28–45). Hershey, PA: IGI Global. doi:10.4018/978-1-4666-1954-8.ch004

Shen, K. N. (2012). Identification vs. self-verification in virtual communities (VC): Theoretical gaps and design implications. In C. El Morr & P. Maret (Eds.), *Virtual community building and the information society: Current and future directions* (pp. 208–236). Hershey, PA: IGI Global. doi:10.4018/978-1-60960-869-9.ch011

Shi, Y., & Liu, Z. (2013). Cultural models and variations. In *Industrial engineering: Concepts, methodologies, tools, and applications* (pp. 1560–1573). Hershey, PA: IGI Global. doi:10.4018/978-1-4666-1945-6.ch083

Shiferaw, A., Sehai, E., Hoekstra, D., & Getachew, A. (2013). Enhanced knowledge management: Knowledge centers for extension communication and agriculture development in Ethiopia. In B. Maumbe & C. Patrikakis (Eds.), *E-agriculture and rural development: Global innovations and future prospects* (pp. 103–116). Hershey, PA: IGI Global. doi:10.4018/978-1-4666-2655-3.ch010

Simão de Vasconcellos, M., & Soares de Araújo, I. (2013). Massively multiplayer online role playing games for health communication in Brazil. In K. Bredl & W. Bösche (Eds.), *Serious games and virtual worlds in education, professional development, and healthcare* (pp. 294–312). Hershey, PA: IGI Global. doi:10.4018/978-1-4666-3673-6.ch018

Simour, L. (2012). Networking identities: Geographies of interaction and computer mediated communication1. In S. Dasgupta (Ed.), *Technical, social, and legal issues in virtual communities: Emerging environments: Emerging environments* (pp. 235–246). Hershey, PA: IGI Global. doi:10.4018/978-1-4666-1553-3.ch016

Singh, G. R. (2013). Cyborg in the village: Culturally embedded resistances to blended teaching and learning. In E. Jean Francois (Ed.), *Transcultural blended learning and teaching in postsecondary education* (pp. 75–90). Hershey, PA: IGI Global. doi:10.4018/978-1-4666-2014-8.ch005

Singh, M., & Iding, M. K. (2013). Does credibility count?: Singaporean students' evaluation of social studies web sites. In R. Zheng (Ed.), *Evolving psychological and educational perspectives on cyber behavior* (pp. 230–245). Hershey, PA: IGI Global. doi:10.4018/978-1-4666-1858-9.ch014

Singh, S. (2013). Information and communication technology and its potential to transform Indian agriculture. In B. Maumbe & C. Patrikakis (Eds.), *E-agriculture and rural development: Global innovations and future prospects* (pp. 140–168). Hershey, PA: IGI Global. doi:10.4018/978-1-4666-2655-3.ch012

Siqueira, S. R., Rocha, E. C., & Nery, M. S. (2012). Brazilian occupational therapy perspective about digital games as an inclusive resource to disabled people in schools. In M. Cruz-Cunha (Ed.), *Handbook of research on serious games as educational, business and research tools* (pp. 730–749). Hershey, PA: IGI Global. doi:10.4018/978-1-4666-0149-9.ch037

Siti-Nabiha, A., & Salleh, D. (2013). Public sector transformation in Malaysia: Improving local governance and accountability. In N. Pomazalová (Ed.), *Public sector transformation processes and internet public procurement: Decision support systems* (pp. 276–290). Hershey, PA: IGI Global. doi:10.4018/978-1-4666-2665-2.ch013

Siwar, C., & Abdulai, A. (2013). Sustainable development and the digital divide among OIC countries: Towards a collaborative digital approach. In *Digital literacy: Concepts, methodologies, tools, and applications* (pp. 242–261). Hershey, PA: IGI Global. doi:10.4018/978-1-4666-1852-7.ch013

Smith, P. A. (2013). Strengthening and enriching audit practice: The socio-technical relevance of "decision leaders". In J. Abdelnour-Nocera (Ed.), *Knowledge and technological development effects on organizational and social structures* (pp. 97–108). Hershey, PA: IGI Global. doi:10.4018/978-1-4666-2151-0.ch006

Smith, P. A., & Cockburn, T. (2013). Generational demographics. In *Dynamic leadership models for global business: Enhancing digitally connected environments* (pp. 230–256). Hershey, PA: IGI Global. doi:10.4018/978-1-4666-2836-6.ch009

Smith, P. A., & Cockburn, T. (2013). Leadership, global business, and digitally connected environments. In *Dynamic leadership models for global business: Enhancing digitally connected environments* (pp. 257–296). Hershey, PA: IGI Global. doi:10.4018/978-1-4666-2836-6.ch010

Sohrabi, B., Gholipour, A., & Amiri, B. (2013). The influence of information technology on organizational behavior: Study of identity challenges in virtual teams. In N. Kock (Ed.), *Interdisciplinary applications of electronic collaboration approaches and technologies* (pp. 79–95). Hershey, PA: IGI Global. doi:10.4018/978-1-4666-2020-9.ch006

Soitu, L., & Paulet-Crainiceanu, L. (2013). Student-faculty communication on Facebook: Prospective learning enhancement and boundaries. In B. Pătruţ, M. Pătruţ, & C. Cmeciu (Eds.), *Social media and the new academic environment: Pedagogical challenges* (pp. 40–67). Hershey, PA: IGI Global. doi:10.4018/978-1-4666-2851-9.ch003

Solvoll, T. (2013). Mobile communication in hospitals: What is the problem? In C. Rückemann (Ed.), *Integrated information and computing systems for natural, spatial, and social sciences* (pp. 287–301). Hershey, PA: IGI Global. doi:10.4018/978-1-4666-2190-9.ch014

Somboonviwat, K. (2013). Topic modeling for web community discovery. In G. Xu & L. Li (Eds.), *Social media mining and social network analysis: Emerging research* (pp. 72–89). Hershey, PA: IGI Global. doi:10.4018/978-1-4666-2806-9.ch005

Speaker, R. B., Levitt, G., & Grubaugh, S. (2013). Professional development in a virtual world. In J. Keengwe & L. Kyei-Blankson (Eds.), *Virtual mentoring for teachers: Online professional development practices* (pp. 122–148). Hershey, PA: IGI Global. doi:10.4018/978-1-4666-1963-0.ch007

Stevenson, G., & Van Belle, J. (2013). Using social media technology to improve collaboration: A case study of micro-blogging adoption in a South African financial services company. In N. Azab (Ed.), *Cases on web 2.0 in developing countries: Studies on implementation, application, and use* (pp. 313–341). Hershey, PA: IGI Global. doi:10.4018/978-1-4666-2515-0.ch012

Strang, K. D. (2013). Balanced assessment of flexible e-learning vs. face-to-face campus delivery courses at an Australian university. In M. Khosrow-Pour (Ed.), *Cases on assessment and evaluation in education* (pp. 304–339). Hershey, PA: IGI Global. doi:10.4018/978-1-4666-2621-8.ch013

Strömberg-Jakka, M. (2013). Social assistance via the internet: The case of Finland in the European context. In J. Lannon & E. Halpin (Eds.), *Human rights and information communication technologies: Trends and consequences of use* (pp. 177–195). Hershey, PA: IGI Global. doi:10.4018/978-1-4666-1918-0.ch011

Sultanow, E., Weber, E., & Cox, S. (2013). A semantic e-collaboration approach to enable awareness in globally distributed organizations. In N. Kock (Ed.), *Interdisciplinary applications of electronic collaboration approaches and technologies* (pp. 1–16). Hershey, PA: IGI Global. doi:10.4018/978-1-4666-2020-9.ch001

Sun, H., Gui, N., & Blondia, C. (2013). A generic adaptation framework for mobile communication. In V. De Florio (Ed.), *Innovations and approaches for resilient and adaptive systems* (pp. 196–207). Hershey, PA: IGI Global. doi:10.4018/978-1-4666-2056-8.ch011

Surgevil, O., & Özbilgin, M. F. (2012). Women in information communication technologies. In C. Romm Livermore (Ed.), *Gender and social computing: Interactions, differences and relationships* (pp. 87–97). Hershey, PA: IGI Global. doi:10.4018/978-1-60960-759-3.ch006

Sylaiou, S., White, M., & Liarokapis, F. (2013). Digital heritage systems: The ARCO evaluation. In M. Garcia-Ruiz (Ed.), *Cases on usability engineering: Design and development of digital products* (pp. 321–354). Hershey, PA: IGI Global. doi:10.4018/978-1-4666-4046-7.ch014

Sylvester, O. A. (2013). Impact of information and communication technology on livestock production: The experience of rural farmers in Nigeria. In B. Maumbe & C. Patrikakis (Eds.), *E-agriculture and rural development: Global innovations and future prospects* (pp. 68–75). Hershey, PA: IGI Global. doi:10.4018/978-1-4666-2655-3.ch007

Taha, K., & Elmasri, R. (2012). Social search and personalization through demographic filtering. In I. Ting, T. Hong, & L. Wang (Eds.), *Social network mining, analysis, and research trends: Techniques and applications* (pp. 183–203). Hershey, PA: IGI Global. doi:10.4018/978-1-61350-513-7.ch012

Tai, Z. (2012). Fame, fantasy, fanfare and fun: The blossoming of the Chinese culture of blogmongering. In T. Dumova & R. Fiordo (Eds.), *Blogging in the global society: Cultural, political and geographical aspects* (pp. 37–54). Hershey, PA: IGI Global. doi:10.4018/978-1-60960-744-9.ch003

Taifi, N., & Gharbi, K. (2013). Technology integration in strategic management: The case of a micro-financing institutions network. In T. Torres-Coronas & M. Vidal-Blasco (Eds.), *Social e-enterprise: Value creation through ICT* (pp. 263–279). Hershey, PA: IGI Global. doi:10.4018/978-1-4666-2667-6.ch015

Talib, S., Clarke, N. L., & Furnell, S. M. (2013). Establishing a personalized information security culture. In I. Khalil & E. Weippl (Eds.), *Contemporary challenges and solutions for mobile and multimedia technologies* (pp. 53–69). Hershey, PA: IGI Global. doi:10.4018/978-1-4666-2163-3.ch004

Tamura, H., Sugasaka, T., & Ueda, K. (2012). Lovely place to buy!: Enhancing grocery shopping experiences with a human-centric approach. In A. Lugmayr, H. Franssila, P. Näränen, O. Sotamaa, J. Vanhala, & Z. Yu (Eds.), *Media in the ubiquitous era: Ambient, social and gaming media* (pp. 53–65). Hershey, PA: IGI Global. doi:10.4018/978-1-60960-774-6.ch003

Tawileh, W., Bukvova, H., & Schoop, E. (2013). Virtual collaborative learning: Opportunities and challenges of web 2.0-based e-learning arrangements for developing countries. In N. Azab (Ed.), *Cases on web 2.0 in developing countries: Studies on implementation, application, and use* (pp. 380–410). Hershey, PA: IGI Global. doi:10.4018/978-1-4666-2515-0.ch014

Teixeira, P. M., Félix, M. J., & Tavares, P. (2012). Playing with design: The universality of design in game development. In M. Cruz-Cunha (Ed.), *Handbook of research on serious games as educational, business and research tools* (pp. 217–231). Hershey, PA: IGI Global. doi:10.4018/978-1-4666-0149-9.ch011

Teusner, P. E. (2012). Networked individualism, constructions of community and religious identity: The case of emerging church bloggers in Australia. In F. Comunello (Ed.), *Networked sociability and individualism: Technology for personal and professional relationships* (pp. 264–288). Hershey, PA: IGI Global. doi:10.4018/978-1-61350-338-6.ch013

Tezcan, M. (2013). Social e-entrepreneurship, employment, and e-learning. In T. Torres-Coronas & M. Vidal-Blasco (Eds.), *Social e-enterprise: Value creation through ICT* (pp. 133–147). Hershey, PA: IGI Global. doi:10.4018/978-1-4666-2667-6.ch008

Thatcher, B. (2012). Approaching intercultural rhetoric and professional communication. In *Intercultural rhetoric and professional communication: Technological advances and organizational behavior* (pp. 1–38). Hershey, PA: IGI Global. doi:10.4018/978-1-61350-450-5.ch001

Thatcher, B. (2012). Borders and etics as units of analysis for intercultural rhetoric and professional communication. In *Intercultural rhetoric and professional communication: Technological advances and organizational behavior* (pp. 39–74). Hershey, PA: IGI Global. doi:10.4018/978-1-61350-450-5.ch002

Thatcher, B. (2012). Core competencies in intercultural teaching and research. In *Intercultural rhetoric and professional communication: Technological advances and organizational behavior* (pp. 318–342). Hershey, PA: IGI Global. doi:10.4018/978-1-61350-450-5.ch011

Thatcher, B. (2012). Distance education and e-learning across cultures. In *Intercultural rhetoric and professional communication: Technological advances and organizational behavior* (pp. 186–215). Hershey, PA: IGI Global. doi:10.4018/978-1-61350-450-5.ch007

Thatcher, B. (2012). Information and communication technologies and intercultural professional communication. In *Intercultural rhetoric and professional communication: Technological advances and organizational behavior* (pp. 97–123). Hershey, PA: IGI Global. doi:10.4018/978-1-61350-450-5.ch004

Thatcher, B. (2012). Intercultural rhetorical dimensions of health literacy and medicine. In *Intercultural rhetoric and professional communication: Technological advances and organizational behavior* (pp. 247–282). Hershey, PA: IGI Global. doi:10.4018/978-1-61350-450-5.ch009

Thatcher, B. (2012). Legal traditions, the universal declaration of human rights, and intercultural professional communication. In *Intercultural rhetoric and professional communication: Technological advances and organizational behavior* (pp. 216–246). Hershey, PA: IGI Global. doi:10.4018/978-1-61350-450-5.ch008

Thatcher, B. (2012). Organizational theory and communication across cultures. In *Intercultural rhetoric and professional communication: Technological advances and organizational behavior* (pp. 159–185). Hershey, PA: IGI Global. doi:10.4018/978-1-61350-450-5.ch006

Thatcher, B. (2012). Teaching intercultural rhetoric and professional communication. In *Intercultural rhetoric and professional communication: Technological advances and organizational behavior* (pp. 343–378). Hershey, PA: IGI Global. doi:10.4018/978-1-61350-450-5.ch012

Thatcher, B. (2012). Website designs as an indicator of globalization. In *Intercultural rhetoric and professional communication: Technological advances and organizational behavior* (pp. 124–158). Hershey, PA: IGI Global. doi:10.4018/978-1-61350-450-5.ch005

Thatcher, B. (2012). Writing instructions and how-to-do manuals across cultures. In *Intercultural rhetoric and professional communication: Technological advances and organizational behavior* (pp. 283–317). Hershey, PA: IGI Global. doi:10.4018/978-1-61350-450-5.ch010

Thirumal, P., & Tartakov, G. M. (2013). India's Dalits search for a democratic opening in the digital divide. In *Digital literacy: Concepts, methodologies, tools, and applications* (pp. 852–871). Hershey, PA: IGI Global. doi:10.4018/978-1-4666-1852-7.ch044

Thomas, G. E. (2013). Facilitating learning with adult students in the transcultural classroom. In E. Jean Francois (Ed.), *Transcultural blended learning and teaching in postsecondary education* (pp. 193–215). Hershey, PA: IGI Global. doi:10.4018/978-1-4666-2014-8.ch011

Tripathi, S. N., & Siddiqui, M. H. (2013). Designing effective mobile advertising with specific reference to developing markets. In I. Lee (Ed.), *Strategy, adoption, and competitive advantage of mobile services in the global economy* (pp. 299–324). Hershey, PA: IGI Global. doi:10.4018/978-1-4666-1939-5.ch017

Truong, Y. (2013). Antecedents of consumer acceptance of mobile television advertising. In A. Mesquita (Ed.), *User perception and influencing factors of technology in everyday life* (pp. 128–141). Hershey, PA: IGI Global. doi:10.4018/978-1-4666-1954-8.ch010

Tsuneizumi, I., Aikebaier, A., Ikeda, M., Enokido, T., & Takizawa, M. (2013). Design and implementation of hybrid time (HT) group communication protocol for homogeneous broadcast groups. In N. Bessis (Ed.), *Development of distributed systems from design to application and maintenance* (pp. 282–293). Hershey, PA: IGI Global. doi:10.4018/978-1-4666-2647-8.ch017

Tzoulia, E. (2013). Legal issues to be considered before setting in force consumer-centric marketing strategies within the European Union. In H. Kaufmann & M. Panni (Eds.), *Customer-centric marketing strategies: Tools for building organizational performance* (pp. 36–56). Hershey, PA: IGI Global. doi:10.4018/978-1-4666-2524-2.ch003

Underwood, J., & Okubayashi, T. (2013). Comparing the characteristics of text-speak used by English and Japanese students. In R. Zheng (Ed.), *Evolving psychological and educational perspectives on cyber behavior* (pp. 258–271). Hershey, PA: IGI Global. doi:10.4018/978-1-4666-1858-9.ch016

Unoki, M., & Miyauchi, R. (2013). Method of digital-audio watermarking based on cochlear delay characteristics. In K. Kondo (Ed.), *Multimedia information hiding technologies and methodologies for controlling data* (pp. 42–70). Hershey, PA: IGI Global. doi:10.4018/978-1-4666-2217-3.ch003

Usman, L. M. (2013). Adult education and sustainable learning outcome of rural widows of central northern Nigeria. In V. Wang (Ed.), *Technological applications in adult and vocational education advancement* (pp. 215–231). Hershey, PA: IGI Global. doi:10.4018/978-1-4666-2062-9.ch017

Usoro, A., & Khan, I. U. (2013). Trust as an aspect of organisational culture: Its effects on knowledge sharing in virtual communities. In R. Colomo-Palacios (Ed.), *Enhancing the modern organization through information technology professionals: Research, studies, and techniques* (pp. 182–199). Hershey, PA: IGI Global. doi:10.4018/978-1-4666-2648-5.ch013

Utz, S. (2012). Social network site use among Dutch students: Effects of time and platform. In F. Comunello (Ed.), *Networked sociability and individualism: Technology for personal and professional relationships* (pp. 103–125). Hershey, PA: IGI Global. doi:10.4018/978-1-61350-338-6.ch006

Vasilescu, R., Epure, M., & Florea, N. (2013). Digital literacy for effective communication in the new academic environment: The educational blogs. In B. Pătruţ, M. Pătruţ, & C. Cmeciu (Eds.), *Social media and the new academic environment: Pedagogical challenges* (pp. 368–390). Hershey, PA: IGI Global. doi:10.4018/978-1-4666-2851-9.ch018

Vladimirschi, V. (2013). An exploratory study of cross-cultural engagement in the community of inquiry: Instructor perspectives and challenges. In Z. Akyol & D. Garrison (Eds.), *Educational communities of inquiry: Theoretical framework, research and practice* (pp. 466–489). Hershey, PA: IGI Global. doi:10.4018/978-1-4666-2110-7.ch023

Vuokko, R. (2012). A practice perspective on transforming mobile work. In *Wireless technologies: Concepts, methodologies, tools and applications* (pp. 1104–1116). Hershey, PA: IGI Global. doi:10.4018/978-1-61350-101-6.ch501

Wall, M., & Kirdnark, T. (2012). The blogosphere in the "land of smiles": Citizen media and political conflict in Thailand. In T. Dumova & R. Fiordo (Eds.), *Blogging in the global society: Cultural, political and geographical aspects* (pp. 19–36). Hershey, PA: IGI Global. doi:10.4018/978-1-60960-744-9.ch002

Warburton, S. (2013). Space for lurking: A pattern for designing online social spaces. In S. Warburton & S. Hatzipanagos (Eds.), *Digital identity and social media* (pp. 149–158). Hershey, PA: IGI Global. doi:10.4018/978-1-4666-1915-9.ch011

Warren, S. J., & Lin, L. (2012). Ethical considerations for learning game, simulation, and virtual world design and development. In H. Yang & S. Yuen (Eds.), *Handbook of research on practices and outcomes in virtual worlds and environments* (pp. 1–18). Hershey, PA: IGI Global. doi:10.4018/978-1-60960-762-3.ch001

Wasihun, T. A., & Maumbe, B. (2013). Information and communication technology uses in agriculture: Agribusiness industry opportunities and future challenges. In B. Maumbe & C. Patrikakis (Eds.), *E-agriculture and rural development: Global innovations and future prospects* (pp. 235–251). Hershey, PA: IGI Global. doi:10.4018/978-1-4666-2655-3.ch017

Webb, L. M., Fields, T. E., Boupha, S., & Stell, M. N. (2012). U.S. political blogs: What aspects of blog design correlate with popularity? In T. Dumova & R. Fiordo (Eds.), *Blogging in the global society: Cultural, political and geographical aspects* (pp. 179–199). Hershey, PA: IGI Global. doi:10.4018/978-1-60960-744-9.ch011

Weeks, M. R. (2012). Toward an understanding of online community participation through narrative network analysis. In H. Li (Ed.), *Virtual community participation and motivation: Cross-disciplinary theories* (pp. 90–102). Hershey, PA: IGI Global. doi:10.4018/978-1-4666-0312-7.ch006

White, J. R. (2013). Language economy in computer-mediated communication: Learner autonomy in a community of practice. In B. Zou, M. Xing, Y. Wang, M. Sun, & C. Xiang (Eds.), *Computer-assisted foreign language teaching and learning: Technological advances* (pp. 75–90). Hershey, PA: IGI Global. doi:10.4018/978-1-4666-2821-2.ch005

Whitworth, B., & Liu, T. (2013). Politeness as a social computing requirement. In J. Bishop (Ed.), *Examining the concepts, issues, and implications of internet trolling* (pp. 88–104). Hershey, PA: IGI Global. doi:10.4018/978-1-4666-2803-8.ch008

Wichowski, D. E., & Kohl, L. E. (2013). Establishing credibility in the information jungle: Blogs, microblogs, and the CRAAP test. In M. Folk & S. Apostel (Eds.), *Online credibility and digital ethos: Evaluating computer-mediated communication* (pp. 229–251). Hershey, PA: IGI Global. doi:10.4018/978-1-4666-2663-8.ch013

Williams, J. (2013). Social cohesion and free home internet in New Zealand. In A. Abdelaal (Ed.), *Social and economic effects of community wireless networks and infrastructures* (pp. 135–159). Hershey, PA: IGI Global. doi:10.4018/978-1-4666-2997-4.ch008

Williams, S., Fleming, S., Lundqvist, K., & Parslow, P. (2013). This is me: Digital identity and reputation on the internet. In S. Warburton & S. Hatzipanagos (Eds.), *Digital identity and social media* (pp. 104–117). Hershey, PA: IGI Global. doi:10.4018/978-1-4666-1915-9.ch008

Winning, R. (2013). Behind the sonic veil: Considering sound as the mediator of illusory life in variable and screen-based media. In D. Harrison (Ed.), Digital media and technologies for virtual artistic spaces (pp. 117-134). Hershey, PA: IGI Global. doi:10.4018/978-1-4666-2961-5.ch009

Wolfe, A. (2012). Network perspective on structures related to communities. In M. Safar & K. Mahdi (Eds.), *Social networking and community behavior modeling: Qualitative and quantitative measures* (pp. 26–50). Hershey, PA: IGI Global. doi:10.4018/978-1-61350-444-4.ch002

Worden, S. (2013). The earth sciences and creative practice: Exploring boundaries between digital and material culture. In D. Harrison (Ed.), *Digital media and technologies for virtual artistic spaces* (pp. 186–204). Hershey, PA: IGI Global. doi:10.4018/978-1-4666-2961-5.ch014

Xing, M., Zou, B., & Wang, D. (2013). A wiki platform for language and intercultural communication. In B. Zou, M. Xing, Y. Wang, M. Sun, & C. Xiang (Eds.), *Computer-assisted foreign language teaching and learning: Technological advances* (pp. 1–15). Hershey, PA: IGI Global. doi:10.4018/978-1-4666-2821-2.ch001

Xu, G., Gu, Y., & Yi, X. (2013). On group extraction and fusion for tag-based social recommendation. In G. Xu & L. Li (Eds.), *Social media mining and social network analysis: Emerging research* (pp. 211–223). Hershey, PA: IGI Global. doi:10.4018/978-1-4666-2806-9.ch014

Yakura, E. K., Soe, L., & Guthrie, R. (2012). Women in IT careers: Investigating support for women in the information technology workforce. In C. Romm Livermore (Ed.), *Gender and social computing: Interactions, differences and relationships* (pp. 35–49). Hershey, PA: IGI Global. doi:10.4018/978-1-60960-759-3.ch003

Yang, Y., Rahim, A., & Karmakar, N. C. (2013). 5.8 GHz portable wireless monitoring system for sleep apnea diagnosis in wireless body sensor network (WBSN) using active RFID and MIMO technology. In N. Karmakar (Ed.), *Advanced RFID systems, security, and applications* (pp. 264–303). Hershey, PA: IGI Global. doi:10.4018/978-1-4666-2080-3.ch012

Yu, Z., Liang, Y., Yang, Y., & Guo, B. (2013). Supporting social interaction in campus-scale environments by embracing mobile social networking. In G. Xu & L. Li (Eds.), *Social media mining and social network analysis: Emerging research* (pp. 182–201). Hershey, PA: IGI Global. doi:10.4018/978-1-4666-2806-9.ch012

Zaman, M., Simmers, C. A., & Anandarajan, M. (2013). Using an ethical framework to examine linkages between "going green" in research practices and information and communication technologies. In B. Medlin (Ed.), *Integrations of technology utilization and social dynamics in organizations* (pp. 243–262). Hershey, PA: IGI Global. doi:10.4018/978-1-4666-1948-7.ch015

Zarmpou, T., Saprikis, V., & Vlachopoulou, M. (2013). Examining behavioral intention toward mobile services: An empirical investigation in Greece. In A. Scupola (Ed.), *Mobile opportunities and applications for e-service innovations* (pp. 37–56). Hershey, PA: IGI Global. doi:10.4018/978-1-4666-2654-6.ch003

Zavala Pérez, J. M. (2012). Registry culture and networked sociability: Building individual identity through information records. In F. Comunello (Ed.), *Networked sociability and individualism: Technology for personal and professional relationships* (pp. 41–62). Hershey, PA: IGI Global. doi:10.4018/978-1-61350-338-6.ch003

Zemliansky, P., & Goroshko, O. (2013). Social media and other web 2.0 technologies as communication channels in a cross-cultural, web-based professional communication project. In B. Pătruţ, M. Pătruţ, & C. Cmeciu (Eds.), *Social media and the new academic environment: Pedagogical challenges* (pp. 256–272). Hershey, PA: IGI Global. doi:10.4018/978-1-4666-2851-9.ch013

Zervas, P., & Alexandraki, C. (2013). The realisation of online music services through intelligent computing. In D. Kanellopoulos (Ed.), *Intelligent multimedia technologies for networking applications: Techniques and tools* (pp. 291–317). Hershey, PA: IGI Global. doi:10.4018/978-1-4666-2833-5.ch012

Zhang, J., & Mao, E. (2013). The effects of consumption values on the use of location-based services on smartphones. In I. Lee (Ed.), *Strategy, adoption, and competitive advantage of mobile services in the global economy* (pp. 1–18). Hershey, PA: IGI Global. doi:10.4018/978-1-4666-1939-5.ch001

Zhang, S., Köbler, F., Tremaine, M., & Milewski, A. (2012). Instant messaging in global software teams. In N. Kock (Ed.), *Advancing collaborative knowledge environments: New trends in e-collaboration* (pp. 158–179). Hershey, PA: IGI Global. doi:10.4018/978-1-61350-459-8.ch010

Zhang, T., Wang, C., Luo, Z., Han, S., & Dong, M. (2013). RFID enabled vehicular network for ubiquitous travel query. In D. Chiu (Ed.), *Mobile and web innovations in systems and service-oriented engineering* (pp. 348–363). Hershey, PA: IGI Global. doi:10.4018/978-1-4666-2470-2.ch019

Zhang, W. (2012). Virtual communities as subaltern public spheres: A theoretical development and an application to the Chinese internet. In H. Li (Ed.), *Virtual community participation and motivation: Cross-disciplinary theories* (pp. 143–159). Hershey, PA: IGI Global. doi:10.4018/978-1-4666-0312-7.ch009

Zhang, X., Wang, L., Li, Y., & Liang, W. (2013). Global community extraction in social network analysis. In G. Xu & L. Li (Eds.), *Social media mining and social network analysis: Emerging research* (pp. 156–171). Hershey, PA: IGI Global. doi:10.4018/978-1-4666-2806-9.ch010

Zhang, X., Wang, L., Li, Y., & Liang, W. (2013). Local community extraction in social network analysis. In G. Xu & L. Li (Eds.), *Social media mining and social network analysis: Emerging research* (pp. 172–181). Hershey, PA: IGI Global. doi:10.4018/978-1-4666-2806-9.ch011

Zulu, S. F. (2013). Emerging information and communication technology policy framework for Africa. In B. Maumbe & J. Okello (Eds.), *Technology, sustainability, and rural development in Africa* (pp. 236–256). Hershey, PA: IGI Global. doi:10.4018/978-1-4666-3607-1.ch016

Compilation of References

Aaker, J., & Smith, A. (2010). *The dragonfly effect: Quick, effective, and powerful ways to use social media to drive social change*. San Francisco, CA: Jossey-Bass.

About Serial. (n.d.). Retrieved from https://serialpodcast.org/about

Abrahamson, D. (Ed.). (1995). *The American magazine. Research perspectives and prospects*. Ames, IA: Iowa State University Press.

Abreu e Lima, L. (2016). *A linguagem do telejornal. Um estudo sobre os modos de organização a partir dos principais telejornais da Rede Globo* [The language of newscast. A study on the modes of organization based on Rede Globo's main newscasts] (Unpublished doctoral dissertation). Federal University of Pernambuco, Recife.

Adaval, R., & Wyer, R. S. Jr. (1998). The role of narratives in consumer information processing. *Journal of Consumer Psychology*, *7*(3), 207–245. doi:10.1207/s15327663jcp0703_01

Aguado, J. (2013). La industria del contenido en la era Post-PC: Horizontes, amenazas y oportunidades [The industry of content in the post-PC era. Horizons, threats and opportunities]. In J. Canavilhas (Ed.), *Noticias e mobilidade: O jornalismo, na era dos dispositivos moveis* [News and mobility. Journalism in the era of mobile devices] (pp. 5–31). Covilha, Portugal: Livros Labcom.

Aguado, J. M., & Güere, H. (2013). Comunicación móvil: Ecosistema digital e industrias culturales [Mobile communication: Digital ecosystem and cultural industries] In J. M. Aguado, C. Feijoó, C. Martínez, & I. Martínez (Eds.), *La comunicación móvil: Hacia un nuevo ecosistema digital* [Mobile communication: Towards a new digital ecosystem] (pp. 57–87). Barcelona: Editorial Gedisa.

Aitamurto, T. (2015). Crowdsourcing as a knowledge-search method in digital journalism. *Digital Journalism*, *4*(2), 280–297. doi:10.1080/21670811.2015.1034807

Alexander, B. (2011). *The new digital storytelling: Creating narratives with new media*. Santa Barbara, CA: Praeger.

Allan, S., & Thorsen, E. (2009). *Citizen journalism: Global perspectives*. New York, NY: Peter Lang.

Allcott, H., & Gentzkow, M. (2017). *Social media and fake news in the 2016 election*. Retrieved from https://web.stanford.edu/~gentzkow/research/fakenews.pdf

Alzamora, G. (2017). El periodismo multiplataforma de TV3 en Facebook sobre el 9-N: Prácticas intermedia o transmedia? [TV3's multiplatform journalism on Facebook over 9-N—intermedia or transmedia practices?]. *Comunicació: Revista de Recerca i d'Anàlisi, 34,* 83–115. Retrieved from http://www.raco.cat/index.php/Comunicacio/article/view/326128

Alzamora, G., & Andrade, L. (2016). A representação do Impeachment Day mediada por hashtags no Twitter e no Facebook: semiose em redes híbridas [The representation of Impeachment Day mediated by hashtags on Twitter and Facebook: Semiosis on hybrid networks]. *Revista Interin, 21*(2), 100–121. Retrieved January 20, 2017, from http://interin.utp.br/index.php/vol11/article/view/478/pdf

Alzamora, G., & Bicalho, L. (2016). A representação do Impeachment Day mediada por hashtags no Twitter e no Facebook: Semiose em redes híbridas [The representation of Impeachment Day mediated by hashtags on Twitter and Facebook: Semiosis in hybrid networks]. *Revista Ínterin, 21*(2), 100–121. Retrieved from http://interin.utp.br/index.php/vol11/article/view/478/pdf

Alzamora, G., & Gambarato, R. (2014). Peircean semiotics and transmedia dynamics. Communicational potentiality of the model of semiosis. *Ocula - Occhio semiotico sui medi, 15*(1), 1–13.

Alzamora, G., Barros, V., & Malta, J. (2015). A narrativa transmídia de iReporter for CNN acerca dos protestos brasileiros de 2013 [iReporter for CNN's transmedia narrative about the 2013 Brazilian protests]. *Brazilian Journalism Research, 11*(2), 204–221. Retrieved from https://bjr.sbpjor.org.br/bjr/article/view/710

Alzamora, G. (2016). A dinâmica transmidiática de #9NTV3 [The transmedia dynamics of #9NTV3]. In A. Angeluci (Ed.), *Comunicação Transmídia* [Transmedia communication] (pp. 112–149). Porto Alegre, Brazil: Editora Universitária da PUCRS. Retrieved from http://www3.pucrs.br/portal/page/portal/edipucrs/Capa/PubEletrEbook

Alzamora, G., & Tárcia, L. (2012). Convergence and transmedia: Semantic galaxies and emergent narratives in journalism. *Brazilian Journalism Research, 8*, 22–34.

Alzamora, G., & Tárcia, L. (2012). Convergence and transmedia: Semantic galaxies and emerging narratives in journalism. *Brazilian Journalism Research, 8*(1), 23–34.

Amado, A. (2016a). *Periodismos argentinos. Modelos y tensiones del siglo XXI* [Argentine journalisms. Models and tensions in the 21st century]. Buenos Aires, Argentina: Infociudadana, KAS.

Amado, A. (2016b). Del newsroom al cloudsroom. El periodista y los productores de información [From the newsroom to the cloudsroom. Journalists and the information producers]. In L. Luchessi & L. Videla (Eds.), *Desafíos del periodismo en la sociedad del conocimiento. Discusiones a partir del tercer Seminario Brasil–Argentina de Pesquisa em jornalismo* [Challenges of journalism in the society of knowledge. Reflections from the 3rd Seminar Brazil-Argentina on Research in Journalism] (pp. 13–21). Viedma, Argentina: Editorial UNRN.

Anderson, R., Dardenne, R., & Killenberg, G. (1994). *The conversation of journalism: Communication, community, and news*. Westport, CT: Praeger.

Andrejevic, M. (2009). Exploiting YouTube: Contradictions of user-generated labor. In P. Snickars & P. Vonderau (Eds.), *The YouTube reader* (pp. 406–423). Stockholm, Sweden: National Library of Sweden.

Andrews, M., Squire, C., & Tamboukou, M. (Eds.). (2013). *Doing narrative research* (2nd ed.). London: Sage. doi:10.4135/9781526402271

Appadurai, A. (1990). Disjuncture and difference in the global cultural economy. *Theory, Culture & Society, 7*(2), 295–310. doi:10.1177/026327690007002017

Avilés, J. A. G., Meier, K., Kaltenbrunner, A., Carvajal, M., & Kraus, D. (2009). Newsroom integration in Austria, Spain and Germany: Models of media convergence. *Journalism Practice*, (3): 1–19.

Bachelard, G. (1997). *The poetics of space*. Boston, MA: Beacon Press.

Bak, J. S., & Reynolds, B. (Eds.). (2011). *Literary journalism across the globe. Journalistic traditions and transnational influences*. Amherst, MA: University of Massachusetts Press.

Banks, J., & Deuze, M. (2009). Co-creative labour. *International Journal of Cultural Studies*, *12*(5), 419–431. doi:10.1177/1367877909337862

Barbeiro, H. (2016, July 13). A estrada da salvação [The road to salvation]. *Notícias R7*. Retrieved from http://noticias.r7.com/blogs/herodoto-barbeiro/2016/07/13/a-estrada-da-salvacao/

Barkho, G. (2016, August 11). How social media changed the Olympics, and what it means for #Rio2016. *Later*. Retrieved from https://later.com/blog/how-social-media-changed-the-olympics-and-rio-2016/

Barnathan, J. (2014). *Why Serial is important for journalism*. Retrieved March 17, 2017, from http://archives.cjr.org/the_kicker/serial_sarah_koenig_journalism.php

Batson, C. D., Batson, J. G., Slingsby, J. K., Harrell, K. L., Peekna, H. M., & Todd, R. M. (1991). Empathic joy and the empathy-altruism hypothesis. *Journal of Personality and Social Psychology*, *61*(3), 413–426. doi:10.1037/0022-3514.61.3.413 PMID:1941512

Batson, C. D., Chang, J., Orr, R., & Rowland, J. (2002). Empathy, attitudes, and action: Can feeling for a member of a stigmatized group motivate one to help the group? *Personality and Social Psychology Bulletin*, *28*(12), 1656–1666. doi:10.1177/014616702237647

Batson, C. D., Lishner, D. A., Cook, J., & Sawyer, S. (2005). Similarity and nurturance: Two possible sources of empathy for strangers. *Basic and Applied Social Psychology*, *27*(1), 15–25. doi:10.1207/s15324834basp2701_2

Bauman, Z. (2000). *Liquid modernity*. Cambridge, MA: Polity Press.

Bauman, Z. (2004). *Identity: Conversations with Benedectto Vecchi*. Cambridge, UK: Polity Press.

Baym, N. K., & Burnett, R. (2009). Amateur experts: International fan labour in Swedish independent music. *International Journal of Cultural Studies*, *12*(5), 433–449. doi:10.1177/1367877909337857

Bazán, C. (2015). Periodismo hiperlocal: El valor de contar lo que está cerca [Hyperlocal journalism. The value of telling stories from nearby] In G. Roitberg & F. Piccato (Eds.), *Periodismo disruptivo. Dilemas y estrategias para la innovación* [Disruptive journalism. Dilemmas and strategies for innovation] (pp. 53–60). Buenos Aires, Argentina: La Crujía.

Bechmann, A. (2012). Towards cross-platform value creation. *Information Communication and Society*, *15*(6), 888–908. doi:10.1080/1369118X.2012.680483

Beckett, C. (2008). *SuperMedia: Saving journalism so it can save the world*. Chichester, UK: Wiley-Blackwell.

Benecchi, E. (2014). L'economia del Fandom [The Economy of Fandom]. In M. Cucco (Ed.), *La trama dei media* (pp. 75–96). Milan, Italy: Carocci.

Benecchi, E., & Colapinto, C. (2010). Engaging with Glee! Transmedia storytelling for a television in transition. In *Business models for a digital economy: The Value of Content* (pp. 201–218). Navarra, Spain: University Press of Navarra.

Benecchi, E., & Colapinto, C. (2011). Television and social media in the era of convergence and participation. In P. Faustino & Z. Vukanovic (Eds.), *Managing media economy, Media content and technology in the age of digital convergence* (pp. 321–344). Lisbon, Portugal: Media XXL.

Bentes, I. (2015). *Mídia-Multidão. Estéticas da comunicação e biopolíticas* [Multitude-media. Aesthetics of communication and biopolitics]. Rio de Janeiro, Brazil: Mauad.

Bergman, M. (2010). C. S. Peirce on interpretation and collateral experience. *Signs (Chicago, Ill.)*, *4*, 134–161.

Bernardo, N. (2014). *Transmedia 2.0 – How to create an entertainment brand using a transmedial approach to storytelling* [Kindle version]. Lisbon, Portugal: BeActive Books.

Berning, N. (2010). *Narrative means to journalistic ends. A narratological analysis of selected journalistic reportages*. Wiesbaden: VS Research.

Berry, R. (2015b). Serial and ten years of podcasting: has the medium grown up? In M. Oliveira & F. Ribeiro (Eds.), *Radio, sound and Internet Proceedings of Net Station International Conference* (pp. 299–309). Braga: CECS - Universidade do Minho.

Berry, R. (2015a). A golden age of podcasting? Evaluating Serial in the context of podcast histories. *Journal of Radio & Audio Media*, *22*(2), 170–178. doi:10.1080/19376529.2015.1083363

Bialy, B., & Svetoka, S. (2016). *New trends in social media*. Riga, Latvia: NATO Strategic Communications Centre of Excellence. Retrieved from http://www.stratcomcoe.org/new-trends-social-media

Bilandzic, H., & Kinnebrock, S. (2009). Narrative experiences and effects of media stories. *Communications*, *34*(4). doi:10.1515/COMM.2009.022

Binge-worthy journalism – Backstage with the creators of Serial. (n.d.). Retrieved from https://www.ctforum.org/binge-worthy-journalism

Blaustein, E. (2013). *Años de rabia. El periodismo, los medios y las batallas del kirchnerismo* [Years of rage. Journalism, media and the battles of Kirchnerism]. Buenos Aires, Argentina: Ediciones B.

Boczkowski, P., & Michelstein, E. (2017). Noticias fusión [Merging News]. *Anfibia*. Retrieved from http://www.revista-anfibia.com/ensayo/noticias-fusion/

Boczkowski, P., & Michelstein, E. (2013). *The news gap. When the information preferences of the media and the public diverge*. London: MIT Press. doi:10.7551/mitpress/9780262019835.001.0001

Bolin, G. (2007). Media technologies, transmedia storytelling and commodification. In T. Storsul & D. Stuedahl (Eds.), *Ambivalence towards convergence: Digitalization and media change* (pp. 237–248). Gothenburg, Sweden: Nordicom.

Bolter, J. D., & Grusin, R. (2000). *Remediation: Understanding new media*. Cambridge, MA: The MIT Press.

Bona, R. F., & Souza, M. P. (2013). A narrativa transmidia na era da convergência: Análise das transposições midiáticas de the Walking Dead [Transmedia narrative in the age of convergence: Analysis of the media transpositions in the Walking Dead]. *Razón y Palabra*, *82*, 1–16.

Borges, J. L. (1974). *Evaristo Carriego. Obras Completas*. Buenos Aires, Argentina: Emecé. (Original work published 1930)

Boumans, J. (2004). *Cross-media, e-content report 8, ACTeN — Anticipating content technology needs*. Retrieved from http://www.sociologia.unimib.it/DATA/Insegnamenti/13_3299/materiale/04%20-%20jak%20boumans%20cross-media%20acten%20aug%202004.pdf

Boumans, J. (2004). *Cross-media: E-Content Report 8*. ACTeN—Anticipating Content Technology Needs. Retrieved from http://www.sociologia.unimib.it/DATA/Insegnamenti/13_3299/materiale/04%20-%20jak%20boumans%20cross-media%20acten%20aug%202004.pdf

Bourne, J.K. (2014a). How to farm a better fish. The world now produces more farmed fish than beef–and that's just the beginning. *National Geographic Tablet Magazine, 225*(6).

Bourne, J.K. (2014b). The next breadbasket. Why big companies are grabbing up land on the planet's hungriest continent. *National Geographic Tablet Magazine, 226*(1).

Bowden, M. (1997). *Black Hawk Down.* Retrieved from http://inquirer.philly.com/packages/somalia/

Bowman, S., & Willis, C. (2003). *We media: How audiences are shaping the future of news and information.* Reston, VA: The Media Center at the American Press Institute.

Boynton, R. S. (2005). *The New New Journalism. Conversations with America's best nonfiction writers on their craft.* New York: Vintage.

Bradham, D. (2013). Crowdsourcing: A model for leveraging online communities. In A. Delwiche & J. Henderson (Eds.), *The participatory culture handbook* (pp. 120–129). New York, NY: Routledge.

Bradley, T. (2017, July 29). *The death of Adobe Flash is long overdue.* Retrieved from https://www.forbes.com/sites/tonybradley/2017/07/29/the-death-of-adobe-flash-is-long-overdue/#7893ee536f8b

Bradshaw, P. (2017). *The online journalism handbook: Skills to survive and thrive in the digital age* (2nd ed.). London: Routledge.

Branch, J. (2012, December 20). Snow fall. The avalanche at Tunnel Creek. *The New York Times.* Retrieved from http://www.nytimes.com/projects/2012/snow-fall/#/?part=tunnel-creek

Brewer, W. F., & Lichtenstein, E. H. (1982). Stories are to entertain. A structural-affect theory of stories. *Journal of Pragmatics, 6*(5–6), 473–486. doi:10.1016/0378-2166(82)90021-2

Bromwich, J. E. (2016, August 9). "The girl from Ipanema" goes walking again, with Gisele Bundchen's help. *The New York Times.* Retrieved from https://www.nytimes.com/2016/08/10/arts/music/the-girl-from-ipanema-goes-walking-again-with-gisele-bundchens-help.html

Brooks, C., & Warren, R. P. (1979). *Modern rhetoric* (4th ed.). New York: Harcourt Brace Jovanovich.

Brown, T. (2008). Design thinking. *Harvard Business Review, 86*(6), 84–92. PMID:18605031

Brüggemann, M. (2002). *The missing link: Crossmediale Vernetzung von Print und Online; Fallstudien führender Print-Medien in Deutschland und den USA* [The missing link: Cross media linking in print and online; Case studies of leading print media in Germany and the USA]. Munich, Germany: Fischer.

Bruns, A. (2008). Reconfiguring television for a networked, produsage context. *Media International Australia Incorporation.* Retrieved from https://eprints.qut.edu.au/

Bruns, A. (2008). *Blogs, Wikipedia, Second Life, and beyond: From production to produsage.* New York, NY: Peter Lang.

Bruns, A., & Burgess, J. (2015). Twitter hashtags from ad hoc to calculated publics. In N. Rambukkana (Ed.), *Hashtag publics: The power and politics of discursive networks* (pp. 13–27). New York, NY: Peter Lang.

Bruzzi, S. (2016). Making a genre: The case of the contemporary true crime documentary. *Law and Humanities, 10*(2), 249–280. doi:10.1080/17521483.2016.1233741

Bull, A. (2010). *Multimedia journalism. A practical guide.* London: Routledge.

Buozis, M. (2017). Giving voice to the accused: Serial and the critical potential of true crime. *Communication and Critical/Cultural Studies, 14*(3), 254–270. doi:10.1080/14791420.2017.1287410

Calabresi, M. (2016). Il piano editoriale di Mario Calabresi: Un giornale trasparente, racconteremo l'Italia che si impegna [The editorial plan of Mario Calabresi: A transparent newspaper, we will tell the commitments undertaken by Italy]. *Repubblica TV*. Retrieved from http://video.repubblica.it/cronaca/il-piano-editoriale-di-mario-calabresi--un-giornale-trasparente-racconteremo-l-italia-che-si-impegna/225390/224653

Calvino, I. (1974). *Invisible cities*. New York, NY: Harcourt Brace & Company.

Calvo, E. (2015). *Anatomía política de twitter en Argentina. Tuiteando #Nisman* [Political anatomy of Twitter in Argentina. Twitting #Nisman]. Buenos Aires, Argentina: Capital Intelectual.

Canavihas, J. (2009). Ensino do jornalismo: O digital como oportunidade [Journalism: digitality as an opportunity]. In J. Fidalgo, & S. Marinho (Eds.), *Actas do Seminário Jornalismo, Mudanças na Profissão, Mudanças na Formação* [Proceedings of the seminar Journalism: changes in the profession and in the training] (pp. 49–56). Braga, Portugal: Universidade do Minho.

Canavilhas, J. (2013). Jornalismo Transmedia: Um desafio ao velho ecossistema mediático [Transmedia journalism: A challenge to the old media ecosystem]. In D. Renó, C. Campalans, S. Ruiz, & V. Gosciola (Eds.), *Periodismo Transmedia: Miradas múltiples* [Transmedia journalism: Multiple views] (pp. 53–68). Bogotá: Editorial Universidad del Rosario.

Canavilhas, J. (2014). Jornalismo transmídia: Um desafio ao velho ecossistema midiático [Transmedia journalism: A challenge to old media ecosystem]. In D. Renó, C. Campalans, S. Ruiz, & V. Gosciola (Eds.), *Periodismo transmedia: Miradas múltiples* [Transmedia journalism: Multiple perspectives] (pp. 53–67). Barcelona, Spain: Editorial UOC.

Carabajal, G. (2012, December 30). Cromagnon: El sufrimiento aún sigue [Cromagnon. The suffering still remains]. *La Nación*. Retrieved from http://www.lanacion.com.ar/1541601-cromagnon-el-sufrimiento-aun-sigue

Carpentier, N., & Dahlgren, P. (2014). The social relevance of participatory theory. In G. Patriarche, H. Bilandzic, N. Carpentier, C. Ponte, K. C. Schrøder, & F. Zeller (Eds.), Building bridges: Pathways to a greater societal significance for audience research (pp. 37–52). Brussels, Belgium: COST Action ISO906.

Carpentier, N., & Dahlgren, P. (2013). The social relevance of participatory theory. *Comunicazioni Sociali*, *3*, 301–315.

Carriere, K., & Richard, E. (1989). Crime stoppers: A study in the organization of community policing. Research Report of the Centre of Criminology, University of Toronto.

Carvalho, A. M. (2016, April 13). O nosso racismo subtil [Our subtil racism]. *Visão*. Retrieved from http://visao.sapo.pt/actualidade/sociedade/2016-04-13-O-nosso-racismo-subtil

Casella, J., & Ridgeway, J. (2013, September 22). New project: Photo requests from solitary. *Solitary Watch*. Retrieved from http://solitarywatch.com/2013/09/22/new-project-photo-requests-solitary/

Castells, M. (2008). *A era da informação: Economia, sociedade e cultura* [The age of information: Economy, society and culture] (11th ed.). São Paulo: Paz e Terra.

Castells, M. (2012). *Networks of outrage and hope. Social movements in the Internet age*. Cambridge, UK: Polity.

Catmull, E. (2014). *Creativity, Inc.: Overcoming the unseen forces that stand in the way of true inspiration*. New York, NY: Random House Publishing Group.

Cavalcanti, G. (2016). *Televisão e redes sociais: Configurações de TV Social em Malhação* [Television and social networks: Social TV configurations in Malhação] (Unpublished master's thesis). Federal University of Pernambuco, Recife.

Channel 4. (n.d.a). *The Great British Property Scandal*. Retrieved from http://www.channel4.com/programmes/the-great-british-property-scandal/videos

Channel 4. (n.d.b). *Campaign results*. Retrieved from http://www.channel4.com/programmes/the-great-british-property-scandal/articles/all/campaign-results

Chávez, F. A. (1974). *My penitente land: Reflections on Spanish New Mexico*. Santa Fe, NM: Museum of New Mexico Press.

Chávez, F. A. (2012). *Origins of New Mexico families: A genealogy of the Spanish colonial period*. Albuquerque, NM: University of New Mexico Press.

Chillón, A. (1999). *Literatura y periodismo. Una tradición de relaciones promiscuas* [Literature and journalism. A tradition of promiscuous relationships]. Barcelona, Spain: Universitat Autónoma de Barcelona.

Ciancia, M. (2016). *Transmedia Design Framework. Un approccio design-oriented alla transmedia practice* [Transmedia Design Framework. Design-oriented approach to transmedia practice]. Milan, Italy: FrancoAngeli.

Cizek, K. (Director). (2010). Out My Window [Web documentary]. Canada: National Film Board of Canada.

Clendenin, L., & Stuckey, D. (2016). *Transmedia journalism expands storytelling for deeper impact*. Retrieved from http://current.org/2016/10/transmedia-journalism-expands-storytelling-for-deeper-impact/

CNN. (2017). *2011 Libya Civil War fast facts*. Retrieved from http://edition.cnn.com/2013/09/20/world/libya-civil-war-fast-facts/index.html

Colapietro, V. (2011). Ubiquitous mediation and critical interventions: Reflections on the function of signs and purposes of Peirce's semiotic. *International Journal of Signs and Semiotic Systems*, *2*(1), 1–27. doi:10.4018/ijsss.2011070101

Colapinto, C., & Benecchi, E. (2012). Movie industry goes viral. In I. Ibrus & C. Scolari (Eds.), *Cross media innovation* (pp. 161–178). Berlin: Peter Lang.

Collie, N. (2013). Walking in the city: Urban space, stories, and gender. *Gender Forum: An Internet Platform for Gender and Women's Studies*, *42*, 1–5.

Connery, T. B. (1990). A third way to tell the story. American literary journalism at the turn of the century. In N. Sims (Ed.), *Literary journalism in the twentieth century* (pp. 3–20). New York: Oxford University Press.

Cooper, M. (2002). Narrative spaces. *Screen*, *43*(2), 139–157. doi:10.1093/screen/43.2.139

Couldry, N., & Curran, J. (2003). *Contesting media power: Alternative media in a networked world*. Lanham, MD: Rowman and Littlefield.

Cracco, G., Galli, G., & Pinardi, D. (2011). Narrare: Tra controinformazione, storia e rappresentazioni di realtà [Telling stories: Between counterinformation, history and representations of reality]. *Paginauno*, *22*, 26–27.

Cramer, T. (2014). Lessons from serial: The myth of the shrinking attention span. *EContent (Wilton, Conn.)*, *37*(10). Retrieved from http://www.econtentmag.com/Articles/Column/T.0/Lessons-from-Serial-The-Myth-of-the-Shrinking-Attention-Span-100832.htm

Crook, T. (2014). *Serial breaks iTunes records – and it's easy to see why*. Retrieved from https://theconversation.com/serial-breaks-itunes-records-and-its-easy-to-see-why-34388

Cruz, D. F., Junior. (2006). *O Éthos do enunciador nos romances de Machado de Assis: Uma abordagem semiótica* [The enunciator's Éthos in Machado de Assis' novels: A semiotic approach] (Unpublished doctoral's dissertation). São Paulo University. Retrieved from www.teses.usp.br/teses/disponiveis/8/.../TESE_DILSON_FEREIRA_CRUZ_JUNIOR.pdf

D'Andrea, C. (2014, May). Conexões intermidiáticas entre transmissões audiovisuais e redes sociais online: Possibilidades e tensionamentos [Intermedia connections between live audiovisual transmissions and online social networks: Possibilities and challenges]. *Anais do XXIII Encontro Anual da Compós—Associação Nacional de Programas de Pós-Graduação em Comunicação Social*. Universidade Federal do Pará. Retrieved from http://www.compos.org.br/biblioteca/_artigodandreacompos2014_2130.pdf

D'Andréa, C., Alzamora, G., & Ziller, J. (2015). Hashtags as intermedia agency resources before FIFA World Cup 2014 in Brazil. In N. Rambukkana (Ed.), *Hashtag publics: The power and politics of discursive networks* (pp. 115–125). New York, NY: Peter Lang.

D'Andrea, C., Alzamora, G., & Ziller, J. (2015). Hashtags as intermedia agency resources before FIFA World Cup 2014 in Brazil. In N. Rambukkana (Ed.), *Hashtag publics—The power and politics of discursive networks* (pp. 115–125). New York, NY: Lang.

Danesi, M. (2009). *Dictionary of media and communications*. New York: M. E. Sharpe.

Davis, C. H. (2013). Audience value and transmedia products. In T. Storsul & A. Krumsvik (Eds.), *Media Innovations* (pp. 175–190). Goteborg: Nordicom.

Dayan, D., & Katz, E. (1992). *Media events: The live broadcasting of history*. Cambridge, MA: Harvard University Press.

de Certeau, M. (1980). L'Invention du quotidien. Vol. 1, arts de faire [The practice of everyday life]. Paris, France: Union générale d'éditions.

de Certeau, M. (1984). *The practice of everyday life*. Berkeley, CA: University of California Press.

De Certeau, M. (1984). *The practices of everyday life*. Berkeley, CA: University of California Press.

De Kosnik, A. (2012). Fandom as free labor. In T. Scholz (Ed.), *Digital labor: The Internet as playground and factory* (pp. 98–111). New York, NY: Routledge.

De la Peña, N. & Virtual Pyedog (Producers) & De la Peña (Director) (2012). *Hunger in Los Angeles* [VR Documentary]. USA: Sand Castle Studios.

De La Peña, N. (Author), Licht, M., MxR Studio, USC School of Cinematic Arts, Vangelis Lympcuridis, World Economic Forum (Producers). (2014). *Project Syria* [VR Documentary]. USA: MxR Studio.

De la Peña, N., Weil, P., Llobera, J., Giannopoulos, E., Pomés, A., Spanlang, B., & Slater, M. (2010). Immersive journalism: Immersive virtual reality for the first-person experience of news. *Presence (Cambridge, Mass.)*, *19*(4), 291–301. doi:10.1162/PRES_a_00005

Deak, J. (2016, May 19). *Laughing Chewbacca Mask Lady* [Video file]. Retrieved from https://www.youtube.com/watch?v=y3yRv5Jg5TI

DeBarros, A. (2014, September 17). *Harvest of Change: Virtual reality project is a journalism first*. Retrieved from http://www.desmoinesregister.com/story/money/agriculture/2014/09/17/harvest-of-change-virtual-farm-virtual-reality/15785377/

Decety, J., & Ickes, W. (2011). *The social neuroscience of empathy*. Cambridge, MA: The MIT Press.

Delwiche, A. A., & Henderson, J. J. (2013). *The participatory cultures handbook*. London: Routledge.

Dena, C. (2009). *Transmedia Practice: Theorizing the practice of expressing a fictional world across distinct media and environments* (Doctoral dissertation). Retrieved from http://ciret-transdisciplinarity.org/biblio/biblio_pdf/Christy_DeanTransm.pdf

Denson, S. (2011). To be continued…: Seriality and serialization in interdisciplinary perspective. *Conference Proceedings of: What Happens Next: The Mechanics of Serialization. Graduate Conference at the University of Amsterdam.* Retrieved March 1, 2017, from http://www.jltonline.de/index.php/conferences/article/view/346/1004

Des Moines Register. (2014). *Harvest of Change: Iowa farm families confront a nation in transition.* Retrieved from http://www.desmoinesregister.com/pages/interactives/harvest-of-change/

Desta, Y. (2016). *Ira Glass on 'Serial' and the 'secret sauce' that makes 'This American Life' so special.* Retrieved March 20, 2017, from http://mashable.com/2016/04/26/ira-glass-pandora/#VkTREMWWzgqD

Deuze, M. (2003). The Web and its journalisms: Considering the consequences of different types of newsmedia online. *New Media & Society*, *5*(2), 203–230. doi:10.1177/1461444803005002004

Deuze, M. (2005). What is journalism? Professional identity and ideology of journalists reconsidered. *Journalism*, *6*(4), 442–464. doi:10.1177/1464884905056815

Deuze, M. (2008). The changing context of news work: Liquid journalism and monitorial citizenship. *International Journal of Communication*, *2*, 848–865.

Devana, C. (2015, April 16). Adiós para una leona de ambo verde [Goodbye to a lioness with a green uniform]. *Infojus Noticias.* Retrieved from http://infojusnoticias.gov.ar/nacionales/adios-para-una-leona-de-ambo-verde-8195.html

Dickson, E. J. (2014). How reddit ruined 'Serial' - and journalism. *The Daily Dot.* Retrieved February 22, 2017, from http://www.dailydot.com/opinion/serial-podcast-reddit-media/

Dinehart, S. (2008). Transmedial play: Cognitive and cross-platform narrative. *The Narrative Design Explorer.* Retrieved from http://narrativedesign.org/2008/05/transmedial-play-cognitive-and-cross-platform-narrative/

Dinehart, S. (2010). DAREtoENGAGE. *TEDx Transmedia Talk.* Retrieved from https://www.youtube.com/watch?v=gz9fZJatIQw

Documedia Mujeres. (n.d.) In *Twitter.* Retrieved August 15, 2017, from https://twitter.com/mujeresenventa

DocuMedia. (n.d.). In *Facebook.* Retrieved August 15, 2017, from https://www.facebook.com/documedia.unr

Dodson, P. C. (2015, October 21). Why Snapchat's Live Stories are the most powerful new social media. *Fast Company.* Retrieved from https://www.fastcompany.com/3052322/why-snapchats-live-stories-are-the-most-powerful-new-social-media

Dohle, M., & Loosen, W. (2014). Journalismusforschung und Rezeptions- und Wirkungsforschung: Intradisziplinäre Trennung oder selbstverständliche Verbindung? [Journalism studies and research about media reception and effects: Intradisciplinary division or natural link?]. In W. Loosen & M. Dohle (Eds.), *Journalismus und (sein) Publikum. Schnittstellen zwischen Journalismusforschung und Rezeptions- und Wirkungsforschung* [Journalism and (its) audience. Gateways between journalism studies and research about media reception and effects] (pp. 1–13). Wiesbaden: Springer VS. doi:10.1007/978-3-531-19821-7_1

Dominguez, E. (2012). Periodismo transmedia, ¿nuevo o renovado? [Transmedia journalism, new or renewed?]. *Revista de los Estudios de Ciencias de la Informacion e Comunicacion,* 13. Retrieved from http://comein.uoc.edu/divulgacio/comein/es/numero13/articles/Article-Eva-Dominguez.html

Donsbach, W., Rentsch, M., Schielicke, A.-M., & Degen, S. (2009). *Entzauberung eines Berufs. Was die Deutschen vom Journalismus erwarten und wie sie enttäuscht werden* [Disenchantment of a profession. What Germans expect from journalism and how they are disappointed]. Constance: UVK.

Doughty, M., Rowland, D., & Lawson, S. (2012). *Who is on your sofa?: TV audience communities and second screening social networks. In Proceedings of the 10th European conference on interactive TV and video—EuroiTV 2012* (pp. 79–86). New York, NY: Association for Computing Machinery. doi:10.1145/2325616.2325635

Dowdy, C. (2015, October 14). A new NLA project proposes solutions for London's housing problems. *Wallpaper*. Retrieved from http://www.wallpaper.com/architecture/a-new-nla-project-proposes-solutions-for-londons-housing-problems#md2tCYfCPqVcmmw0.99

DRNC. (2015, December 16). *State of the Subreddit survey results*. Retrieved from: https://www.reddit.com/r/serialpodcast/comments/3x333w/state_of_the_subreddit_survey_results/

Durrani, M., Gotkin, K., & Laughlin, C. (2015). Serial, seriality, and the possibilities for the podcast format. *American Anthropologist*, *117*(3), 593–596. doi:10.1111/aman.12302

Eberwein, T. (2015c). Der "andere" Journalismus. Verselbständigung und Differenzierung an der Grenze von Journalismus und Literatur [The "other" journalism. Autonomization and differentiation on the border between journalism and literature]. *medien & zeit*, *30*(1), 5–16.

Eberwein, T. (2013). *Literarischer Journalismus. Theorie – Traditionen – Gegenwart* [Literary journalism. Theory – traditions – present]. Cologne: Halem.

Eberwein, T. (2015a). Der Widerspruch von Schnelligkeit und Aktualität. Medienethische Überlegungen zum gegenwärtigen Geschwindigkeitswahn im Journalismus [The contradiction between quickness and timeliness. Media-ethical reflections on the current obsession with speed in journalism]. *Communicatio Socialis*, *48*(4), 407–411. doi:10.5771/0010-3497-2015-4-407

Eberwein, T. (2015b). Journalistisches Erzählen im Wandel. Ergebnisse einer Mehrmethodenstudie [Journalistic storytelling in transition. Results from a multi-method study] In O. Hahn, R. Hohlfeld, & T. Knieper (Eds), *Digitale Öffentlichkeit* (pp. 107–120). Constance: UVK.

Eberwein, T., Fengler, S., & Karmasin, M. (Eds.). (in press). *Media accountability in the era of post-truth politics: European challenges and perspectives*. London: Routledge.

Eberwein, T., & Porlezza, C. (2016). Both sides of the story. *Journal of Communication*, *66*(2), 328–342. doi:10.1111/jcom.12216

Echterhoff, G., & Straub, J. (2003). Narrative Psychologie. Facetten eines Forschungsprogramms. Erster Teil [Narrative psychology. Facets of a research program. First part]. *Handlung Kultur Interpretation*, *12*(2), 317–346.

Echterhoff, G., & Straub, J. (2004). Narrative Psychologie. Facetten eines Forschungsprogramms. Zweiter Teil [Narrative psychology. Facets of a research program. Second part]. *Handlung Kultur Interpretation*, *13*(1), 151–186.

Edmond, M. (2015). All platforms considered: Contemporary radio and transmedia engagement. *New Media & Society*, *17*(9), 1566–1582. doi:10.1177/1461444814530245

Elleström, L. (2010). The modalities of media: A model for understanding intermedial relations. In L. Elleström (Ed.), *Media borders, multimodality and intermediality* (pp. 11–50). New York, NY: Palgrave Macmillian. doi:10.1057/9780230275201_2

Erdal, I. J. (2009). Repurposing of content in multi-platform news production. *Journalism Practice*, *3*(2), 178–195. doi:10.1080/17512780802681223

Erdal, I. J. (2011). Coming to terms with convergence journalism: Cross-media as a theoretical and analytical concept. *Convergence (London)*, *17*(2), 213–223. doi:10.1177/1354856510397109

Esporte e Mídia. (2016, July 13). Globoesporte.com detalha cobertura dos Jogos Olímpicos; saiba mais [Globoesporte.com presents the details of the Olympic Games coverage; learn more]. *Esporte e Mídia*. Retrieved from http://www.esporteemidia.com/2016/07/globoesportecom-detalha-cobertura-dos.html

Ettema, J. S., & Glasser, T. L. (1984). *On the epistemology of investigative journalism.* Paper presented at the annual meeting of the AEJMC, Gainesville, FL.

Evans, E. (2011). *Transmedia television. Audiences, new media, and Daily Life*. New York: Routledge.

Evans, E. (2011). *Transmedia television: Audiences, new media, and daily life*. New York, NY: Routledge.

Expresso. (2016a, April 16). *Mais de 16% dos portugueses dizem que são racistas* [More than 16% of Portugueses declare that they are racist]. Retrieved from http://expresso.sapo.pt/sociedade/2016-04-16-Mais-de-16-dos-portugueses-dizem-que-sao-racistas

Expresso. (2016b, April 16). *Não sou racista, até tenho um amigo….* [I am not racist, I even have a friend…]. Retrieved from http://expresso.sapo.pt/sociedade/2016-04-18-Nao-sou-racista-ate-tenho-um-amigo

Fast, K., & Örnebring, H. (2015). Transmedia world-building: The Shadow (1931–present) and Transformers (1984–present). *International Journal of Cultural Studies*. doi:10.1177/1367877915605887

Fechine, Y. (2008a). Performance dos apresentadores dos telejornais: A construção do *éthos* [The performance of the presenters of a newscast: The building of the *éthos*]. *Famecos*, *1*(36), 69–76. Retrieved from http://revistaseletronicas.pucrs.br/ojs/index.php/revistafamecos/article/view/4417/3317

Fechine, Y. (2013). *Televisão transmídia: conceituações em torno de novas estratégias e práticas interacionais da TV* [Television transmedia: conceptualizations centered on the new interactional strategies and practices of TV]. Paper presented at Anais do XXIII Encontro Anual da Compós (Associação Nacional dos Programas de Pós-graduação em Comunicação). Universidade Federal da Bahia (UFBA), Salvador. Retrieved from http://compos.org.br/data/biblioteca_2109.pdf

Fechine, Y. (2014). Transmidiação e cultura participativa: Pensando as práticas textuais de agenciamento dos fãs de telenovelas brasileiras [Transmediation and participatory culture: Thinking about the textual practices of mediation from Brazilian soap operas fans]. *Revista Contracampo, 31*(1), 5–22. Retrieved from www.contracampo.uff.br/index.php/revista/article/viewFile/694/430

Fechine, Y. (2008b). *Televisão e presença: Uma abordagem semiótica da transmissão direta* [Television and presence: A semiotic approach about direct transmission]. São Paulo: Estação das Letras e Cores/Centro de Pesquisas Sociossemióticas.

Fechine, Y. (2012). Transmidiação, entre o lúdico e o narrativo [Transmediation, between the ludic and the narrative]. In C. Campalans, D. Renó, & V. Gosciola (Eds.), *Narrativas Transmedia. Entre Teorías y Prácticas* [Transmedia narratives. Between Theories and Practices] (pp. 69–84). Bogotá, Colombia: Editoral Universidad de Rosario.

Fechine, Y., Gouveia, D., Almeida, C., Costa, M., & Estevão, F. (2013). Como pensar os conteúdos transmídias na teledramaturgia brasileira? Uma proposta de abordagem a partir das telenovelas da Globo [How transmedia contents in Brazilian soap operas should be thought? A proposal of approach based on Globo's productions]. In M. I. V. Lopes (Ed.), *Estratégias de Transmidiação na Ficção Televisiva Brasileira* [Transmediation Strategies in Brazilian Fiction Television] (pp. 19–60). Porto Alegre: Sulina. Retrieved from http://obitelbrasil.blogspot.com.br/p/publicacoes.html

Fechine, Y., Gouveia, D., Teixeira, C., Almeida, C., Costa, M., & Cavalcanti, G. (2015). Governo da participação: Uma discussão sobre processos interacionais em ações transmídias [Participation management: A discussion over the interactional procedures in transmedia actions]. In M. I. V. Lopes (Ed.), *Por uma teoria de fãs da ficção televisiva brasileira* [On a theory of the fans of Brazilian fiction television] (pp. 321–355). Porto Alegre: Sulina. Retrieved from http://obitelbrasil.blogspot.com.br/p/publicacoes.html

Feltrin, R. (2016, August 21). Exclusivo: Globo investiu US$ 250 milhões na Rio 2016 [Exclusive: Globo invested US$250 million on Rio 2016]. *UOL*. Retrieved from https://tvefamosos.uol.com.br/noticias/ooops/2016/08/21/exclusivo-globo-investiu-us-250-mi-na-rio-2016-veja-gastos-de-outras-tvs.htm?cmpid=copiaecola

Ferrer Conill, R., & Karlsson, M. (2015). The gamification of journalism. In H. Gangadharbatla & D. Z. Davis (Eds.), *Emerging research and trends in gamification* (pp. 356–383). Hershey, PA: IGI Global.

Fink, K., & Schudson, M. (2014). The rise of contextual journalism, 1950s–2000s. *Journalism*, *15*(1), 3–20. doi:10.1177/1464884913479015

Finnegan, W. (1999, March 14). *A million enemies*. Retrieved from http://www.nytimes.com/books/99/03/14/reviews/990314.14finnegt.html

Fiorin, J. L. (2004). O *Éthos* do enunciador [The enunciator's *éthos*]. In A. Cortina & R. Marchezan (Eds.), *Razões e sensibilidades: a semiótica em foco* [Senses and sensibilities: Semiotic at issue] (pp. 117–138). Araraquara: Laboratório Editorial FLC/UNESP/Cultura Acadêmica Editora.

Fisher, M. (2011, March 26). In Tunisia, act of one fruit vendor sparks wave of revolution through Arab world. *The Washington Post*. Retrieved from https://www.washingtonpost.com/world/in-tunisia-act-of-one-fruit-vendor-sparks-wave-of-revolution-through-arab-world/2011/03/16/AFjfsueB_story.html?utm_term=.582d6f8b9fd1

Fishman, M., & Cavender, G. (Eds.). (1998). *Entertaining crime. Television reality programs*. New York: Aldine De Gruyter.

Flath, H. (2013). *Storytelling im Journalismus. Formen und Wirkungen narrativer Berichterstattung* [Storytelling in journalism. Forms and effects of narrative coverage]. (Diss.). TU Ilmenau.

Fleming, M. J. (2015, December 18). *"Star Wars" legacy II: An architect of Hollywood's greatest deal recalls how George Lucas won sequel rights*. Retrieved April 27, 2017, from http://deadline.com/2015/12/star-wars-franchise-george-lucas-historic-rights-deal-tom-pollock-1201669419/

Fludernik, M. (2009). *An introduction to narratology*. London: Routledge.

Fog, K., Budtz, C., Munch, P., & Blanchette, S. (2010). *Storytelling. Branding in practice* (2nd ed.). Berlin: Springer.

Foley, J. (2014). A five step plan to feed the world. It doesn't have to be industrial farms versus small, organic ones. There's another way. *National Geographic Tablet Magazine, 225*(5).

Folger, T. (2014). The next green revolution. Modern supercrops will be a big help. But agriculture can't be fixed by biotechnology alone. *National Geographic Tablet Magazine, 226*(4).

Ford, S. (2007, April 5). Transmedia journalism: A story-based approach to convergence. *Futures of Entertainment*. Retrieved from http://www.convergenceculture.org/weblog/2007/04/transmedia_journalism_a_storyb.php

Ford, S. (2007, April 5). Transmedia Journalism: A story-based approach to convergence. *MIT Convergence Culture Consortium*. Retrieved from http://www.convergenceculture.org/weblog/2007/04/transmedia_journalism_a_storyb.php

Ford, S. (2007, April 7). *Transmedia journalism: A story-based approach to convergence*. MIT Convergence Culture Consortium. Retrieved from http://www.convergenceculture.org/weblog/2007/04/transmedia_journalism_a_storyb.php

Ford, A. (1994). *Navegaciones. Comunicación, cultura y crisis* [Navigations. Communication, culture and crisis]. Buenos Aires, Argentina: Amorrortu.

Foster, A. D. (1978). *Splinter of the mind's eye*. New York, NY: Warner Books.

Fox, A. (Ed.). (2016). *Global perspectives on media events in contemporary society*. Hershey, PA: IGI Global. doi:10.4018/978-1-4666-9967-0

Franklin, B. (2006). *Letter to Peter Collinson, the support of the poor, May 9, 1753*. Retrieved April 26, 2017, from http://teachingamericanhistory.org/library/document/letter-to-peter-collinson/

Freeman, M. (2014). Advertising the Yellow Brick Road: Historicizing the industrial emergence of transmedia storytelling. *International Journal of Communication*, *8*, 2362–2381.

Freeman, M. (2016a). *Industrial approaches to media: A methodological gateway to industry studies*. London: Palgrave Macmillan. doi:10.1057/978-1-137-55176-4

Freeman, M. (2016b). *Historicising transmedia storytelling: Early twentieth-century transmedia story worlds*. New York, NY: Routledge.

Freeman, M., & Proctor, W. (2018). *Global convergence cultures: Transmedia earth*. London: Routledge.

Frey, F. (2014). Wirkungen des Narrativen. Ein systematischer Forschungsüberblick zu Effekten narrativer Kommunikationsformen [Impacts of narrative. A systematic synopsis of research on effects of narrative forms of communication]. In W. Früh & F. Frey (Eds.), *Narration und Storytelling. Theorie und empirische Befunde* [Narration and storytelling. Theory and empirical findings] (pp. 120–192). Cologne: Halem.

Frey, F., & Früh, W. (2014). Die Vielfalt der Erzählung: Eine Inhaltsanalyse zur Definition von "Narration," "Geschichte" und "Narrativität" in wissenschaftlichen Fachzeitschriften [The diversity of story: A content analysis on the definition of "narration," "story" and "narrativity" in scientific journals]. In W. Früh & F. Frey (Eds.), *Narration und Storytelling. Theorie und empirische Befunde* [Narration and storytelling. Theory and empirical findings] (pp. 14–62). Cologne: Halem.

Fuchs, C. (2010). Labor in informational capitalism and on the Internet. *The Information Society*, *26*(3), 179–196. doi:10.1080/01972241003712215

Fuchs, C. (2012). Class and exploitation on the Internet. In T. Scholz (Ed.), *Digital labor: The Internet as playground and factory* (pp. 211–224). New York, NY: Routledge.

Fulton, A., McKenna, M., McMillan, T., & Rupp, R. (2014, April 1). The plate [blog]. Retrieved April 28, 2017, from http://www.nationalgeographic.com/people-and-culture/food/the-plate/

G1. (2016, August 28). Rio 2016 é evento mais "instagramado" da história [Rio 2016 is the most "instagramed" event in history]. *G1*. Retrieved from http://g1.globo.com/tecnologia/noticia/2016/08/rio-2016-e-evento-mais-instagramado-da-historia-foto-de-neymar-bomba.html

Gallivan, M. (2010). *Median ages across NPR Platforms*. Retrieved March 3, 2017, from: http://www.npr.org/sections/gofigure/2010/04/05/125578017/median-ages-across-npr-platforms

Gambarato, R. R. (2013). Transmedia project design: Theoretical and analytical considerations. *Baltic Screen Media Review*, (1), 80–100.

Gambarato, R. R. (2012). Signs, systems and complexity of transmedia storytelling. *Communication Studies*, *12*, 69–83.

Gambarato, R. R. (2013). Transmedia project design: Theoretical and analytical considerations. *Baltic Screen Media Review*, *1*, 80–100.

Gambarato, R. R. (2014). Transmedia storytelling in analysis: The case of Final Punishment. *Journal of Print and Media Technology Research*, *3*(2), 95–106.

Gambarato, R. R. (2016). The Sochi Project: Slow Journalism within the transmedia space. *Digital Journalism*, *4*(4), 445–461. doi:10.1080/21670811.2015.1096746

Gambarato, R. R., Alzamora, G. C., & Tàrcia, L. P. T. (2016). Russian news coverage of 2014 Sochi Winter Olympic Games: A transmedia analysis. *International Journal of Communication*, *10*, 1446–1469.

Gambarato, R. R., Alzamora, G., & Tárcia, L. (2016). Russian news coverage of the 2014 Sochi Winter Olympic Games: A transmedial analysis. *International Journal of Communication*, *10*, 1446–1469.

Gambarato, R. R., Alzamora, G., Tárcia, L., & Jurno, A. (2017). 2014 FIFA World Cup on the Brazilian Globo Network: A transmedia dynamics? *Global Media and Communication*. doi:10.1177/1742766517734256

Gambarato, R. R., & Medvedev, S. (2015a). Grassroots political campaign in Russia: Alexei Navalny and transmedia strategies for democratic development. In J. Svensson & V. Kumar (Eds.), *Promoting social change and democracy through information technology* (pp. 165–192). Hershey, PA: IGI Global. doi:10.4018/978-1-4666-8502-4.ch008

Gambarato, R. R., & Medvedev, S. (2015b). Fish Fight: Transmedia storytelling strategies for food policy change. *International Journal of E-Politics*, *6*(3), 43–59. doi:10.4018/IJEP.2015070104

Gambarato, R. R., & Medvedev, S. (2017). Transmedia storytelling impact on government policy change. In Y. Ibrahim (Ed.), *Politics, protest, and empowerment in digital spaces* (pp. 31–51). Hershey, PA: IGI Global. doi:10.4018/978-1-5225-1862-4.ch003

Gambarato, R. R., & Nanì, A. (2016). Blurring boundaries, transmedia storytelling and the ethics of C.S. Peirce. In S. Maras (Ed.), *Ethics in screenwriting: New perspective* (pp. 147–175). Melbourne, Australia: Palgrave Macmillan. doi:10.1057/978-1-137-54493-3_7

Gambarato, R. R., & Tárcia, L. P. T. (2017). Transmedia strategies in journalism. An analytical model for the news coverage of planned events. *Journalism Studies*, *18*(11), 1381–1399. doi:10.1080/1461670X.2015.1127769

Gans, H. (1979). *Deciding What's News. A study of CBS Evening news, NBC Nightly news, Newsweek and Time.* New York, NY: Random House.

García Canclini, N. (1990). *Culturas híbridas. Estrategias para entrar y salir de la Modernidad* [Hybrid cultures. Strategies to entering and leaving Modernity] Mexico City, Mexico: Grijalbo.

García, J. S. (2013). Nuevas exigencias para el periodismo: gobiernos en la calle y ciudadanos en las redes sociales [New demands for journalism: Governments on the street and citizens in social networks]. *Telos: Cuadernos de Comunicación e Innovación*, 58–67. Retrieved from https://dialnet.unirioja.es/servlet/articulo?codigo=4255542

García, L. (2008). Distribución y promoción del producto informativo [Distribution and promotion of the news product]. In *Organización y gestión de la empresa informativa* [Organization and management of news companies] (pp. 129–141). Madrid, Spain: Síntesis.

Gaskell, E. (2003). *The complete guide to digital video*. London: Cengage Learning.

Gaudenzi, S. (2013). *The living documentary: From representing reality to co-creating reality in digital interactive documentary* (Unpublished doctoral thesis). University of London.

Gayomali, C. (2014, September 22). *How an Iowa newspaper is using Oculus Rift for big, ambitious journalism*. Retrieved from https://www.fastcompany.com/3035851/world-changing-ideas/how-an-iowa-newspaper-is-using-oculus-rift-for-big-ambitious-journalism

Getz, D. (2012). *Event studies: Theory, research and policy for planned events*. New York, NY: Routledge.

Gibbons, A. (2014). The evolution of diet. Some experts say modern humans should eat from a Stone Age menu. What's on it may surprise you. *National Geographic Tablet Magazine, 226*(3).

Gifreu, A. (2011). El documental multimedia interactivo como discurso de la no ficción interactiva. Por una propuesta de definición y categorización del nuevo género emergente [The interactive multimedia documentary as a discourse of interactive nonfiction. For a proposal of definition and categorization of the new emerging genre]. *Hipertext, 9*. Retrieved from http://www.upf.edu/hipertextnet/numero-9/documental-multimedia.html

Gifreu, A. (2012). Nuevo Modelo de No Ficción interactiva Móvil. Caracterización del reportaje y el documental Interactivo [New model of mobile non-fiction. Characterization of the report and the interactive documentary]. *Tendencias y Oportunidades de la Movilidad Digital*, 59–66. Retrieved from http://dialnet.unirioja.es/servlet/articulo;jsessionid=51B9CB65639F1302FE2A8CB2B38B28A4.dialnet01?codigo=4555307

Gifreu, A. (2014). El documental interactivo en la estrategia de la multidifusión digital. Evaluación del estado del arte en relación con la temática, las plataformas y la experiencia del usuario [The interactive documentary in the strategy of the digital multicast. Assessment of the state of the art in relation to the theme, platforms and user experience]. *Revista,* 96. Retrieved from http://telos.fundaciontelefonica.com/seccion=1268&idioma=es_ES&id=2013102313510003&activo=6.do

Gifreu, A. (2016). Inmersión en narrativas inmersivas y transmedia [Immersion in immersive and transmedia narratives]. In F. Irigaray & D. Renó (Eds.), *Transmediaciones. Creatividad, innovación y estrategias en nuevas narrativas* [Transmediations. Creativity, innovation and strategies in new narratives] (pp. 55–69). Buenos Aires, Argentina: Editorial La Crujía.

Gilder, G. (2000). *Telecosm*. New York: Free Press.

Gitlin, T. (2005). *Enfermos de información. De cómo el torrente mediático está saturando nuestras vidas* [Sick of news. How the torrent of images and sounds overwhelms our lives]. Barcelona, Spain: Paidós.

Godulla, A., & Wolf, C. (2016). Visuelle Grammatik im Fotojournalismus: Eine Untersuchung der Bildsprache von Pressefotos am Beispiel des National Geographic Magazins [Visual grammar in photojournalism: An examination of the imagery of press photos using the example of the National Geographic magazine]. In K. Arnold, T. Birkner, S. Geise, K. Lobinger, & M. Löblich (Eds.), *Historische Perspektiven auf den Iconic Turn. Die Entwicklung der öffentlichen visuellen Kommunikation* [Historic perspectives on the iconic turn. The development of public visual communication] (pp. 166–183). Cologne, Germany: Herbert von Halem Verlag.

Godulla, A., & Wolf, C. (2017). *Digitale Langformen in Journalismus und Corporate Publishing: Scrollytelling – Webdokumentationen – Multimediastorys* [Digital longforms in journalism and corporate media: Scrollytelling—Web documentations—multimedia stories]. Wiesbaden, Germany: Springer VS. doi:10.1007/978-3-658-17556-6

Goldstein, J. (2014). *The Complicated Ethics Of 'Serial,' The Most Popular Podcast of All Time.* Retrieved February 22, 2017, from https://thinkprogress.org/the-complicated-ethics-of-serial-the-most-popular-podcast-of-all-time-6f84043de9a9#.yfkebqnk8

Gomez, J. (2010). Pergunta: Esse modelo de narrativa transmídia storytelling pode ser aplicado ao jornalismo? Você conhece algum caso? [Issue: Can transmedia storytelling be applied to journalism? Do you know of any cases?]. *Tá Rolando*. Retrieved from http://redeglobo.globo.com/platb/tarolando/category/workshop-transmedia-storytelling-jeff-gomez/

Gomez, J. (2012). The 10 commandments of 21st century franchise production. *Business Insider.* Retrieved from http://www.businessinsider.com/10-commandments-of-21st-century-franchise-production-2012-10

Goode, L. (2009). Social news, citizen journalism and democracy. *New Media & Society, 11*(8), 1287–1305. doi:10.1177/1461444809341393

Google Analytics Solutions. (2017). Retrieved April 28, 2017, from https://www.google.com/analytics/#?modal_active=none

Gosciola, V. (2012). A máquina de narrativa transmídia: Transmidiação e literatura fantástica [The transmedia narrative machine: Transmission and fantastic literature]. *Revista Comunicación, 10*(1), 131–139.

Gosciola, V. (2012). Narrativa transmedia: Concepto y orígenes [Transmedia Narrative. Concept and origins]. In C. Campalans, D. Renó, & V. Gosciola (Eds.), *Narrativas transmedia entre teorías y prácticas* [Transmedia narratives. Theories and practices] (pp. 7–14). Bogotá, Colombia: Editorial Universidad del Rosario.

Gosciola, V. (2012). Narrativa transmídia: conceituação e origens [Transmedia narrative: conception and origins English translation of the title]. In C. Campalans, D. Renó, & V. Gosciola (Eds.), *Narrativa transmedia: entre teorías y practices* [Transmedia narrative: Between theories and practices] (pp. 7–14). Bogotá, Colombia: Editorial Universidad del Rosario.

Gosciola, V. (2014). Narrativa transmídia: conceituação e origens [Transmedia Storytelling: conceptualization and origins]. In C. Campalans, D. Renó, & V. Gosciola (Eds.), *Narrativas transmedia: entre teorías y prácticas* [Transmedia storytelling: Between theories and practices] (pp. 7–14). Barcelona, Spain: Editorial UOC.

Gottfried, J., & Shearer, E. (2016). *News use across social media platforms 2016*. Washington, DC: Pew Research Center. Retrieved from http://www.journalism.org/2016/05/26/news-use-across-social-media-platforms-2016/

Gouveia, D. (2015). *Cultura participativa na TV Globo*: *Governo da audiência a partir de dispositivos midiáticos de participação* [Participatory culture on Globo Network: Audience management based on participation media devices] (Unpublished doctoral dissertation). Federal University of Pernambuco, Recife.

Granados, N. (2016, October 3). What is media in the digital age? *Forbes*. Retrieved from https://www.forbes.com/sites/nelsongranados/2016/10/03/what-is-media-in-the-digital-age/#4989549a51ea

Greenberg, S. (2007). Slow journalism. *Prospect*, (2), 15–16.

Greenberg, S. (2012). Slow journalism in the digital fast lane. In R. L. Keeble & J. Tulloch (Eds.), *Global literaly journalism: Exploring the journalistic imagination* (pp. 381–393). New York: Peter Lang.

Greenberg, S. (2012). Slow journalism in the digital fast lane. In R. Keeble & J. Tulloch (Eds.), *Global literary journalism: Exploring the journalistic imagination* (pp. 381–393). New York: Peter Lang.

Green, M. C., Strange, J. J., & Brock, T. C. (Eds.). (2013). *Narrative impact. Social and cognitive foundations*. New York: Psychology Press.

Groshek, J., & Groshek, M. C. (2013). Agenda trending: Reciprocity and the predictive capacity of social network sites in intermedia agenda setting across issues over time. *Media and Communication, 1*(1), 15–27. doi:10.2139/ssrn.2199144

Grüner, U., Kretschmer, B., & Täubig, K. (2010). *Praxisbuch Crossmedia: Das Arbeitsbuch für Konzeption, Produktion und Evaluation* [Cross media practice book: The work book for concepts, production, and evaluation]. Norderstedt, Germany: Books on Demand.

Grupo Globo. (2016, June 22). Grupo Globo announces media sponsorship of the Rio 2016 Olympic Games. *Grupo Globo*. Retrieved from http://grupoglobo.globo.com/ingles/news/grupo_globo_sponsorship_olympic_games.php

Habermas, J. (1981). *Historia y crítica de la opinión pública* [History and criticism of public opinion]. Barcelona, Spain: Gustavo Gilli.

Haglund, D. (2014). *Was there an ending? We discuss the final episode of Serial*. Retrieved March 17, 2017, from http://www.slate.com/blogs/browbeat/2014/12/18/serial_podcast_last_episode_what_we_know_was_a_worthy_finale_slate_discuses.html

Harary, F., & Norman, R. (1953). *Graph Theory as a mathematical model in the social sciences*. Ann Arbor, MI: ISR.

Harding, D. C. W. (1963). *Experience into words*. CUP Archive.

Hardt, M., & Negri, A. (2004). *Multitude: War and democracy in the age of empire*. New York, NY: Penguin.

Hartsock, J. C. (2000). *A history of American literary journalism. The emergence of a modern narrative form*. Amherst, MA: University of Massachusetts Press.

Hayes, G. (2011). *How to write a transmedia production bible*. Retrieved from https://speakerdeck.com/jodieinblack/how-to-write-a-transmedia-production-bible

Hayes, G. P. (2011). *How to write a transmedia production bible*. Retrieved from http://videoturundus.ee/bible.pdf

Hayes, G. P. (2011). How to write a transmedia production bible. *Screen Australia*. Retrieved from http://videoturundus.ee/bible.pdf

Hayes, G. P. (2011). How to write a transmedia production bible. *Screen Australia*. Retrieved from https://www.screenaustralia.gov.au/getmedia/33694e05-95c2-4a05-8465-410fb8a224aa/Transmedia-production-bible-template.pdf

Heinrich, A. (2011). *Network Journalism: Journalistic practice in interactive spheres*. New York, NY: Routledge.

Henley, J. (2013, May 23). Firestorm. *The Guardian*. Retrieved from https://www.theguardian.com/world/interactive/2013/may/26/firestorm-bushfire-dunalley-holmes-family

Hepp, A., & Couldry, N. (2010). Introduction: Media events in globalized media cultures. In N. Couldry, A. Hepp, & F. Krotz (Eds.), *Media events in a global age* (pp. 1–20). London: Routledge.

Here Be Dragons (Producer), Arora, G., & Milk, C. (Directors). (2015). *Clouds over Sidra* [VR Documentary]. USA: The United Nations.

Herkman, J. (2012). Convergence or intermediality? Finnish political communication in the New Media. *Convergence (London)*, *18*(4), 369–384. doi:10.1177/1354856512448727

Herms, J. M. (2003). *"La Nostra": Vint anys de TV3* ["Ours": Twenty years of TV3]. Barcelona: Proa.

Hesmondhalgh, D. (2010). User-generated content, free labour, and the cultural industries. *Ephemera: Theory and Politics in Organization*, *10*(3/4), 267–284.

Highfield, T., Harrington, S., & Bruns, A. (2013). Twitter as a technology for audiencing and fandom: The #Eurovision phenomenon. *Information Communication and Society*, *16*(3), 315–339. doi:10.1080/1369118X.2012.756053

Hiippala, T. (2016). The multimodality of digital longform journalism. *Digital Journalism*, 1–23. doi:10.1080/21670811.2016.1169197

Hinyard, L. J., & Kreuter, M. W. (2007). Using narrative communication as a tool for health behavior change. A conceptual, theoretical, and empirical overview. *Health Education & Behavior*, *34*(5), 777–792. doi:10.1177/1090198106291963 PMID:17200094

Hochberg, A. (2014, November 04). *News for the Minecraft generation: Gannett experiments with virtual reality*. Retrieved from http://www.poynter.org/2014/news-for-the-minecraft-generation-gannett-experiments-with-virtual-reality/270633/

Hopewell, J. (2016, August 2). Brazil's Globo hopes to vault to future with Rio Games. *Variety*. Retrieved from http://variety.com/2016/tv/global/brazil-globo-network-rio-olympics-technology-1201828462/

Hornstra, R., & van Bruggen, A. (2013). *The Sochi project*. Retrieved from http://www.thesochiproject.org/en/chapters/the-summer-capital/

Houston, B. (2010). The future of investigative journalism. *Daedalus*, *139*(2), 45–56. doi:10.1162/daed.2010.139.2.45

Howe, J. (2008). *Crowdsourcing: How the power of the crowd is driving the future of business*. New York, NY: Crown Business.

Humphries, C. (1991). On Quakerism, trans-media and democracy: Thoughts of Stuart Saunders Smith. *Ex-tempore*. Retrieved from http://www.ex-tempore.org/Humphrie.htm

Hunicke, R., LeBlanc, M., & Zubek, R. (2004, July). MDA: A formal approach to game design and game research. *Proceedings of the AAAI Workshop on Challenges in Game AI*, *4*(1).

Igarza, R. (2009). *Burbujas de ocio. Nuevas formas de consumo cultural* [Leisure Bubbles. New forms of cultural consumption]. Buenos Aires, Argentina: La Crujía.

Igarza, R. (2010). *Burbujas de Ocio. Nuevas formas de consumo cultural* [Bubbles of leisure. New forms of cultural consumption]. Buenos Aires, Argentina: La Crujía Ediciones. Col. Futuribles.

Infobae. (2012, July 17). *Cronología del conflicto agropecuario por la resolución 125* [Cronology of the agricultural conflict over Resolution No. 125]. Retrieved from http://www.infobae.com/2012/07/17/659506-cronologia-del-conflicto-agropecuario-la-resolucion-125/

Infobae. (2015, May 21). *La Argentina, entre los 25 países con mayor cantidad de usuarios de smartphones* [Argentina, among the 25 countries with more smartphone users]. Retrieved from http://www.infobae.com/2015/05/21/1730171-la-argentina-los-25-paises-mayor-cantidad-usuarios-smartphones/

Institut für Demoskopie Allensbach. (2013). Hohes Ansehen für Ärzte und Lehrer – Reputation von Hochschulprofessoren und Rechtsanwälten rückläufig [High esteem for doctors and teachers – Reputation of university professors and lawyers on the decline]. *Allensbacher Berufsprestige-Skala 2013*. Retrieved from http://www.ifd-allensbach.de/uploads/tx_reportsndocs/PD_2013_05.pdf

International Association for Literary Journalism Studies. (2011). Selected bibliography of scholarship and criticism examining literary journalism. *Literary Journalism Studies*, *3*(1), 123–141.

International Olympic Committee. (2015). *IOC social and digital media guidelines for persons accredited to the Games of the XXXI Olympiad Rio 2016*. Retrieved from https://stillmed.olympic.org/media/Document%20Library/OlympicOrg/Games/Summer-Games/Games-Rio-2016-Olympic-Games/Social-Media-Blogging-Internet-Guidelines-and-News-Access-Rules/IOC-Social-and-Digital-Media-Guidelines-Rio-2016.pdf#_ga=1.124100364.74130809.1484839460

International Olympic Committee. (2016). *Editorial use of the Olympic properties by media organisations*. Retrieved from https://stillmed.olympic.org/Documents/THE%20IOC/IOC_guide_media_web%2029.11.13.pdf

Irigaray, F. (2014). La ciudad como plataforma narrativa: El Documental Transmedia Tras los pasos de El Hombre Bestia [The city as a narrative platform: The transmedia documentary Following the footsteps of The Beast Man]. In F. Irigaray & A. Lovato (Eds.), *Hacia una comunicación transmedia* [Towards a transmedia communication] (pp. 113–131). Rosario, Argentina: UNR Editora. Retrieved from http://hdl.handle.net/2133/3610

Irigaray, F. (2015). Navegación territorial. Entramado narrativo urbano [Territorial navigation. Urban narrative lattice]. In F. Irigaray & A. Lovato (Eds.), *Producciones transmedia de no ficción. Análisis, experiencias y tecnologías* [Transmedia non-fiction productions. Analysis, experiences and technologies] (pp. 115–126). Rosario, Argentina: UNR Editora. Retrieved from http://hdl.handle.net/2133/5666

Irigaray, F. (2016). Documental transmedia: narrativas espaciales y relatos expandidos [Transmedia documentary: Spatial narratives and expanded stories]. In F. Irigaray & D. Renó (Eds.), *Transmediaciones. Creatividad, innovación y estrategias en nuevas narrativas* [Transmediations. Creativity, innovation and strategies in new narratives] (pp. 39–53). Buenos Aires, Argentina: Editorial La Crujía.

Irisarri, P., & Loja, M. (2017). *¿Qué pasa después? Aportes y desafíos para la construcción de derechos de víctimas de trata y explotación sexual* [What happens next? Contributions and challenges for the construction of rights of victims of trafficking and sexual exploitation]. Rosario, Argentina: UNR Editora. Retrieved from https://www.academia.edu/31773338/_Qu%C3%A9_pasa_despu%C3%A9s_Aportes_y_desaf%C3%ADos_para_la_construcci%C3%B3n_de_derechos_de_v%C3%ADctimas_de_trata_y_explotaci%C3%B3n_sexual

Izquierdo Labella, L. (2012). El nuevo periodismo de proximidad, una ventana abierta al mundo [The new proximity journalism. An open window to the world]. In J. Correia (Ed.), *Ágora, jornalismo de poximidade: Limites, desafios e oportunidades* [Journalism and proximity: Boundaries, challenges and opportunities] (pp. 87–98). Covilha, Portugal: Labcom Books.

Jansson, A. (2013). Mediatization and social space: Reconstructing mediatization for the transmedia age. *Communication Theory*, *23*(3), 279–296. doi:10.1111/comt.12015

Jansson, A., & Lindell, J. (2015). News media consumption in the transmedia age. Amalgamations, orientations and geo-social structuration. *Journalism Studies*, *16*(1), 79–96. doi:10.1080/1461670X.2014.890337

Jarvis, J. (2009). *The future of journalism is an entrepreneurial, collaborative process*. Keynote given at the Medientage München. Retrieved March 4, 2017, from: http://www.carta.info/17734/jarvis-keynote-medientage/

Jaxxon. (n.d.). [Fan Wiki]. Retrieved April 28, 2017, from http://starwars.wikia.com/wiki/Jaxxon

Jenkins, H. (2002). Game design as narrative architecture. *MIT*. Retrieved from http://web.mit.edu/21fms/People/henry3/games&narrative.html

Jenkins, H. (2003). Transmedia storytelling. *MIT Technology Review*. Retrieved from https://www.technologyreview.com/s/401760/transmedia-storytelling

Jenkins, H. (2003). Transmedia Storytelling. *MIT Technology Review*. Retrieved from https://www.technologyreview.com/s/401760/transmedia-storytelling/

Jenkins, H. (2003). *Transmedia storytelling*. Retrieved from MIT Technology Review: https://www.technologyreview.com/s/401760/transmedia-storytelling/

Jenkins, H. (2003). Transmedia storytelling: Moving characters from books to films to video games can make them stronger and more compelling. *MIT Technology Review*. Retrieved from http://www.technologyreview.com/news/401760/transmedia-storytelling/

Jenkins, H. (2003). *Transmedia storytelling: Moving characters from books to films to video-games can make them stronger and more compelling*. Retrieved from https://www.technologyreview.com/s/401760/transmedia-storytelling/

Jenkins, H. (2003). Transmedia storytelling—moving characters from books to films to video games can make them stronger and more compelling. *MIT Technology Review*. Retrieved from https://www.technologyreview.com/s/401760/transmedia-storytelling/

Jenkins, H. (2003, January 15). Transmedia storytelling. *Technology Review*. Retrieved from http://www.technologyreview.com/news/401760/transmedia-storytelling/

Jenkins, H. (2007). Transmedia Storytelling 101. *Blog Confessions of an Aca-Fan*. Retrieved from http://henryjenkins.org/2007/03/transmedia_storytelling_101.html

Jenkins, H. (2009). The revenge of the origami unicorn: Seven principles of transmedia storytelling. *Blog Confessions of an Aca-Fan*. Retrieved from http://henryjenkins.org/2009/12/the_revenge_of_the_origami_uni.html

Jenkins, H. (2009, December 12). The revenge of the origami unicorn: Seven principles of transmedia storytelling (Well, two actually. Five more on Friday). *Blog Confessions of an aca-fan*. Retrieved from http://henryjenkins.org/2009/12/the_revenge_of_the_origami_uni.html

Jenkins, H. (2009, December 12). The revenge of the origami unicorn: Seven principles of transmedia storytelling (Well, two actually. Five more on Friday). *Confession of an Aca-fan Blog*. Retrieved October 10, 2010, from http://henryjenkins.org/2009/12/the_revenge_of_the_origami_uni.html

Jenkins, H. (2009, December 12). The revenge of the origami unicorn: Seven principles of transmedia storytelling. *Blog Confessions of an Aca-Fan*. Retrieved from: http://henryjenkins.org/blog/2009/12/the_revenge_of_the_origami_uni.html

Jenkins, H. (2009, December 12). *The revenge of the origami unicorn: Seven principles of transmedia storytelling*. Retrieved from http://henryjenkins.org/2009/12/the_revenge_of_the_origami_uni.html

Jenkins, H. (2009, December 21). *The revenge of the origami unicorn: The remaining seven principles of transmedia storytelling*. Retrieved December 12, 2017, from http://www.convergenceculture.org/weblog/2009/12/the_revenge_of_the_origami_uni.php

Jenkins, H. (2009a, December 12). The revenge of the origami unicorn: Seven principles of transmedia storytelling (Well, two actually. Five more on Friday). *Confession of an Aca-Fan*. Retrieved from http://henryjenkins.org/blog/2009/12/the_revenge_of_the_origami_uni.html

Jenkins, H. (2009a, December 12). The revenge of the origami unicorn: Seven principles of transmedia storytelling (Well, two actually. Five more on Friday). *Confessions of an Aca-fan Blog*. Retrieved from http://henryjenkins.org/2009/12/the_revenge_of_the_origami_uni.html

Jenkins, H. (2009b December 12). The revenge of the origami unicorn: The remaining four principles of transmedia storytelling. *Confession of an Aca-Fan*. Retrieved from http://henryjenkins.org/blog/2009/12/revenge_of_the_origami_unicorn.html

Jenkins, H. (2009b, December 12). The revenge of the origami unicorn: The remaining four principles of transmedia storytelling. *Confessions of an Aca-fan Blog*. Retrieved from http://henryjenkins.org/2009/12/revenge_of_the_origami_unicorn.html

Jenkins, H. (2011, January 26). "Deep media," transmedia, what's the difference? An interview with Frank Rose (Part one). *Blog Confessions of an aca-fan*. Retrieved from http://henryjenkins.org/blog/2011/01/deep_media_transmedia_whats_th.html

Jenkins, H. (2013). *Transmedia storytelling: Moving characters from books to films to video-games can make them stronger and more compelling*. Retrieved from http://www.technologyreview.com/biotech/13052

Jenkins, H., Ito, M., & boyd, d. (2015). *Participatory culture in a networked era: A conversation on youth, learning, commerce, and politics.* Cambridge, UK: Polity Press.

Jenkins, H. (1992). *Textual Poachers: Television fans and participatory culture.* New York: Routledge.

Jenkins, H. (1992). *Textual pochers: Television fans & participatory culture.* New York: Routledge.

Jenkins, H. (2003). Transmedia storytelling. Moving characters from books to films to video games can make them stronger and more compelling. *Technology Review*, *15*(January). Retrieved from http://www.technologyreview.com/biotech/13052/

Jenkins, H. (2004). Game design as narrative architecture. In N. Wardrip-Fruin & P. Harrigan (Eds.), *First person: New media as story, performance and game* (pp. 118–130). Cambridge, MA: The MIT Press.

Jenkins, H. (2006). *Convergence culture. Where old and new media collide.* New York: New York University.

Jenkins, H. (2006). *Convergence culture: Where old and new media collide.* New York, NY: New York University Press.

Jenkins, H. (2006). *Convergence Culture: Where old and new media collide.* New York: New York University Press.

Jenkins, H. (2006). Searching for the origami unicorn. In *Convergence Culture: Where Old and New Media Collide* (pp. 93–130). New York, NY: NYU Press.

Jenkins, H. (2008). *Convergence culture: Where old and new media collide (Updated and with a new afterword).* New York, NY: New York Univ. Press.

Jenkins, H. (2010). Transmedia storytelling 101. In *Cross-media communications. An introduction of creating integrated media experiences* (pp. 188–193). Lexington: ETC Press.

Jenkins, H., Ford, S., & Green, J. (2013). *Spreadable media: Creating value and meaning in a networked culture.* New York, NY: New York University Press.

Jenkins, H., Ford, S., & Green, J. (2013). *Spreadable Media: Creating value and meaning in a networked culture.* New York: New York University Press.

Jensen, J. F. (1998). *Interactivity, tracking a new concept in Media and Communication Studies.* Retrieved March 3, 2017, from http://www.nordicom.gu.se/en/tidskrifter/nordicom-review-11998/interactivity-tracking-new-concept-media-and-communication-studies

Johansson-Sköldberg, U., Woodilla, J., & Çetinkaya, M. (2013). Design thinking: Past, present and possible futures. *Creativity and Innovation Management*, *22*(2), 121–146. doi:10.1111/caim.12023

Johns, C. (2014). Editor's note: Food for thought. *National Geographic Tablet Magazine*, (5).

Jornal da Record News. (n.d.). *Home* [YouTube Channel]. Retrieved August 5, 2017, from https://www.youtube.com/playlist?list=PLt5YPA-Y-vppPke8WsreLH6DuVz7FPTQc

Jost, F. (2010). *Compreender a televisão* [Understanding television]. Porto Alegre, Brazil: Sulina.

Joven Pan. (2016, August 5). Rio 2016: Ex-BBB Ana Paula vence desafio e terá tweet projetado em monumento [Rio 2016: Ex-BBB Ana Paul won the challenge and her tweet will be projected onto monument]. *Joven Pan.* Retrieved from https://beta.jovempan.uol.com.br/esportes/rio-2016-ex-bbb-ana-paula-vence-desafio-e-tera-tweet-projetado-em-monumento.html

Kafka, P., & Molla, R. (2017, May 4). How The New York Times saved itself. *Recode.* Retrieved from https://www.recode.net/2017/5/4/15550052/new-york-times-subscription-advertising-revenue-chart?curator=theedge

Kammer, A. (2013). Audience participation in the production of online news: Towards a typology. *Nordicom Review*, *3*, 113–126.

Karlsson, M. (2010). Rituals of transparency. *Journalism Studies*, *11*(4), 535–545. doi:10.1080/14616701003638400

Karlsson, M. (2011). The immediacy of online news, the visibility of journalistic processes and a restructuring of journalistic authority. *Journalism*, *12*(3), 279–295. doi:10.1177/1464884910388223

Keeble, R. L., & Tulloch, J. (Eds.). (2012). *Global literary journalism. Exploring the journalistic imagination*. New York: Lang.

Keen, S. (2006). A theory of narrative empathy. *Narrative*, *14*(3), 207–236. doi:10.1353/nar.2006.0015

Kerrigan, S., & Velikovsky, J. T. (2016). Examining documentary transmedia narratives through The Living History of Fort Scratchley Project. *Convergence (London)*, *22*(3), 250–268. doi:10.1177/1354856514567053

Kim, J., & Hong, J. (2013). Analysis of trans-media storytelling strategies. *International Journal of Multimedia and Ubiquitous Engineering*, *8*(3), 1–10.

Kinder, M. (1991). *Playing with power in movies, television, and video games: From Muppet Babies to Teenage Mutant Ninja Turtles*. Berkeley, CA: University of California Press.

Kleine Wieskamp, P. (Ed.). (2016). *Storytelling: Digital – Multimedial – Social. Formen und Praxis für PR, Marketing, TV, Game und Social Media* [Storytelling: Digital – multimedia – social. Forms and practice for PR, marketing, TV, game, and social media]. Munich: Hanser.

Kolodzy, J. (2012). *Convergence Journalism: Writing and reporting across the news media*. London: Routledge.

Kottasova, I. (2016, December 6). The top hashtag of the year had nothing to do with Donald Trump. *CNN*. Retrieved from http://money.cnn.com/2016/12/06/technology/twitter-top-events-hashtags-2016/

Kramer, M., & Call, W. (Eds.). (2007). *Telling true stories. A nonfiction writers' guide from the Nieman Foundation at Harvard University*. New York: Plume.

Kress, G., & van Leeuwen, T. (2001). *Multimodal discourse: the modes and media of contemporary communication*. London: Hodder Education.

Krüger, U. (2014, March). *Acceleration in journalism: A theoretical approach to a complex phenomenon*. Paper presented at the conference "Journalism in Transition: Crisis or Opportunity?" of the Journalism Studies Section within the European Communication Research and Education Association (ECREA) in Thessaloniki.

Kunzig, R. (2014). Carnivore's dilemma. Unhealthy. Nutritious. Cruel. Delicious. Unsustainable. All-American. In the beef debate there are so many sides. *National Geographic Tablet Magazine, 226*(5).

Kushner, D. (2008, May 1). Rebel alliance: How a small band of sci-fi geeks is leading Hollywood into a new era. *Fast Company*. Retrieved from http://www.fastcompany.com/798975/rebel-alliance

La Nación. (2014, September 15). *La tragedia de LAPA. Una causa judicial de la que fue absuelto por prescripción* [The LAPA tragedy. An action barred and an acquitted person]. Retrieved from http://www.lanacion.com.ar/1727346-la-tragedia-de-lapa-una-carga-judicial-de-la-que-fue-absuelto-por-prescripcion

La Vanguardia. (2014a, September 11). *Las cifras de la Via Catalana 2014: 1,8 millones—La marcha ha tenido su vértice en la plaza de las Glòries, ha cubierto 11 kilómetros y ha contado también con 54 "colles" de "castellers"* [The figures of the Catalan Road 2014: 1.8 million—The march has had its vertex in the Plaza de las Glòries, has covered 11 kilometers and has also had 54 "colles" of "castellers"]. Retrieved from http://www.lavanguardia.com/politica/20140911/54414923722/cifras-via-catalana.html

La Vanguardia. (2014b, November 10). *TV3, referente informativo en la jornada del 9N—Más de un millón de personas vieron el "Telenoticies' cap de setmana vesper" que se emitía de forma conjunta por TV3 y el 3/24* [TV3, informative reference in the day of 9N—More than one million people saw the "Telenoticies" main of week evening, that was emitted jointly by TV3 and 3/24]. Retrieved from http://www.lavanguardia.com/television/audiencias/20141110/54419751982/audiencia-tv3-9n.html#ixzz3buH0nioP

Labov, W., & Waletzky, J. (1967). Narrative analysis. Oral versions of personal experience. In J. Helm (Ed.), *Essays on the verbal and visual arts* (pp. 12–44). Seattle, WA: University of Washington Press.

Landi, O. (1992). *Devórame otra vez. Qué hizo la televisión con la gente. Qué hace la gente con la televisión* [Swallow me again. What did television do to people? What does people do with television?]. Buenos Aires, Argentina: Planeta.

Laurel, B. (2000). *Creating core content in a post-convergence world*. New York, NY: Tauzero.

Lausberg, H. (1998). *Handbook of literary rhetoric. A foundation for literary study*. Leiden: Brill.

Le Masurier, M. (2015). What is slow journalism? *Journalism Practice*, *9*(2), 138–152. doi:10.1080/17512786.2014.916471

Lee, A. M.-C. (2014). *How fast is too fast? Examining the impact of speed-driven journalism on news production and audience reception* (PhD thesis). University of Texas, Austin, TX.

Lee, I. (2017, March 24). Six years ago the Arab Spring came to Egypt -- and Hosni Mubarak fell. *CNN*. Retrieved from http://edition.cnn.com/2017/03/24/middleeast/egypt-six-years-after/index.html

Lee, W., & Gretzel, U. (2012). Designing persuasive destination websites. A mental imagery processing perspective. *Tourism Management*, *33*(5), 1270–1280. doi:10.1016/j.tourman.2011.10.012

Lessig, L. (2009). *Remix: Making art and commerce thrive in the hybrid economy*. London: Penguin.

Levin, B. (1970). *The pendulum years: Britain and the sixties*. London: Jonathan Cape.

Lévy, P. (1997). *Collective intelligence: Mankind's emerging world in cyberspace*. Cambridge, MA: Perseus Books.

Lévy, P. (1997). *Collective Intelligence: Mankind's emerging world in cyberspace*. Cambridge, MA: Perseus Books.

Lewis, S. (2012). The tension between professional control and open participation. *Information Communication and Society*, *15*(6), 836–866. doi:10.1080/1369118X.2012.674150

Lewis, S. C., Holton, A. E., & Coddington, M. (2017). From participation to reciprocity in the journalist-audience relationship. In C. Peters & M. Broersma (Eds.), *Rethinking journalism again* (pp. 161–174). London: Routledge.

Lippmann, W. (1965). *Public Opinion*. New York, NY: The Free Press. (Original work published 1922)

Liuzzi, A. (2014). Transmedia "historytelling." De Documentales Interactivos y Géneros Híbridos [Transmedia "historytelling." From interactive documentaries and hybrid genres]. In F. Irigaray & A. Lovato (Eds.), *Hacia una comunicación transmedia* [Towards a transmedia communication] (pp. 65–86). Rosario, Argentina: UNR Editora. Retrieved from http://hdl.handle.net/2133/3610

Liuzzi, A. (2014). Transmedia storytelling. De documentales interactivos y géneros híbridos. [Transmedia storytelling. Interactive documentaries and hybrid genres] In F. Irigaray & A. Lovato (Eds.), *Hacia una comunicación transmedia* [Toward a transmedia communication system]. (pp. 65–86). Rosario, Argentina: UNR.

Livingstone, S. (2004). The challenge of challenging audiences, or, what is the audience researcher to do in the age of the Internet? *European Journal of Communication*, *19*(1), 75–86. doi:10.1177/0267323104040695

Lobo, A. P. (2016, August 8). Globo usa DWDM nacional para transmitir em 8K na Rio 2016 [Globo uses national DWDM to broadcast in 8K in Rio 2016]. *Convergência Digital*. Retrieved from http://www.convergenciadigital.com.br/cgi/cgilua.exe/sys/start.htm?UserActiveTemplate=site&%25252525253Butm%252525252525252525255Fmedium=&UserActiveTemplate=site%252Csite&infoid=43182&sid=4

Lockwood, T. (2010). *Design thinking: Integrating innovation, customer experience, and brand value*. New York, NY: Skyhorse Publishing, Inc.

Long, G. (2007). *Transmedia Storytelling: Business, aesthetics and production at the Jim Henson Company* (Master of Science Degree thesis). Retrieved from http://cmsw.mit.edu/transmedia-storytelling-jim-henson-company/

Long, M. (2016, August 4). Globo gathering: How Brazil's biggest broadcaster is tackling Rio 2016. *SportsPro*. Retrieved from http://www.sportspromedia.com/magazine_features/globo_gathering_how_brazils_biggest_broadcaster_is_gearing_up_for_rio_2016

Lorenz, M. (2014). Personalização: Análise aos 6 graus [Customization: 6 degrees analysis]. In J. Canavilhas (Ed.), *Webjornalismo: 7 caraterísticas que marcam a diferença* [Webjournalism: 7 characteristics that make a difference] (pp. 137–158). Covilhã: Livros Labcom.

Lovato, A. (2015). Del periodismo multimedia al periodismo transmedia. Guiones para pensar nuevas narrativas [From multimedia journalism to transmedia journalism. Scripts for thinking about new narratives]. In F. Irigaray & A. Lovato (Eds.), *Producciones transmedia de no ficción. Análisis, experiencias y tecnologías* [Transmedia non-fiction productions. Analysis, experiences and technologies] (pp. 33–52). Rosario, Argentina: UNR Editora.

Lovato, A. (2016). Guión transmedia en narrativas de no ficción [Transmedia script in nonfiction narratives]. In F. Irigaray & D. Renó (Eds.), *Transmediaciones. Creatividad, innovación y estrategias en nuevas narrativas* [Transmediations. Creativity, innovation and strategies in new narratives] (pp. 23–37). Buenos Aires, Argentina: Editorial La Crujía.

Luchessi, L. (2016a). Descentramientos, influencias y reacomodamientos en el ejercicio periodístico [Off-centerings, influencies and readaptations of the journalistic activity]. In A. Amado (Ed.), Periodismos argentinos. Modelos y tensiones del siglo XXI [Argentine journalisms. Models and tensions in the 21st century] (pp.37–49). Buenos Aires, Argentina: Infociudadana, KAS.

Luchessi, L. (2006). *Informe final del Seminario de Política y Medios* [Final report of the Seminar on politics and media]. Buenos Aires, Argentina: Universidad de Buenos Aires.

Luchessi, L. (2013). *Calidad informativa. Escenarios de postcrisis* [Information quality. Post-crisis scenarios]. Buenos Aires, Argentina: La Crujía.

Luchessi, L. (2016b). *PI UNRN 40-C-153. Información y periodismo en contextos transmediáticos. Informe final* [Journalism and information in transmedia contexts. Final report]. Viedma, Argentina: UNRN.

Luchessi, L., & Cetkovich, G. (2007). Punto Ciego. [Blind spot] In L. Luchessi & M. Rodriguez (Eds.), *Fronteras globales. Cultura, política y medios de comunicación* [Global borders. Culture, politics and mass media]. Buenos Aires, Argentina: La Crujía.

Lugo, N. (2016). *Diseño de narrativas transmedia para la transalfabetización* [Design of transmedia narratives for the transalphabetization] (Unpublished PhD dissertation). Universidad Pompeu Fabra, Barcelona, Spain.

Lunenfeld, P. (2003). The Design Cluster. In B. Laurel (Ed.), *Design Research. Methods and Perspectives* (pp. 10–15). Cambridge, MA: MIT Press.

Lurie, J. (2014). *"This American Life" channels "True Detective" in a new podcast*. Retrieved February 20, 2017, from http://www.motherjones.com/media/2014/09/ira-glass-sarah-koenig-julie-snyder-serial-podcast-this-american-life

Machill, M., Köhler, S., & Waldhauser, M. (2006). Narrative Fernsehnachrichten. Ein Experiment zur Innovation journalistischer Darstellungsformen [Narrative television news. An experiment on the innovation of journalistic genres]. *Publizistik*, *51*(4), 479–497. doi:10.1007/s11616-006-0241-x

MacLuhan, M. (1994). *Understanding media: The extensions of Man*. Cambridge, MA: MIT Press.

Madianou, M., & Miller, D. (2013). Polymedia: Towards a new theory of digital media in interpersonal communication. *International Journal of Cultural Studies*, *16*(2), 169–187. doi:10.1177/1367877912452486

Maier, S. R. (2015). Compassion fatigue and the elusive quest for journalistic impact: A content and reader-metrics analysis assessing audience response. *Journalism & Mass Communication Quarterly*, *92*(3), 700–722. doi:10.1177/1077699015599660

Malini, F., & Antoun, H. (2013). *A internet e as ruas: Ciberativismo e mobilização nas redes sociais* [The Internet and the streets: Cyber-mobilization and mobilization on social networks]. Porto Alegre, Brazil: Editora Sulina.

Malmelin, N., & Villi, M. (2015). Co-creation of what? Modes of audience community collaboration in media work. *Convergence (London)*. doi:10.1177/1354856515592511

Manzini, E. (2015). *Design, when everybody designs. An introduction to design for social innovation*. Cambridge, MA: The MIT Press.

Marcondes Filho, C. (2000). *A saga dos cães perdidos* [The long history of lost dogs]. São Paulo, Brazil: Hacker Editores.

Marshall, L. (Producer), & Macdonald, K. (Director). (2011). *Life in a Day* [Motion picture]. United Kingdom, United States: National Geographic Films.

Martín Barbero, J. (1987). *De los medios a las mediaciones. Comunicación, cultura y hegemonía* [From media to mediations. Communication, culture and hegemony]. Mexico City, Mexico: Gustavo Gili.

Martin, E. (2013). *Reflections on the recent Boston crisis*. Retrieved from https://redditblog.com/2013/04/22/reflections-on-the-recent-boston-crisis/

Martini, S. (2000). Periodismo, noticia y noticiabilidad [Journalism, news and newsworthiness]. Bogotá, Colombia: Norma.

Mastrini, G., & Becerra, M. (2017). *Medios en Guerra. Balance, crítica y desguace de las políticas de comunicación 2003-2016* [Media at war. Assessment, criticism and destruction of communication policies]. Buenos Aires, Argentina: Biblos.

Mattei, M. (2016). *Transmedia News. Un approccio alternativo per affrontare la svolta digitale del giornalismo* (Master of Science Degree thesis). Retrieved from POLITesi. (https://www.politesi.polimi.it/bitstream/10589/122020/3/Tesi.pdf)

Mayring, P. (2014). *Qualitative content analysis: Theoretical foundation, basic procedures and software solution*. Klagenfurt: SSOAR.

McCombs, M. (2004). *Setting the agenda*. Cambridge, MA: Polity Press.

McMillan, T. (2014). The new face of hunger. Millions of working Americans don't know where their next meal is coming from. *National Geographic Tablet Magazine*, *226*(2).

Menke, M., Kinnebrock, S., Kretzschmar, S., Aichberger, I., Broersma, M., Hummel, R., & Salaverría, R. et al. (2016). Convergence culture in European newsrooms: Comparing editorial strategies for cross-media news production in six countries. *Journalism Studies*, 1–24. doi:10.1080/1461670X.2016.1232175

Mermelstein, A. (2016, August 26). Olimpíada impulsionou Globo em diversas plataformas [Olympics boosted Globo Network in various platforms]. *Converge Comunicações*. Retrieved from http://convergecom.com.br/telaviva/paytv/26/08/2016/olimpiadas-impulsionaram-globo-em-diversas-plataformas/

Micó, J., & Barbosa, S. (2009). Models of business convergence in the information industry: A mapping of cases in Brazil and Spain. *Brazilian Journalism Research*, *2*(1), 1–18. doi:10.25200/BJR.v.5n1.2009.198

Mídia Ninja Site. (n.d.). Retrieved March, 30, 2017 from https://ninja.oximity.com/

Miller, V. (2011). *Understanding digital culture*. London: Sage.

Mioli, T. (2015, October 26). Rio 2016 Olympic Games communications director explains how the city is getting ready for 30,000 journalists. *Journalism in the Americas*. Retrieved from https://knightcenter.utexas.edu/blog/00-16397-rio2016-olympic-games-communications-director-explains-how-city-getting-ready-30000-jo

Mittell, J. (2014). Strategies of storytelling on transmedia television. In M.-L. Ryan & J.-N. Thon (Eds.), *Storyworlds across media: Toward a media-conscious narratology* (pp. 253–277). Lincoln, NE: University of Nebraska Press. doi:10.2307/j.ctt1d9nkdg.16

Mittell, J. (2015). *Complex TV: The poetics of contemporary television storytelling*. London: NYU Press.

Mitu, B., & Poulakidakos, S. (Eds.). (2016). *Media events: A critical contemporary approach*. Basingstoke, UK: Palgrave Macmillan. doi:10.1057/9781137574282

Moloney, K. (2010). *Building transmedia journalism*. Retrieved February 20, 2017, from http://transmediajournalism.org/contexts/building-transmedia-journalism/

Moloney, K. (2011). *Porting transmedia storytelling to journalism* (Unpublished master's thesis). University of Denver, Denver, CO.

Moloney, K. (2011). *Transmedia journalism in principle*. Retrieved from https://transmediajournalism.org/2011/11/23/transmedia-journalism-in-principle/

Moloney, K. (2013). *Breaking news as native transmedia journalism*. Retrieved July 1, 2017, from https://transmedia-journalism.org/2013/10/

Moloney, K. (2014). *Multimedia, crossmedia, transmedia... What's in a name?* Retrieved from https://transmediajournalism.org/2014/04/21/multimedia-crossmedia-transmedia-whats-in-a-name/

Moloney, K. (2015). *Future of story: Transmedia journalism and National Geographic's Future of Food Project* (dissertation). University of Colorado, Boulder, CO.

Moloney, K. (2015). *Future of story: Transmedia journalism and National Geographic's Future of Food project* (Unpublished doctoral dissertation). University of Colorado Boulder, Boulder, CO.

Moloney, K. (2015). *Future of story: Transmedia journalism and National Geographic's future of food project*. ATLAS Institute Graduate Theses & Dissertations, University of Colorado Boulder. Retrieved December 20, 2017, from http://scholar.colorado.edu/atlas_gradetds/6

Moloney, K. (n.d.). *What is transmedia storytelling?* Retrieved from https://transmediajournalism.org/contexts/what-is-transmedia-storytelling/

Moloney, K. T. (2011). *Porting transmedia storytelling to journalism* (MA thesis). University of Denver.

Moloney, K. T. (2011). *Porting transmedia storytelling to journalism* (Unpublished master's thesis). University of Denver, Denver, CO.

Moloney, K. (2011). *Porting transmedia storytelling to journalism (M.A. Thesis).* Denver, CO: University of Denver. Retrieved from http://0-proquest.umi.com.bianca.penlib.du.edu/pqdlink?did=2510689501&Fmt=2&rqt=309

Moloney, K. (2011). *Porting transmedia storytelling to journalism (Master of Arts Degree thesis).* Denver, CO: University of Colorado. Retrieved from http://www.colorado.edu/journalism/photojournalism/Transmedia_Journalism.pdf

Moloney, K. (2012). *Transmedia Journalism as a post-digital narrative.* Denver, CO: University of Colorado Press.

Monteiro, H. (2016, April 19). O racismo do português suave [The racism of the soft Portuguese]. *Expresso Online.* Retrieved from http://expresso.sapo.pt/blogues/blogue_chamem_me_o_que_quiserem/2016-04-19-O-racismo-do-portugues-suave

Müller, J. (2010). Intermediality revisited: Some reflections about basic principles of this axe de pertinence. In L. Elleström (Ed.), *Media borders, multimodality and intermediality* (pp. 237–252). London: Palgrave Macmillan. doi:10.1057/9780230275201_17

Muntsand, A. (2014). Televisión pública y era digital: las emisoras de proximidad en Cataluña como caso paradigmático en su adaptación a Internet [Public television and the digital age: The proximity stations in Catalonia as a paradigmatic case in its adaptation to the Internet]. *Obra digital – Revista de Comunicación, 7,* 9–26. Retrieved from http://www.raco.cat/index.php/ObraDigital/article/view/283078

Murphy, T. (2014). Solitary confinement is cruel and all too usual. Why is it only getting worse? *The Guardian.* Retrieved from https://www.theguardian.com/commentisfree/2014/oct/13/solitary-confinement-us-prisoners-rehabilitation

Murray, J. H. (1997). *Hamlet on the holodeck: The future of narrative in cyberspace.* Cambridge, MA: The MIT Press.

Nanì, A. (2013). *Crossmedia practices for the enhancement of civic engagement* (Unpublished master's thesis). Tallinn University Baltic Film and Media School, Tallinn, Estonia.

National Geographic Channel. (2013). *Killing Kennedy.* Retrieved from http://kennedyandoswald.com

National Geographic Society. (1987). *The National Geographic Society—100 Years of adventure and discovery.* Washington, DC: National Geographic Society.

National Geographic Society. (2013a). *National Geographic 125 Years: Legendary photographs, adventures and discoveries that changed the world.* Washington, DC: National Geographic Society.

National Geographic Society. (2013b). *The photography issue. 125th anniversary collector's edition.* Washington, DC: National Geographic Society.

National Geographic Society. (2014a). *'FOOD: Our global kitchen' Exhibition to Open at National Geographic Museum Oct. 16.* Retrieved from http://press.nationalgeographic.com/2014/10/02/food-our-global-kitchen-exhibition-to-open-at-national-geographic-museum-oct-16/

National Geographic Society. (2014b). Eat. The new food revolution: Serving more than 7 billion every day. *National Geographic Tablet Magazine, 225*(5).

National Geographic Society. (2016). *About the National Geographic Society.* Retrieved from http://press.nationalgeographic.com/about-national-geographic/

National Geographic Society. (2017a). *About The Plate.* Retrieved from http://www.theplate.nationalgeographic.com/

National Geographic Society. (2017b). *About us*. Retrieved from http://www.nationalgeographic.com/about/

Negroponte, N. (1995). *Being digital*. New York: Alfred A. Knopf.

Newman, N. (2009, September 3). *The rise of social media and its impact on mainstream journalism*. Reuters Institute for the Study of Journalism, University of Oxford. Retrieved from: http://reutersinstitute.politics.ox.ac.uk/our-research/rise-social-media-and-its-impact-mainstream-journalism

Newman, N. (2015). *Journalism, media and technology predictions 2016*. Oxford, UK: University of Oxford, Reuters Institute.

Newman, N. (2016). *Journalism, media and technology predictions 2017*. Oxford, UK: University of Oxford, Reuters Institute.

Newman, N., Fletcher, R., Levy, D. A. L., & Nielsen, R. K. (2016). *Reuters Institute digital news report 2016*. Oxford, UK: Reuters Institute for the Study of Journalism. Retrieved from http://reutersinstitute.politics.ox.ac.uk/sites/default/files/Digital-News-Report-2016.pdf

Nichols, B. (1997). *La representación de la realidad. Cuestiones y conceptos del documental* [The representation of reality. Issues and concepts of the documentary]. Barcelona, Spain: Paidos.

Normann, R. (2001). *Reframing business: When the map changes the landscape*. New York: John Wiley & Sons.

North, M. M., & North, S. M. (2016). A comparative study of sense of presence of traditional virtual reality and immersive environments. *AJIS. Australasian Journal of Information Systems*, *20*, 1–15. doi:10.3127/ajis.v20i0.1168

Notícia R7. (2015, October 20). *Jornal da Record News será o primeiro telejornal transmídia da TV brasileira* [Jornal da Record News will be first transmedia news show on Brazilian TV]. Retrieved from http://noticias.r7.com/record-news/jornal-da-record-news/videos/jornal-da-record-news-sera-o-primeiro-telejornal-transmidia-da-tv-brasileira-20102015

Notícia R7. (2016a, April 13). *JR News transmite reunião de pauta ao vivo pelo Facebook* [JR News transmits live on Facebook the editorial meeting]. Retrieved from http://noticias.r7.com/blogs/herodoto-barbeiro/2016/04/13/jr-news-transmite-reuniao-de-pauta-ao-vivo-pelo-facebook/

Notícia R7. (2016b, August 1). *Mais de meio milhão de pessoas conectadas no JR News* [More than a half million people connected to JR News]. Retrieved from http://noticias.r7.com/blogs/herodoto-barbeiro/2016/08/01/mais-de-meio-milhao-de-pessoas-conectadas-no-jr-news/

Notícias, S. I. C. (2016a, June 14). *E se fosse consigo?* [What if it were you?]. Retrieved from http://sicnoticias.sapo.pt/programas/e-se-fosse-consigo

Notícias, S. I. C. (2016b, April 15). *Há ou não racismo em Portugal?* [Is there or not racism in Portugal?]. Retrieved from http://sicnoticias.sapo.pt/programas/e-se-fosse-consigo/racismo/2016-04-15-Ha-ou-nao-racismo-em-Portugal--1

Notícias, S. I. C. (2016c, April 17). *O racismo explicado às crianças* [Racism explaned to children]. Retrieved from http://sicnoticias.sapo.pt/programas/e-se-fosse-consigo/racismo/2016-04-17-O-racismo-explicado-por-criancas

O'Meara, J. (2017). *"Like movies for radio": Media convergence and the Serial podcast sensation*. Retrieved March 17, 2017, from http://framescinemajournal.com/article/like-movies-for-radio-media-convergence-and-the-serial-podcast-sensation/#_edn3

O'Riordan, C. (2012, August 13). The story of the digital Olympics: Streams, browsers, most watched, four screens. *BBC*. Retrieved from http://www.bbc.co.uk/blogs/bbcinternet/2012/08/digital_olympics_reach_stream_stats.html

Oliver, M. B., Dillard, J. P., Bae, K., & Tamul, D. J. (2012). The effect of narrative news format on empathy for stigmatized groups. *Journalism & Mass Communication Quarterly, 89*(2), 205–224. doi:10.1177/1077699012439020

Ondine, A. (2012, September 3). *What is transmedia?* [Video file]. Retrieved from https://vimeo.com/48763753

Opgenhaffen, M., & d'Haenens, L. (2011). The impact of online news features on learning from news. A knowledge experiment. *International Journal of Internet Science, 6*(1), 8–28.

Orme, W. (2014, February 19). *"Crypto-Jews" in the Southwest find faith in a shrouded legacy*. Retrieved April 26, 2017, from http://www.npr.org/sections/codeswitch/2014/02/19/275862633/crypto-jews-in-the-southwest-find-faith-in-a-shrouded-legacy

Osborne, H. (2015, September 23). Downsizing could free up to 2.5m home. *The Guardian*. Retrieved from http://www.theguardian.com/money/2015/sep/23/downsizing-could-free-up-25m-homes?CMP=fb_gu

Owen, J. (2014, May 29). More than a million homes currently lie empty in Britain. *Independent*. Retrieved from http://www.independent.co.uk/news/uk/politics/more-than-a-million-homes-currently-lie-empty-in-britain-9456263.html

Owens, J. (2007). *Television sports production*. New York: Focal Press.

Panis, K., van den Bulck, H., Verschraegen, B., van der Burg, M., & Paulussen, S. (2014). Does media cross-ownership translate into cross-promotion? *Journalism Studies, 16*(6), 868–886. doi:10.1080/1461670X.2014.953780

Pariser, E. (2011). *The filter bubble: What the Internet is hiding from you*. New York, NY: Penguin Press.

Pase, A. (2008). *Vídeo online, alternativa para as mudanças da TV na cultura digital* [Online video, alternative for the transformation of TV inside digital culture] (Unpublished doctoral dissertation). Pontifícia Universidade Católica do Rio Grande do Sul.

Pase, A., Nunes, A. C., & Fontoura, M. (2012). One subject, many paths: Transmedia communication in journalism. *Brazilian Journalism Research, 8*(1), 63–76.

Pastor, D. (2014, November 10). Datos Audiencia 09 de noviembre de 2014 [Audience data on November 9, 2014]. *Focus Media*. Retrieved from http://www.focusmedia.es/datos-audiencia-09-de-noviembre-de-2014/

Payne, C. (2016, May 19). *It's the simple joys in life...* [Video file]. Retrieved from https://www.facebook.com/candaceSpayne/videos/10209653193067040/

Peirce, C. S. (1932). Collected Papers of Charles Sanders Peirce (Vol. 2; C. Hartshorne & P. Weiss, Eds.). Cambridge, MA: Harvard University Press.

Penn, W. S. (2013). *Storytelling in the digital age*. New York: Palgrave Macmillan. doi:10.1057/9781137365293

Pequenza, N. (2010). Production story. In PTV Productions. *Inside Disaster: Press Kit*. Retrieved from http://insidedisaster.com/outreach/IDH-PressKit_Dec2010.pdf

Pérez Latorre, Ó. (2015). The social discourse of video games analysis model and case study: GTA IV. *Games and Culture, 10*(5), 415–437. doi:10.1177/1555412014565639

Peters, C., & Broersma, M. (Eds.). (2013). *Rethinking journalism. Trust and participation in a transformed news landscape*. London: Routledge.

Phillips, A. (2012). *A creator's guide to transmedia storytelling*. New York: McGraw-Hill.

Phillips, A. (2012). *A creator's guide to transmedia storytelling: How to captivate and engage audiences across multiple platforms*. New York, NY: McGraw Hill Professional.

Poell, T., & van Dijck, J. (2015). Social media and activist communication. In C. Atton (Ed.), *The Routledge companion to alternative and community media* (pp. 527–537). London: Routledge.

Polak, P., & Warwick, M. (2013). *The business solution to poverty. Designing products and services for three billion new customers.* San Francisco, CA: Berrett-Koehler Publishers.

Ponce, I. (2012). *Monográfico: Redes sociales. Historia de las redes sociales* [Monograph: Social networks. The history of social networks]. Retrieved from http://recursostic.educacion.es/observatorio/web/es/internet/web-20/1043-redes-sociales?start=2

Pope, V. (2014). The joy of food. Food is more than survival. With it we make friends, court lovers, and count our blessings. *National Geographic Tablet Magazine, 226*(6).

Pöttker, H., & Kornilov, E. A. (2010). Genre-Systematik [Taxonomy of genres]. In A. G. Bespalova, E. A. Kornilov, & H. Pöttker (Eds.), *Journalistische Genres in Deutschland und Russland. Handbuch* [Journalistic genres in Germany and Russia. Handbook] (pp. 46–52). Cologne: Halem.

Pratten, R. (2011). *Getting started in transmedia storytelling: A practical guide for beginners.* London: CreativeSpace. Retrieved from http://www.tstoryteller.com/getting-started-in-transmedia-storytelling

Pratten, R. (2015). *Getting Started in Transmedia Storytelling: A Practical Guide for Beginners* (2nd ed.). London: CreateSpace.

Pratten, R. (2015). *Getting started with transmedia storytelling: A practical guide for beginners* (2nd ed.). CreateSpace Independent Publishing Platform.

Pratten, R. (2015). *Getting started with Transmedia Storytelling: A practical guide for beginners* (2nd ed.). CreateSpace Independent Publishing Platform.

Price, V. (1994). *La opinión pública. Esfera pública y comunicación* [Public opinion. Public sphere and communication]. Barcelona, Spain: Paidós.

Prince, G. (1987). *A dictionary of narratology.* Lincoln, NE: University of Nebraska Press.

Prinzing, M. (Ed.). (2015). *Die Kunst der Story* [The art of story]. Thun: Werd & Weber.

Propmark. (2016, June 28). Infoglobo prepara ambiente digital para cobertura da Rio 2016 [Infoglobo prepares digital environment for the coverage of the Rio 2016]. *Propmark.* Retrieved from http://propmark.com.br/midia/infoglobo-prepara-ambiente-digital-para-cobertura-da-rio-2016

PTV Productions. (2010a). *Inside Disaster.* Retrieved from http://insidedisaster.com/haiti/

PTV Productions. (2010b). *Inside Disaster: Press Kit.* Retrieved from http://insidedisaster.com/outreach/IDH-PressKit_Dec2010.pdf

Puccini, S. (2015). *Guión de documentales: De la preproducción a la posproducción* [Documentary script: From pre-production to post-production]. Buenos Aires, Argentina: La marca editora.

Quandt, T. (2008). (No) news on the world wide web? *Journalism Studies, 9*(5), 717–738. doi:10.1080/14616700802207664

Quantcast. (2017). Retrieved April 28, 2017, from https://www.quantcast.com/

Quirk, V. (2015). *Guide to podcasting. Report from the Tow Center for digital journalism.* Retrieved March 3, 2017, from http://towcenter.org/research/guide-to-podcasting/

Rajewski, I. O. (2005). Intermediality, intertextuality, and remediation: A literary perspective on intermediality. *Intermédialités*, *6*, 43–64.

Ralph Lawrence Carr. (2017, April 4). In *Wikipedia*. Retrieved from https://en.wikipedia.org/w/index.php?title=Ralph_Lawrence_Carr&oldid=773864607

Raphael, C., Bachen, C., Lynn, K. M., Baldwin-Philippi, J., & McKee, K. A. (2010). Games for civic learning: A conceptual framework and agenda for research and design. *Games and Culture*, *5*(2), 199–235. doi:10.1177/1555412009354728

Record New. (2016a, July 11). Pauta JR News [JR News editorial meeting] [Facebook post]. Retrieved from https://www.facebook.com/recordnews/videos/1035902746457964/

Record New. (2016b, July 13). Pauta JR News [JR News editorial meeting] [Facebook post]. Retrieved from https://www.facebook.com/recordnews/videos/1037194792995426

Record News. (2016c, July 20). Como será que o Heródoto Barbeiro se prepara antes do JR News ir ao ar? Nós mostramos para você. [How Heródoto Barbeiro prepares himself before going on air on JR News? We show you] [Facebook post]. Retrieved from https://www.facebook.com/recordnews/videos/1040753445972894

Record News. (n.d.). In *Facebook*. Retrieved August 5, 2017, from https://www.facebook.com/recordnews

Rede Globo. (2016a, August 3). Rio 2016: Globo e Snapchat fecham parceria para produção de conteúdo [Rio 2016: Globo and Snapchat agree on partnership for content production]. *Rede Globo*. Retrieved from http://redeglobo.globo.com/novidades/noticia/2016/08/rio-2016-globo-e-snapchat-fecham-parceria-para-producao-de-conteudo.html

Rede Globo. (2016b, July 29). Aplicativo Globo Rio 2016: Guia de serviços e realidade aumentada; baixe [Rio 2016 Globo Application: Service guide and augmented reality; download it]. *Rede Globo*. Retrieved from http://redeglobo.globo.com/novidades/noticia/2016/07/aplicativo-globo-rio-2016-guia-de-servicos-e-realidade-aumentada-baixe.html

Rede Globo. (2016c, July 29). Globo estreia estúdio no coração dos Jogos Olímpicos no domingo, dia 31 [Globo launches studio in the heart of the Olympic Games on Sunday, 31]. *Rede Globo*. Retrieved from http://redeglobo.globo.com/novidades/noticia/2016/07/globo-estreia-estudio-no-coracao-dos-jogos-olimpicos-no-domingo-dia-31.html

Reno, D. (2014). Diversidade de modelos narrativos para documentários transmedia [Diversity of narrative models for transmedia documentaries]. *Revista, 14*, 93–112. Retrieved from http://www.doc.ubi.pt/14/dossier_denis_reno.pdf

Reno, D. (2014). Formatos y técnicas para la producción de documentales transmedia [Formats and techniques for the production of transmedia documentaries]. In *Hacia una comunicación transmedia* [Towards a transmedia communication]. Rosario: UNR Editora. Retrieved from https://es.scribd.com/doc/244926680/Hacia-una-Comunicacion-Transmedia

Renó, D. (2014). Transmedia journalism and the new media ecology: Possible languages. In D. Renó, C. Campalans, S. Ruiz, & V. Gosciola (Eds.), *Periodismo transmedia: Miradas múltiples* [Transmedia journalism: Multiple perspectives] (pp. 3–19). Barcelona, Spain: Editorial UOC.

Renó, D. (2014). Transmedia Journalism and the new media ecology: Possible languages. In D. Renó, C. Campalans, S. Ruiz, & V. Gosciola (Eds.), *Periodismo Transmedia: Miradas Múltiples* [Transmedia journalism: Multiple perspectives] (pp. 3–19). Barcelona, Spain: Editorial UOC.

Renó, D., & Flores, J. (2012). *Periodismo transmedia* [Transmedia journalism]. Madrid, Spain: Fragua Editorial.

Renó, D., & Flores, J. (2012). *Periodismo transmedia. Reflexiones y técnicas para el ciberperiodista desde los laboratorios de medios interactivos* [Transmedia journalism. Reflections and techniques for the cyberjournalist from the interactive media labs]. Madrid: Fragua.

Renó, D., & Ruiz, S. (2012). Reflexiones sobre periodismo ciudadano y narrativa transmedia [Reflections over citizen journalism and transmedia narrative]. In C. Campalans, D. Renó, & V. Gosciola (Eds.), *Narrativas Transmedia. Entre Teorías y Prácticas* [Transmedia Narratives. Between Theories and Practices] (pp. 49–67). Bogotá: Editoral Universidad de Rosario.

Resler, R. (2015). The race to dominate the world of podcasting. *Jacobs Media Strategy*. Retrieved March 3, 2017, from http://jacobsmedia.com/the-race-to-dominate-the-world-of-podcasting/

Reuters Institute digital news report 2014: España. (2014). Navarra, Spain: Universidad de Navarra. Retrieved from https://www.unav.edu/documents/3786985/0/Reuters-Institute-Digital-News-Report-2014-Espana.pdf

Reuters Institute. (2015). *Digital News Report 2015*. Retrieved from https://reutersinstitute.politics.ox.ac.uk/sites/default/files/Reuters%20Institute%20Digital%20News%20Report%202015_Full%20Report.pdf

Reuters Institute. (2017). *Digital news report*. Retrieved from http://www.digitalnewsreport.org/

Ricaurte, P., & Ramos-Vidal, I. (2015). Investigación en redes sociales digitales: Consideraciones metodológicas desde el paradigma estructural [Research on digital social networks. Methodological reflexions from the structural paradigm]. *Revista Virtualis*, *11*(1), 165–194.

Ricketts, M. S. (2007). *The use of narratives in safety and health communication* (Diss.). Kansas State University, Manhattan, KS.

Rincón, O. (2013). El periodista DJ es el medio [The DJ journalist is the medium]. In L. Luchessi (Ed.), *Calidad informativa. Escenarios de postcrisis* [News quality. Post-crisis scenarios] (pp. 9–31). Buenos Aires, Argentina: La Crujía.

Roberts, A. (2014). *The Serial podcast: By the numbers*. Retrieved March 3, 2017, from http://edition.cnn.com/2014/12/18/showbiz/feat-serial-podcast-btn

Rodríguez, C. (2001). *Fissures in the mediascape: An international study of citizens' media*. New York, NY: Hampton Press.

Rose, M. (2011, November 30). *Four categories of collaborative documentary*. Retrieved from https://collabdocs.wordpress.com/2011/11/30/four-categories-of-collaborative-documentary/

Rose, F. (2011). *The art of immersion: How the digital generation is remaking Hollywood, Madison avenue, and the way we tell stories*. New York, NY: W. W. Norton & Company.

Rosenstiel, T., & Mitchell, A. (2012). *Future of mobile news. The explosion in mobile audiences and a close look at what it means for news*. Retrieved from http://www.journalism.org/files/legacy/Futureofmobilenews%20_final1.pdf

Rost, A., Bernardi, M. T., & Bergero, I. (2017). *Transmedia: La narración distribuida de la noticia* [Transmedia: The distributed narration of the news]. Neuquén: PubliFadecs.

Ruiz, S., Stokes, B., & Watson, J. (2012). Mobile and Locative Games in the "Civic Tripod:" Activism, Art and Learning. *International Journal of Learning and Media*, *3*(3). doi:10.1162/IJLM_a_00078

Ryan, M.-L. (2013, October). *Transmedia storytelling: Myth or reality?* Keynote Speech (from author transcript) presented at the Rethinking Intermediality in the Digital Age, Cluj, Romania. Retrieved from http://www.youtube.com/watch?v=zqFsg8zqcLA&feature=youtube_gdata_player

Ryan, M. L. (2015). *Narrative as virtual reality 2: Revisiting immersion and interactivity in literature and electronic media* [Kindle version]. Baltimore, MD: Johns Hopkins University Press.

Ryan, M.-L. (2006). *Avatars of story* (Vol. 17). Minneapolis, MN: University of Minnesota Press.

Ryan, M.-L. (2014). Story/worlds/media: Tuning the instruments of a media-conscious narratology. In *Storyworlds across media: Toward a media-conscious narratology* (pp. 25–49). Lincoln, NE: University of Nebraska Press. doi:10.2307/j.ctt1d9nkdg.6

Salaverría, R., & Negredo, S. (2008). *Periodismo integrado: Convergencia de medios y reorganización de redacciones* [Integrated journalism: Media convergence and reorganization of newsrooms]. Barcelona: Sol90.

Salaverría, R. (2005). *Redacción periodística en Internet* [Newspaper writing techniques on the Internet]. Pamplona: EUNSA.

Salaverría, R. (2014). Multimedialidade: Informar para cinco sentidos [Multimediality: To inform to five senses] In J. Canavilhas (Ed.), *Webjornalismo: 7 caraterísticas que marcam a diferença* [Webjournalism: 7 characteristics that make a difference] (pp. 25–52). Covilhã: Livros Labcom.

Saldre, M., & Torop, P. (2012). Transmedia space. In I. Ibrus & C. A. Scolari (Eds.), *Crossmedia innovations: Texts, markets, institutions* (pp. 25–44). New York, NY: Peter Lang.

Saleh, S. H. (2015). Freedom from freedom: The beneficial role of constraints in collaborative creativity. *Dissertation Abstracts International.*

Salmon, C. (2010). *Storytelling: Bewitching the modern mind.* New York, NY: Verso Books.

Salvatores, G. (Director). (2014). *Italy in a Day* [Motion picture]. Italy, United Kingdom: Indiana Production Company, Rai Cinema, Scott Free Production.

San Cornelio, G., & Roig Telo, A. (2015). Being Lucky. Transmedia and co-creation practices in music video-clips. *International Journal of Transmedia Literacy*, *1*(1), 131–145.

Sánchez, N. (2017, February 22). Tragedia de Once: Familiares y sobrevivientes pidieron cárcel común para los funcionarios [Once Station tragedy. Relatives and survivors demand for the public officers to be put in regular jails]. *Clarín.* Retrieved from https://www.clarin.com/ciudades/tragedia-once-familiares-sobrevivientes-pidieron-carcel-comun-funcionarios_0_rJl-v8sFl.html

Sánchez, C., Rodríguez-Vásquez, A., & López-García, X. (2015). Del periodismo transmedia al replicante. Cobertura informativa del contagion del ébola en España por Elpais.com [From journalism transmedia to the replicant. Ebola contagion information coverage in Spain by Elpais.com]. *El Profesional de la Información*, *24*(3), 2820290. Retrieved from https://www.academia.edu/12777757/Del_periodismo_transmedia_al_replicante._Cobertura_informativa_del_contagio_de_%C3%89bola_en_Espa%C3%B1a_por_Elpais.com

Schlichting, L. (2015). Transmedia storytelling and the challenge of knowledge transfer in contemporary digital journalism. A look at the interactive documentary *Hollow* (2012–). *Image*, *21*, 81–95.

Schmid, W. (2010). *Narratology. An introduction.* Berlin: De Gruyter.

Schneider, A. (1997). Jump cut! Memoirs of a pioneer television editor. Jefferson: McFarland.

Schuemie, M. J., Van Der Straaten, P., Krijn, M., & Van Der Mast, C. A. (2001). Research on presence in virtual reality: A survey. *Cyberpsychology & Behavior*, *4*(2), 183–201. doi:10.1089/109493101300117884 PMID:11710246

Scolari, C. (2011). *Narrativas Transmidiáticas: mundos de ficción y prosumidores en la ecología de los médios* [Transmedia storytelling: fiction worlds and prosumers in the ecology of the middle]. Retrieved December 20, 2017, from http://www.slideshare.net/cscolari/02-transmedia

Scolari, C. (2013, June 27). Spreadable media. Entre la cultura de masas y la colaborativa (II) [Between the mass and the collaborative culture]. *Blog Hipermediaciones*. Retrieved from https://hipermediaciones.com/2013/06/27/spreadable-media-entre-la-cultura-de-masas-y-la-colaborativa-ii/

Scolari, C. (2017). El translector. Lectura y narrativas transmedia en la nueva ecología de la comunicación [The transreader. Reading and transmedia storytelling in the new ecology of communication]. *Hipermediaciones*. Retrieved from https://hipermediaciones.com/2017/03/02/el-translector-lectura-y-narrativas-transmedia-en-la-nueva-ecologia-de-la-comunicacion/

Scolari, C. A. (2014). Transmedia storytelling: New ways of communicating in the digital age. *ACE digital culture annual report 2014*. Madri: Acción Cultural Espanhóla. Retrieved from https://www.accioncultural.es/media/Default%20Files/activ/2014/Adj/Anuario_ACE_2014/EN/6Storytelling_CScolari.pdf

Scolari, C. (2008). *Hipermediaciones. Elementos para una teoría de la comunicación digital interactiva* [Hypermediations. Elements for a theory on interactive digital communication]. Barcelona, Spain: Gedisa.

Scolari, C. (2009). Transmedia storytelling. Implicit consumers, narrative worlds and branding in contemporary media production. *International Journal of Communication*, *3*, 586–606.

Scolari, C. (2013). *Narrativa transmedia – cuando todos los medios cuentan* [Transmedia narrative - when all the media count]. Bilbao, Spain: Deustos.

Scolari, C. (2013). *Narrativas transmedia. Cuando todos los medios cuentan* [Transmedia narratives. When all media count]. Barcelona: Deusto.

Scolari, C. (2014). Lostología: Narrativa transmediática, estrategias crossmedia e hipertelevisión [Lostology: Transmedia narrative, crossmedia strategies and hypertelevision]. In C. Campalans, D. Renó, & V. Gosciola (Eds.), *Narrativas transmedia: Entre teorías y prácticas* [Transmedia narratives: Between theory and praxis] (pp. 137–163). Bogotá: Editorial UOC.

Scolari, C. A. (2009). Transmedia Storytelling: Implicit consumers, narrative worlds, and branding in contemporary media production. *International Journal of Communication*, *3*, 586–606. Retrieved from http://ijoc.org/index.php/ijoc/article/view/477

Scolari, C. A. (2013). *Narrativas transmedia: Cuando todos los medios cuentan* [Transmedia narratives: When all media count]. Barcelona, Spain: Deusto-Planeta.

Scott, S. (2013). Textual poachers, twenty years later: A conversation between Henry Jenkins and Suzanne Scott. In H. Jenkins (Ed.), *Textual Poachers: Television fans and participatory culture* (pp. vii–I). New York, NY: Routledge.

Scruton, R. (1996). The eclipse of listening. *The New Criterion*, *15*(3), 5–13.

Se Fosse Consigo, E. (2016a, April 8). Bem-vindo à página do E Se Fosse Consigo no Facebook [Welcome to the E Se Fosse Consigo Facebook page] [Facebook post]. Retrieved from https://www.facebook.com/esefosseconsigo/posts/983757405065882

Se Fosse Consigo, E. (2016b, April 19). O Snap-Expresso (nome do canal Snapchat do Expresso) foi para a rua perguntar aos jovens "E Se Fosse Con(s)tigo?" [The Snap-Expresso (name of the Snapchat channel of Expresso) went to the streets to ask youngsters "What if it Were You?"] [Facebook post]. Retrieved from https://www.facebook.com/esefosseconsigo/videos/990130521095237

Se Fosse Consigo, E. (n.d.). In *Facebook*. Retrieved August 03, 2017, from https://www.facebook.com/esefosseconsigo

Serious Science. (2016, October 28). *Transmedia storytelling: Media scientist Renira Rampazzo Gambarato on multi-platform production, crossmedia and the world of Harry Potter* [video file]. Retrieved from http://serious-science.org/transmedia-storytelling-7392

Serrano Tellería, A. (2016). Transmedia journalism: Exploring genres and interface design. *Trípodos*, *38*, 67–85.

Shankland, S. (2015). *The death of Adobe's Flash is lingering, not sudden*. Retrieved from https://www.cnet.com/news/the-death-of-adobes-flash-is-lingering-not-sudden/

Shelter. (n.d.). *The shortage of affordable homes*. Retrieved from http://england.shelter.org.uk/campaigns/why_we_campaign/the_housing_crisis

Shirky, C. (2010). *Cognitive surplus: Creativity and generosity in a connected age*. New York, NY: Penguin.

Sibilia, P. (2012). *La intimidad como espectáculo* [Intimacy as spectacle]. Buenos Aires, Argentina: FCE.

Siegelman, P. (2016). *An economist listens to serial*. Retrieved February 20, 2017, from http://works.bepress.com/peter_siegelman/43/

Sillesen, L. B., Ip, C., & Uberti, D. (2015). Journalism and the power of emotions. *Columbia Journalism Review*, *54*(1). Retrieved from https://www.cjr.org/analysis/journalism_and_the_power_of_emotions.php

Silverstein, J. (2015, November 5). The displaced. *The New York Times*. Retrieved from https://www.nytimes.com/2015/11/08/magazine/the-displaced-introduction.html?_r=0

Simmons Research. (2017). Retrieved April 28, 2017, from https://simmonsresearch.com/product-portfolio/

Simmons, M. (1993). *The last conquistador: Juan de Onate and the settling of the Far Southwest*. Norman, OK: University of Oklahoma Press.

Simo, F. (2017, January 11). Introducing: The Facebook Journalism Project. *Media*. Retrieved from https://media.fb.com/2017/01/11/facebook-journalism-project/

Sims, N. (2007). *True stories. A century of literary journalism*. Evanston, IL: Northwestern University Press.

Skinner, C. (2012, January 10). Best iPhone app: Five property-related apps. *PC Advisor*. Retrieved from http://www.pcadvisor.co.uk/feature/software/best-iphone-apps-five-property-related-apps-3328918/

Smith, A., Stavros, C., & Westberg, K. (2017). *Brand fans: Lessons from the world's greatest sporting brands*. Melbourne, Australia: Palgrave Macmillan. doi:10.1007/978-3-319-48854-7

Soengas, X. (2013). El papel de Internet y de las redes sociales en las revueltas árabes: Una alternativa a la censura de la prensa oficial [The Role of the Internet and social networks in the Arab spring. An alternative to official press censorship]. *Comunicar*, *41*(21), 147–155.

Sofri, L. (2015, August 20). *Il Fottuto Storytelling* [The fucking storytelling] [Blog Post]. Retrieved from http://www.wittgenstein.it/2015/08/20/storytelling-giornalismo

Sokolova, N. (2012). Co-opting transmedia consumers: User content as entertainment or free labour? The cases of S.T.A.L.K.E.R. and Metro 2033. *Europe-Asia Studies*, *64*(8), 1565–1583. doi:10.1080/09668136.2012.712253

Sousa, R. B. F. (2015). *As estratégias transmídias em Big Brother Brasil* [Transmedia strategies in Big Brother Brazil] (Unpublished master's thesis). Federal University of Pernambuco, Recife.

Soutelo, N. (2016, August 26). O que as redes sociais fizeram pelas Olimpíadas e o que também podem fazer pela sua marca [What have social media networks done for the Olympics and what they can also do for your brand]. *SocialBrain*. Retrieved from http://www.socialbrain.com.br/inbound-marketing/o-que-as-redes-sociais-fizeram-pelas-olimpiadas-e-que-tambem-podem-fazer-pela-sua-marca/

Spor, T. V. (2016, July 8). SporTV entrega a maior cobertura dos Jogos Olímpicos Rio 2016 [SporTV delivers the biggest coverage of the 2016 Rio Olympic Games]. *SporTV*. Retrieved from http://sportv.globo.com/site/programas/rio-2016/noticia/2016/07/sportv-entrega-maior-cobertura-dos-jogos-olimpicos-rio-2016.html

SRDS media planning platform. (2017). Retrieved April 28, 2017, from http://www.kantarmedia.com/us/our-solutions/media-planning-tools/srds-media-planning-platform

Srivastava, L. (2009). *Transmedia activism: Telling your story across media platforms to create effective social change*. Retrieved March 30, 2017, from http://www.mediarights.org/news/Transmedia_Activism_Telling_Your_Story_Across_Media_Platforms_to_Create_Eff

Stanfill, M., & Condis, M. (2014). Fandom and/as labor. *Transformative Works and Cultures*, *15*. doi:10.3983/twc.2014.0593

Stanzel, F. K. (1984). *A theory of narrative*. Cambridge, UK: Cambridge University Press.

Statista. (2017). Retrieved April 28, 2017, from https://www.statista.com/

Steensen, S. (2011). Online journalism and the promises of new technology. A critical review and look ahead. *Journalism Studies*, *12*(3), 311–327. doi:10.1080/1461670X.2010.501151

Steensen, S., & Ahva, L. (2017). *Theories of journalism in a digital age*. London: Routledge.

Storkman, F. N., & Sprenger, C. J. A. (1989). GRADAP. Graph definition and analysis package: User's manual. Groningen, The Netherlands: Iec ProGAMMA.

Stycer, M. (2016, August 25). Audiência do SporTV na Rio-2016 foi maior que a soma de todos os concorrentes [SporTV's audience during the 2016 Rio Olympics was bigger than the sum of all other concurrents]. *Blog do Mauricio Stycer*. Retrieved from https://mauriciostycer.blogosfera.uol.com.br/2016/08/25/audiencia-do-sportv-na-rio-2016-foi-maior-que-a-soma-de-todos-concorrentes/

Suleiman, S. R., & Crosman, I. (Eds.). (1980). *The reader in the text*. Princeton, NJ: Princeton University Press. doi:10.1515/9781400857111

Syndicut. (n.d.). *The Great British Property Scandal*. Retrieved from http://www.syndicut.com/Posts/Channel-4/Great-British-Property-Scandal

Tanforan Racetrack. (2017, February 13). In *Wikipedia*. Retrieved from https://en.wikipedia.org/w/index.php?title=Tanforan_Racetrack&oldid=765226913

Tanz, J. (2017). Journalism fights for survival in the post-truth era. *Wired*. Retrieved from https://www.wired.com/2017/02/journalism-fights-survival-post-truth-era/

Targino, M. G. (2009). *Jornalismo cidadão: informa ou deforma?* [Citizen journalism: it informs or it deforms?]. Brasília: Ibict/UNESCO. Retrieved from http://unesdoc.unesco.org/images/0018/001823/182399por.pdf

Taylor, M., Hodges, S. D., & Kohányi, A. (2003). The illusion of independent agency: Do adult fiction writers experience their characters as having minds of their own? *Imagination, Cognition and Personality*, *22*(4), 361–380. doi:10.2190/FTG3-Q9T0-7U26-5Q5X

TED. (2015). *Chris Milk: How virtual reality can create the ultimate empathy machine* [Video file]. Retrieved from https://www.youtube.com/watch?v=iXHil1TPxvA

Telenoche. (2015, April 17). *Murió Estela Morandi, una heroína anónima* [Estela Morandi died, an anonimous hero] [Video file]. Retrieved from https://www.youtube.com/watch?v=sy1SiG6mfrk

Tenderic, B., & Williams, J. (2015). *Transmedia branding—Engage your audience*. Los Angeles, CA: USC Annenberg Press.

Tenenboim-Weinblatt, K., & Neiger, M. (2017). Temporal affordances in the news. *Journalism*, *1*(19), 1–19.

Terranova, T. (2000). Free labor: Producing culture for the digital economy. *Social Text*, *18*(2), 33–58. doi:10.1215/01642472-18-2_63-33

The Economist. (2015, September 26). *Through the Roof*. Retrieved from http://www.economist.com/news/britain/21667973-britain-has-one-booming-market-could-do-crash-through-roof

The Guardian. (2016). *6x9: A virtual experience of solitary confinement*. Retrieved from https://www.theguardian.com/world/ng-interactive/2016/apr/27/6x9-a-virtual-experience-of-solitary-confinement

The Guardian. (2016, November 10). *Underworld: – Trailer for latest virtual reality experience from the Guardian* [Video file]. Retrieved from https://www.youtube.com/watch?v=rgQJH9_xgpo

The Guardian. (2017a, January 3). *Arctic 360: A virtual experience of a disappearing landscape* [Video file]. Retrieved from https://www.youtube.com/watch?v=ncEj8rZaQs8

The Guardian. (2017b, April 3). *First impressions: A virtual experience of the first year of life* [Video file]. Retrieved from https://www.youtube.com/watch?v=QKhZYZfq8Zk

The Late Show with James Corden. (2016, May 23). *Chewbacca mom takes James Corden to work* [Video file]. Retrieved from https://www.youtube.com/watch?v=uQereoIxioI

The Mill. & The Guardian, (Producers), Panetta, F., & Poulton, L. (Directors). (2016). *6x9: A virtual experience of solitary confinement* [VR Documentary]. United Kingdom: *The Mill*.

The New York Times. (2014, March 24). *The full New York Times innovation report*. Retrieved from http://mashable.com/2014/05/16/full-new-york-times-innovation-report/#SAhU_lDTkPqo

The Project Factory. (n.d.). *The Great British Property Scandal*. Retrieved from http://www.theprojectfactory.com/great-british-property-scandal

Thorson, E., Wicks, R., & Leshner, G. (2012). Experimental methodology in journalism and mass communication research. *Journalism & Mass Communication Quarterly*, *89*(1), 112–124. doi:10.1177/1077699011430066

Time 100. (2017). Retrieved from http://time.com/collection/2017-time-100/

Toffler, A. (1980). *The third wave*. London, UK: Pan Books.

Top Nonprofits, L. (2017). *Top 100 nonprofits on the web*. Retrieved from https://topnonprofits.com/lists/best-nonprofits-on-the-web/

Topaz War Relocation Center. (2017, April 26). In *Wikipedia*. Retrieved from https://en.wikipedia.org/w/index.php?title=Topaz_War_Relocation_Center&oldid=777385616

Tuchman, G. (1978). *Making news. A study in the construction of reality*. New York, NY: The Free Press.

TV3. (2014, November 10). *TV3 i el 3/24, líders el 9-N un 24,3%* d'audiència [TV3 and 3/24, leading the 9-N 24.3% audience]. Retrieved from http://www.ccma.cat/tv3/TV3-i-el-324-liders-el-9-N-amb-un-243-daudiencia/noticia-arxiu/659460/

UOL. (2015, December 10). *Globo assegura direitos de transmissão das Olimpíadas até 2032* [Globo ensures the Olympic broadcast rights until 2032]. Retrieved from https://olimpiadas.uol.com.br/noticias/2015/12/10/globo-assegura-direitos-de-transmissao-das-olimpiadas-ate-2032.htm

Uricchio, W., Wolozin, S., Bui, L., Flynn, S., & Tortum, D. (2015). *Mapping the intersection of two cultures: Interactive documentary and digital journalism*. Cambridge, MA: MIT Open Documentary Lab and MacArthur Foundation.

Usher, N. (2010). *Why spreadable doesn't equal viral: A conversation with Henry Jenkins*. Retrieved from http://www.niemanlab.org/2010/11/why-spreadable-doesnt-equal-viral-a-conversation-with-henry-jenkins/

Van der Haak, B., Parks, M., & Castells, M. (2012). The future of journalism: Networked journalism. *International Journal of Communication*, *6*(16), 2923–2938.

VanCour, S. G. (2008). *The sounds of Radio*. Wisconsin, MA: ProQuest.

Vanoost, M. (2017, May). *Reading news as narrative or as inverted pyramid: The role of gender on the reading experience*. Paper presented at the 12th annual conference of the International Association of Literary Journalism Studies (IALJS), Halifax, Nova Scotia, Canada.

Veglis, A. (2012). From cross media to transmedia reporting in newspaper articles. *Publishing Research Quarterly*, *28*(4), 313–324. doi:10.1007/s12109-012-9294-z

Verdú, D. (2016, May 1). *Fukushima, vidas contaminadas* [Fukushima, contaminated lives] [Video file]. Retrieved from http://elpaissemanal.elpais.com/documentos/fukushima-vidas-contaminadas/

Visual Timeline. (n.d.). Retrieved February 20, 2016 from https://www.reddit.com/r/serialpodcast/comments/2k3o0h/visual_timeline/

Vogelsberg, D. (2006). Crossmedia. In O. Altendorfer & L. Hilmer (Eds.), *Medienbetriebswirtschaftslehre - Marketing* [Media business management—marketing]. Opladen, Germany: Westdt. Verlag.

Wasserman, S., & Faust, K. (1992). *Social network analysis: Methods and applications, structural analysis in the social sciences*. Cambridge, MA: Cambridge University Press.

Weiler, L. (2009). Lance Weiler explains why filmmakers should expand their films into a "storyworld." *Filmmaker Magazine*. Retrieved April 27, 2017, from http://www.filmmakermagazine.com/archives/issues/summer2009/culture_hacker.php#.WQJzGcm1s3E

Weissberg, J. L. (2004). Paradoxos da teleinformática [Paradoxes of teleinformatics]. In A. Parente (Ed.), *Tramas da Rede* [Network frames] (pp. 113–141). Porto Alegre, Brazil: Sulina.

Wenz, K. (2004). As formas intermidiáticas em textos [The intermedia forms in texts]. In L. Santaella & W. Nöth (Eds.), *Palavra e imagem nas mídias: Um estudo intercultural* [Word and image in the media: An intercultural study] (pp. 251–269). Belém, Brazil: Editora Universitária UFPA.

Wenzlaff, K. (2013). Bezahlbarer Journalismus in der digitalen Moderne [Affordable journalism in the modern digital]. In L. Kramp, L. Novy, D. Ballwieser, & K. Wenzlaff (Eds.), *Journalismus in der digitalen Moderne. Einsichten – Ansichten – Aussichten* [Journalism in the modern digital. Insights—viewpoints—perspectives] (pp. 147–158). Wiesbaden, Germany: Springer VS. doi:10.1007/978-3-658-01144-4_12

Westlund, O. (2011). *Cross-media news work*. Gothenburg, Sweden: JMG.

Williams, N. (2016, December 27). "Chewbacca Mom" on winning Facebook in 2016. *BBC*. Retrieved from http://www.bbc.com/news/world-us-canada-38348401

Wilson, C. J., & Soranzo, A. (2015). The use of virtual reality in psychology: A case study in visual perception. *Computational and Mathematical Methods in Medicine*, *2015*, 1–7. doi:10.1155/2015/151702 PMID:26339281

Witzel, A. (2000). Das problemzentrierte Interview [The problem-centered interview]. *Forum Qualitative Social Research*, *1*(1), 22. Retrieved from http://www.qualitativeresearch.net/index.php/fqs/article/view/1132/2522

Wolf, C. (2010). Drehscheibe (mobiles) Internet: Integration mobiler Dienste in online basierte Crossmedia-Umwelten [Hub (mobile) Internet: Integration of mobile services into online based cross media environments]. In R. Hohlfeld, P. Müller, A. Richter, & F. Zacher (Eds.), Passauer Schriften zur Kommunikationswissenschaft. Crossmedia - Wer bleibt auf der Strecke? Beiträge aus Wissenschaft und Praxis [Cross media—Who is going to lose? Contributions from science and the practical field] (pp. 111–122). Berlin, Germany: Lit.

Wolf, C., & Godulla, A. (2016). Potentials of digital longforms in journalism. A survey among mobile Internet users about the relevance of online devices, Internet-specific qualities, and modes of payment. *Journal of Media Business Studies*, 1–23. 10.1080/16522354.2016.1184922

Wolf, C. (2014). *Mobiler Journalismus. Angebote, Produktionsroutinen und redaktionelle Strategien deutscher Print- und Rundfunkredaktionen. Aktuell. Studien zum Journalismus* [Mobile journalism. Content, production routines, and editorial strategies of German print and broadcasting editorial offices] (Vol. 8). Baden-Baden, Germany: Nomos.

Wolf, C., & Schnauber, A. (2015). News consumption in the mobile era: The role of mobile devices and traditional journalism's content within the user's information repertoire. *Digital Journalism*, *3*(5), 759–776. doi:10.1080/21670811.2014.942497

Wolf, M. J. P. (2012). *Building imaginary worlds. The theory and history of subcreation*. New York, NY: Routledge.

Women for Sale. (2015a). Retrieved from http://www.documedia.com.ar/mujeres/index-en.html

Women for Sale. (2015b). *Transmedia tour*. Retrieved from http://www.documedia.com.ar/mujeres/universotransmedia-en.html

Yang, G. (2016). Narrative agency in hashtag activism: The case of #BlackLivesMatter. *Media and Communication*, *4*(4), 13–17. doi:10.17645/mac.v4i4.692

Yin, R. K. (2009). *Case study research: Design and methods* (4th ed.). London: Sage Publication.

Youngblood, G. (1970). *Expanded Cinema*. New York: P. Dutton & Co. Inc.

Zacher, F. (2010). Die normative Bewertung von Cross-Promotion: Eine akzeptable Marketing-Strategie für crossmedial aufgestellte Medienkonzerne? [The normative assessment of cross-promotion: an acceptable marketing strategy for cross media media groups?]. In R. Hohlfeld, P. Müller, A. Richter, & F. Zacher (Eds.), Passauer Schriften zur Kommunikationswissenschaft. Crossmedia - Wer bleibt auf der Strecke? Beiträge aus Wissenschaft und Praxis [Cross media—Who is going to lose? Contributions from science and the practical field] (pp. 210–227). Berlin, Germany: Lit.

Zelizer, B. (2004). When facts, truth, and reality are God-terms: On journalism's uneasy place in cultural studies. *Communication and Critical/Cultural Studies*, *1*(1), 100–119. doi:10.1080/1479142042000180953

Zhang, S. I. (2012). The newsroom of the future. *Journalism Practice*, *6*(5-6), 776–787. doi:10.1080/17512786.2012.667281

Zirondi, M. (2016, August 11). Snapchat se destaca na Olimpíada com transmissões ao vivo [Snapchat excels in the Olympics with live broadcasts]. *Propmark*. Retrieved from http://propmark.com.br/rio-2016/snapchat-se-destaca-na-olimpiada-com-transmissoes-ao-vivo

Zorrilla Abascal, M. L. (2016). Transmedia intertextualities in educational media resources: The case of BBC Schools in the United Kingdom. *New Media & Society*, *18*(11), 2629–2648. doi:10.1177/1461444815590140

About the Contributors

Renira Rampazzo Gambarato is Assistant Professor in the Faculty of Communications, Media and Design at the National Research University Higher School of Economics, in Moscow, Russia. Her Post-doctorate in Film Studies is from Concordia University, Canada and she holds a PhD in Communication and Semiotics from Pontifical Catholic University of São Paulo, Brazil; a MA in Communication and Semiotics also from Pontifical Catholic University of São Paulo and a BA in Industrial Design from São Paulo State University, Brazil.

Geane Carvalho Alzamora is Professor in the Social Communication Department at the Federal University of Minas Gerais, Brazil and Researcher of CNPq, Brazil (CNPq Productivity Scholarship, process: 311914/2016). Her Post-doctorate is from Pompeu Fabra University, Spain. She holds a PhD in Communication and Semiotics from Pontifical Catholic University of São Paulo, Brazil; a MA in Communication and Semiotics also from Pontifical Catholic University of São Paulo and a BA in Journalism from Pontifical Catholic University of Minas Gerais, Brazil.

* * *

Eleonora Benecchi is a post-doctoral fellow and lecturer at the Institute of Media and Journalism at the Università della Svizzera italiana in Lugano, Switzerland. She teaches courses and carries out research on digital culture and social media. She also published in the field of Internet fandom and participatory cultures.

Luciana Andrade Gomes Bicalho is a PhD candidate in Social Communication at Federal University of Minas Gerais (CAPES/PROEX Fellow), Brazil. Researcher at The Intermedia Connections Research Group (NucCon), which is linked to the New Media Convergence Center (CCNM). She has experience in Communication, with emphasis on Narrative and Theories of Communication, acting on the following topics: new media, cyberculture, semiotics and transmedia.

João Canavilhas, associate professor, has done his PhD at the Universidad de Salamanca (Spain). He teaches at the University of Beira Interior (Covilhã, Portugal), where he is vice-rector and researcher at Labcom: Laboratory of Online Communication. He is the author or co-author of 4 books, 20 book chapters and 30 papers in national and international scientific journals. His most important contribution to online journalism is the "Tumbled Pyramid Theory." His research work focuses on various aspects of "Communication and New Technologies," particularly in the fields of online journalism, e-politics, social media and journalism for portable devices.

Mariana Ciancia holds a PhD in Design from Politecnico di Milano, Italy. She is currently researcher (Design Department, Politecnico di Milano) and lecturer (School of Design, Politecnico di Milano and Università Cattolica del Sacro Cuore). Her research activity deals with new media and participatory culture, with the aim of understanding how multichannel phenomena (crossmedia and transmedia) are changing the processes of production, distribution and consumption of narrative environments. National and international publications include articles and book chapters on transmedia phenomena, narrative formats, and audiovisual artefacts.

Cinzia Colapinto (PhD) is Assistant Professor of Management at Ca' Foscari University of Venice, Italy. Her research interests lie in the area of strategy-innovation interface, and decision making. She published in international refereed journals (including European Journal of Operational Research, Annals of Operations Research, International Journal of Media Management and Media Culture and Society). Cinzia has been a visiting scholar at London School of Economics and Political Science, United Kingdom, University of Canberra, Australia, Laurentian University, Canada, and Queensland University of Technology, Australia.

Tobias Eberwein, PhD, is a Senior Scientist at the Institute for Comparative Media and Communication Studies of the Austrian Academy of Sciences and the Alpen-Adria-Universität in Vienna, Austria. His research focuses on the fields of media accountability and media change, print and online journalism, methods of media and communication studies as well as comparative media and communication studies. He was visiting professor at Dresden University of Technology and at Dortmund University of Technology, Germany. Currently, he acts as a visiting lecturer at Hamburg Media School and at Cologne University of Applied Sciences, Germany.

Yvana Fechine has a PhD in Communication and Semiotics, she is a journalist and a professor both at the Graduated Program in Communication and of the Communication Department at the Federal University of Pernambuco, Brazil. With the support of Conselho Nacional de Desenvolvimento Científico e Tecnológico (CNPq), her research and publications are currently focused on the transformations of television formats resulting from media convergence.

Alexander Godulla received his Diploma in Journalism at the Catholic University Eichstätt-Ingolstadt, Germany. His PhD is from the same University. From 2009 to 2015, he worked as a Research fellow at the Chair for Communication Science at the University of Passau. In 2015, he finished his post-doctoral thesis on the prospects for modeling in public communication in the digital era. In the same year, he started to work as a full professor at the University of Applied Sciences Würzburg-Schweinfurt, Germany. Since 2017 he is a full professor for Empirical Communication and Media Research at the University of Leipzig, Germany.

Bruna Marcon Goss, MsC, Journalist, former researcher at Ubilab laboratory (http://ubilab.pucrs.br/), Brazil. Marketing Manager for Mailee.me and RedeHost companies, specialized in content marketing, marketing strategies and startup communications. Specialist in online journalism, digital divide, mobile communication, user eXperience, digital accessibility and Agile software development for marketing and social communication. Interested in researching journalism and software, mobile interfaces, newsgames and serious games.

Anahí Lovato is studying for a Master's degree in Digital Interactive Communication at National University of Rosario (UNR), Argentina. Member of the Multimedia Communication Department, where she works as a multimedia content coordinator, TV, multimedia and transmedia scriptwriter. Among her projects are "Women for sale: human trafficking in Argentina" (transmedia documentary, 2015), "Lost Streets" (interactive documentary, 2013) and "Following the footsteps of The Beast Man" (transmedia documentary, 2013). She teaches at National University of Rosario. Member of the Latin American Chair of Transmedia Storytelling, she has published several books and articles on digital journalism and transmedia storytelling.

Lila Luchessi is the Director of the Institute for Public Policy and Government Research of the National University of Río Negro, Argentina. Since 2009, she is a Tenured Professor at the UNRN and UBA (1997). She is a member of the Academic Committees of the Latin American Professorship of Transmedia Narratives and the Technopolitics and Culture at CIESPAL. She is the author of many books and articles, and she is a member of several academic and editorial committees in the field of social communication. She has a PhD in Political Sciences (UB) and a Bachelor's Degree in Communication Sciences (UBA).

Michele Mattei graduated in Communication Design at Politecnico di Milano, Italy, with a thesis on transmedia approach to the digital journalism in Italy. Currently, he is User Experience Designer at Intesa Sanpaolo bank, with the task to redesign the main processes in order to speed up the internal workflow of the company and make the customer journey totally digital. His area of interest concerns the study of the human behavior during the everyday-process of information on multi-channel platforms, how the news industry is facing the digital turn around the world and how it can improve the relationship with his readers.

Kevin Moloney is an assistant professor of Emerging Media Design and Development at Ball State University, United States. He holds a Ph.D. in Technology, Media and Society from the interdisciplinary ATLAS Institute at the University of Colorado. He lectures internationally on photojournalism, documentary photography and transmedia storytelling. As a second-generation photojournalist, he has visually reported more than 960 stories pole to pole and on three continents for the New York Times. He has worked for scores of other international publications including National Geographic, Time, Newsweek, U.S. News and World Report, Stern, Paris Match and others.

André Fagundes Pase, PhD, Journalist and Professor at Pontifical Catholic University of Rio Grande do Sul, Brazil, for undergraduate and graduate students enrolled in Journalism and Creative Writing courses. Researcher at Ubilab laboratory (http://ubilab.pucrs.br/). Specialist in online journalism, mobile communication, videogames, virtual reality, online video, graphic novels, and processes that involve the combination of information with entertainment. Collaborated in research projects for Globo.com, MIT Mobile Experience Lab, WAN-IFRA, dbServer, and RBS. Developed games and apps for smartphones and tablets.

Colin Porlezza is Senior Research and Teaching Associate at the Institute of Mass Communication and Media Research IPMZ, University of Zurich, Switzerland. He is also Visiting Professor for entrepreneurial journalism at the Academy of Journalism and Media, University of Neuchâtel, Switzerland. Previously he worked as a lecturer of journalism innovation at the Department of Journalism at City, University of London. His main fields of research are journalism innovation, data journalism as well as accountability and transparency of the media. His main publications appeared in the Journal of Communication, Journalism, Journalism Practice and Media and Communication.

Sofia Costa Rêgo is a journalist and has a master's degree in Communication at the Federal University of Pernambuco, Brazil. She investigates transmedia experiences in Brazilian television journalism and had inventoried the strategies of articulation between TV and Internet, in order to propose a categorization of the transmedia contents produced, along with their respective functions. The study also found that the transmedia strategies in television news have a minor role in the journalistic qualification and have a more decisive part in building the program ethos, by reinforcing its communicative contracts with the audience.

Nohemí Lugo Rodríguez, Professor in the Department of Creative Industries at Tecnológico de Monterrey, Queretaro Campus in Mexico. She obtained a PhD in Communications at Pompeu Fabra University, Spain.It involves ethnography and design based research. Her Master's Degree in Spanish is from Western Michigan University, United States, in 2002. She is interested in participating in multidisciplinary teams in order to design and develop methods, processes, materials and applications that promote social change through education, social inclusion, health and similar fields by using storytelling and game principles.

Lorena Tárcia is Professor in Social Communication Department at the University Center of Belo Horizonte, Minas Gerais, Brazil. She holds a PhD in Communication from the Federal University of Minas Gerais; a MA in Education from Pontifical Catholic University of Minas Gerais and a BA in Journalism also from Pontifical Catholic University of Minas Gerais, Brazil.

Roberto Tietzmann, PhD, is a professor and researcher at Pontifical Catholic University of Rio Grande do Sul, Brazil, for Communication Studies and Creative Writing postgraduate programmes. Coordinates two research initiatives, ViDiCa (Digital Audiovisual Culture research group) and DaVint (Data Visualization and Interaction Lab). Investigates interfaces between audiovisual storytelling, design and technology. Specialist in advertising, worked in visual communication, and directed fictional and non-fictional movies. Also developed CD-ROMs and digital interactive pieces during the first ten years of commercial Internet in Brazil.

Cornelia Wolf received her Diploma in Journalism at the Catholic University Eichstätt-Ingolstadt, Germany in 2008. From 2009 to 2014 she worked as a Research Associate at the University of Passau, Germany at the Chair for Communication Science and the Chair for Computer-mediated Communication. In 2014, she received her PhD at the same University for her work about mobile journalism in Germany. Since 2014 she is a junior professor for Online Communication at the University of Leipzig, Germany. Her research and teaching focuses in the areas of cross media strategies and new online and mobile formats in journalism.

Index

L

M

N

O

P

R

S

T

U

V

Z

Printed in the United States
By Bookmasters